TEEN TITANS

ROBIN NO MORE

writers

ROBBIE THOMPSON
ADAM GLASS

artists

EDUARDO PANSICA
JÚLIO FERREIRA
JAVIER FERNANDEZ
JESÚS MERINO
CAM SMITH

colorists

MARCELO MAIOLO
HI-FI

letterer

ROB LEIGH

collection cover artists

BERNARD CHANG
and **MARCELO MAIOLO**

SUPERBOY created by JERRY SIEGEL
By special arrangement with the Jerry Siegel family

VOL.

4

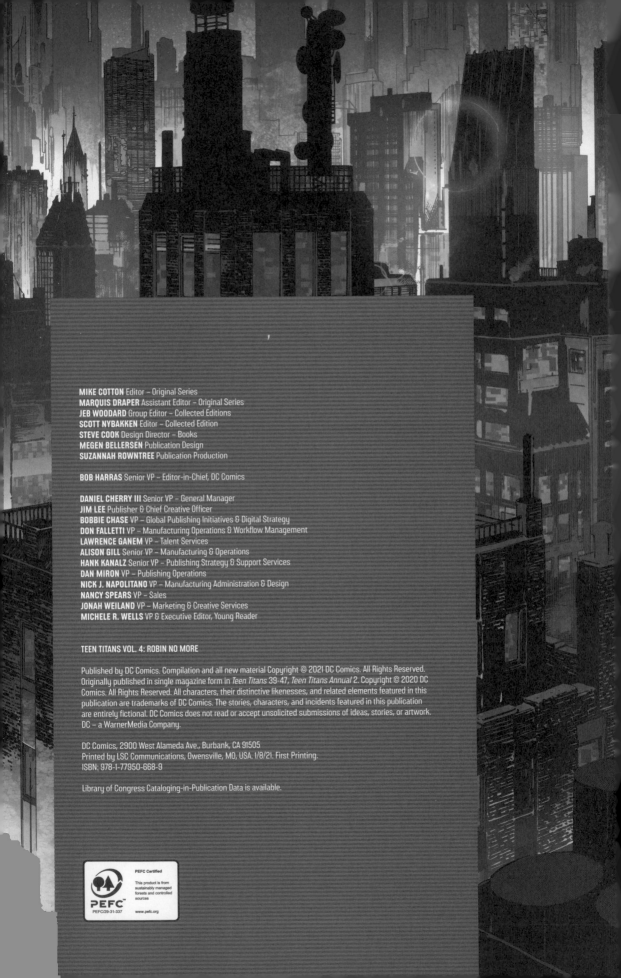

MIKE COTTON Editor – Original Series
MARQUIS DRAPER Assistant Editor – Original Series
JEB WOODARD Group Editor – Collected Editions
SCOTT NYBAKKEN Editor – Collected Edition
STEVE COOK Design Director – Books
MEGEN BELLERSEN Publication Design
SUZANNAH ROWNTREE Publication Production

BOB HARRAS Senior VP – Editor-in-Chief, DC Comics

DANIEL CHERRY III Senior VP – General Manager
JIM LEE Publisher & Chief Creative Officer
BOBBIE CHASE VP – Global Publishing Initiatives & Digital Strategy
DON FALLETTI VP – Manufacturing Operations & Workflow Management
LAWRENCE GANEM VP – Talent Services
ALISON GILL Senior VP – Manufacturing & Operations
HANK KANALZ Senior VP – Publishing Strategy & Support Services
DAN MIRON VP – Publishing Operations
NICK J. NAPOLITANO VP – Manufacturing Administration & Design
NANCY SPEARS VP – Sales
JONAH WEILAND VP – Marketing & Creative Services
MICHELE R. WELLS VP & Executive Editor, Young Reader

TEEN TITANS VOL. 4: ROBIN NO MORE

DC Comics, 2900 West Alameda Ave., Burbank, CA 91505
Printed by LSC Communications, Owensville, MO, USA. 1/8/21. First Printing.
ISBN: 978-1-77950-668-9

Library of Congress Cataloging-in-Publication Data is available.

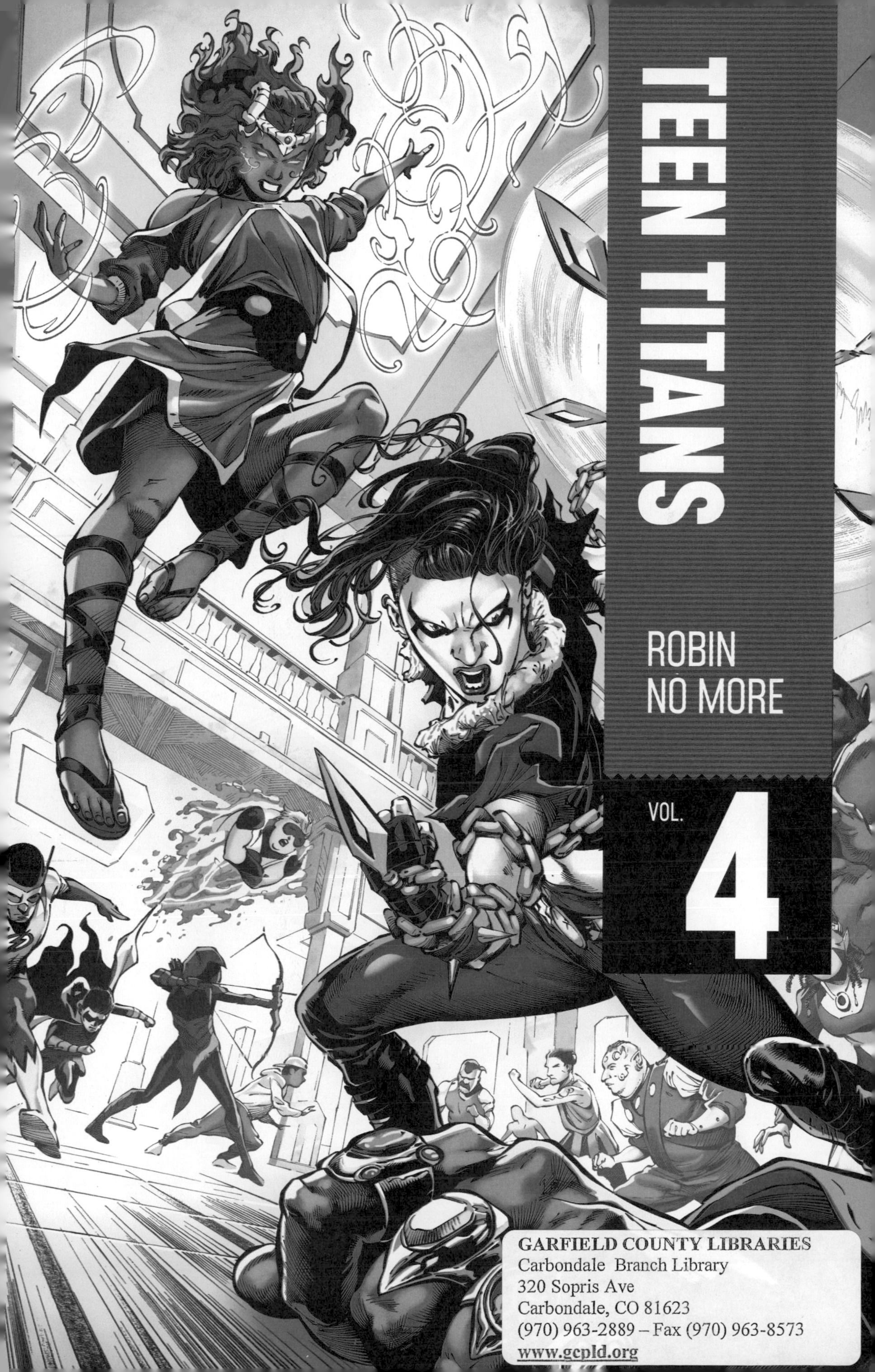
TEEN TITANS
ROBIN
NO MORE
VOL.
4

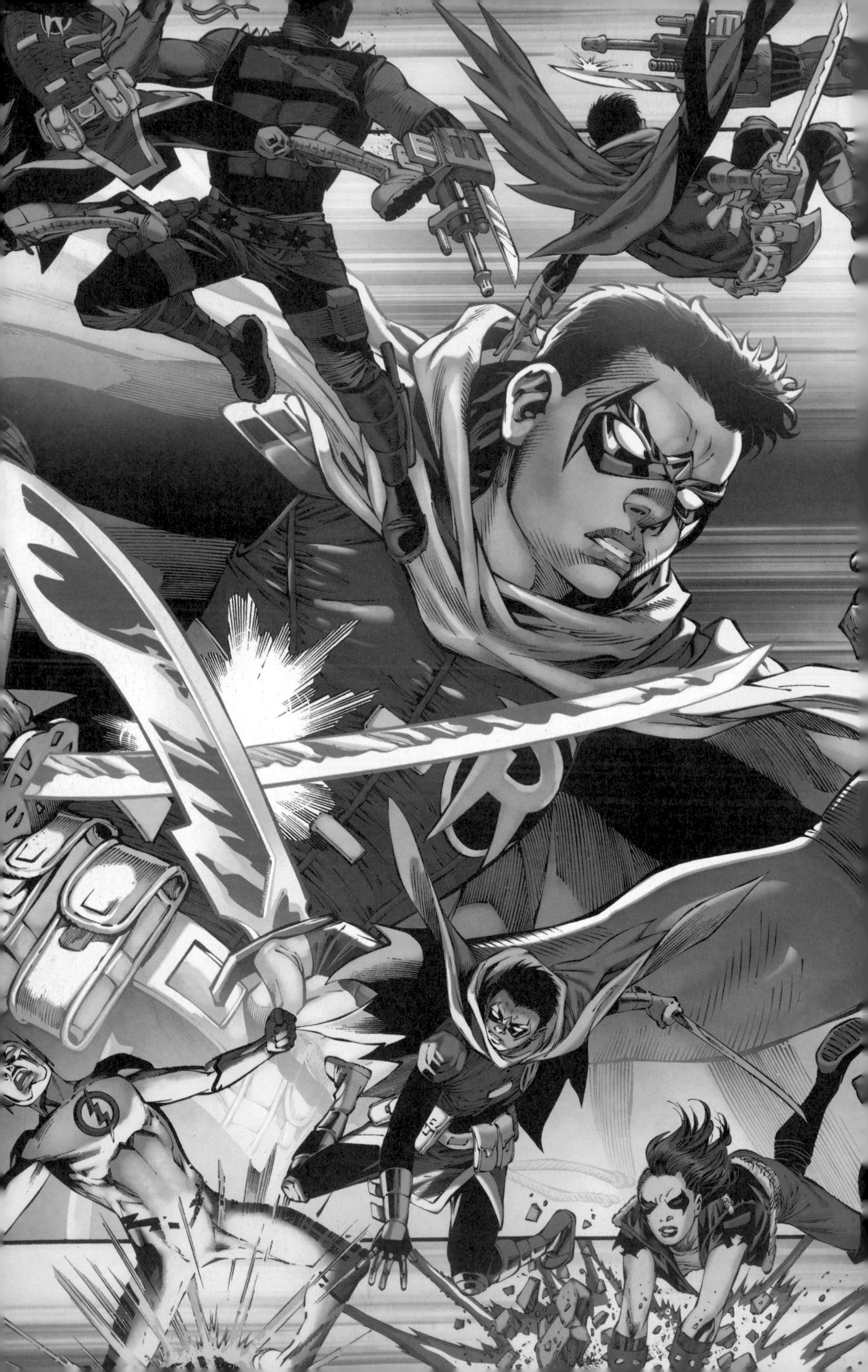

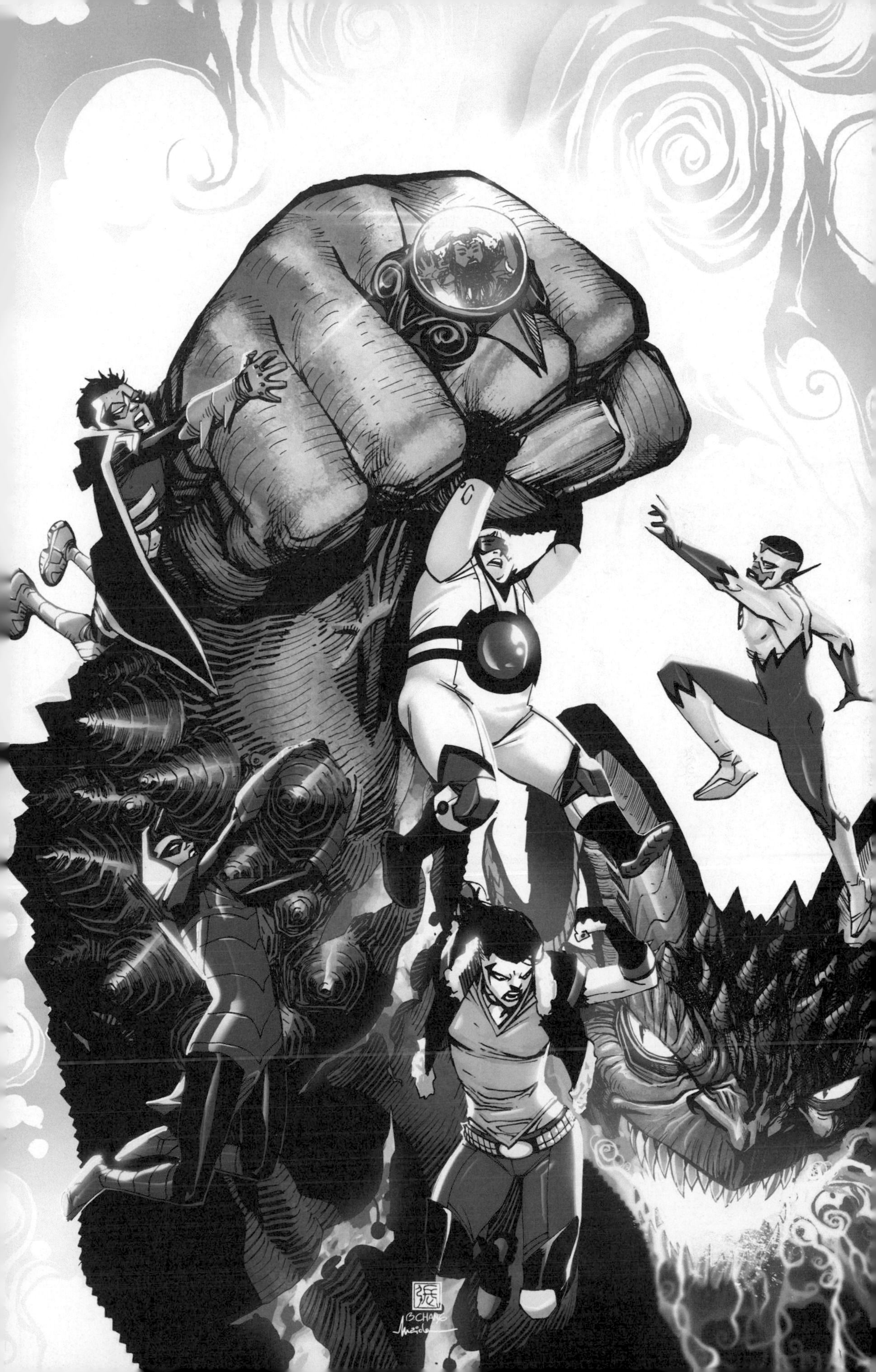
BCHANG

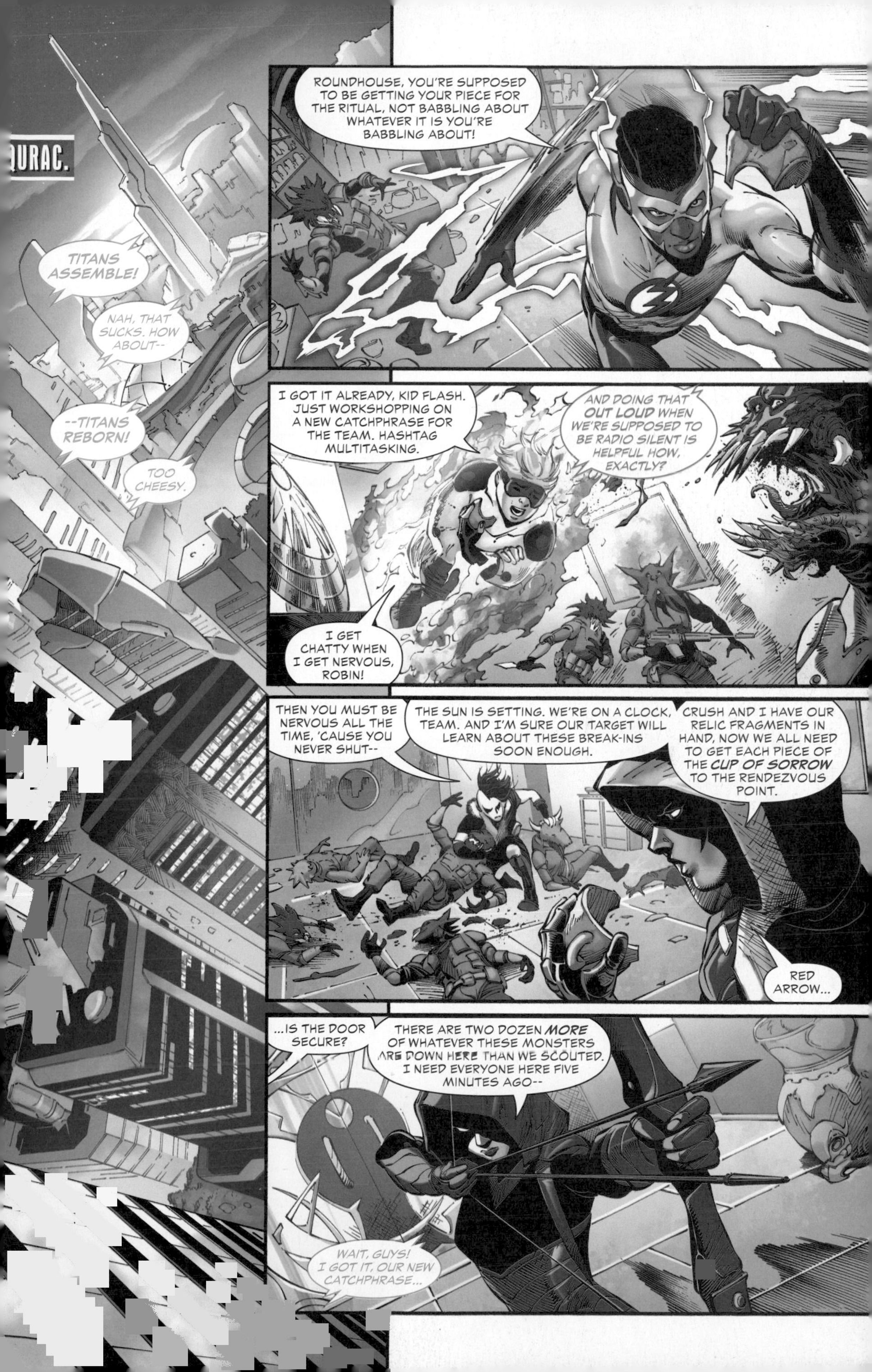
QURAC.
TITANS ASSEMBLE!
NAH, THAT SUCKS. HOW ABOUT--
--TITANS REBORN!
TOO CHEESY.
ROUNDHOUSE, YOU'RE SUPPOSED TO BE GETTING YOUR PIECE FOR THE RITUAL, NOT BABBLING ABOUT WHATEVER IT IS YOU'RE BABBLING ABOUT!
I GOT IT ALREADY, KID FLASH. JUST WORKSHOPPING ON A NEW CATCHPHRASE FOR THE TEAM. HASHTAG MULTITASKING.
AND DOING THAT OUT LOUD WHEN WE'RE SUPPOSED TO BE RADIO SILENT IS HELPFUL HOW, EXACTLY?
I GET CHATTY WHEN I GET NERVOUS, ROBIN!
THEN YOU MUST BE NERVOUS ALL THE TIME, 'CAUSE YOU NEVER SHUT--
THE SUN IS SETTING. WE'RE ON A CLOCK, TEAM. AND I'M SURE OUR TARGET WILL LEARN ABOUT THESE BREAK-INS SOON ENOUGH.
CRUSH AND I HAVE OUR RELIC FRAGMENTS IN HAND, NOW WE ALL NEED TO GET EACH PIECE OF THE CUP OF SORROW TO THE RENDEZVOUS POINT.
RED ARROW...
...IS THE DOOR SECURE?
THERE ARE TWO DOZEN MORE OF WHATEVER THESE MONSTERS ARE DOWN HERE THAN WE SCOUTED. I NEED EVERYONE HERE FIVE MINUTES AGO--
WAIT, GUYS! I GOT IT, OUR NEW CATCHPHRASE...

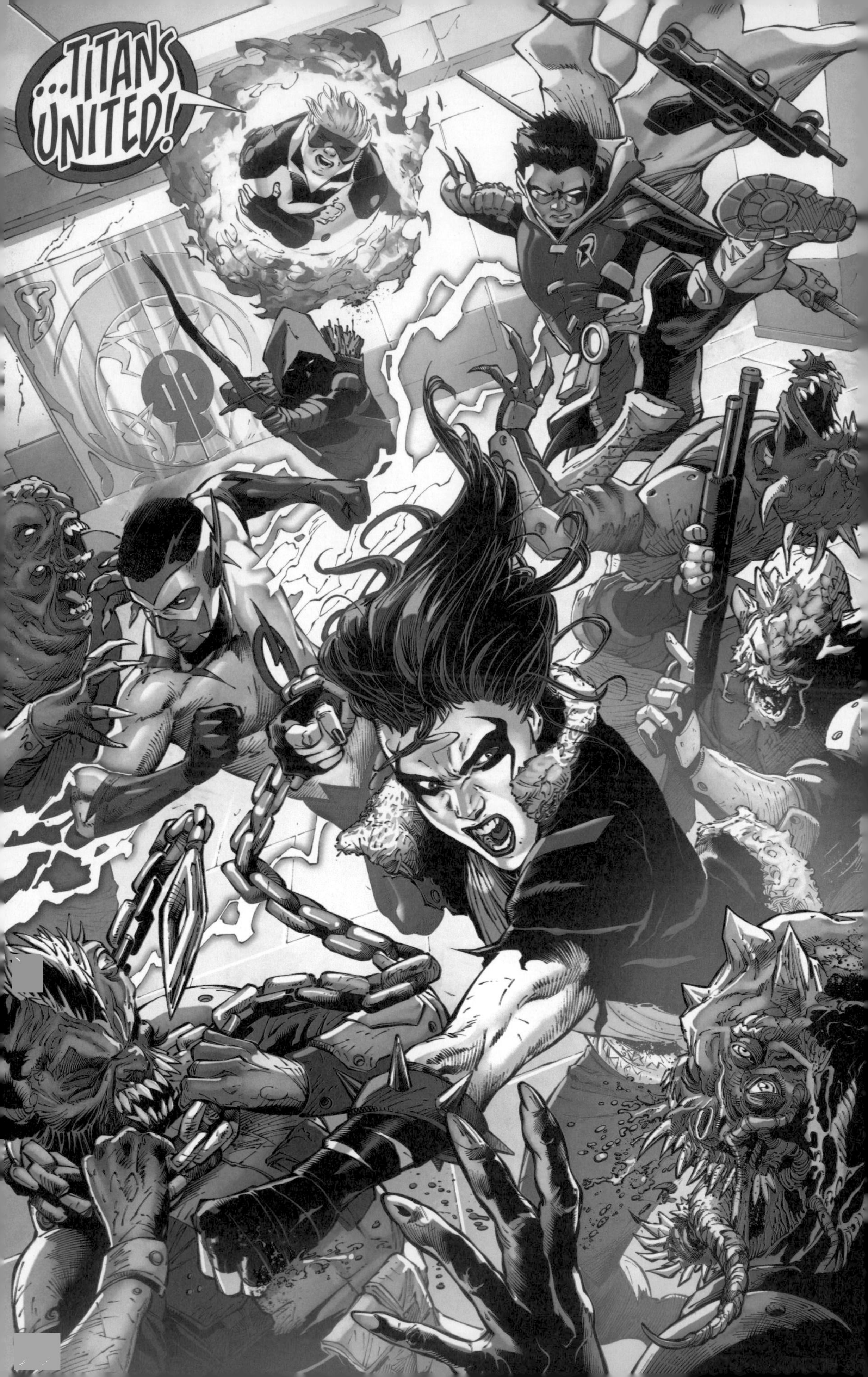
...TITANS UNITED!

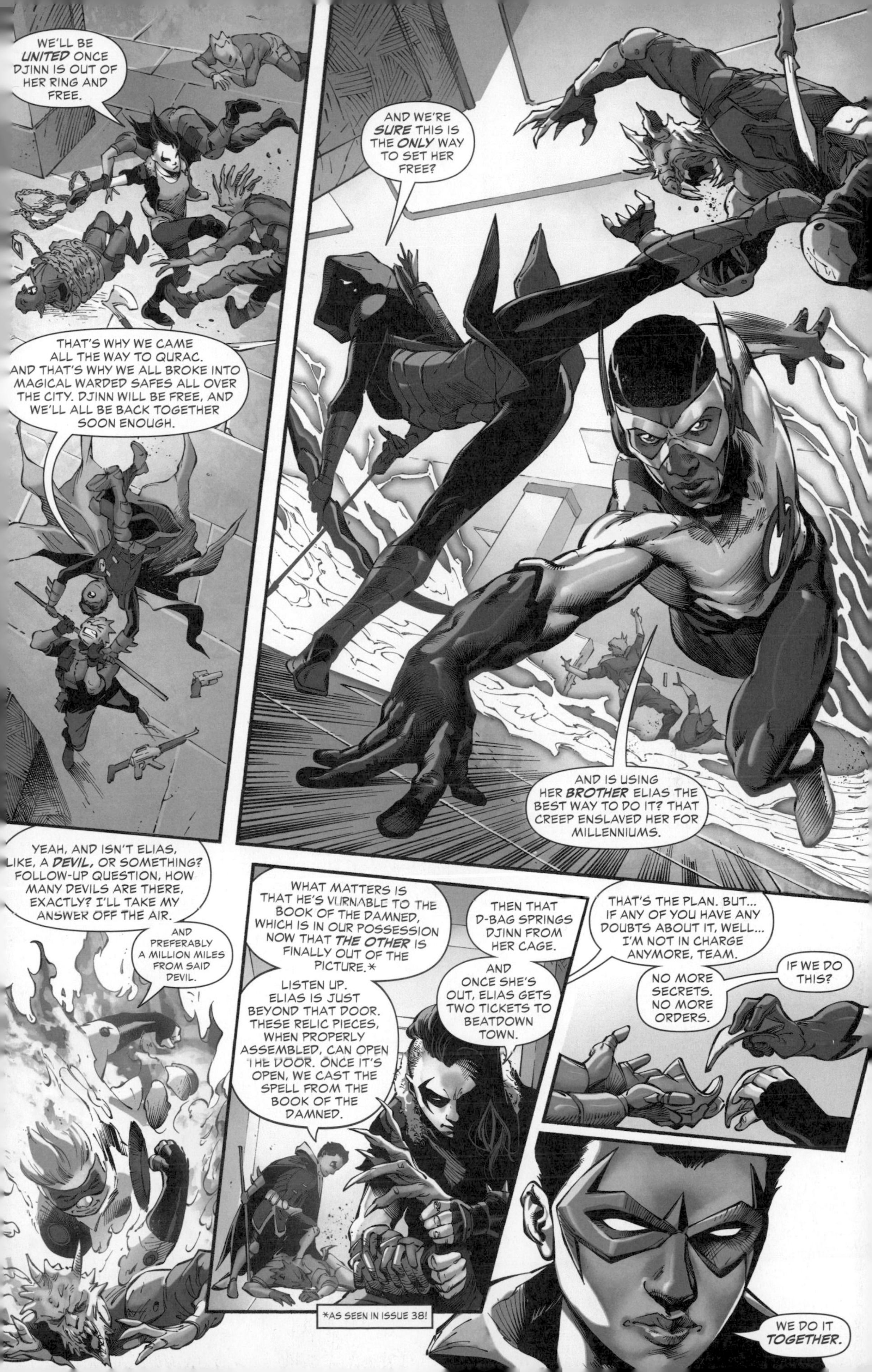
WE'LL BE UNITED ONCE DJINN IS OUT OF HER RING AND FREE.
AND WE'RE SURE THIS IS THE ONLY WAY TO SET HER FREE?
THAT'S WHY WE CAME ALL THE WAY TO QURAC. AND THAT'S WHY WE ALL BROKE INTO MAGICAL WARDED SAFES ALL OVER THE CITY. DJINN WILL BE FREE, AND WE'LL ALL BE BACK TOGETHER SOON ENOUGH.
AND IS USING HER BROTHER ELIAS THE BEST WAY TO DO IT? THAT CREEP ENSLAVED HER FOR MILLENNIUMS.
YEAH, AND ISN'T ELIAS, LIKE, A DEVIL, OR SOMETHING? FOLLOW-UP QUESTION, HOW MANY DEVILS ARE THERE, EXACTLY? I'LL TAKE MY ANSWER OFF THE AIR.
AND PREFERABLY A MILLION MILES FROM SAID DEVIL.
WHAT MATTERS IS THAT HE'S VURNABLE TO THE BOOK OF THE DAMNED, WHICH IS IN OUR POSSESSION NOW THAT THE OTHER IS FINALLY OUT OF THE PICTURE.*
LISTEN UP. ELIAS IS JUST BEYOND THAT DOOR. THESE RELIC PIECES, WHEN PROPERLY ASSEMBLED, CAN OPEN THE DOOR. ONCE IT'S OPEN, WE CAST THE SPELL FROM THE BOOK OF THE DAMNED.
THEN THAT D-BAG SPRINGS DJINN FROM HER CAGE.
AND ONCE SHE'S OUT, ELIAS GETS TWO TICKETS TO BEATDOWN TOWN.
THAT'S THE PLAN. BUT... IF ANY OF YOU HAVE ANY DOUBTS ABOUT IT, WELL... I'M NOT IN CHARGE ANYMORE, TEAM.
NO MORE SECRETS. NO MORE ORDERS.
IF WE DO THIS?
WE DO IT TOGETHER.
*AS SEEN IN ISSUE 38!

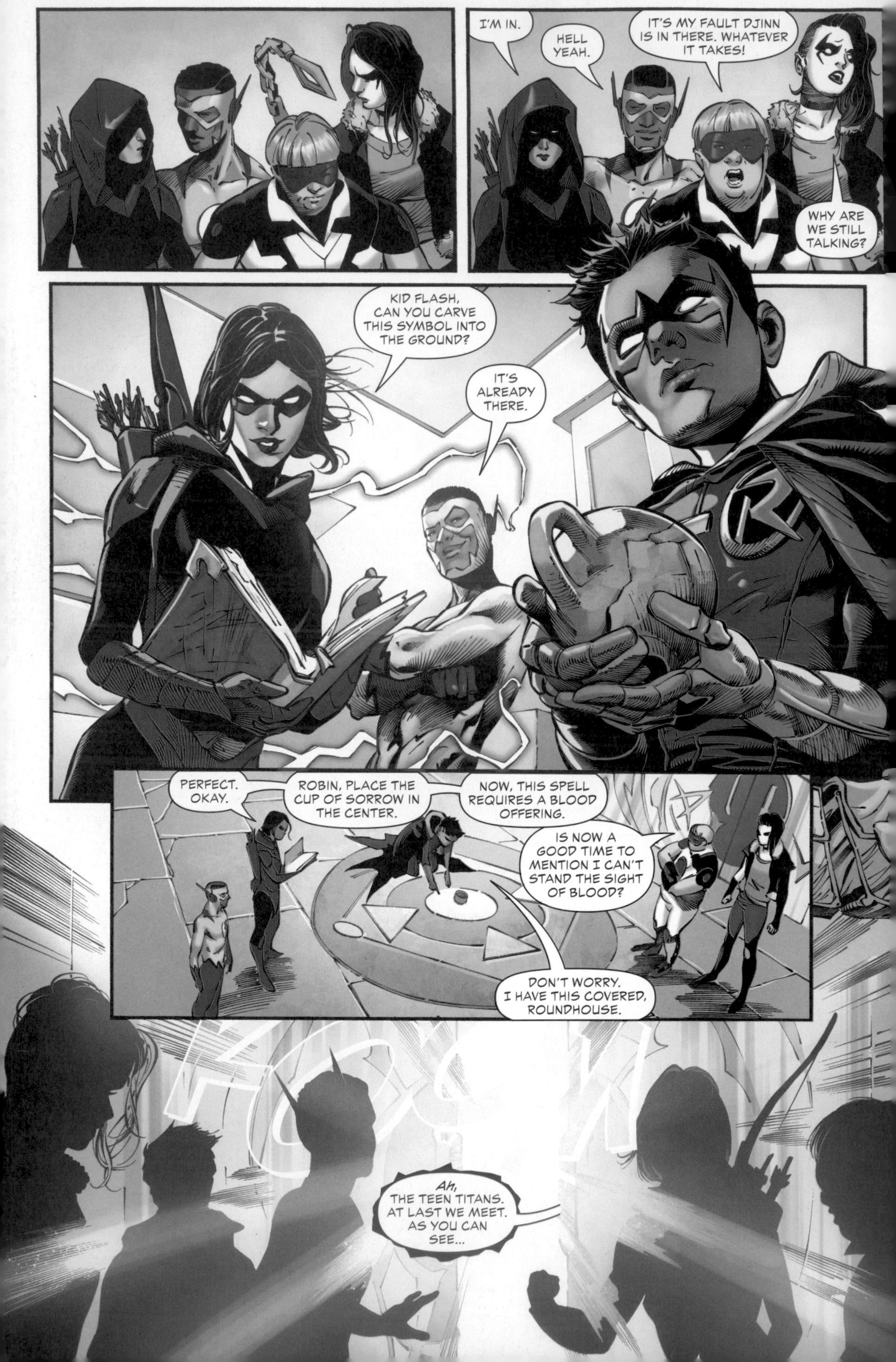
I'M IN.
HELL YEAH.
IT'S MY FAULT DJINN IS IN THERE. WHATEVER IT TAKES!
WHY ARE WE STILL TALKING?
KID FLASH, CAN YOU CARVE THIS SYMBOL INTO THE GROUND?
IT'S ALREADY THERE.
PERFECT. OKAY.
ROBIN, PLACE THE CUP OF SORROW IN THE CENTER.
NOW, THIS SPELL REQUIRES A BLOOD OFFERING.
IS NOW A GOOD TIME TO MENTION I CAN'T STAND THE SIGHT OF BLOOD?
DON'T WORRY. I HAVE THIS COVERED, ROUNDHOUSE.
Ah, THE TEEN TITANS. AT LAST WE MEET. AS YOU CAN SEE...

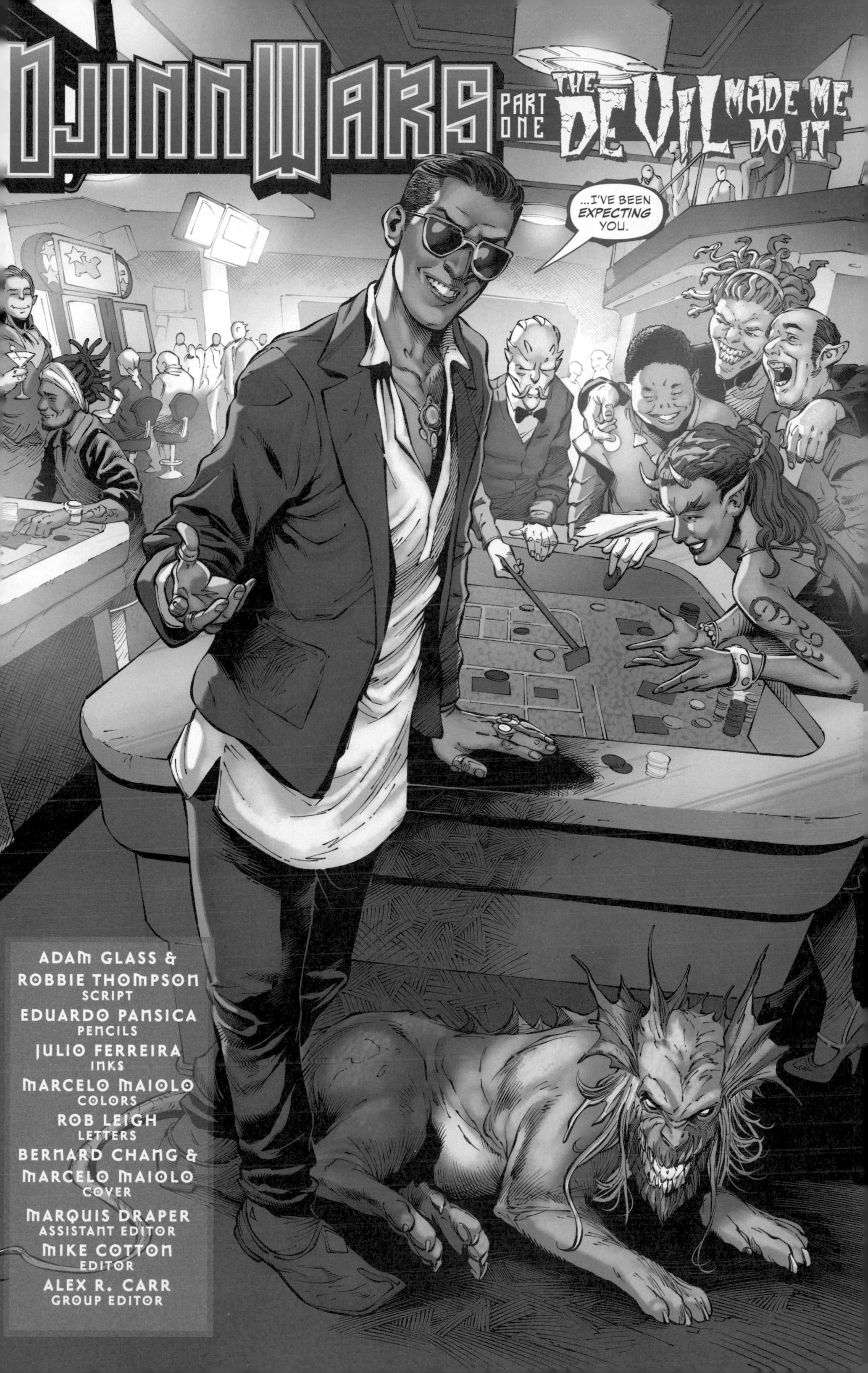
DJINN WARS
PART ONE
THE DEVIL MADE ME DO IT
...I'VE BEEN EXPECTING YOU.
ADAM GLASS & ROBBIE THOMPSON
SCRIPT
EDUARDO PANSICA
PENCILS
JULIO FERREIRA
INKS
MARCELO MAIOLO
COLORS
ROB LEIGH
LETTERS
BERNARD CHANG & MARCELO MAIOLO
COVER
MARQUIS DRAPER
ASSISTANT EDITOR
MIKE COTTON
EDITOR
ALEX R. CARR
GROUP EDITOR

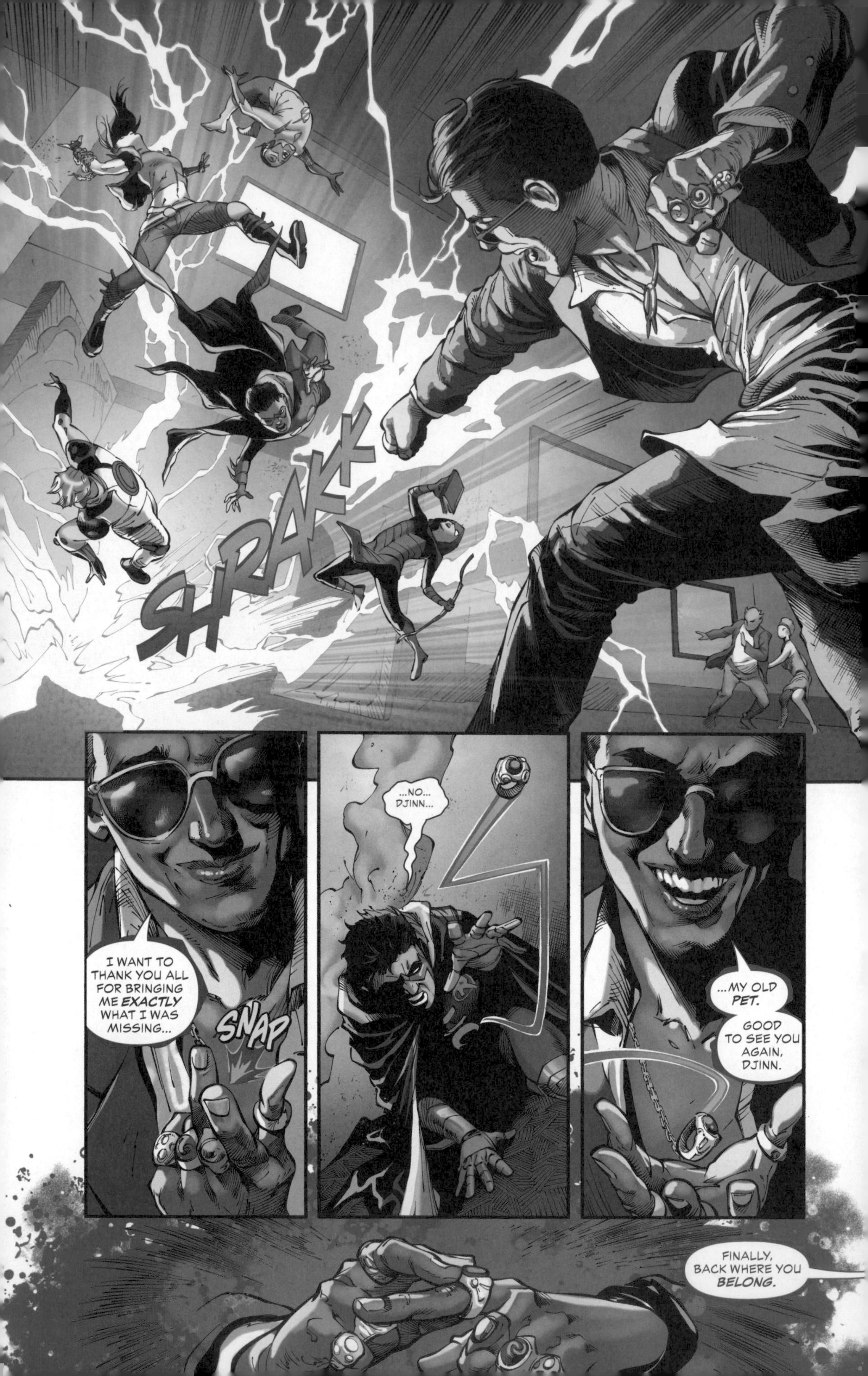
SHRAKK
I WANT TO THANK YOU ALL FOR BRINGING ME EXACTLY WHAT I WAS MISSING...
SNAP
...NO... DJINN...
...MY OLD PET.
GOOD TO SEE YOU AGAIN, DJINN.
FINALLY, BACK WHERE YOU BELONG.

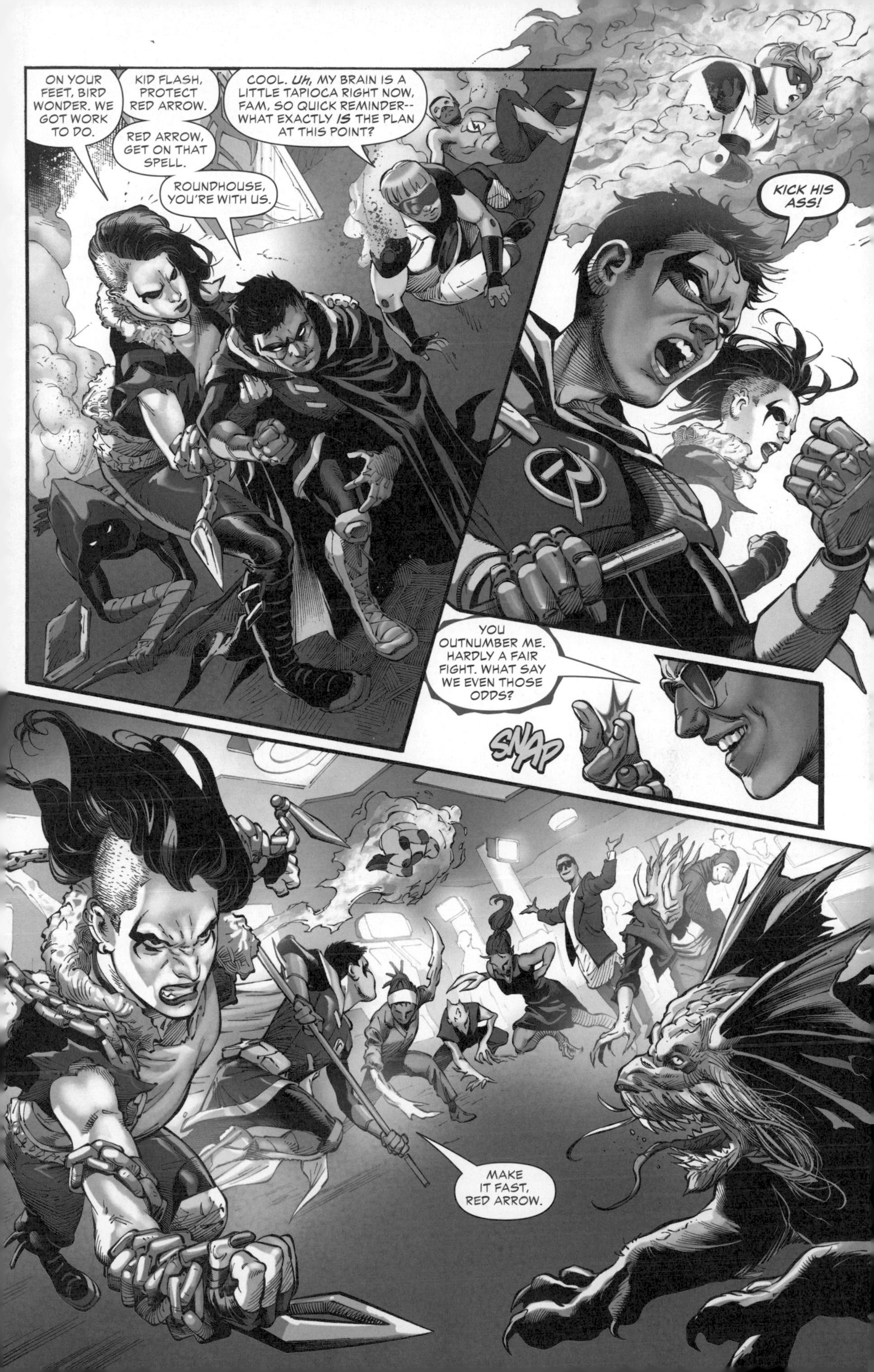
ON YOUR FEET, BIRD WONDER. WE GOT WORK TO DO.
KID FLASH, PROTECT RED ARROW.
RED ARROW, GET ON THAT SPELL.
ROUNDHOUSE, YOU'RE WITH US.
COOL. *UH*, MY BRAIN IS A LITTLE TAPIOCA RIGHT NOW, FAM, SO QUICK REMINDER-- WHAT EXACTLY *IS* THE PLAN AT THIS POINT?
KICK HIS ASS!
YOU OUTNUMBER ME. HARDLY A FAIR FIGHT. WHAT SAY WE EVEN THOSE ODDS?
SNAP
MAKE IT FAST, RED ARROW.

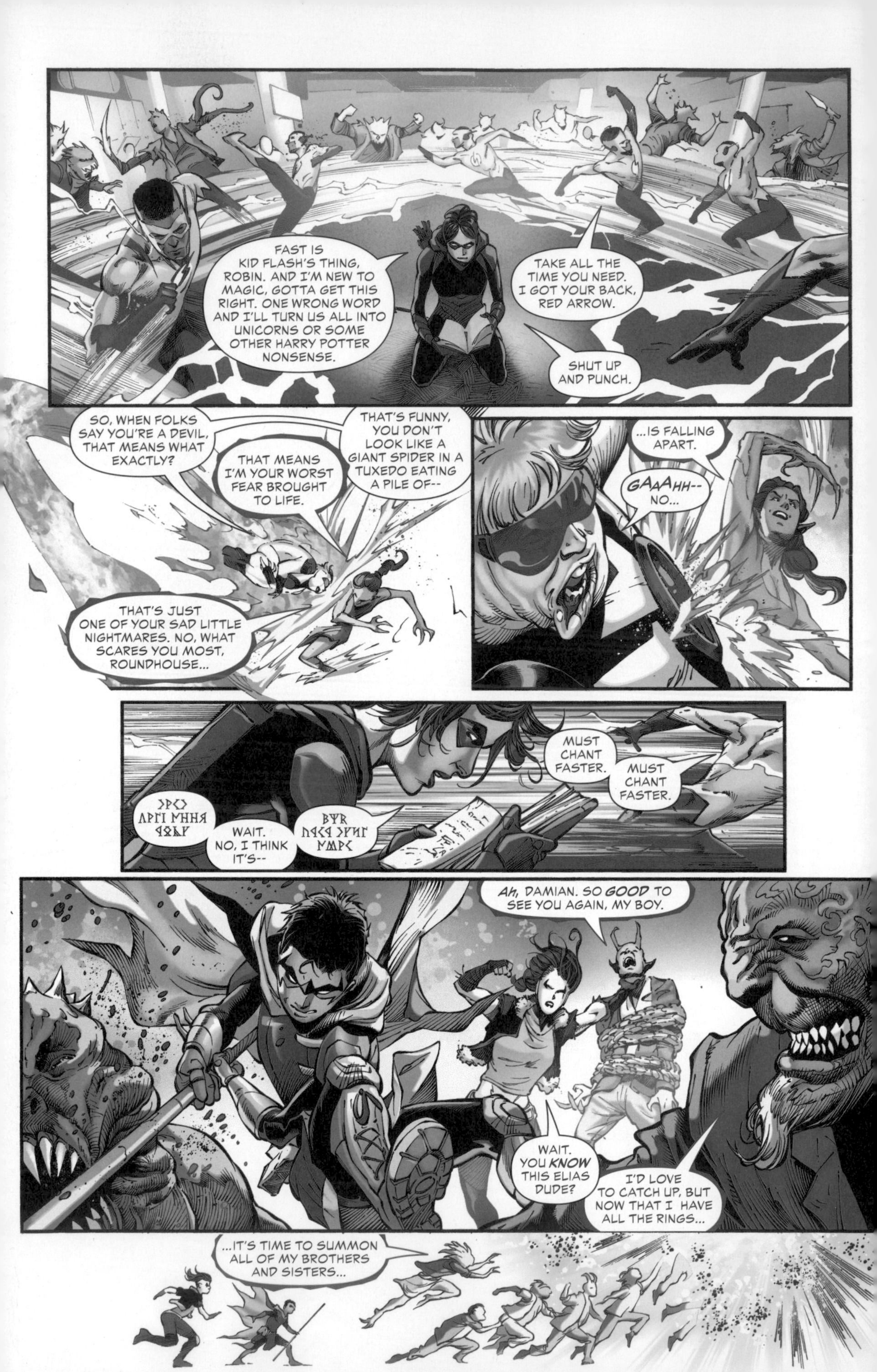
FAST IS KID FLASH'S THING, ROBIN. AND I'M NEW TO MAGIC, GOTTA GET THIS RIGHT. ONE WRONG WORD AND I'LL TURN US ALL INTO UNICORNS OR SOME OTHER HARRY POTTER NONSENSE.
TAKE ALL THE TIME YOU NEED. I GOT YOUR BACK, RED ARROW.
SHUT UP AND PUNCH.
SO, WHEN FOLKS SAY YOU'RE A DEVIL, THAT MEANS WHAT EXACTLY?
THAT MEANS I'M YOUR WORST FEAR BROUGHT TO LIFE.
THAT'S FUNNY, YOU DON'T LOOK LIKE A GIANT SPIDER IN A TUXEDO EATING A PILE OF--
THAT'S JUST ONE OF YOUR SAD LITTLE NIGHTMARES. NO, WHAT SCARES YOU MOST, ROUNDHOUSE...
...IS FALLING APART.
GAAAHH-- NO...
MUST CHANT FASTER.
MUST CHANT FASTER.
WAIT. NO, I THINK IT'S--
Ah, DAMIAN. SO GOOD TO SEE YOU AGAIN, MY BOY.
WAIT. YOU KNOW THIS ELIAS DUDE?
I'D LOVE TO CATCH UP, BUT NOW THAT I HAVE ALL THE RINGS...
...IT'S TIME TO SUMMON ALL OF MY BROTHERS AND SISTERS...

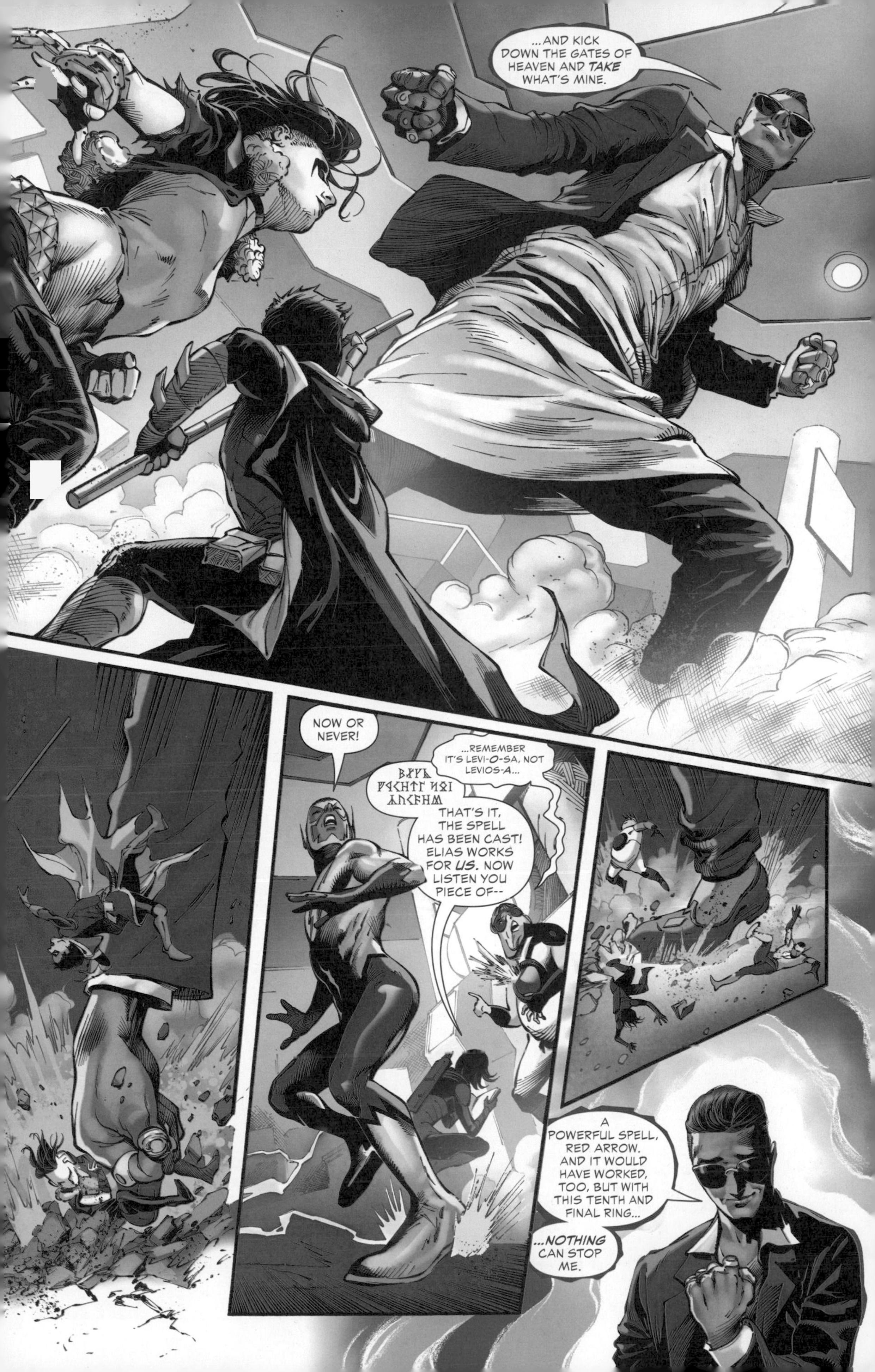
...AND KICK DOWN THE GATES OF HEAVEN AND *TAKE* WHAT'S MINE.
NOW OR NEVER!
...REMEMBER IT'S LEVI-*O*-SA, NOT LEVIOS-*A*...
THAT'S IT, THE SPELL HAS BEEN CAST! ELIAS WORKS FOR *US*. NOW LISTEN YOU PIECE OF--
A POWERFUL SPELL, RED ARROW. AND IT WOULD HAVE WORKED, TOO, BUT WITH THIS TENTH AND FINAL RING...
...NOTHING CAN STOP ME.

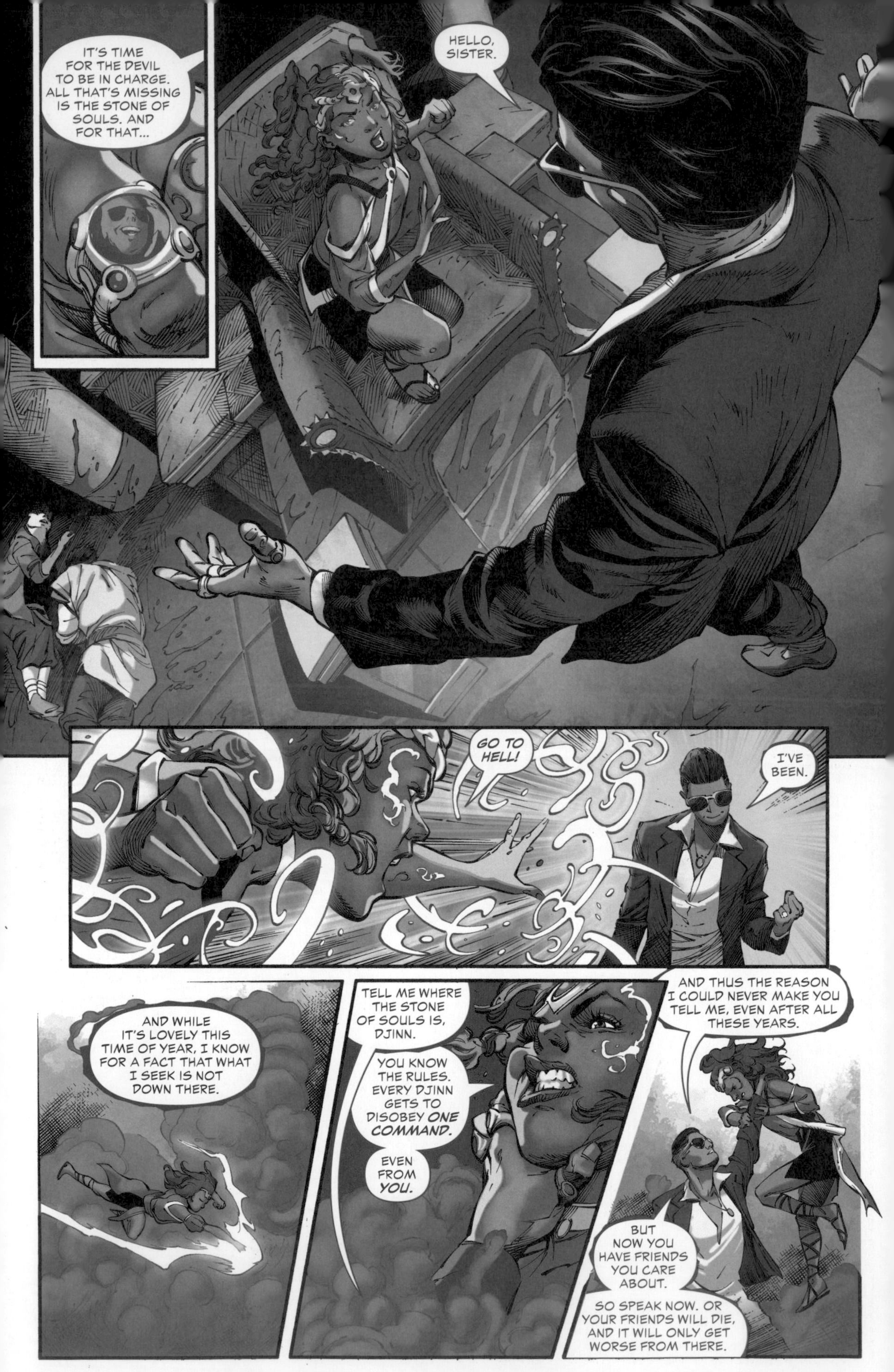
IT'S TIME FOR THE DEVIL TO BE IN CHARGE. ALL THAT'S MISSING IS THE STONE OF SOULS. AND FOR THAT...
HELLO, SISTER.
GO TO HELL!
I'VE BEEN.
AND WHILE IT'S LOVELY THIS TIME OF YEAR, I KNOW FOR A FACT THAT WHAT I SEEK IS NOT DOWN THERE.
TELL ME WHERE THE STONE OF SOULS IS, DJINN.
YOU KNOW THE RULES. EVERY DJINN GETS TO DISOBEY ONE COMMAND.
EVEN FROM YOU.
AND THUS THE REASON I COULD NEVER MAKE YOU TELL ME, EVEN AFTER ALL THESE YEARS.
BUT NOW YOU HAVE FRIENDS YOU CARE ABOUT.
SO SPEAK NOW. OR YOUR FRIENDS WILL DIE, AND IT WILL ONLY GET WORSE FROM THERE.

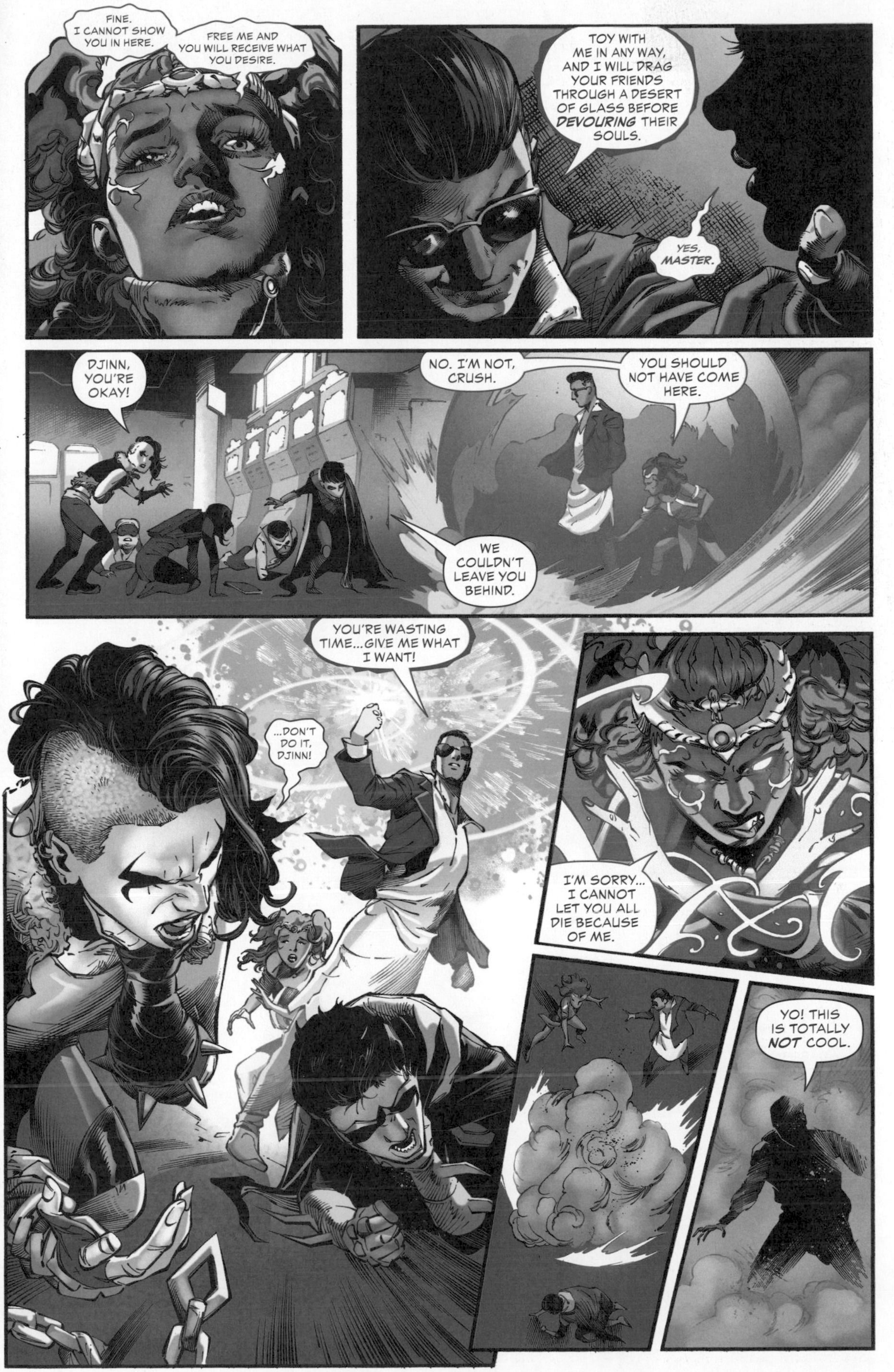
FINE. I CANNOT SHOW YOU IN HERE.
FREE ME AND YOU WILL RECEIVE WHAT YOU DESIRE.
TOY WITH ME IN ANY WAY, AND I WILL DRAG YOUR FRIENDS THROUGH A DESERT OF GLASS BEFORE DEVOURING THEIR SOULS.
YES, MASTER.
DJINN, YOU'RE OKAY!
NO. I'M NOT, CRUSH.
YOU SHOULD NOT HAVE COME HERE.
WE COULDN'T LEAVE YOU BEHIND.
YOU'RE WASTING TIME...GIVE ME WHAT I WANT!
...DON'T DO IT, DJINN!
I'M SORRY... I CANNOT LET YOU ALL DIE BECAUSE OF ME.
YO! THIS IS TOTALLY NOT COOL.

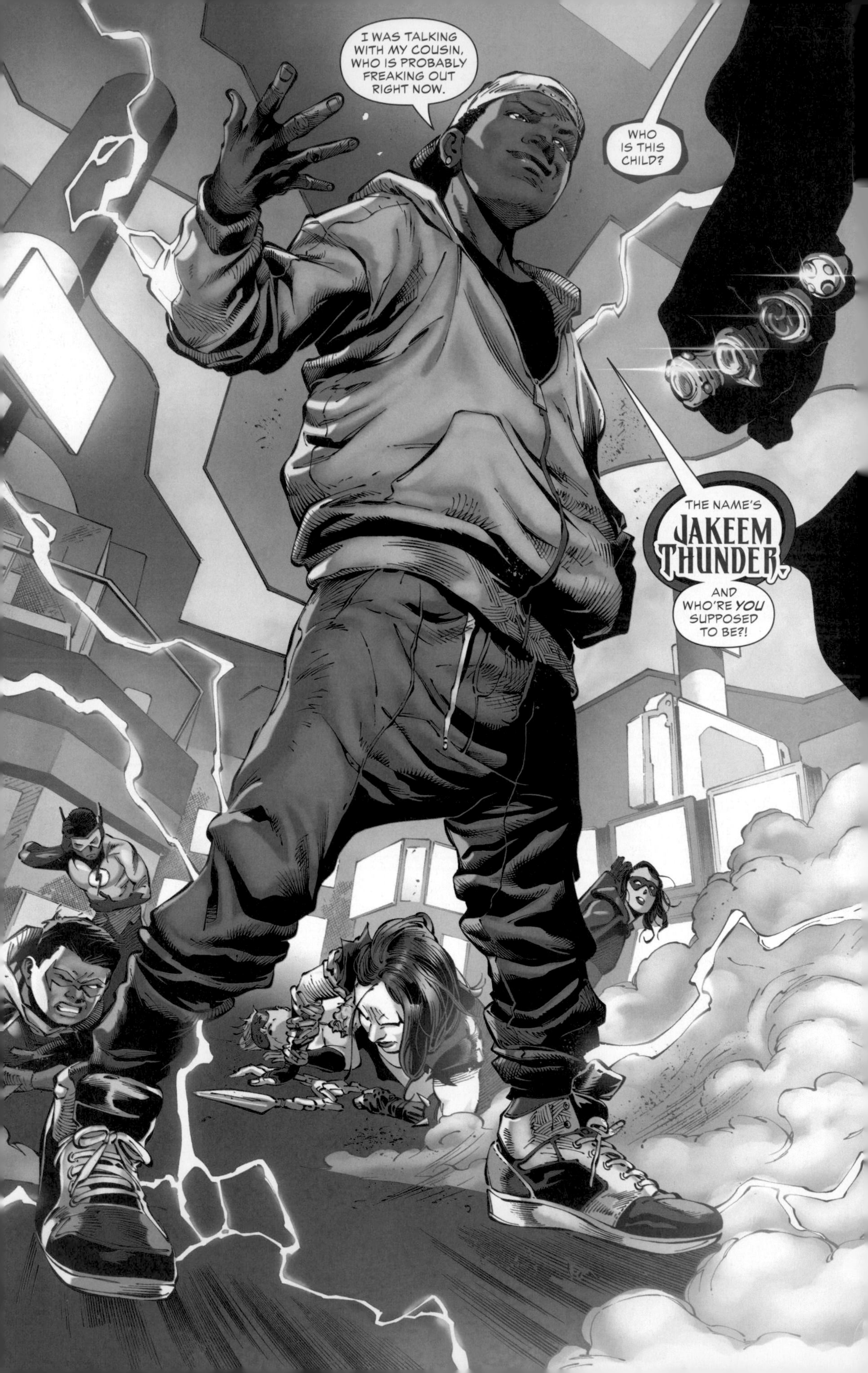
I WAS TALKING WITH MY COUSIN, WHO IS PROBABLY FREAKING OUT RIGHT NOW.
WHO IS THIS CHILD?
THE NAME'S JAKEEM THUNDER.
AND WHO'RE YOU SUPPOSED TO BE?!

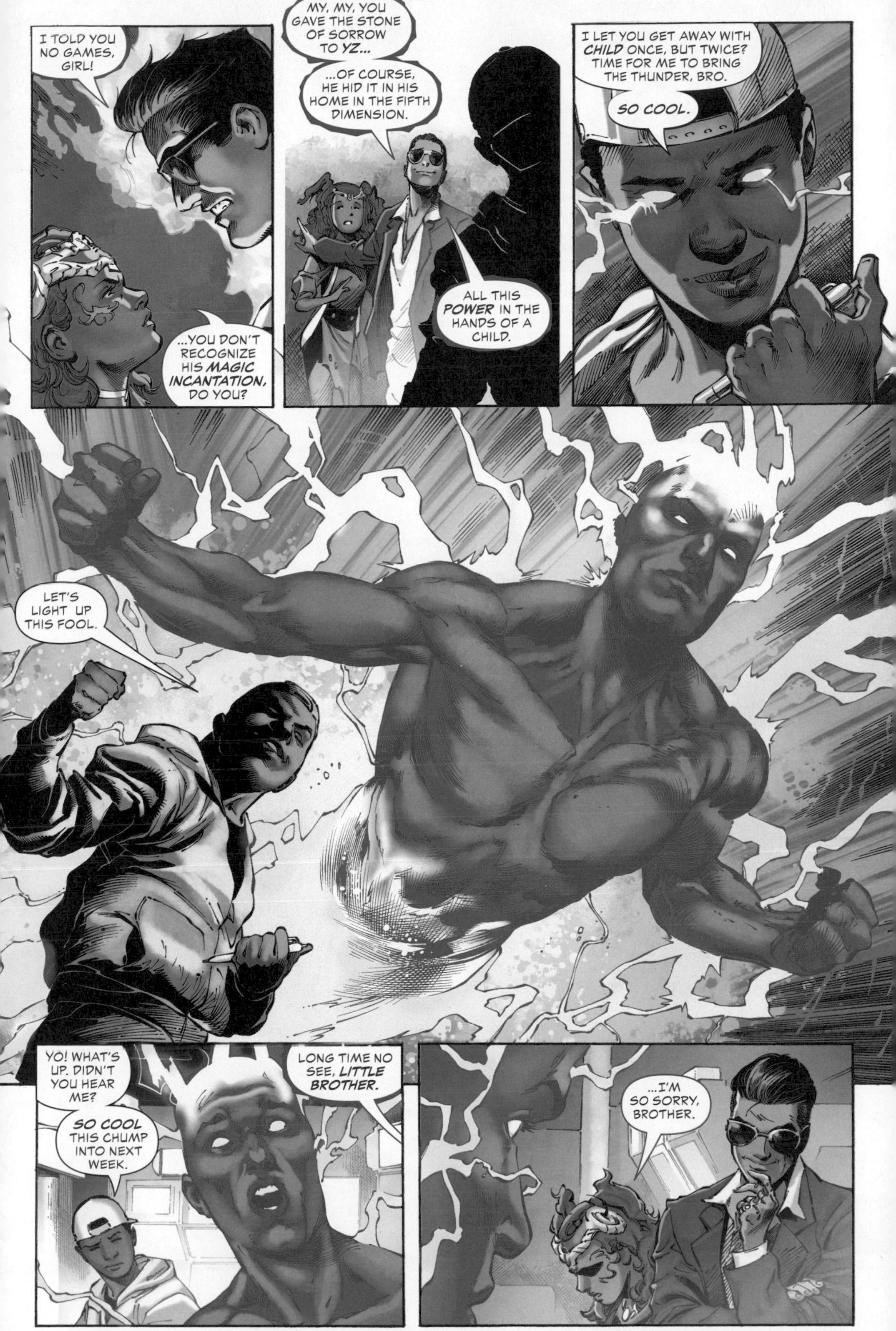

I TOLD YOU NO GAMES, GIRL!
...YOU DON'T RECOGNIZE HIS MAGIC INCANTATION, DO YOU?
MY, MY, YOU GAVE THE STONE OF SORROW TO YZ...
...OF COURSE, HE HID IT IN HIS HOME IN THE FIFTH DIMENSION.
ALL THIS POWER IN THE HANDS OF A CHILD.
I LET YOU GET AWAY WITH CHILD ONCE, BUT TWICE? TIME FOR ME TO BRING THE THUNDER, BRO.
SO COOL.
LET'S LIGHT UP THIS FOOL.
YO! WHAT'S UP. DIDN'T YOU HEAR ME?
SO COOL THIS CHUMP INTO NEXT WEEK.
LONG TIME NO SEE, LITTLE BROTHER.
...I'M SO SORRY, BROTHER.

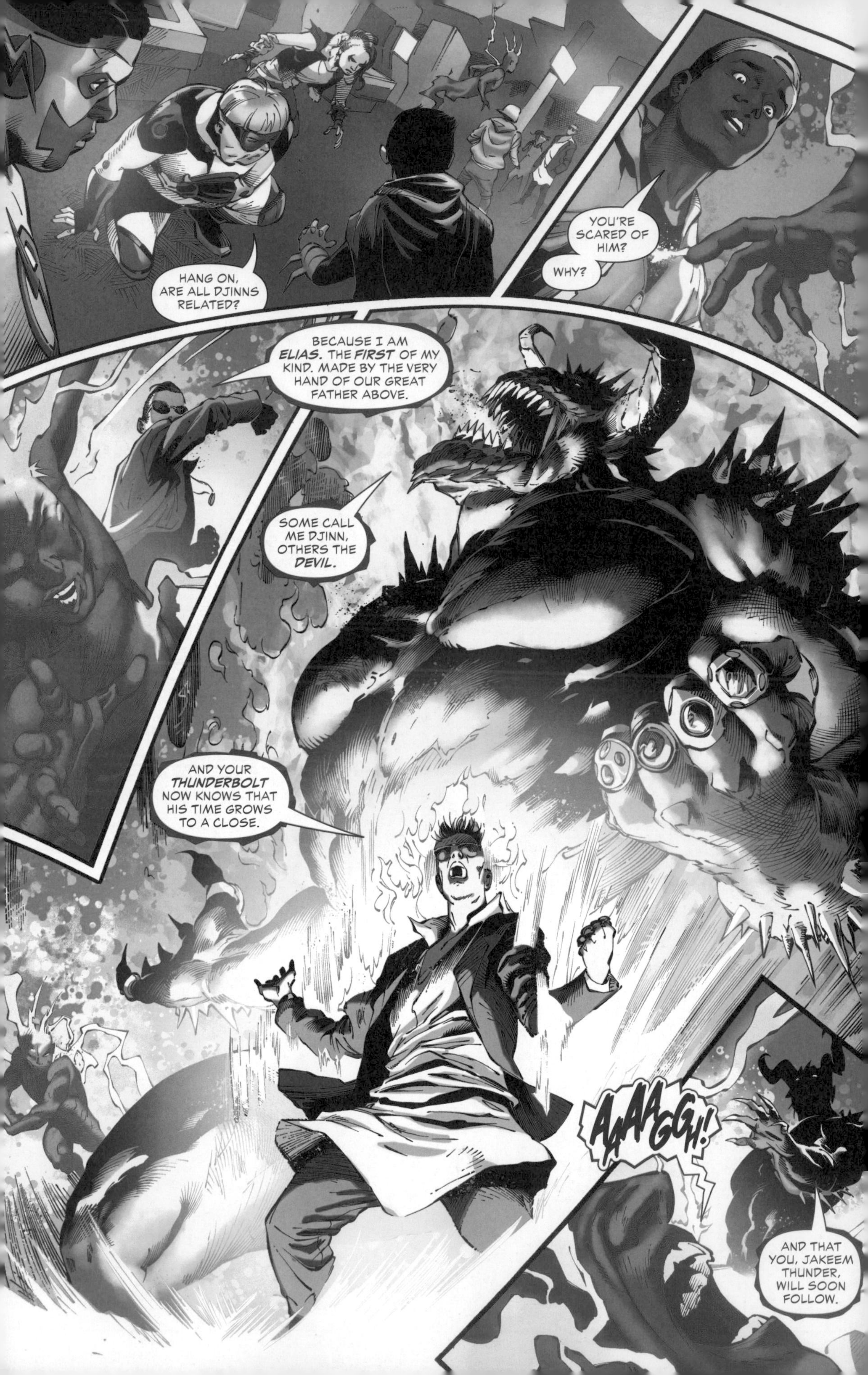
HANG ON, ARE ALL DJINNS RELATED?
YOU'RE SCARED OF HIM?
WHY?
BECAUSE I AM ELIAS. THE FIRST OF MY KIND. MADE BY THE VERY HAND OF OUR GREAT FATHER ABOVE.
SOME CALL ME DJINN, OTHERS THE DEVIL.
AND YOUR THUNDERBOLT NOW KNOWS THAT HIS TIME GROWS TO A CLOSE.
AAAAGGH!
AND THAT YOU, JAKEEM THUNDER, WILL SOON FOLLOW.

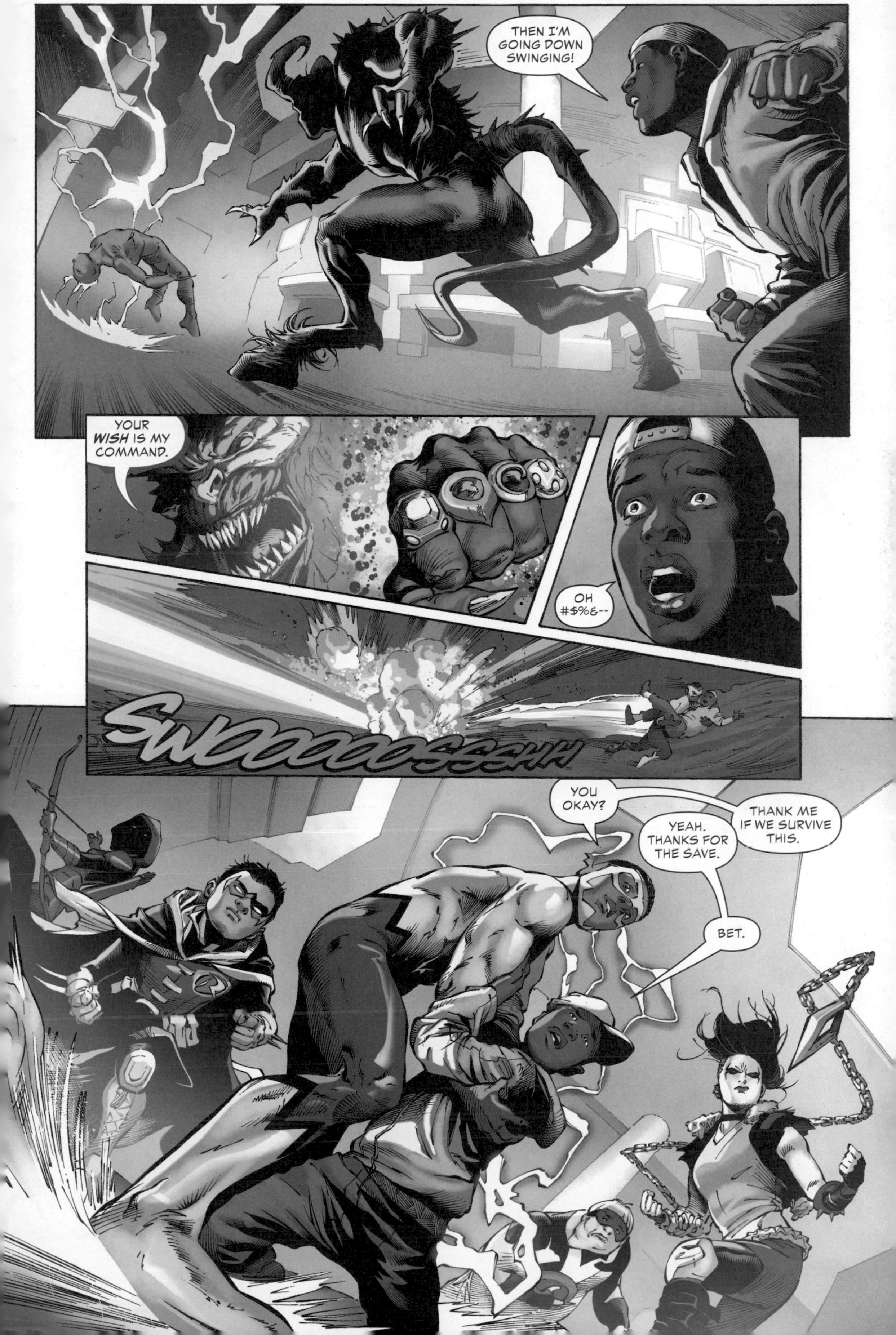
THEN I'M GOING DOWN SWINGING!
YOUR *WISH* IS MY COMMAND.
OH #$%&--
SWOOOOOSSSHH
YOU OKAY?
YEAH. THANKS FOR THE SAVE.
THANK ME IF WE SURVIVE THIS.
BET.

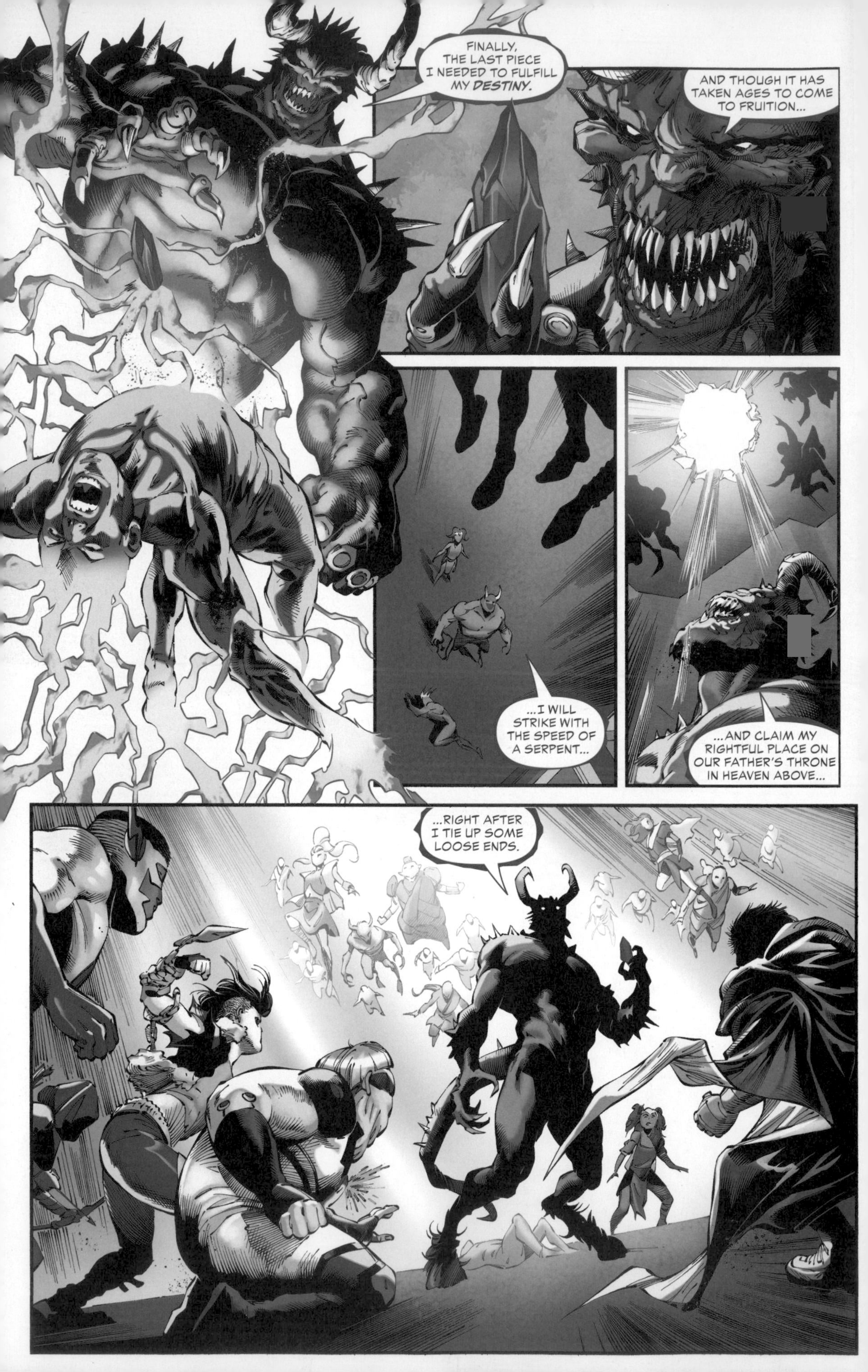
FINALLY, THE LAST PIECE I NEEDED TO FULFILL MY *DESTINY*.
AND THOUGH IT HAS TAKEN AGES TO COME TO FRUITION...
...I WILL STRIKE WITH THE SPEED OF A SERPENT...
...AND CLAIM MY RIGHTFUL PLACE ON OUR FATHER'S THRONE IN HEAVEN ABOVE...
...RIGHT AFTER I TIE UP SOME LOOSE ENDS.

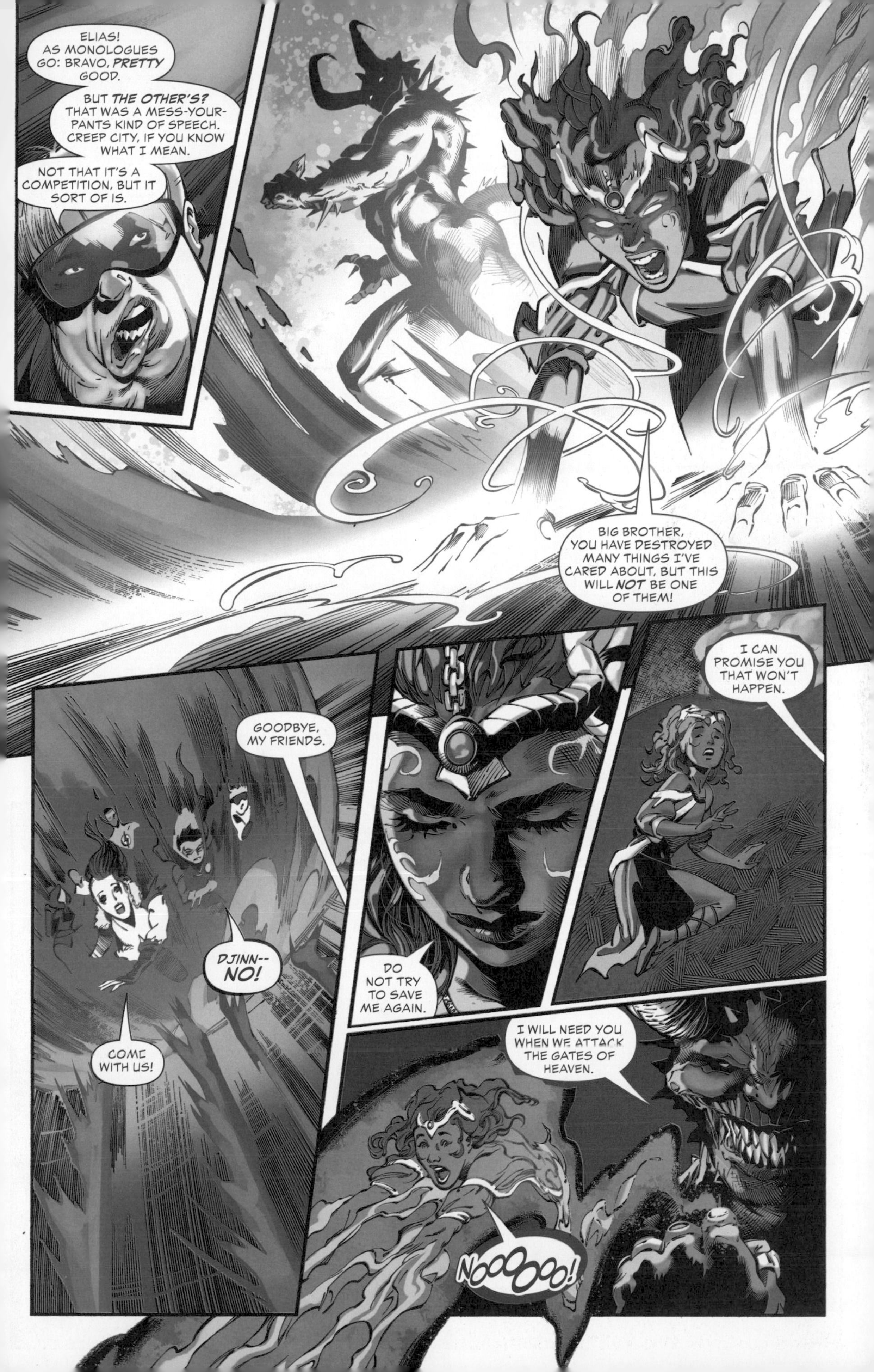
ELIAS! AS MONOLOGUES GO: BRAVO, PRETTY GOOD.
BUT THE OTHER'S? THAT WAS A MESS-YOUR-PANTS KIND OF SPEECH. CREEP CITY, IF YOU KNOW WHAT I MEAN.
NOT THAT IT'S A COMPETITION, BUT IT SORT OF IS.
BIG BROTHER, YOU HAVE DESTROYED MANY THINGS I'VE CARED ABOUT, BUT THIS WILL NOT BE ONE OF THEM!
GOODBYE, MY FRIENDS.
DJINN-- NO!
COME WITH US!
DO NOT TRY TO SAVE ME AGAIN.
I CAN PROMISE YOU THAT WON'T HAPPEN.
I WILL NEED YOU WHEN WE ATTACK THE GATES OF HEAVEN.
NOOOOOO!

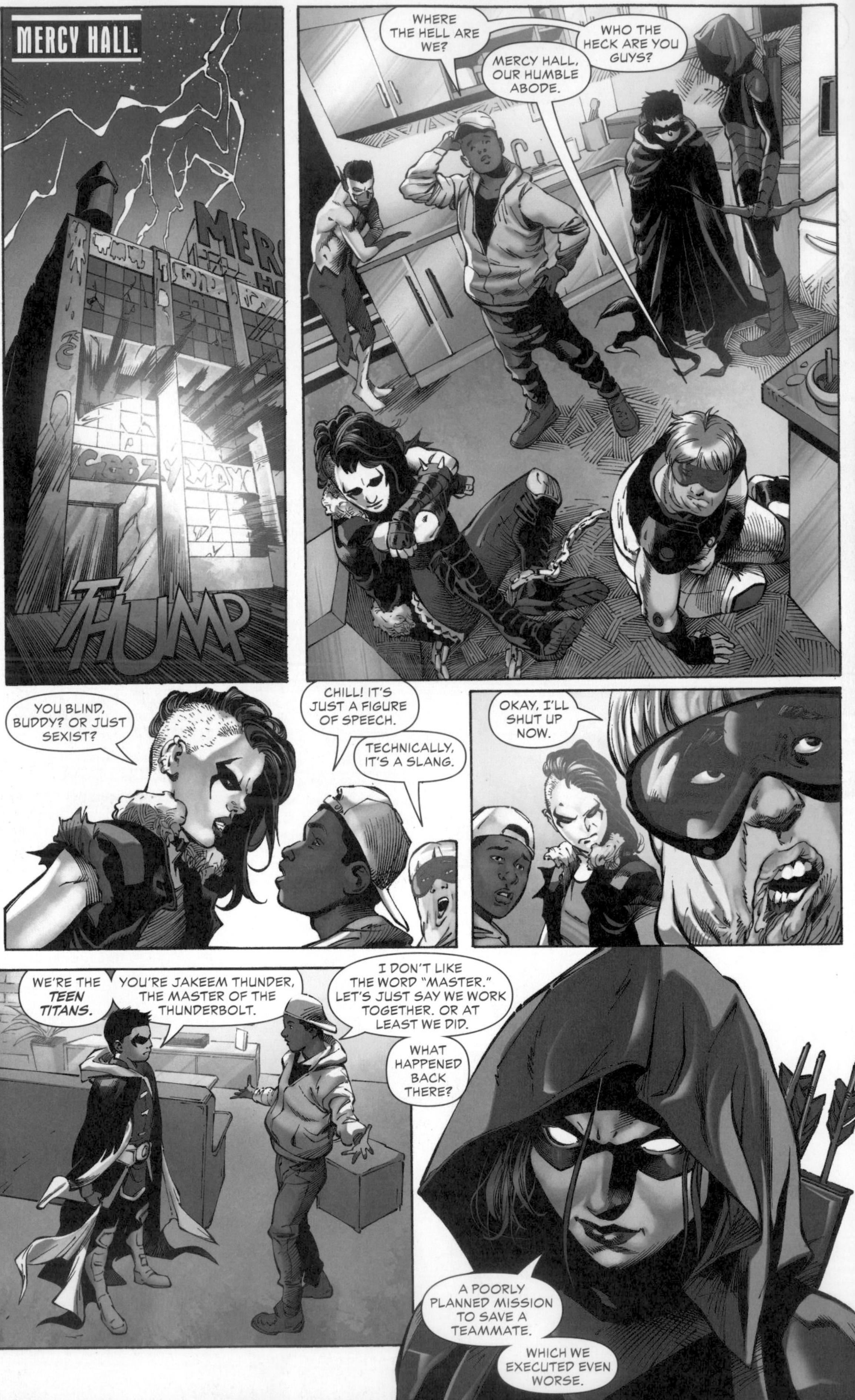
MERCY HALL.
THUMP
WHERE THE HELL ARE WE?
WHO THE HECK ARE YOU GUYS?
MERCY HALL, OUR HUMBLE ABODE.
YOU BLIND, BUDDY? OR JUST SEXIST?
CHILL! IT'S JUST A FIGURE OF SPEECH.
TECHNICALLY, IT'S A SLANG.
OKAY, I'LL SHUT UP NOW.
WE'RE THE *TEEN TITANS.*
YOU'RE JAKEEM THUNDER, THE MASTER OF THE THUNDERBOLT.
I DON'T LIKE THE WORD "MASTER." LET'S JUST SAY WE WORK TOGETHER. OR AT LEAST WE DID.
WHAT HAPPENED BACK THERE?
A POORLY PLANNED MISSION TO SAVE A TEAMMATE.
WHICH WE EXECUTED EVEN WORSE.

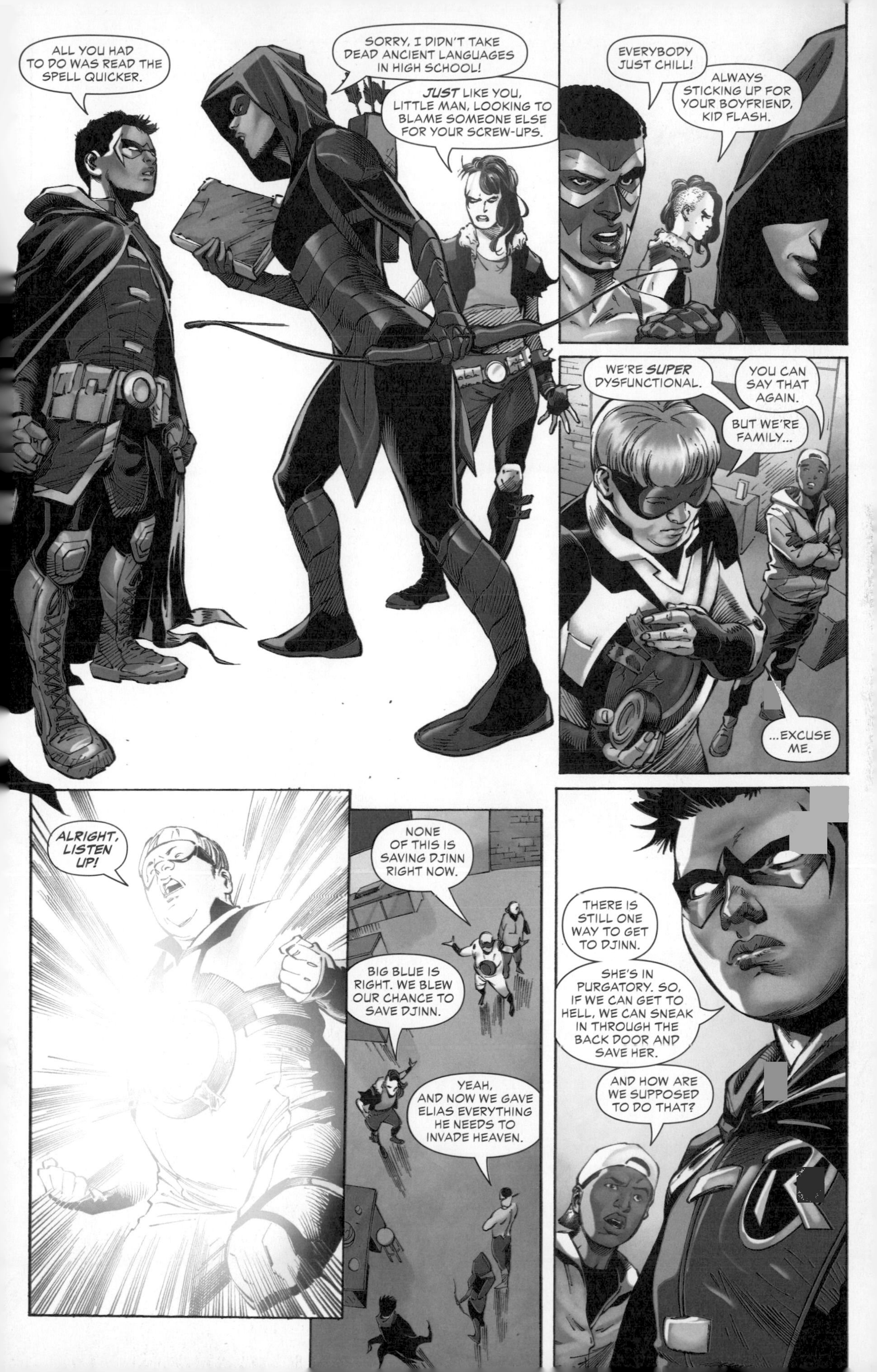
ALL YOU HAD TO DO WAS READ THE SPELL QUICKER.
SORRY, I DIDN'T TAKE DEAD ANCIENT LANGUAGES IN HIGH SCHOOL!
JUST LIKE YOU, LITTLE MAN, LOOKING TO BLAME SOMEONE ELSE FOR YOUR SCREW-UPS.
EVERYBODY JUST CHILL!
ALWAYS STICKING UP FOR YOUR BOYFRIEND, KID FLASH.
WE'RE SUPER DYSFUNCTIONAL.
YOU CAN SAY THAT AGAIN.
BUT WE'RE FAMILY...
...EXCUSE ME.
ALRIGHT, LISTEN UP!
NONE OF THIS IS SAVING DJINN RIGHT NOW.
BIG BLUE IS RIGHT. WE BLEW OUR CHANCE TO SAVE DJINN.
YEAH, AND NOW WE GAVE ELIAS EVERYTHING HE NEEDS TO INVADE HEAVEN.
THERE IS STILL ONE WAY TO GET TO DJINN.
SHE'S IN PURGATORY. SO, IF WE CAN GET TO HELL, WE CAN SNEAK IN THROUGH THE BACK DOOR AND SAVE HER.
AND HOW ARE WE SUPPOSED TO DO THAT?

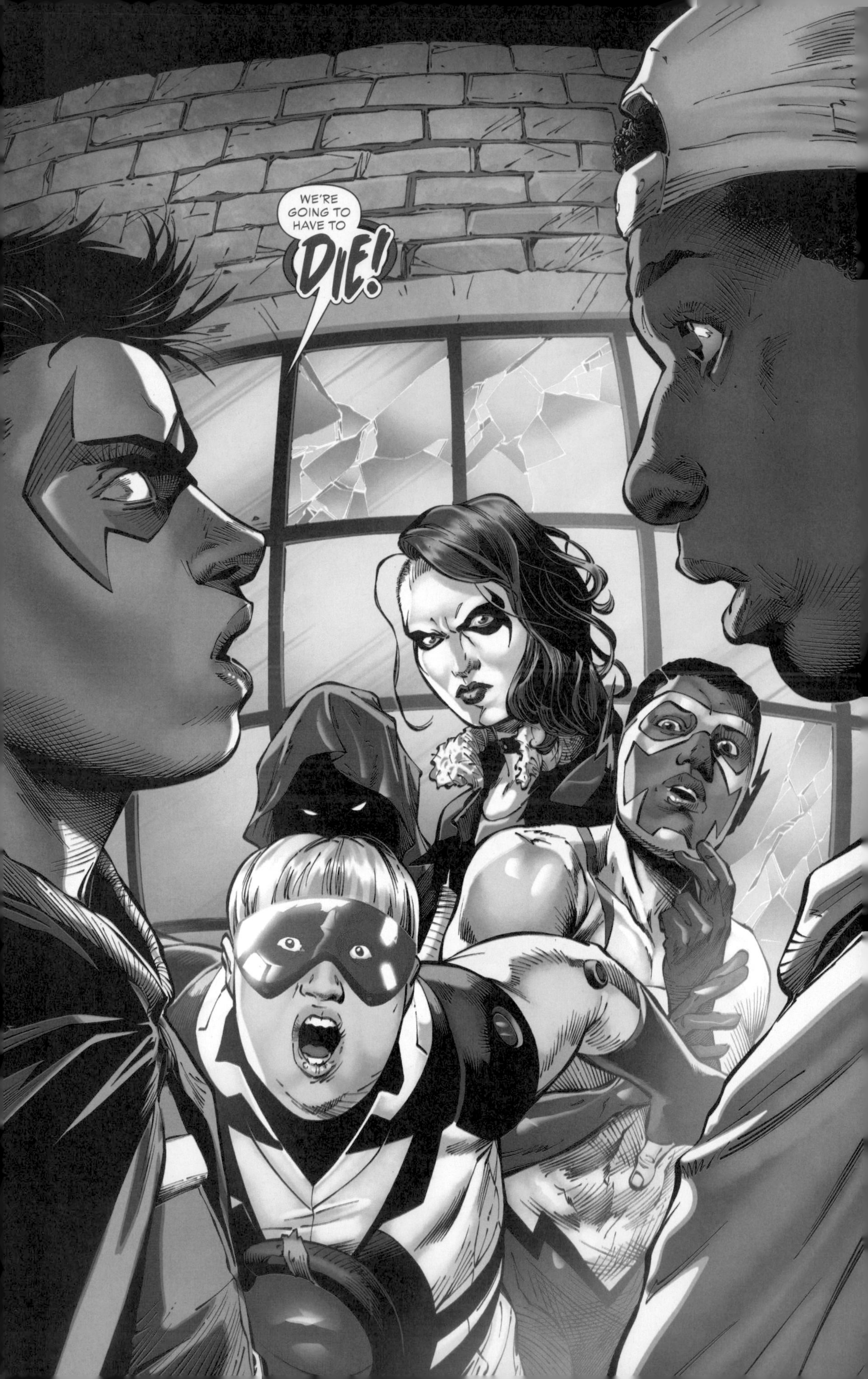
WE'RE GOING TO HAVE TO DIE!

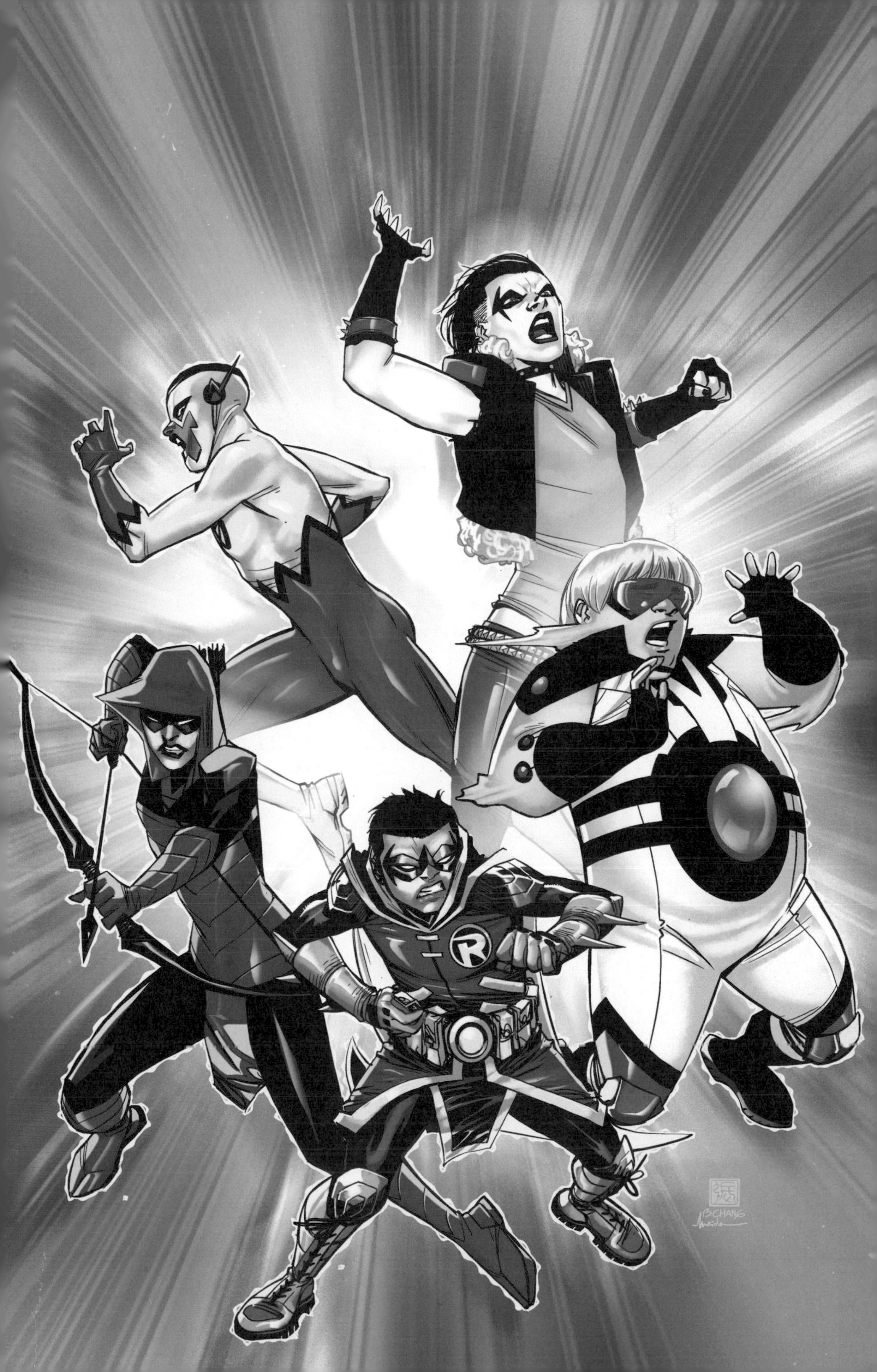
B.CHANG

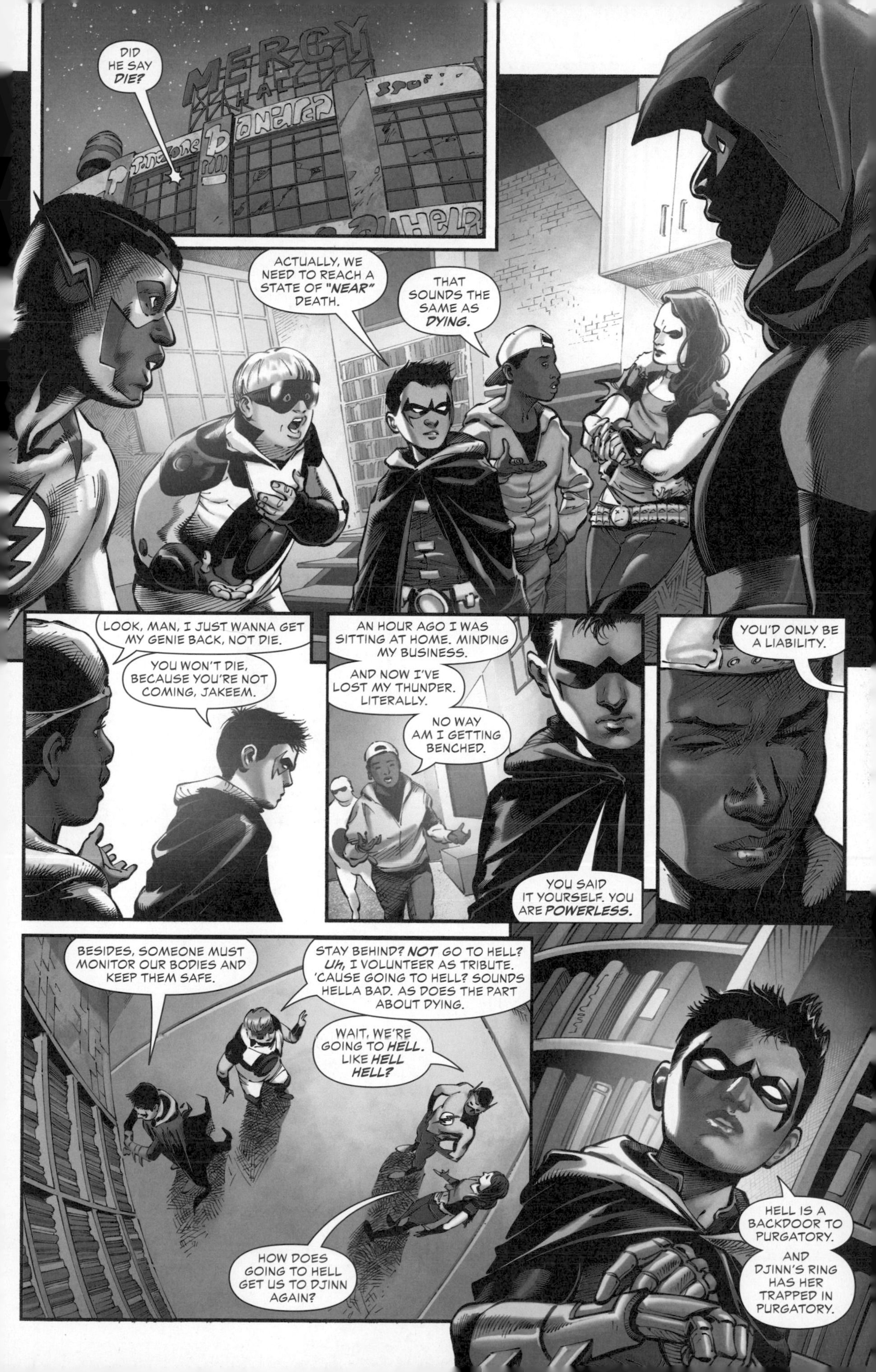

DID HE SAY *DIE?*
MERCY HALL
ACTUALLY, WE NEED TO REACH A STATE OF *"NEAR"* DEATH.
THAT SOUNDS THE SAME AS *DYING.*
LOOK, MAN, I JUST WANNA GET MY GENIE BACK, NOT DIE.
YOU WON'T DIE, BECAUSE YOU'RE NOT COMING, JAKEEM.
AN HOUR AGO I WAS SITTING AT HOME. MINDING MY BUSINESS.
AND NOW I'VE LOST MY THUNDER. LITERALLY.
NO WAY AM I GETTING BENCHED.
YOU SAID IT YOURSELF. YOU ARE *POWERLESS.*
YOU'D ONLY BE A LIABILITY.
BESIDES, SOMEONE MUST MONITOR OUR BODIES AND KEEP THEM SAFE.
STAY BEHIND? *NOT* GO TO HELL? *Uh,* I VOLUNTEER AS TRIBUTE. 'CAUSE GOING TO HELL? SOUNDS HELLA BAD. AS DOES THE PART ABOUT DYING.
WAIT, WE'RE GOING TO *HELL.* LIKE *HELL HELL?*
HOW DOES GOING TO HELL GET US TO DJINN AGAIN?
HELL IS A BACKDOOR TO PURGATORY.
AND DJINN'S RING HAS HER TRAPPED IN PURGATORY.

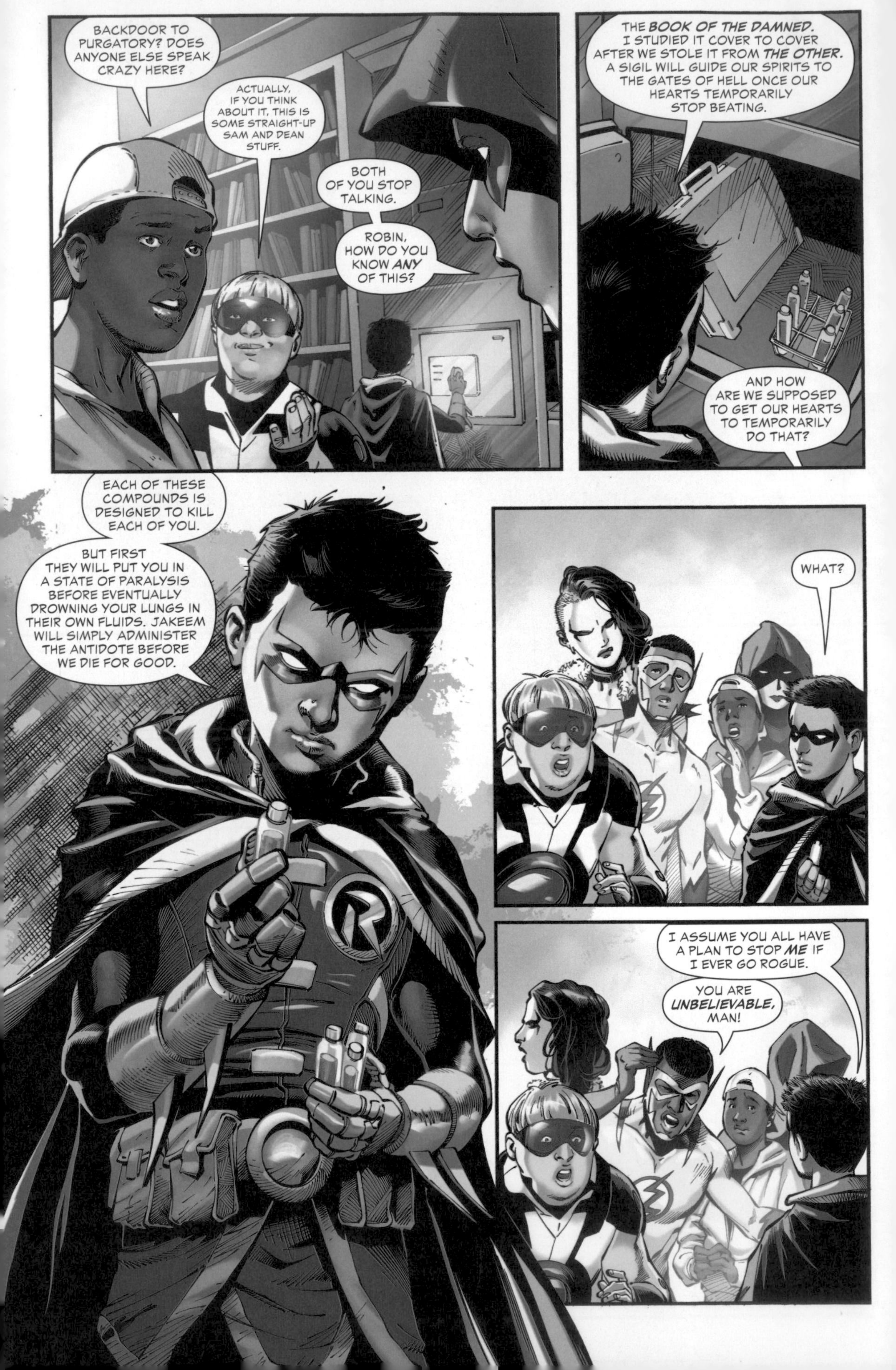
BACKDOOR TO PURGATORY? DOES ANYONE ELSE SPEAK CRAZY HERE?
ACTUALLY, IF YOU THINK ABOUT IT, THIS IS SOME STRAIGHT-UP SAM AND DEAN STUFF.
BOTH OF YOU STOP TALKING.
ROBIN, HOW DO YOU KNOW ANY OF THIS?
THE BOOK OF THE DAMNED. I STUDIED IT COVER TO COVER AFTER WE STOLE IT FROM THE OTHER. A SIGIL WILL GUIDE OUR SPIRITS TO THE GATES OF HELL ONCE OUR HEARTS TEMPORARILY STOP BEATING.
AND HOW ARE WE SUPPOSED TO GET OUR HEARTS TO TEMPORARILY DO THAT?
EACH OF THESE COMPOUNDS IS DESIGNED TO KILL EACH OF YOU.
BUT FIRST THEY WILL PUT YOU IN A STATE OF PARALYSIS BEFORE EVENTUALLY DROWNING YOUR LUNGS IN THEIR OWN FLUIDS. JAKEEM WILL SIMPLY ADMINISTER THE ANTIDOTE BEFORE WE DIE FOR GOOD.
WHAT?
I ASSUME YOU ALL HAVE A PLAN TO STOP ME IF I EVER GO ROGUE.
YOU ARE UNBELIEVABLE, MAN!

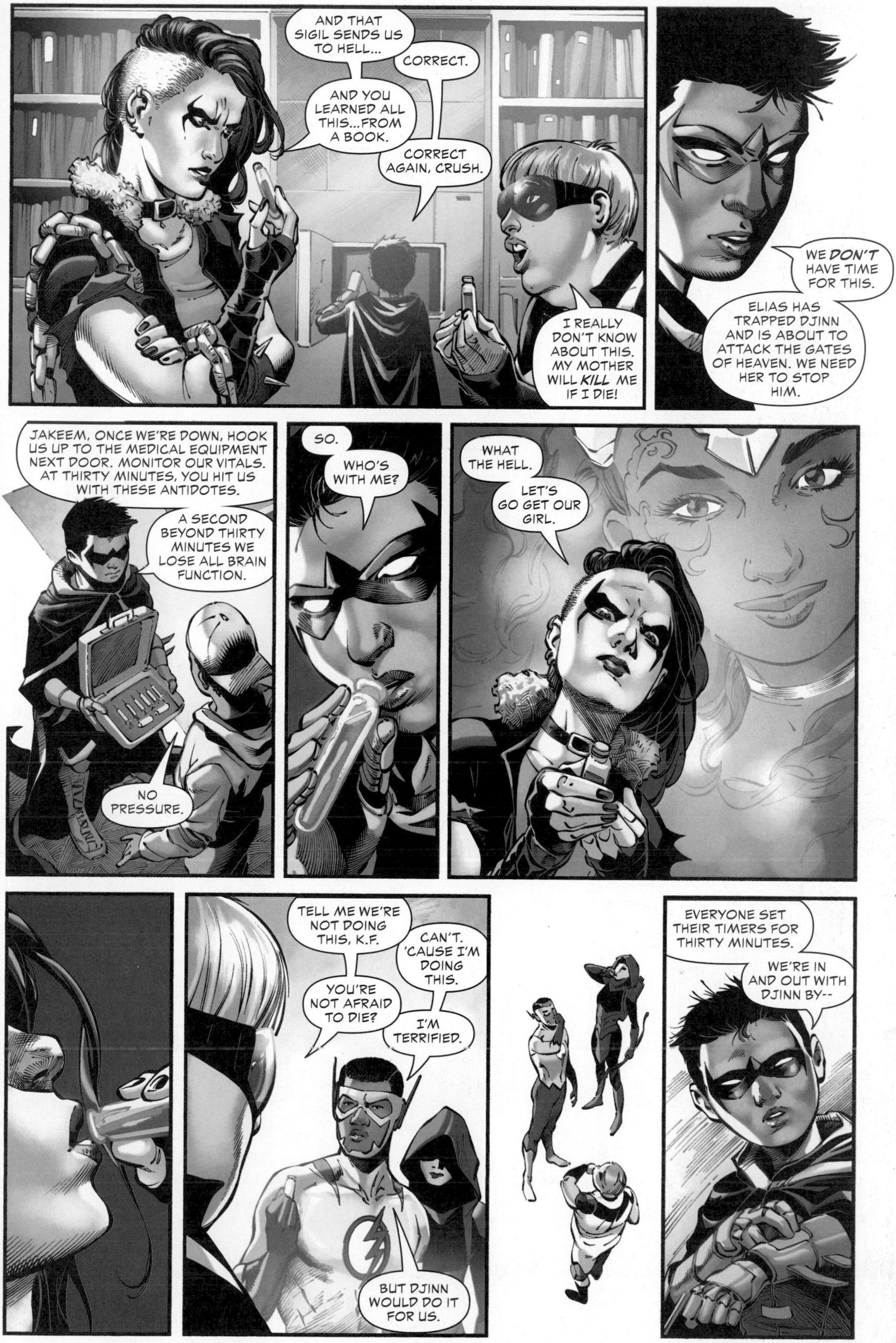
AND THAT SIGIL SENDS US TO HELL...
CORRECT.
AND YOU LEARNED ALL THIS...FROM A BOOK.
CORRECT AGAIN, CRUSH.
I REALLY DON'T KNOW ABOUT THIS. MY MOTHER WILL KILL ME IF I DIE!
WE DON'T HAVE TIME FOR THIS.
ELIAS HAS TRAPPED DJINN AND IS ABOUT TO ATTACK THE GATES OF HEAVEN. WE NEED HER TO STOP HIM.
JAKEEM, ONCE WE'RE DOWN, HOOK US UP TO THE MEDICAL EQUIPMENT NEXT DOOR. MONITOR OUR VITALS. AT THIRTY MINUTES, YOU HIT US WITH THESE ANTIDOTES.
A SECOND BEYOND THIRTY MINUTES WE LOSE ALL BRAIN FUNCTION.
NO PRESSURE.
SO.
WHO'S WITH ME?
WHAT THE HELL.
LET'S GO GET OUR GIRL.
TELL ME WE'RE NOT DOING THIS, K.F.
CAN'T. 'CAUSE I'M DOING THIS.
YOU'RE NOT AFRAID TO DIE?
I'M TERRIFIED.
BUT DJINN WOULD DO IT FOR US.
EVERYONE SET THEIR TIMERS FOR THIRTY MINUTES.
WE'RE IN AND OUT WITH DJINN BY--

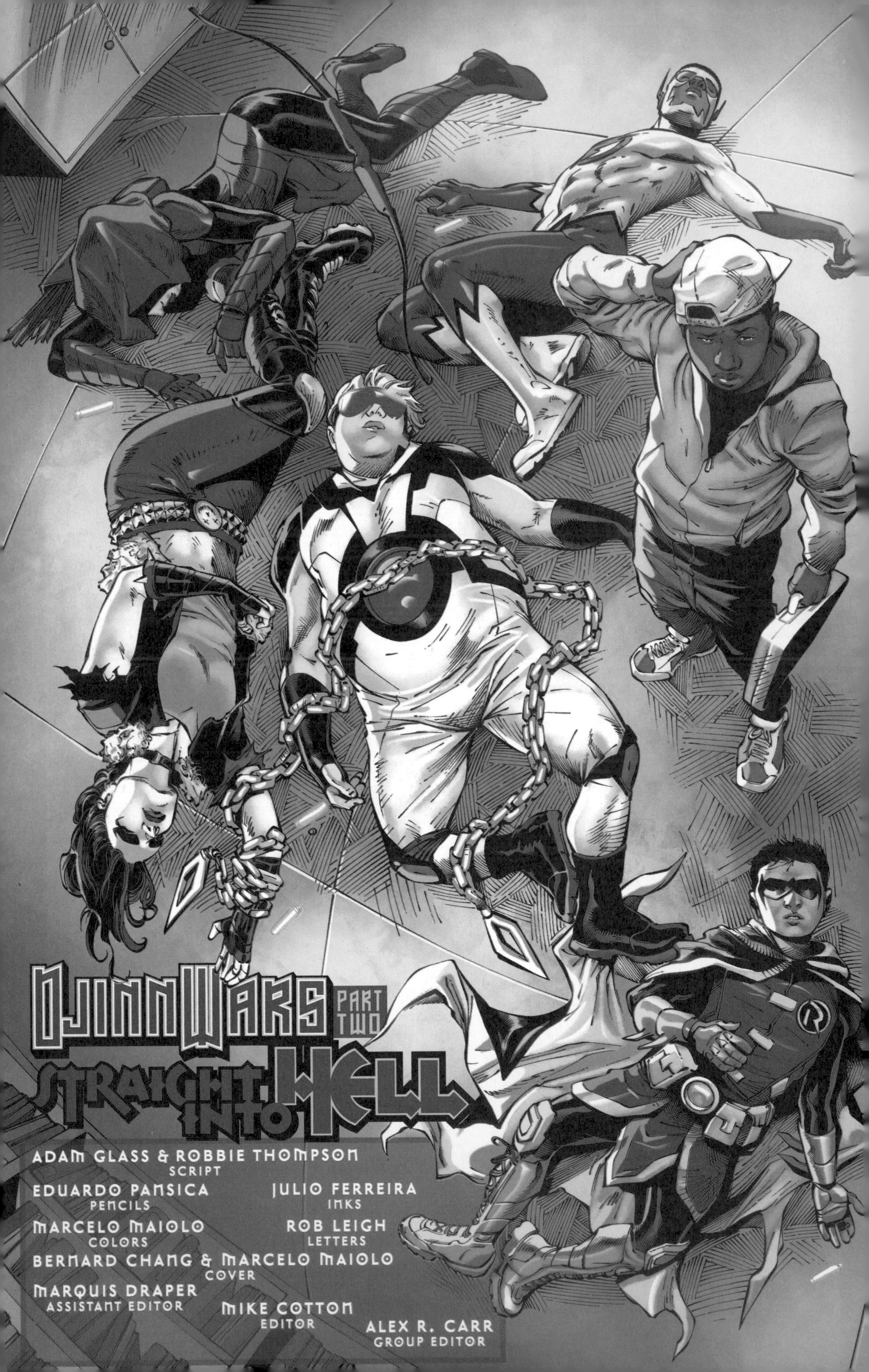
DJINN WARS PART TWO
STRAIGHT INTO HELL
ADAM GLASS & ROBBIE THOMPSON
SCRIPT
EDUARDO PANSICA
PENCILS
JULIO FERREIRA
INKS
MARCELO MAIOLO
COLORS
ROB LEIGH
LETTERS
BERNARD CHANG & MARCELO MAIOLO
COVER
MARQUIS DRAPER
ASSISTANT EDITOR
MIKE COTTON
EDITOR
ALEX R. CARR
GROUP EDITOR

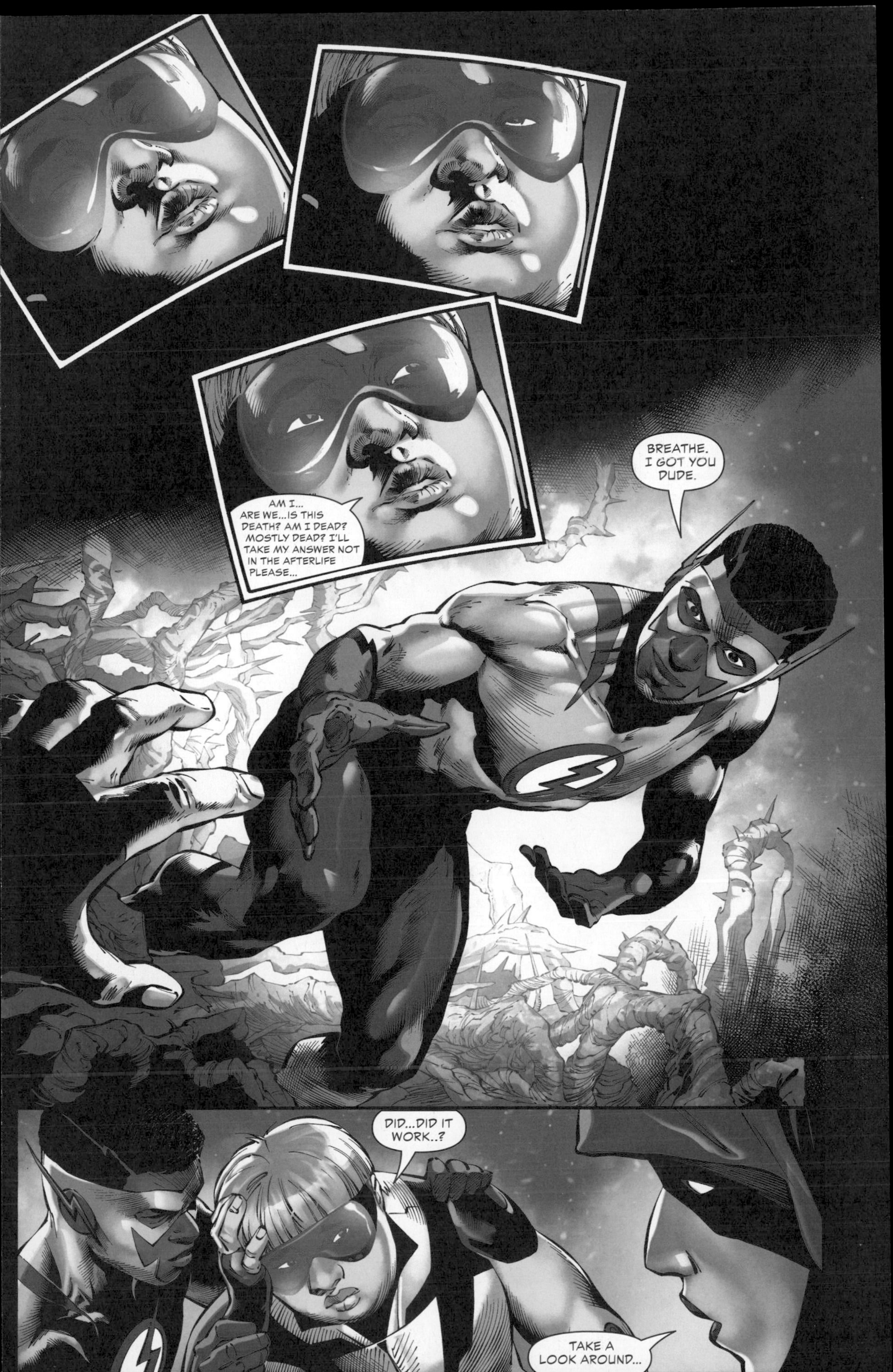
AM I... ARE WE...IS THIS DEATH? AM I DEAD? MOSTLY DEAD? I'LL TAKE MY ANSWER NOT IN THE AFTERLIFE PLEASE...
BREATHE. I GOT YOU DUDE.
DID...DID IT WORK..?
TAKE A LOOK AROUND...

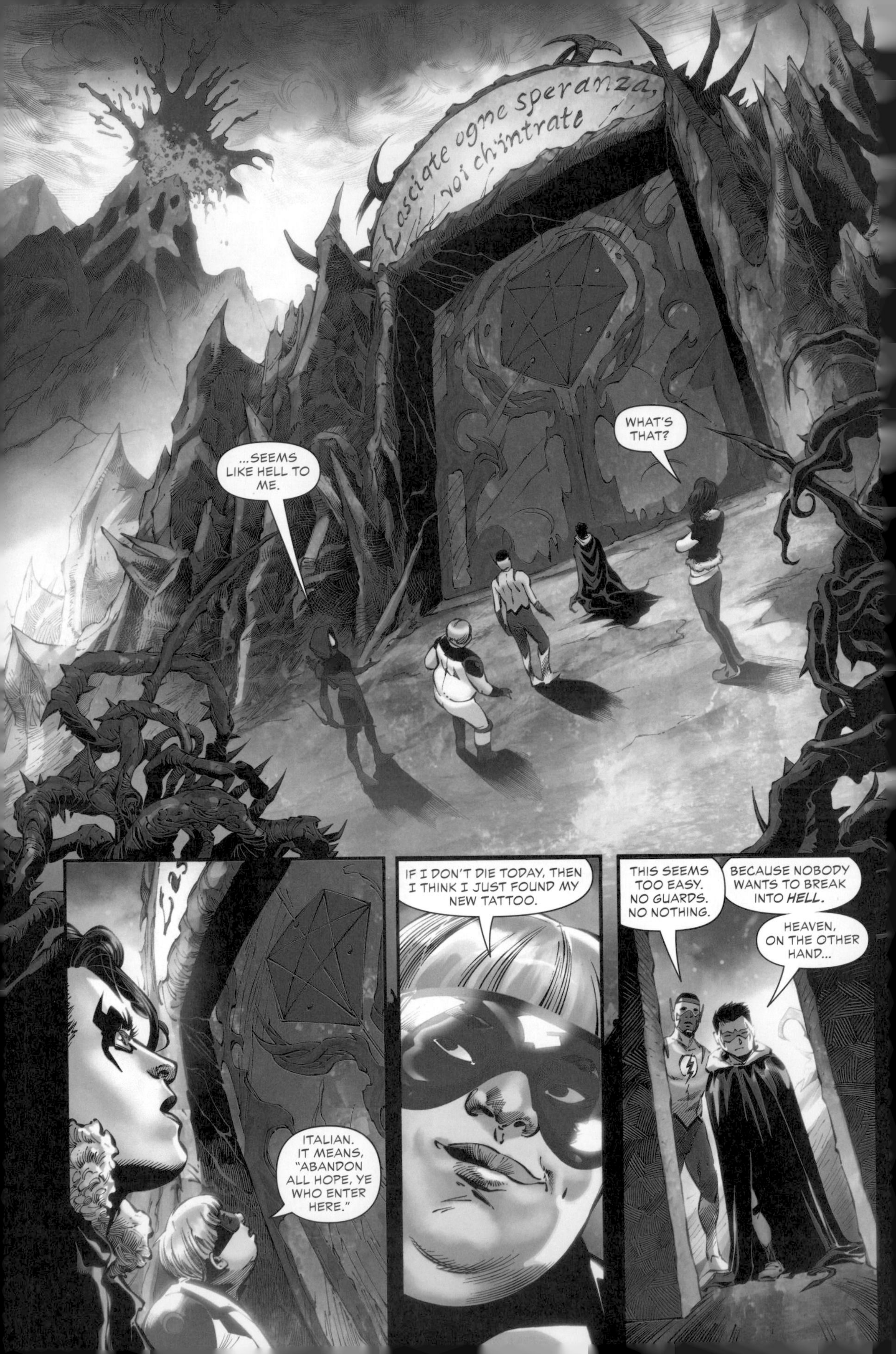
Lasciate ogne speranza, voi ch'intrate
WHAT'S THAT?
...SEEMS LIKE HELL TO ME.
ITALIAN. IT MEANS, "ABANDON ALL HOPE, YE WHO ENTER HERE."
IF I DON'T DIE TODAY, THEN I THINK I JUST FOUND MY NEW TATTOO.
THIS SEEMS TOO EASY. NO GUARDS. NO NOTHING.
BECAUSE NOBODY WANTS TO BREAK INTO HELL.
HEAVEN, ON THE OTHER HAND...

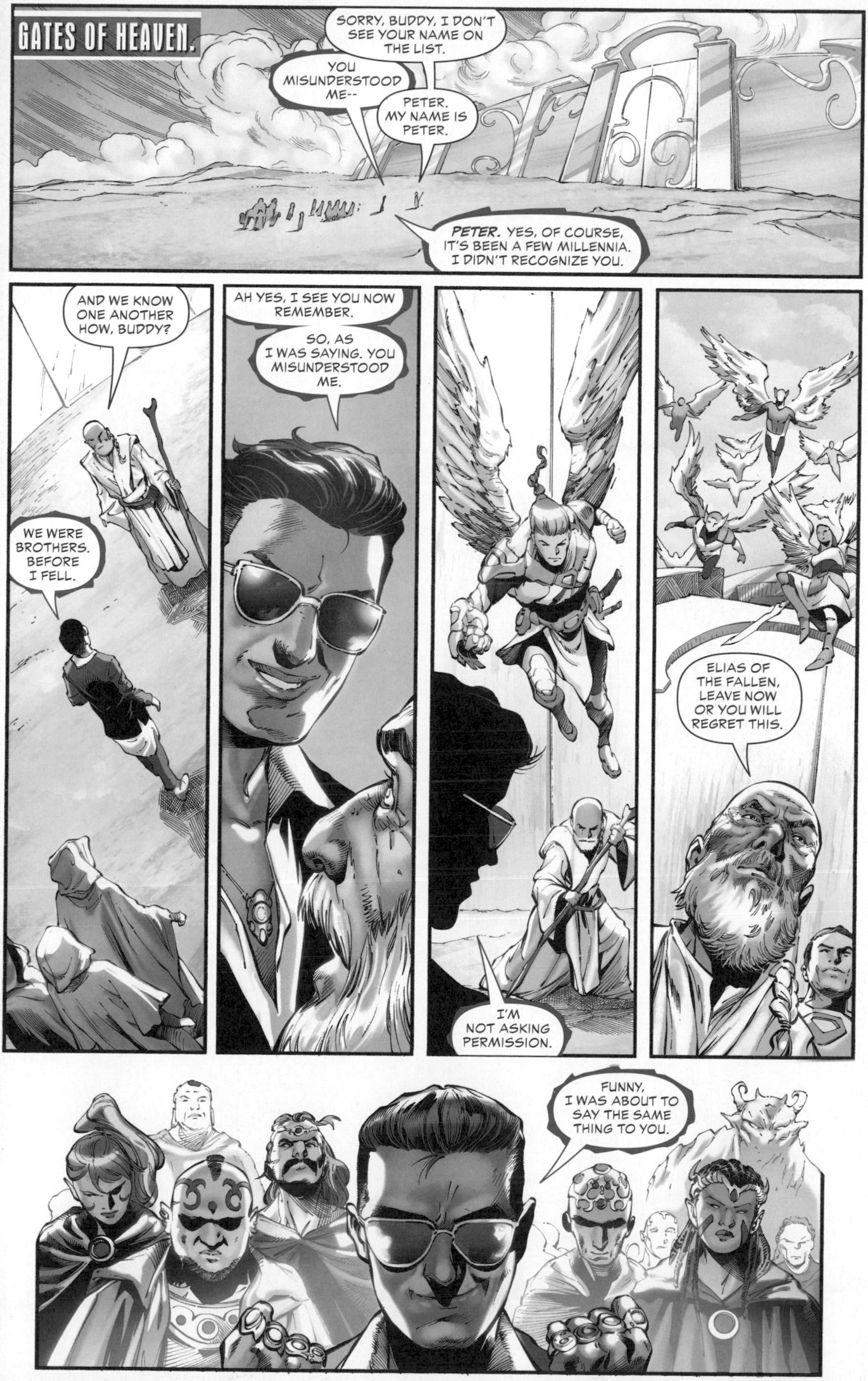
GATES OF HEAVEN.
SORRY, BUDDY, I DON'T SEE YOUR NAME ON THE LIST.
YOU MISUNDERSTOOD ME--
PETER. MY NAME IS PETER.
PETER. YES, OF COURSE, IT'S BEEN A FEW MILLENNIA. I DIDN'T RECOGNIZE YOU.
AND WE KNOW ONE ANOTHER HOW, BUDDY?
WE WERE BROTHERS. BEFORE I FELL.
AH YES, I SEE YOU NOW REMEMBER.
SO, AS I WAS SAYING. YOU MISUNDERSTOOD ME.
I'M NOT ASKING PERMISSION.
ELIAS OF THE FALLEN, LEAVE NOW OR YOU WILL REGRET THIS.
FUNNY, I WAS ABOUT TO SAY THE SAME THING TO YOU.

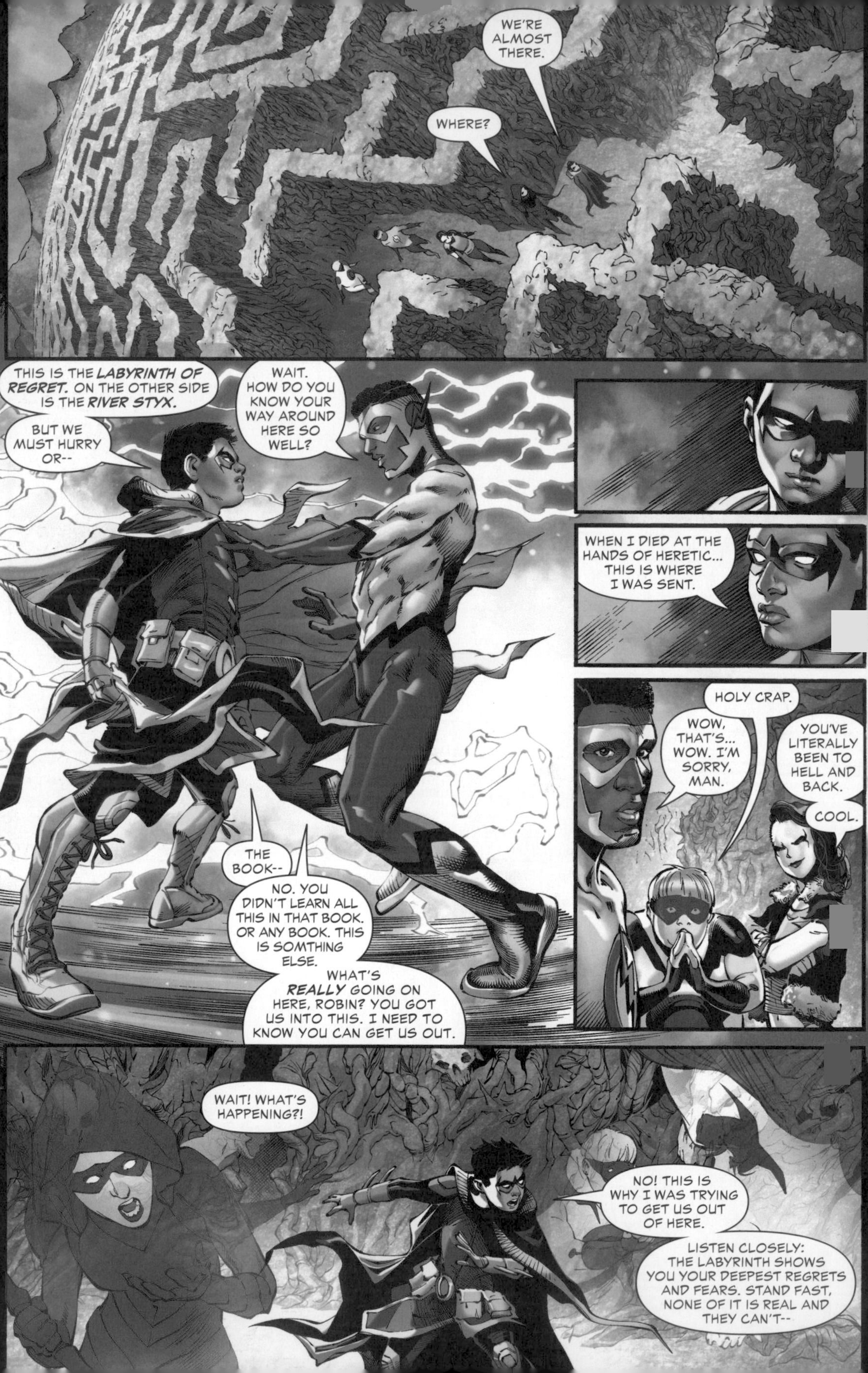

WE'RE ALMOST THERE.
WHERE?
THIS IS THE **LABYRINTH OF REGRET.** ON THE OTHER SIDE IS THE **RIVER STYX.**
BUT WE MUST HURRY OR--
WAIT. HOW DO YOU KNOW YOUR WAY AROUND HERE SO WELL?
WHEN I DIED AT THE HANDS OF HERETIC... THIS IS WHERE I WAS SENT.
HOLY CRAP.
WOW, THAT'S... WOW. I'M SORRY, MAN.
YOU'VE LITERALLY BEEN TO HELL AND BACK.
COOL.
THE BOOK--
NO. YOU DIDN'T LEARN ALL THIS IN THAT BOOK. OR ANY BOOK. THIS IS SOMTHING ELSE.
WHAT'S **REALLY** GOING ON HERE, ROBIN? YOU GOT US INTO THIS. I NEED TO KNOW YOU CAN GET US OUT.
WAIT! WHAT'S HAPPENING?!
NO! THIS IS WHY I WAS TRYING TO GET US OUT OF HERE.
LISTEN CLOSELY: THE LABYRINTH SHOWS YOU YOUR DEEPEST REGRETS AND FEARS. STAND FAST, NONE OF IT IS REAL AND THEY CAN'T--

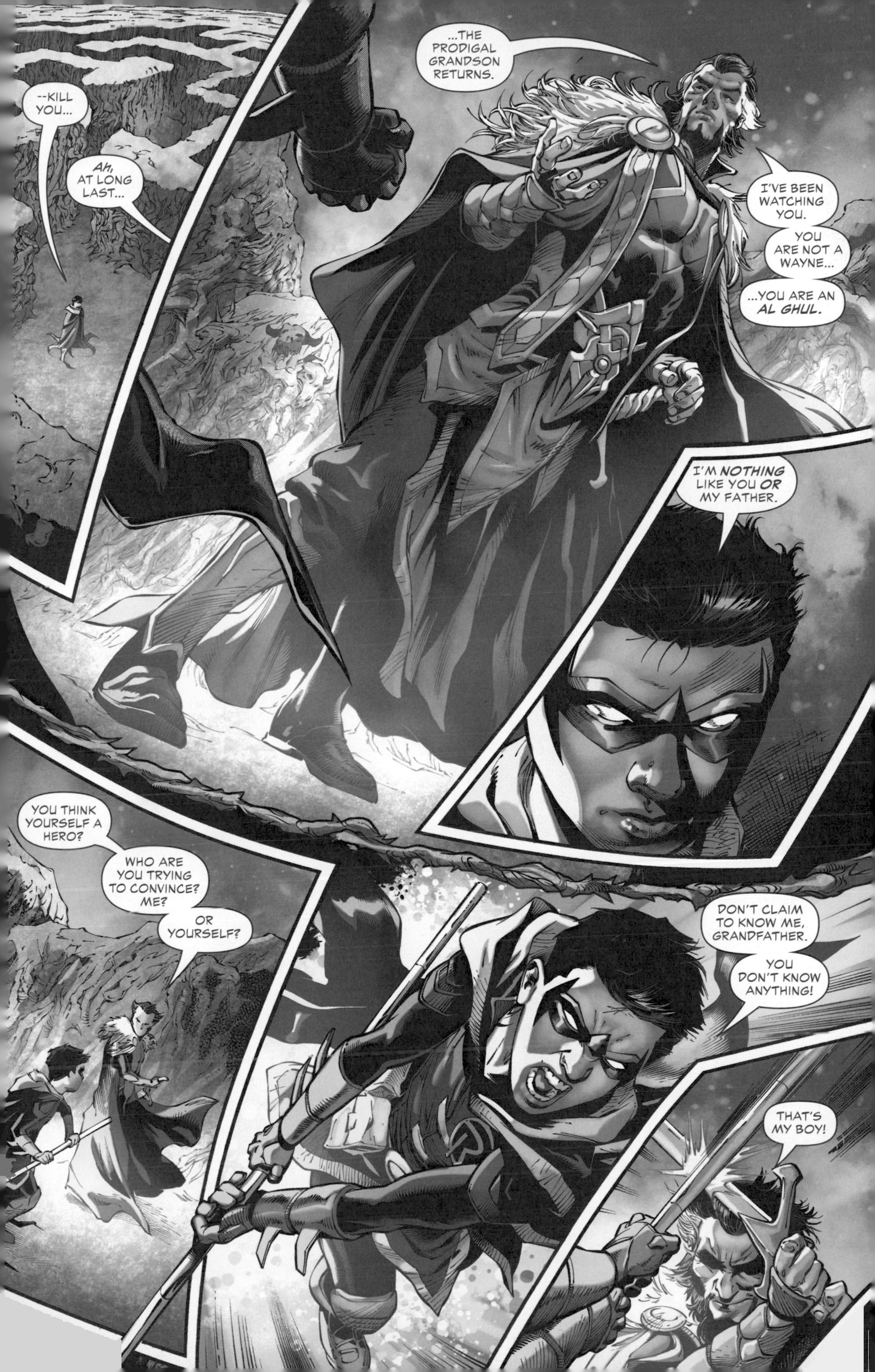
--KILL YOU...
AH, AT LONG LAST...
...THE PRODIGAL GRANDSON RETURNS.
I'VE BEEN WATCHING YOU.
YOU ARE NOT A WAYNE...
...YOU ARE AN AL GHUL.
I'M NOTHING LIKE YOU OR MY FATHER.
YOU THINK YOURSELF A HERO?
WHO ARE YOU TRYING TO CONVINCE? ME?
OR YOURSELF?
DON'T CLAIM TO KNOW ME, GRANDFATHER.
YOU DON'T KNOW ANYTHING!
THAT'S MY BOY!

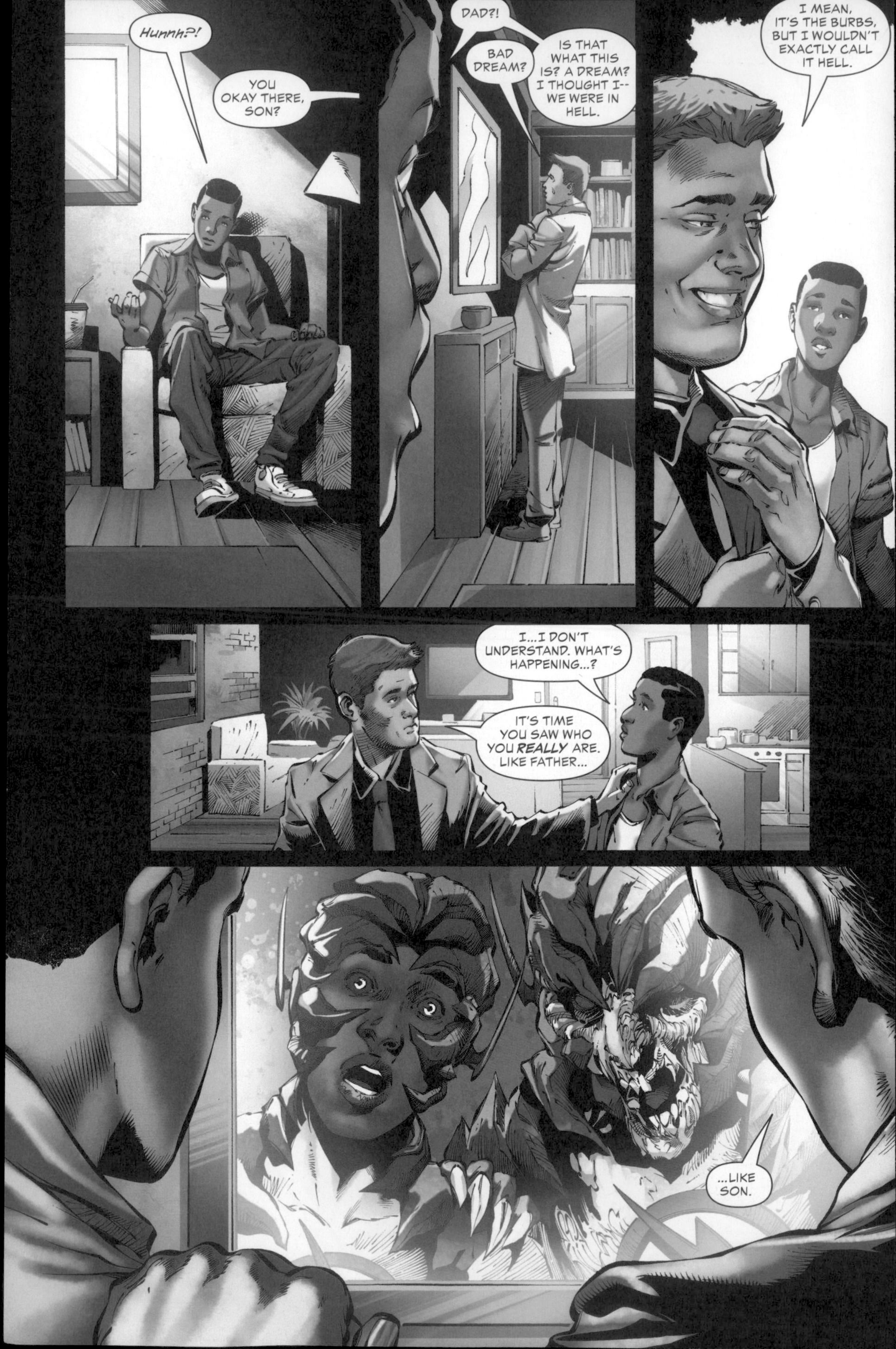

Hunnh?!
YOU OKAY THERE, SON?
DAD?!
BAD DREAM?
IS THAT WHAT THIS IS? A DREAM? I THOUGHT I-- WE WERE IN HELL.
I MEAN, IT'S THE BURBS, BUT I WOULDN'T EXACTLY CALL IT HELL.
I...I DON'T UNDERSTAND. WHAT'S HAPPENING...?
IT'S TIME YOU SAW WHO YOU *REALLY* ARE. LIKE FATHER...
...LIKE SON.

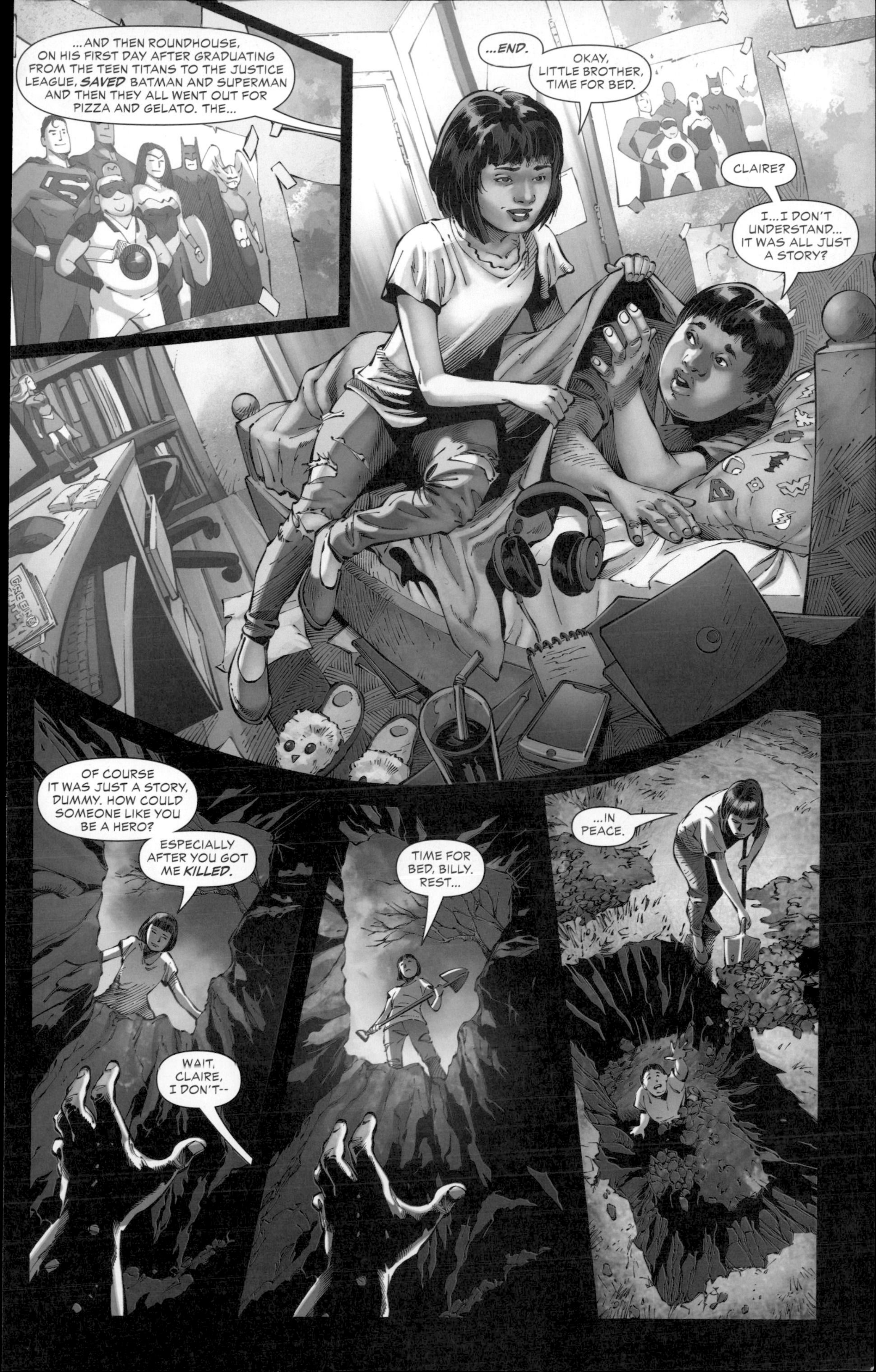
...AND THEN ROUNDHOUSE, ON HIS FIRST DAY AFTER GRADUATING FROM THE TEEN TITANS TO THE JUSTICE LEAGUE, SAVED BATMAN AND SUPERMAN AND THEN THEY ALL WENT OUT FOR PIZZA AND GELATO. THE...
...END.
OKAY, LITTLE BROTHER, TIME FOR BED.
CLAIRE?
I...I DON'T UNDERSTAND... IT WAS ALL JUST A STORY?
OF COURSE IT WAS JUST A STORY, DUMMY. HOW COULD SOMEONE LIKE YOU BE A HERO?
ESPECIALLY AFTER YOU GOT ME KILLED.
WAIT, CLAIRE, I DON'T--
TIME FOR BED, BILLY. REST...
...IN PEACE.

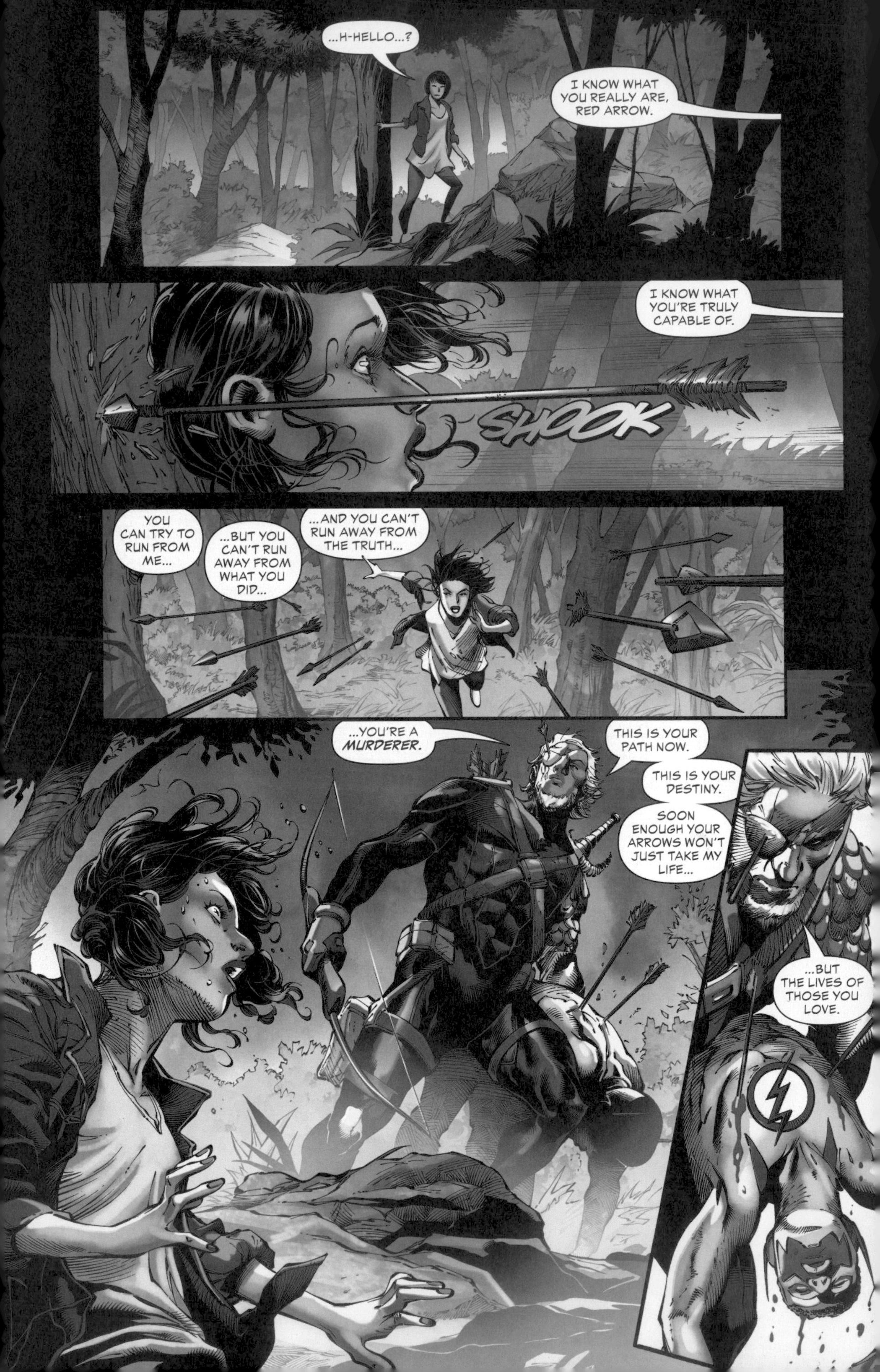
...H-HELLO...?
I KNOW WHAT YOU REALLY ARE, RED ARROW.
I KNOW WHAT YOU'RE TRULY CAPABLE OF.
SHOOK
YOU CAN TRY TO RUN FROM ME...
...BUT YOU CAN'T RUN AWAY FROM WHAT YOU DID...
...AND YOU CAN'T RUN AWAY FROM THE TRUTH...
...YOU'RE A *MURDERER.*
THIS IS YOUR PATH NOW.
THIS IS YOUR DESTINY.
SOON ENOUGH YOUR ARROWS WON'T JUST TAKE MY LIFE...
...BUT THE LIVES OF THOSE YOU LOVE.

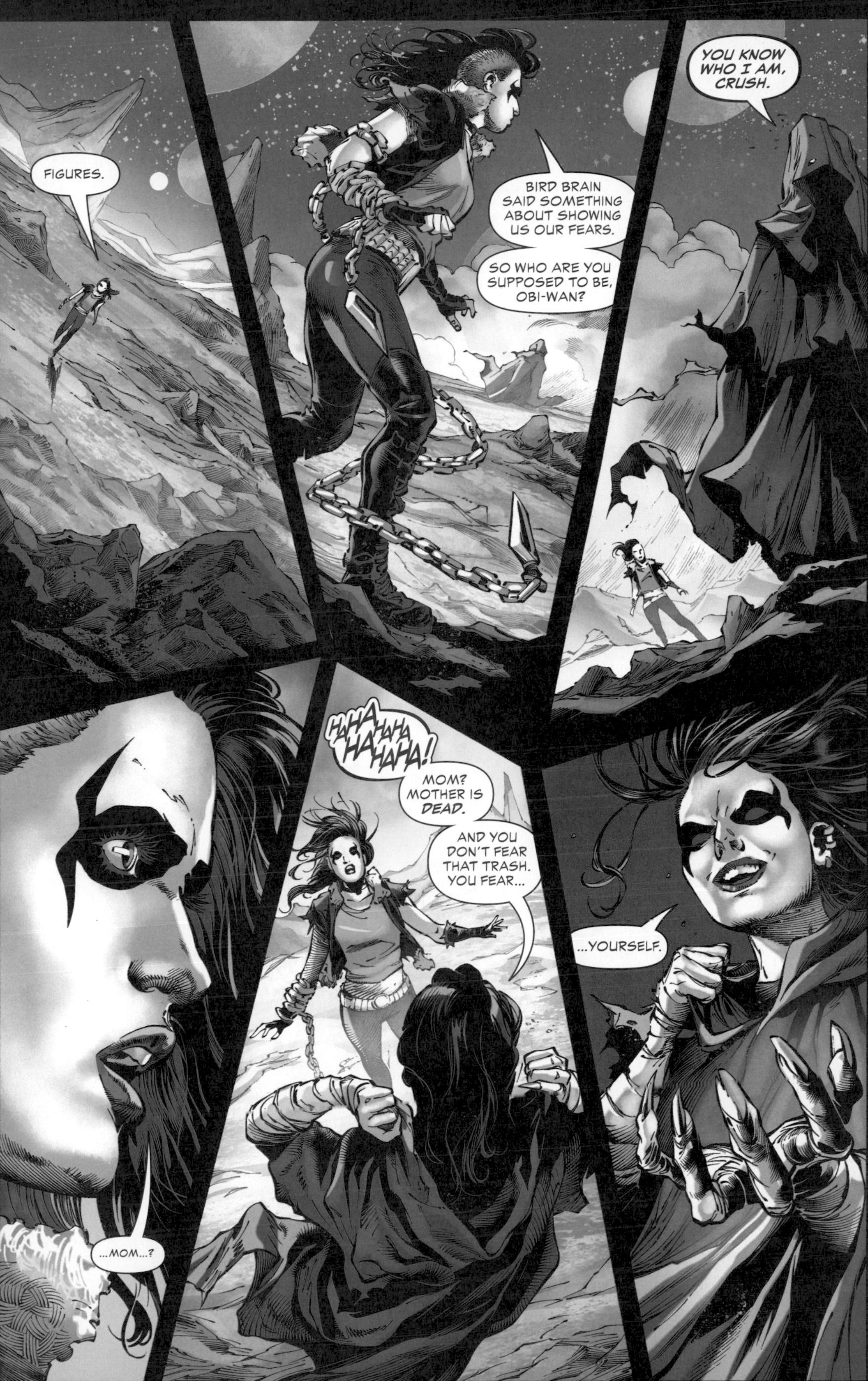
FIGURES.
BIRD BRAIN SAID SOMETHING ABOUT SHOWING US OUR FEARS.
SO WHO ARE YOU SUPPOSED TO BE, OBI-WAN?
YOU KNOW WHO I AM, CRUSH.
...MOM...?
HAHAHAHA HAHAHAHA!
MOM? MOTHER IS DEAD.
AND YOU DON'T FEAR THAT TRASH. YOU FEAR...
...YOURSELF.

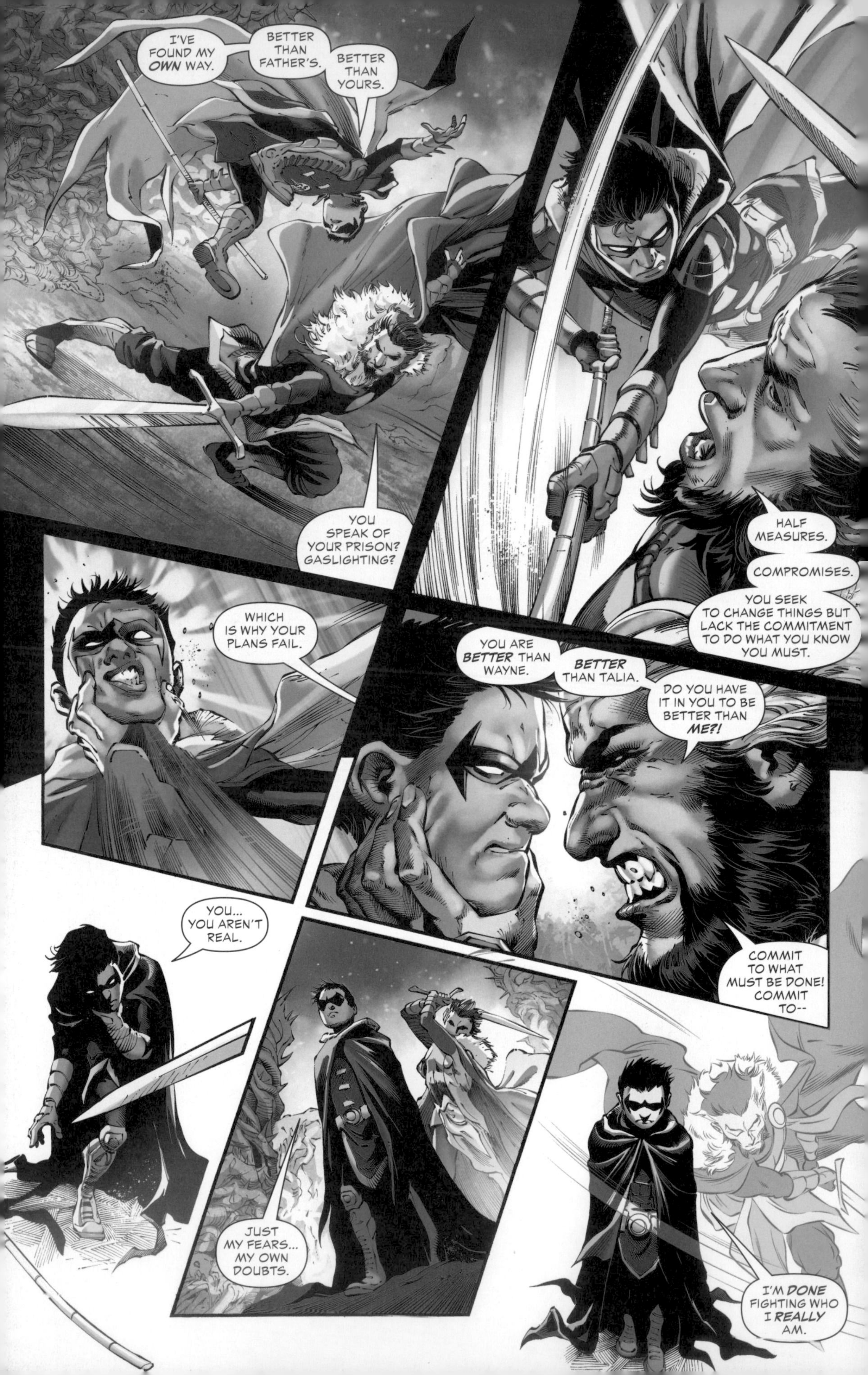
I'VE FOUND MY *OWN* WAY.
BETTER THAN FATHER'S.
BETTER THAN YOURS.
YOU SPEAK OF YOUR PRISON? GASLIGHTING?
HALF MEASURES.
COMPROMISES.
YOU SEEK TO CHANGE THINGS BUT LACK THE COMMITMENT TO DO WHAT YOU KNOW YOU MUST.
WHICH IS WHY YOUR PLANS FAIL.
YOU ARE *BETTER* THAN WAYNE.
BETTER THAN TALIA.
DO YOU HAVE IT IN YOU TO BE BETTER THAN *ME?!*
YOU... YOU AREN'T REAL.
COMMIT TO WHAT MUST BE DONE! COMMIT TO--
JUST MY FEARS... MY OWN DOUBTS.
I'M *DONE* FIGHTING WHO I *REALLY* AM.

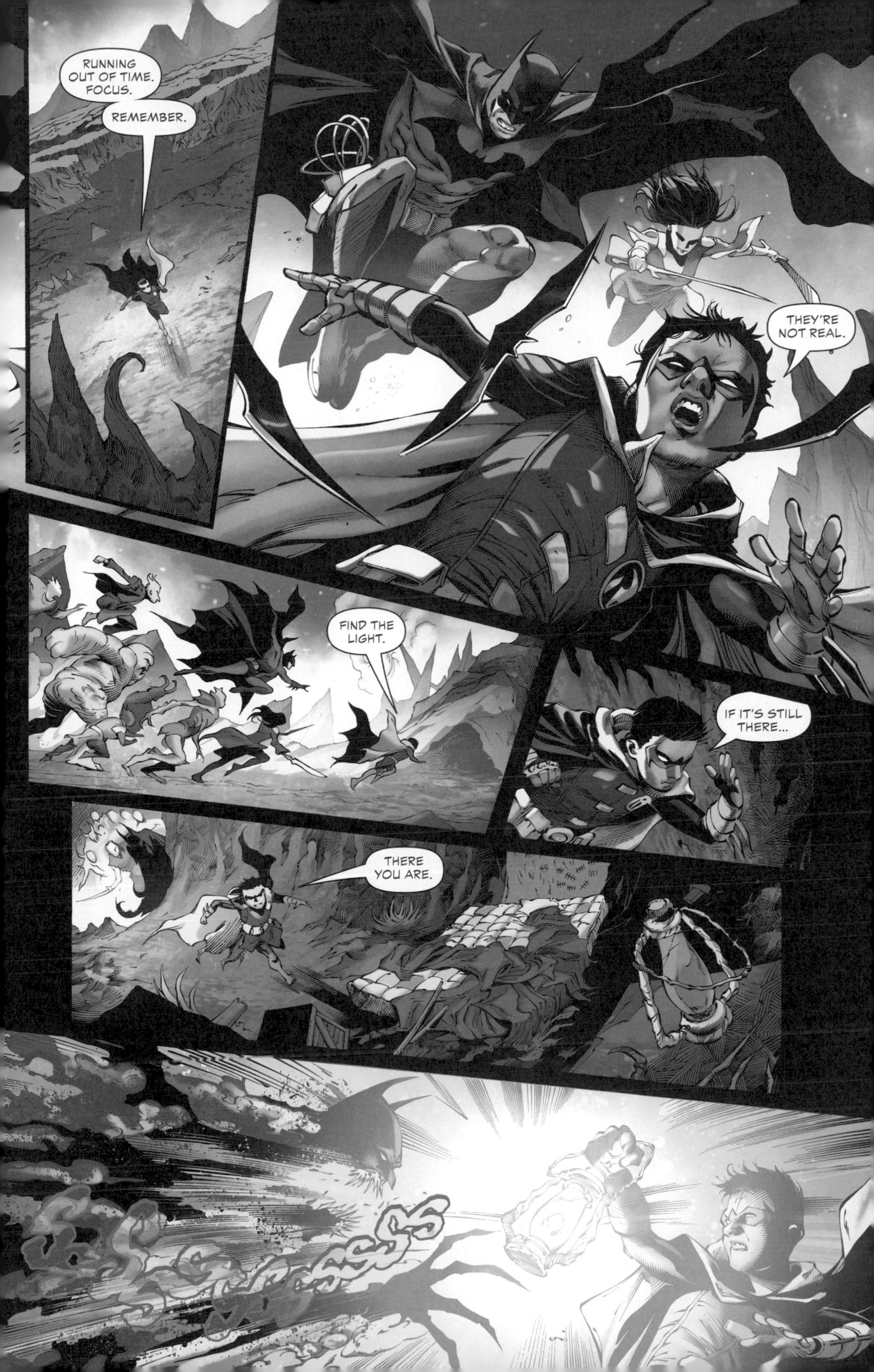
RUNNING OUT OF TIME. FOCUS.
REMEMBER.
THEY'RE NOT REAL.
FIND THE LIGHT.
IF IT'S STILL THERE...
THERE YOU ARE.

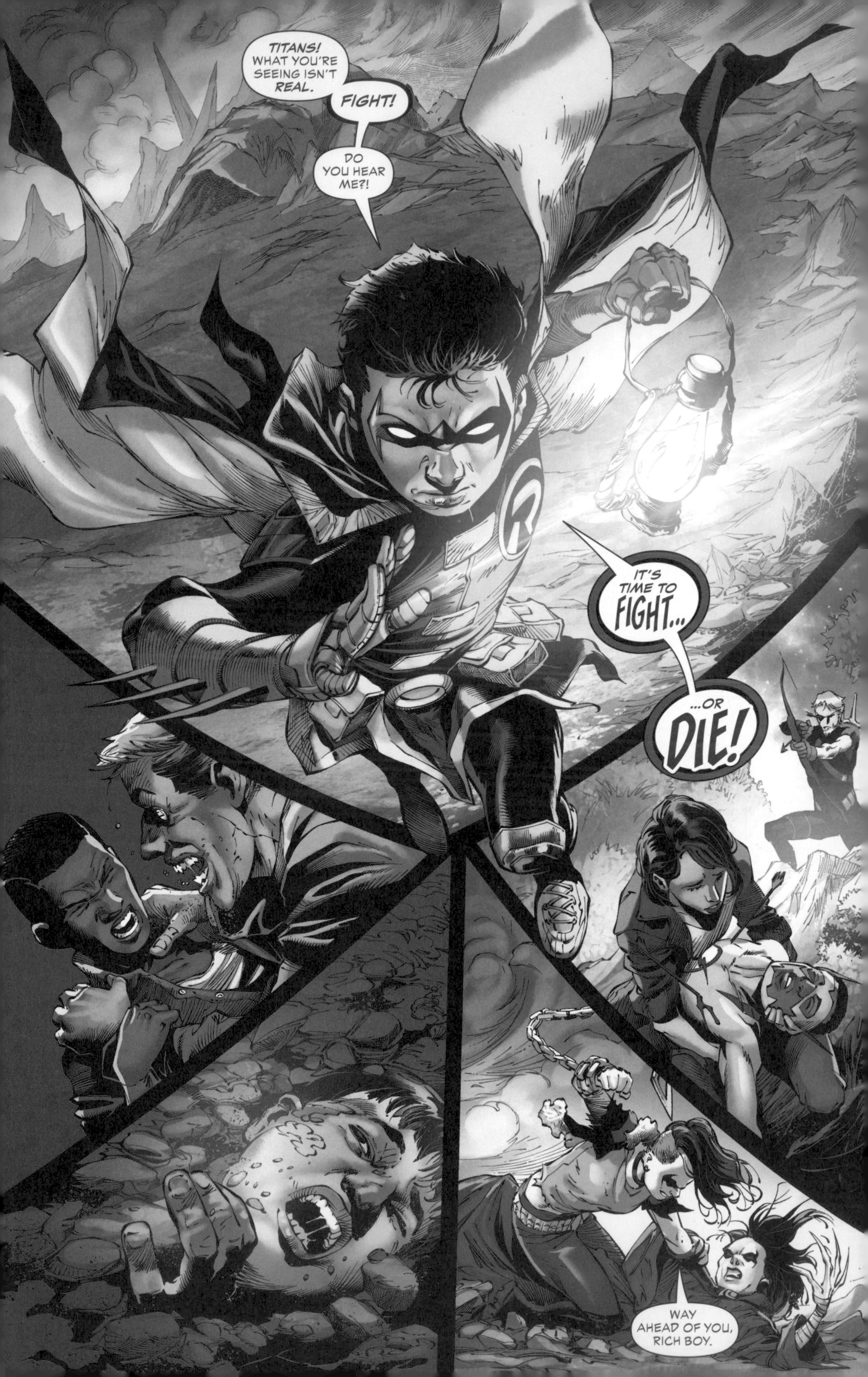
TITANS! WHAT YOU'RE SEEING ISN'T REAL.
FIGHT!
DO YOU HEAR ME?!
IT'S TIME TO FIGHT...
...OR DIE!
WAY AHEAD OF YOU, RICH BOY.

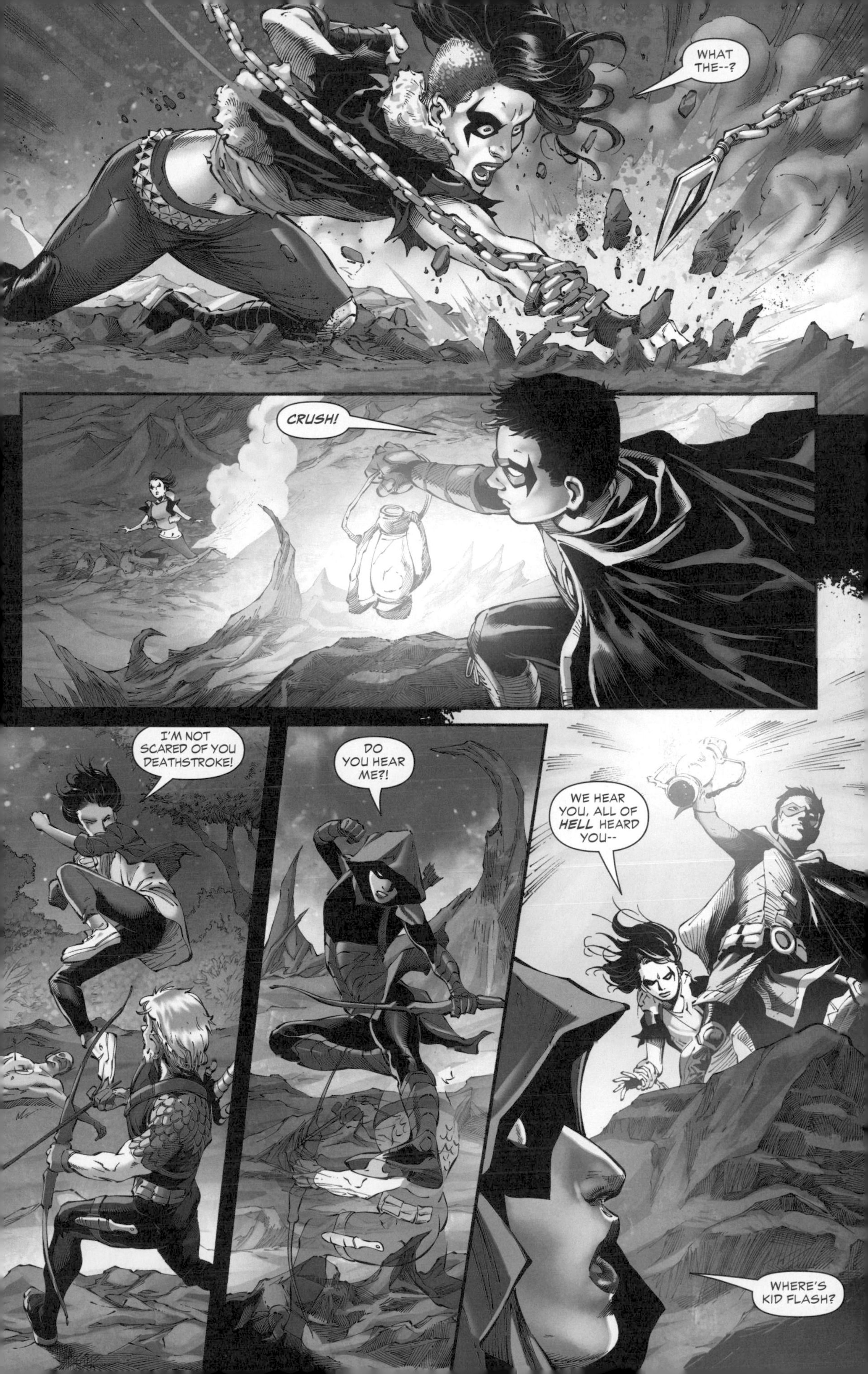
WHAT THE--?
CRUSH!
I'M NOT SCARED OF YOU DEATHSTROKE!
DO YOU HEAR ME?!
WE HEAR YOU, ALL OF HELL HEARD YOU--
WHERE'S KID FLASH?

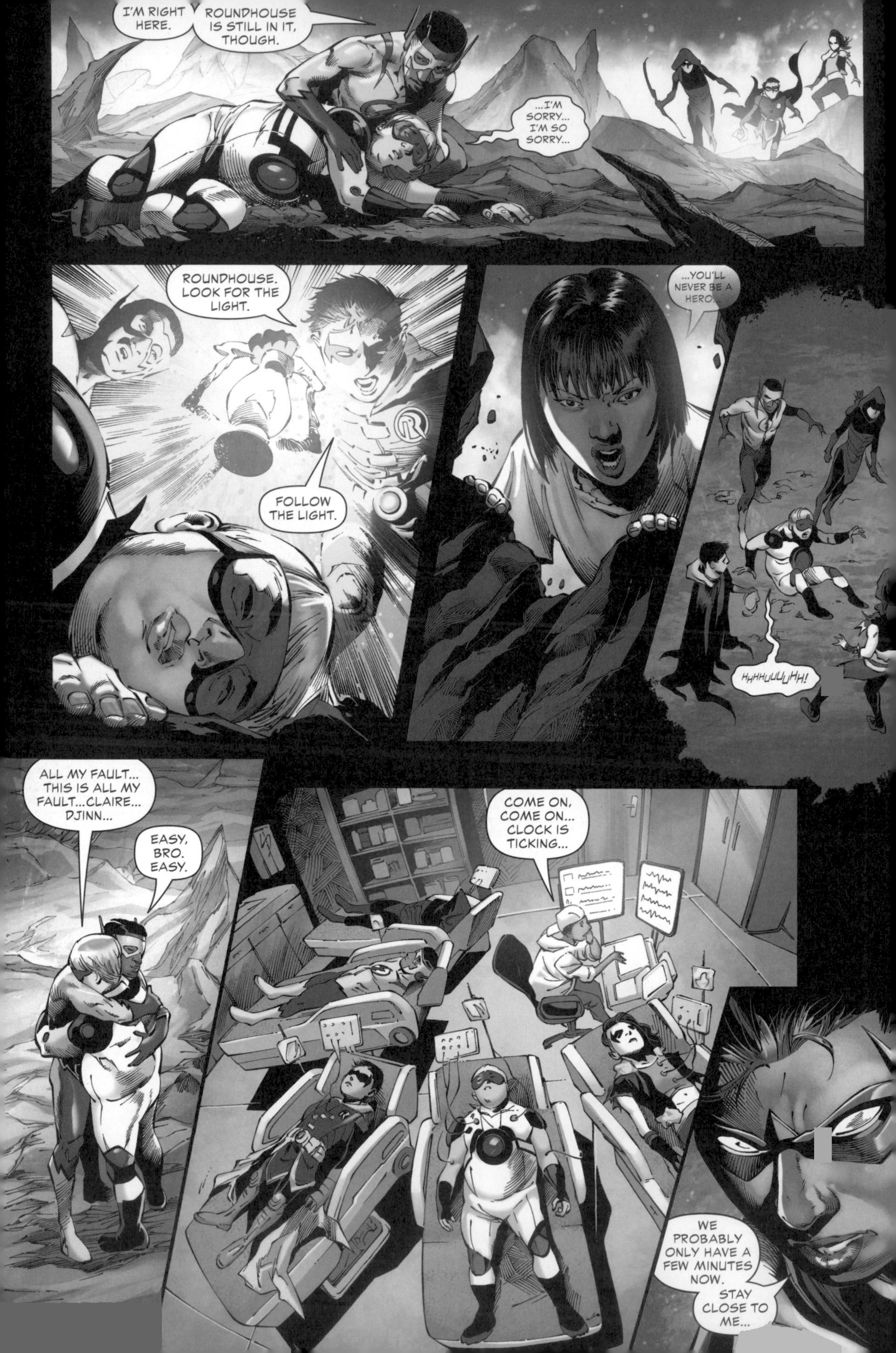
I'M RIGHT HERE.
ROUNDHOUSE IS STILL IN IT, THOUGH.
...I'M SORRY... I'M SO SORRY...
ROUNDHOUSE. LOOK FOR THE LIGHT.
FOLLOW THE LIGHT.
...YOU'LL NEVER BE A HERO...
HHHHUUUUHH!
ALL MY FAULT... THIS IS ALL MY FAULT...CLAIRE... DJINN...
EASY, BRO. EASY.
COME ON, COME ON... CLOCK IS TICKING...
WE PROBABLY ONLY HAVE A FEW MINUTES NOW.
STAY CLOSE TO ME...

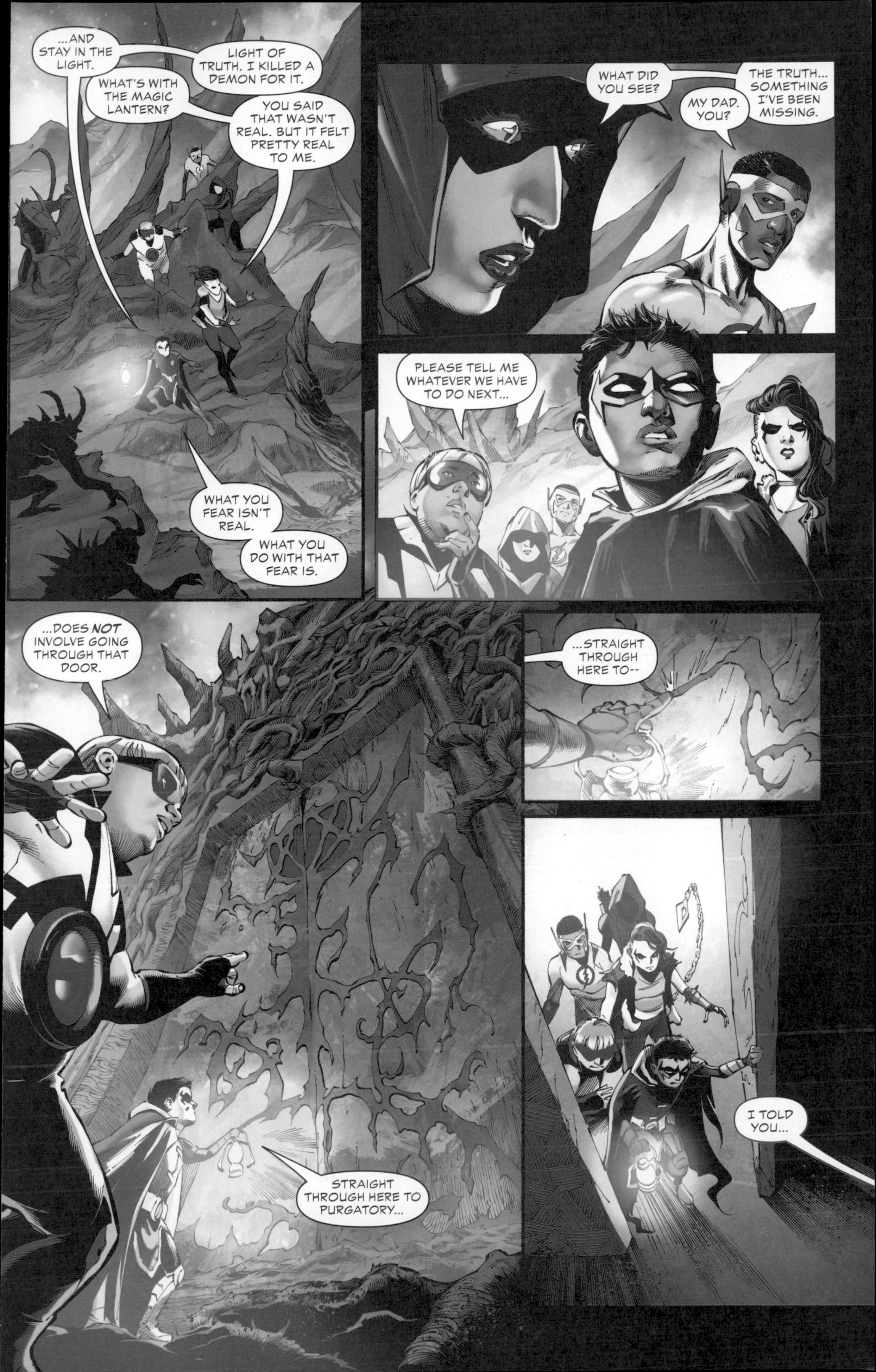

...AND STAY IN THE LIGHT.
WHAT'S WITH THE MAGIC LANTERN?
LIGHT OF TRUTH. I KILLED A DEMON FOR IT.
YOU SAID THAT WASN'T REAL. BUT IT FELT PRETTY REAL TO ME.
WHAT YOU FEAR ISN'T REAL.
WHAT YOU DO WITH THAT FEAR IS.
WHAT DID YOU SEE?
MY DAD. YOU?
THE TRUTH... SOMETHING I'VE BEEN MISSING.
PLEASE TELL ME WHATEVER WE HAVE TO DO NEXT...
...DOES NOT INVOLVE GOING THROUGH THAT DOOR.
STRAIGHT THROUGH HERE TO PURGATORY...
...STRAIGHT THROUGH HERE TO--
I TOLD YOU...

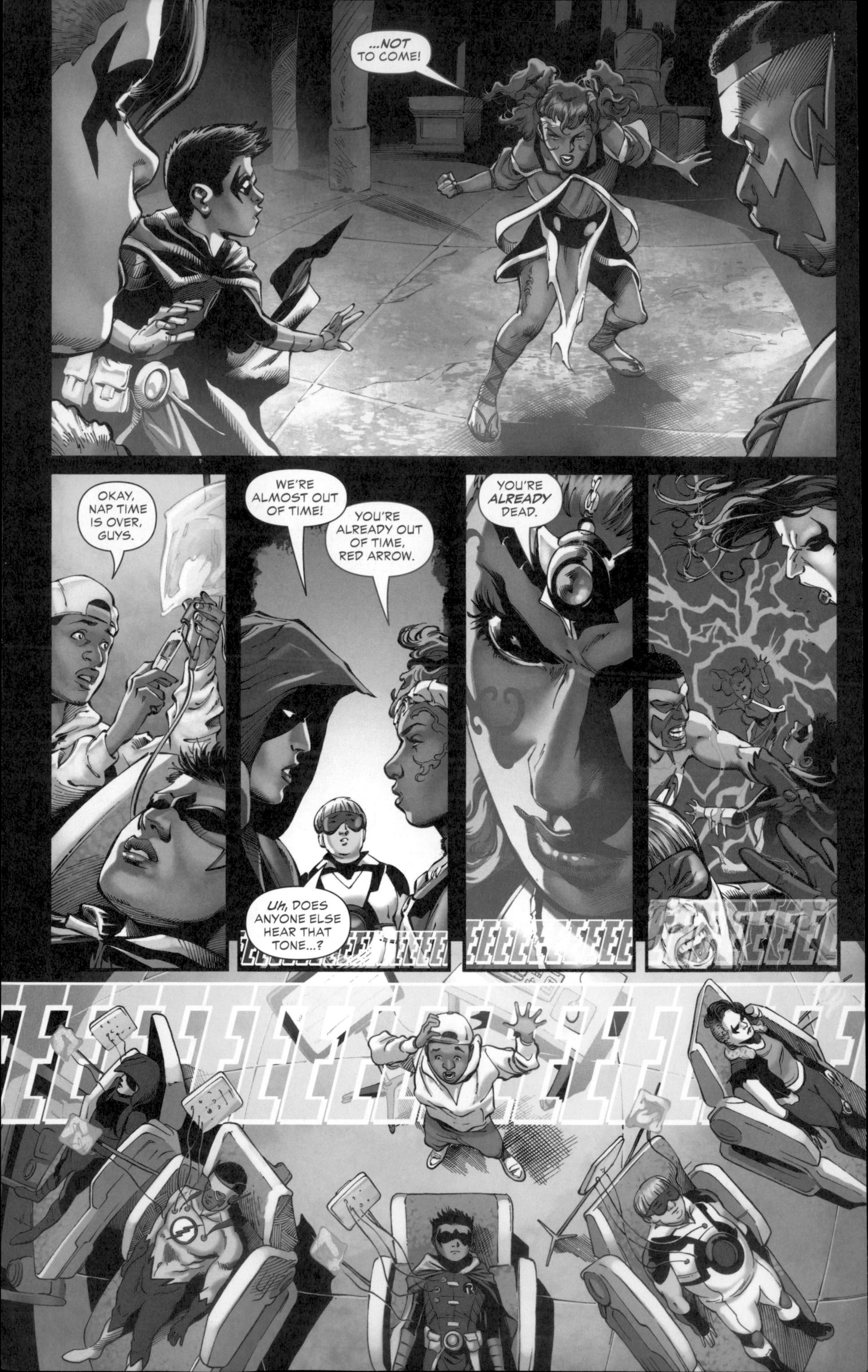
...NOT TO COME!
OKAY, NAP TIME IS OVER, GUYS.
WE'RE ALMOST OUT OF TIME!
YOU'RE ALREADY OUT OF TIME, RED ARROW.
Uh, DOES ANYONE ELSE HEAR THAT TONE...?
YOU'RE ALREADY DEAD.

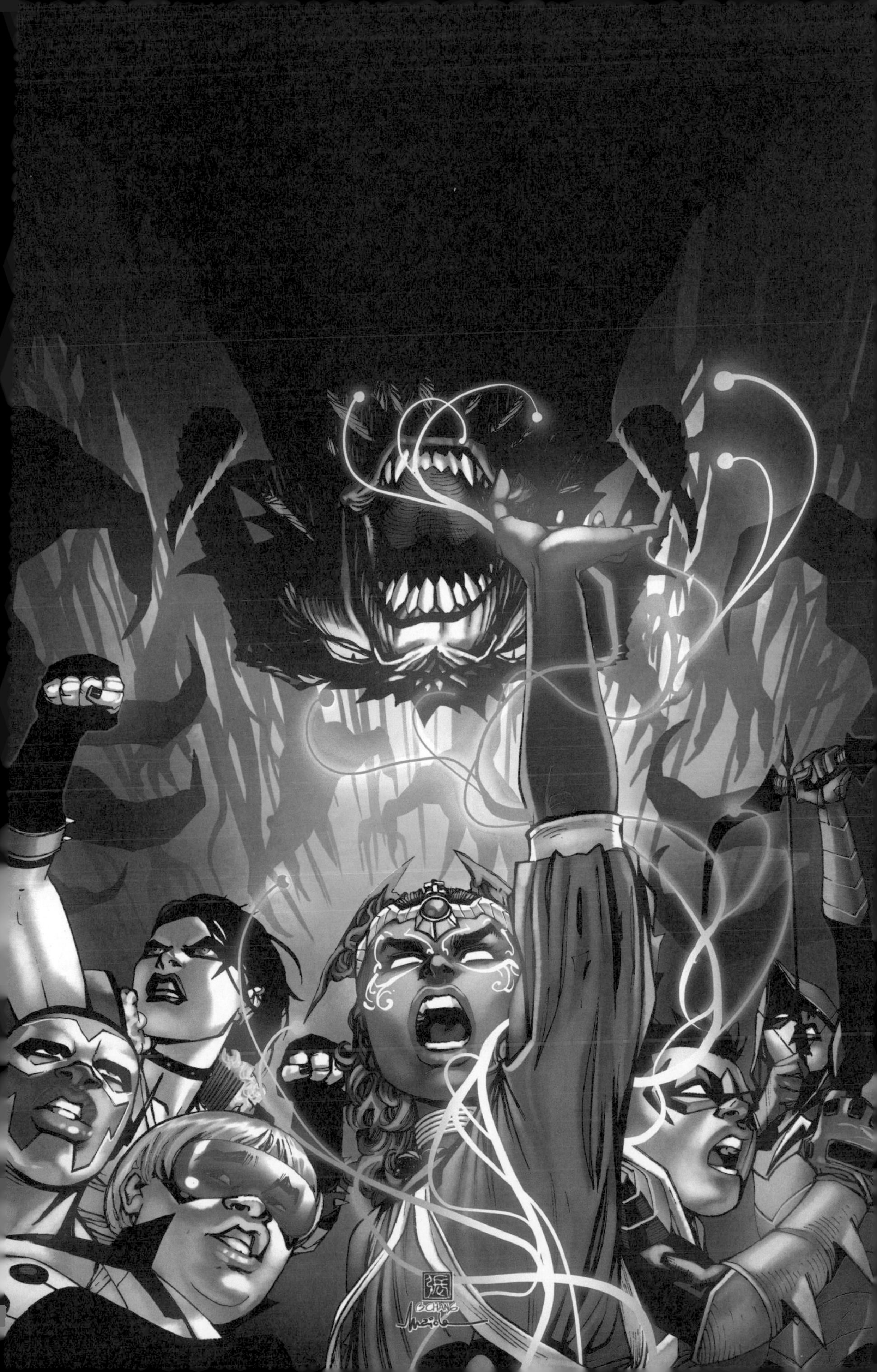
B CHANG

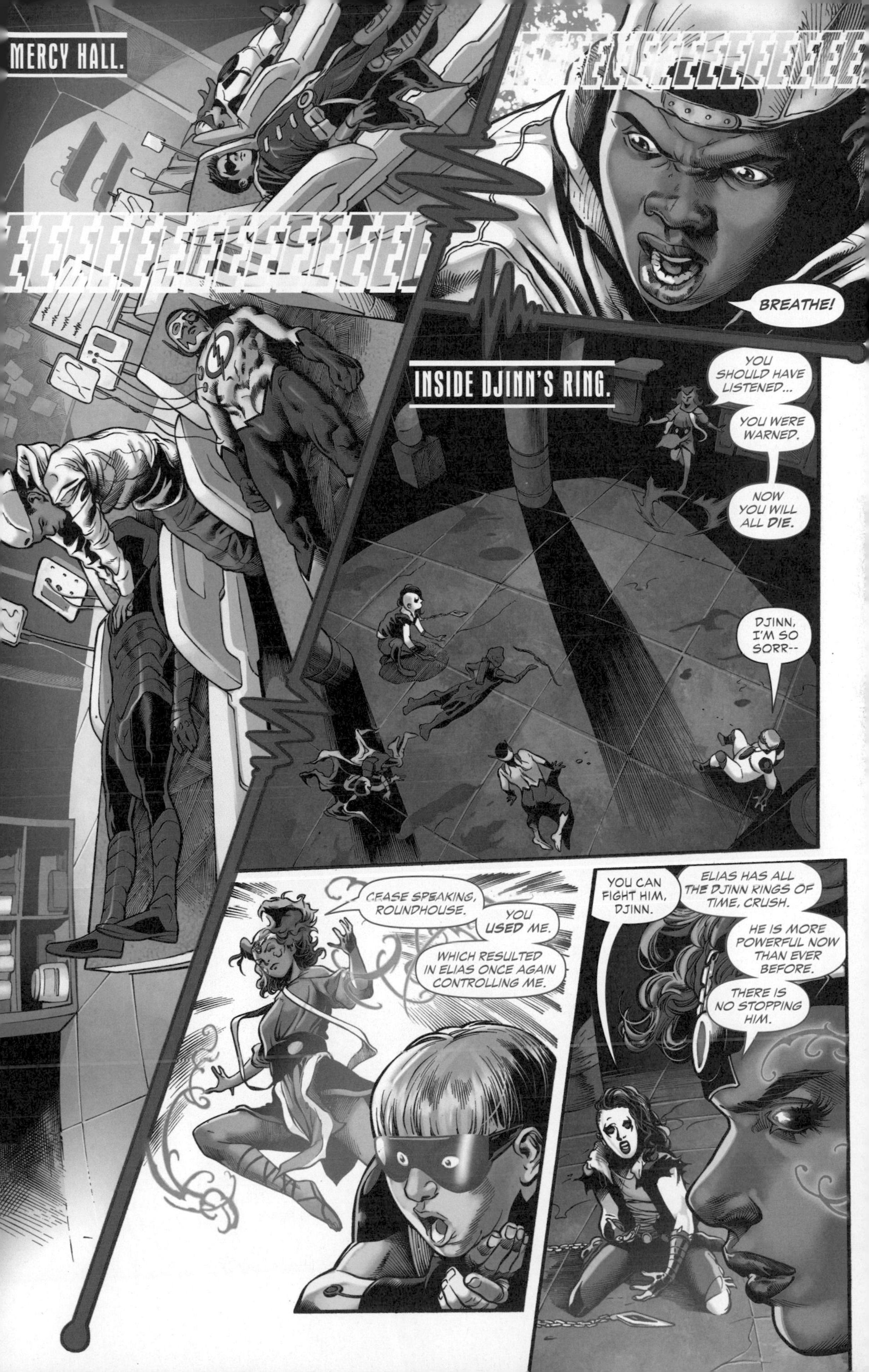

MERCY HALL.
EEEEEEEEEEEEEE
EEEEEEEEEEEEEE
BREATHE!
INSIDE DJINN'S RING.
YOU SHOULD HAVE LISTENED...
YOU WERE WARNED.
NOW YOU WILL ALL DIE.
DJINN, I'M SO SORR--
CEASE SPEAKING, ROUNDHOUSE.
YOU USED ME.
WHICH RESULTED IN ELIAS ONCE AGAIN CONTROLLING ME.
YOU CAN FIGHT HIM, DJINN.
ELIAS HAS ALL THE DJINN RINGS OF TIME, CRUSH.
HE IS MORE POWERFUL NOW THAN EVER BEFORE.
THERE IS NO STOPPING HIM.

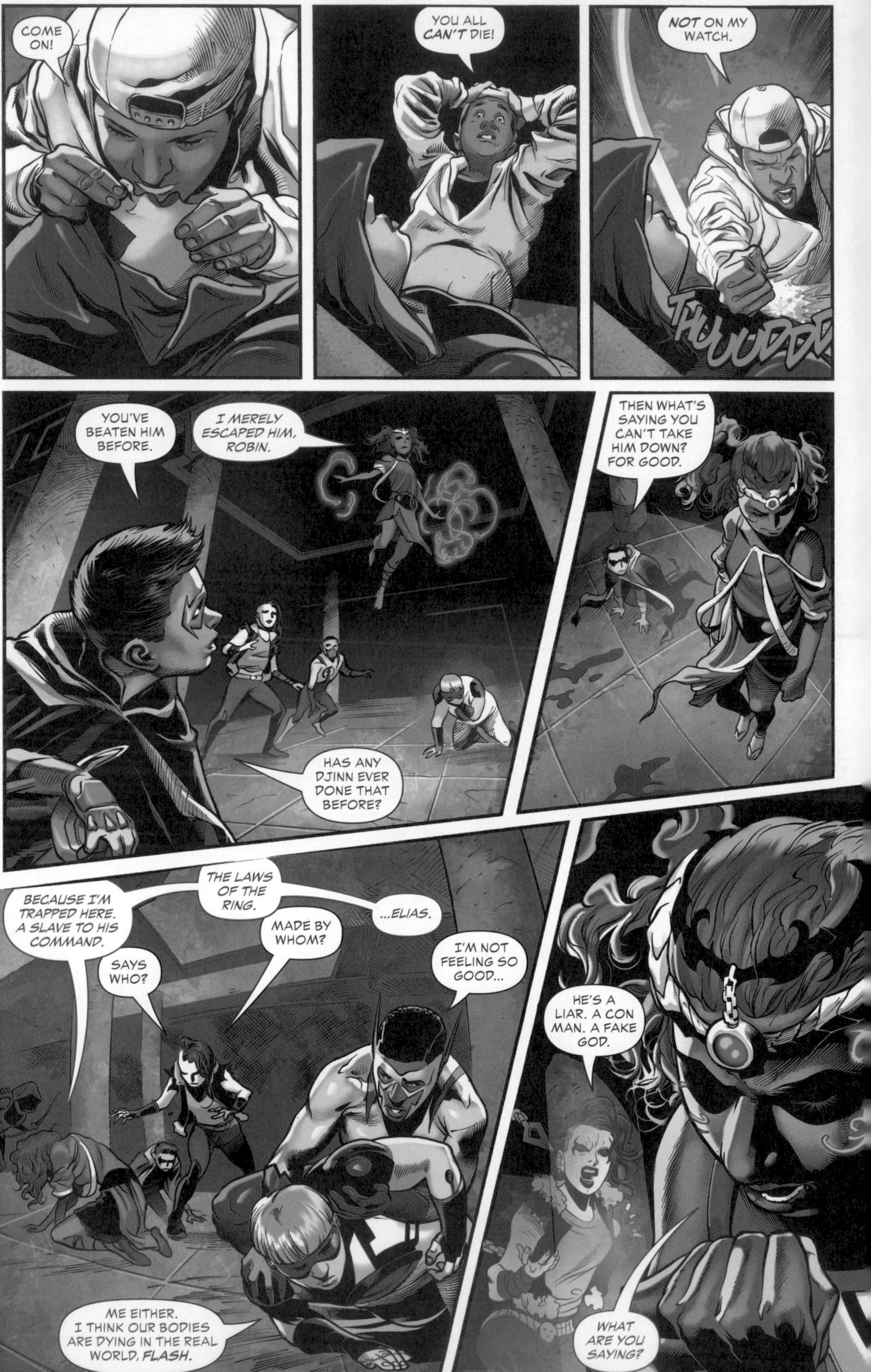
COME ON!
YOU ALL CAN'T DIE!
NOT ON MY WATCH.
THUUDDD
YOU'VE BEATEN HIM BEFORE.
I MERELY ESCAPED HIM, ROBIN.
HAS ANY DJINN EVER DONE THAT BEFORE?
THEN WHAT'S SAYING YOU CAN'T TAKE HIM DOWN? FOR GOOD.
BECAUSE I'M TRAPPED HERE. A SLAVE TO HIS COMMAND.
SAYS WHO?
THE LAWS OF THE RING.
MADE BY WHOM?
...ELIAS.
I'M NOT FEELING SO GOOD...
ME EITHER. I THINK OUR BODIES ARE DYING IN THE REAL WORLD, FLASH.
HE'S A LIAR. A CON MAN. A FAKE GOD.
WHAT ARE YOU SAYING?

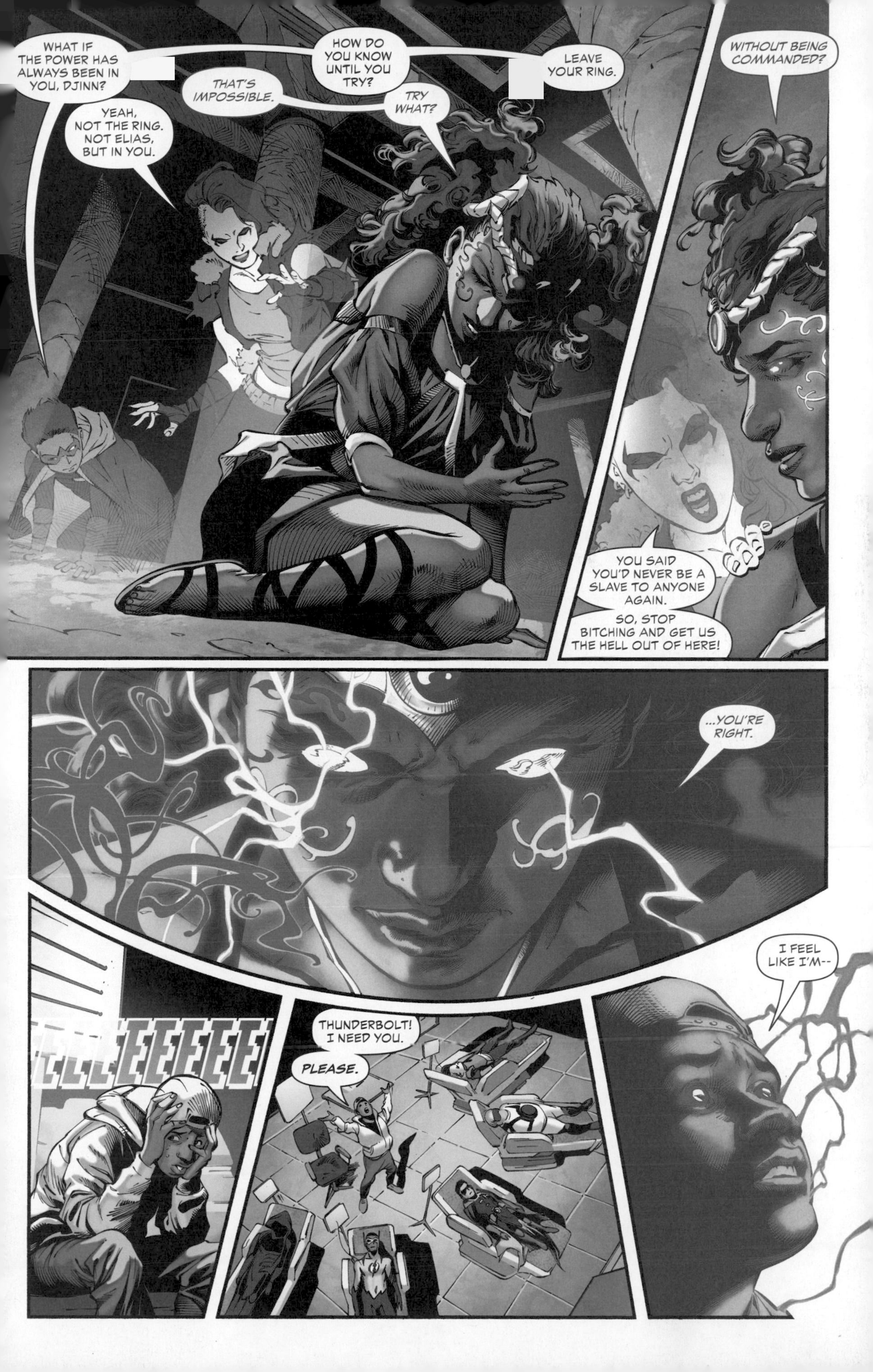
WHAT IF THE POWER HAS ALWAYS BEEN IN YOU, DJINN?
YEAH, NOT THE RING. NOT ELIAS, BUT IN YOU.
THAT'S IMPOSSIBLE.
HOW DO YOU KNOW UNTIL YOU TRY?
TRY WHAT?
LEAVE YOUR RING.
WITHOUT BEING COMMANDED?
YOU SAID YOU'D NEVER BE A SLAVE TO ANYONE AGAIN.
SO, STOP BITCHING AND GET US THE HELL OUT OF HERE!
...YOU'RE RIGHT.
EEEEEEEE
THUNDERBOLT! I NEED YOU.
PLEASE.
I FEEL LIKE I'M--

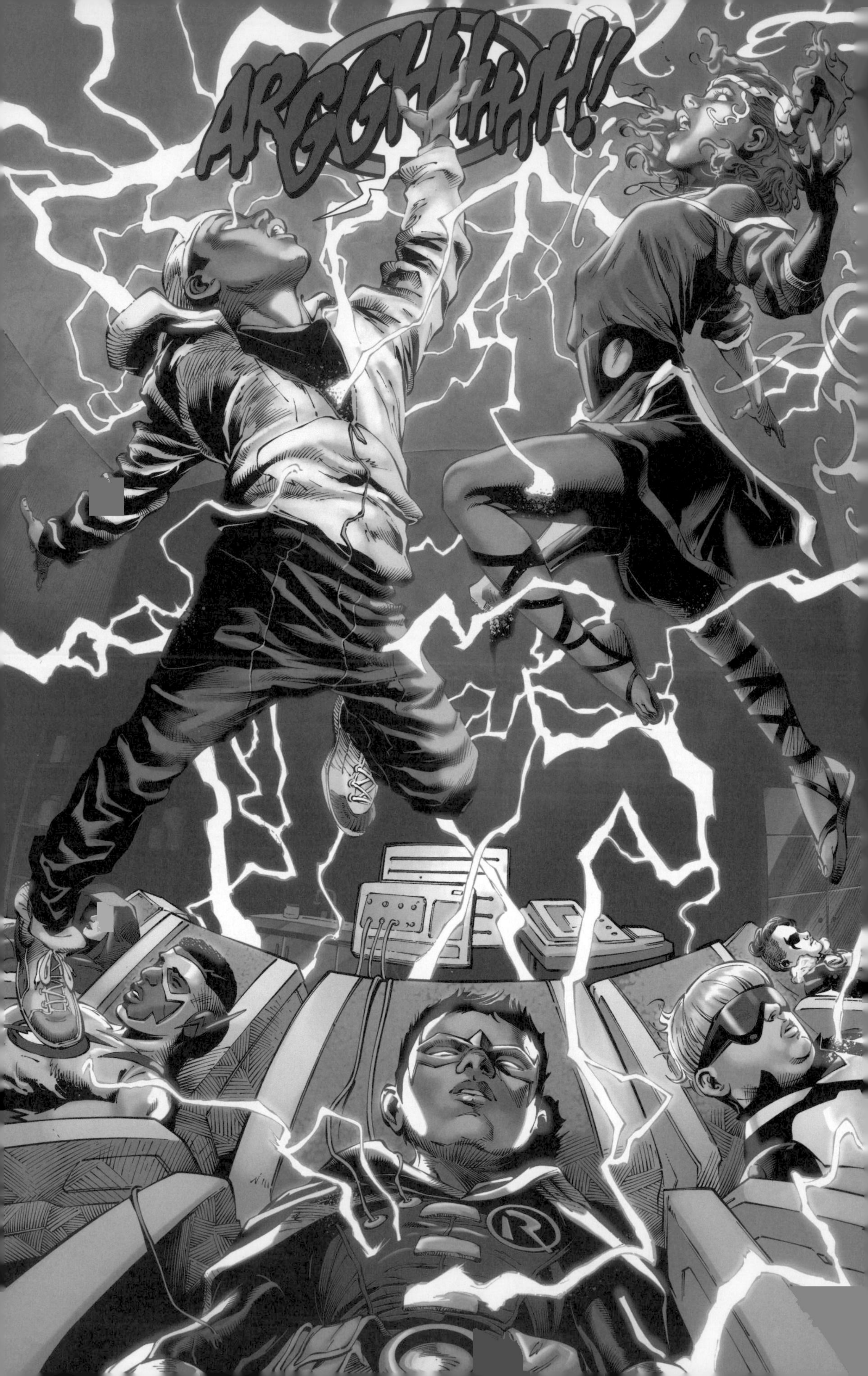
ARGGHHHHH!!

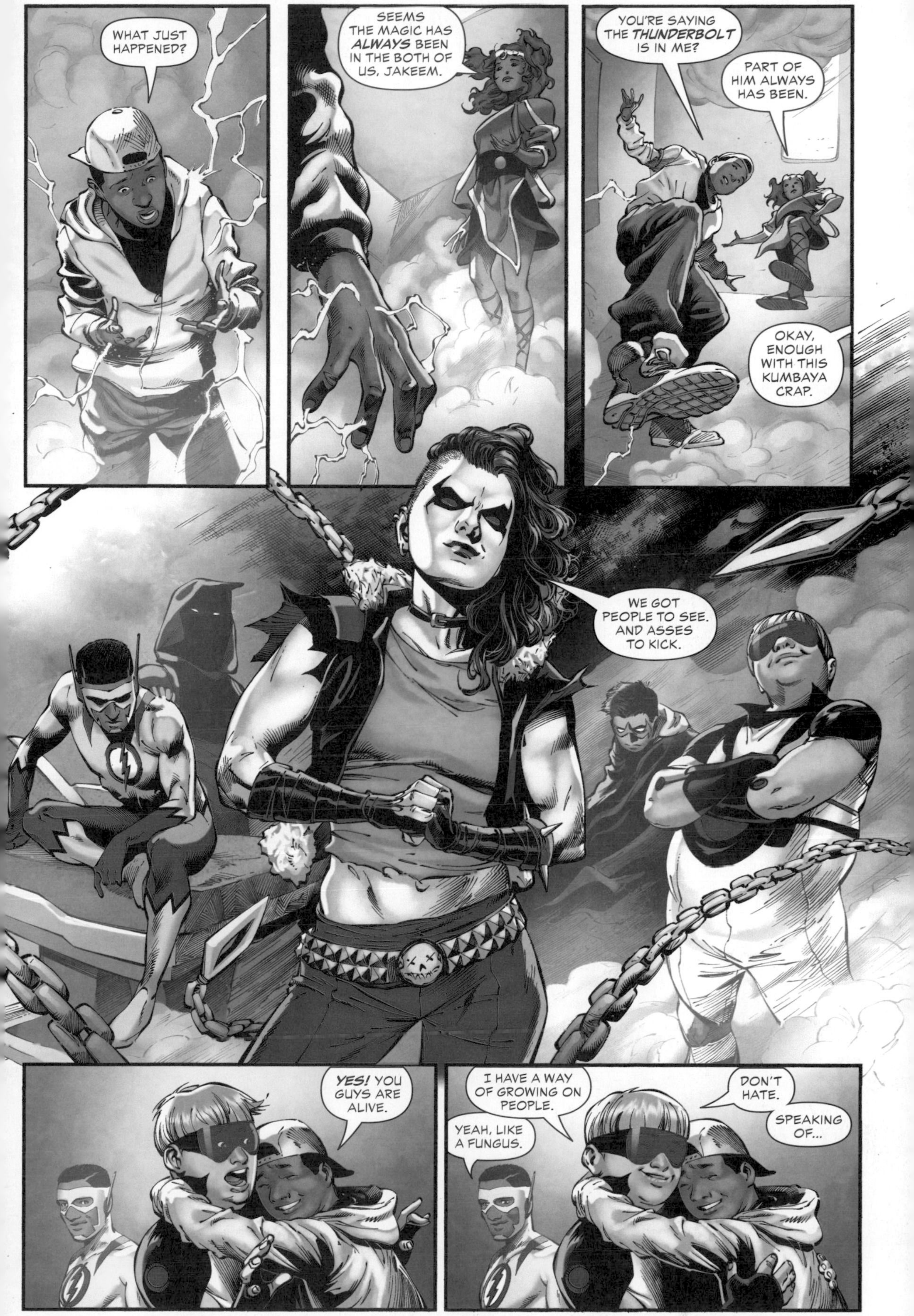
WHAT JUST HAPPENED?
SEEMS THE MAGIC HAS ALWAYS BEEN IN THE BOTH OF US, JAKEEM.
YOU'RE SAYING THE THUNDERBOLT IS IN ME?
PART OF HIM ALWAYS HAS BEEN.
OKAY, ENOUGH WITH THIS KUMBAYA CRAP.
WE GOT PEOPLE TO SEE. AND ASSES TO KICK.
YES! YOU GUYS ARE ALIVE.
I HAVE A WAY OF GROWING ON PEOPLE.
YEAH, LIKE A FUNGUS.
DON'T HATE.
SPEAKING OF...

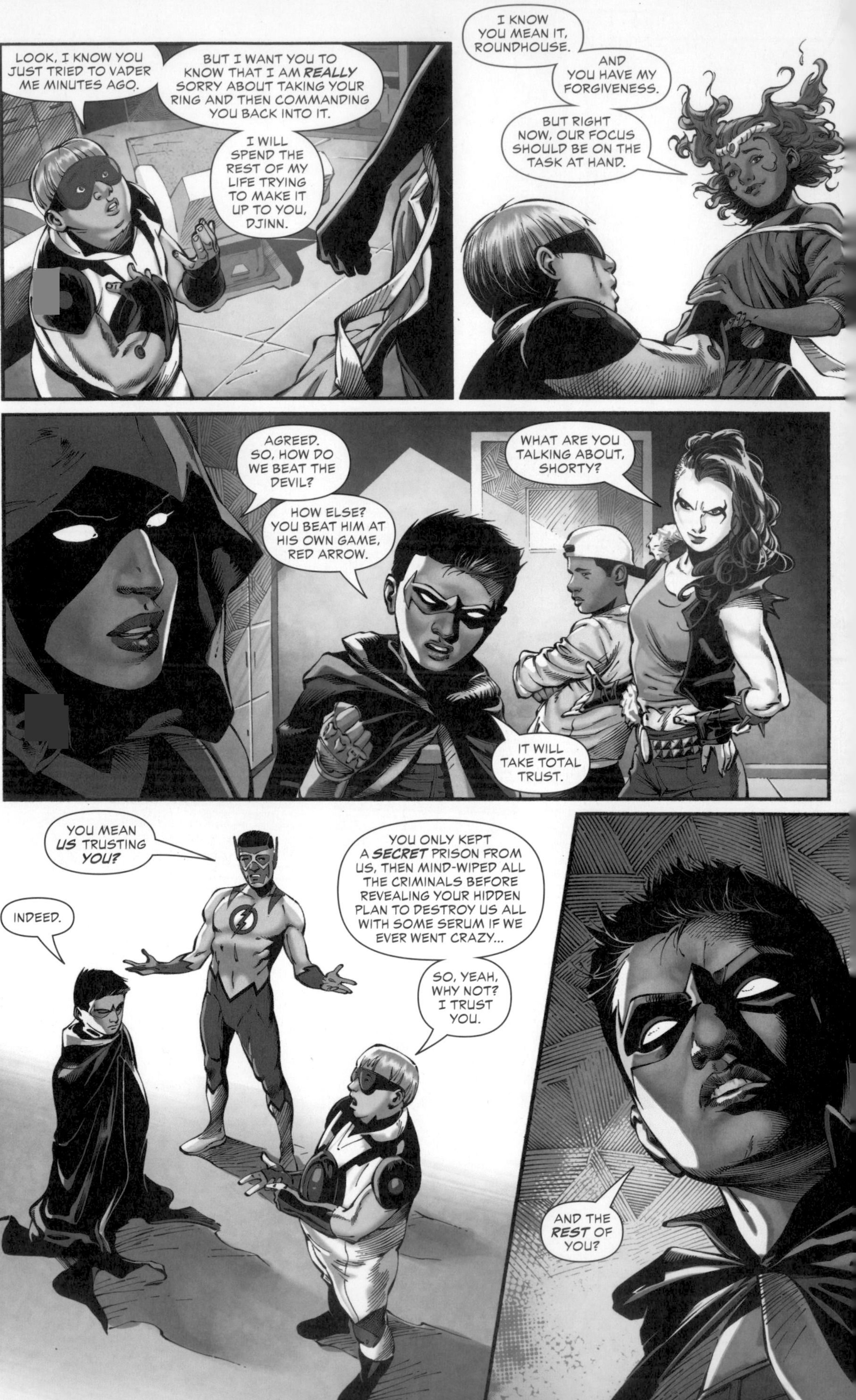
LOOK, I KNOW YOU JUST TRIED TO VADER ME MINUTES AGO.
BUT I WANT YOU TO KNOW THAT I AM REALLY SORRY ABOUT TAKING YOUR RING AND THEN COMMANDING YOU BACK INTO IT.
I WILL SPEND THE REST OF MY LIFE TRYING TO MAKE IT UP TO YOU, DJINN.
I KNOW YOU MEAN IT, ROUNDHOUSE.
AND YOU HAVE MY FORGIVENESS.
BUT RIGHT NOW, OUR FOCUS SHOULD BE ON THE TASK AT HAND.
AGREED. SO, HOW DO WE BEAT THE DEVIL?
HOW ELSE? YOU BEAT HIM AT HIS OWN GAME, RED ARROW.
WHAT ARE YOU TALKING ABOUT, SHORTY?
IT WILL TAKE TOTAL TRUST.
YOU MEAN US TRUSTING YOU?
INDEED.
YOU ONLY KEPT A SECRET PRISON FROM US, THEN MIND-WIPED ALL THE CRIMINALS BEFORE REVEALING YOUR HIDDEN PLAN TO DESTROY US ALL WITH SOME SERUM IF WE EVER WENT CRAZY...
SO, YEAH, WHY NOT? I TRUST YOU.
AND THE REST OF YOU?

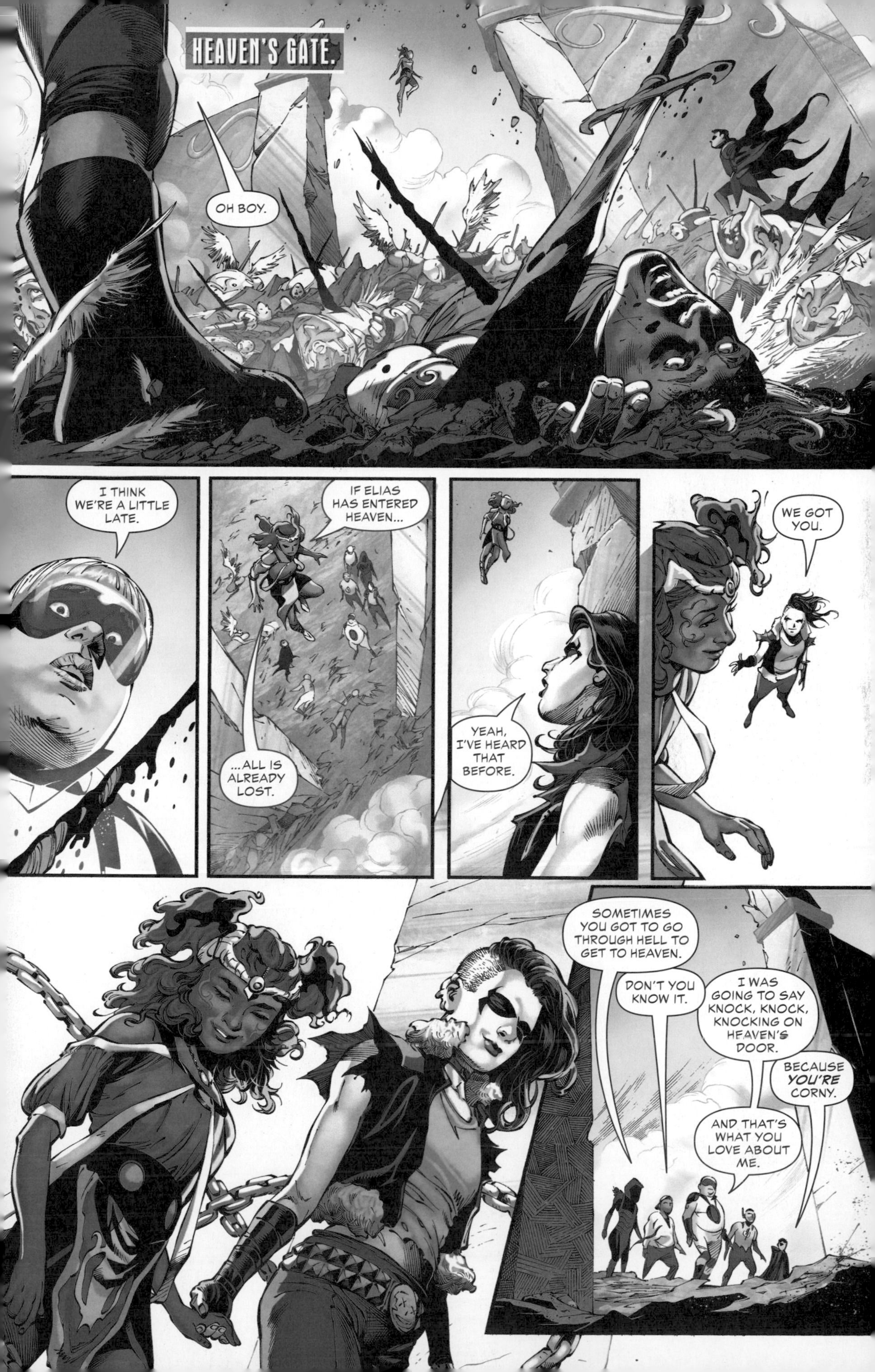
HEAVEN'S GATE.
OH BOY.
I THINK WE'RE A LITTLE LATE.
IF ELIAS HAS ENTERED HEAVEN...
...ALL IS ALREADY LOST.
YEAH, I'VE HEARD THAT BEFORE.
WE GOT YOU.
SOMETIMES YOU GOT TO GO THROUGH HELL TO GET TO HEAVEN.
DON'T YOU KNOW IT.
I WAS GOING TO SAY KNOCK, KNOCK, KNOCKING ON HEAVEN'S DOOR.
BECAUSE *YOU'RE* CORNY.
AND THAT'S WHAT YOU LOVE ABOUT ME.

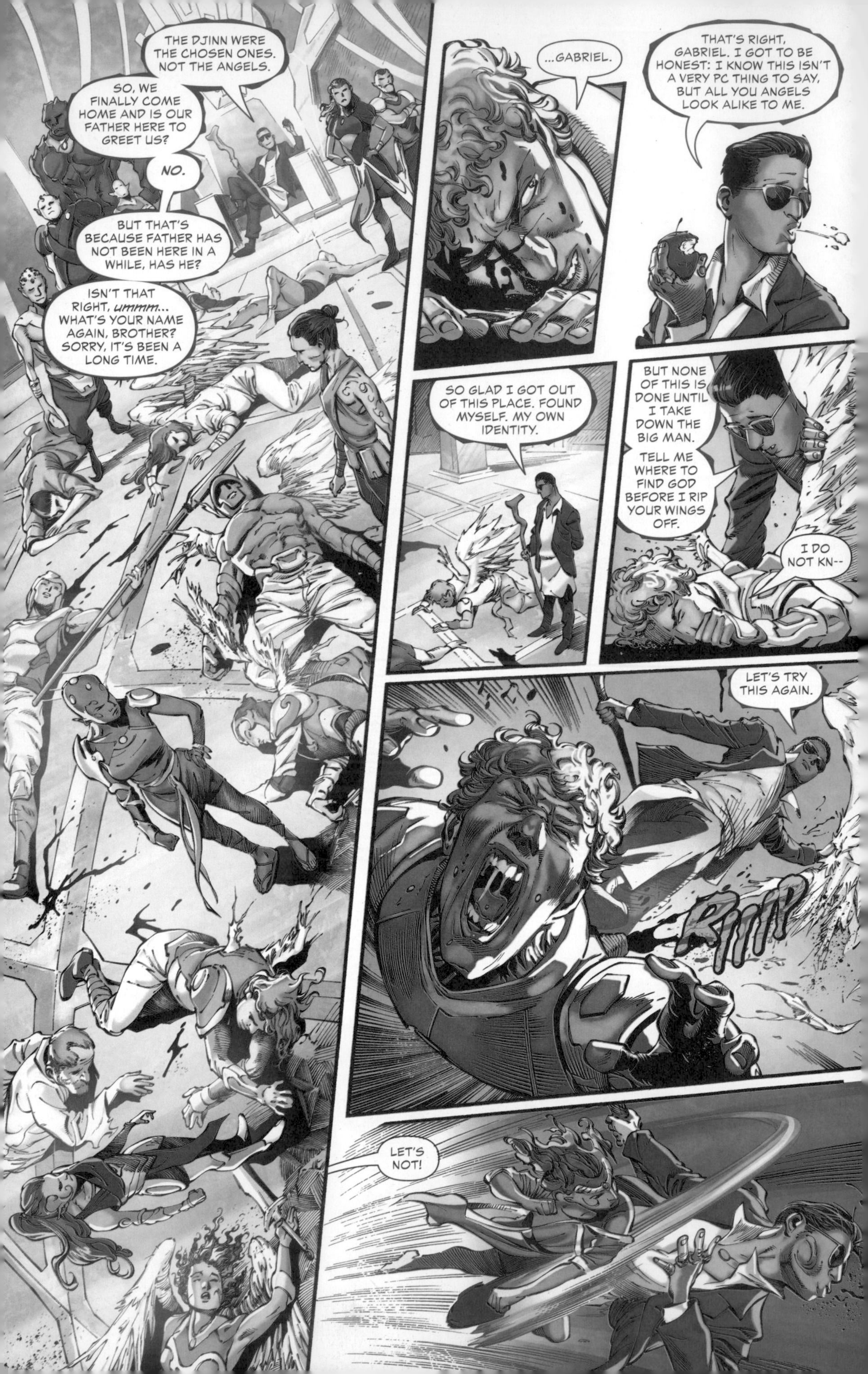
THE DJINN WERE THE CHOSEN ONES. NOT THE ANGELS.
SO, WE FINALLY COME HOME AND IS OUR FATHER HERE TO GREET US?
NO.
BUT THAT'S BECAUSE FATHER HAS NOT BEEN HERE IN A WHILE, HAS HE?
ISN'T THAT RIGHT, *UMMMM*... WHAT'S YOUR NAME AGAIN, BROTHER? SORRY, IT'S BEEN A LONG TIME.
...GABRIEL.
THAT'S RIGHT, GABRIEL. I GOT TO BE HONEST: I KNOW THIS ISN'T A VERY PC THING TO SAY, BUT ALL YOU ANGELS LOOK ALIKE TO ME.
SO GLAD I GOT OUT OF THIS PLACE. FOUND MYSELF. MY OWN IDENTITY.
BUT NONE OF THIS IS DONE UNTIL I TAKE DOWN THE BIG MAN.
TELL ME WHERE TO FIND GOD BEFORE I RIP YOUR WINGS OFF.
I DO NOT KN--
LET'S TRY THIS AGAIN.
RIIIP
LET'S NOT!

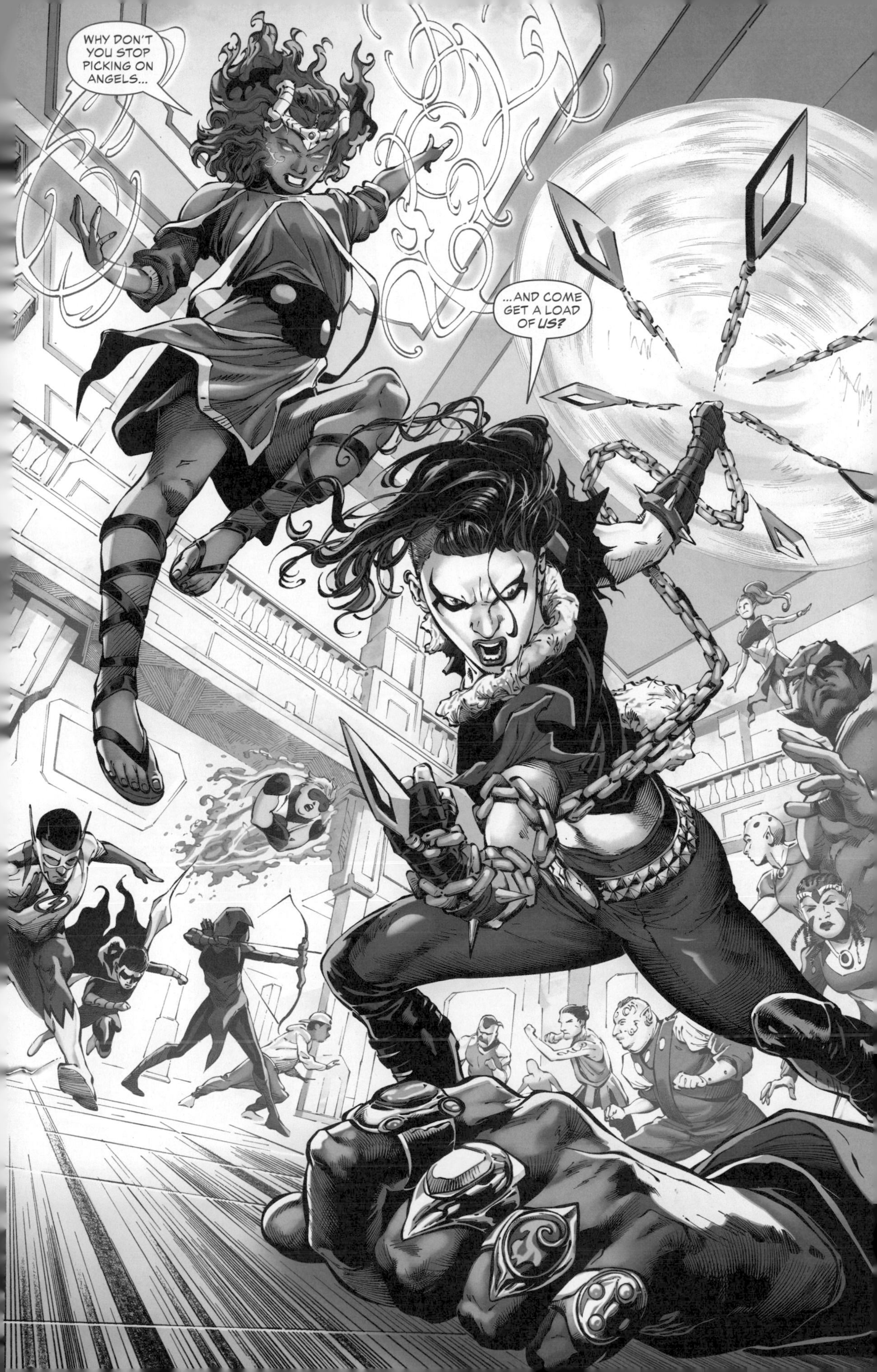
WHY DON'T YOU STOP PICKING ON ANGELS...
...AND COME GET A LOAD OF US?

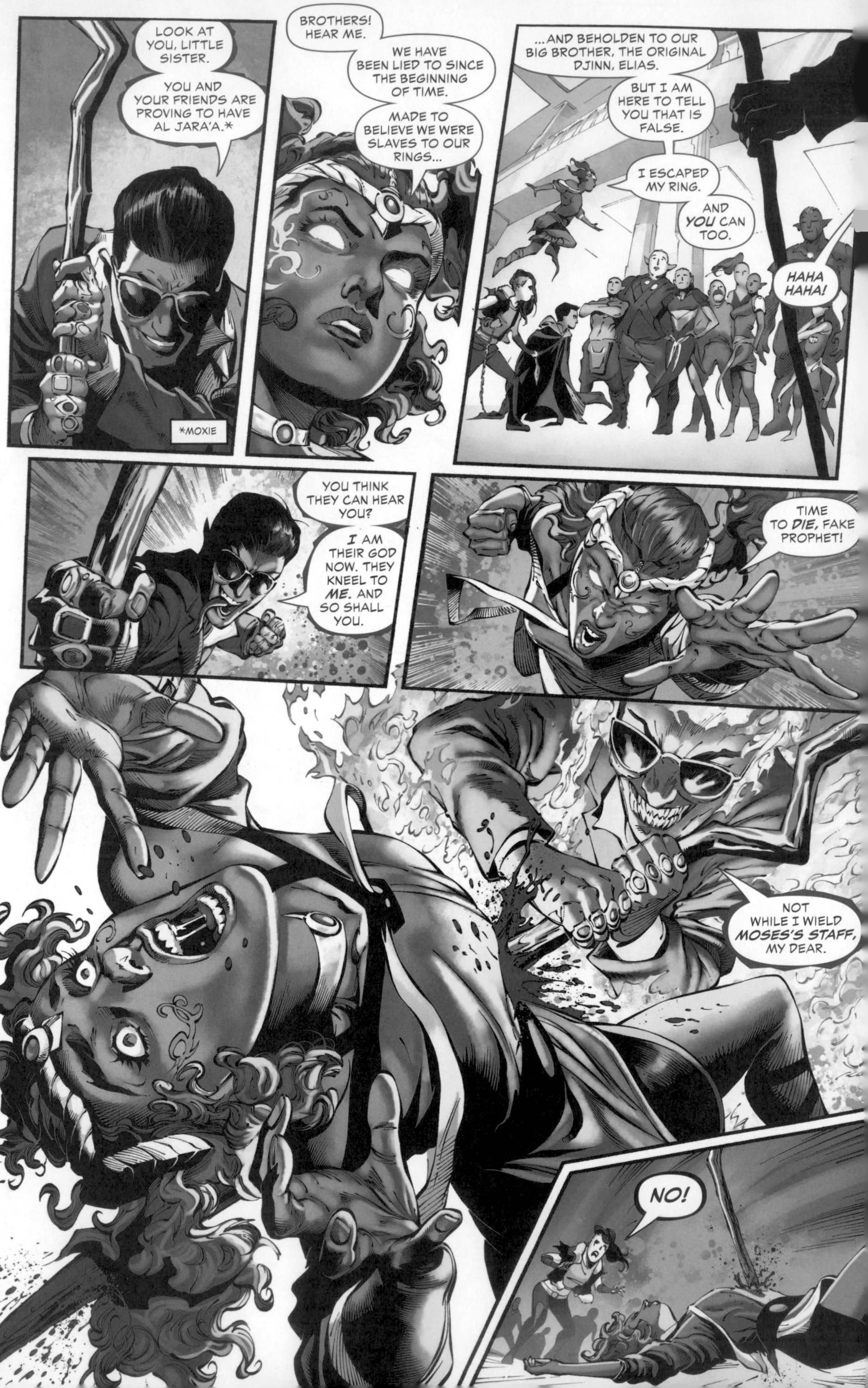
LOOK AT YOU, LITTLE SISTER.
YOU AND YOUR FRIENDS ARE PROVING TO HAVE AL JARA'A.*
*MOXIE
BROTHERS! HEAR ME.
WE HAVE BEEN LIED TO SINCE THE BEGINNING OF TIME.
MADE TO BELIEVE WE WERE SLAVES TO OUR RINGS...
...AND BEHOLDEN TO OUR BIG BROTHER, THE ORIGINAL DJINN, ELIAS.
BUT I AM HERE TO TELL YOU THAT IS FALSE.
I ESCAPED MY RING.
AND YOU CAN TOO.
HAHA HAHA!
YOU THINK THEY CAN HEAR YOU?
I AM THEIR GOD NOW. THEY KNEEL TO ME. AND SO SHALL YOU.
TIME TO DIE, FAKE PROPHET!
NOT WHILE I WIELD MOSES'S STAFF, MY DEAR.
NO!

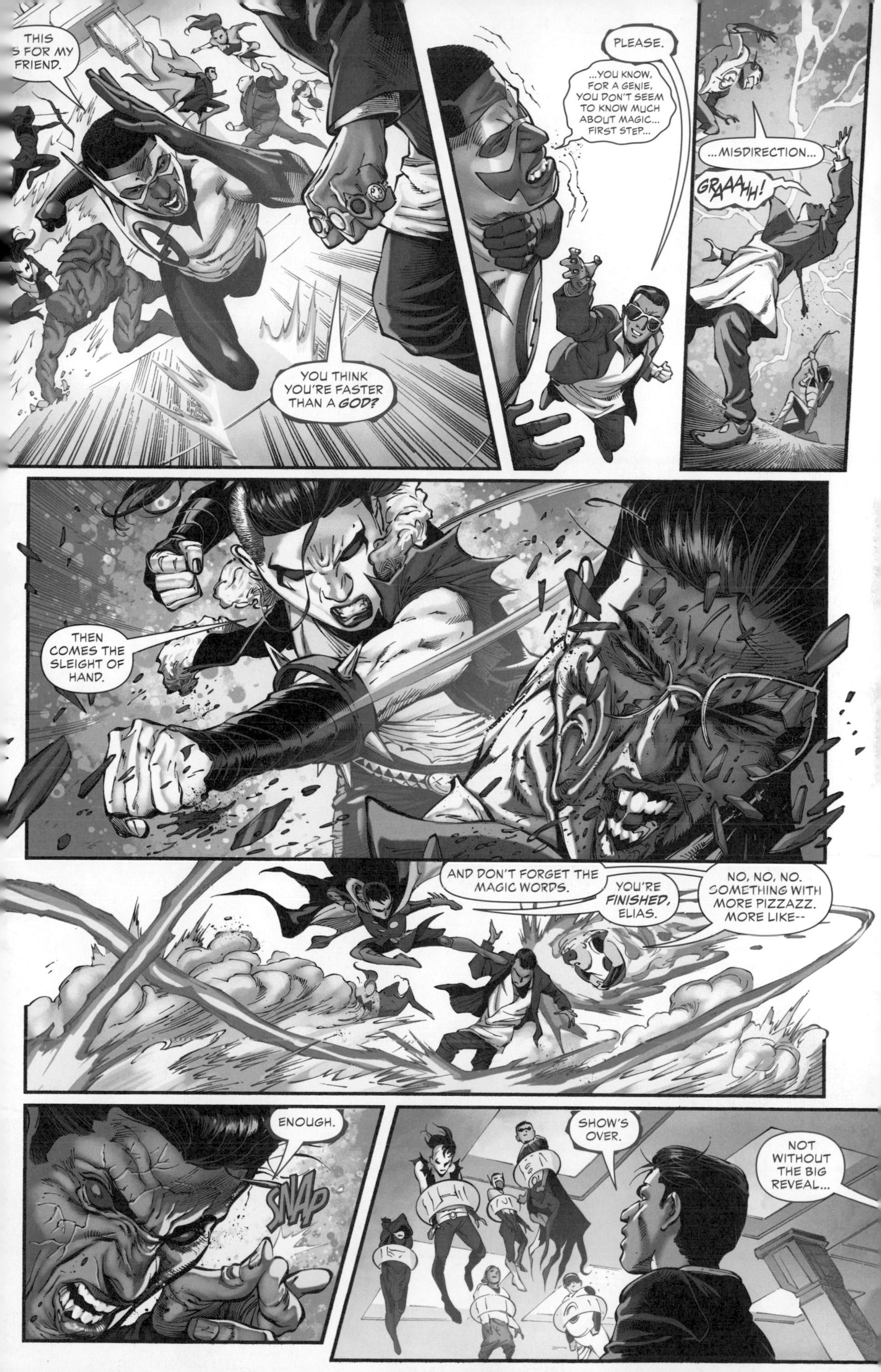
THIS S FOR MY FRIEND.
YOU THINK YOU'RE FASTER THAN A GOD?
PLEASE.
...YOU KNOW, FOR A GENIE, YOU DON'T SEEM TO KNOW MUCH ABOUT MAGIC... FIRST STEP...
...MISDIRECTION...
GRAAAHH!
THEN COMES THE SLEIGHT OF HAND.
AND DON'T FORGET THE MAGIC WORDS.
YOU'RE FINISHED, ELIAS.
NO, NO, NO. SOMETHING WITH MORE PIZZAZZ. MORE LIKE--
ENOUGH.
SNAP
SHOW'S OVER.
NOT WITHOUT THE BIG REVEAL...

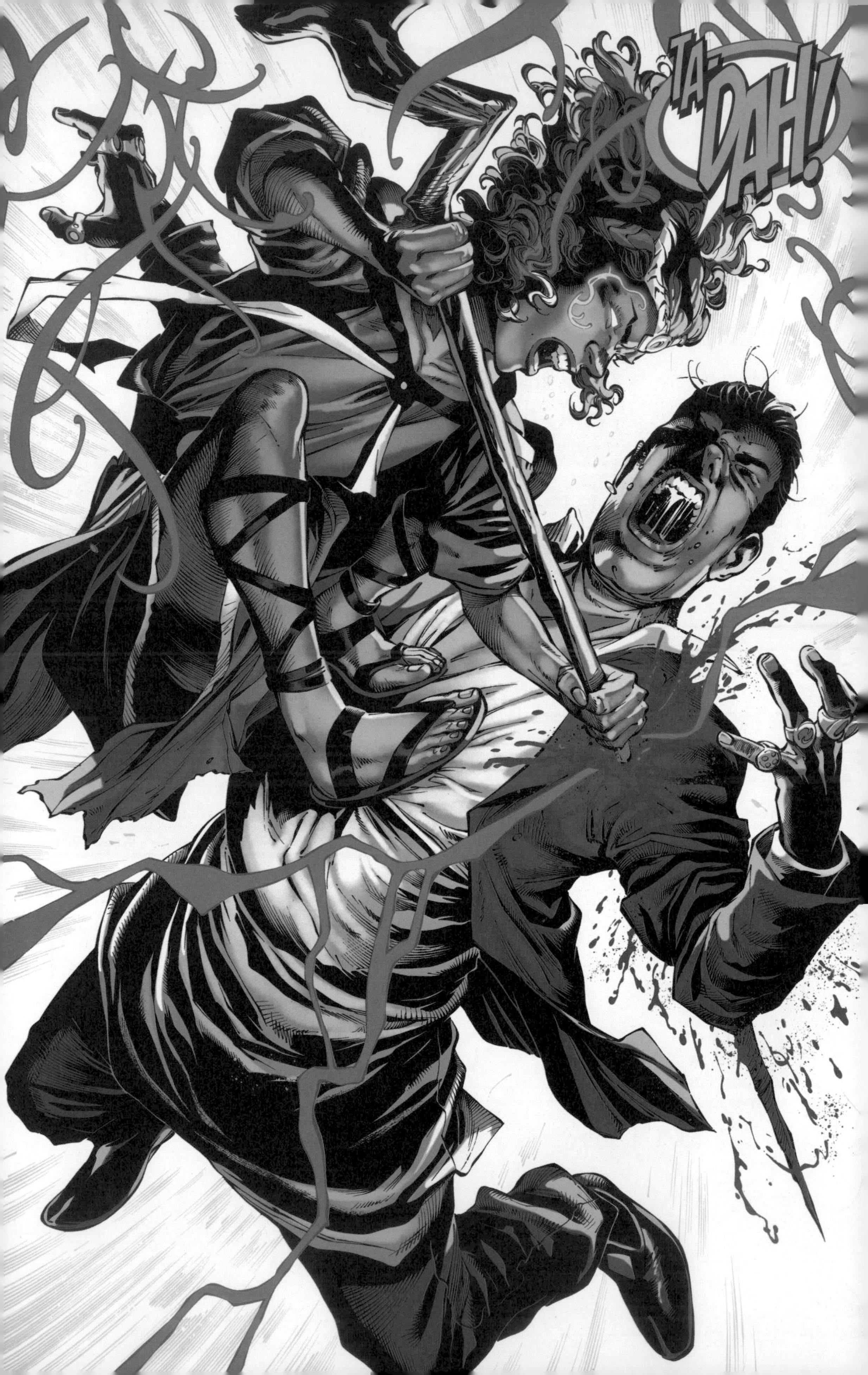
TA-DAH!

IMPOSSIBLE.

I THOUGHT SO, TOO.

BUT ROBIN AND CRUSH KNEW. THE MAGIC WAS IN ME.

YOU'VE BEEN BLINDED BY RAGE. AMBITION. SO MUCH SO THAT YOU SAW WHAT YOU WANTED...

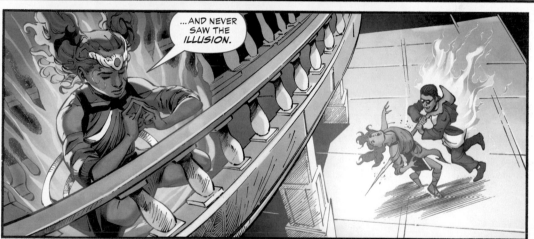

...AND NEVER SAW THE ILLUSION.

BUT YOU NEVER REALLY SAW ME, DID YOU?

WHAT I'M CAPABLE OF.

WHAT ARE WE GONNA DO WITH HIM? I DUNNO IF A MIND WIPE IS GONNA WORK HERE, BROS.

IT'S UP TO DJINN.

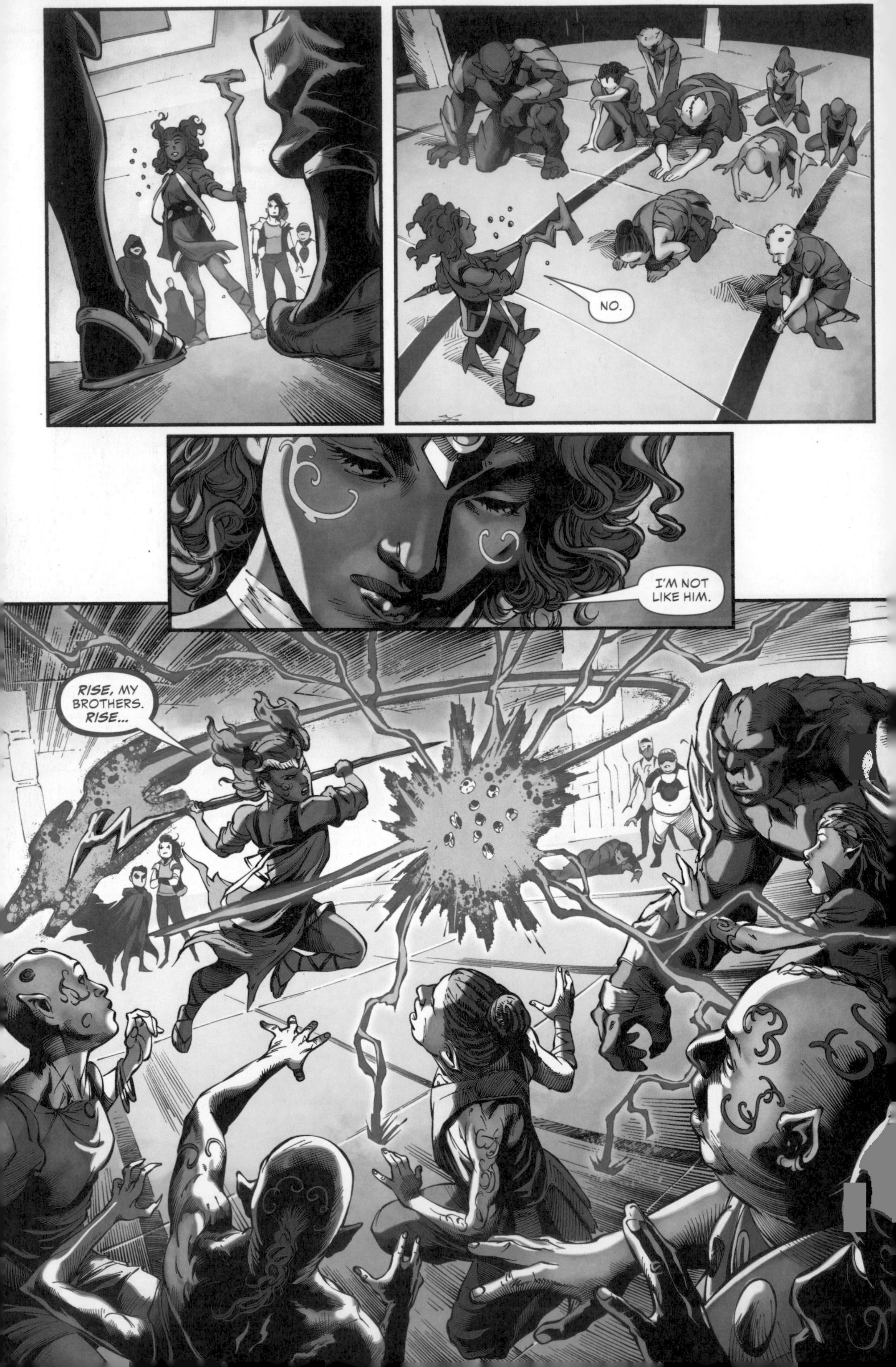
NO.
I'M NOT LIKE HIM.
RISE, MY BROTHERS. RISE...

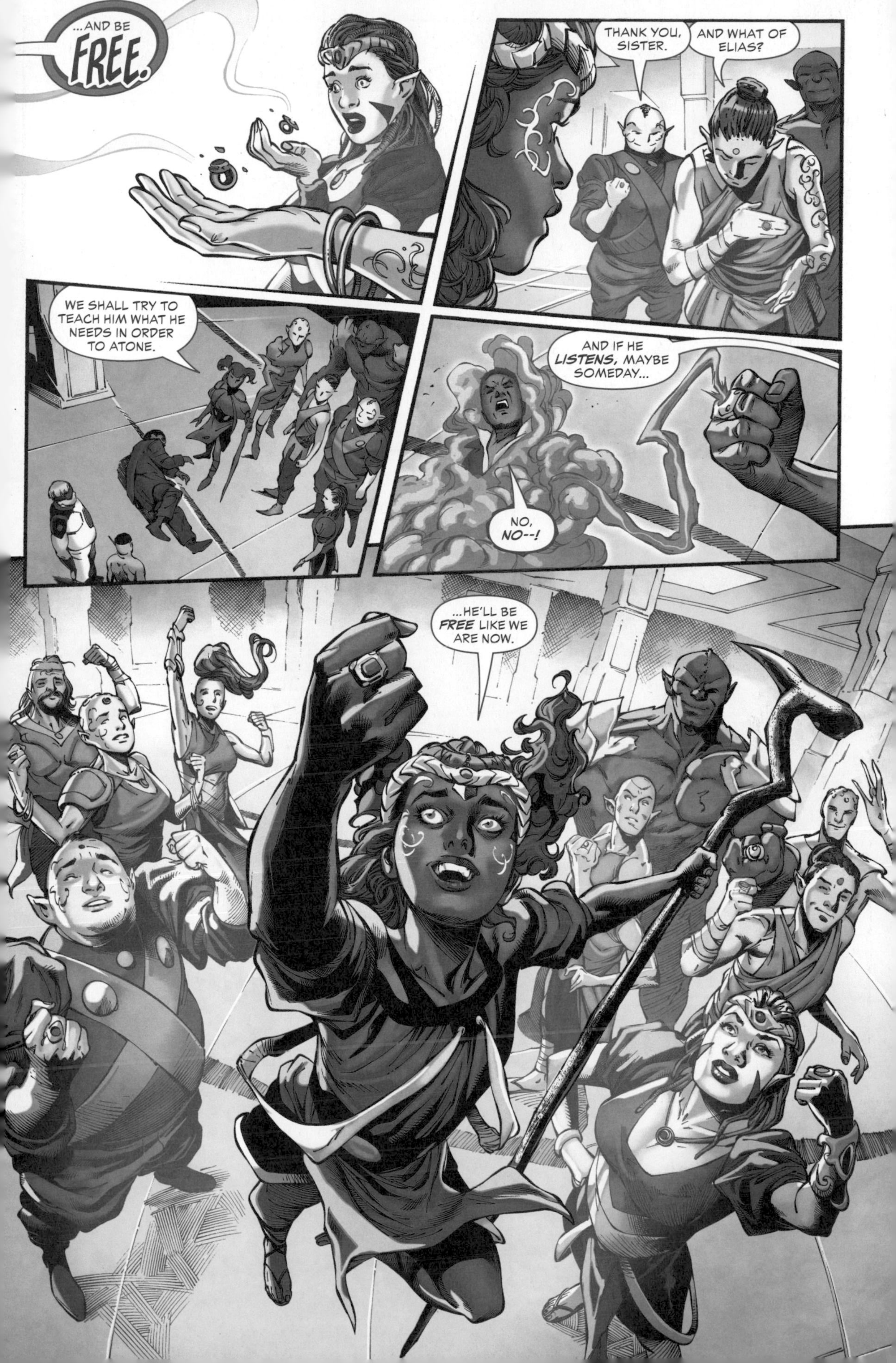
...AND BE FREE.
THANK YOU, SISTER.
AND WHAT OF ELIAS?
WE SHALL TRY TO TEACH HIM WHAT HE NEEDS IN ORDER TO ATONE.
AND IF HE LISTENS, MAYBE SOMEDAY...
NO, NO--!
...HE'LL BE FREE LIKE WE ARE NOW.

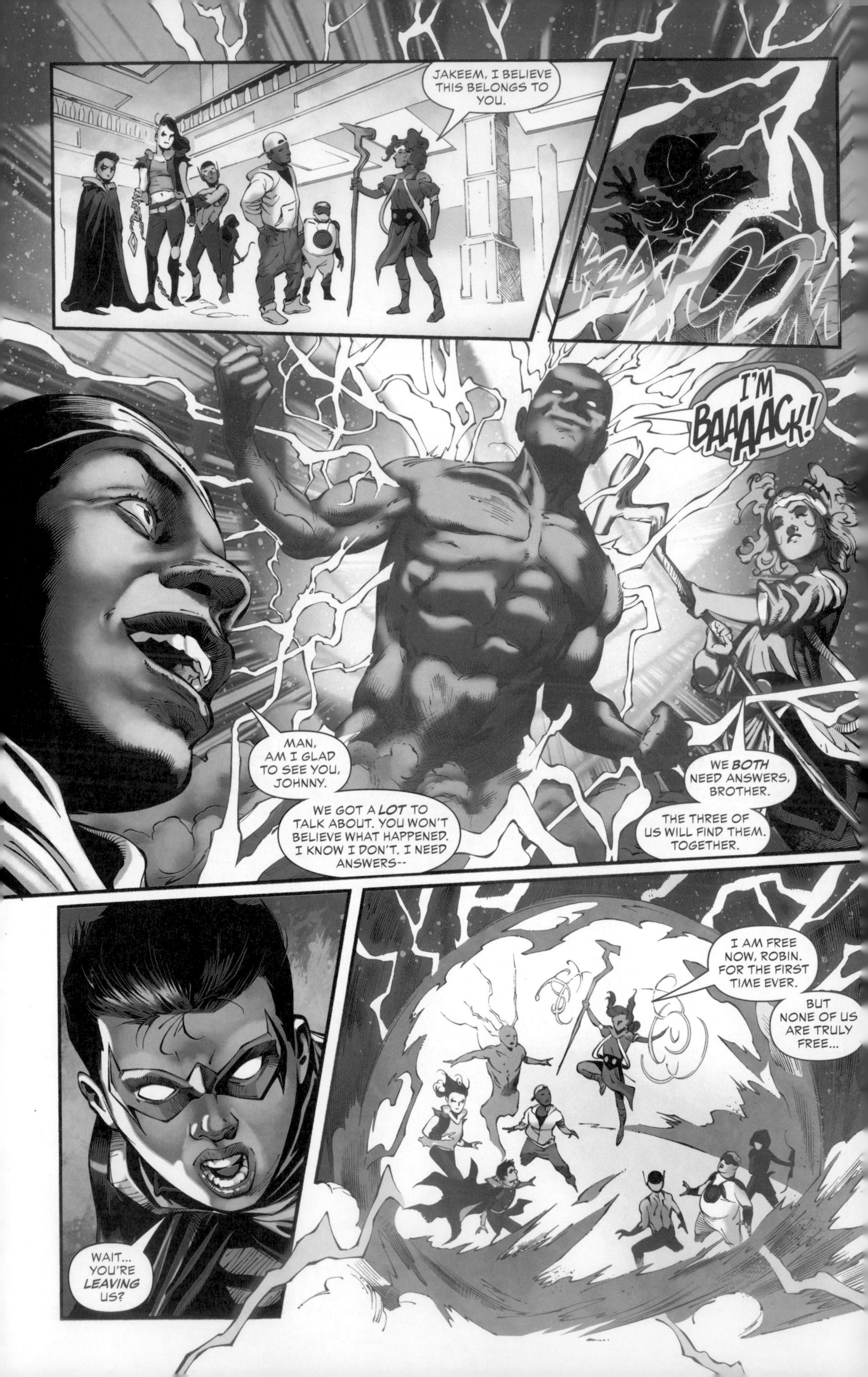

JAKEEM, I BELIEVE THIS BELONGS TO YOU.
I'M BAAAACK!
MAN, AM I GLAD TO SEE YOU, JOHNNY.
WE GOT A *LOT* TO TALK ABOUT. YOU WON'T BELIEVE WHAT HAPPENED. I KNOW I DON'T. I NEED ANSWERS--
WE *BOTH* NEED ANSWERS, BROTHER.
THE THREE OF US WILL FIND THEM. TOGETHER.
WAIT... YOU'RE *LEAVING* US?
I AM FREE NOW, ROBIN. FOR THE FIRST TIME EVER.
BUT NONE OF US ARE TRULY FREE...

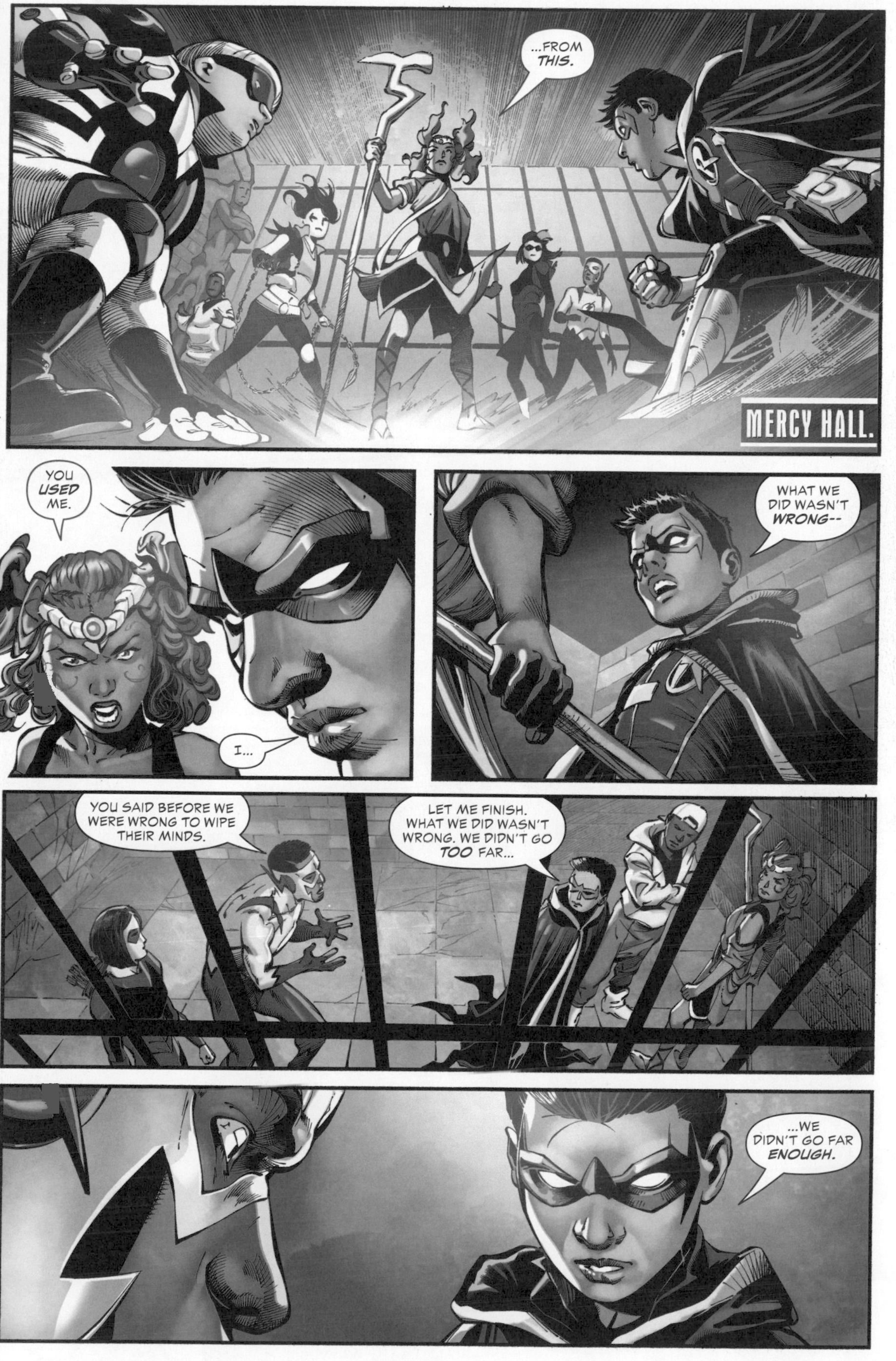
...FROM THIS.
MERCY HALL.
YOU USED ME.
I...
WHAT WE DID WASN'T WRONG--
YOU SAID BEFORE WE WERE WRONG TO WIPE THEIR MINDS.
LET ME FINISH. WHAT WE DID WASN'T WRONG. WE DIDN'T GO TOO FAR...
...WE DIDN'T GO FAR ENOUGH.

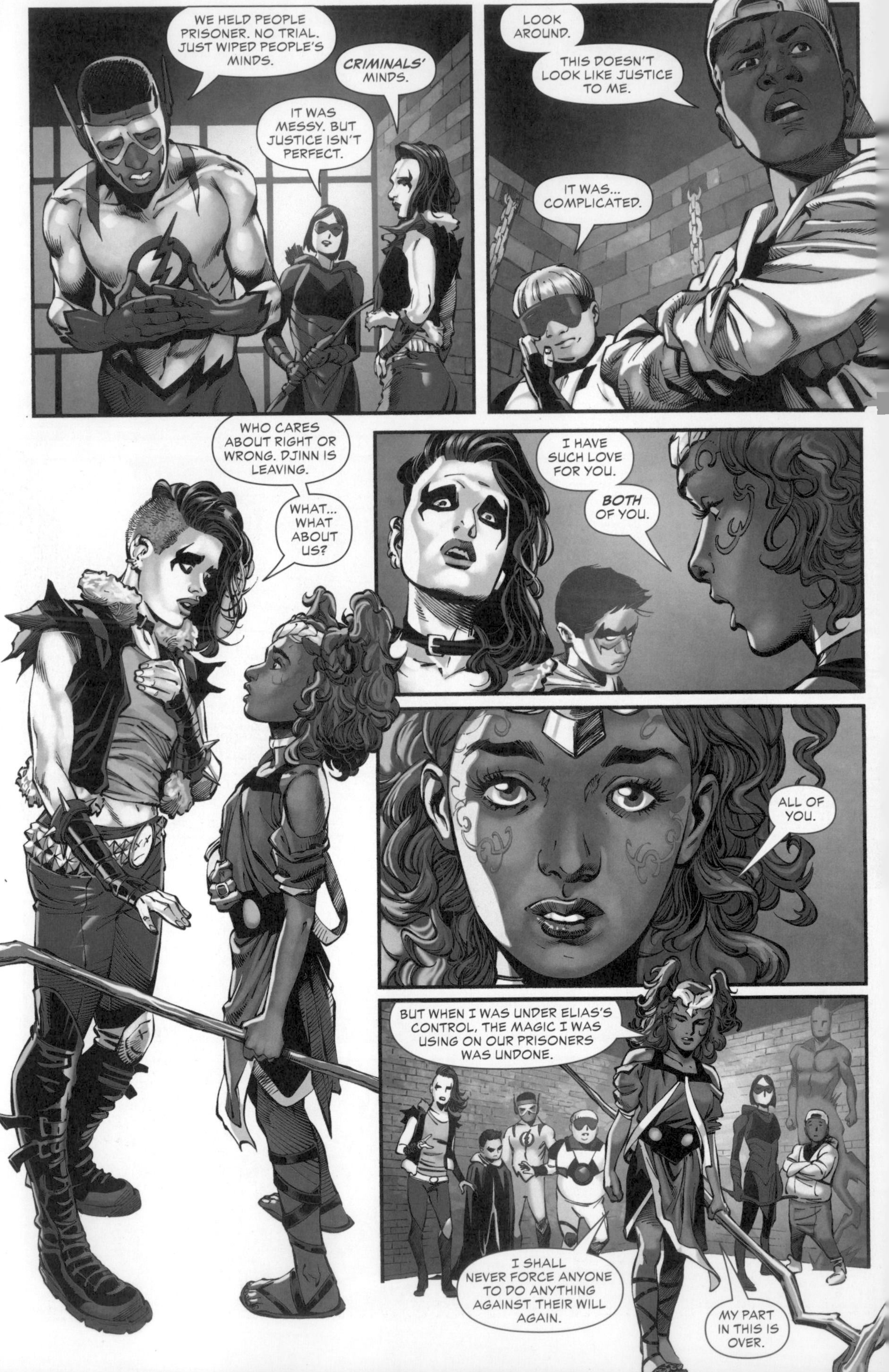
WE HELD PEOPLE PRISONER. NO TRIAL. JUST WIPED PEOPLE'S MINDS.
CRIMINALS' MINDS.
IT WAS MESSY. BUT JUSTICE ISN'T PERFECT.
LOOK AROUND.
THIS DOESN'T LOOK LIKE JUSTICE TO ME.
IT WAS... COMPLICATED.
WHO CARES ABOUT RIGHT OR WRONG. DJINN IS LEAVING.
WHAT... WHAT ABOUT US?
I HAVE SUCH LOVE FOR YOU.
BOTH OF YOU.
ALL OF YOU.
BUT WHEN I WAS UNDER ELIAS'S CONTROL, THE MAGIC I WAS USING ON OUR PRISONERS WAS UNDONE.
I SHALL NEVER FORCE ANYONE TO DO ANYTHING AGAINST THEIR WILL AGAIN.
MY PART IN THIS IS OVER.

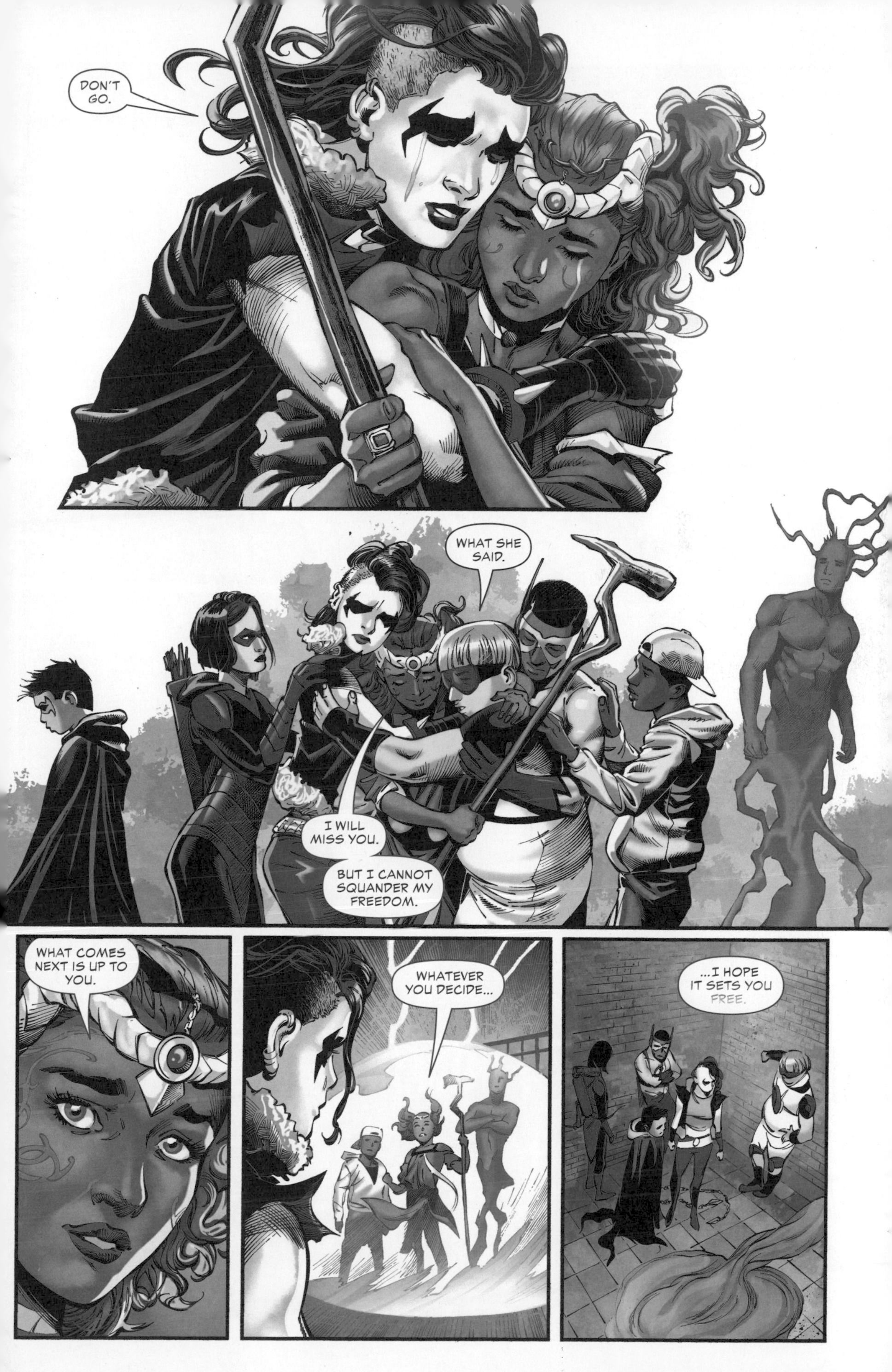
DON'T GO.
WHAT SHE SAID.
I WILL MISS YOU.
BUT I CANNOT SQUANDER MY FREEDOM.
WHAT COMES NEXT IS UP TO YOU.
WHATEVER YOU DECIDE...
...I HOPE IT SETS YOU FREE.

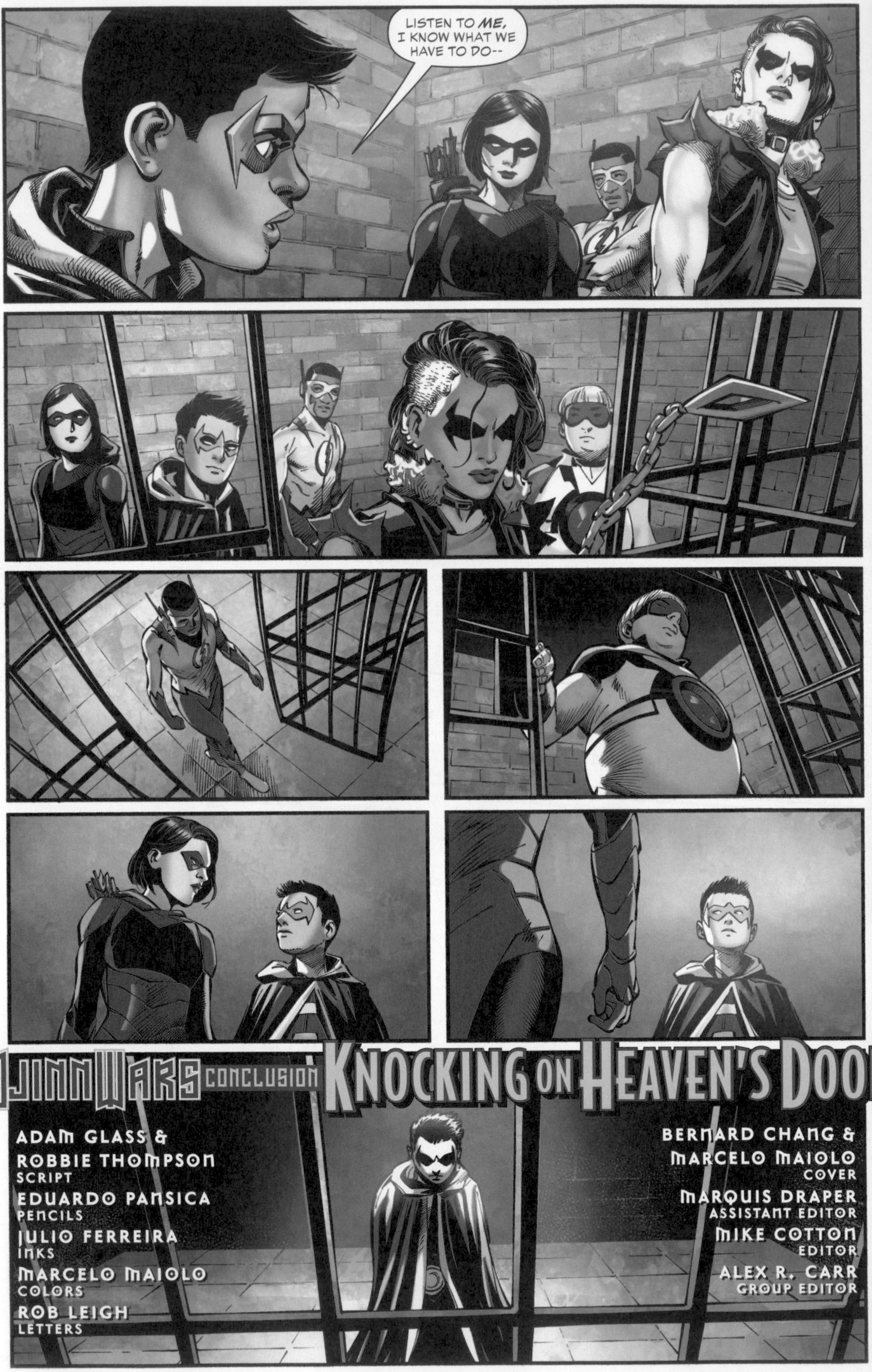
LISTEN TO ME, I KNOW WHAT WE HAVE TO DO--
DJINN WARS CONCLUSION
KNOCKING ON HEAVEN'S DOO
ADAM GLASS & ROBBIE THOMPSON SCRIPT
EDUARDO PANSICA PENCILS
JULIO FERREIRA INKS
MARCELO MAIOLO COLORS
ROB LEIGH LETTERS
BERNARD CHANG & MARCELO MAIOLO COVER
MARQUIS DRAPER ASSISTANT EDITOR
MIKE COTTON EDITOR
ALEX R. CARR GROUP EDITOR

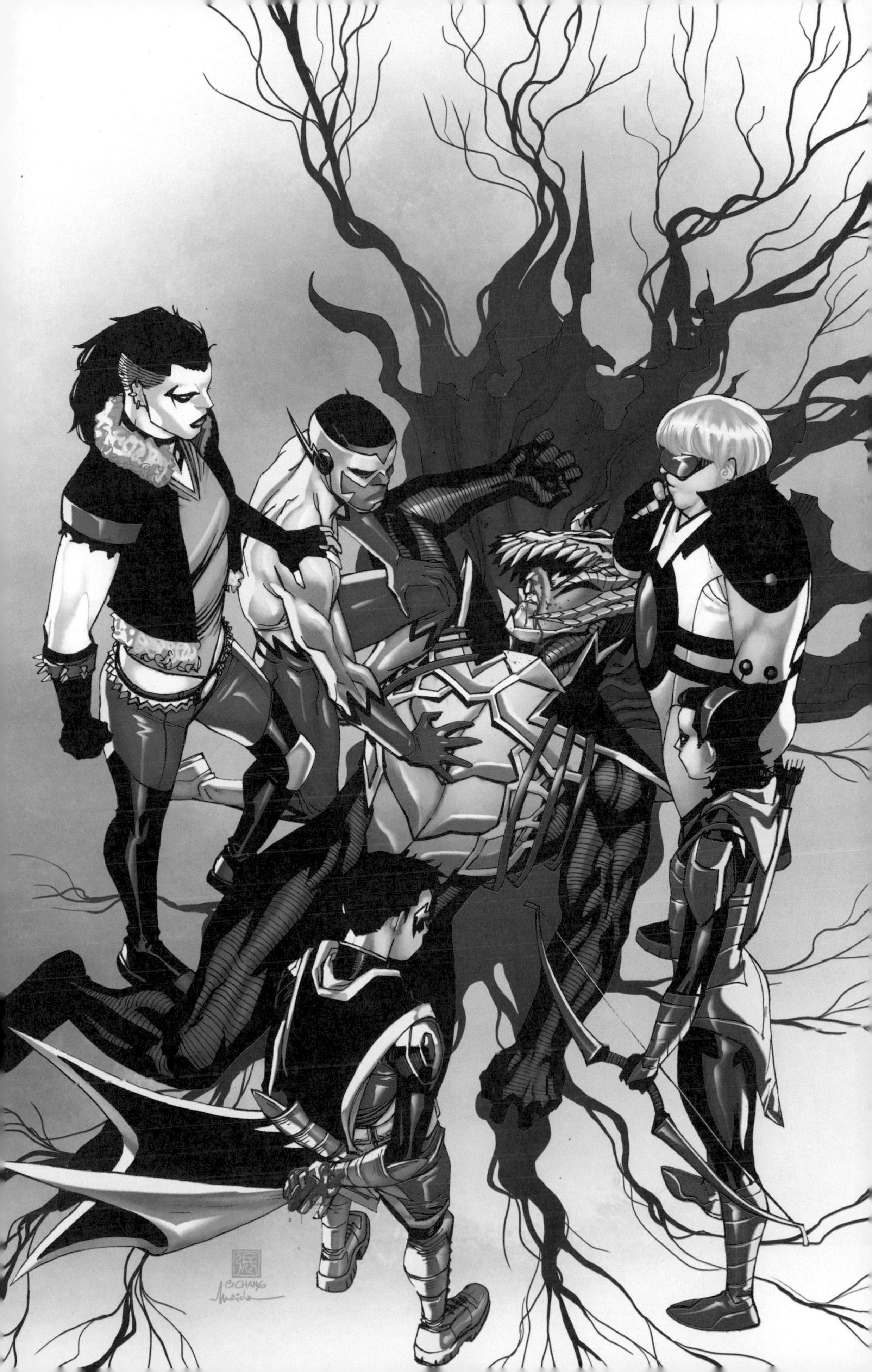

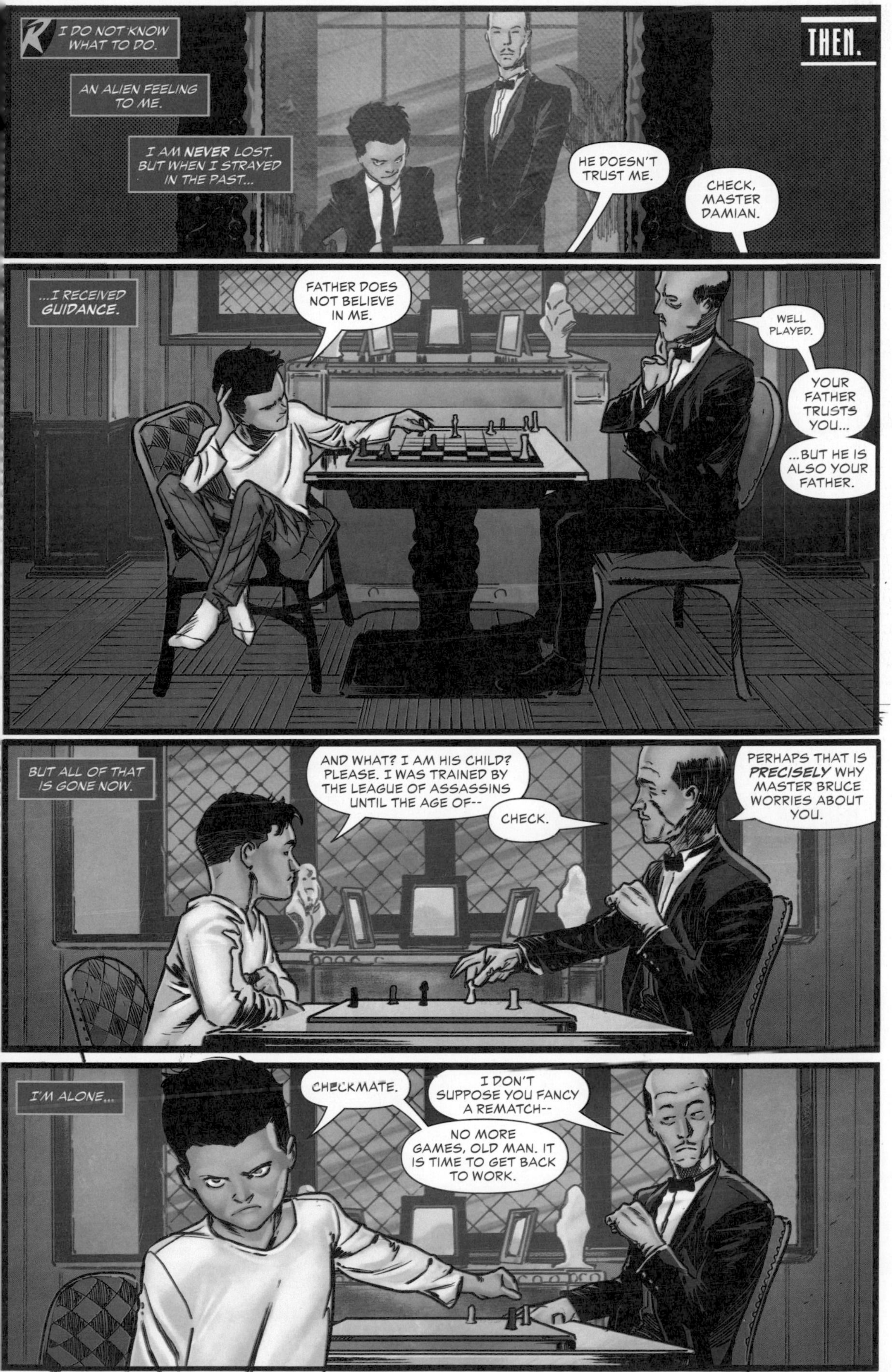
I DO NOT KNOW WHAT TO DO.
AN ALIEN FEELING TO ME.
I AM NEVER LOST. BUT WHEN I STRAYED IN THE PAST...
THEN.
HE DOESN'T TRUST ME.
CHECK, MASTER DAMIAN.
...I RECEIVED GUIDANCE.
FATHER DOES NOT BELIEVE IN ME.
WELL PLAYED.
YOUR FATHER TRUSTS YOU...
...BUT HE IS ALSO YOUR FATHER.
BUT ALL OF THAT IS GONE NOW.
AND WHAT? I AM HIS CHILD? PLEASE. I WAS TRAINED BY THE LEAGUE OF ASSASSINS UNTIL THE AGE OF--
CHECK.
PERHAPS THAT IS PRECISELY WHY MASTER BRUCE WORRIES ABOUT YOU.
I'M ALONE...
CHECKMATE.
I DON'T SUPPOSE YOU FANCY A REMATCH--
NO MORE GAMES, OLD MAN. IT IS TIME TO GET BACK TO WORK.

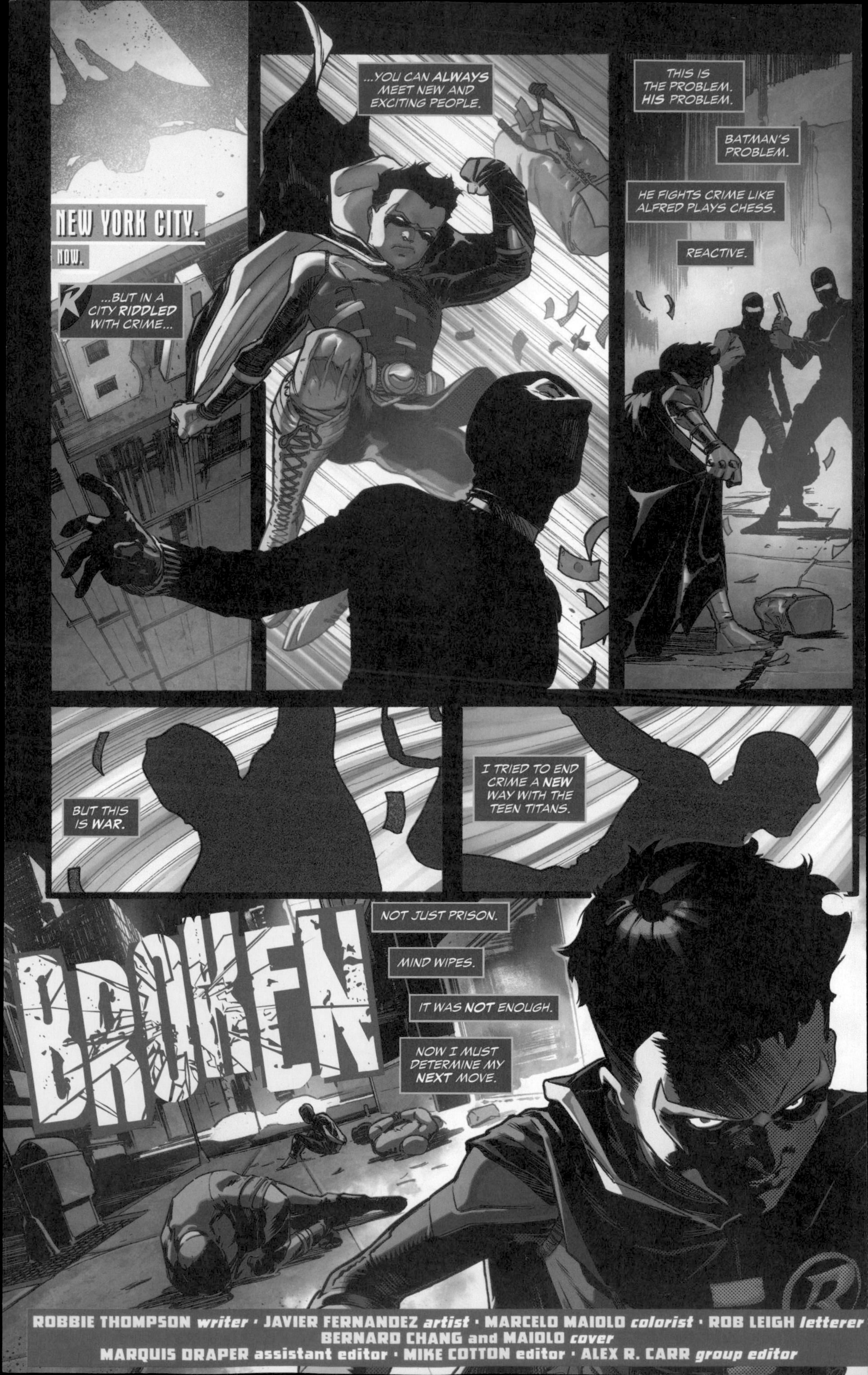
NEW YORK CITY.
NOW.
...BUT IN A CITY RIDDLED WITH CRIME...
...YOU CAN ALWAYS MEET NEW AND EXCITING PEOPLE.
THIS IS THE PROBLEM. HIS PROBLEM.
BATMAN'S PROBLEM.
HE FIGHTS CRIME LIKE ALFRED PLAYS CHESS.
REACTIVE.
BUT THIS IS WAR.
I TRIED TO END CRIME A NEW WAY WITH THE TEEN TITANS.
BROKEN
NOT JUST PRISON.
MIND WIPES.
IT WAS NOT ENOUGH.
NOW I MUST DETERMINE MY NEXT MOVE.
ROBBIE THOMPSON writer · JAVIER FERNANDEZ artist · MARCELO MAIOLO colorist · ROB LEIGH letterer
BERNARD CHANG and MAIOLO cover
MARQUIS DRAPER assistant editor · MIKE COTTON editor · ALEX R. CARR group editor

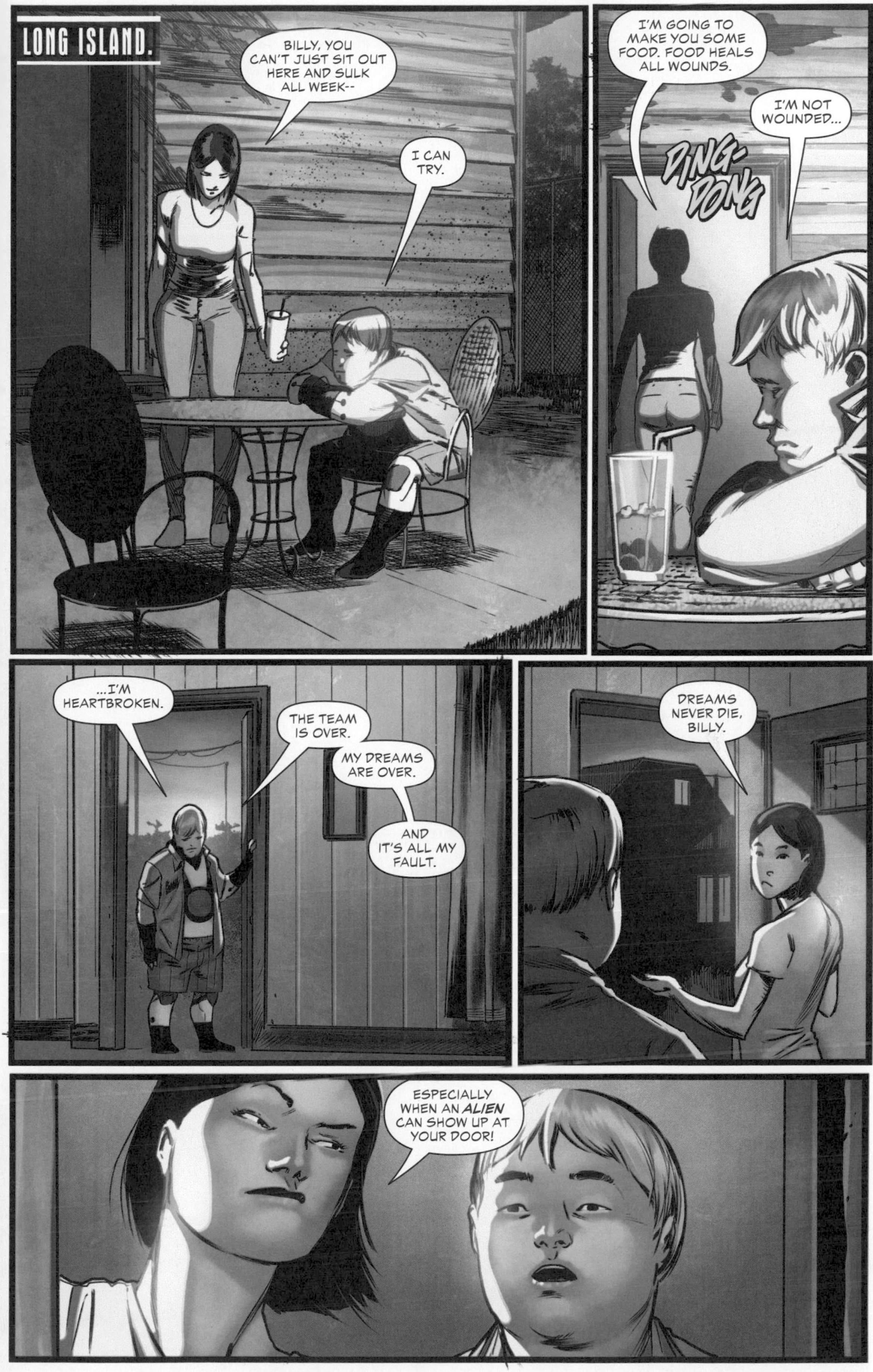
LONG ISLAND.
BILLY, YOU CAN'T JUST SIT OUT HERE AND SULK ALL WEEK--
I CAN TRY.
I'M GOING TO MAKE YOU SOME FOOD. FOOD HEALS ALL WOUNDS.
I'M NOT WOUNDED...
DING-DONG
...I'M HEARTBROKEN.
THE TEAM IS OVER.
MY DREAMS ARE OVER.
AND IT'S ALL MY FAULT.
DREAMS NEVER DIE, BILLY.
ESPECIALLY WHEN AN ALIEN CAN SHOW UP AT YOUR DOOR!

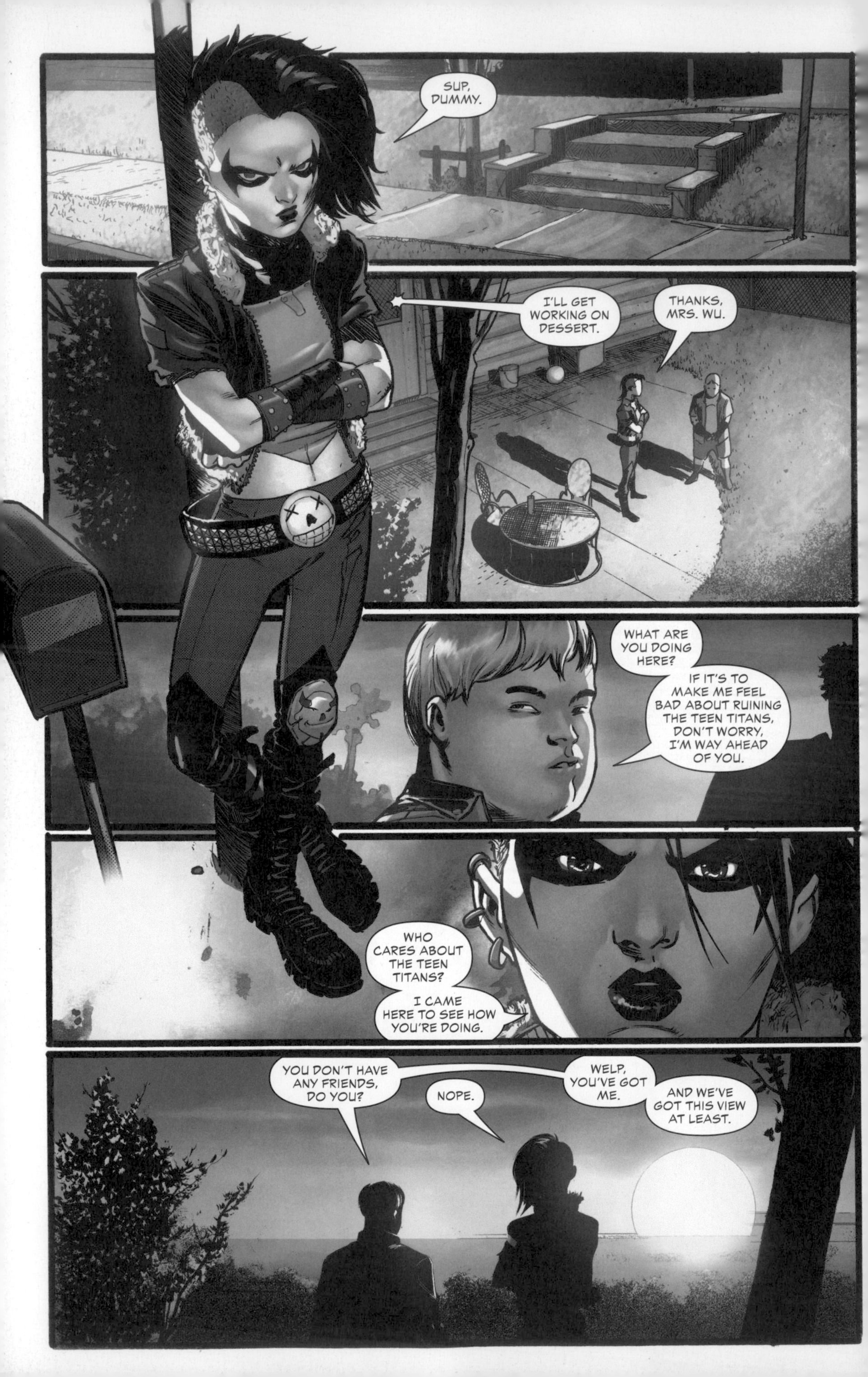
SUP, DUMMY.
I'LL GET WORKING ON DESSERT.
THANKS, MRS. WU.
WHAT ARE YOU DOING HERE?
IF IT'S TO MAKE ME FEEL BAD ABOUT RUINING THE TEEN TITANS, DON'T WORRY, I'M WAY AHEAD OF YOU.
WHO CARES ABOUT THE TEEN TITANS?
I CAME HERE TO SEE HOW YOU'RE DOING.
YOU DON'T HAVE ANY FRIENDS, DO YOU?
NOPE.
WELP, YOU'VE GOT ME.
AND WE'VE GOT THIS VIEW AT LEAST.

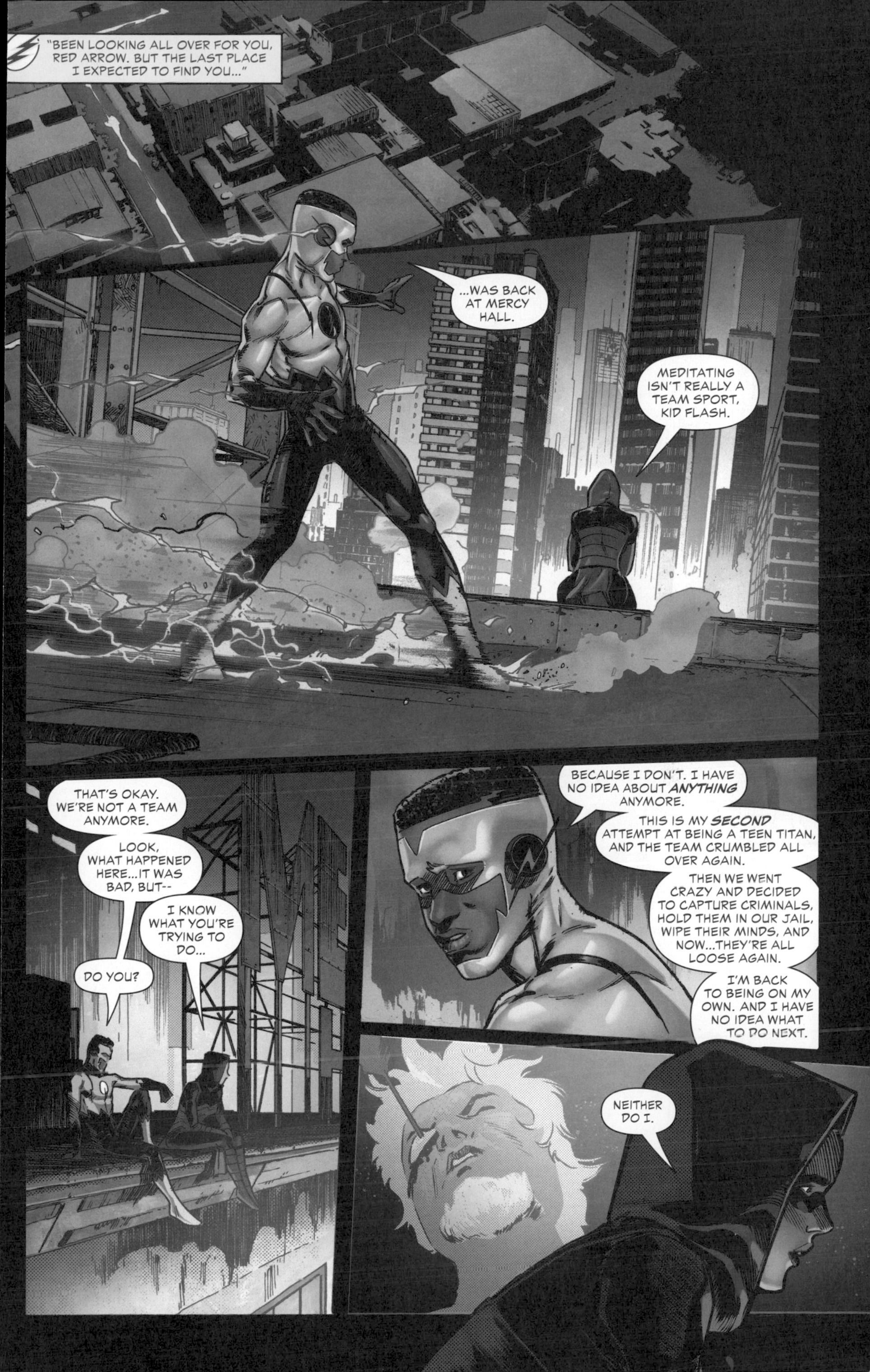
"BEEN LOOKING ALL OVER FOR YOU, RED ARROW. BUT THE LAST PLACE I EXPECTED TO FIND YOU..."
...WAS BACK AT MERCY HALL.
MEDITATING ISN'T REALLY A TEAM SPORT, KID FLASH.
THAT'S OKAY. WE'RE NOT A TEAM ANYMORE.
LOOK, WHAT HAPPENED HERE...IT WAS BAD, BUT--
I KNOW WHAT YOU'RE TRYING TO DO...
DO YOU?
BECAUSE I DON'T. I HAVE NO IDEA ABOUT ANYTHING ANYMORE.
THIS IS MY SECOND ATTEMPT AT BEING A TEEN TITAN, AND THE TEAM CRUMBLED ALL OVER AGAIN.
THEN WE WENT CRAZY AND DECIDED TO CAPTURE CRIMINALS, HOLD THEM IN OUR JAIL, WIPE THEIR MINDS, AND NOW...THEY'RE ALL LOOSE AGAIN.
I'M BACK TO BEING ON MY OWN. AND I HAVE NO IDEA WHAT TO DO NEXT.
NEITHER DO I.

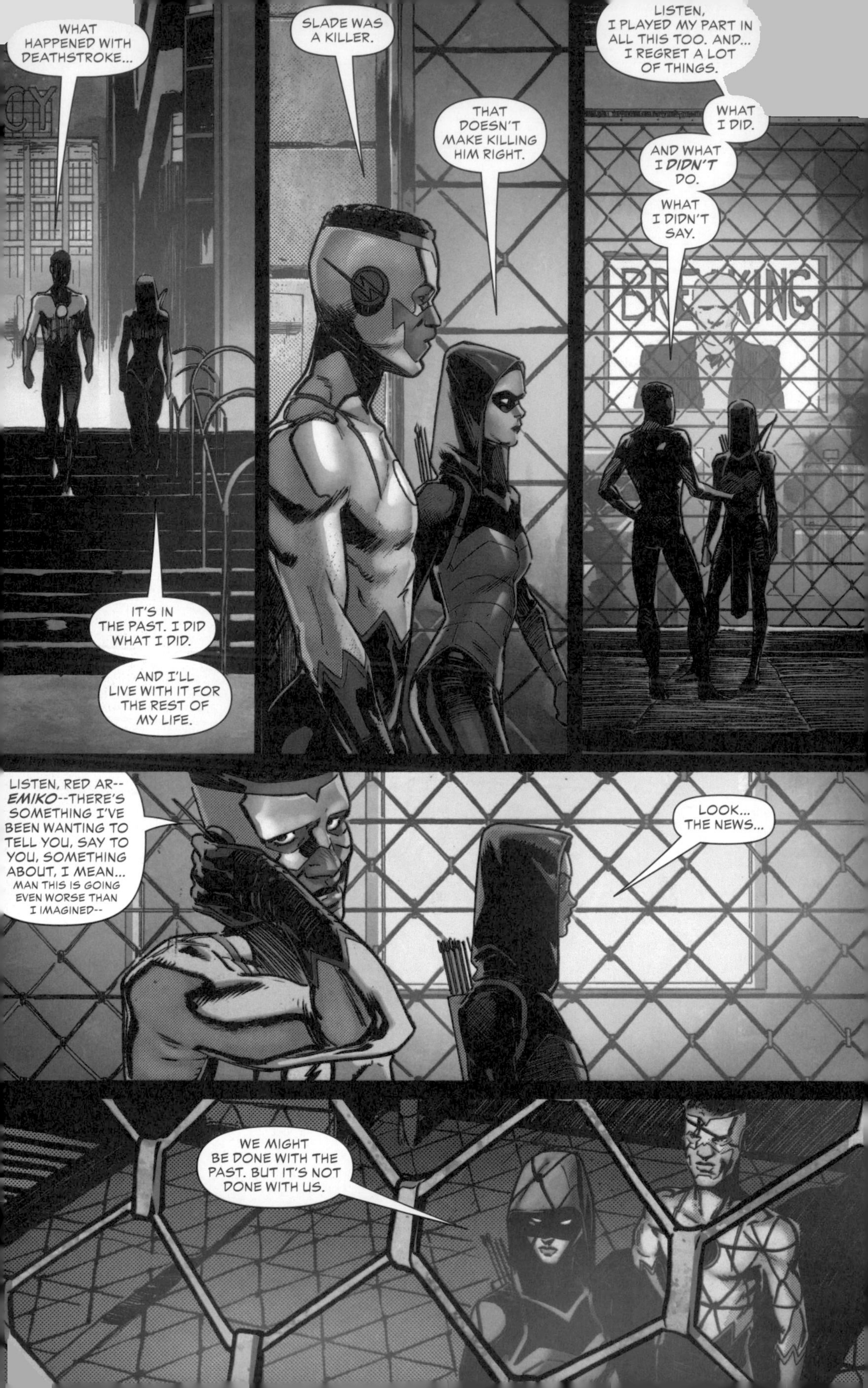
WHAT HAPPENED WITH DEATHSTROKE...
IT'S IN THE PAST. I DID WHAT I DID.
AND I'LL LIVE WITH IT FOR THE REST OF MY LIFE.
SLADE WAS A KILLER.
THAT DOESN'T MAKE KILLING HIM RIGHT.
LISTEN, I PLAYED MY PART IN ALL THIS TOO. AND... I REGRET A LOT OF THINGS.
WHAT I DID.
AND WHAT I *DIDN'T* DO.
WHAT I DIDN'T SAY.
BRE KING
LISTEN, RED AR-- *EMIKO*--THERE'S SOMETHING I'VE BEEN WANTING TO TELL YOU, SAY TO YOU, SOMETHING ABOUT, I MEAN... MAN THIS IS GOING EVEN WORSE THAN I IMAGINED--
LOOK... THE NEWS...
WE MIGHT BE DONE WITH THE PAST. BUT IT'S NOT DONE WITH US.

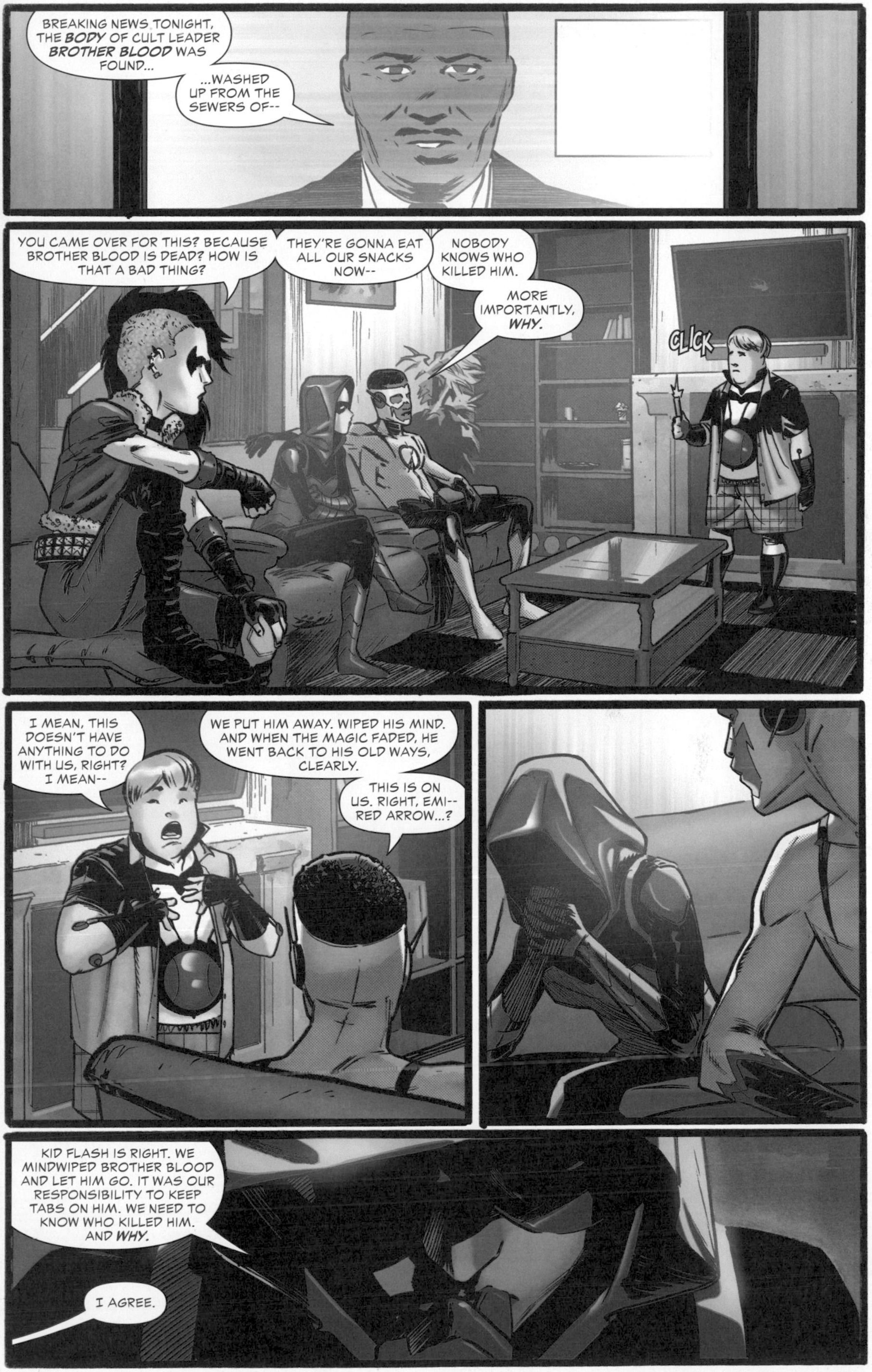
BREAKING NEWS TONIGHT, THE BODY OF CULT LEADER BROTHER BLOOD WAS FOUND...
...WASHED UP FROM THE SEWERS OF--
YOU CAME OVER FOR THIS? BECAUSE BROTHER BLOOD IS DEAD? HOW IS THAT A BAD THING?
THEY'RE GONNA EAT ALL OUR SNACKS NOW--
NOBODY KNOWS WHO KILLED HIM.
MORE IMPORTANTLY, WHY.
CLICK
I MEAN, THIS DOESN'T HAVE ANYTHING TO DO WITH US, RIGHT? I MEAN--
WE PUT HIM AWAY. WIPED HIS MIND. AND WHEN THE MAGIC FADED, HE WENT BACK TO HIS OLD WAYS, CLEARLY.
THIS IS ON US. RIGHT, EMI-- RED ARROW...?
KID FLASH IS RIGHT. WE MINDWIPED BROTHER BLOOD AND LET HIM GO. IT WAS OUR RESPONSIBILITY TO KEEP TABS ON HIM. WE NEED TO KNOW WHO KILLED HIM. AND WHY.
I AGREE.

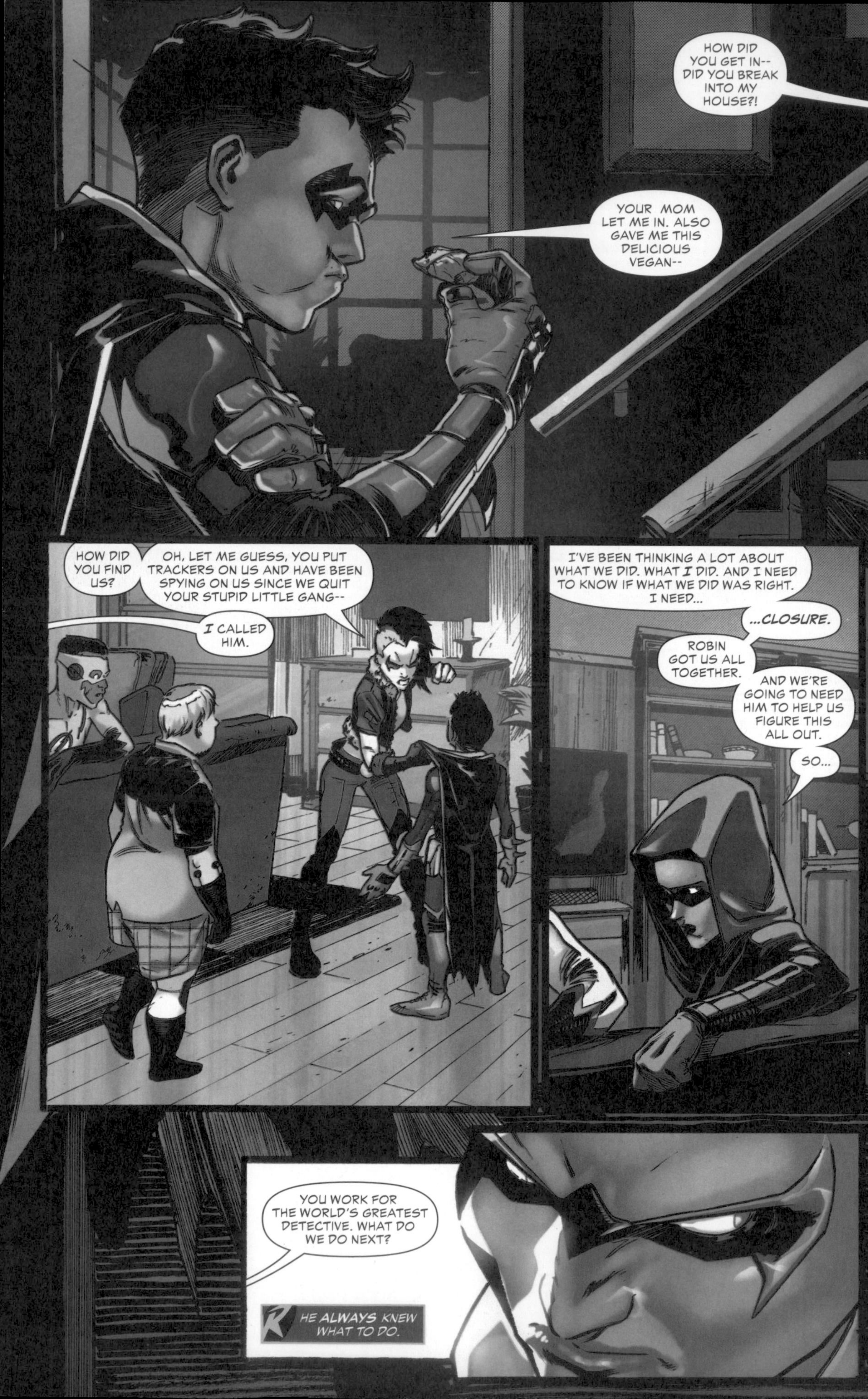
HOW DID YOU GET IN-- DID YOU BREAK INTO MY HOUSE?!
YOUR MOM LET ME IN. ALSO GAVE ME THIS DELICIOUS VEGAN--
HOW DID YOU FIND US?
OH, LET ME GUESS, YOU PUT TRACKERS ON US AND HAVE BEEN SPYING ON US SINCE WE QUIT YOUR STUPID LITTLE GANG--
I CALLED HIM.
I'VE BEEN THINKING A LOT ABOUT WHAT WE DID. WHAT I DID. AND I NEED TO KNOW IF WHAT WE DID WAS RIGHT. I NEED...
...CLOSURE.
ROBIN GOT US ALL TOGETHER.
AND WE'RE GOING TO NEED HIM TO HELP US FIGURE THIS ALL OUT.
SO...
YOU WORK FOR THE WORLD'S GREATEST DETECTIVE. WHAT DO WE DO NEXT?
HE ALWAYS KNEW WHAT TO DO.

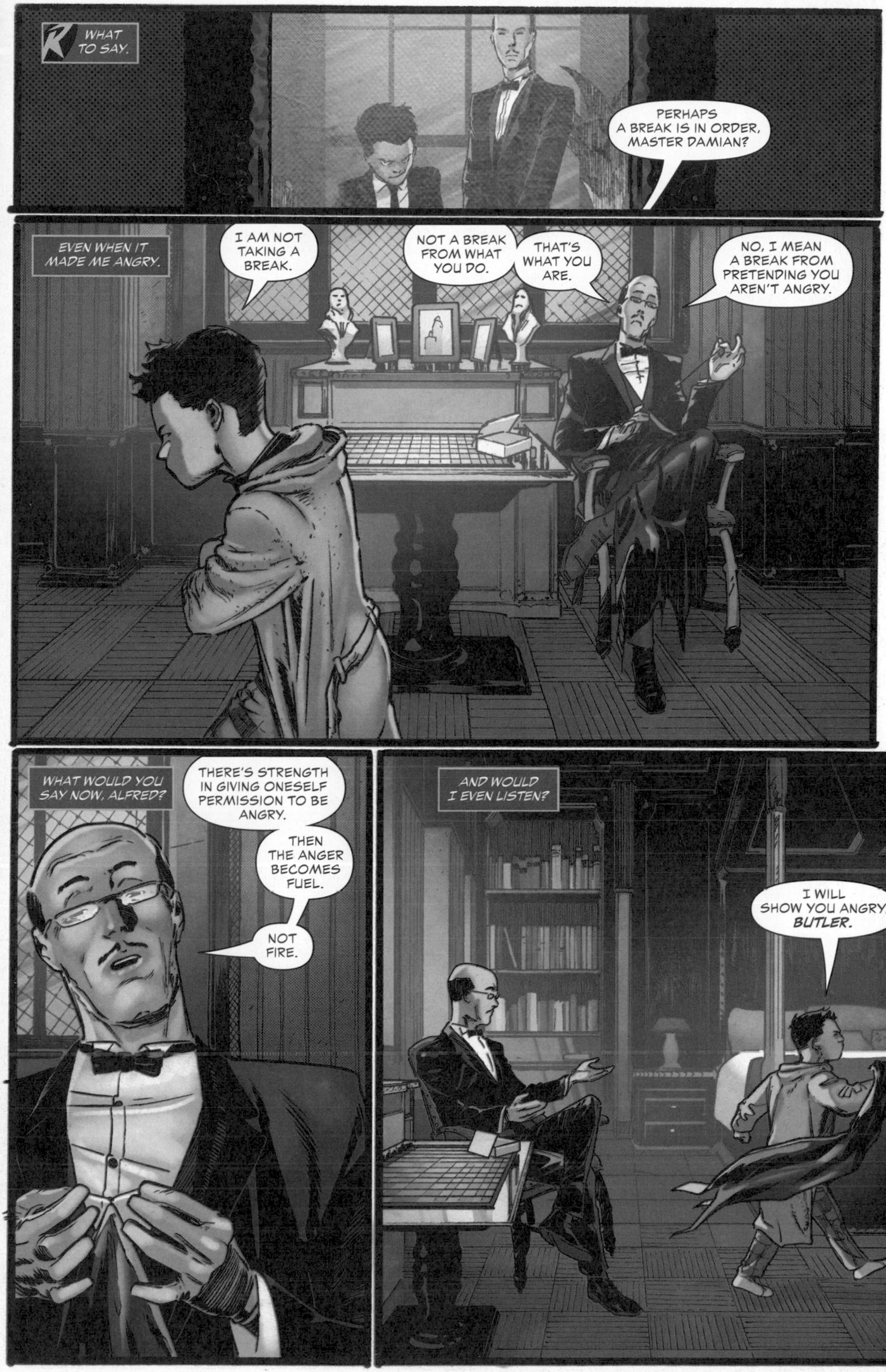
WHAT TO SAY.
PERHAPS A BREAK IS IN ORDER, MASTER DAMIAN?
EVEN WHEN IT MADE ME ANGRY.
I AM NOT TAKING A BREAK.
NOT A BREAK FROM WHAT YOU DO.
THAT'S WHAT YOU ARE.
NO, I MEAN A BREAK FROM PRETENDING YOU AREN'T ANGRY.
WHAT WOULD YOU SAY NOW, ALFRED?
THERE'S STRENGTH IN GIVING ONESELF PERMISSION TO BE ANGRY.
THEN THE ANGER BECOMES FUEL.
NOT FIRE.
AND WOULD I EVEN LISTEN?
I WILL SHOW YOU ANGRY, *BUTLER*.

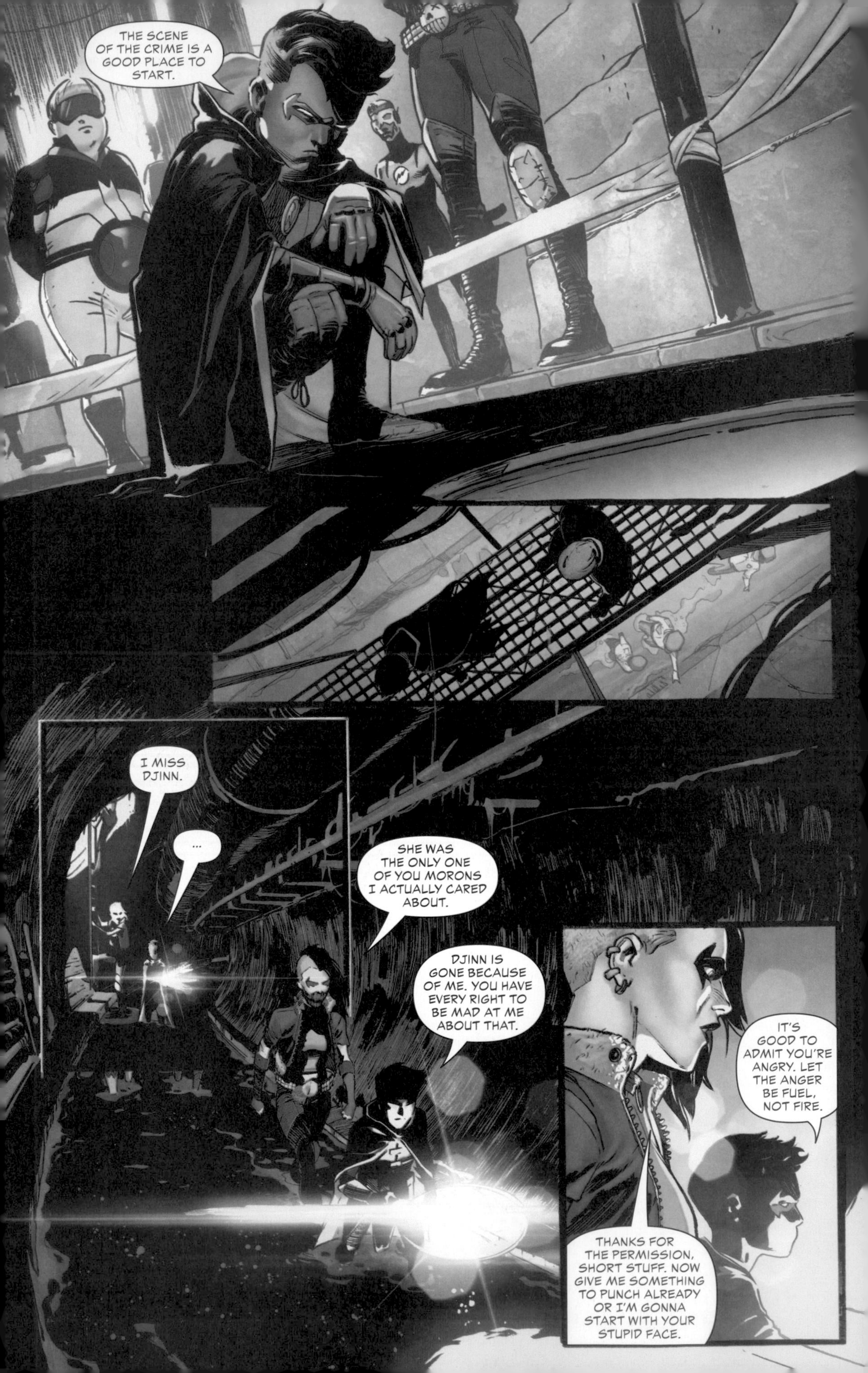
THE SCENE OF THE CRIME IS A GOOD PLACE TO START.
I MISS DJINN.
...
SHE WAS THE ONLY ONE OF YOU MORONS I ACTUALLY CARED ABOUT.
DJINN IS GONE BECAUSE OF ME. YOU HAVE EVERY RIGHT TO BE MAD AT ME ABOUT THAT.
IT'S GOOD TO ADMIT YOU'RE ANGRY. LET THE ANGER BE FUEL, NOT FIRE.
THANKS FOR THE PERMISSION, SHORT STUFF. NOW GIVE ME SOMETHING TO PUNCH ALREADY OR I'M GONNA START WITH YOUR STUPID FACE.

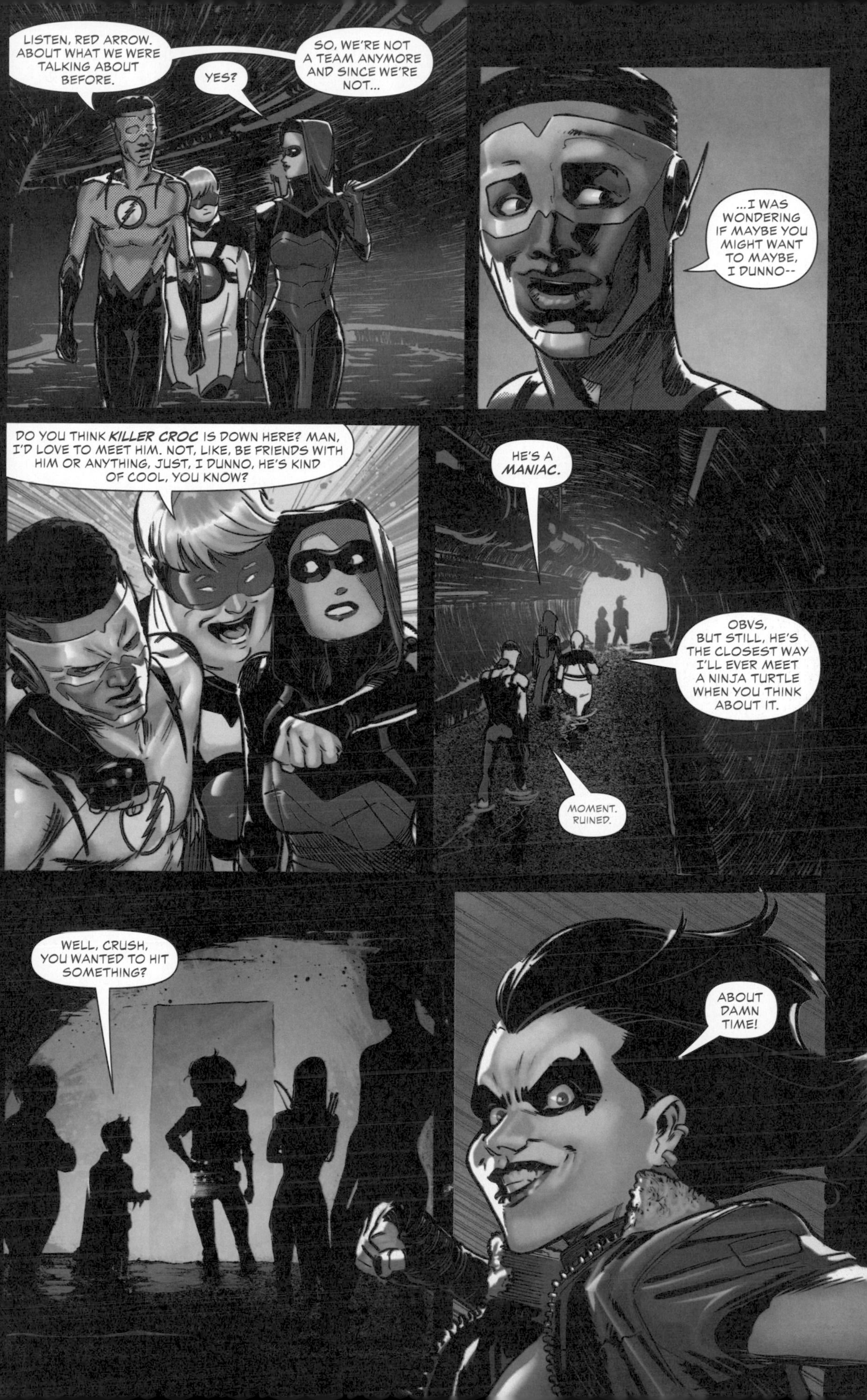
LISTEN, RED ARROW. ABOUT WHAT WE WERE TALKING ABOUT BEFORE.
YES?
SO, WE'RE NOT A TEAM ANYMORE AND SINCE WE'RE NOT...
...I WAS WONDERING IF MAYBE YOU MIGHT WANT TO MAYBE, I DUNNO--
DO YOU THINK KILLER CROC IS DOWN HERE? MAN, I'D LOVE TO MEET HIM. NOT, LIKE, BE FRIENDS WITH HIM OR ANYTHING, JUST, I DUNNO, HE'S KIND OF COOL, YOU KNOW?
HE'S A MANIAC.
OBVS, BUT STILL, HE'S THE CLOSEST WAY I'LL EVER MEET A NINJA TURTLE WHEN YOU THINK ABOUT IT.
MOMENT. RUINED.
WELL, CRUSH, YOU WANTED TO HIT SOMETHING?
ABOUT DAMN TIME!

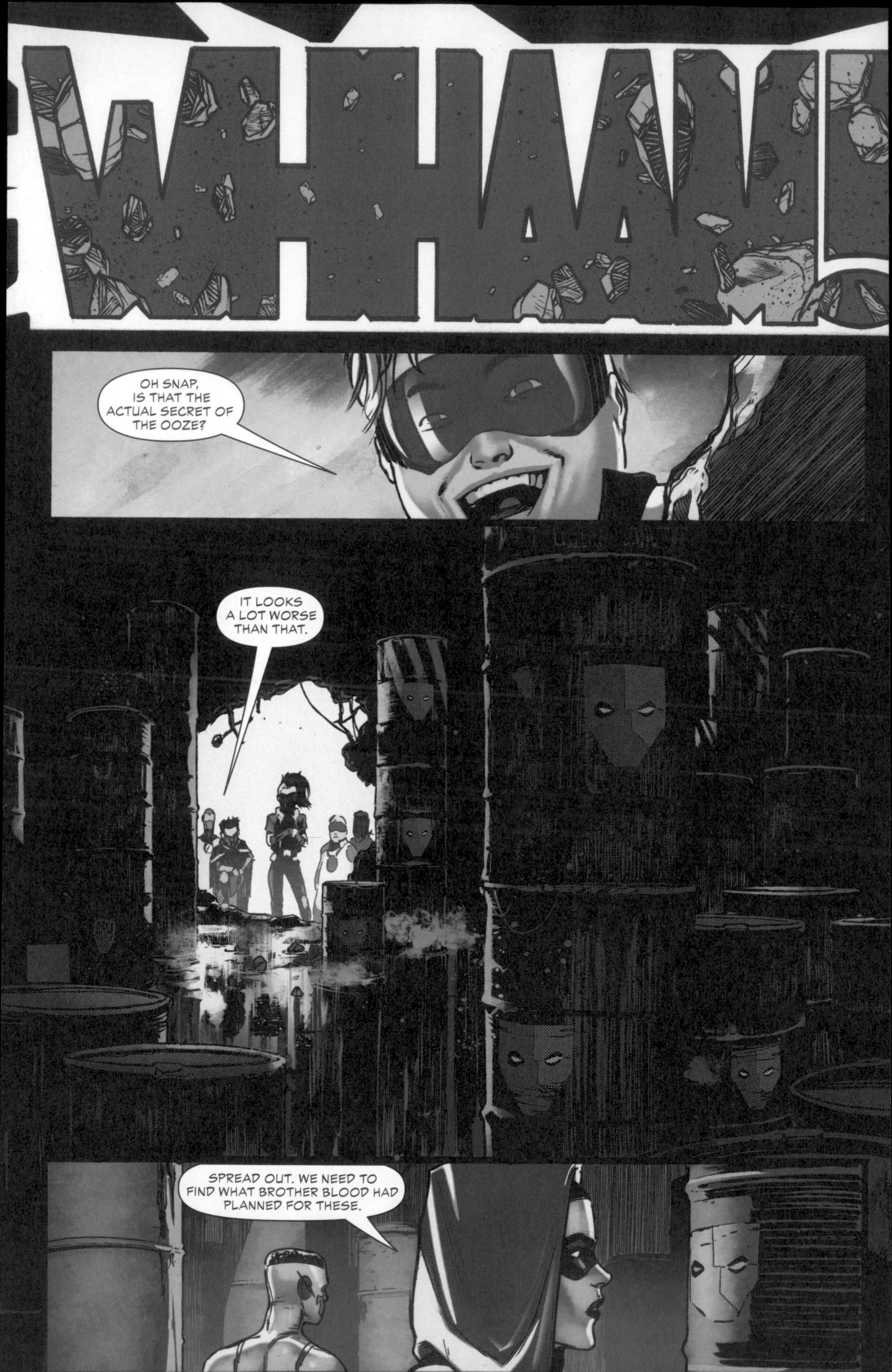
WHAAM
OH SNAP, IS THAT THE ACTUAL SECRET OF THE OOZE?
IT LOOKS A LOT WORSE THAN THAT.
SPREAD OUT. WE NEED TO FIND WHAT BROTHER BLOOD HAD PLANNED FOR THESE.

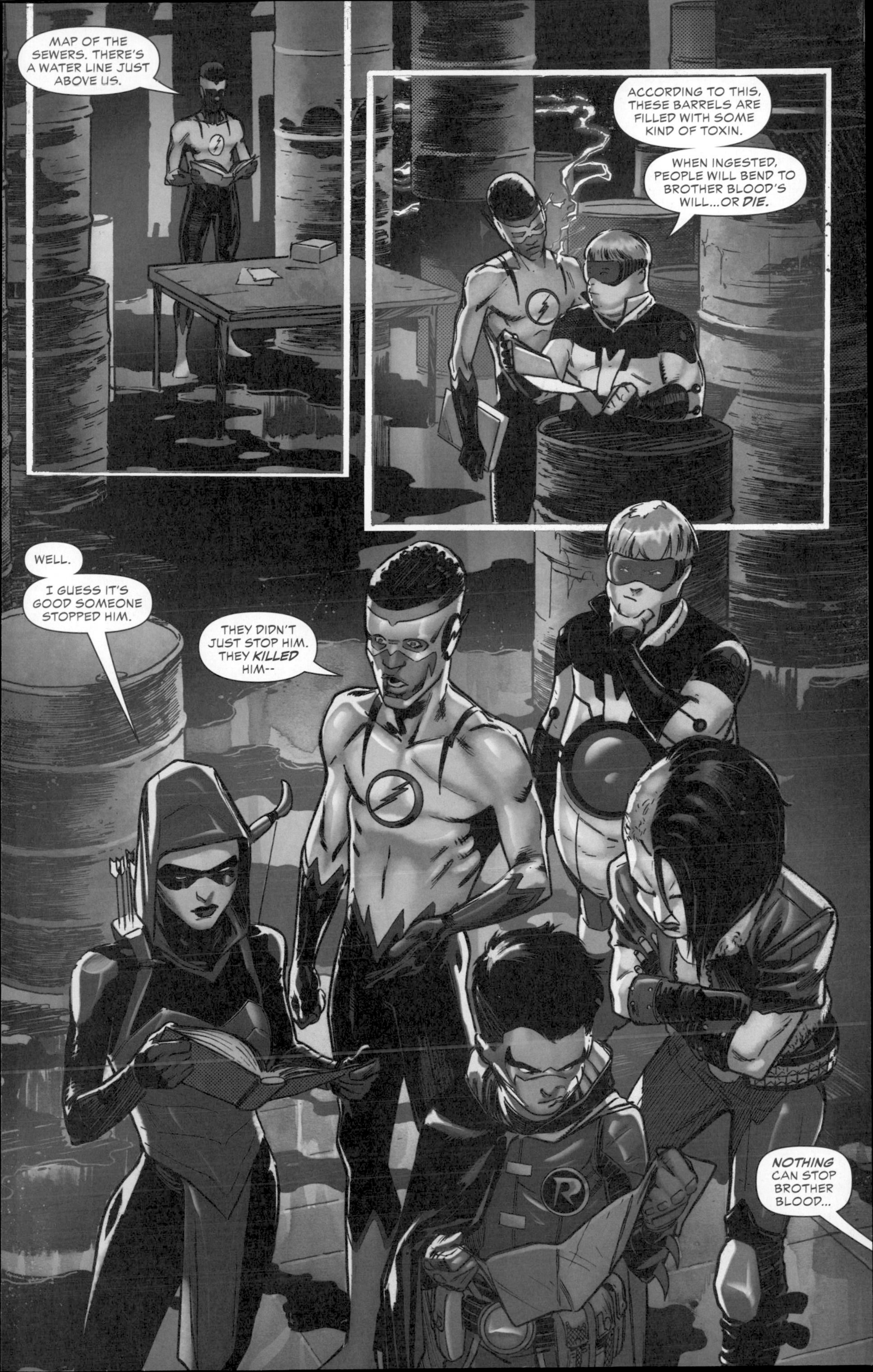
MAP OF THE SEWERS. THERE'S A WATER LINE JUST ABOVE US.
ACCORDING TO THIS, THESE BARRELS ARE FILLED WITH SOME KIND OF TOXIN.
WHEN INGESTED, PEOPLE WILL BEND TO BROTHER BLOOD'S WILL...OR *DIE.*
WELL.
I GUESS IT'S GOOD SOMEONE STOPPED HIM.
THEY DIDN'T JUST STOP HIM. THEY *KILLED* HIM--
NOTHING CAN STOP BROTHER BLOOD...

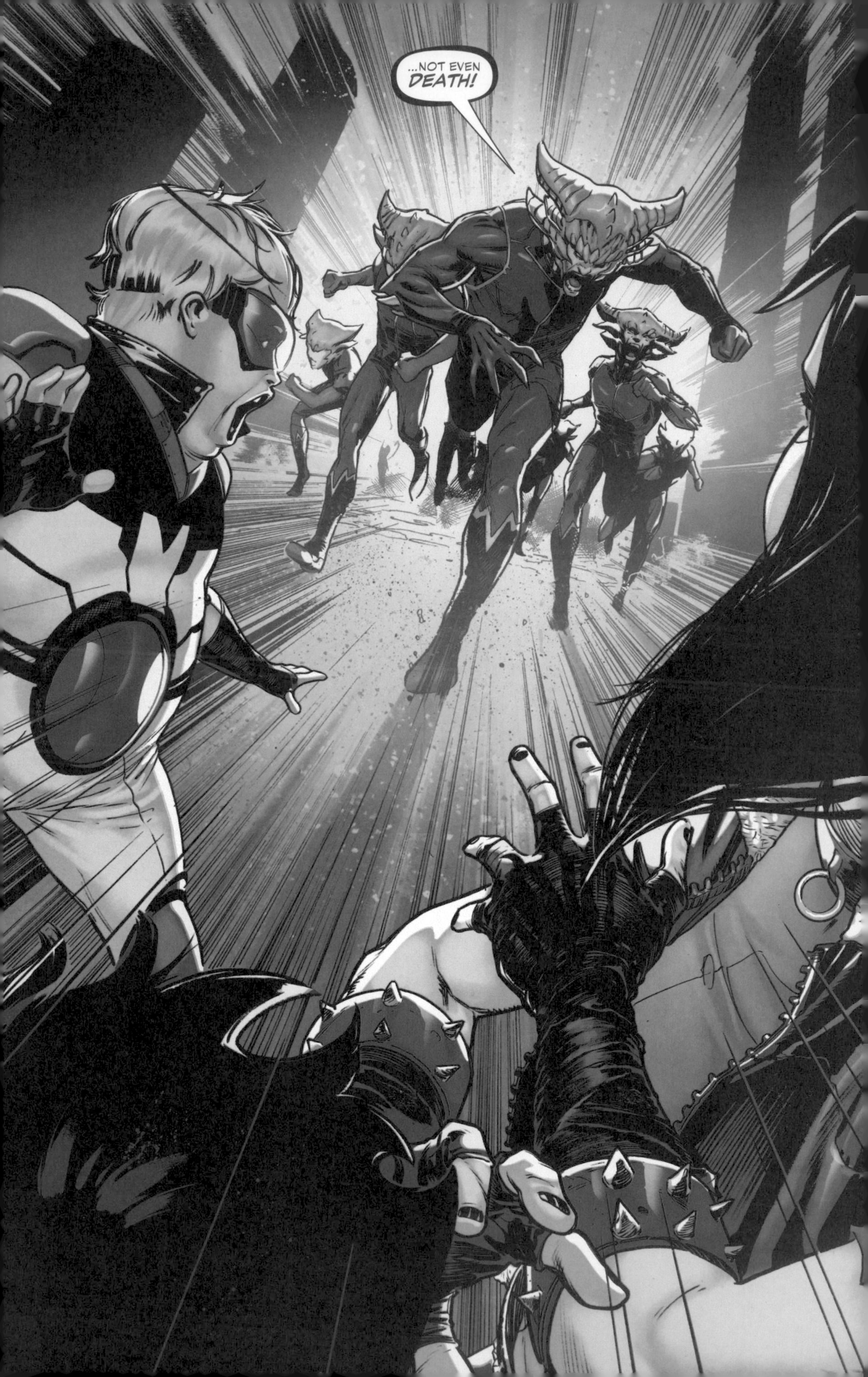
...NOT EVEN DEATH!

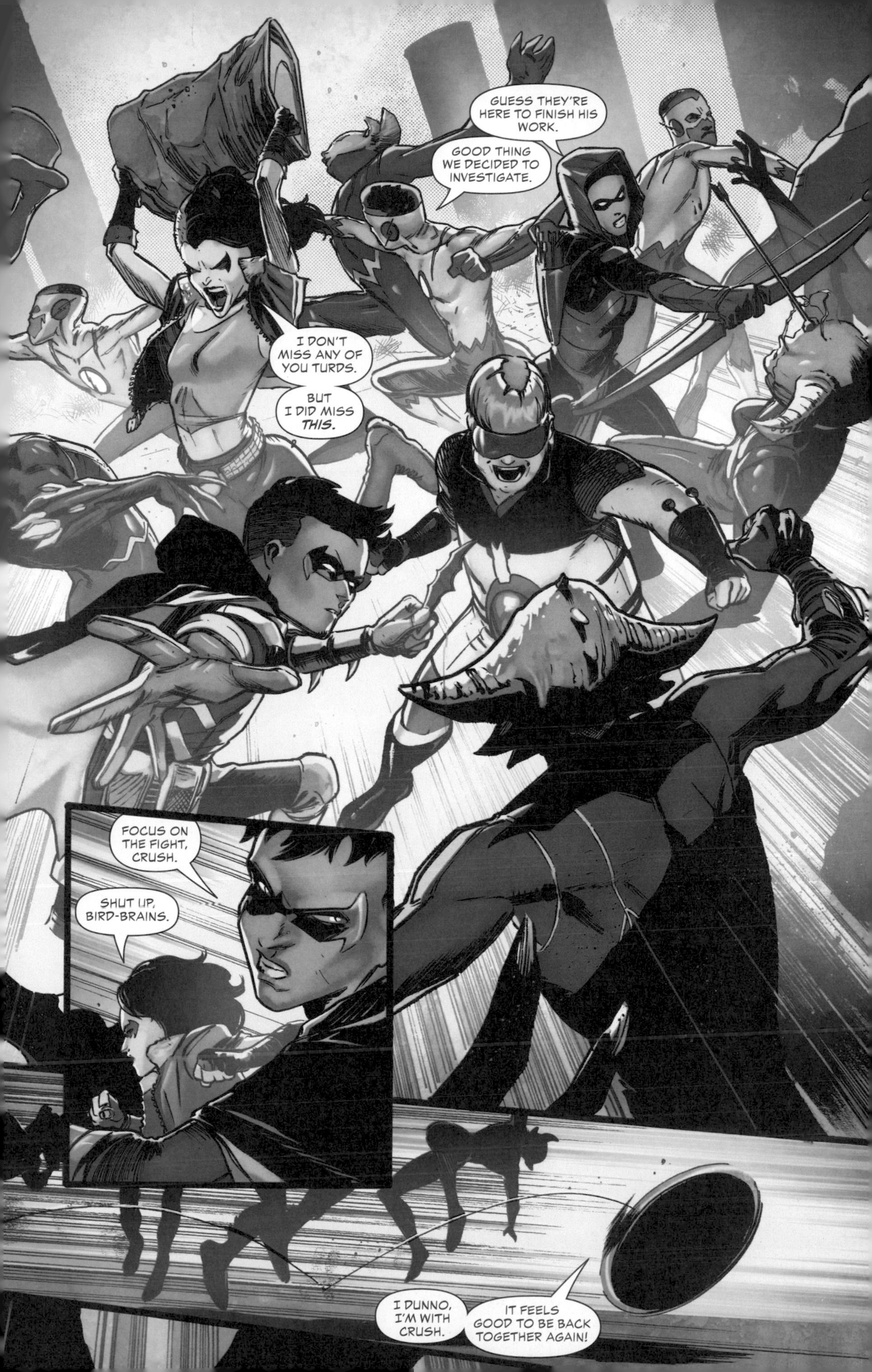
GUESS THEY'RE HERE TO FINISH HIS WORK.
GOOD THING WE DECIDED TO INVESTIGATE.
I DON'T MISS ANY OF YOU TURDS.
BUT I DID MISS *THIS*.
FOCUS ON THE FIGHT, CRUSH.
SHUT UP, BIRD-BRAINS.
I DUNNO, I'M WITH CRUSH.
IT FEELS GOOD TO BE BACK TOGETHER AGAIN!

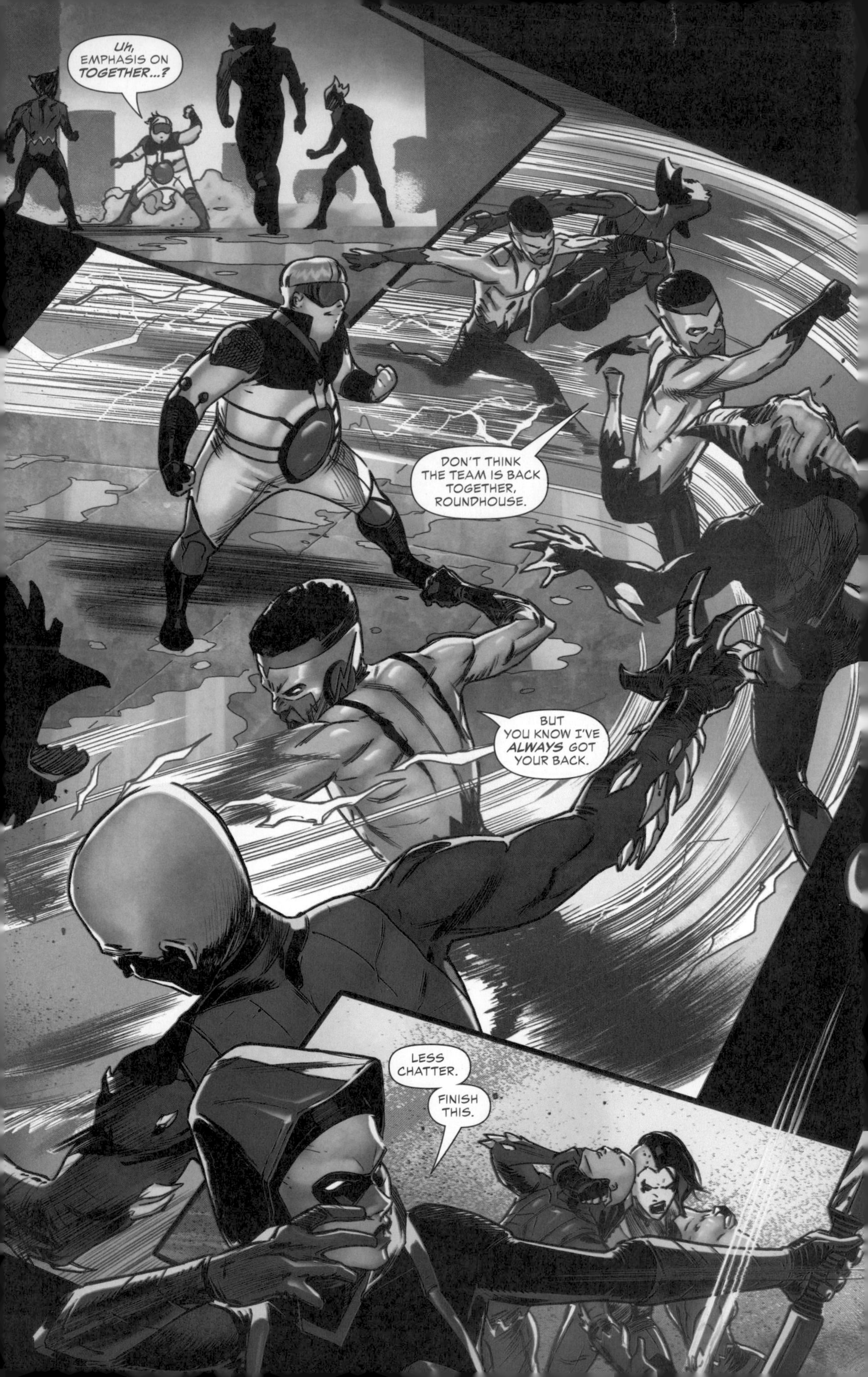

Uh, EMPHASIS ON *TOGETHER...?*
DON'T THINK THE TEAM IS BACK TOGETHER, ROUNDHOUSE.
BUT YOU KNOW I'VE ***ALWAYS*** GOT YOUR BACK.
LESS CHATTER.
FINISH THIS.

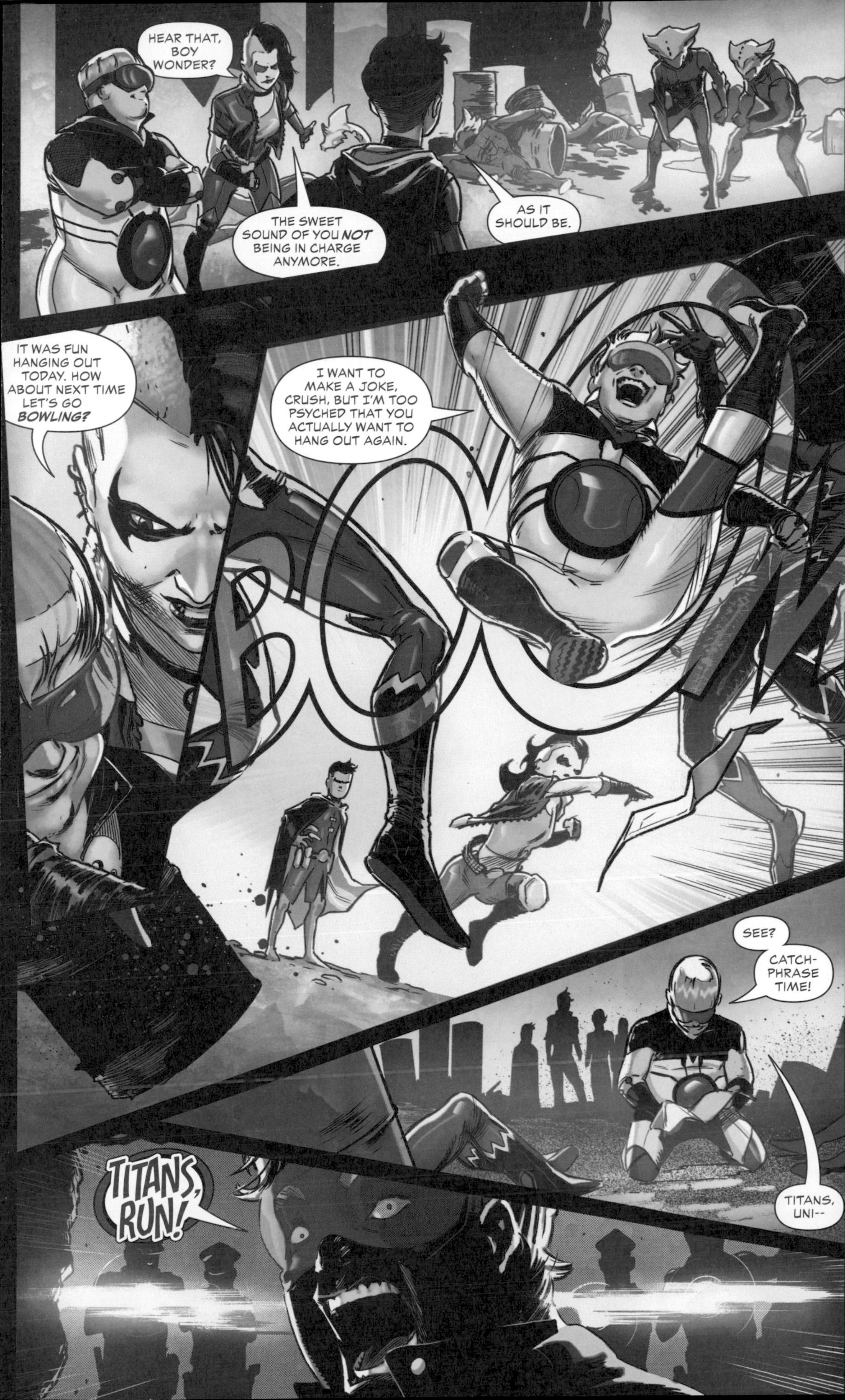
HEAR THAT, BOY WONDER?
THE SWEET SOUND OF YOU NOT BEING IN CHARGE ANYMORE.
AS IT SHOULD BE.
IT WAS FUN HANGING OUT TODAY. HOW ABOUT NEXT TIME LET'S GO BOWLING?
I WANT TO MAKE A JOKE, CRUSH, BUT I'M TOO PSYCHED THAT YOU ACTUALLY WANT TO HANG OUT AGAIN.
BOOM
SEE?
CATCH-PHRASE TIME!
TITANS, UNI--
TITANS, RUN!

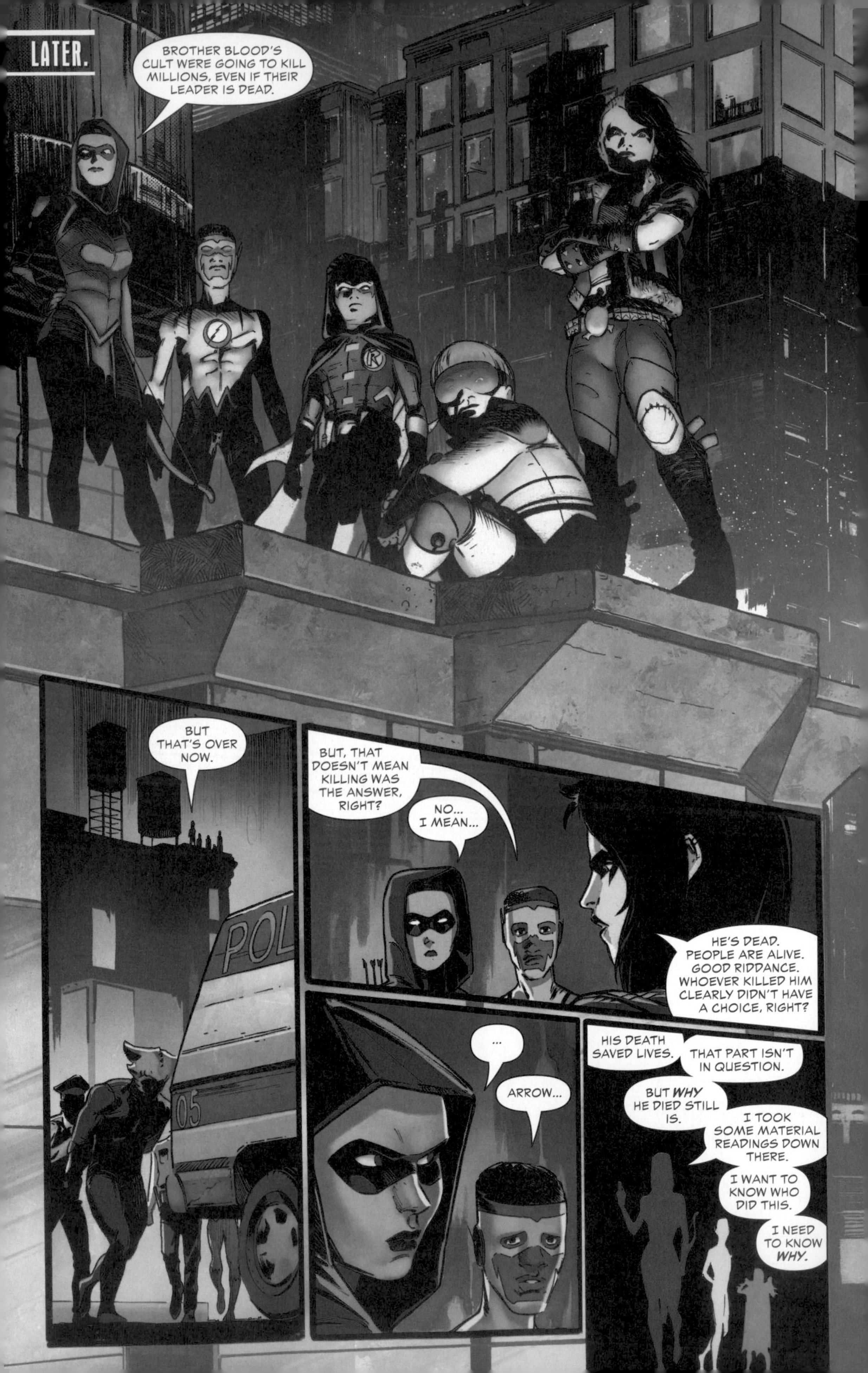
LATER.
BROTHER BLOOD'S CULT WERE GOING TO KILL MILLIONS, EVEN IF THEIR LEADER IS DEAD.
BUT THAT'S OVER NOW.
POL
05
BUT, THAT DOESN'T MEAN KILLING WAS THE ANSWER, RIGHT?
NO... I MEAN...
HE'S DEAD. PEOPLE ARE ALIVE. GOOD RIDDANCE. WHOEVER KILLED HIM CLEARLY DIDN'T HAVE A CHOICE, RIGHT?
...
ARROW...
HIS DEATH SAVED LIVES.
THAT PART ISN'T IN QUESTION.
BUT *WHY* HE DIED STILL IS.
I TOOK SOME MATERIAL READINGS DOWN THERE.
I WANT TO KNOW WHO DID THIS.
I NEED TO KNOW *WHY*.

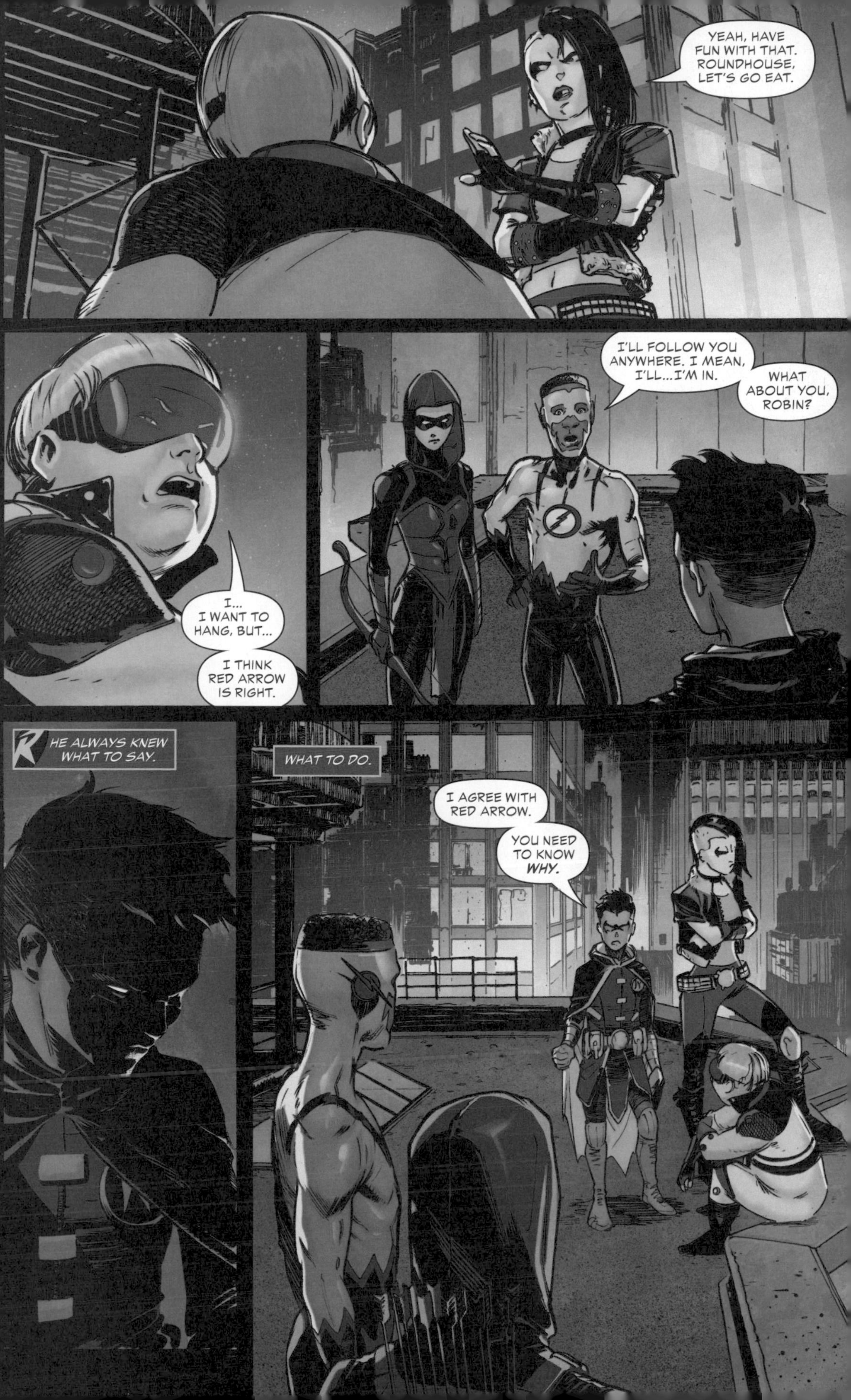
YEAH, HAVE FUN WITH THAT. ROUNDHOUSE, LET'S GO EAT.
I... I WANT TO HANG, BUT...
I THINK RED ARROW IS RIGHT.
I'LL FOLLOW YOU ANYWHERE. I MEAN, I'LL...I'M IN.
WHAT ABOUT YOU, ROBIN?
HE ALWAYS KNEW WHAT TO SAY.
WHAT TO DO.
I AGREE WITH RED ARROW.
YOU NEED TO KNOW WHY.

I WOULDN'T LISTEN.

YET HE PERSISTED. FOUND A WAY TO GUIDE ME.

NO MATTER HOW LOST I BECAME.

BUT HE'S GONE NOW.

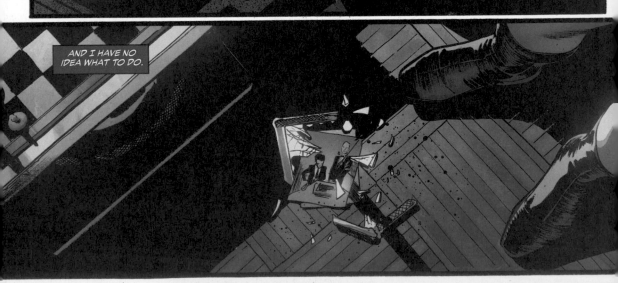

AND I HAVE NO IDEA WHAT TO DO.

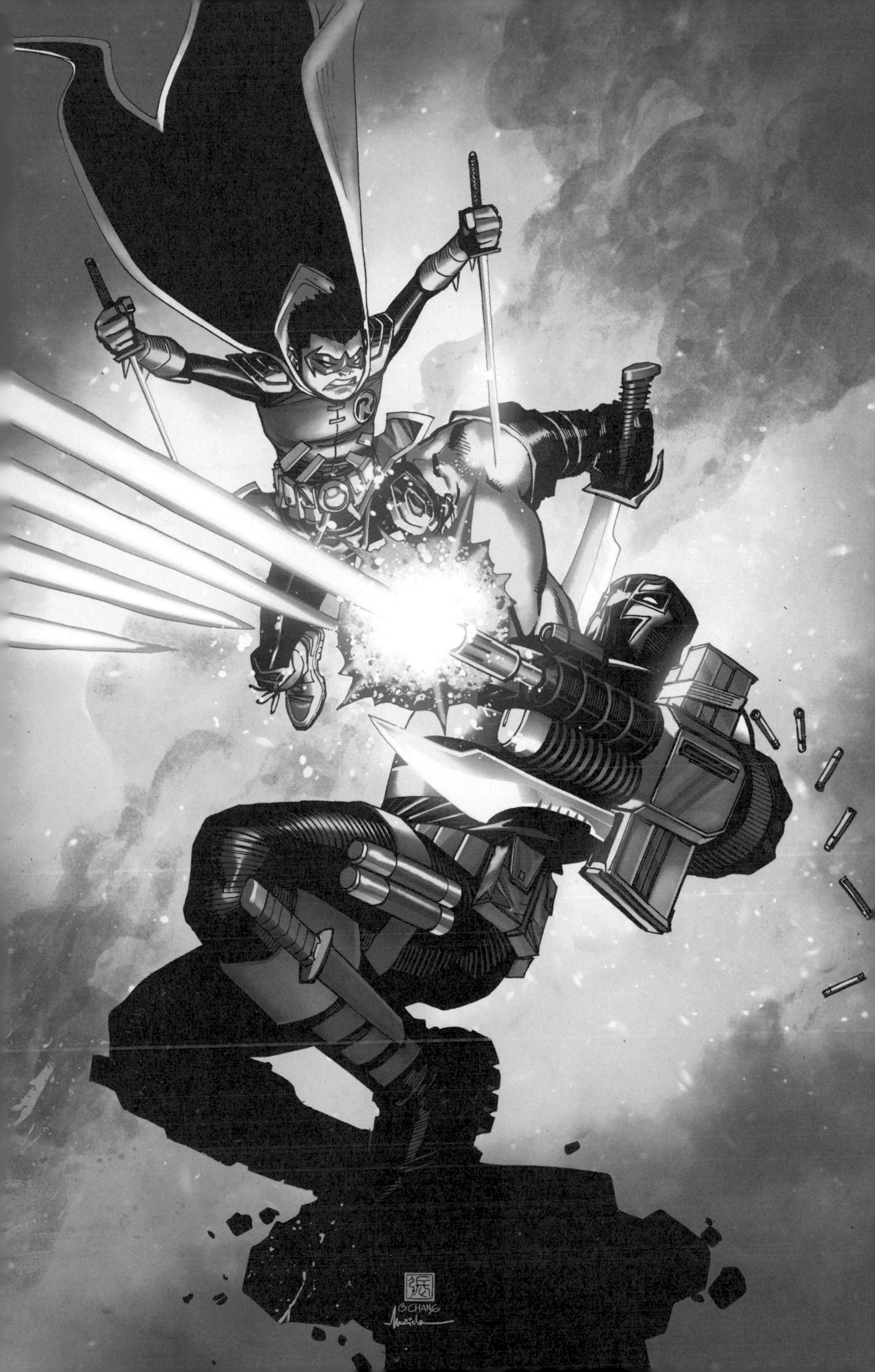

B CHANG

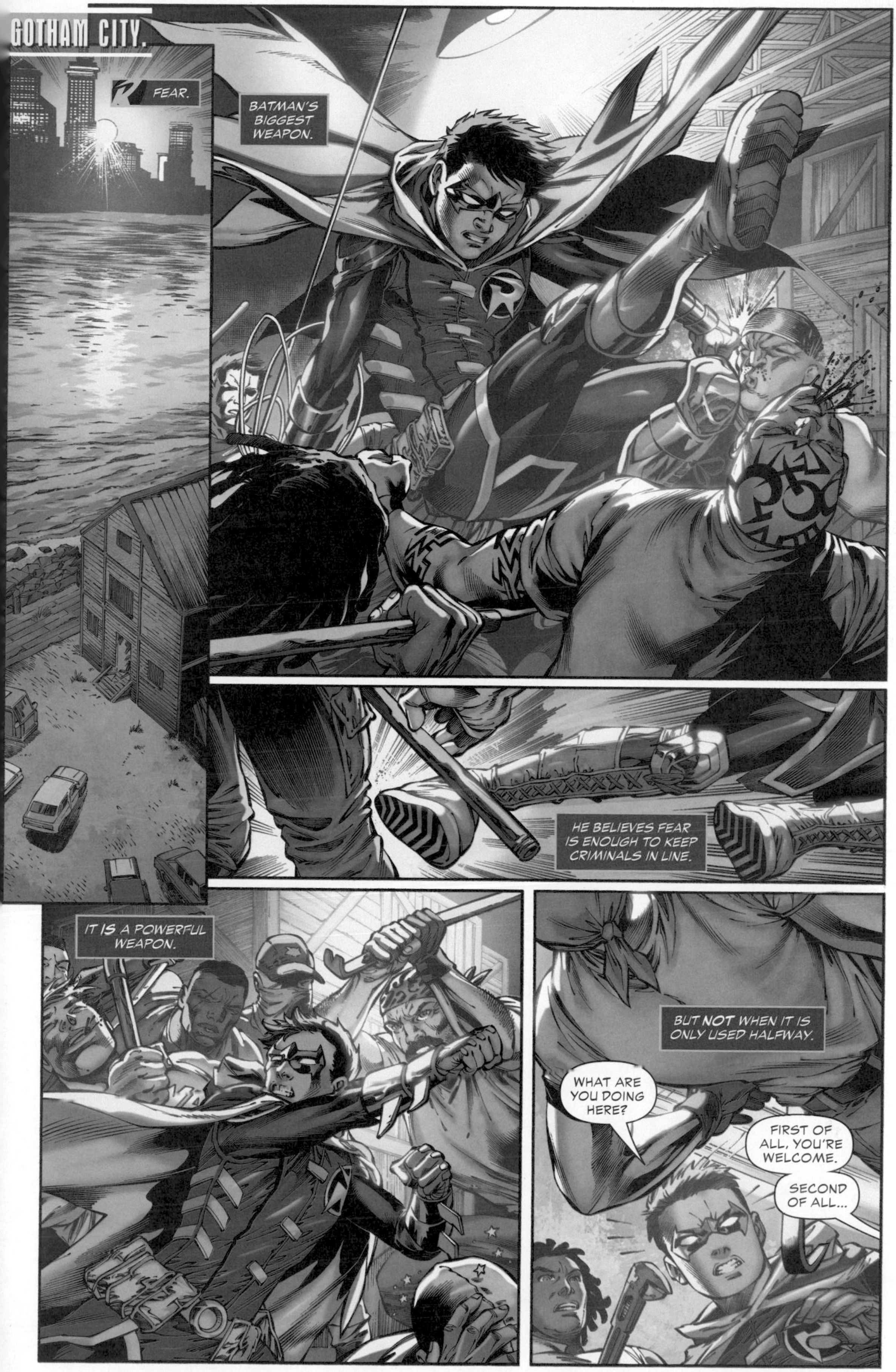

GOTHAM CITY.
FEAR.
BATMAN'S BIGGEST WEAPON.
HE BELIEVES FEAR IS ENOUGH TO KEEP CRIMINALS IN LINE.
IT IS A POWERFUL WEAPON.
BUT NOT WHEN IT IS ONLY USED HALFWAY.
WHAT ARE YOU DOING HERE?
FIRST OF ALL, YOU'RE WELCOME.
SECOND OF ALL...

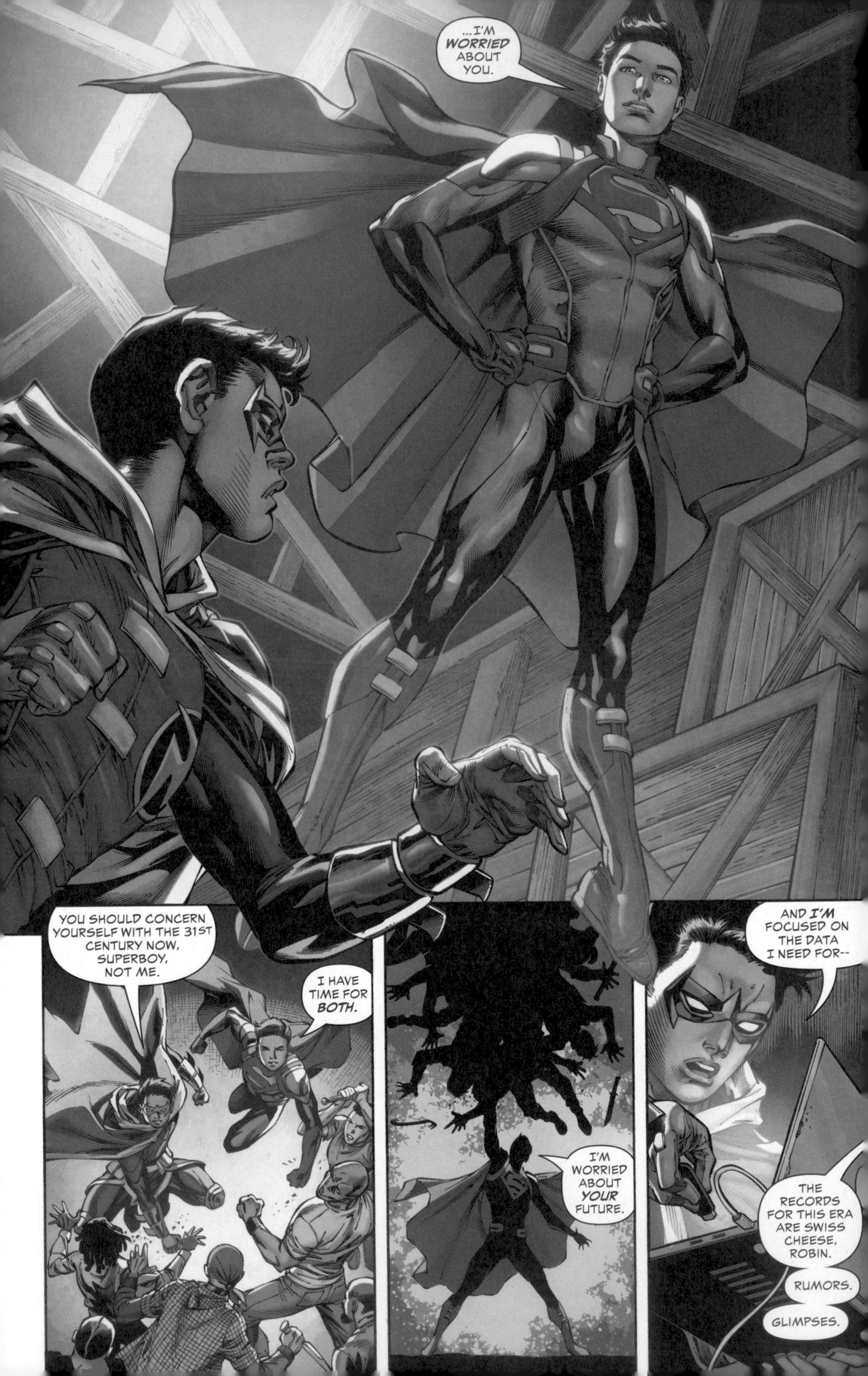
...I'M WORRIED ABOUT YOU.
YOU SHOULD CONCERN YOURSELF WITH THE 31ST CENTURY NOW, SUPERBOY, NOT ME.
I HAVE TIME FOR BOTH.
I'M WORRIED ABOUT YOUR FUTURE.
AND I'M FOCUSED ON THE DATA I NEED FOR--
THE RECORDS FOR THIS ERA ARE SWISS CHEESE, ROBIN.
RUMORS.
GLIMPSES.

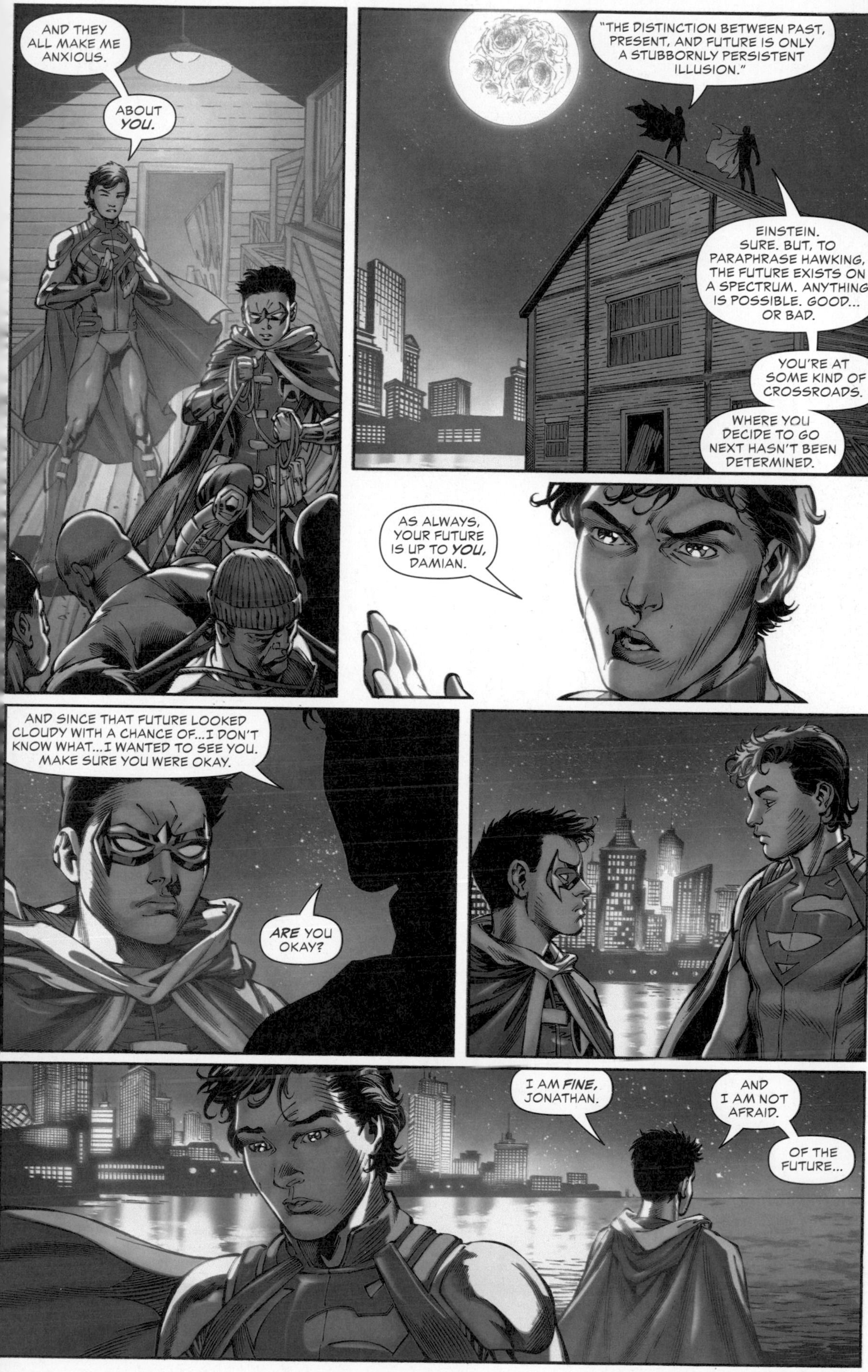
AND THEY ALL MAKE ME ANXIOUS.
ABOUT *YOU.*
"THE DISTINCTION BETWEEN PAST, PRESENT, AND FUTURE IS ONLY A STUBBORNLY PERSISTENT ILLUSION."
EINSTEIN. SURE. BUT, TO PARAPHRASE HAWKING, THE FUTURE EXISTS ON A SPECTRUM. ANYTHING IS POSSIBLE. GOOD... OR BAD.
YOU'RE AT SOME KIND OF CROSSROADS.
WHERE YOU DECIDE TO GO NEXT HASN'T BEEN DETERMINED.
AS ALWAYS, YOUR FUTURE IS UP TO *YOU,* DAMIAN.
AND SINCE THAT FUTURE LOOKED CLOUDY WITH A CHANCE OF...I DON'T KNOW WHAT...I WANTED TO SEE YOU. MAKE SURE YOU WERE OKAY.
ARE YOU OKAY?
I AM *FINE,* JONATHAN.
AND I AM NOT AFRAID.
OF THE FUTURE...

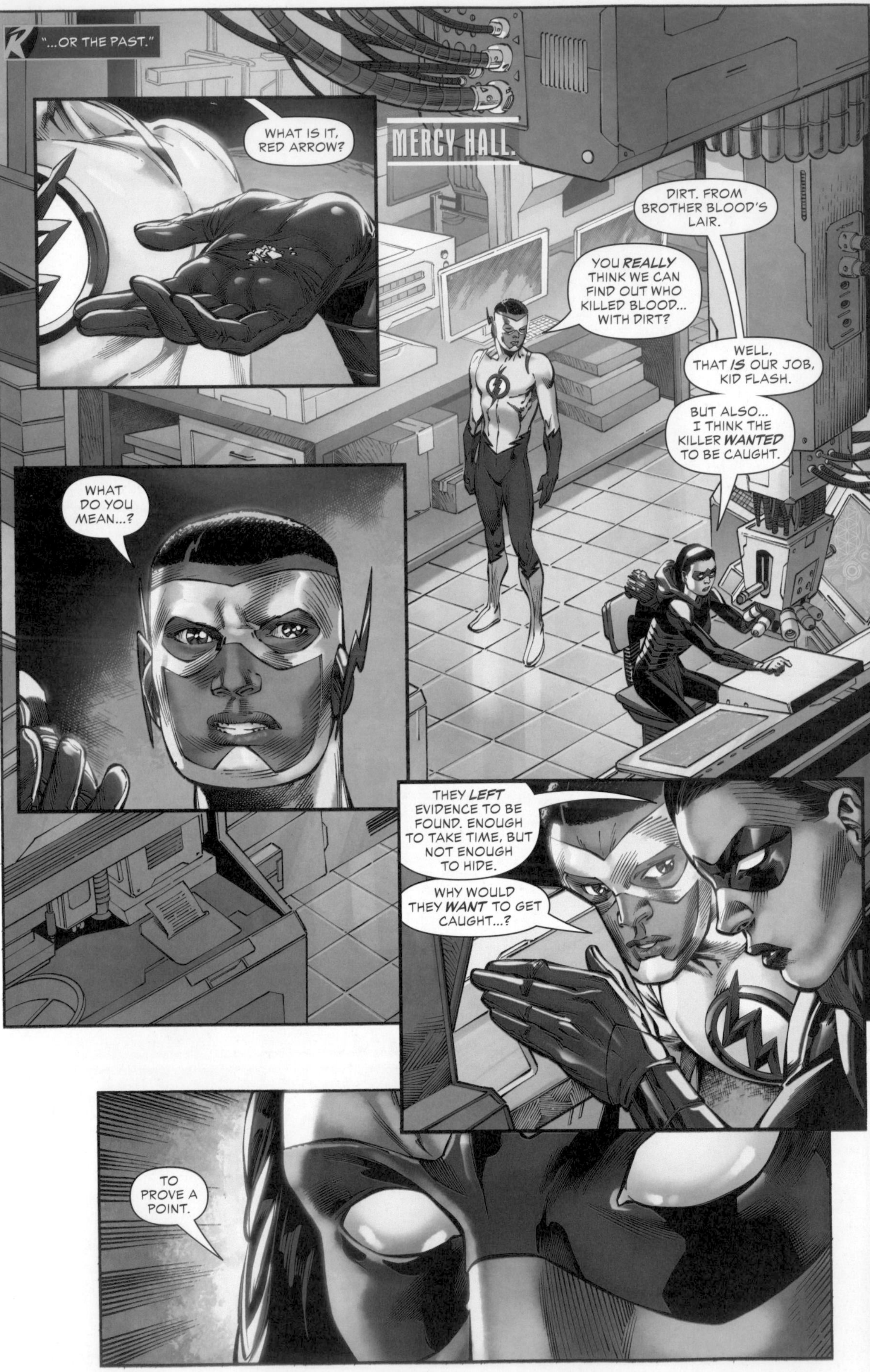
"...OR THE PAST."
MERCY HALL.
WHAT IS IT, RED ARROW?
DIRT. FROM BROTHER BLOOD'S LAIR.
YOU REALLY THINK WE CAN FIND OUT WHO KILLED BLOOD... WITH DIRT?
WELL, THAT IS OUR JOB, KID FLASH.
BUT ALSO... I THINK THE KILLER WANTED TO BE CAUGHT.
WHAT DO YOU MEAN...?
THEY LEFT EVIDENCE TO BE FOUND. ENOUGH TO TAKE TIME, BUT NOT ENOUGH TO HIDE.
WHY WOULD THEY WANT TO GET CAUGHT...?
TO PROVE A POINT.

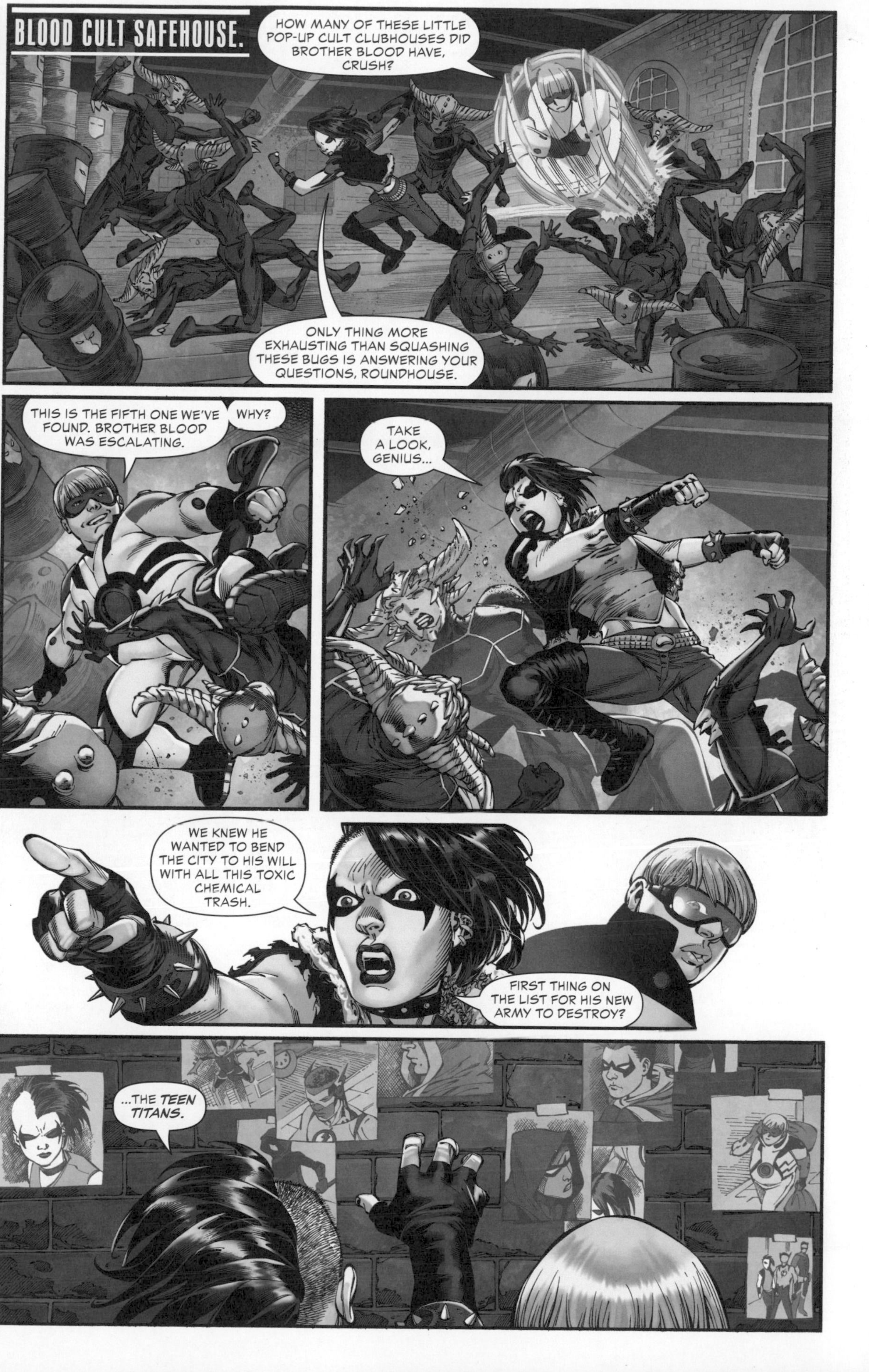
BLOOD CULT SAFEHOUSE.
HOW MANY OF THESE LITTLE POP-UP CULT CLUBHOUSES DID BROTHER BLOOD HAVE, CRUSH?
ONLY THING MORE EXHAUSTING THAN SQUASHING THESE BUGS IS ANSWERING YOUR QUESTIONS, ROUNDHOUSE.
THIS IS THE FIFTH ONE WE'VE FOUND. BROTHER BLOOD WAS ESCALATING.
WHY?
TAKE A LOOK, GENIUS...
WE KNEW HE WANTED TO BEND THE CITY TO HIS WILL WITH ALL THIS TOXIC CHEMICAL TRASH.
FIRST THING ON THE LIST FOR HIS NEW ARMY TO DESTROY?
...THE *TEEN TITANS.*

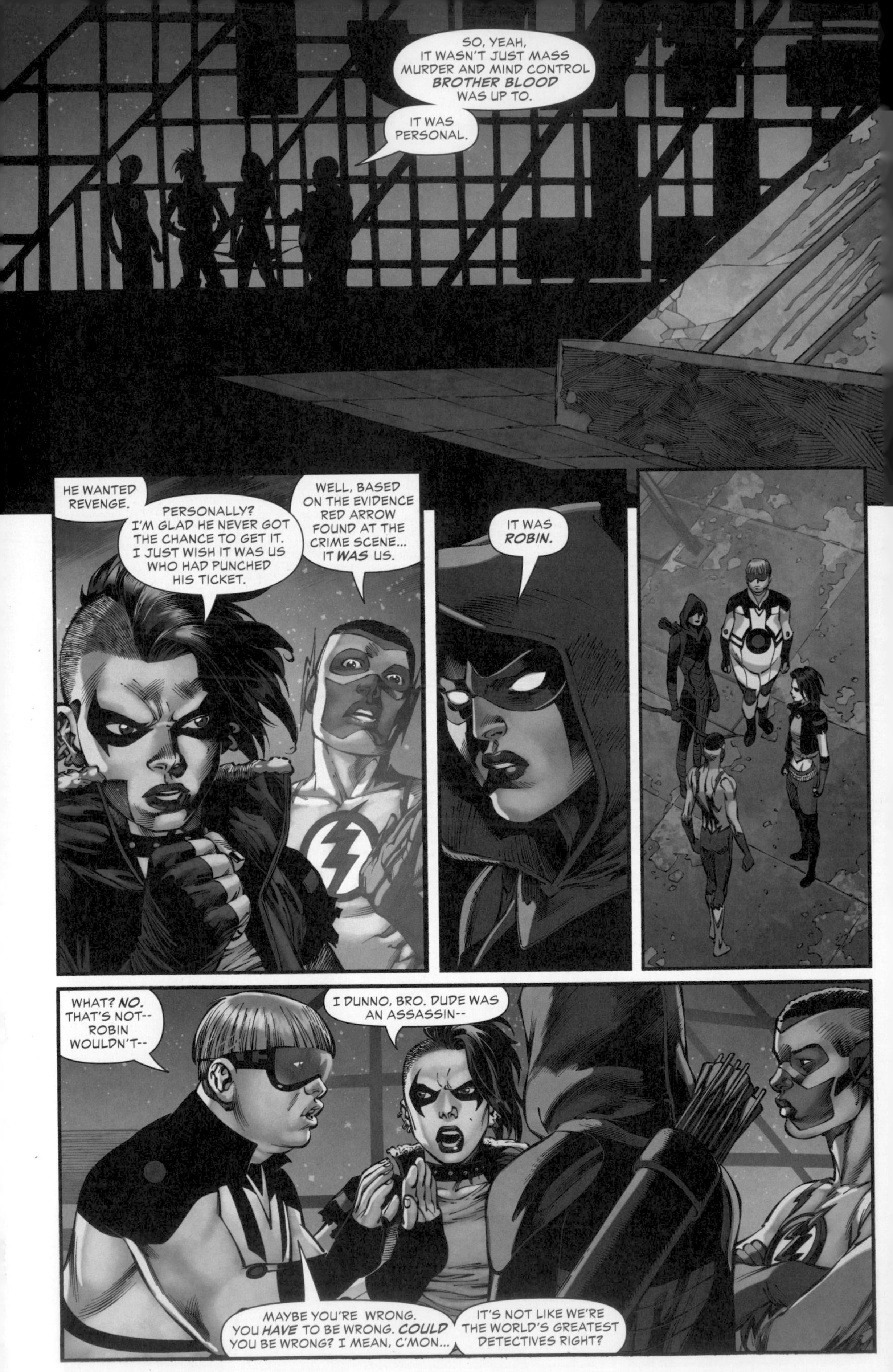
SO, YEAH, IT WASN'T JUST MASS MURDER AND MIND CONTROL BROTHER BLOOD WAS UP TO.
IT WAS PERSONAL.
HE WANTED REVENGE.
PERSONALLY? I'M GLAD HE NEVER GOT THE CHANCE TO GET IT. I JUST WISH IT WAS US WHO HAD PUNCHED HIS TICKET.
WELL, BASED ON THE EVIDENCE RED ARROW FOUND AT THE CRIME SCENE... IT WAS US.
IT WAS ROBIN.
WHAT? NO. THAT'S NOT-- ROBIN WOULDN'T--
I DUNNO, BRO. DUDE WAS AN ASSASSIN--
MAYBE YOU'RE WRONG. YOU HAVE TO BE WRONG. COULD YOU BE WRONG? I MEAN, C'MON...
IT'S NOT LIKE WE'RE THE WORLD'S GREATEST DETECTIVES RIGHT?

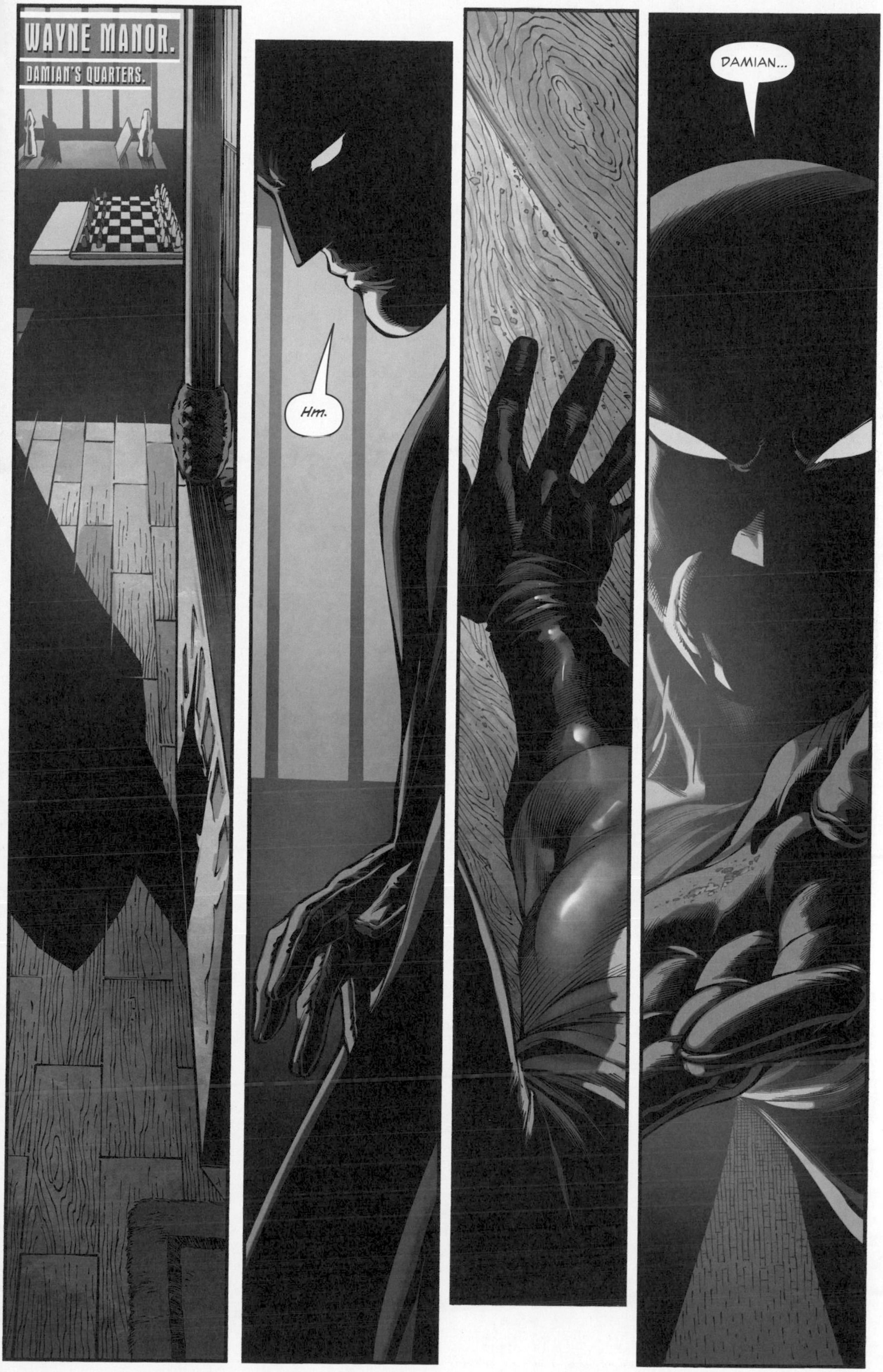
WAYNE MANOR.
DAMIAN'S QUARTERS.
Hm.
DAMIAN...

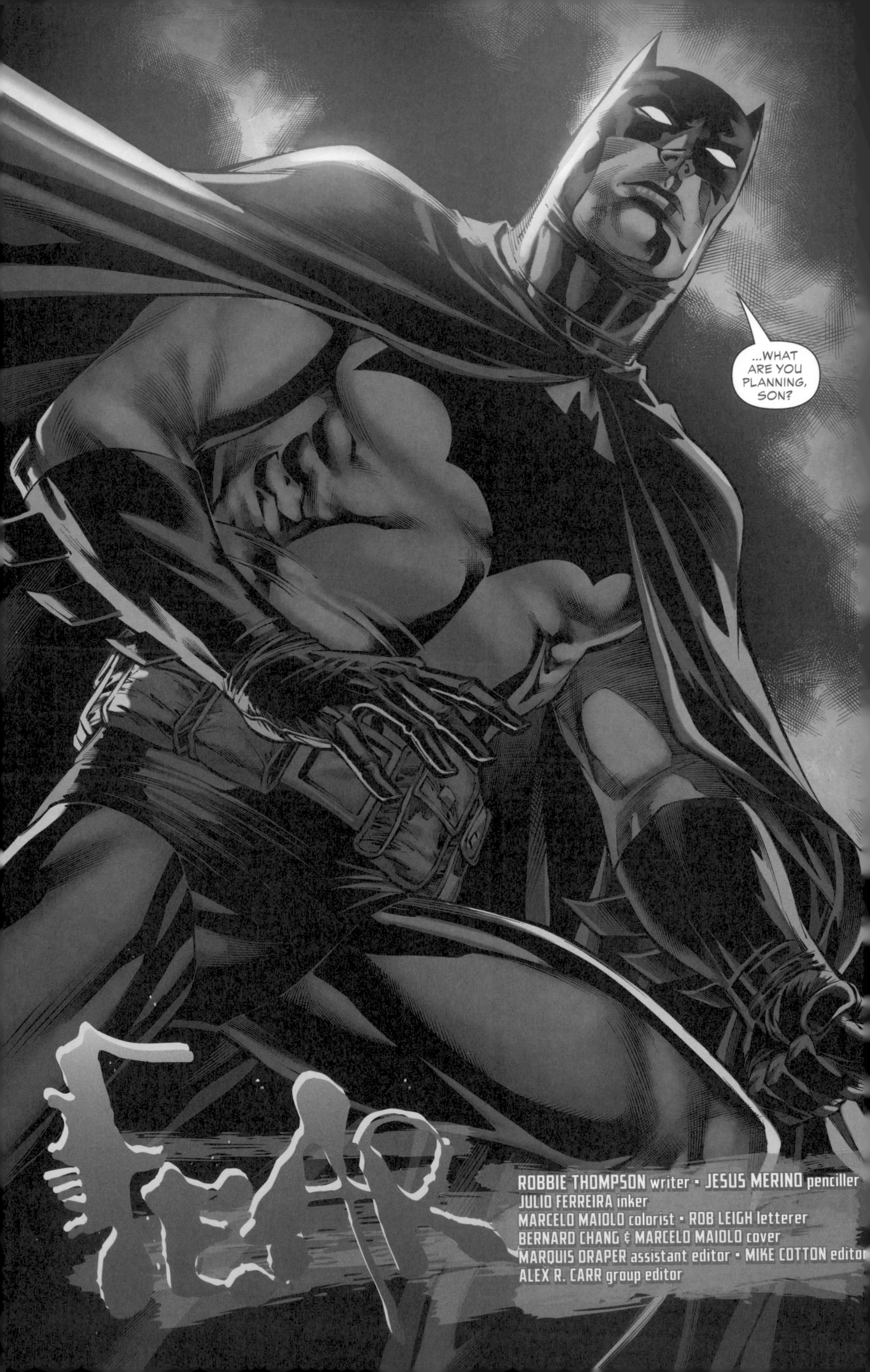

...WHAT ARE YOU PLANNING, SON?
ROBBIE THOMPSON writer • JESUS MERINO penciller
JULIO FERREIRA inker
MARCELO MAIOLO colorist • ROB LEIGH letterer
BERNARD CHANG & MARCELO MAIOLO cover
MARQUIS DRAPER assistant editor • MIKE COTTON editor
ALEX R. CARR group editor

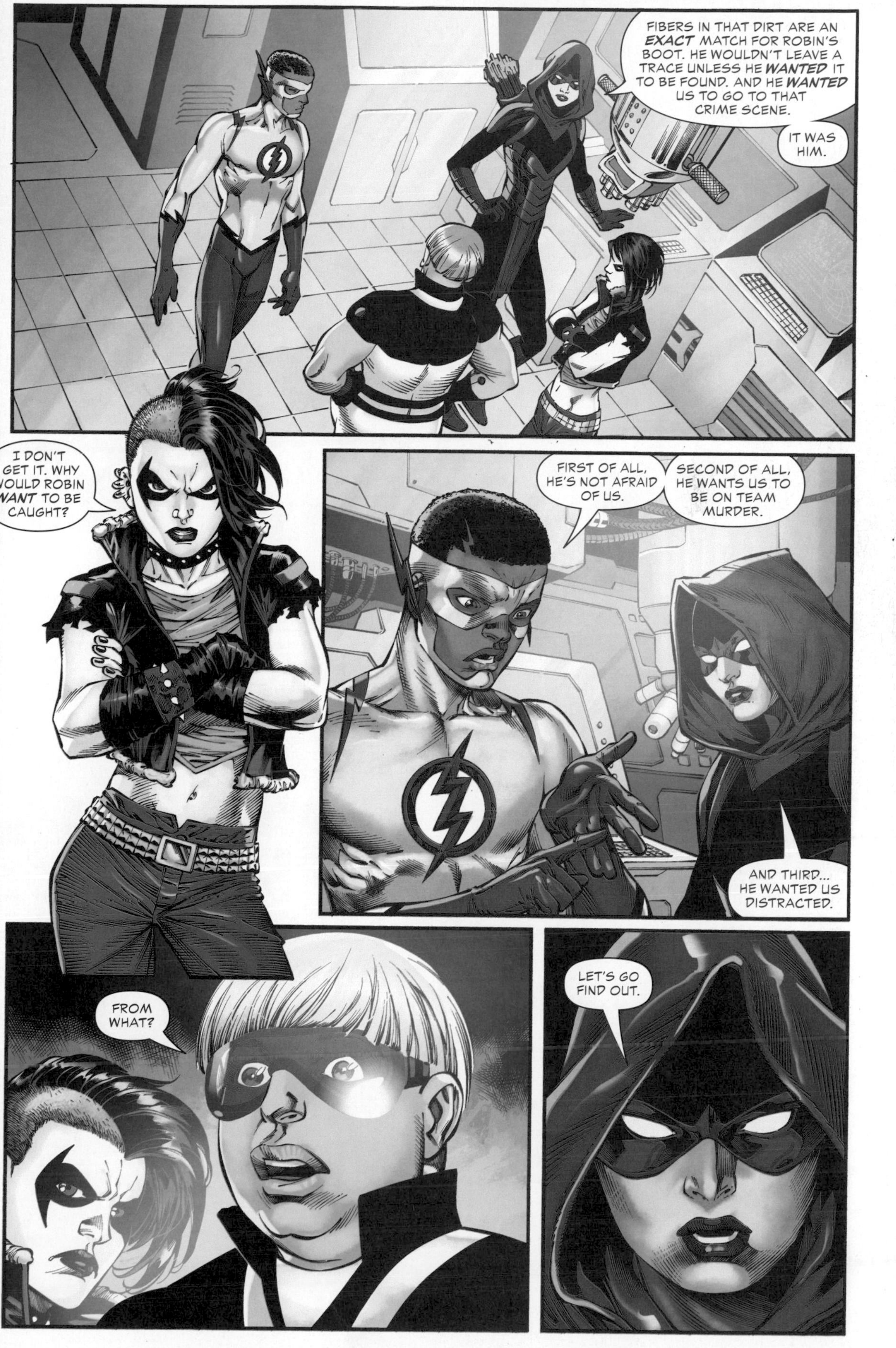
FIBERS IN THAT DIRT ARE AN EXACT MATCH FOR ROBIN'S BOOT. HE WOULDN'T LEAVE A TRACE UNLESS HE WANTED IT TO BE FOUND. AND HE WANTED US TO GO TO THAT CRIME SCENE.
IT WAS HIM.
I DON'T GET IT. WHY WOULD ROBIN WANT TO BE CAUGHT?
FIRST OF ALL, HE'S NOT AFRAID OF US.
SECOND OF ALL, HE WANTS US TO BE ON TEAM MURDER.
AND THIRD... HE WANTED US DISTRACTED.
FROM WHAT?
LET'S GO FIND OUT.

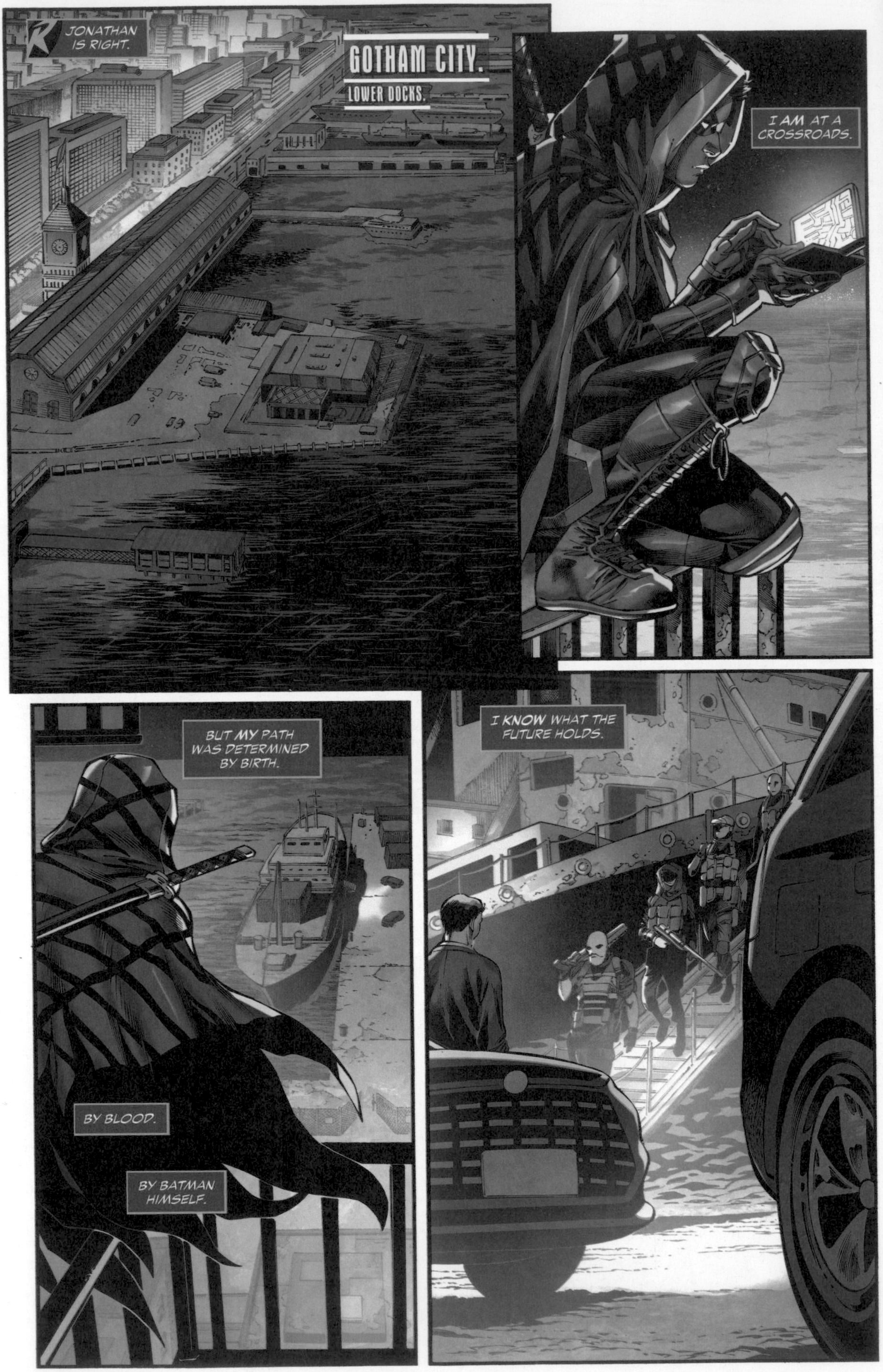
JONATHAN IS RIGHT.
GOTHAM CITY.
LOWER DOCKS.
I AM AT A CROSSROADS.
BUT MY PATH WAS DETERMINED BY BIRTH.
BY BLOOD.
BY BATMAN HIMSELF.
I KNOW WHAT THE FUTURE HOLDS.

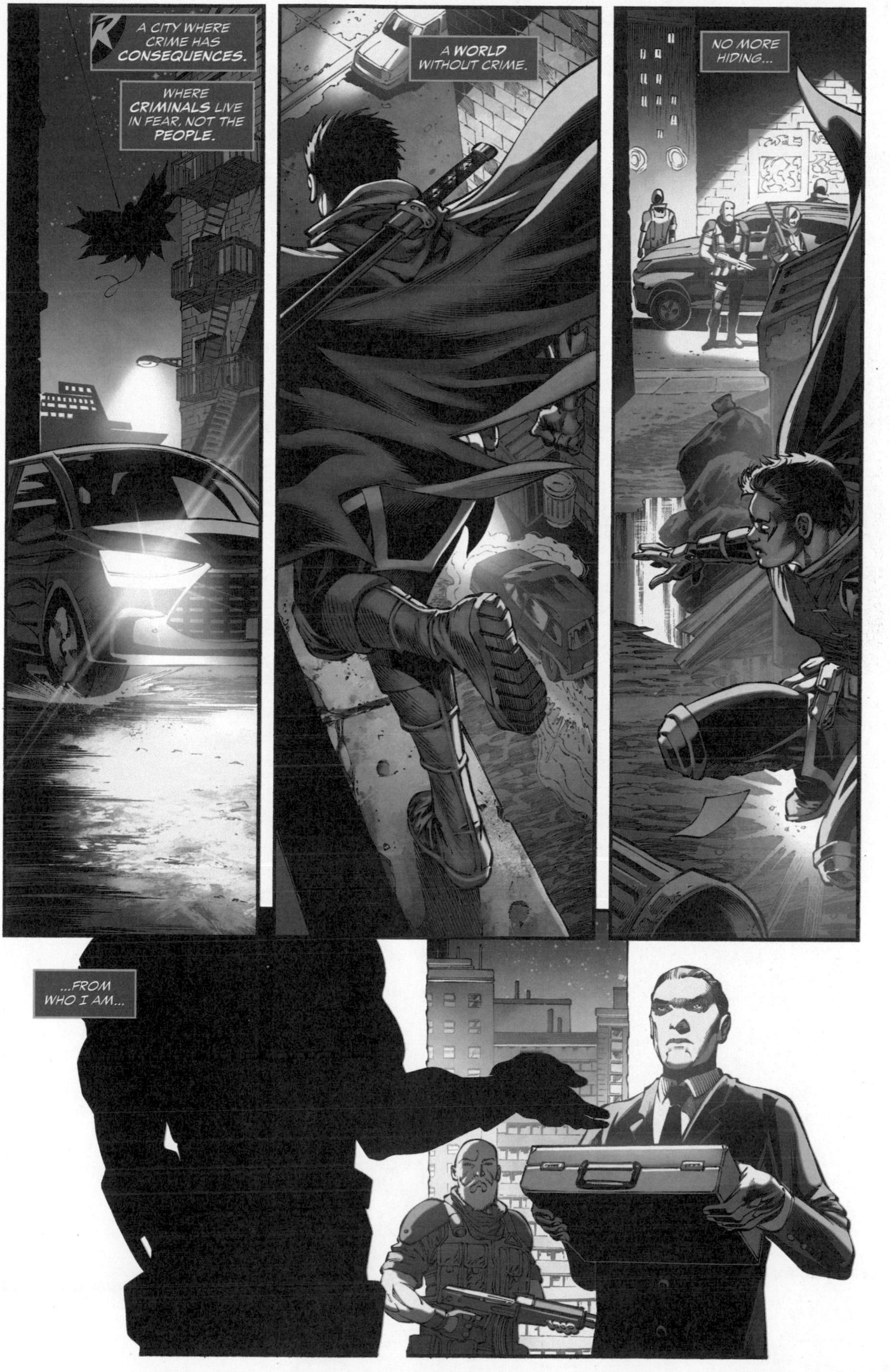
A CITY WHERE CRIME HAS CONSEQUENCES.
WHERE CRIMINALS LIVE IN FEAR, NOT THE PEOPLE.
A WORLD WITHOUT CRIME.
NO MORE HIDING...
...FROM WHO I AM...

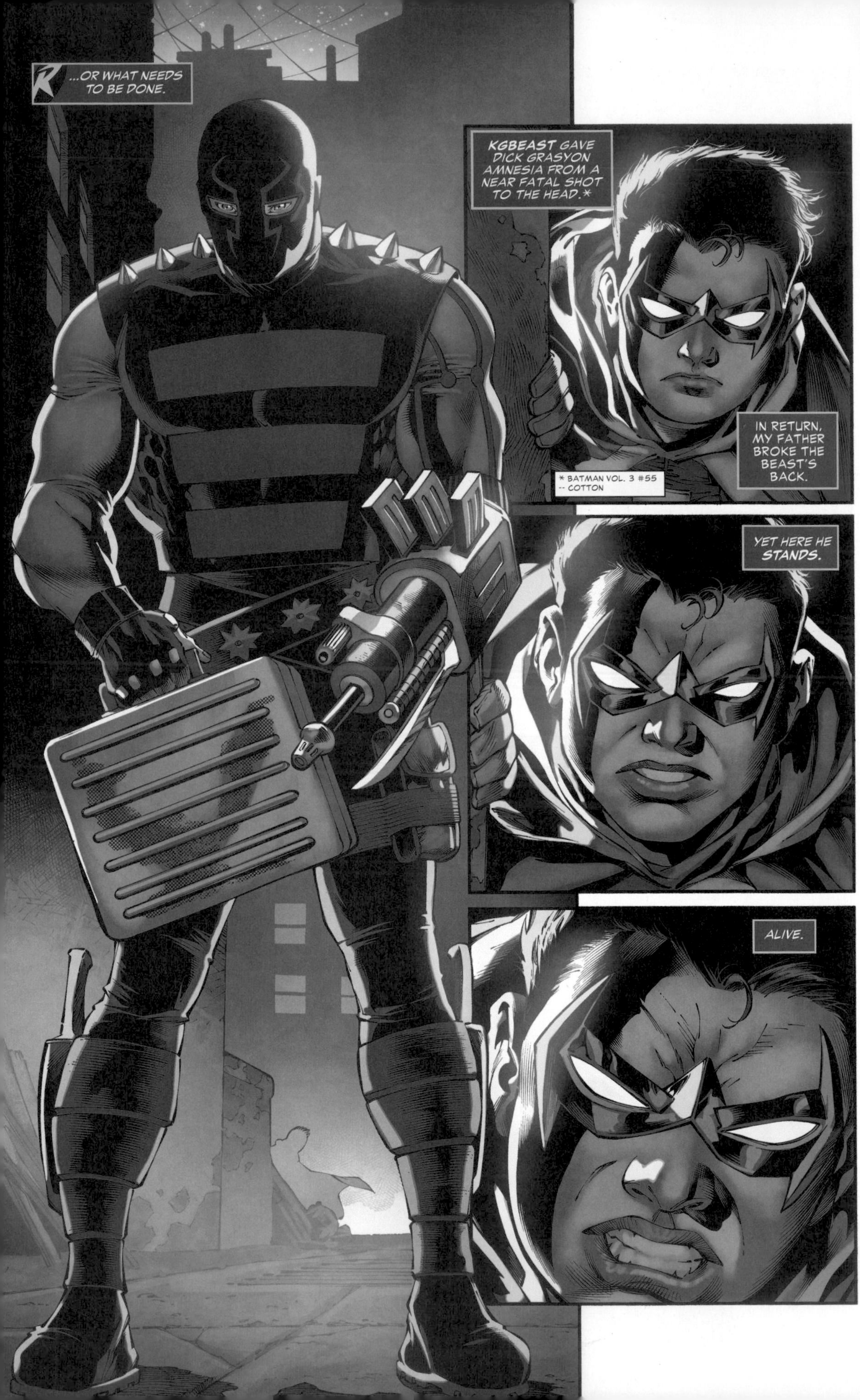
...OR WHAT NEEDS TO BE DONE.
KGBEAST GAVE DICK GRASYON AMNESIA FROM A NEAR FATAL SHOT TO THE HEAD.*
* BATMAN VOL. 3 #55 -- COTTON
IN RETURN, MY FATHER BROKE THE BEAST'S BACK.
YET HERE HE STANDS.
ALIVE.

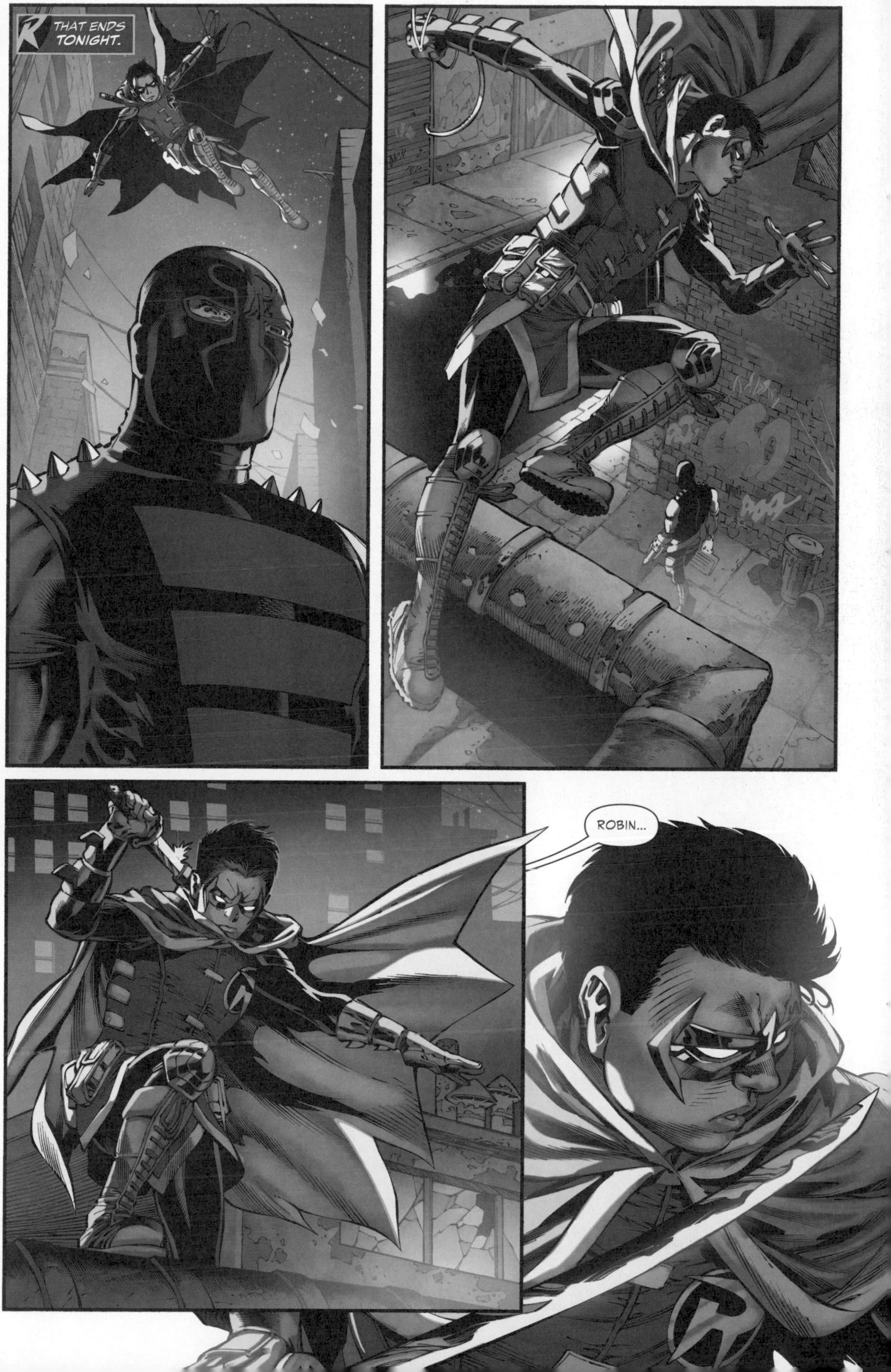
THAT ENDS TONIGHT.
ROBIN...

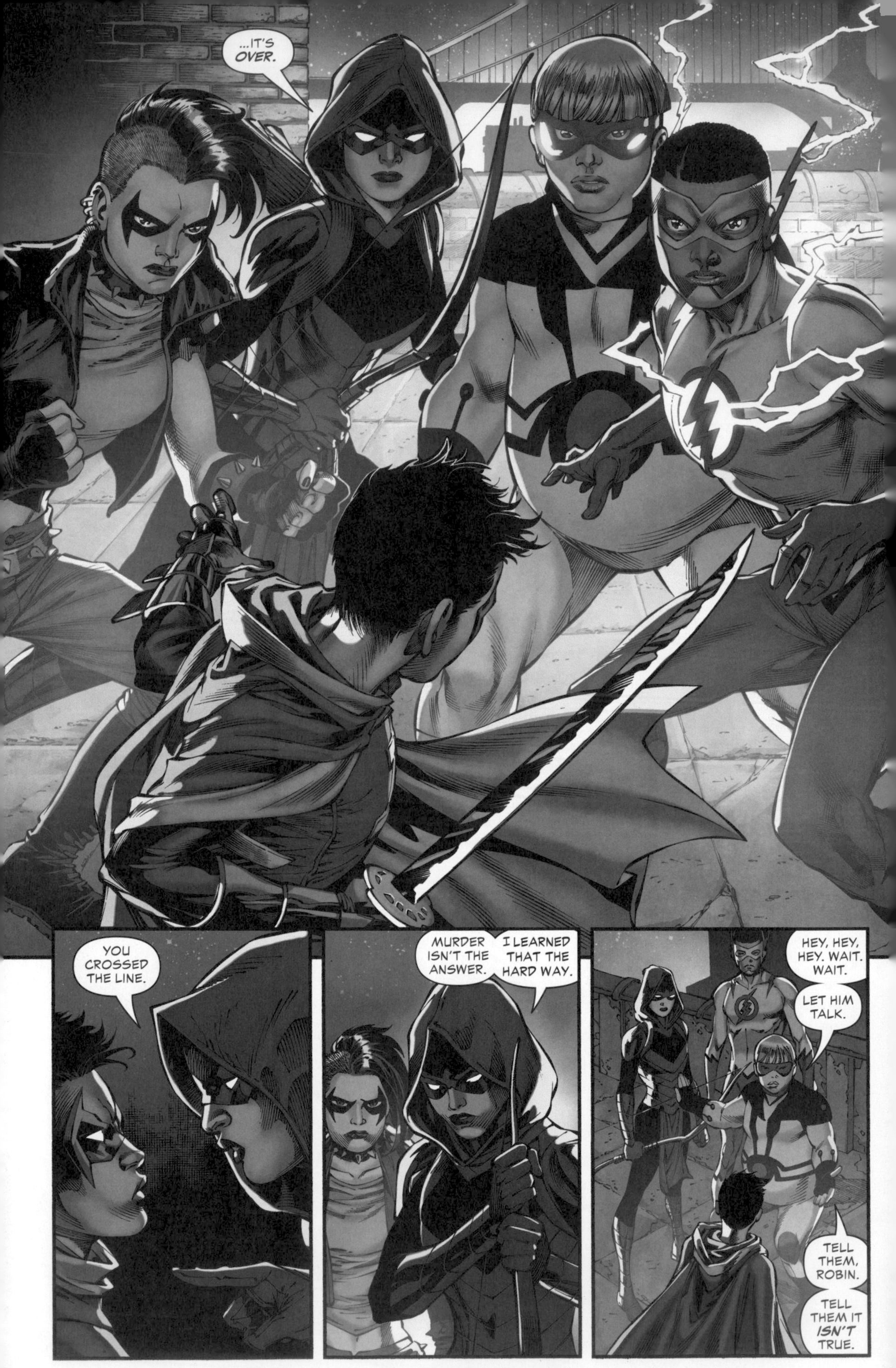
...IT'S OVER.
YOU CROSSED THE LINE.
MURDER ISN'T THE ANSWER.
I LEARNED THAT THE HARD WAY.
HEY, HEY, HEY. WAIT. WAIT.
LET HIM TALK.
TELL THEM, ROBIN.
TELL THEM IT ISN'T TRUE.

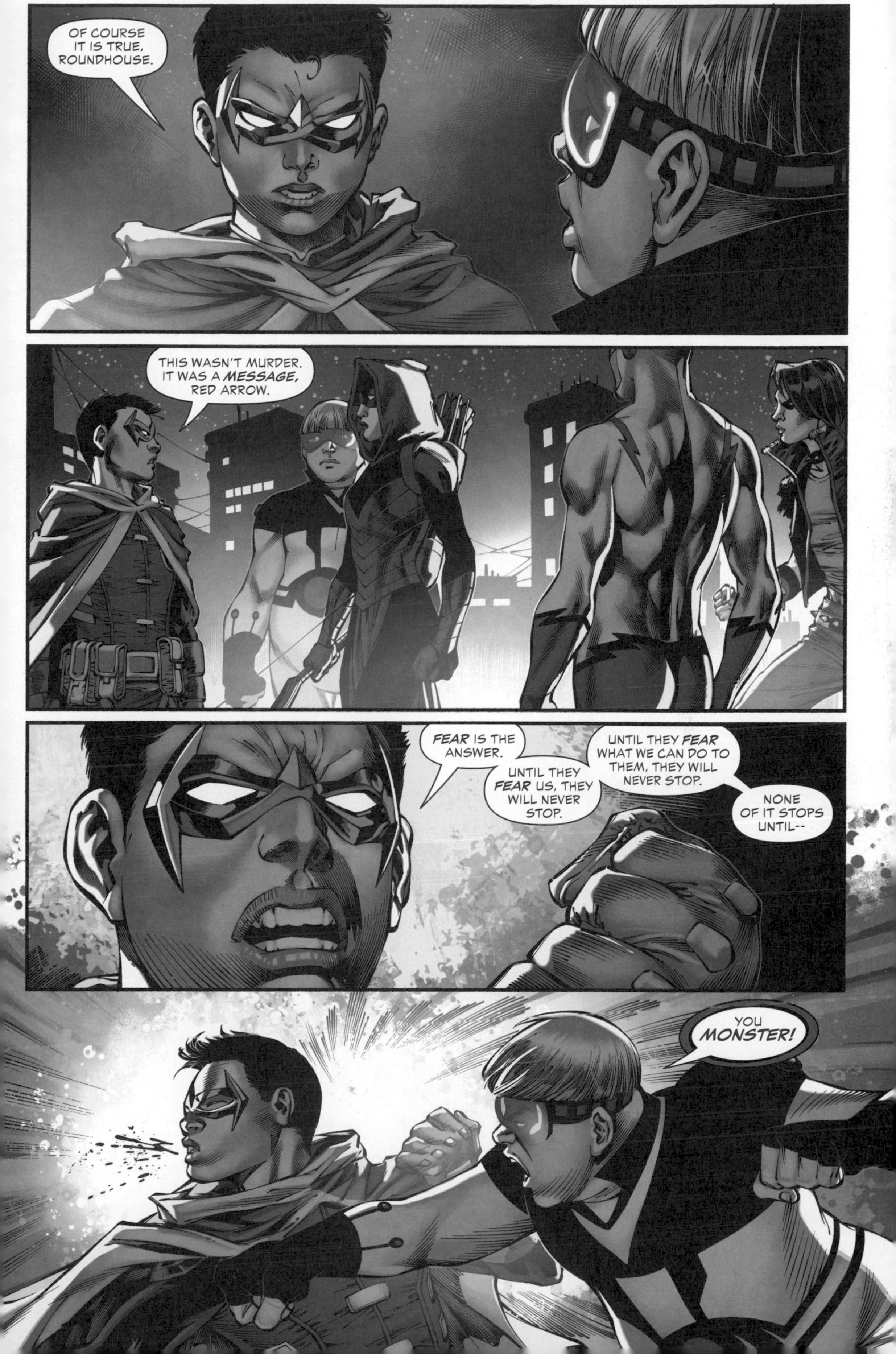
OF COURSE IT IS TRUE, ROUNDHOUSE.
THIS WASN'T MURDER. IT WAS A *MESSAGE,* RED ARROW.
FEAR IS THE ANSWER.
UNTIL THEY *FEAR* US, THEY WILL NEVER STOP.
UNTIL THEY *FEAR* WHAT WE CAN DO TO THEM, THEY WILL NEVER STOP.
NONE OF IT STOPS UNTIL--
YOU *MONSTER!*

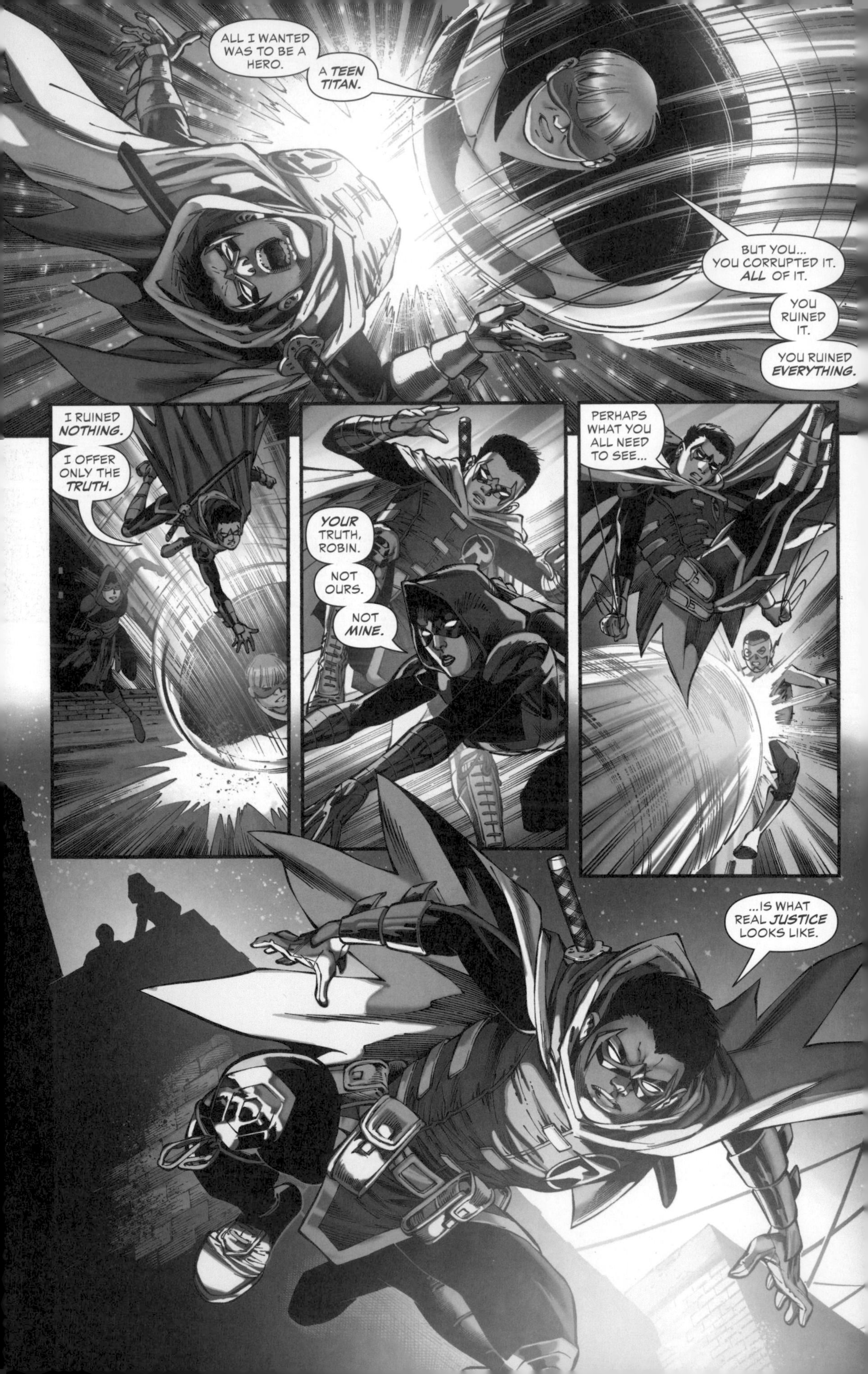
ALL I WANTED WAS TO BE A HERO.
A *TEEN TITAN*.
BUT YOU... YOU CORRUPTED IT. *ALL* OF IT.
YOU RUINED IT.
YOU RUINED *EVERYTHING*.
I RUINED *NOTHING*.
I OFFER ONLY THE *TRUTH*.
YOUR TRUTH, ROBIN.
NOT OURS.
NOT *MINE*.
PERHAPS WHAT YOU ALL NEED TO SEE...
...IS WHAT REAL *JUSTICE* LOOKS LIKE.

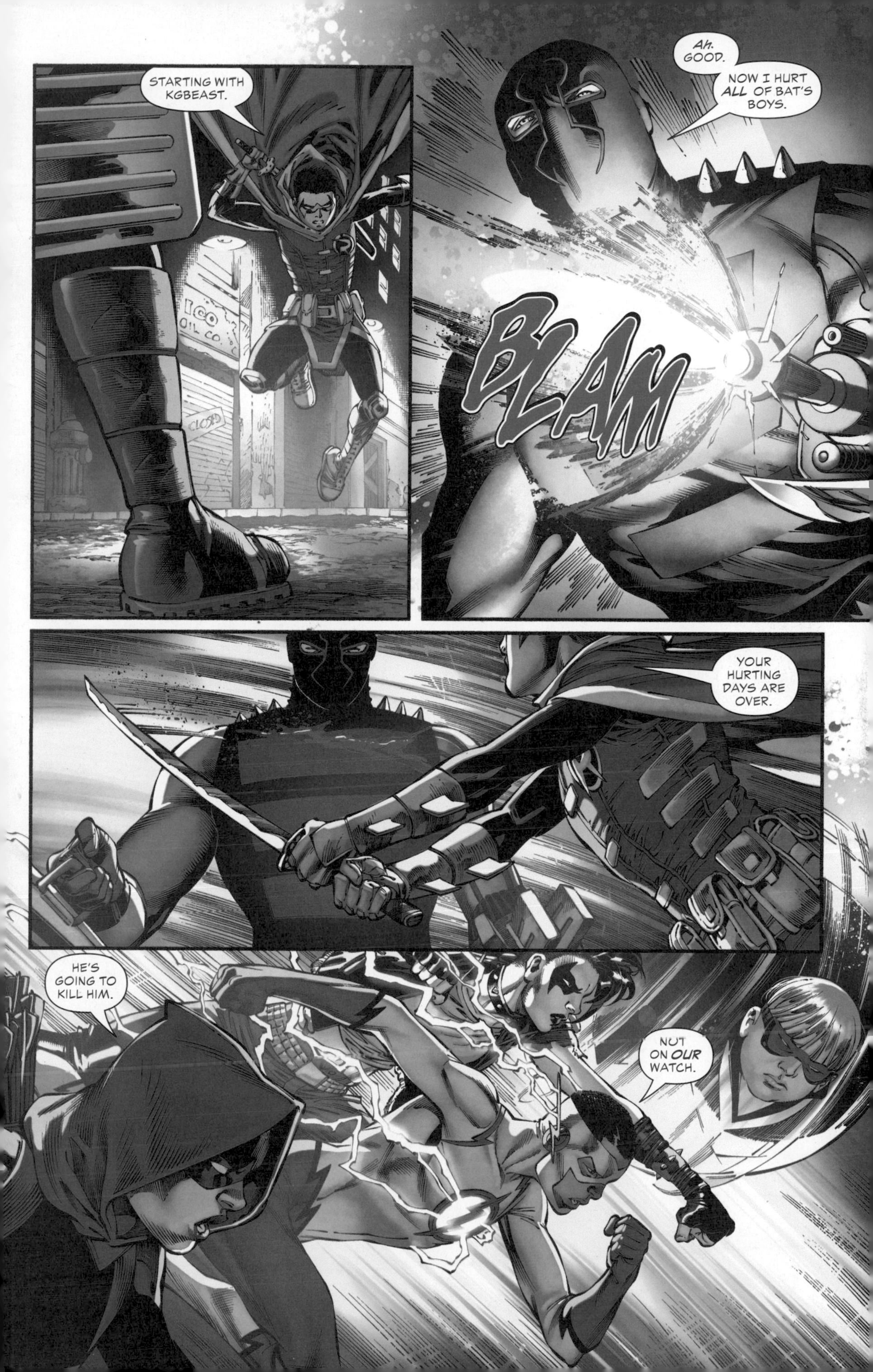
STARTING WITH KGBEAST.
CLOSED
Ah. GOOD.
NOW I HURT ALL OF BAT'S BOYS.
BLAM
YOUR HURTING DAYS ARE OVER.
HE'S GOING TO KILL HIM.
NOT ON OUR WATCH.

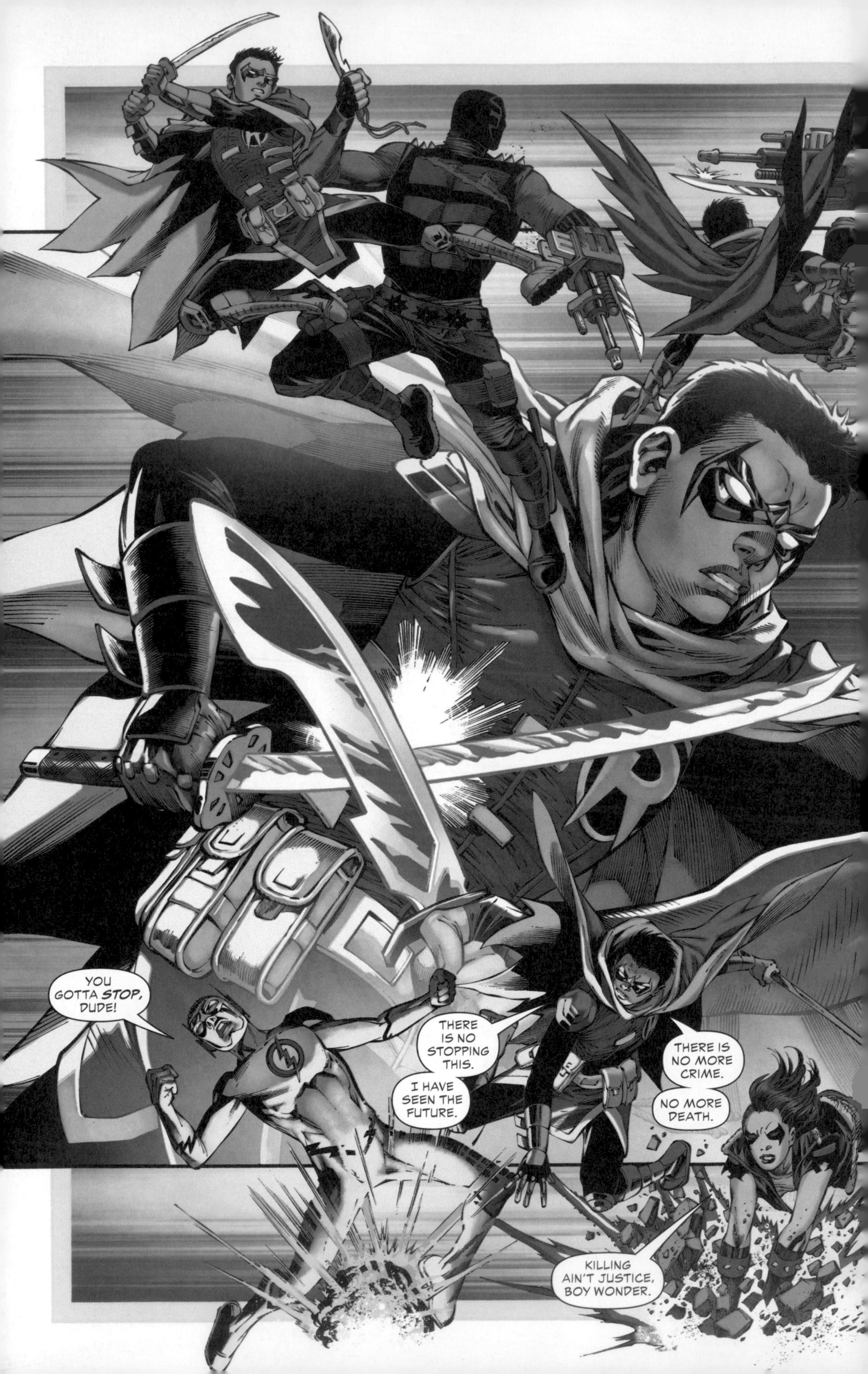
YOU GOTTA STOP, DUDE!
THERE IS NO STOPPING THIS.
I HAVE SEEN THE FUTURE.
THERE IS NO MORE CRIME.
NO MORE DEATH.
KILLING AIN'T JUSTICE, BOY WONDER.

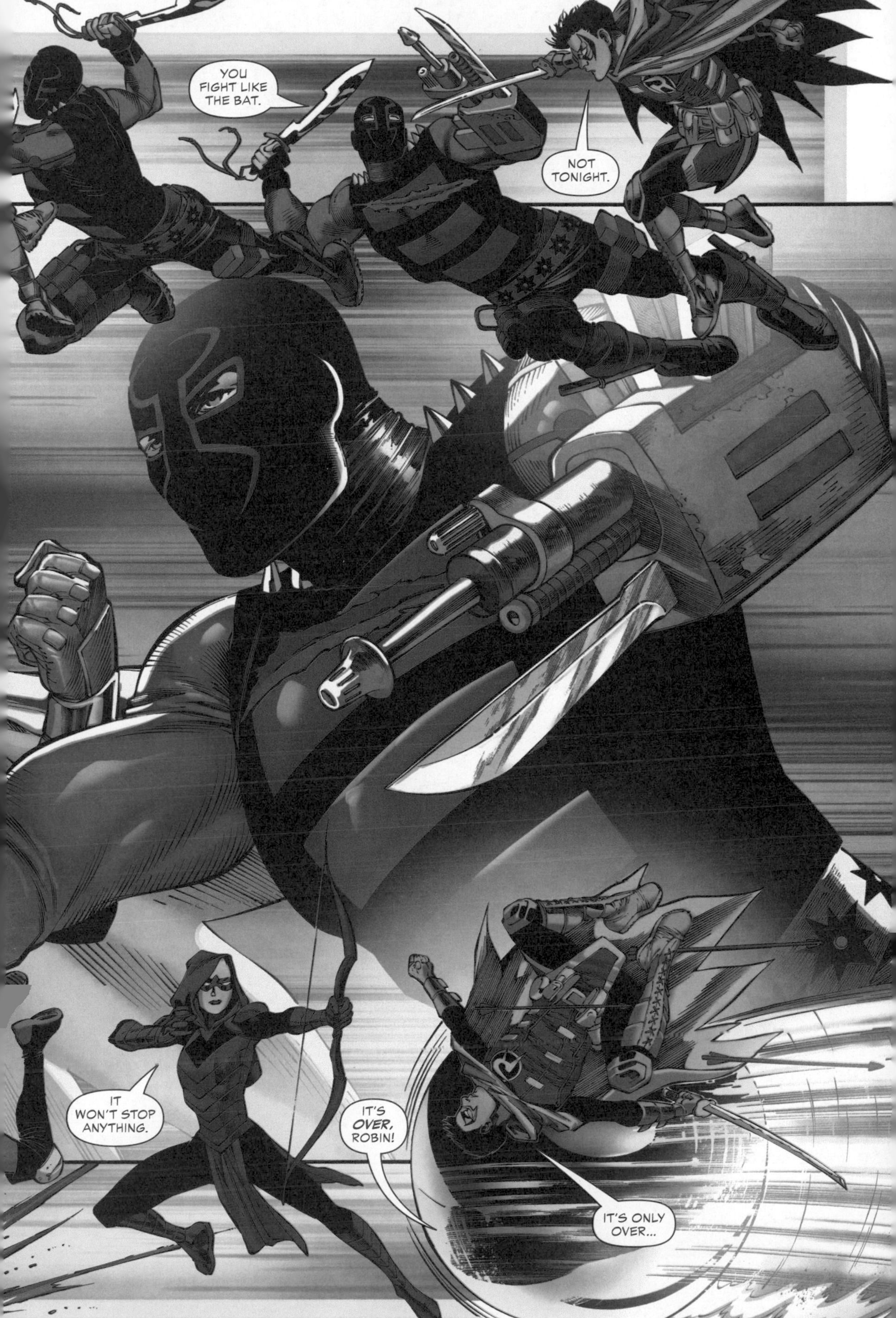
YOU FIGHT LIKE THE BAT.
NOT TONIGHT.
IT WON'T STOP ANYTHING.
IT'S OVER, ROBIN!
IT'S ONLY OVER...

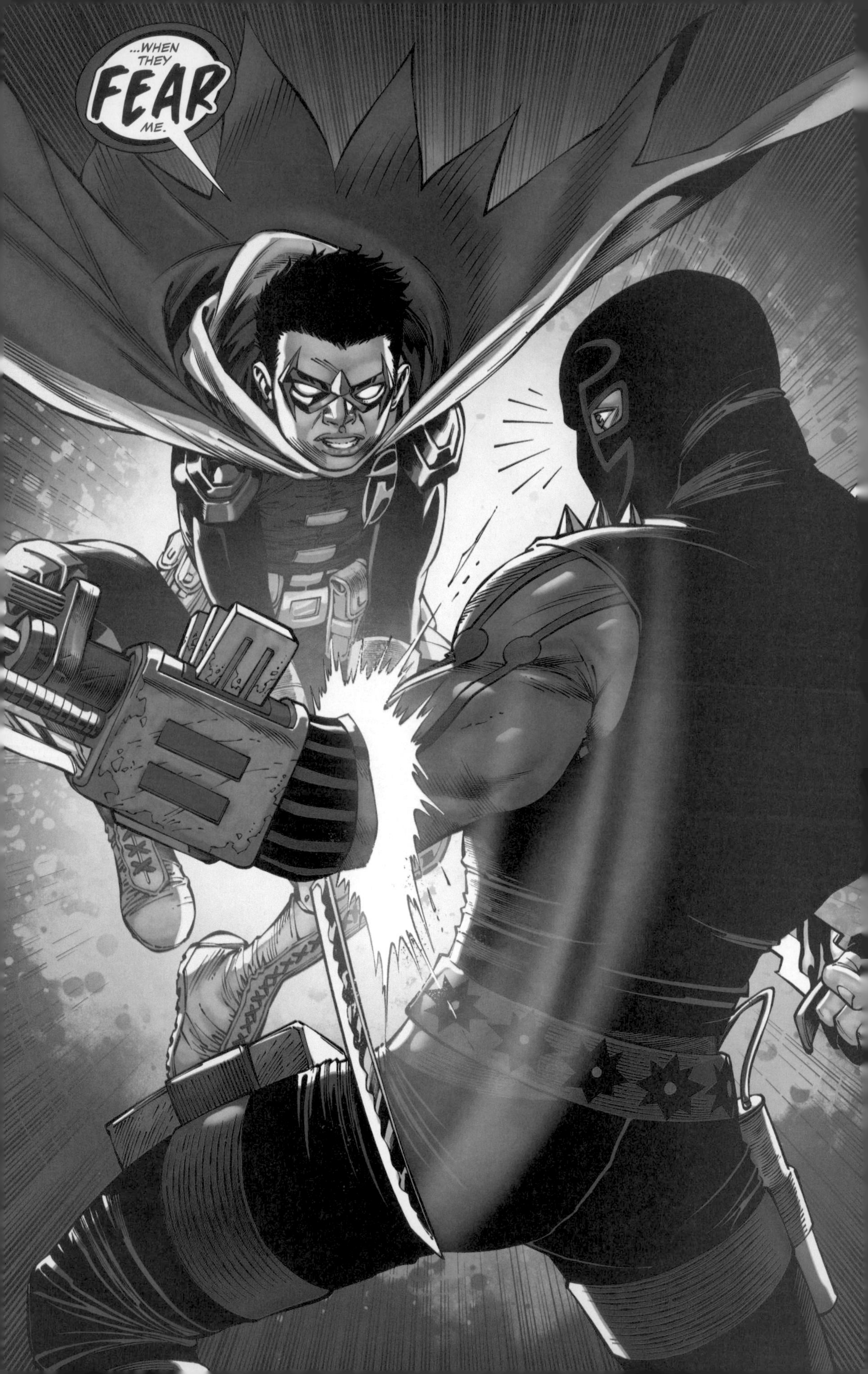
...WHEN THEY FEAR ME.

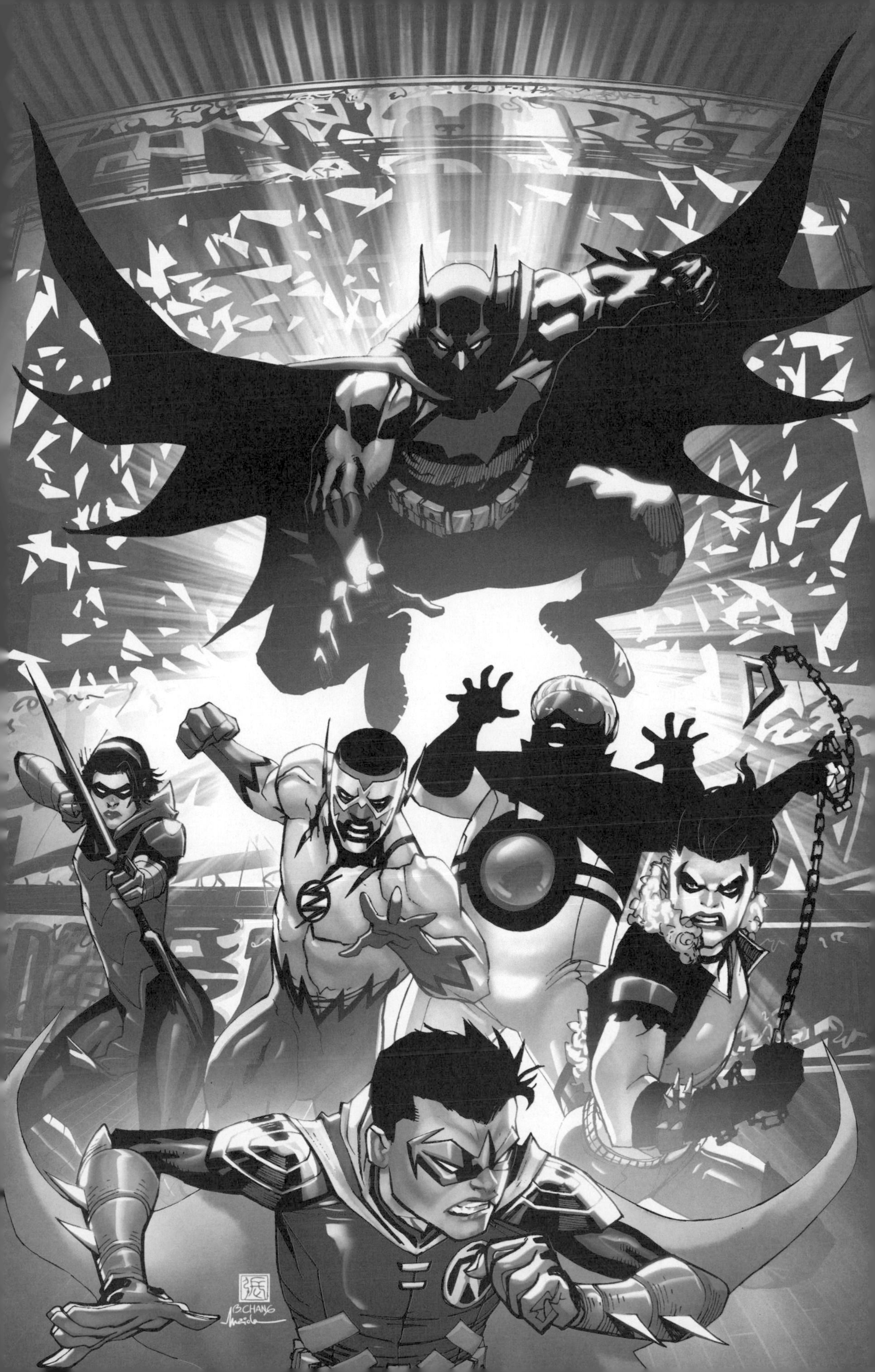
B CHANG

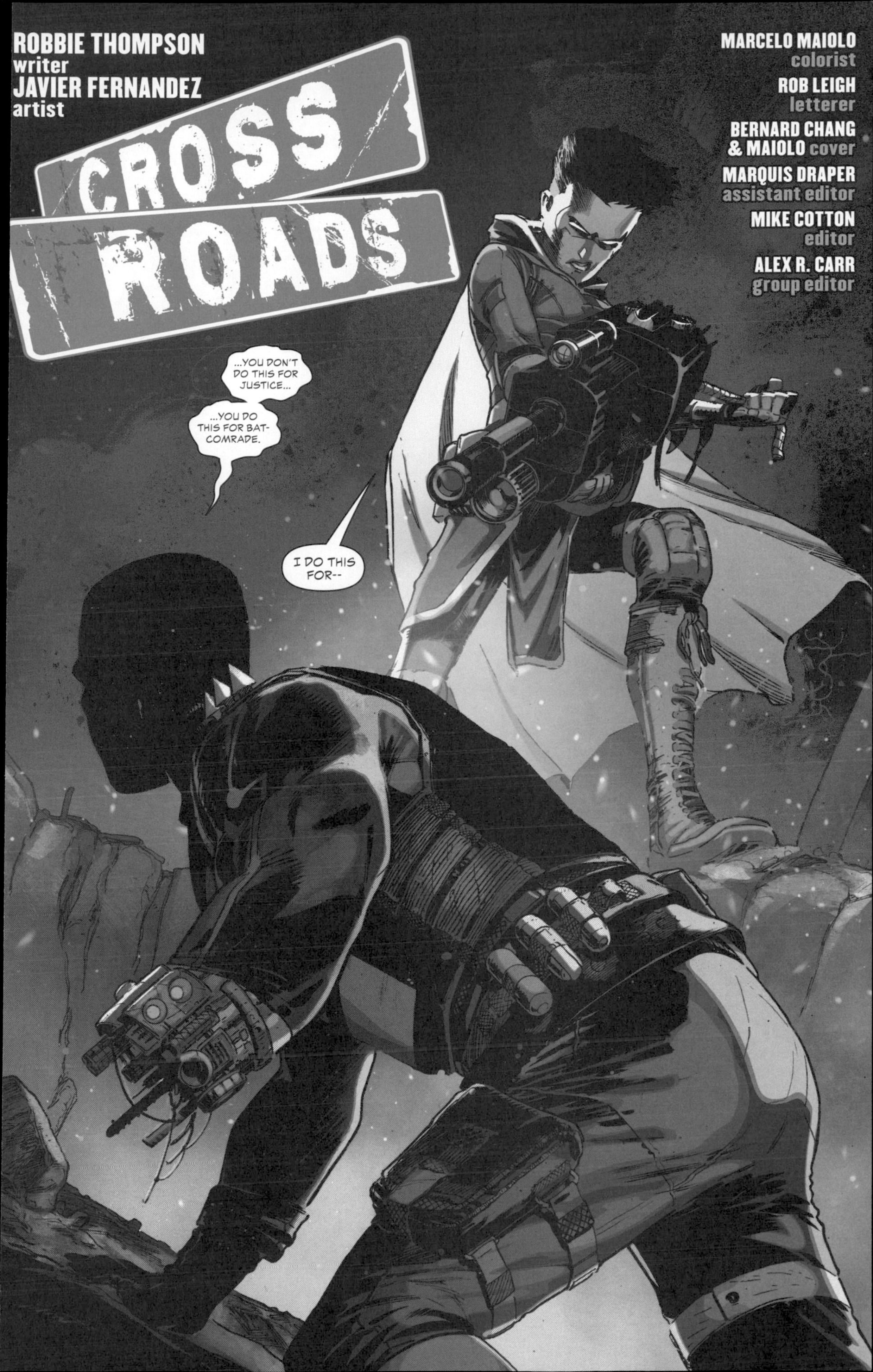
ROBBIE THOMPSON
writer
JAVIER FERNANDEZ
artist
CROSS ROADS
MARCELO MAIOLO
colorist
ROB LEIGH
letterer
BERNARD CHANG & MAIOLO cover
MARQUIS DRAPER
assistant editor
MIKE COTTON
editor
ALEX R. CARR
group editor
...YOU DON'T DO THIS FOR JUSTICE...
...YOU DO THIS FOR BAT-COMRADE.
I DO THIS FOR--

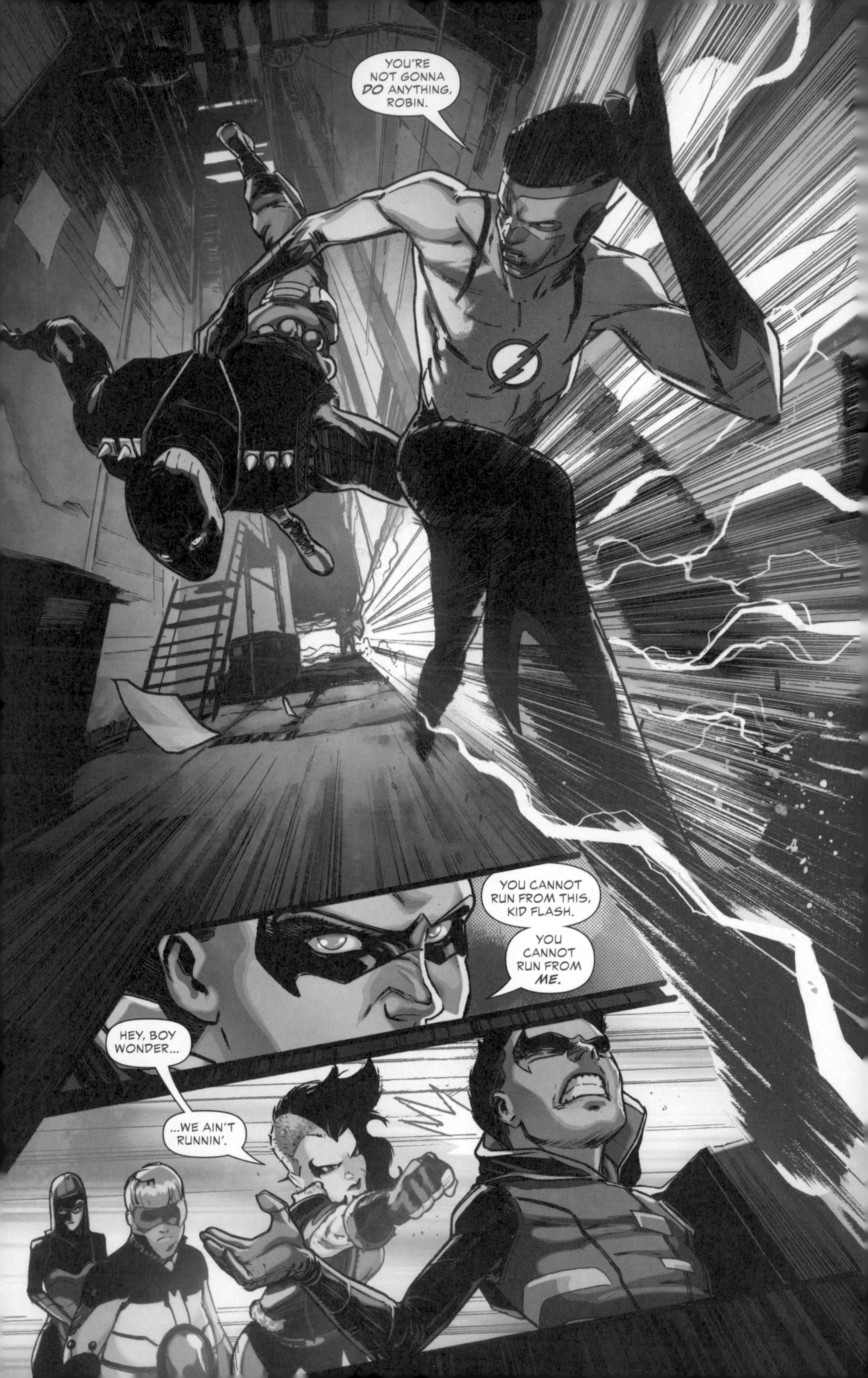
YOU'RE NOT GONNA DO ANYTHING, ROBIN.
YOU CANNOT RUN FROM THIS, KID FLASH.
YOU CANNOT RUN FROM ME.
HEY, BOY WONDER...
...WE AIN'T RUNNIN'.

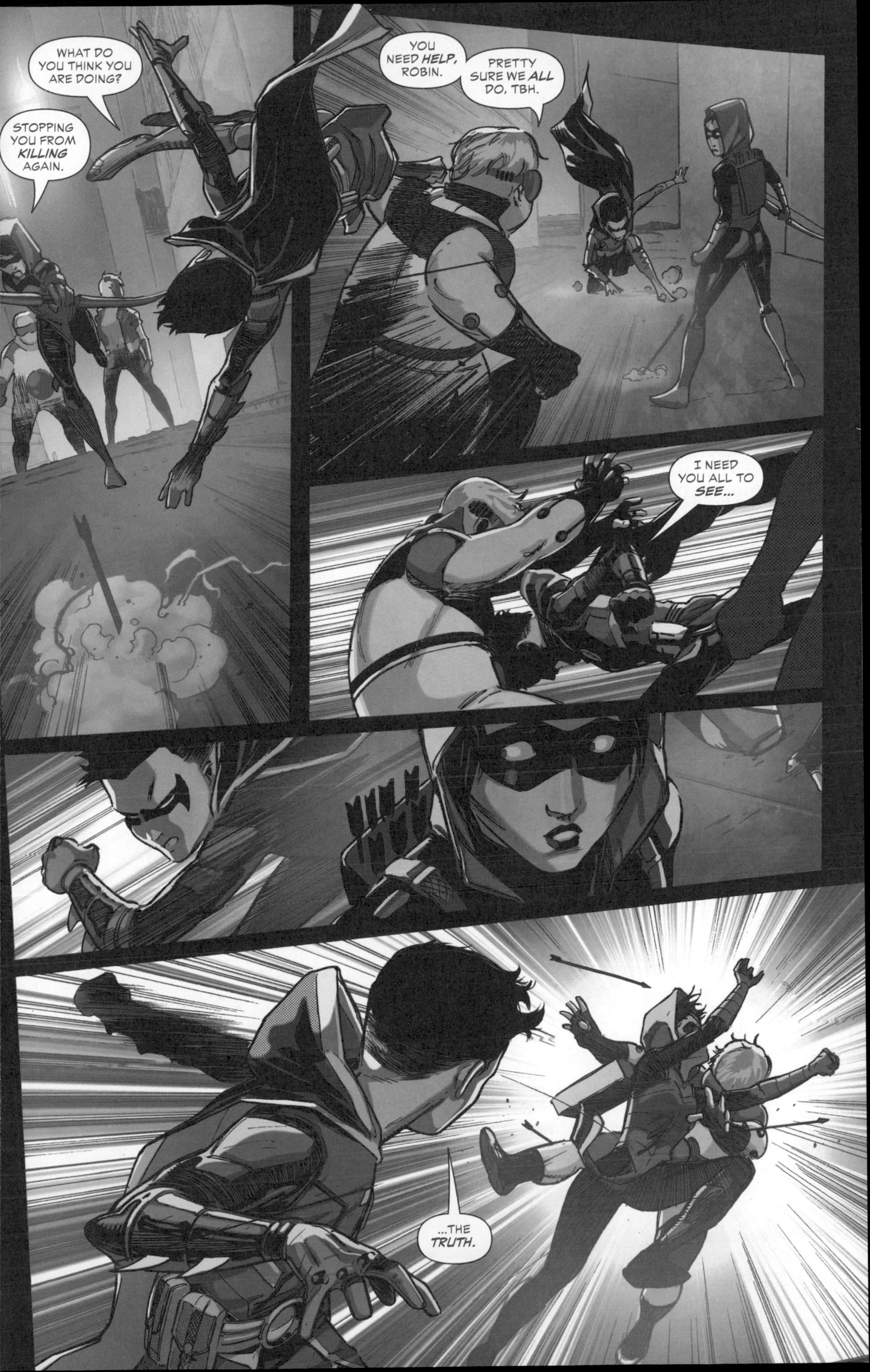
WHAT DO YOU THINK YOU ARE DOING?
STOPPING YOU FROM KILLING AGAIN.
YOU NEED HELP, ROBIN.
PRETTY SURE WE ALL DO, TBH.
I NEED YOU ALL TO SEE...
...THE TRUTH.

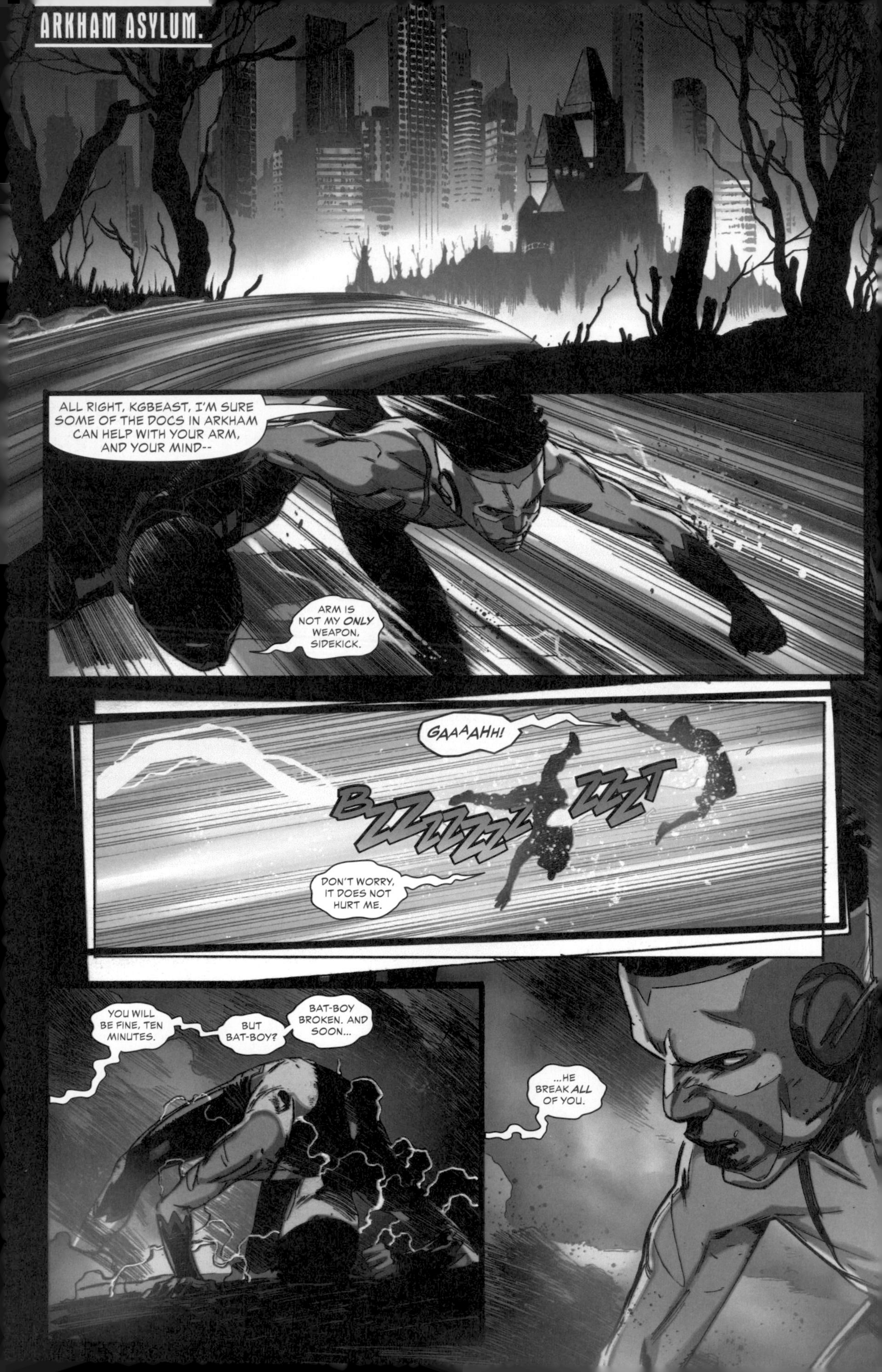
ARKHAM ASYLUM.
ALL RIGHT, KGBEAST, I'M SURE SOME OF THE DOCS IN ARKHAM CAN HELP WITH YOUR ARM, AND YOUR MIND--
ARM IS NOT MY ONLY WEAPON, SIDEKICK.
GAAAAHH!
BZZZZZZZZZZT
DON'T WORRY, IT DOES NOT HURT ME.
YOU WILL BE FINE, TEN MINUTES.
BUT BAT-BOY?
BAT-BOY BROKEN. AND SOON...
...HE BREAK ALL OF YOU.

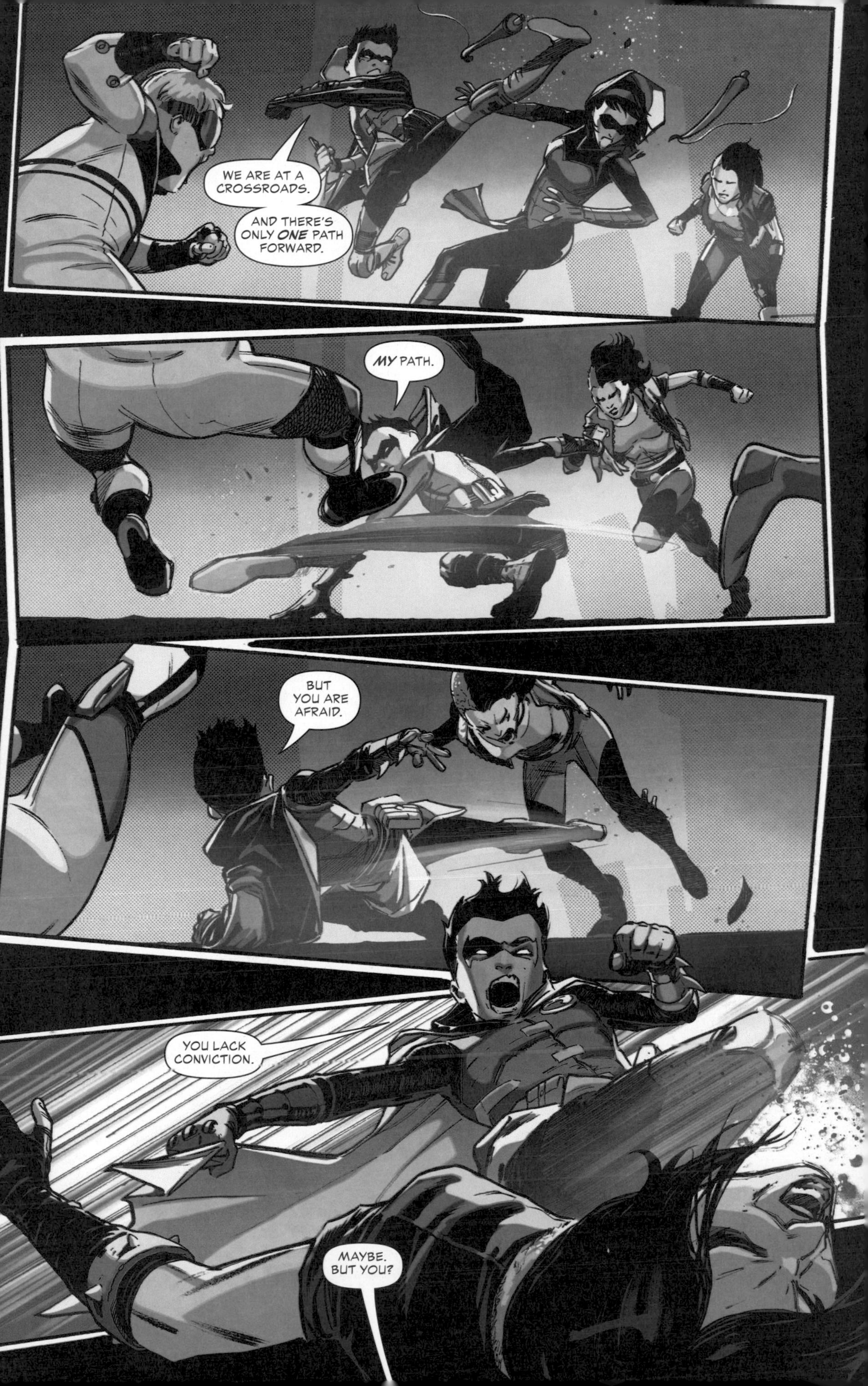
WE ARE AT A CROSSROADS.
AND THERE'S ONLY ONE PATH FORWARD.
MY PATH.
BUT YOU ARE AFRAID.
YOU LACK CONVICTION.
MAYBE. BUT YOU?

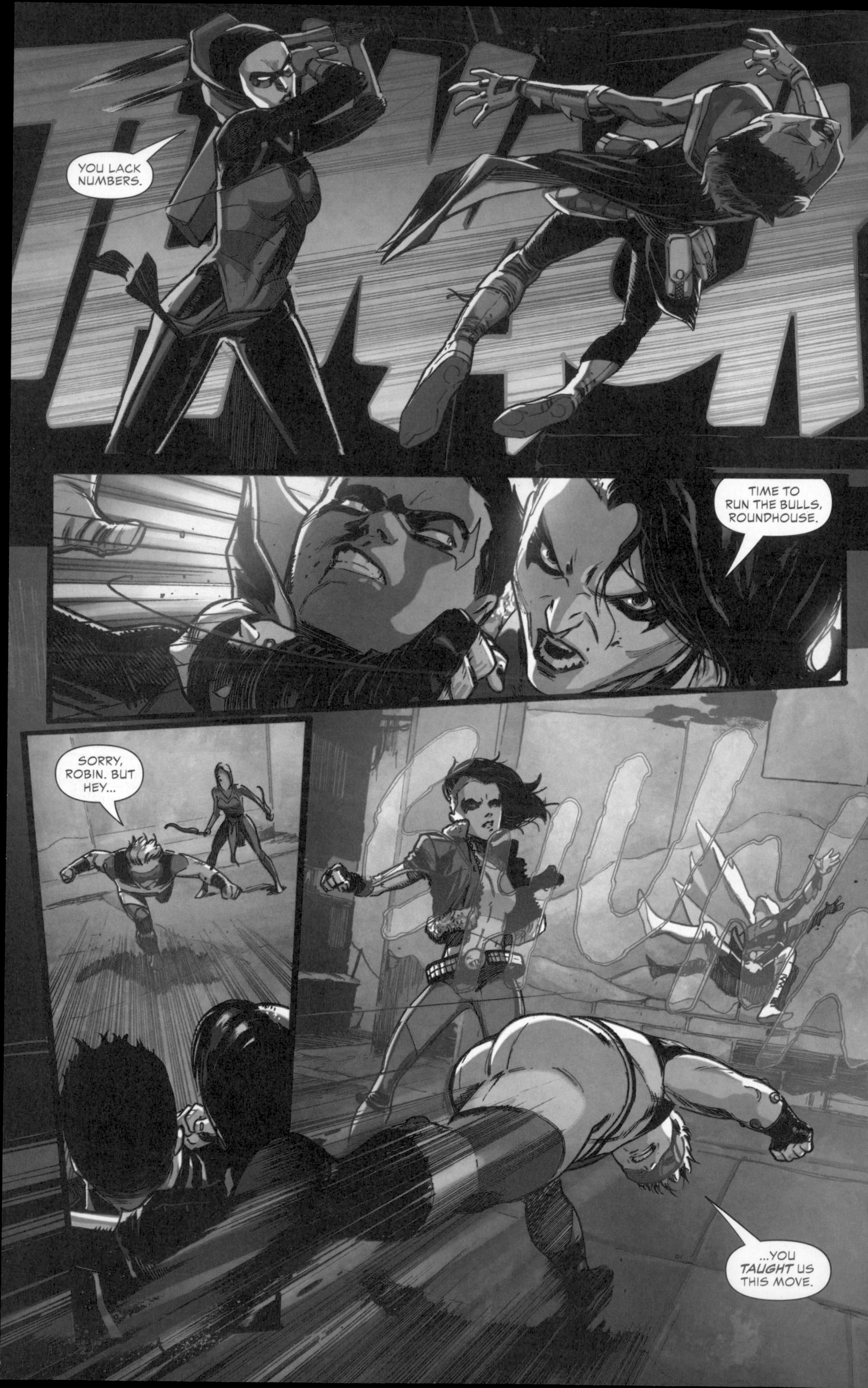
YOU LACK NUMBERS.
TIME TO RUN THE BULLS, ROUNDHOUSE.
SORRY, ROBIN. BUT HEY...
...YOU *TAUGHT* US THIS MOVE.

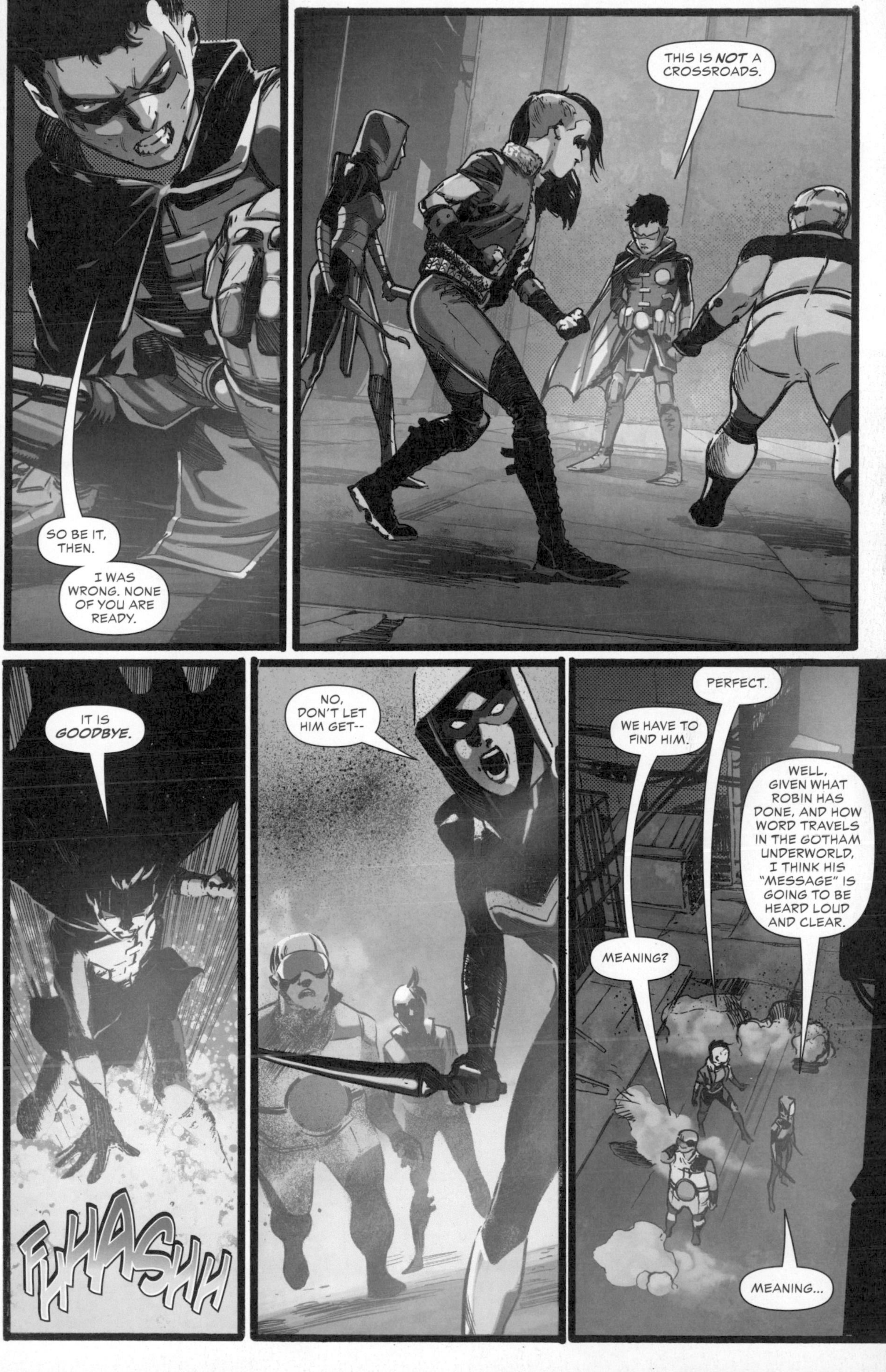

SO BE IT, THEN.
I WAS WRONG. NONE OF YOU ARE READY.
THIS IS NOT A CROSSROADS.
IT IS GOODBYE.
FWHASHH
NO, DON'T LET HIM GET--
PERFECT.
WE HAVE TO FIND HIM.
WELL, GIVEN WHAT ROBIN HAS DONE, AND HOW WORD TRAVELS IN THE GOTHAM UNDERWORLD, I THINK HIS "MESSAGE" IS GOING TO BE HEARD LOUD AND CLEAR.
MEANING?
MEANING...

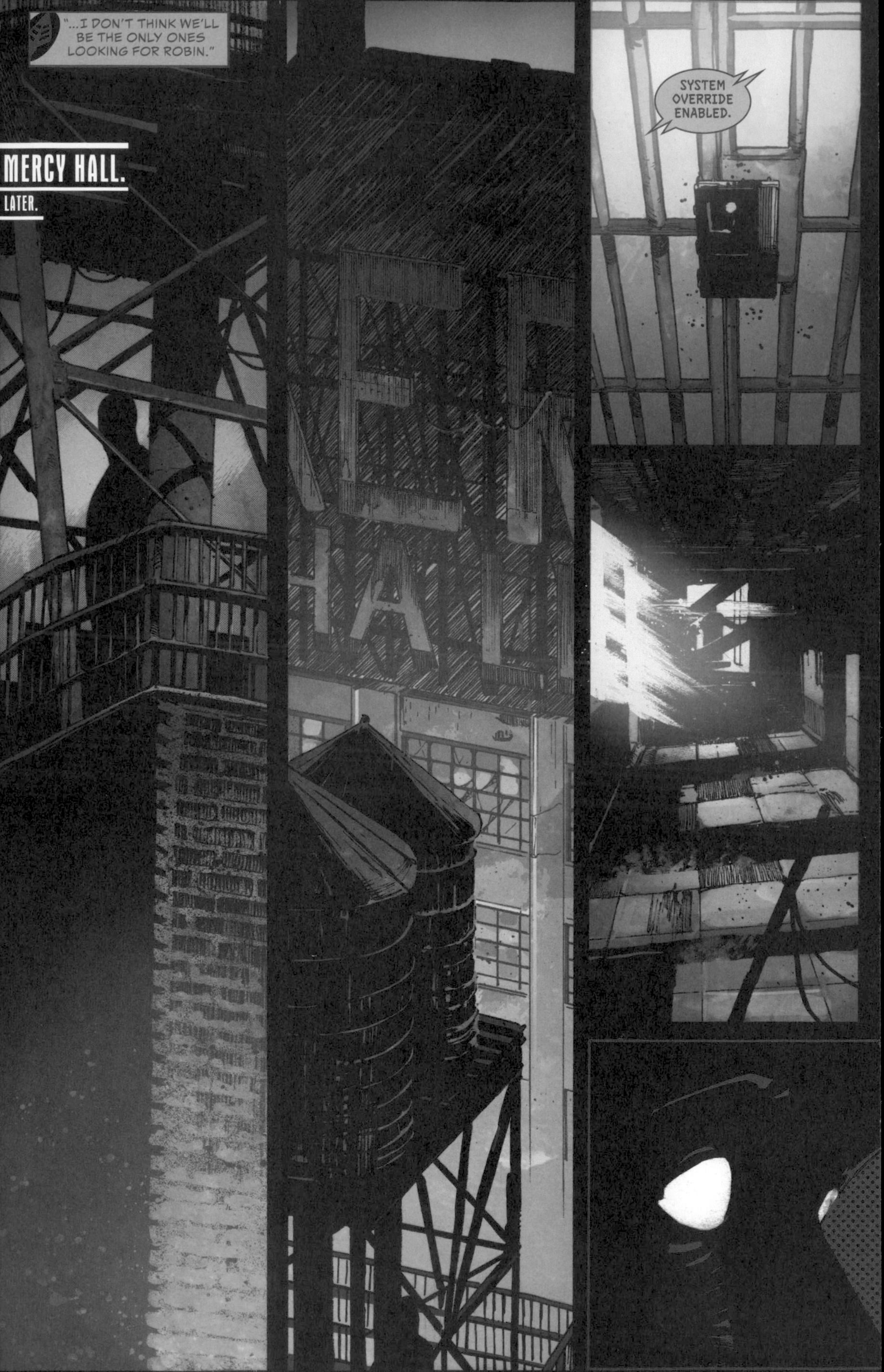
"...I DON'T THINK WE'LL BE THE ONLY ONES LOOKING FOR ROBIN."
MERCY HALL.
LATER.
SYSTEM OVERRIDE ENABLED.

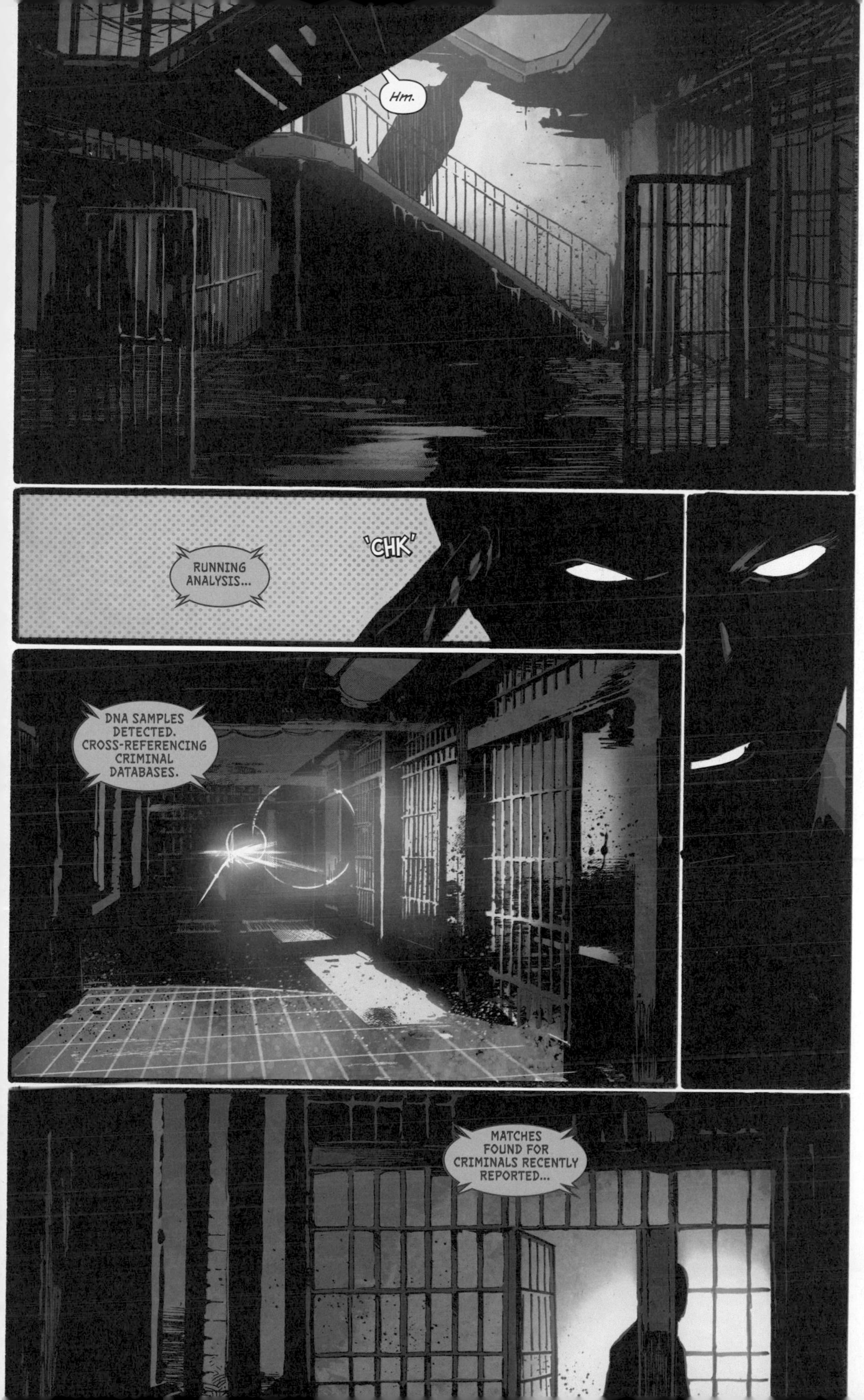
Hm.
'CHK'
RUNNING ANALYSIS...
DNA SAMPLES DETECTED. CROSS-REFERENCING CRIMINAL DATABASES.
MATCHES FOUND FOR CRIMINALS RECENTLY REPORTED...

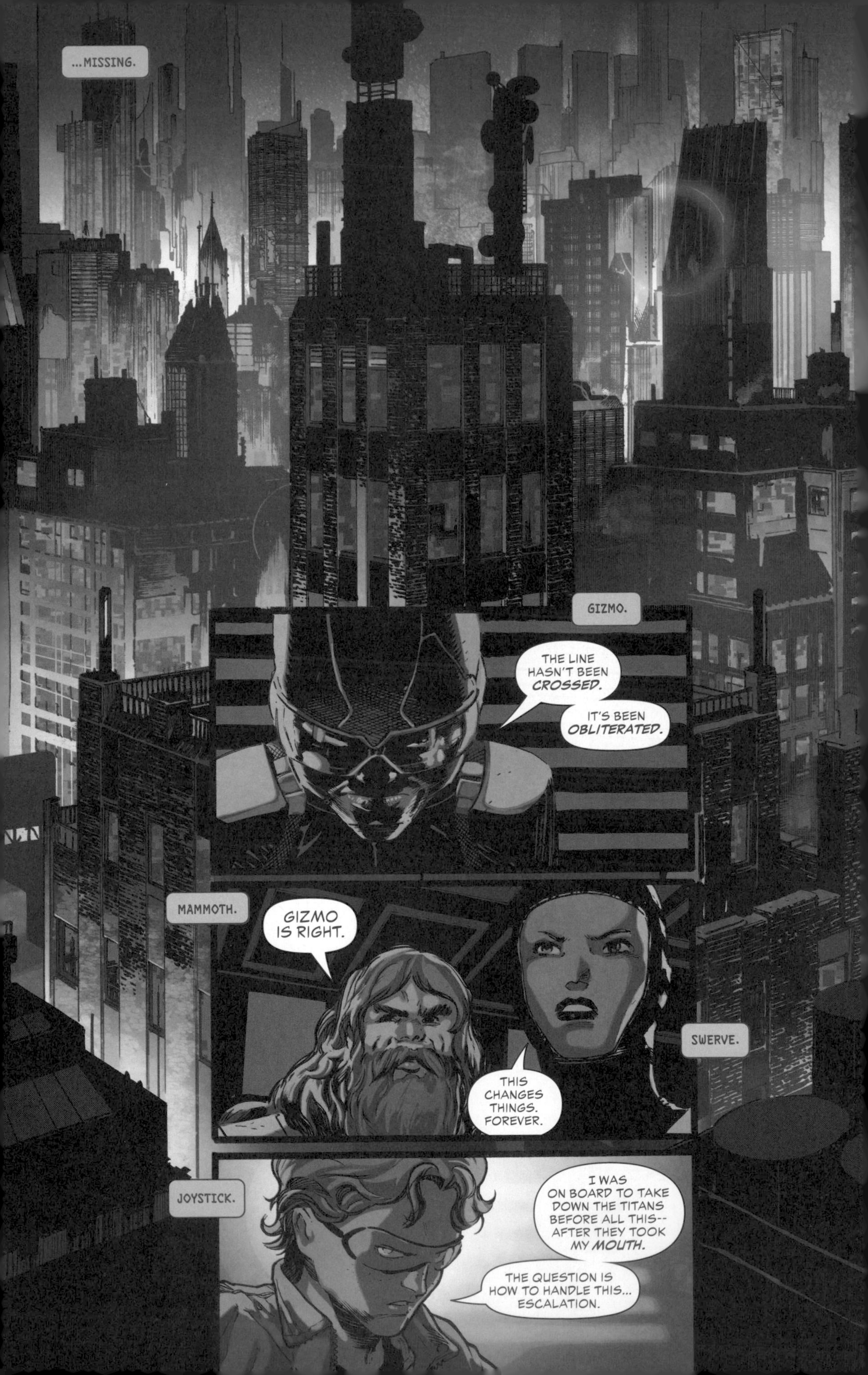
...MISSING.
GIZMO.
THE LINE HASN'T BEEN CROSSED.
IT'S BEEN OBLITERATED.
MAMMOTH.
GIZMO IS RIGHT.
SWERVE.
THIS CHANGES THINGS. FOREVER.
JOYSTICK.
I WAS ON BOARD TO TAKE DOWN THE TITANS BEFORE ALL THIS-- --AFTER THEY TOOK MY MOUTH.
THE QUESTION IS HOW TO HANDLE THIS... ESCALATION.

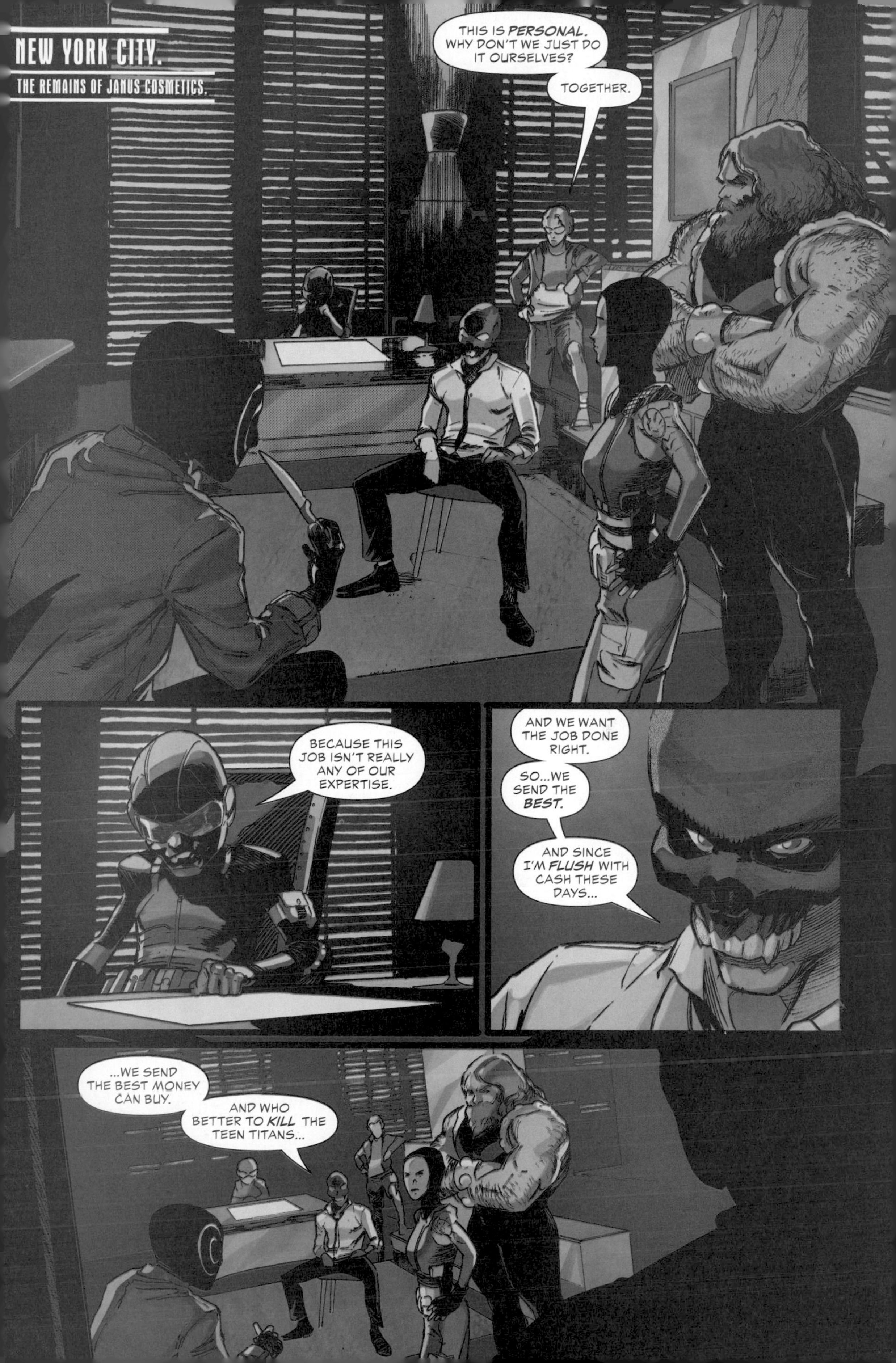
NEW YORK CITY.
THE REMAINS OF JANUS COSMETICS.
THIS IS *PERSONAL.* WHY DON'T WE JUST DO IT OURSELVES?
TOGETHER.
BECAUSE THIS JOB ISN'T REALLY ANY OF OUR EXPERTISE.
AND WE WANT THE JOB DONE RIGHT.
SO...WE SEND THE *BEST.*
AND SINCE I'M *FLUSH* WITH CASH THESE DAYS...
...WE SEND THE BEST MONEY CAN BUY.
AND WHO BETTER TO *KILL* THE TEEN TITANS...

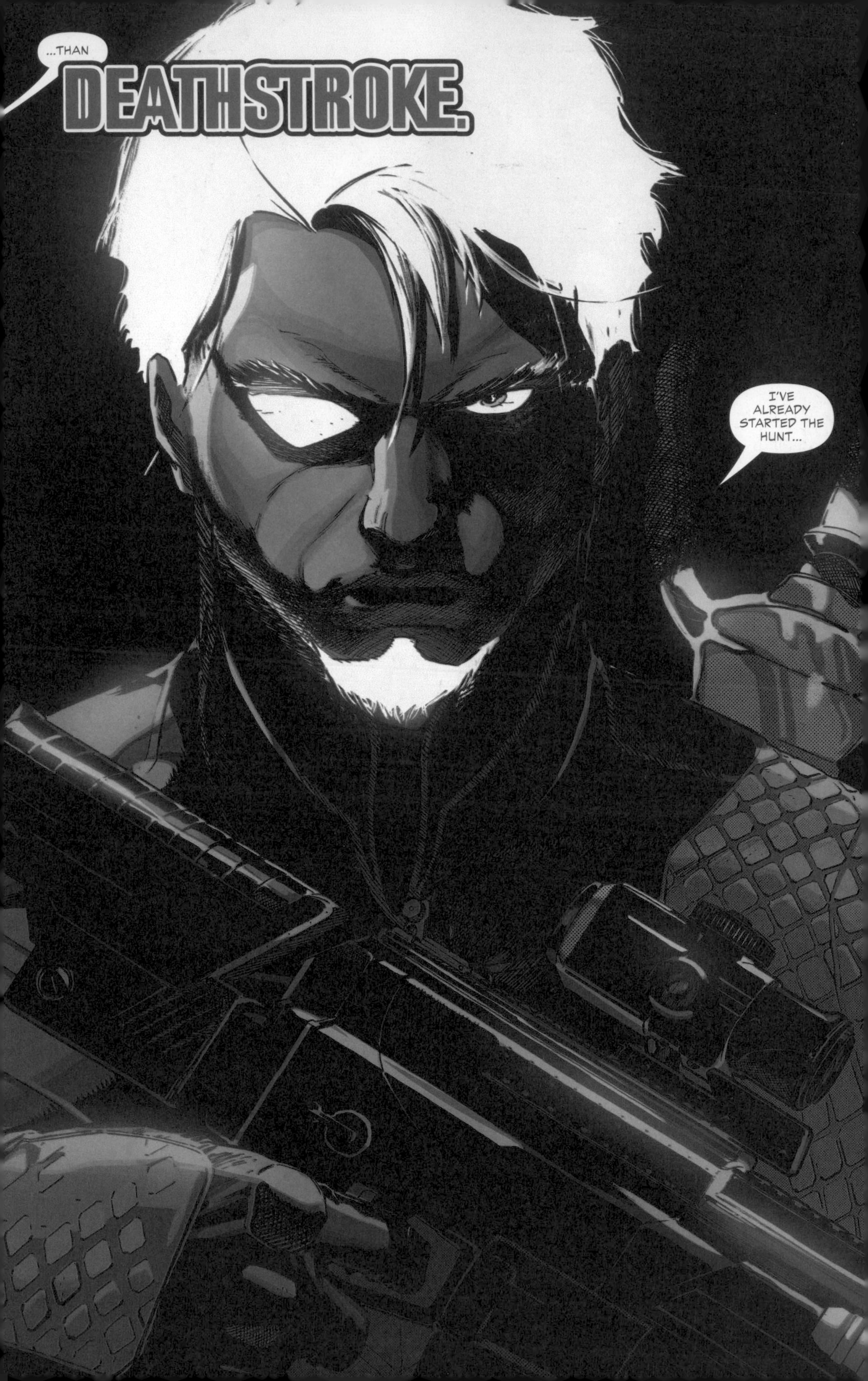
...THAN
DEATHSTROKE.
I'VE ALREADY STARTED THE HUNT...

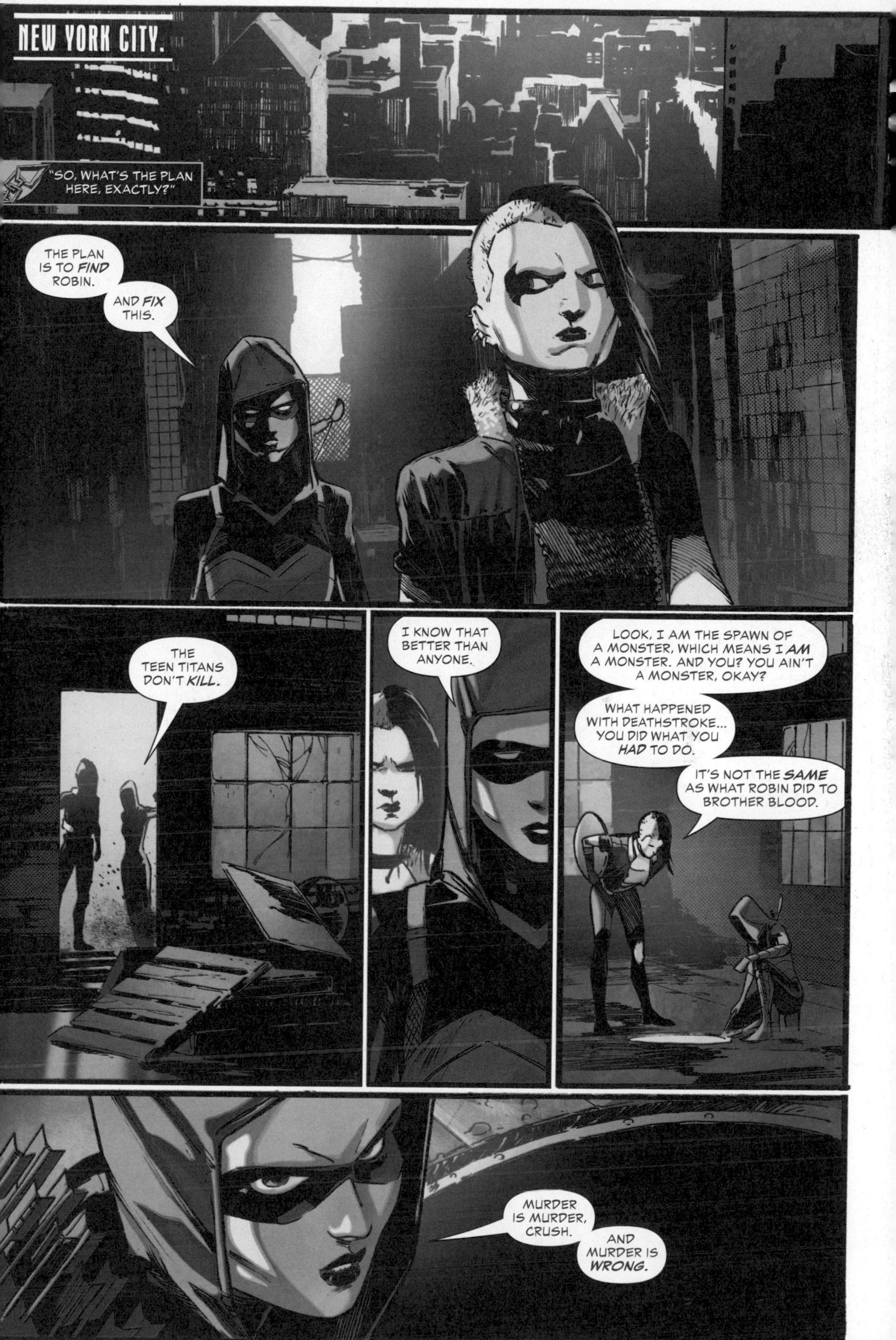
NEW YORK CITY.
"SO, WHAT'S THE PLAN HERE, EXACTLY?"
THE PLAN IS TO FIND ROBIN.
AND FIX THIS.
THE TEEN TITANS DON'T KILL.
I KNOW THAT BETTER THAN ANYONE.
LOOK, I AM THE SPAWN OF A MONSTER, WHICH MEANS I AM A MONSTER. AND YOU? YOU AIN'T A MONSTER, OKAY?
WHAT HAPPENED WITH DEATHSTROKE... YOU DID WHAT YOU HAD TO DO.
IT'S NOT THE SAME AS WHAT ROBIN DID TO BROTHER BLOOD.
MURDER IS MURDER, CRUSH.
AND MURDER IS WRONG.

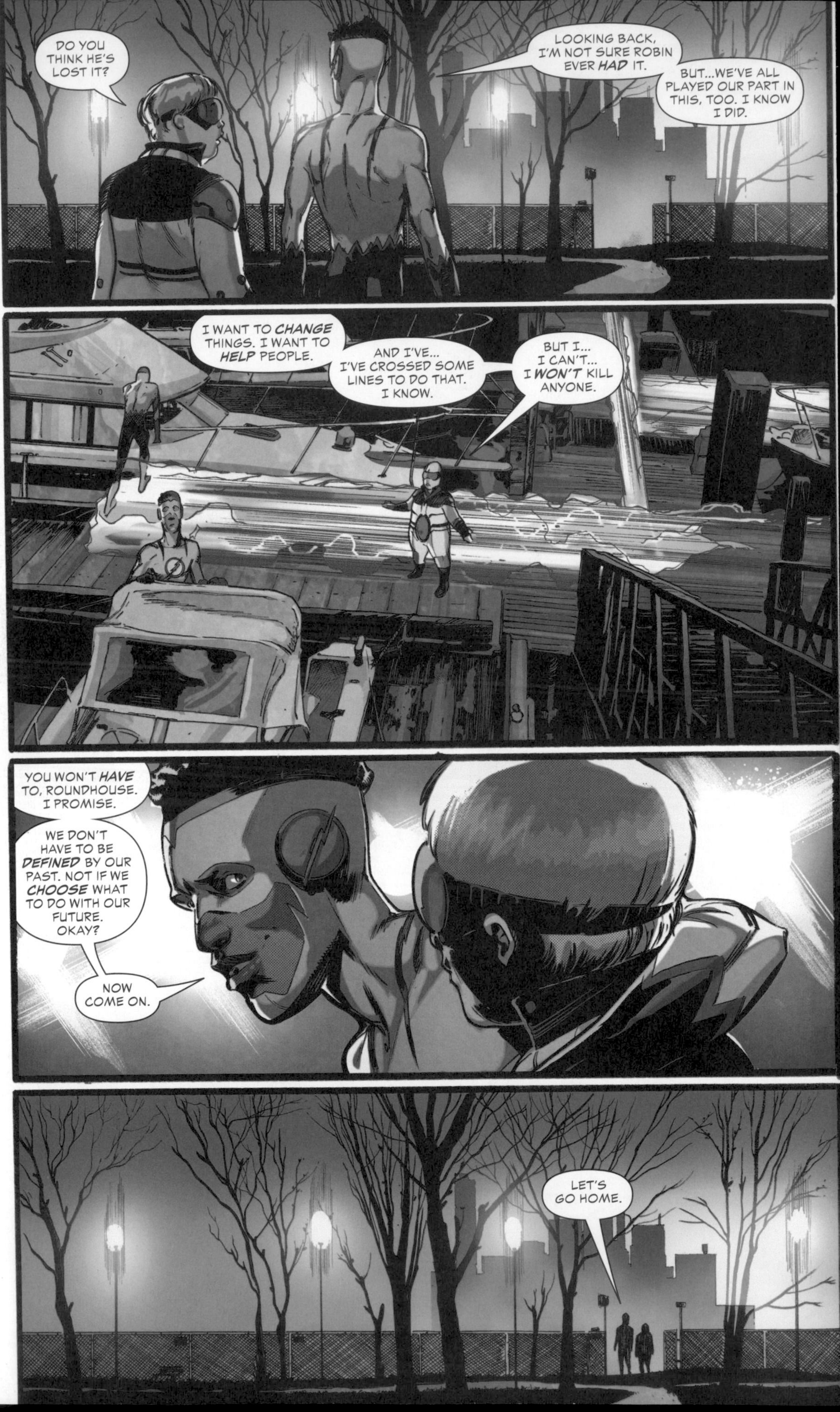
DO YOU THINK HE'S LOST IT?
LOOKING BACK, I'M NOT SURE ROBIN EVER HAD IT.
BUT...WE'VE ALL PLAYED OUR PART IN THIS, TOO. I KNOW I DID.
I WANT TO CHANGE THINGS. I WANT TO HELP PEOPLE.
AND I'VE... I'VE CROSSED SOME LINES TO DO THAT. I KNOW.
BUT I... I CAN'T... I WON'T KILL ANYONE.
YOU WON'T HAVE TO, ROUNDHOUSE. I PROMISE.
WE DON'T HAVE TO BE DEFINED BY OUR PAST. NOT IF WE CHOOSE WHAT TO DO WITH OUR FUTURE. OKAY?
NOW COME ON.
LET'S GO HOME.

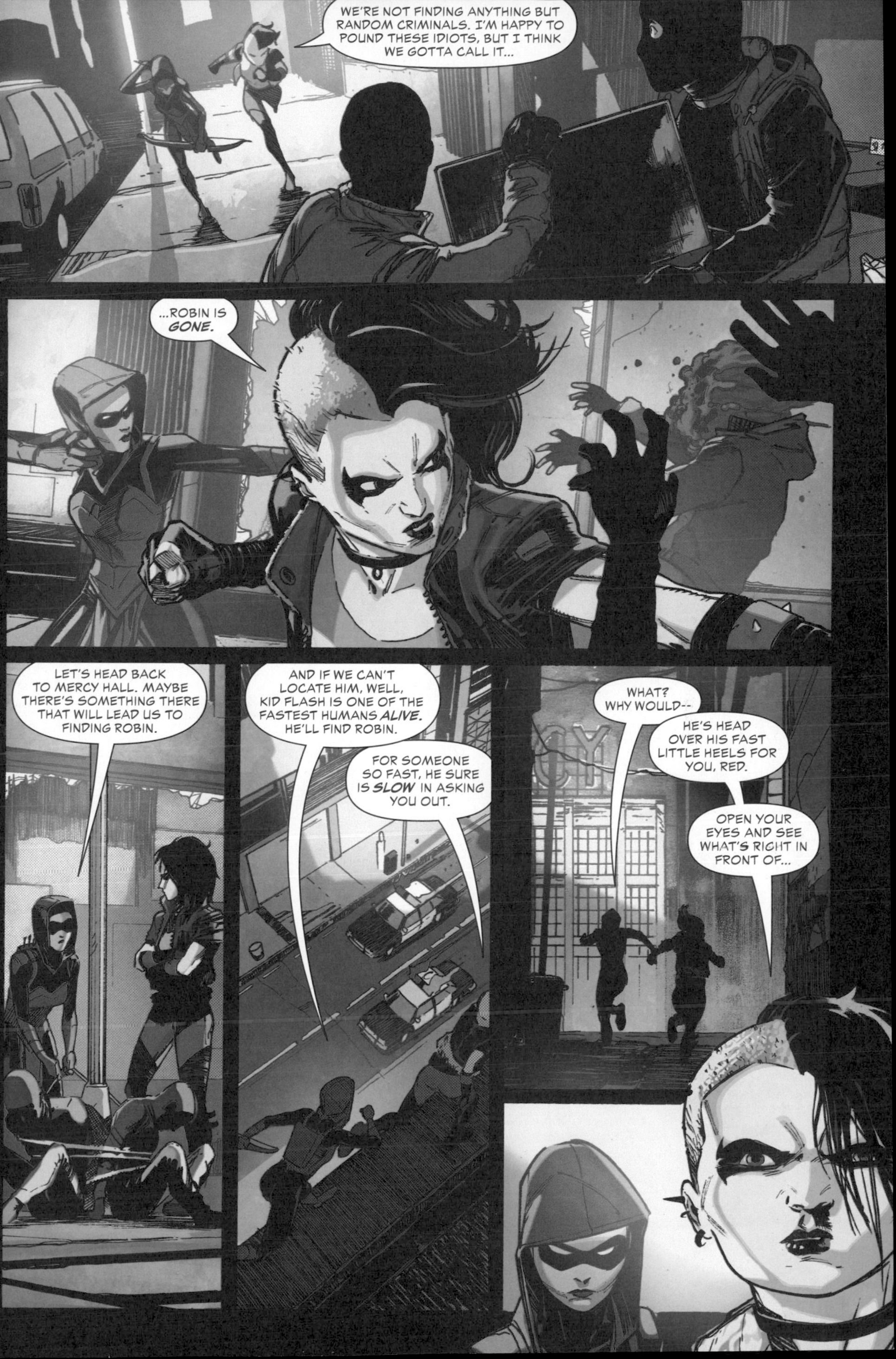
WE'RE NOT FINDING ANYTHING BUT RANDOM CRIMINALS. I'M HAPPY TO POUND THESE IDIOTS, BUT I THINK WE GOTTA CALL IT...
...ROBIN IS *GONE.*
LET'S HEAD BACK TO MERCY HALL. MAYBE THERE'S SOMETHING THERE THAT WILL LEAD US TO FINDING ROBIN.
AND IF WE CAN'T LOCATE HIM, WELL, KID FLASH IS ONE OF THE FASTEST HUMANS *ALIVE.* HE'LL FIND ROBIN.
FOR SOMEONE SO FAST, HE SURE IS *SLOW* IN ASKING YOU OUT.
WHAT? WHY WOULD--
HE'S HEAD OVER HIS FAST LITTLE HEELS FOR YOU, RED.
OPEN YOUR EYES AND SEE WHAT'S RIGHT IN FRONT OF...

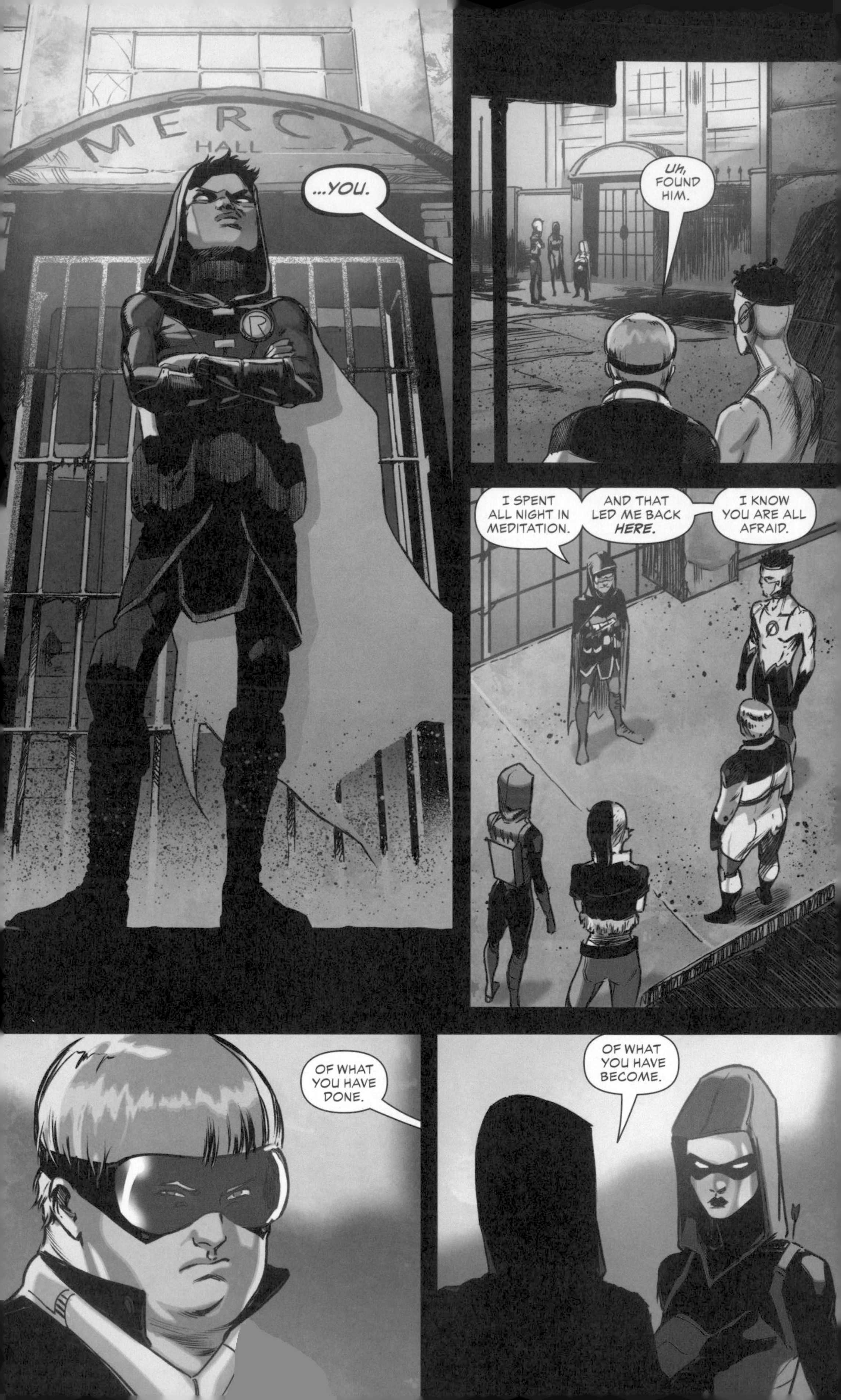
...YOU.
Uh, FOUND HIM.
I SPENT ALL NIGHT IN MEDITATION.
AND THAT LED ME BACK HERE.
I KNOW YOU ARE ALL AFRAID.
OF WHAT YOU HAVE DONE.
OF WHAT YOU HAVE BECOME.

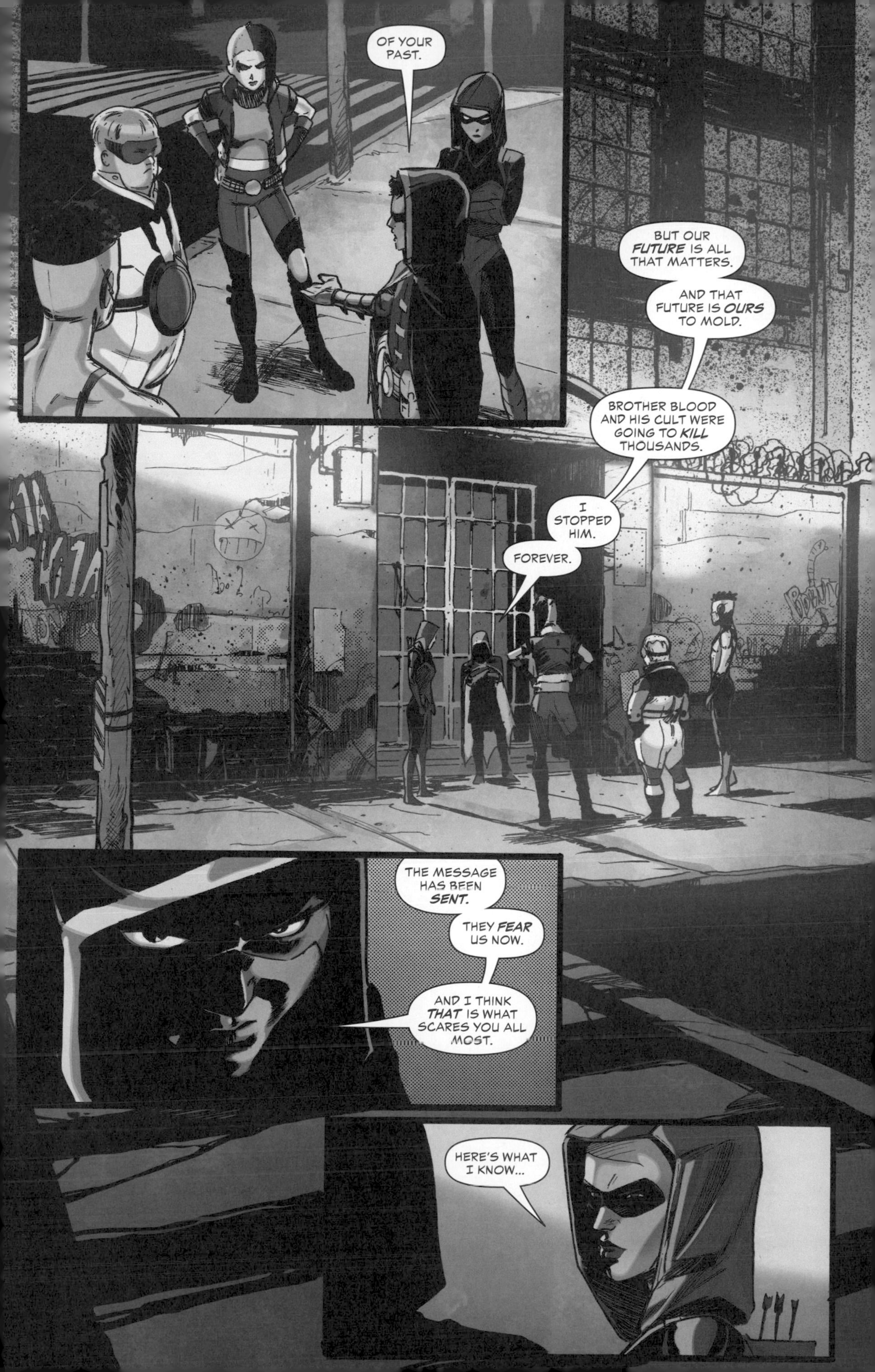
OF YOUR PAST.
BUT OUR *FUTURE* IS ALL THAT MATTERS.
AND THAT FUTURE IS *OURS* TO MOLD.
BROTHER BLOOD AND HIS CULT WERE GOING TO *KILL* THOUSANDS.
I STOPPED HIM.
FOREVER.
THE MESSAGE HAS BEEN *SENT.*
THEY *FEAR* US NOW.
AND I THINK *THAT* IS WHAT SCARES YOU ALL MOST.
HERE'S WHAT I KNOW...

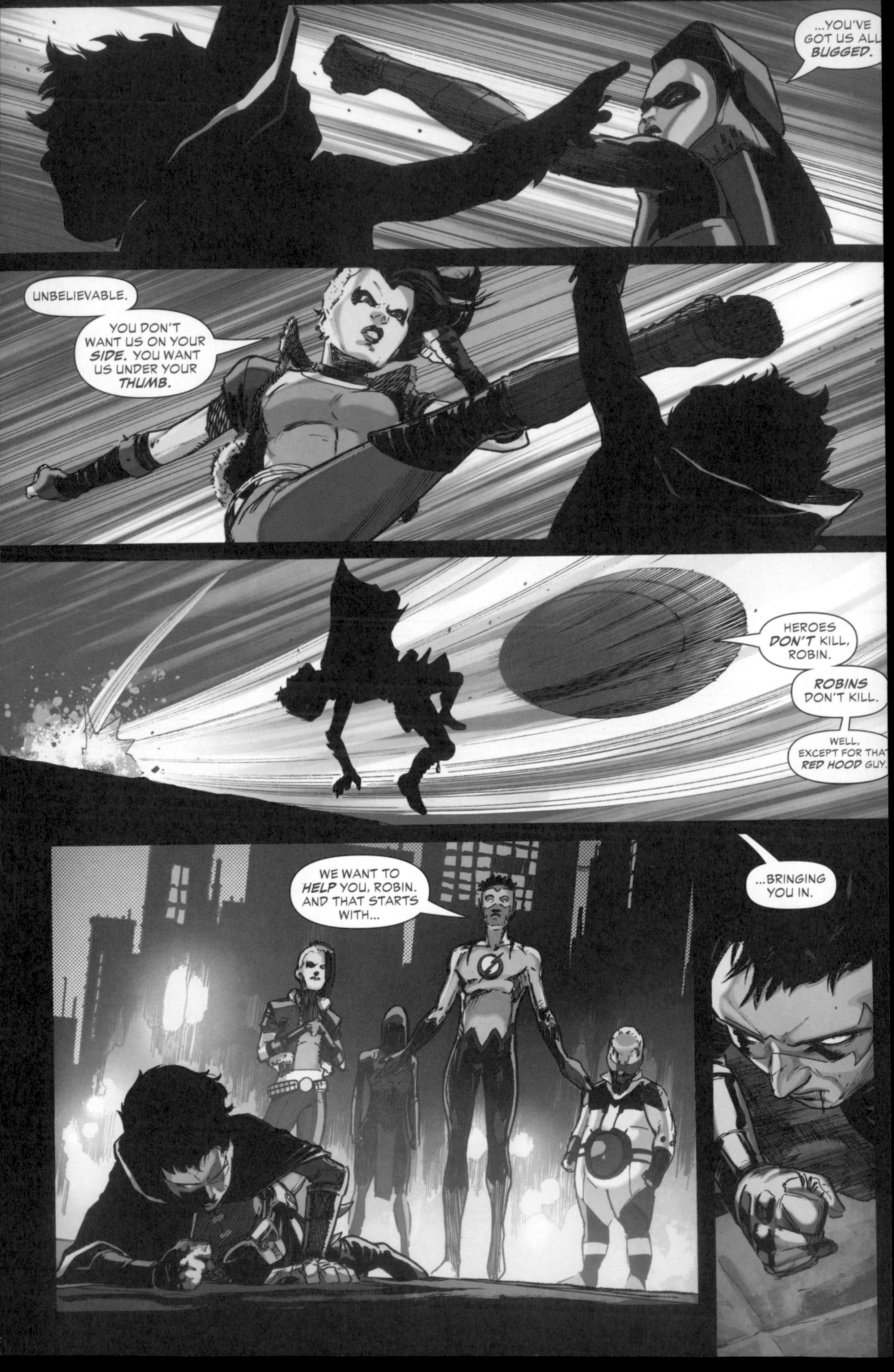
...YOU'VE GOT US ALL *BUGGED.*
UNBELIEVABLE.
YOU DON'T WANT US ON YOUR *SIDE.* YOU WANT US UNDER YOUR *THUMB.*
HEROES *DON'T* KILL, ROBIN.
ROBINS DON'T KILL.
WELL, EXCEPT FOR THAT *RED HOOD* GUY.
WE WANT TO *HELP* YOU, ROBIN. AND THAT STARTS WITH...
...BRINGING YOU IN.

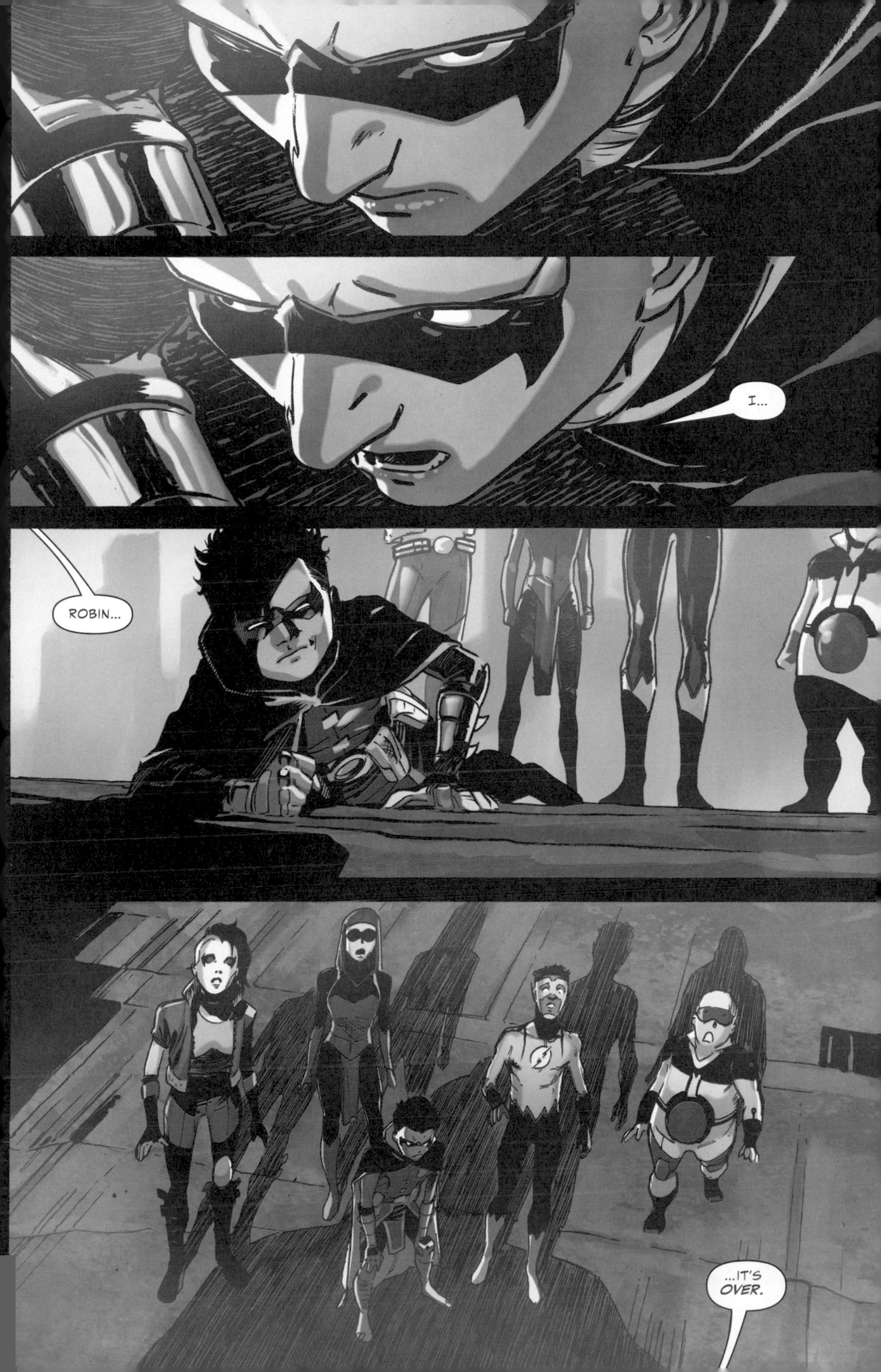
I...
ROBIN...
...IT'S OVER.

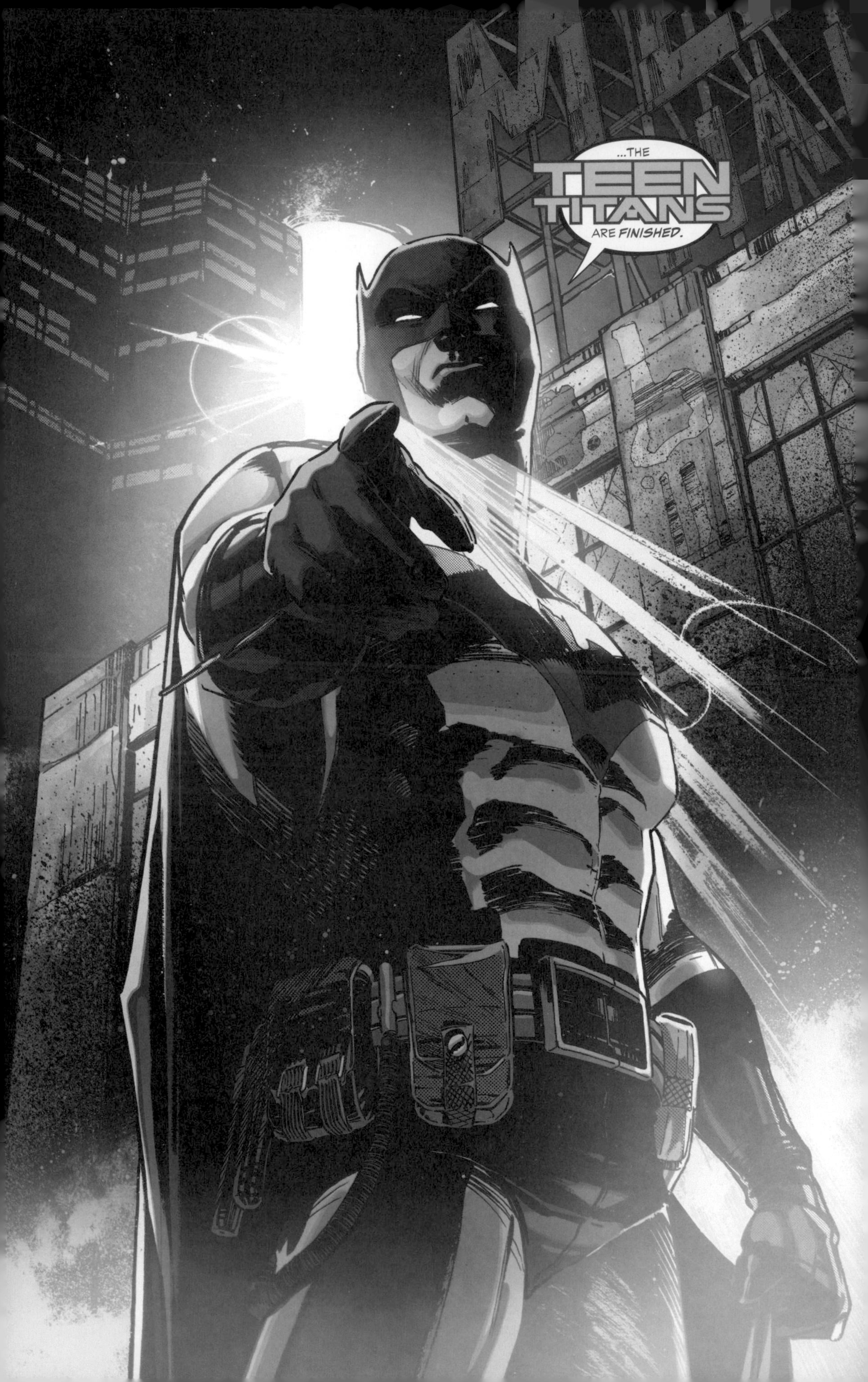
...THE TEEN TITANS ARE FINISHED.

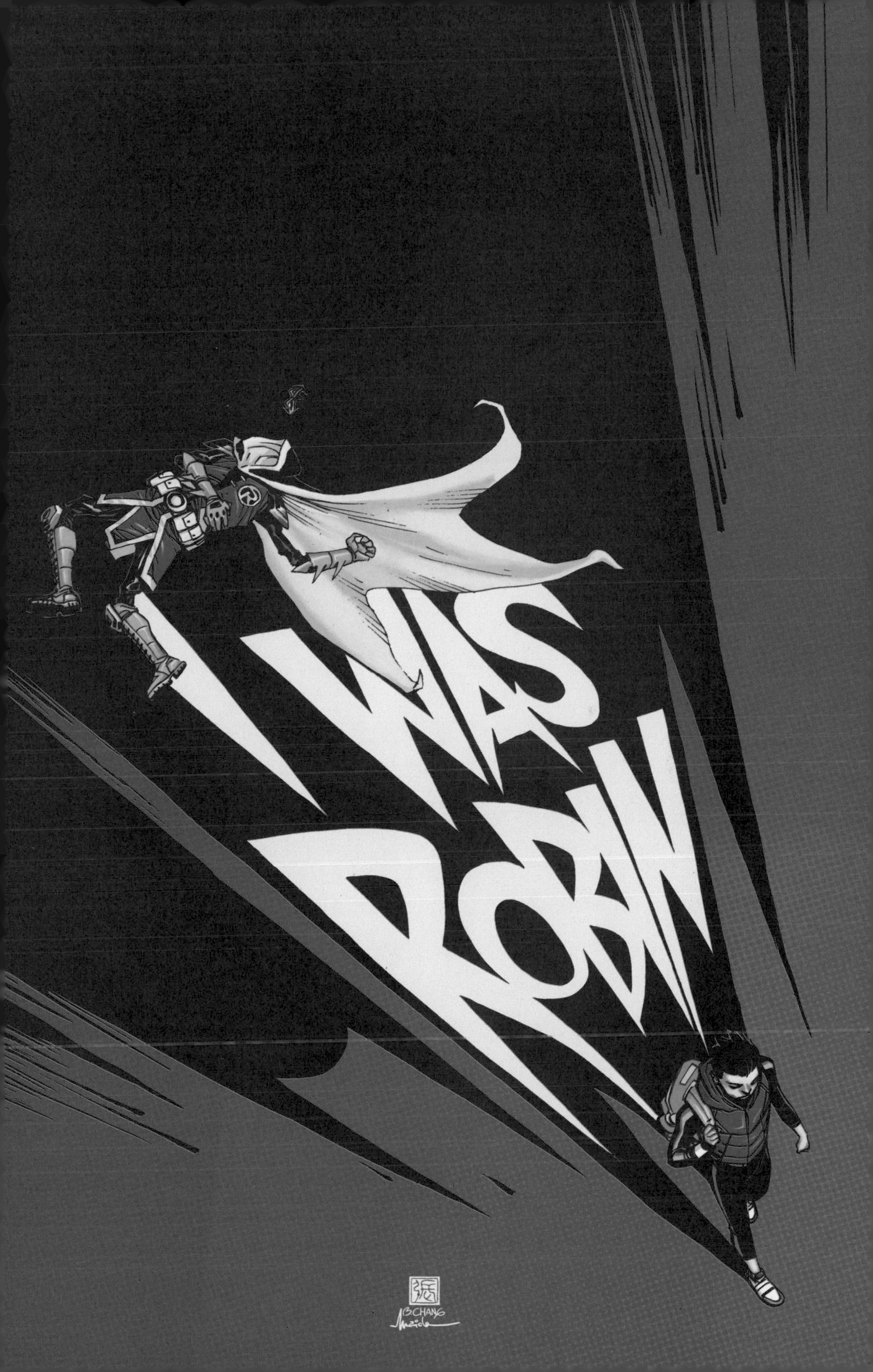
I WAS ROBIN

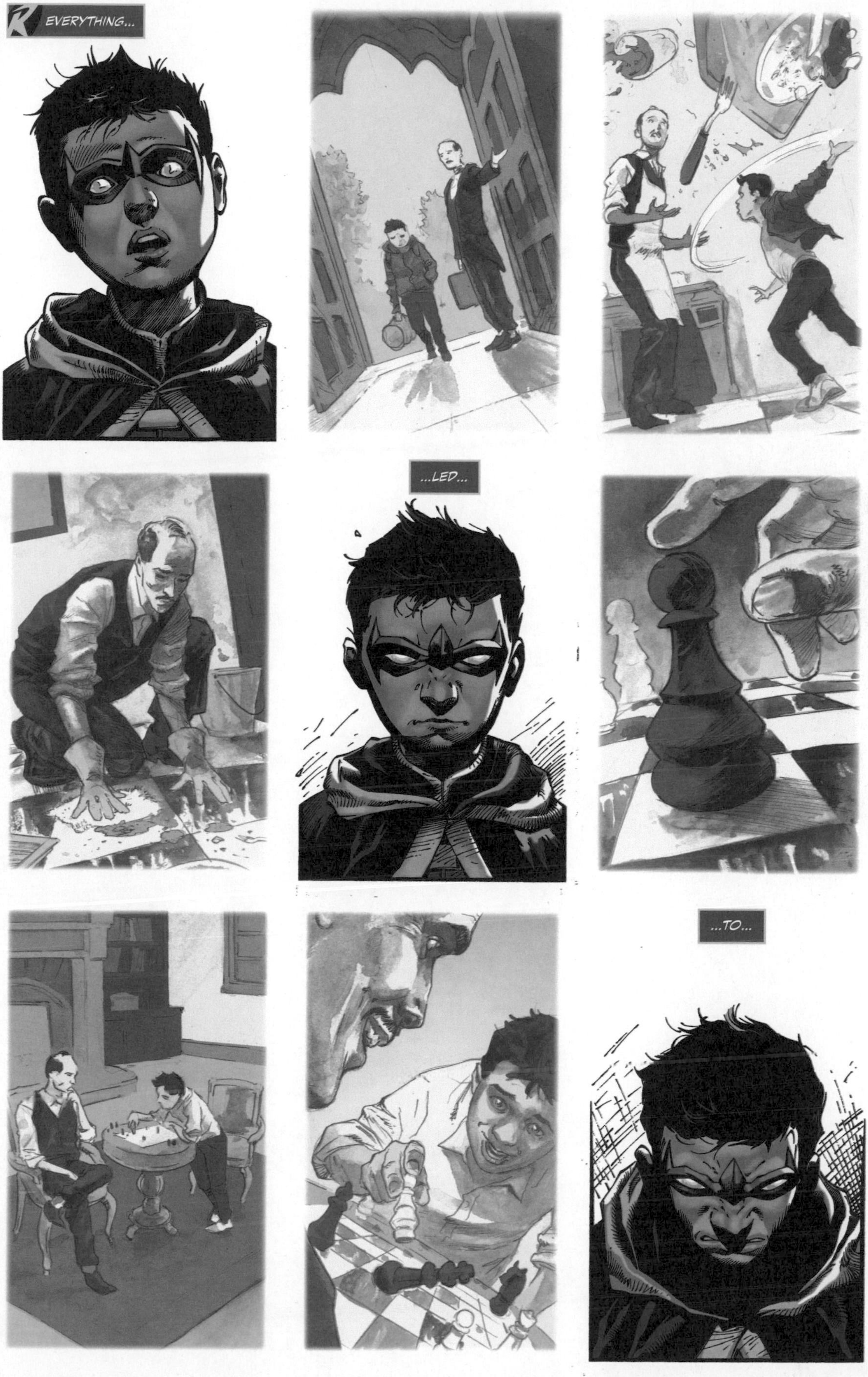
EVERYTHING...
...LED...
...TO...

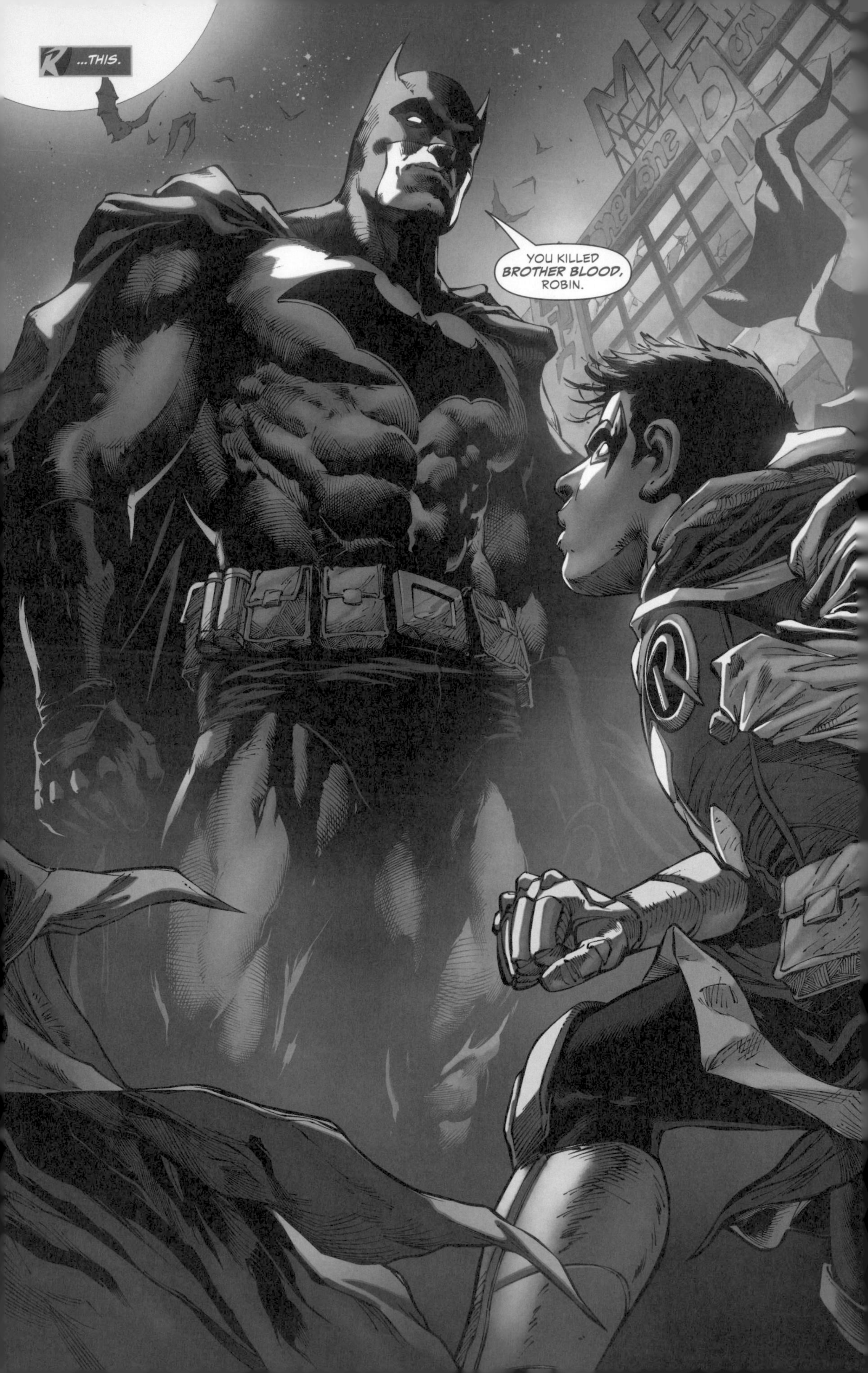
...THIS.
YOU KILLED BROTHER BLOOD, ROBIN.

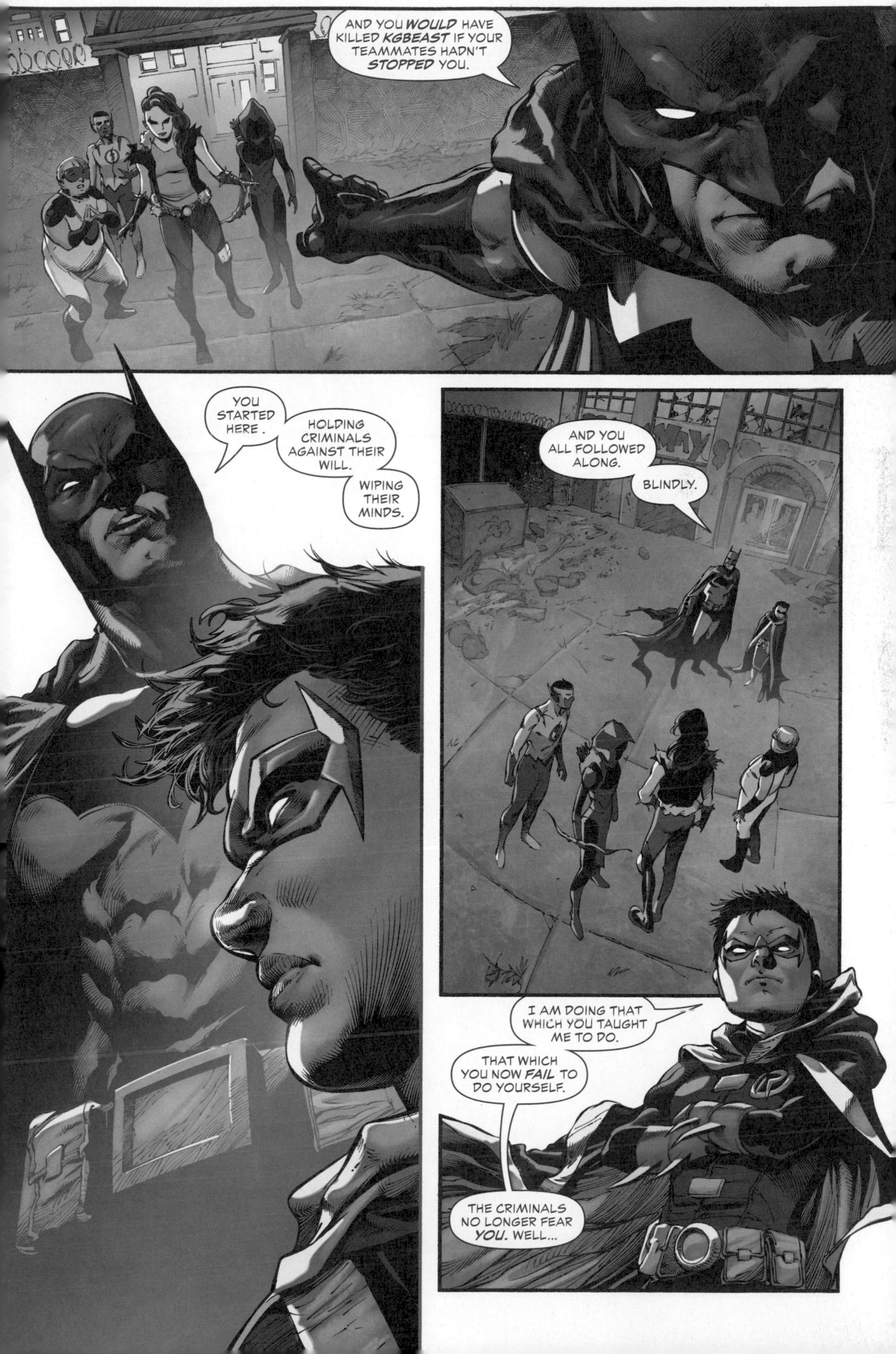
AND YOU WOULD HAVE KILLED KGBEAST IF YOUR TEAMMATES HADN'T STOPPED YOU.
YOU STARTED HERE.
HOLDING CRIMINALS AGAINST THEIR WILL.
WIPING THEIR MINDS.
AND YOU ALL FOLLOWED ALONG.
BLINDLY.
I AM DOING THAT WHICH YOU TAUGHT ME TO DO.
THAT WHICH YOU NOW FAIL TO DO YOURSELF.
THE CRIMINALS NO LONGER FEAR YOU. WELL...

...THEY FEAR THE **TEEN TITANS** NOW.

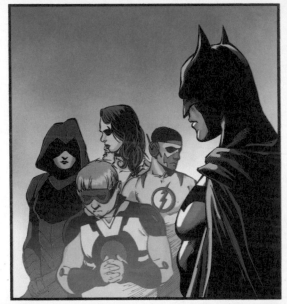

THE ONLY ONE AFRAID OF YOU, *ROBIN...*

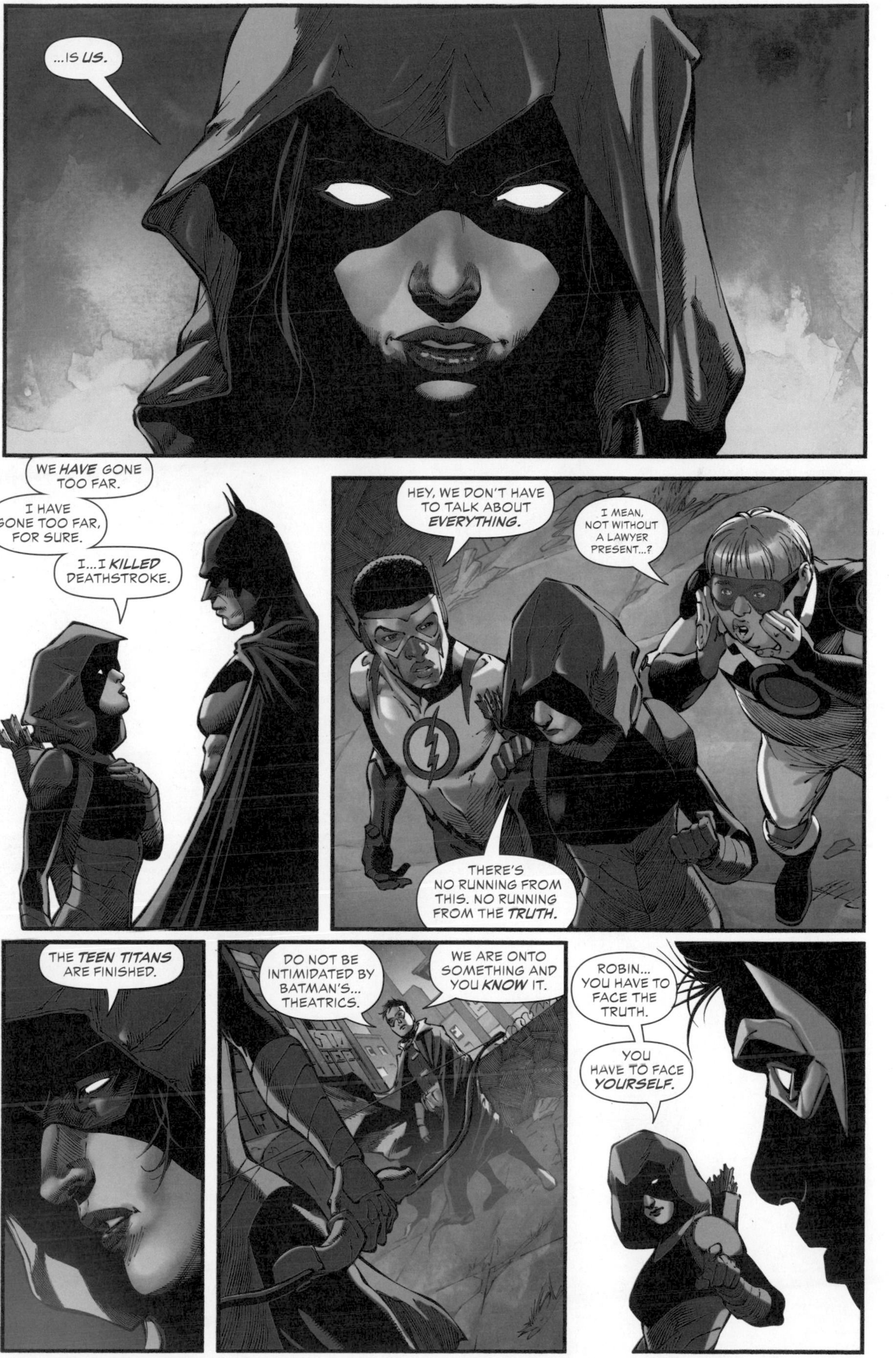
...IS *US.*
WE *HAVE* GONE TOO FAR.
I HAVE GONE TOO FAR, FOR SURE.
I...I *KILLED* DEATHSTROKE.
HEY, WE DON'T HAVE TO TALK ABOUT *EVERYTHING.*
I MEAN, NOT WITHOUT A LAWYER PRESENT...?
THERE'S NO RUNNING FROM THIS. NO RUNNING FROM THE *TRUTH.*
THE *TEEN TITANS* ARE FINISHED.
DO NOT BE INTIMIDATED BY BATMAN'S... THEATRICS.
WE ARE ONTO SOMETHING AND YOU *KNOW* IT.
ROBIN... YOU HAVE TO FACE THE TRUTH.
YOU HAVE TO FACE *YOURSELF.*

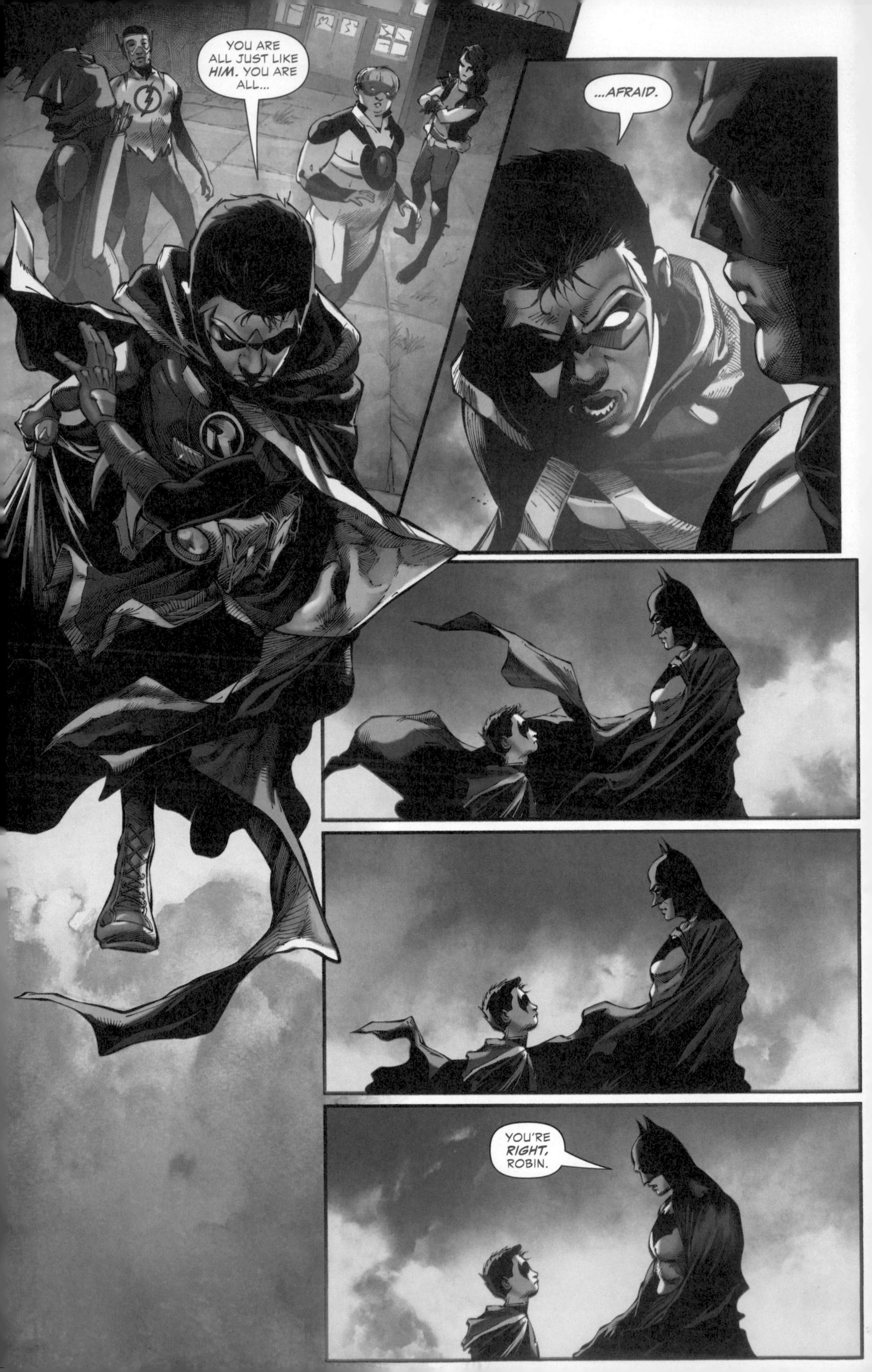
YOU ARE ALL JUST LIKE *HIM*. YOU ARE ALL...
...AFRAID.
YOU'RE *RIGHT*, ROBIN.

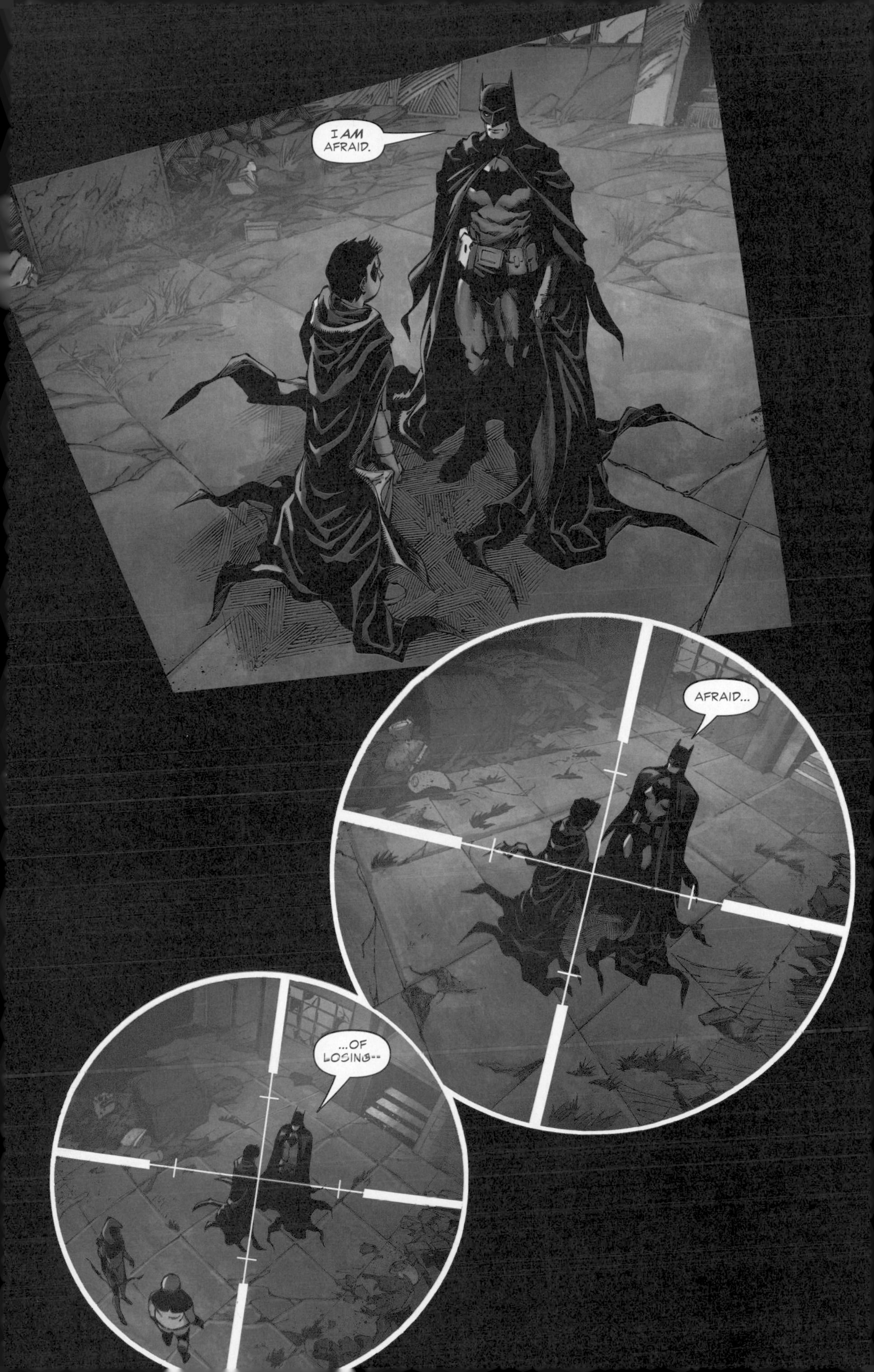
I AM AFRAID.
AFRAID...
...OF LOSING--

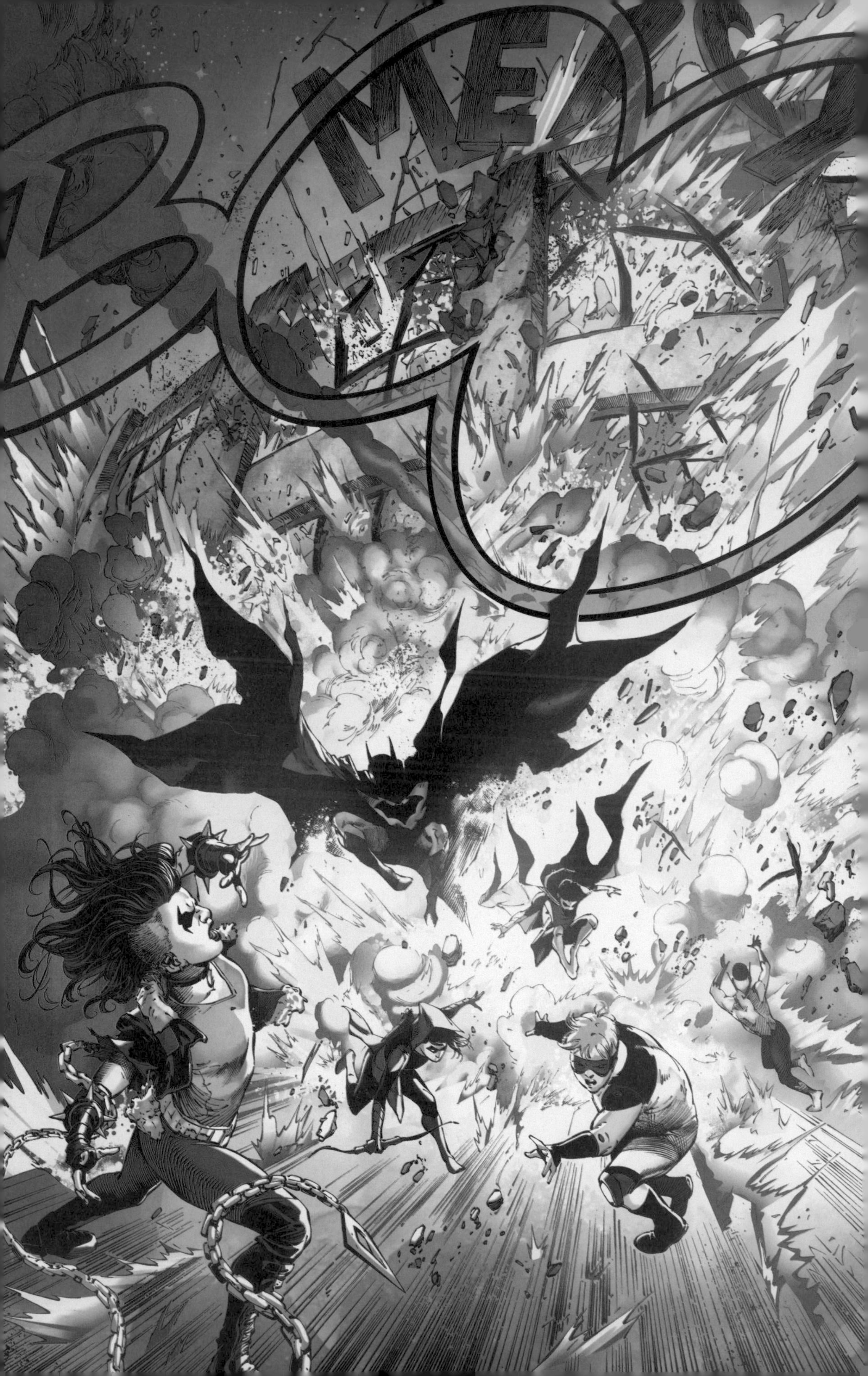

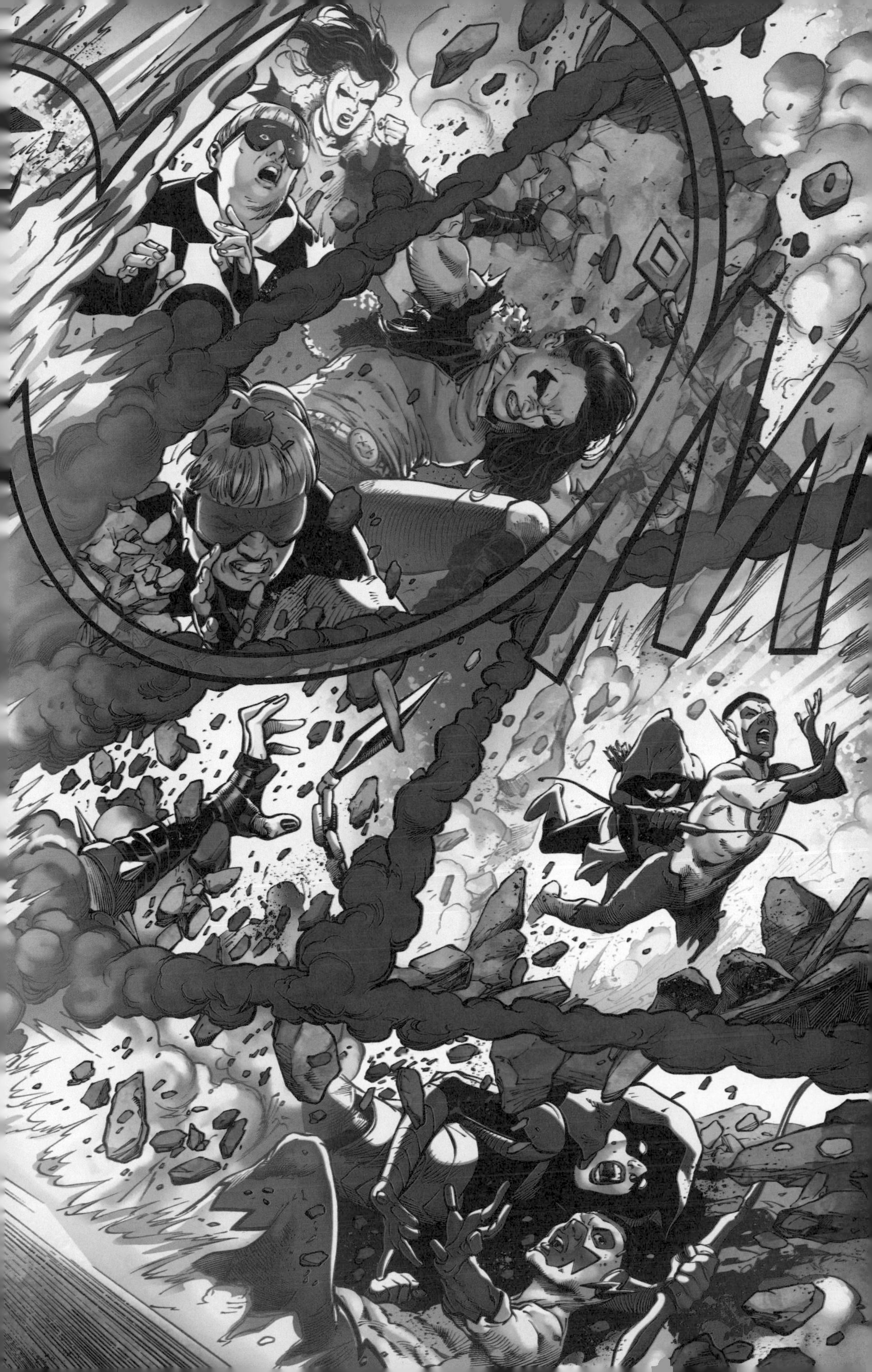

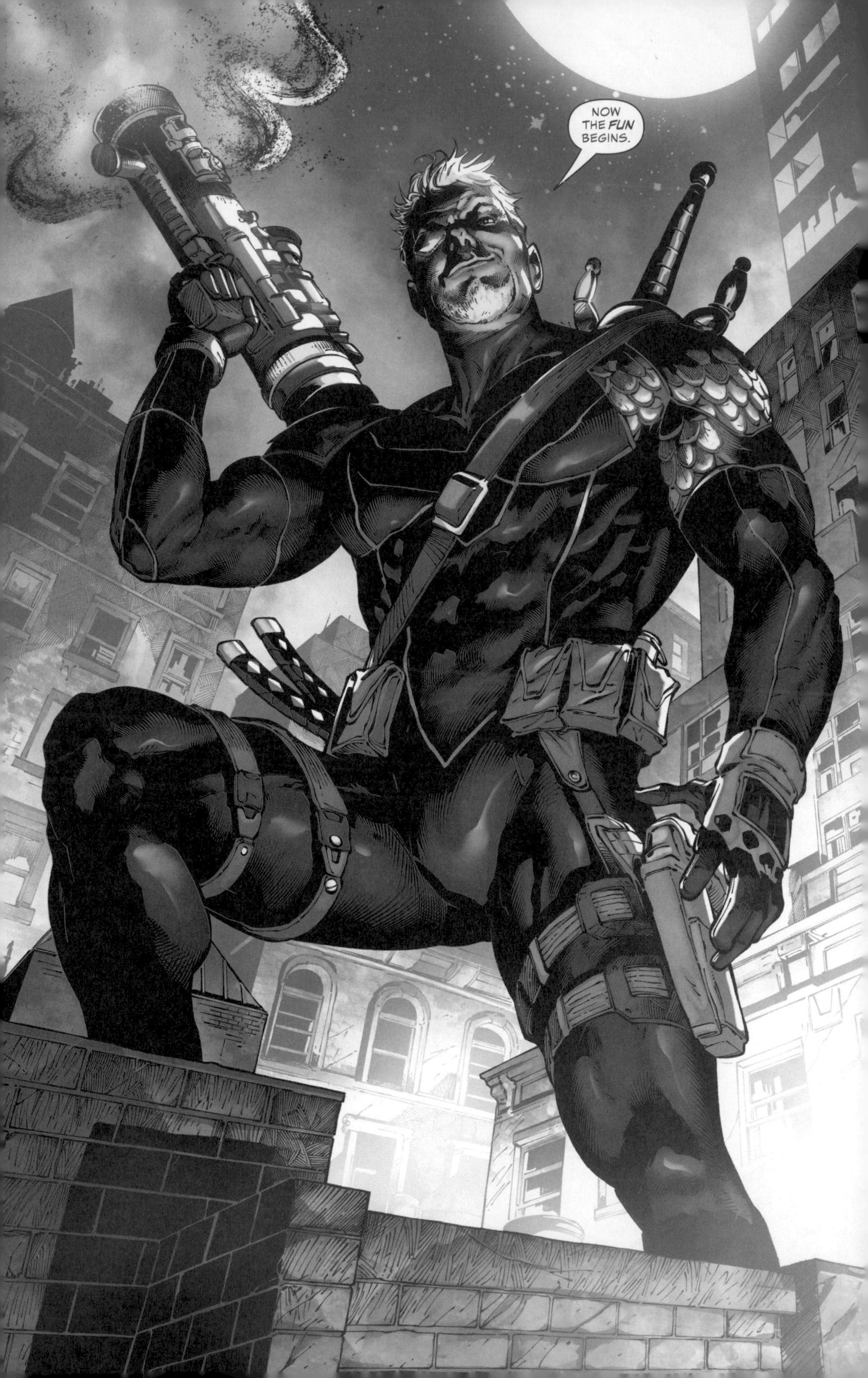
NOW THE *FUN* BEGINS.

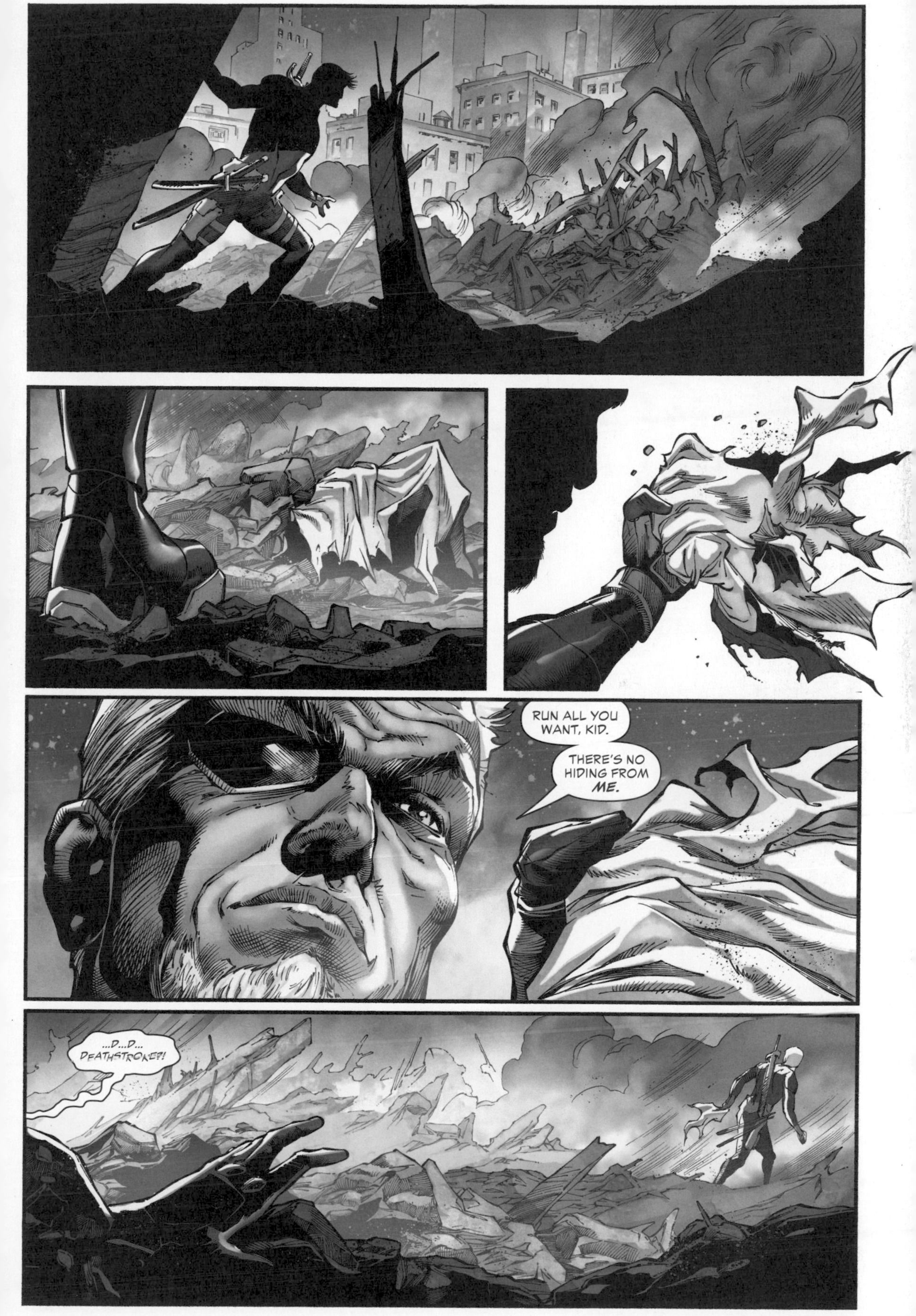
RUN ALL YOU WANT, KID.
THERE'S NO HIDING FROM *ME*.
...D...D... DEATHSTROKE?!

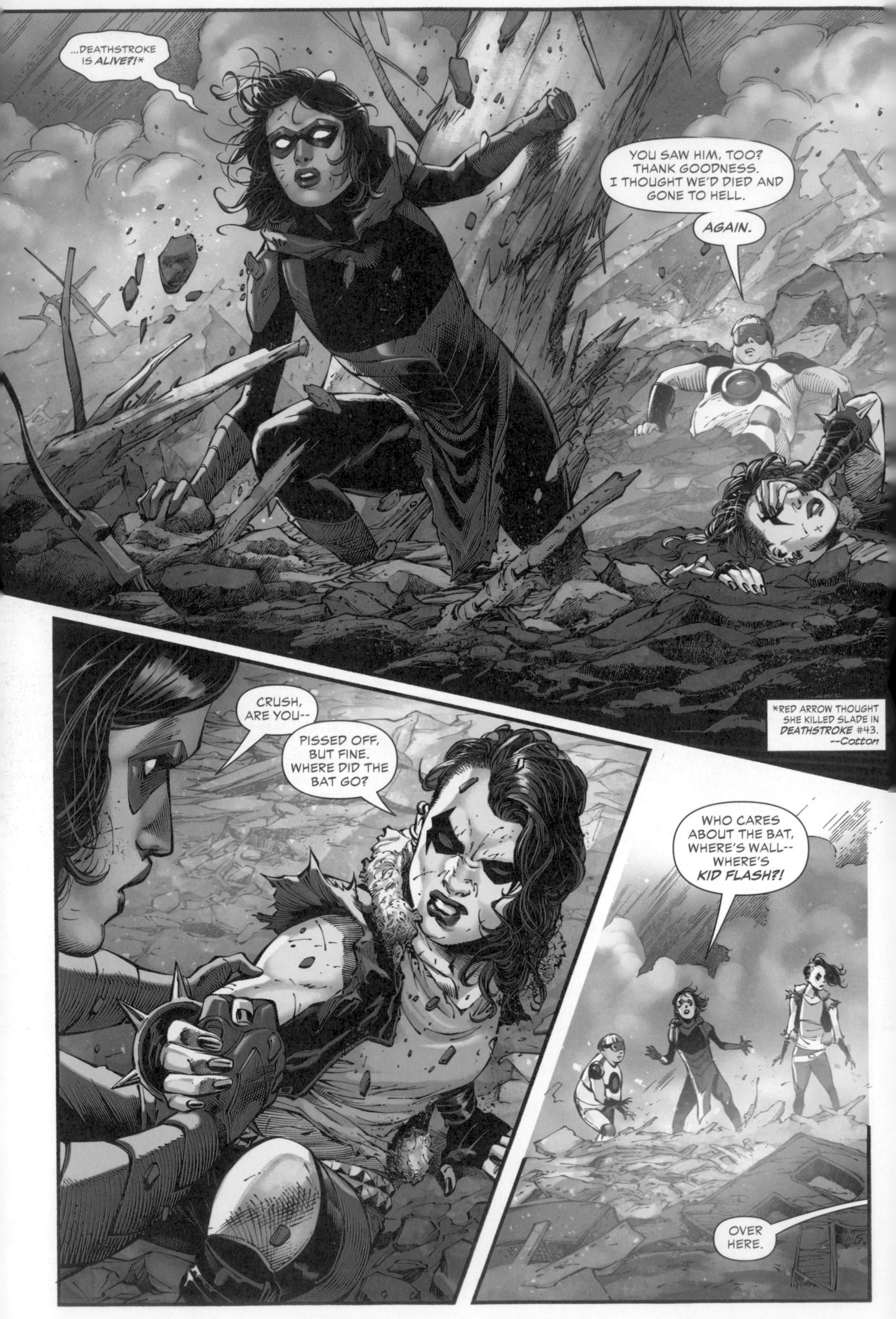

...DEATHSTROKE IS ALIVE?!*
YOU SAW HIM, TOO? THANK GOODNESS. I THOUGHT WE'D DIED AND GONE TO HELL.
AGAIN.
*RED ARROW THOUGHT SHE KILLED SLADE IN DEATHSTROKE #43. --Cotton
CRUSH, ARE YOU--
PISSED OFF, BUT FINE. WHERE DID THE BAT GO?
WHO CARES ABOUT THE BAT, WHERE'S WALL-- WHERE'S KID FLASH?!
OVER HERE.

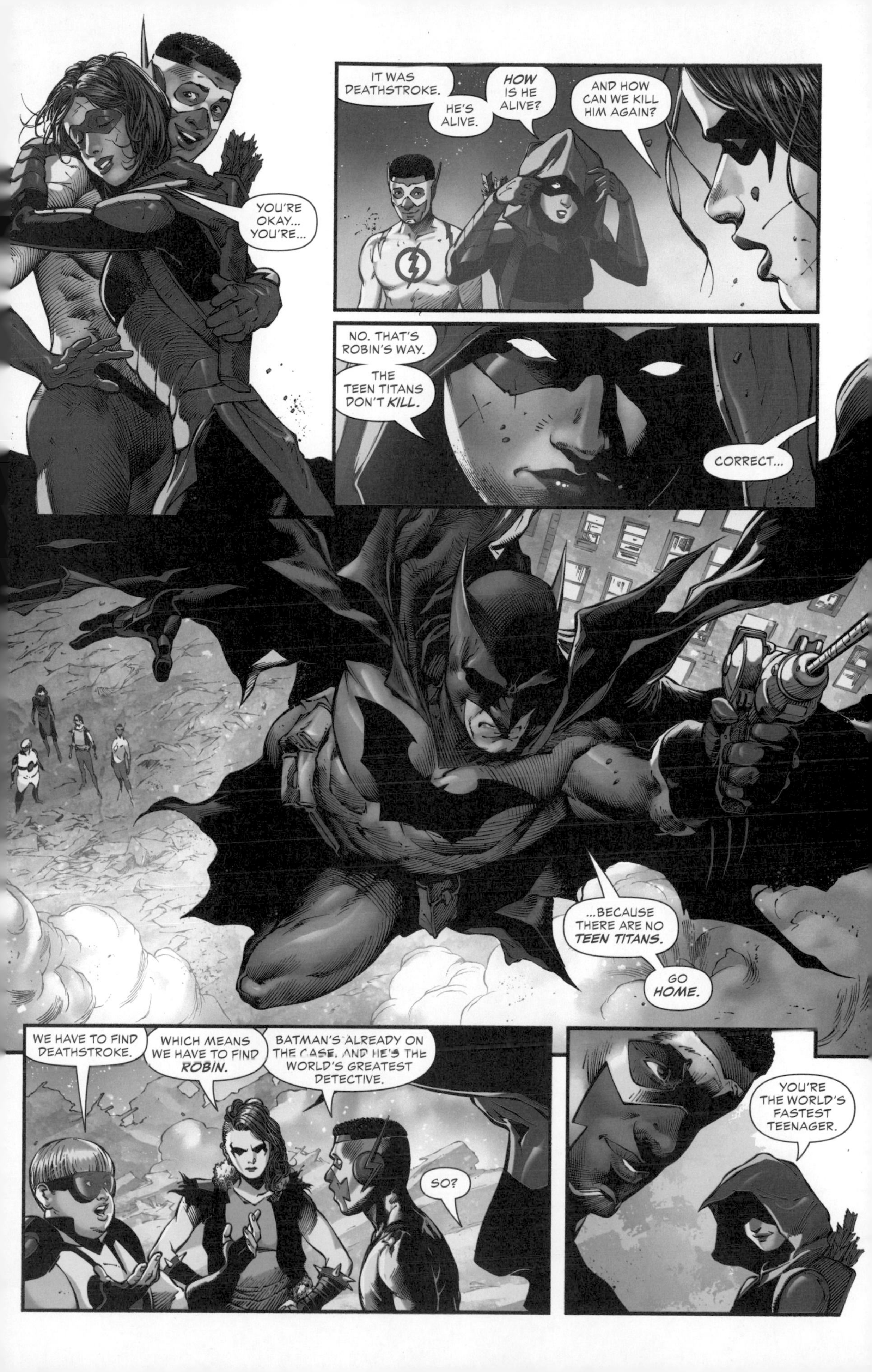
YOU'RE OKAY... YOU'RE...
IT WAS DEATHSTROKE.
HE'S ALIVE.
HOW IS HE ALIVE?
AND HOW CAN WE KILL HIM AGAIN?
NO. THAT'S ROBIN'S WAY.
THE TEEN TITANS DON'T KILL.
CORRECT...
...BECAUSE THERE ARE NO TEEN TITANS.
GO HOME.
WE HAVE TO FIND DEATHSTROKE.
WHICH MEANS WE HAVE TO FIND ROBIN.
BATMAN'S ALREADY ON THE CASE. AND HE'S THE WORLD'S GREATEST DETECTIVE.
SO?
YOU'RE THE WORLD'S FASTEST TEENAGER.

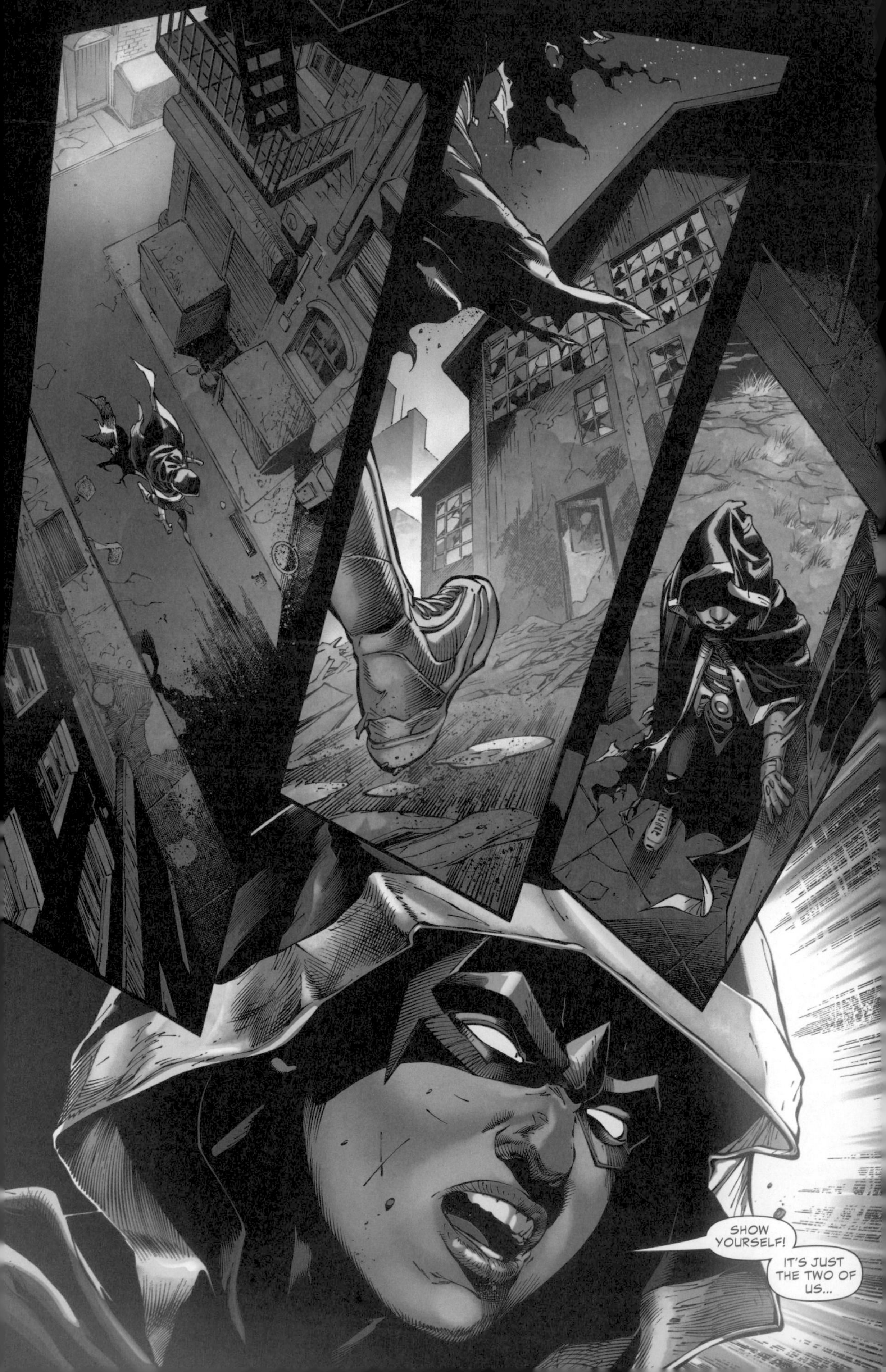
SHOW YOURSELF!
IT'S JUST THE TWO OF US...

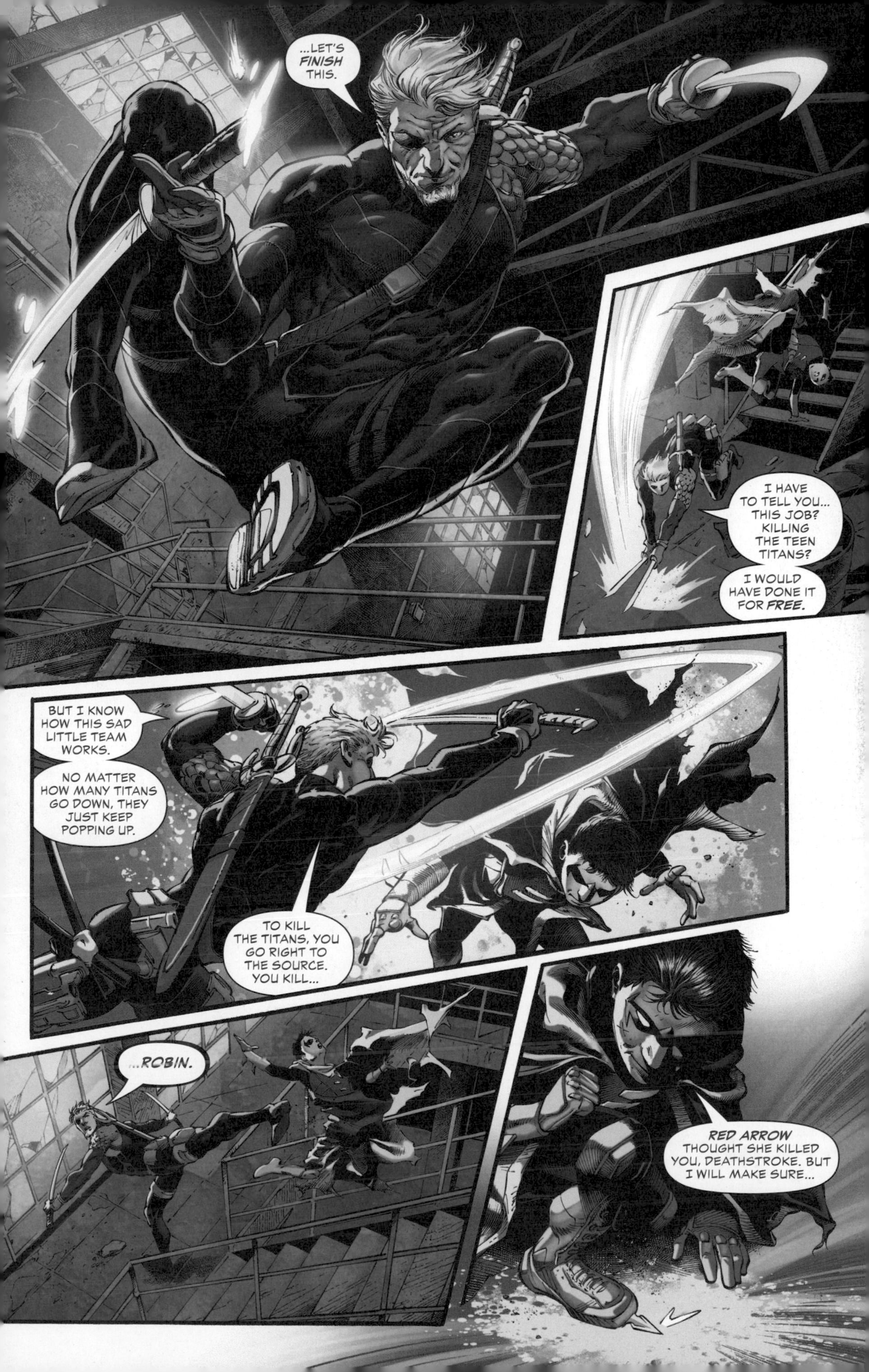
...LET'S *FINISH* THIS.
I HAVE TO TELL YOU... THIS JOB? KILLING THE TEEN TITANS?
I WOULD HAVE DONE IT FOR *FREE.*
BUT I KNOW HOW THIS SAD LITTLE TEAM WORKS.
NO MATTER HOW MANY TITANS GO DOWN, THEY JUST KEEP POPPING UP.
TO KILL THE TITANS, YOU GO RIGHT TO THE SOURCE. YOU KILL...
...*ROBIN.*
RED ARROW THOUGHT SHE KILLED YOU, DEATHSTROKE. BUT I WILL MAKE SURE...

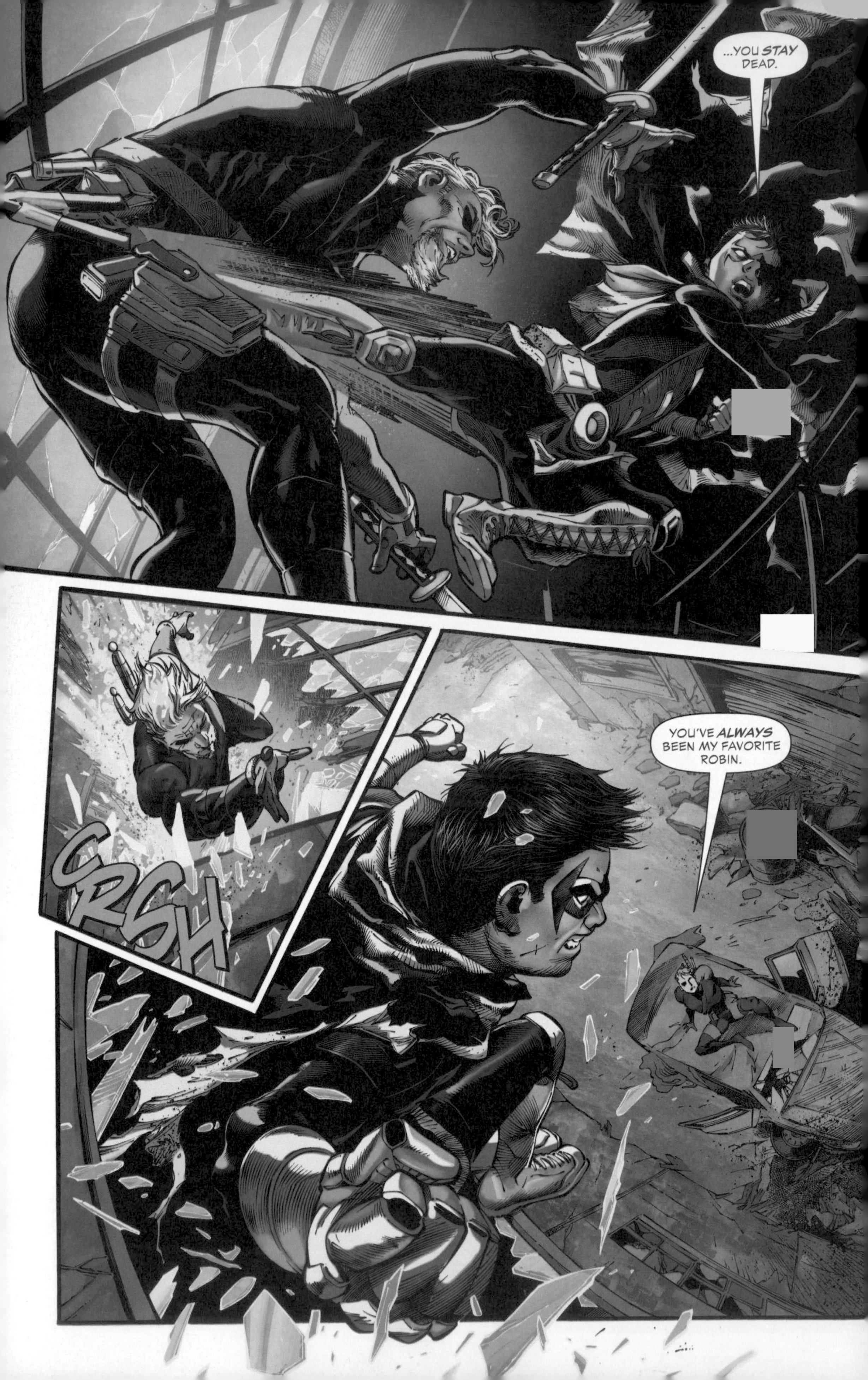
...YOU STAY DEAD.
CRSH
YOU'VE ALWAYS BEEN MY FAVORITE ROBIN.

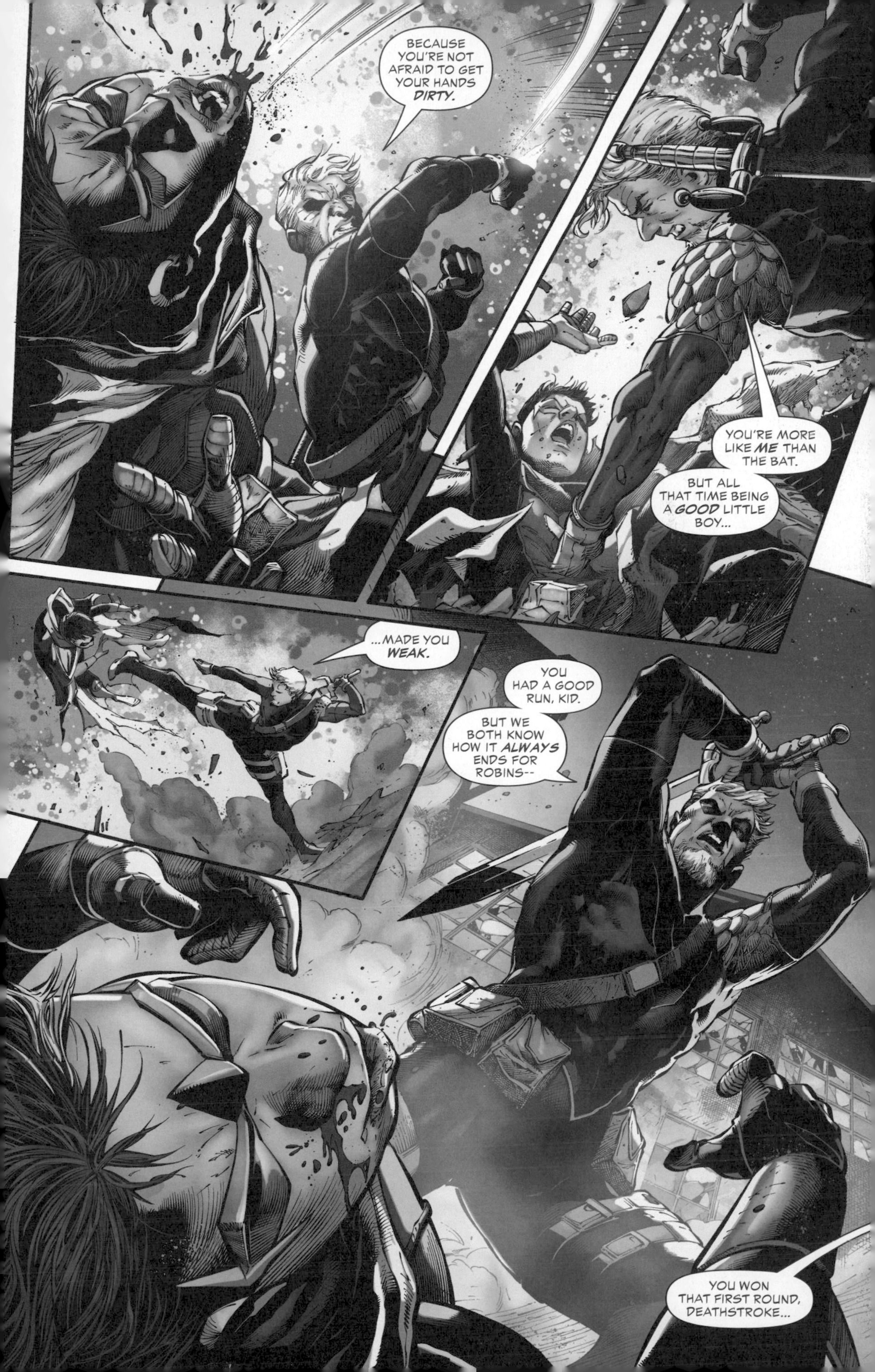
BECAUSE YOU'RE NOT AFRAID TO GET YOUR HANDS DIRTY.
YOU'RE MORE LIKE ME THAN THE BAT.
BUT ALL THAT TIME BEING A GOOD LITTLE BOY...
...MADE YOU WEAK.
YOU HAD A GOOD RUN, KID.
BUT WE BOTH KNOW HOW IT ALWAYS ENDS FOR ROBINS--
YOU WON THAT FIRST ROUND, DEATHSTROKE...

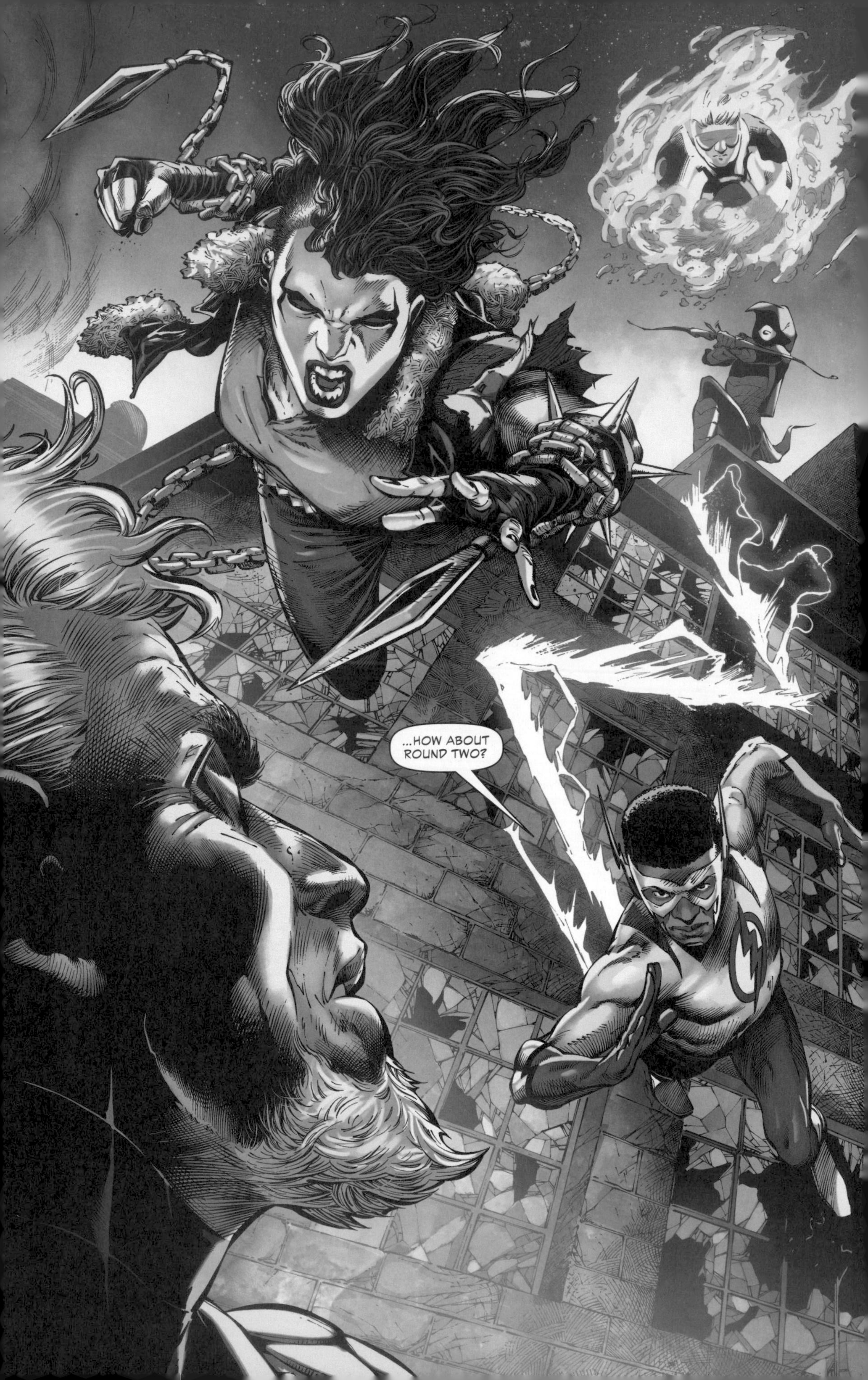
...HOW ABOUT ROUND TWO?

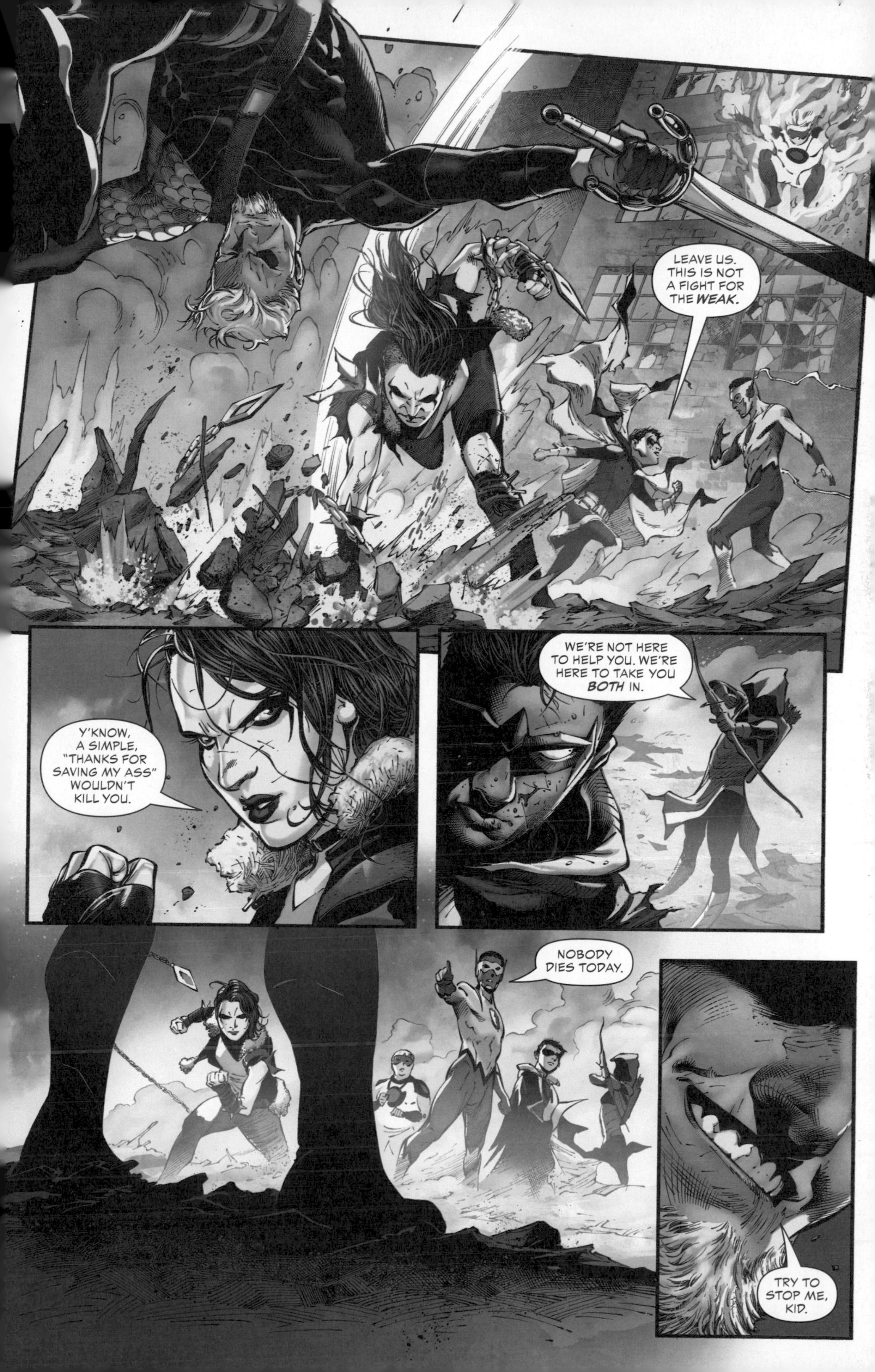
LEAVE US. THIS IS NOT A FIGHT FOR THE *WEAK.*
Y'KNOW, A SIMPLE, "THANKS FOR SAVING MY ASS" WOULDN'T KILL YOU.
WE'RE NOT HERE TO HELP YOU. WE'RE HERE TO TAKE YOU *BOTH* IN.
NOBODY DIES TODAY.
TRY TO STOP ME, KID.

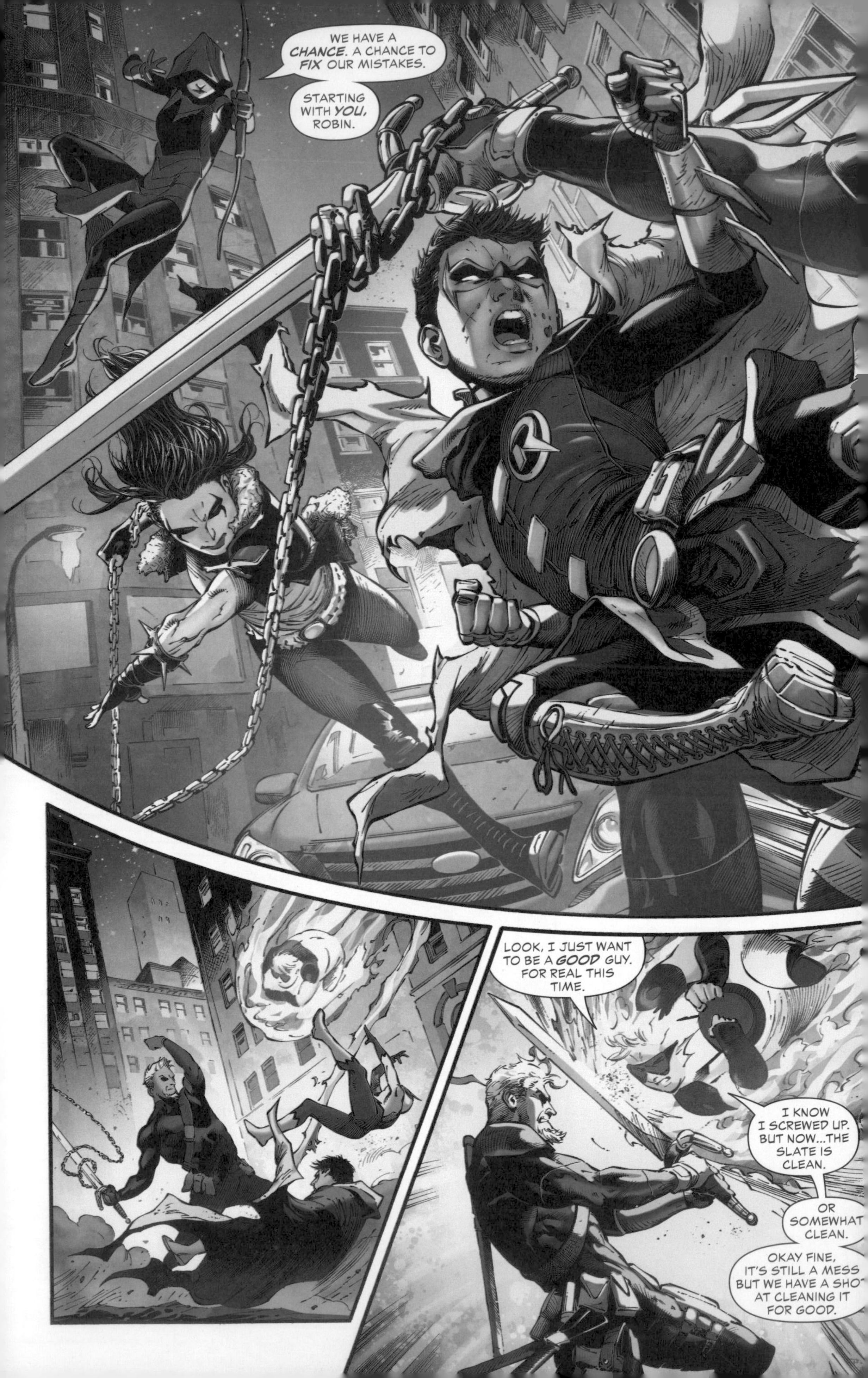
WE HAVE A CHANCE. A CHANCE TO FIX OUR MISTAKES.
STARTING WITH YOU, ROBIN.
LOOK, I JUST WANT TO BE A GOOD GUY. FOR REAL THIS TIME.
I KNOW I SCREWED UP. BUT NOW...THE SLATE IS CLEAN.
OR SOMEWHAT CLEAN.
OKAY FINE, IT'S STILL A MESS BUT WE HAVE A SHOT AT CLEANING IT FOR GOOD.

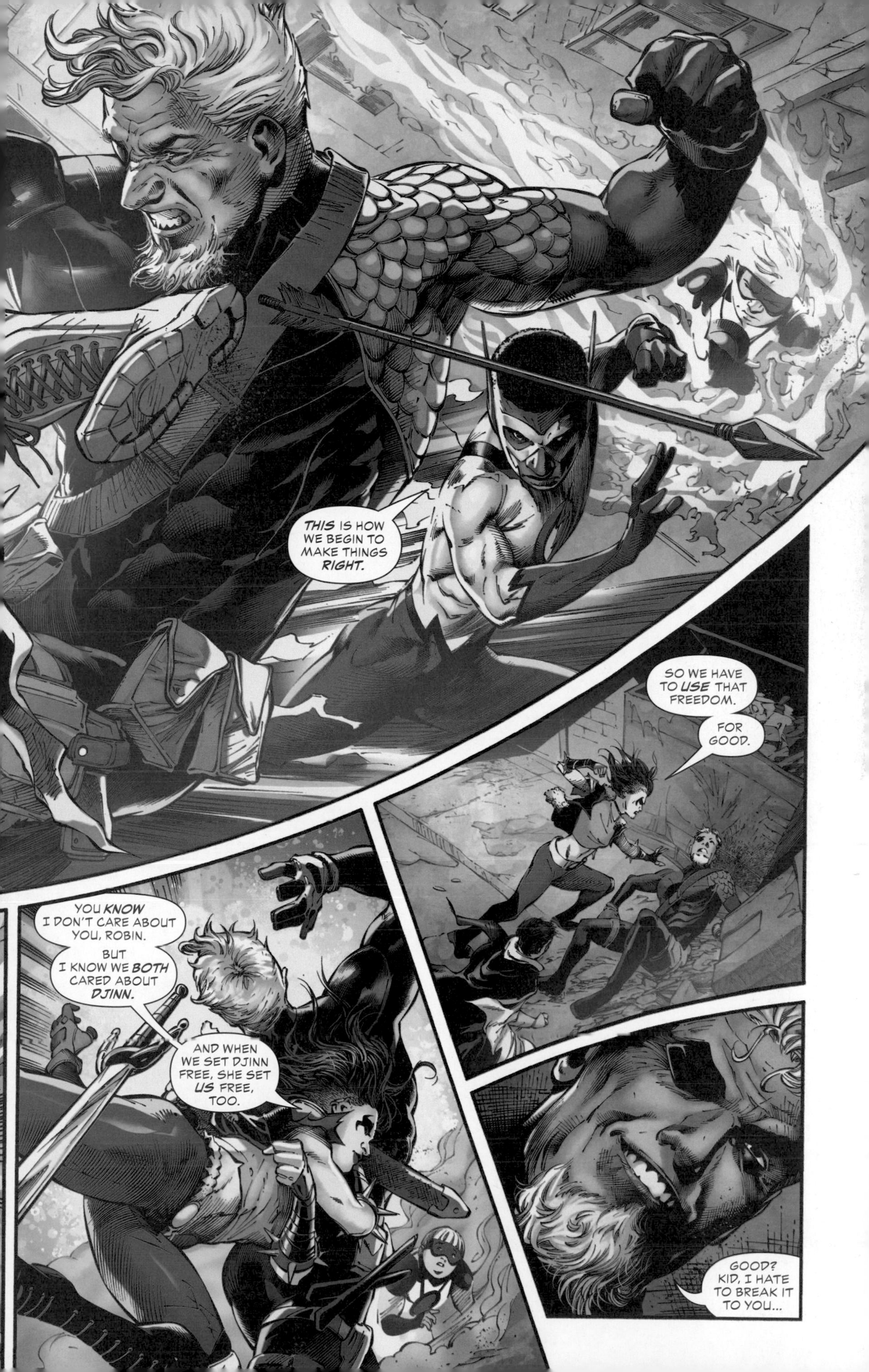
THIS IS HOW WE BEGIN TO MAKE THINGS RIGHT.
SO WE HAVE TO USE THAT FREEDOM.
FOR GOOD.
YOU KNOW I DON'T CARE ABOUT YOU, ROBIN.
BUT I KNOW WE BOTH CARED ABOUT DJINN.
AND WHEN WE SET DJINN FREE, SHE SET US FREE, TOO.
GOOD? KID, I HATE TO BREAK IT TO YOU...

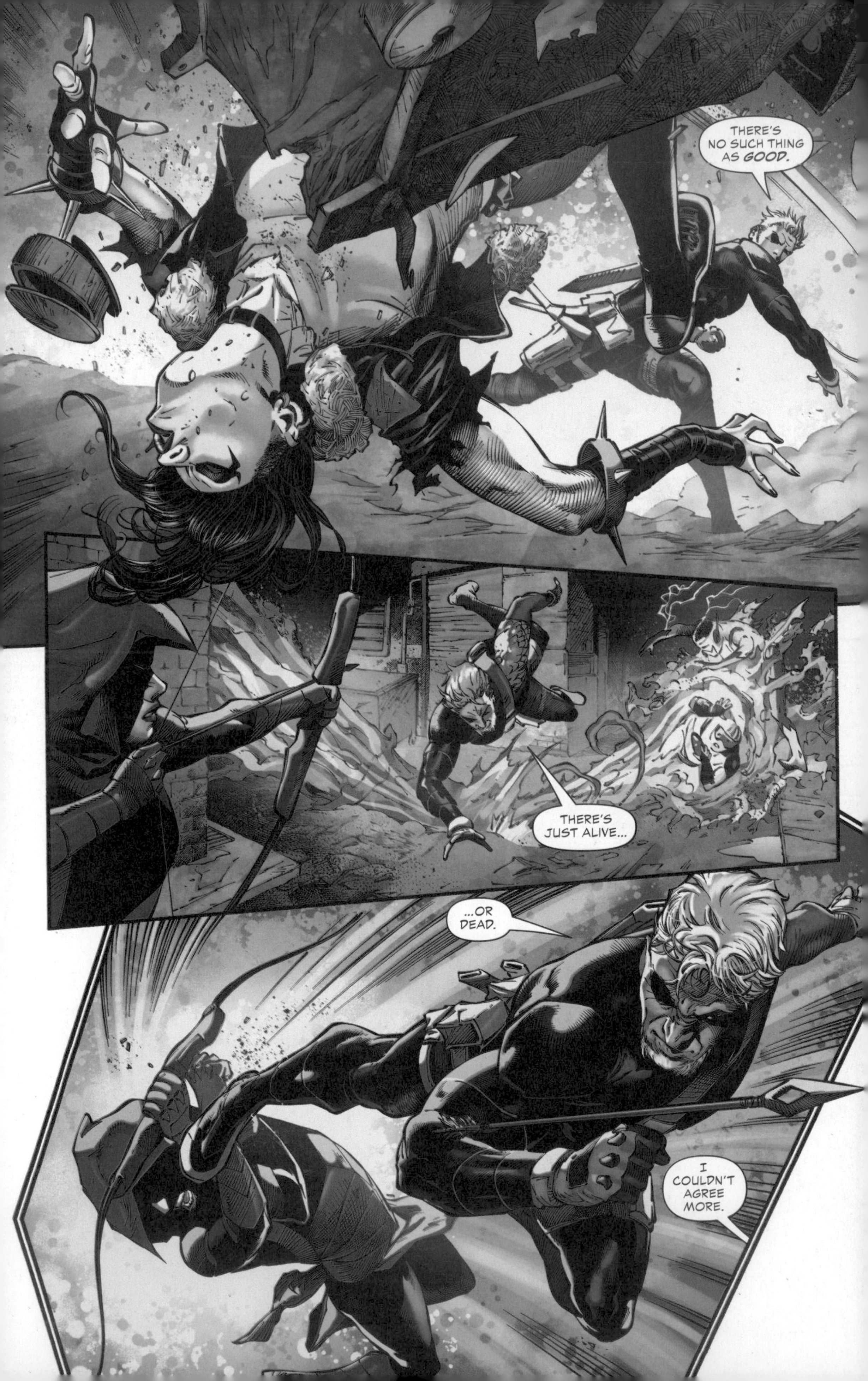
THERE'S NO SUCH THING AS GOOD.
THERE'S JUST ALIVE...
...OR DEAD.
I COULDN'T AGREE MORE.

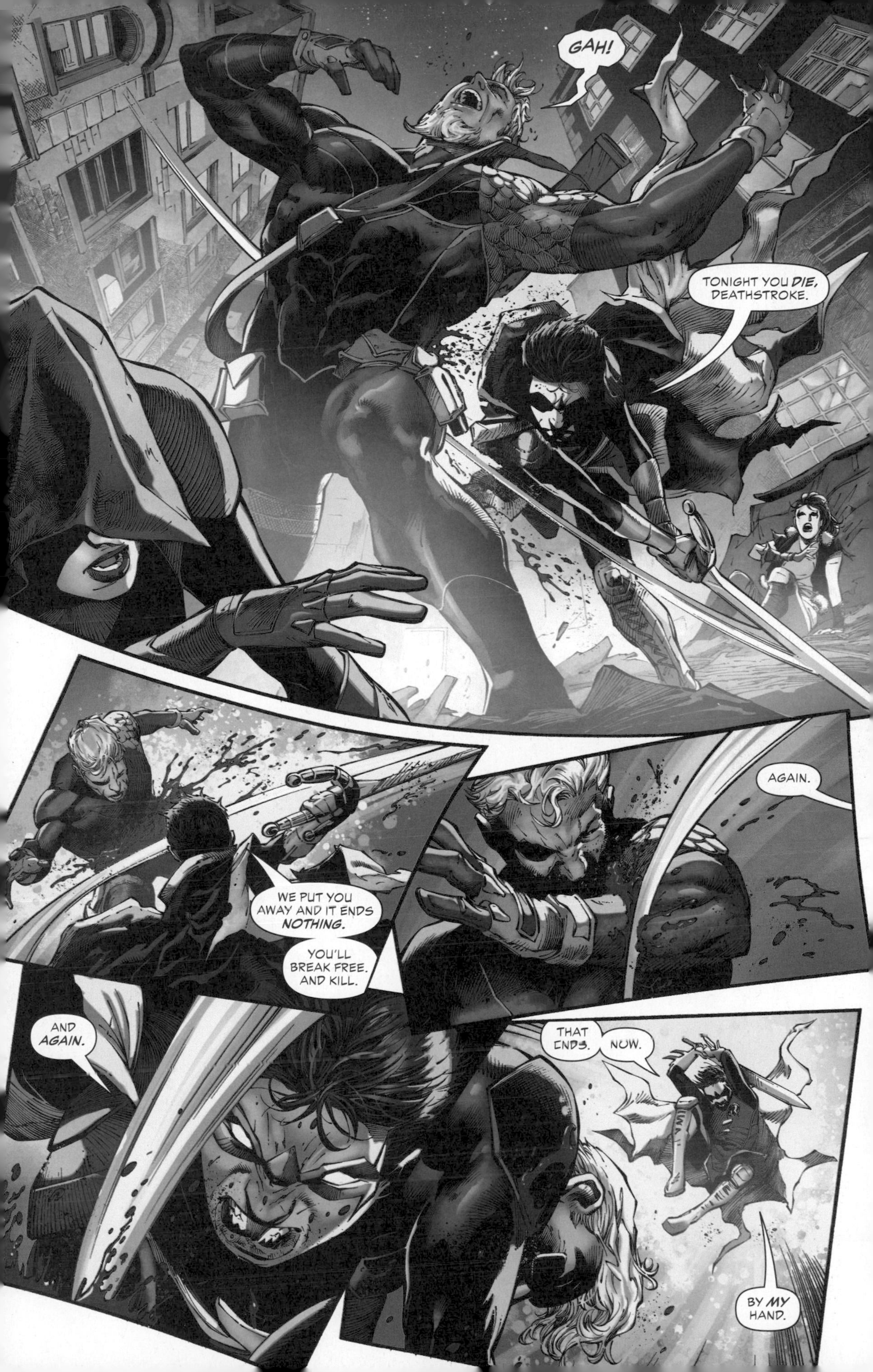
GAH!
TONIGHT YOU *DIE*, DEATHSTROKE.
AGAIN.
WE PUT YOU AWAY AND IT ENDS *NOTHING*.
YOU'LL BREAK FREE. AND KILL.
AND *AGAIN*.
THAT ENDS.
NOW.
BY *MY* HAND.

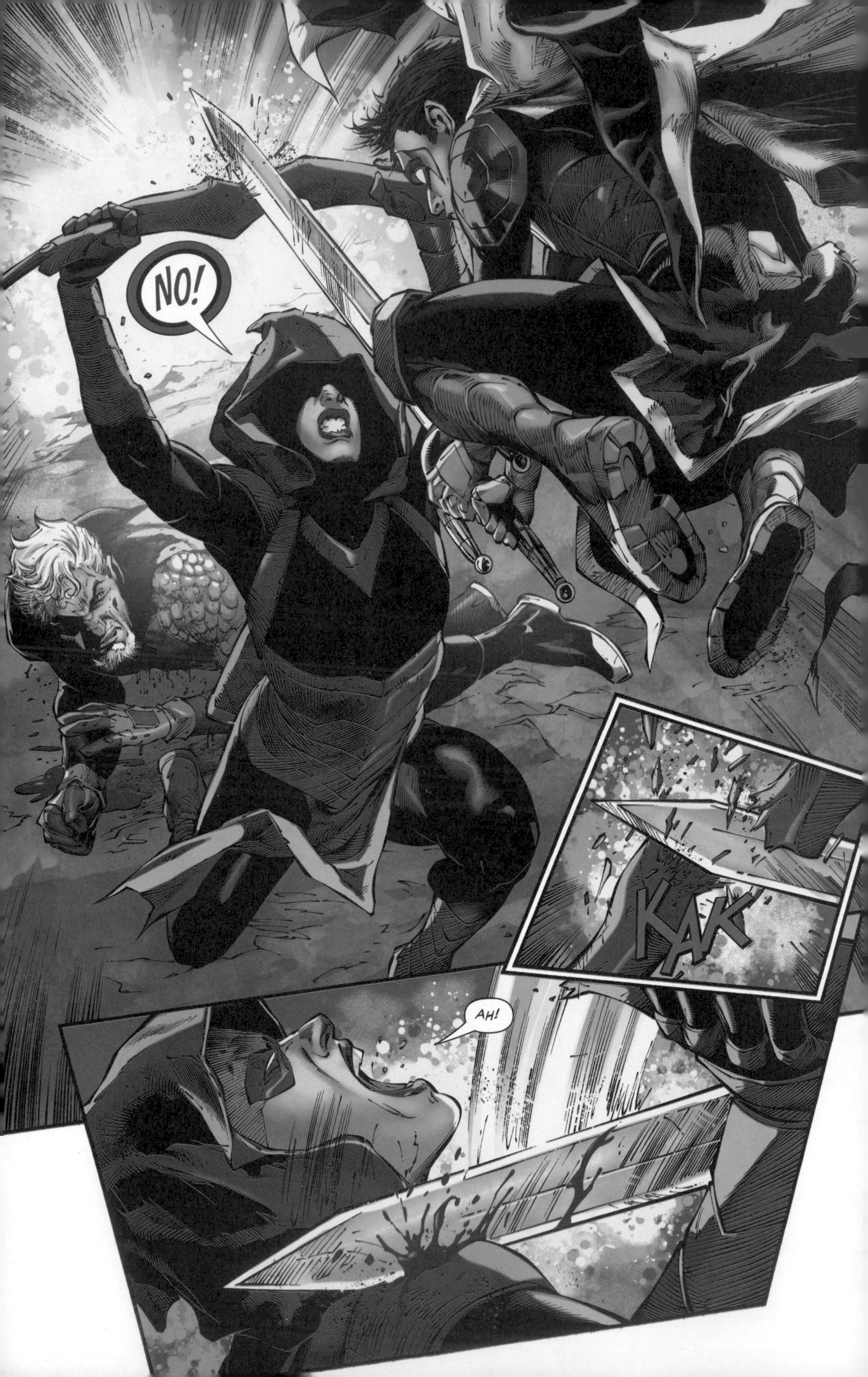
NO!
KAK
AH!

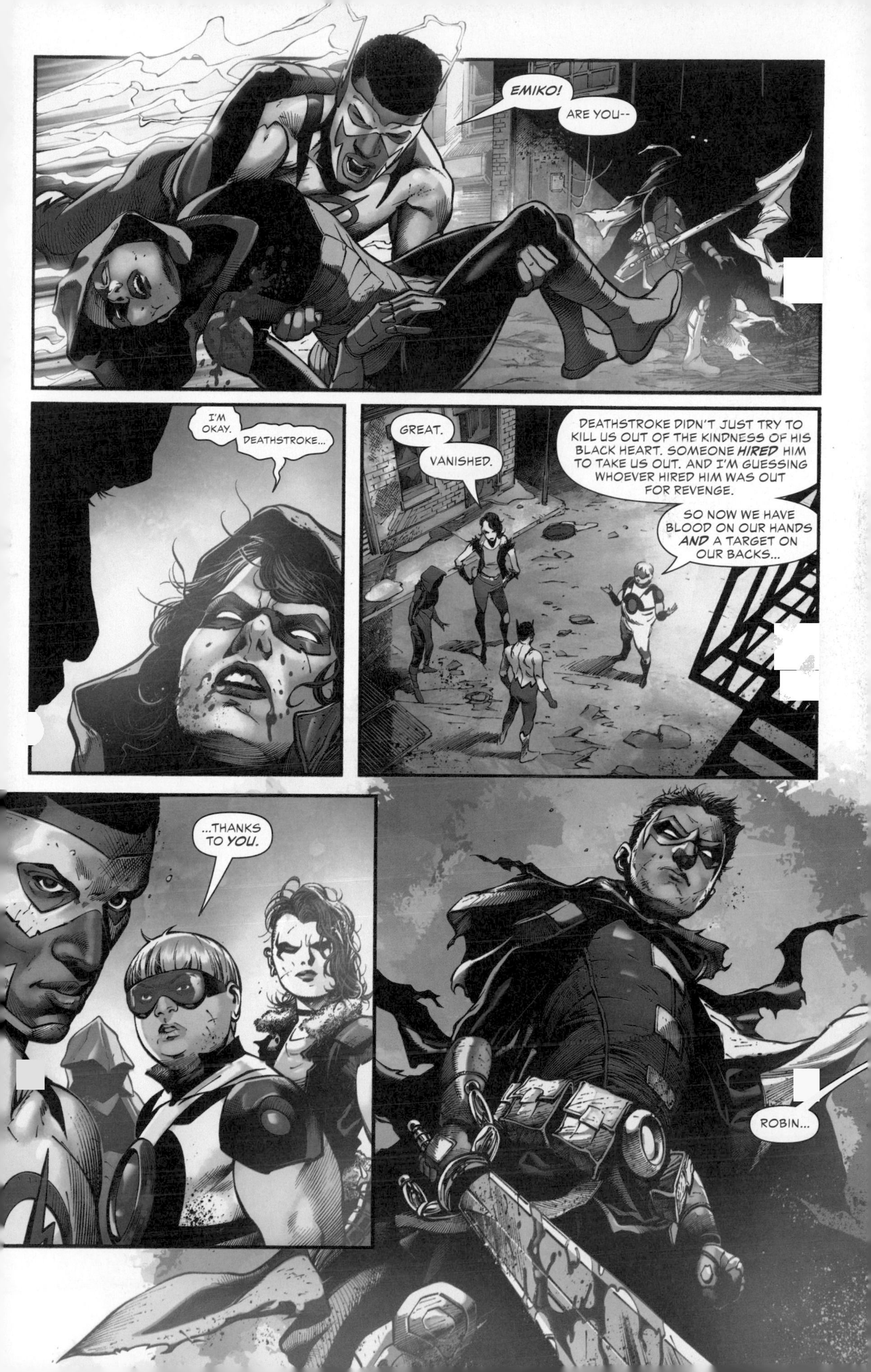
EMIKO!
ARE YOU--
I'M OKAY.
DEATHSTROKE...
GREAT.
VANISHED.
DEATHSTROKE DIDN'T JUST TRY TO KILL US OUT OF THE KINDNESS OF HIS BLACK HEART. SOMEONE HIRED HIM TO TAKE US OUT. AND I'M GUESSING WHOEVER HIRED HIM WAS OUT FOR REVENGE.
SO NOW WE HAVE BLOOD ON OUR HANDS AND A TARGET ON OUR BACKS...
...THANKS TO YOU.
ROBIN...

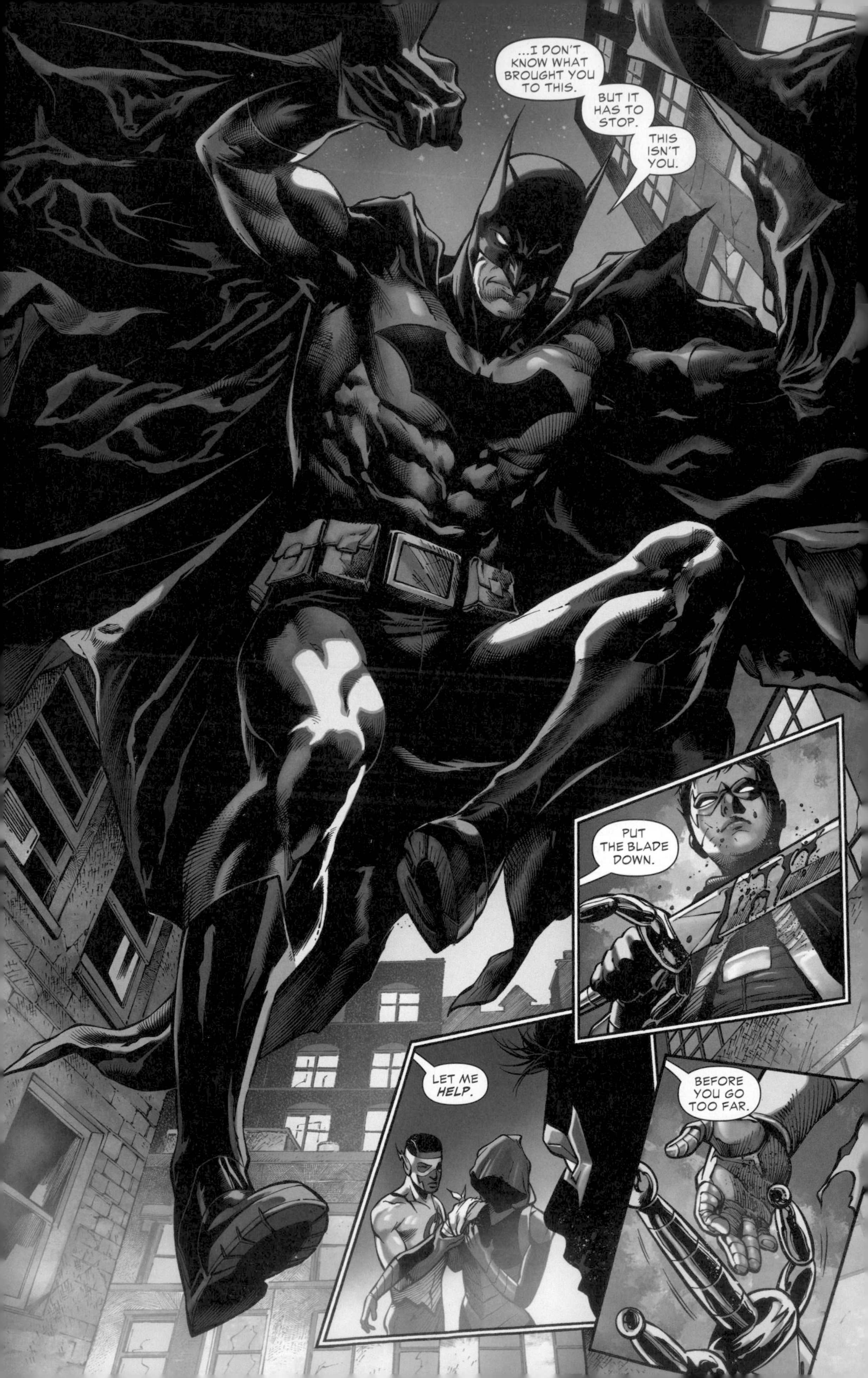
...I DON'T KNOW WHAT BROUGHT YOU TO THIS.
BUT IT HAS TO STOP.
THIS ISN'T YOU.
PUT THE BLADE DOWN.
LET ME *HELP*.
BEFORE YOU GO TOO FAR.

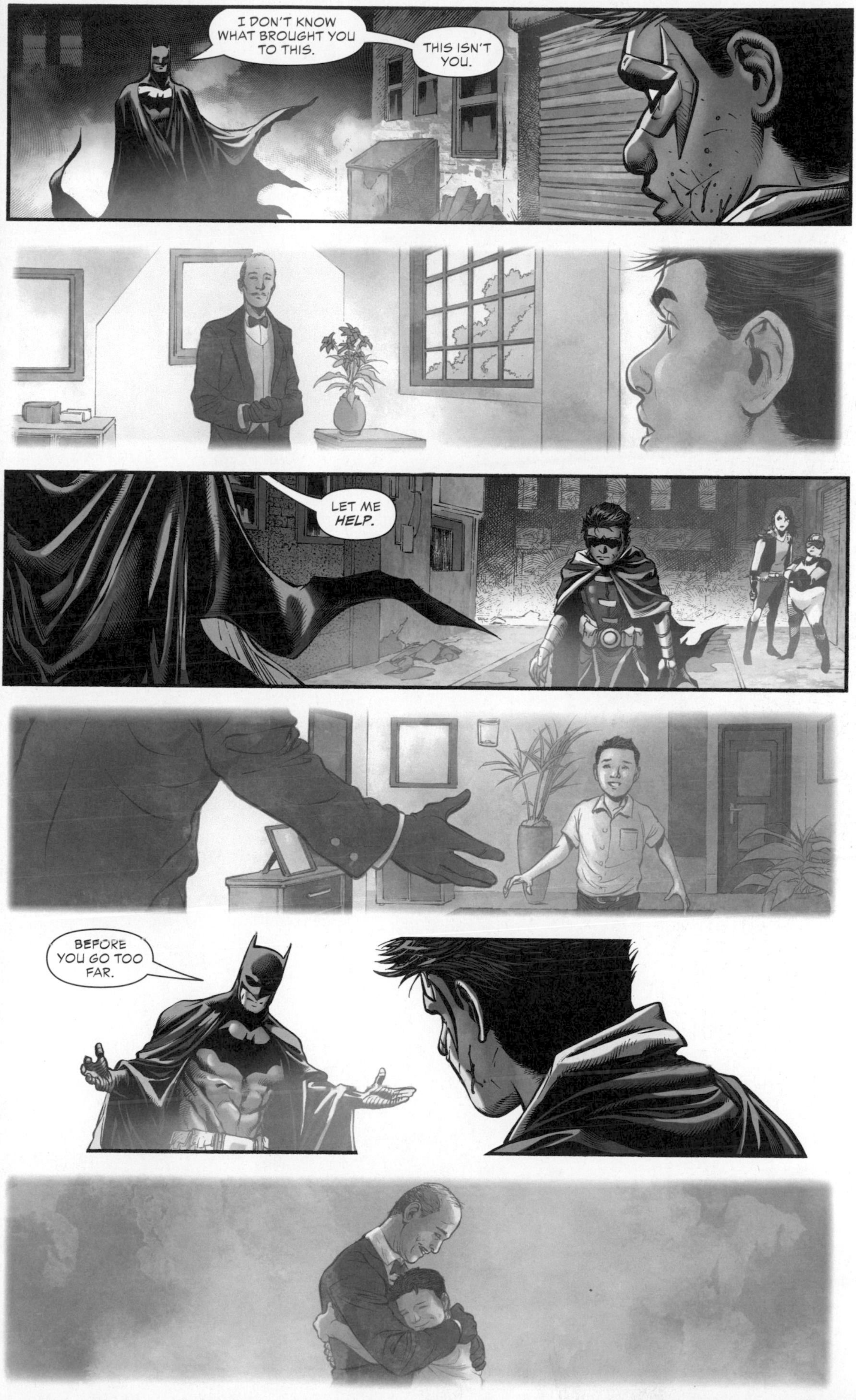
I DON'T KNOW WHAT BROUGHT YOU TO THIS.
THIS ISN'T YOU.
LET ME *HELP.*
BEFORE YOU GO TOO FAR.

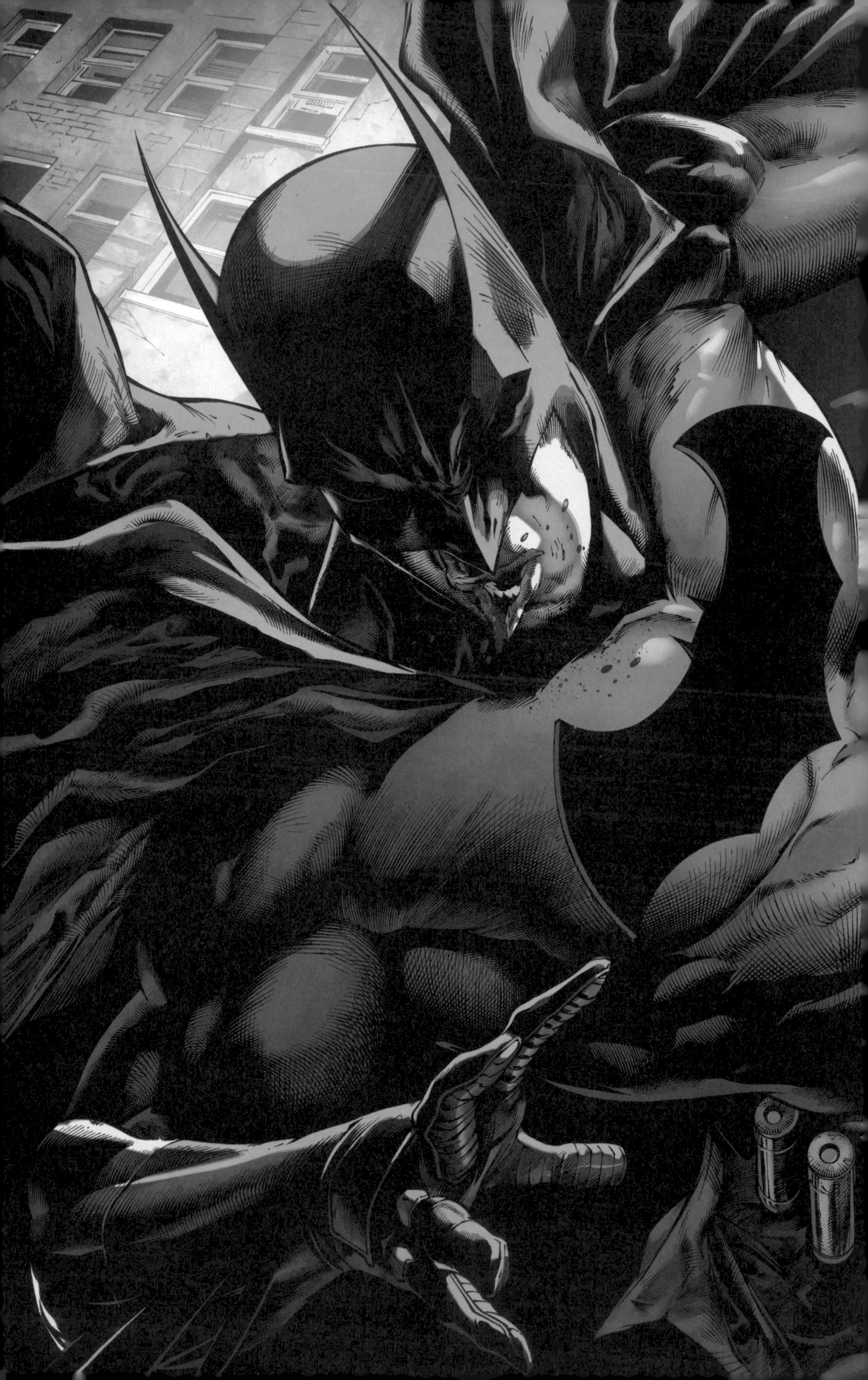

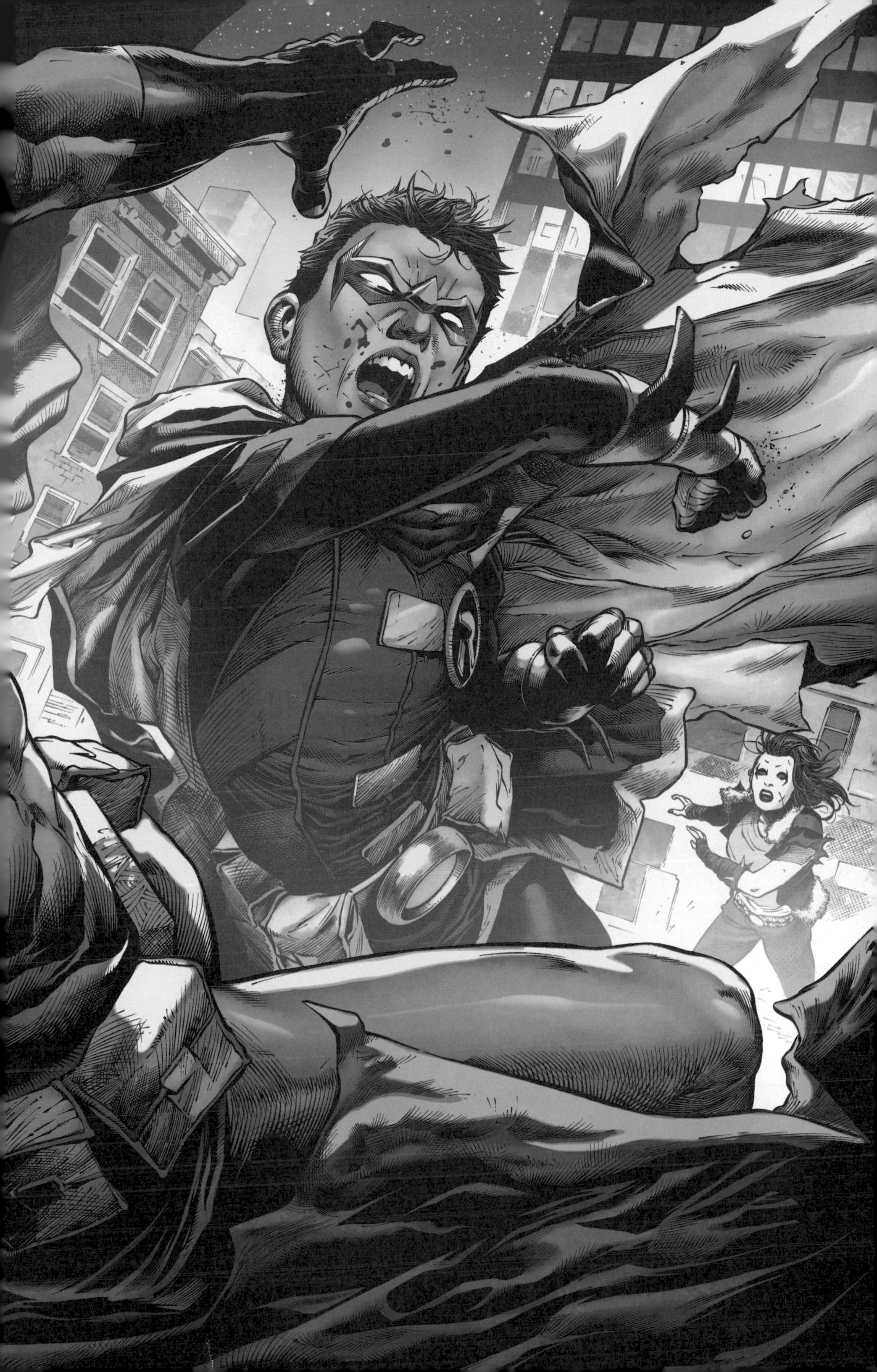

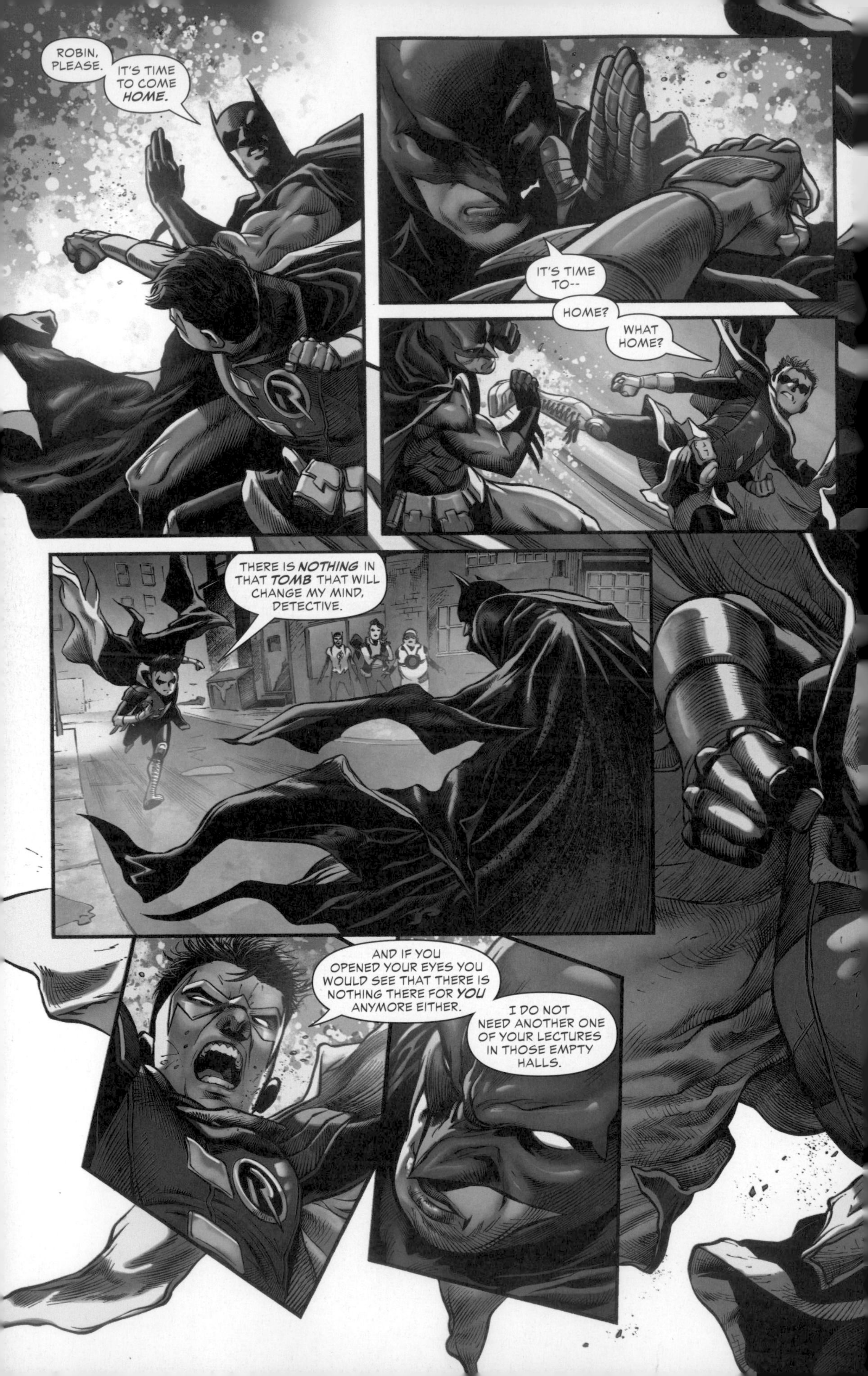

ROBIN, PLEASE.
IT'S TIME TO COME HOME.
IT'S TIME TO--
HOME?
WHAT HOME?
THERE IS NOTHING IN THAT TOMB THAT WILL CHANGE MY MIND, DETECTIVE.
AND IF YOU OPENED YOUR EYES YOU WOULD SEE THAT THERE IS NOTHING THERE FOR YOU ANYMORE EITHER.
I DO NOT NEED ANOTHER ONE OF YOUR LECTURES IN THOSE EMPTY HALLS.

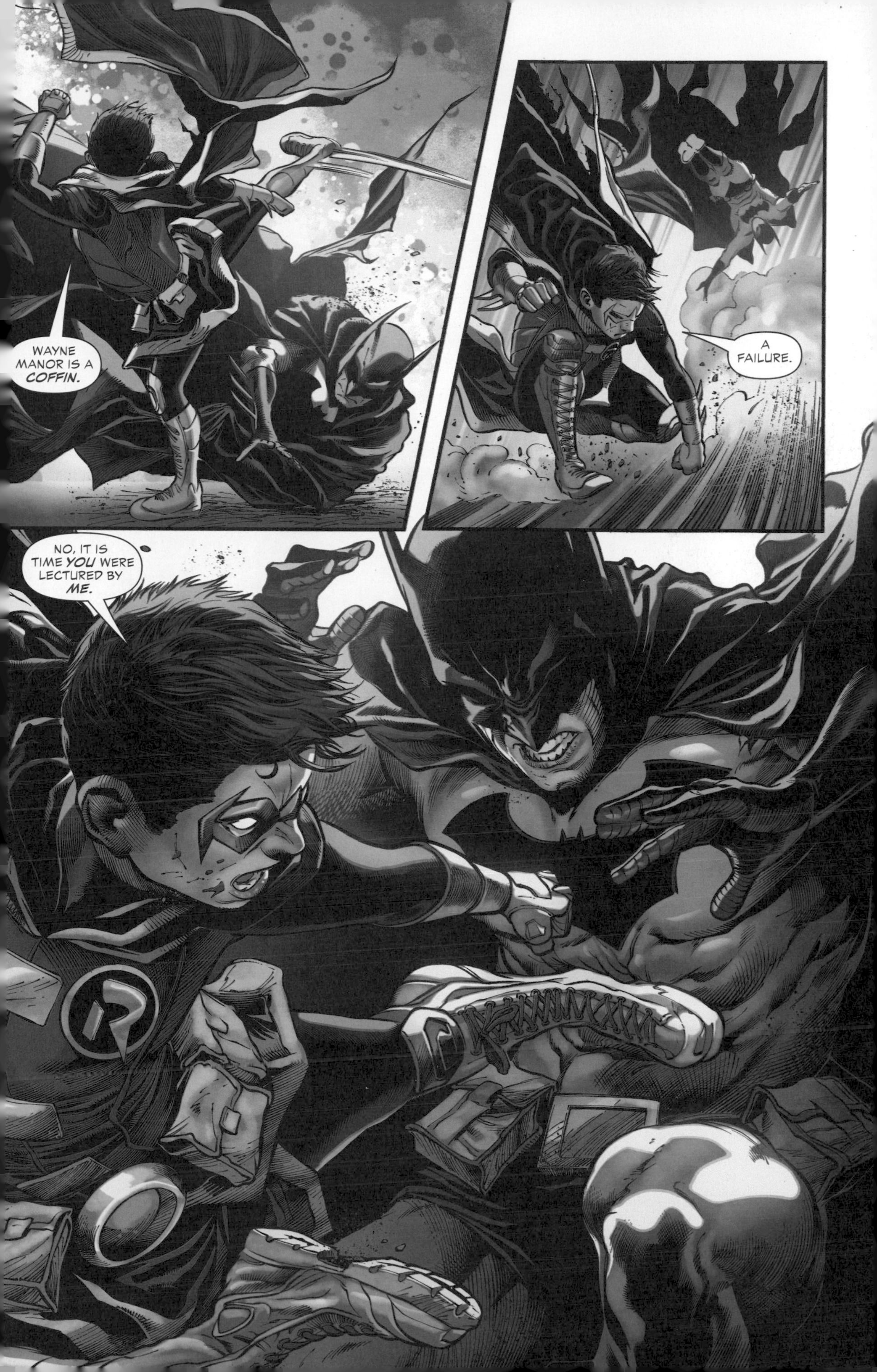
WAYNE MANOR IS A *COFFIN*.
A FAILURE.
NO, IT IS TIME *YOU* WERE LECTURED BY *ME*.

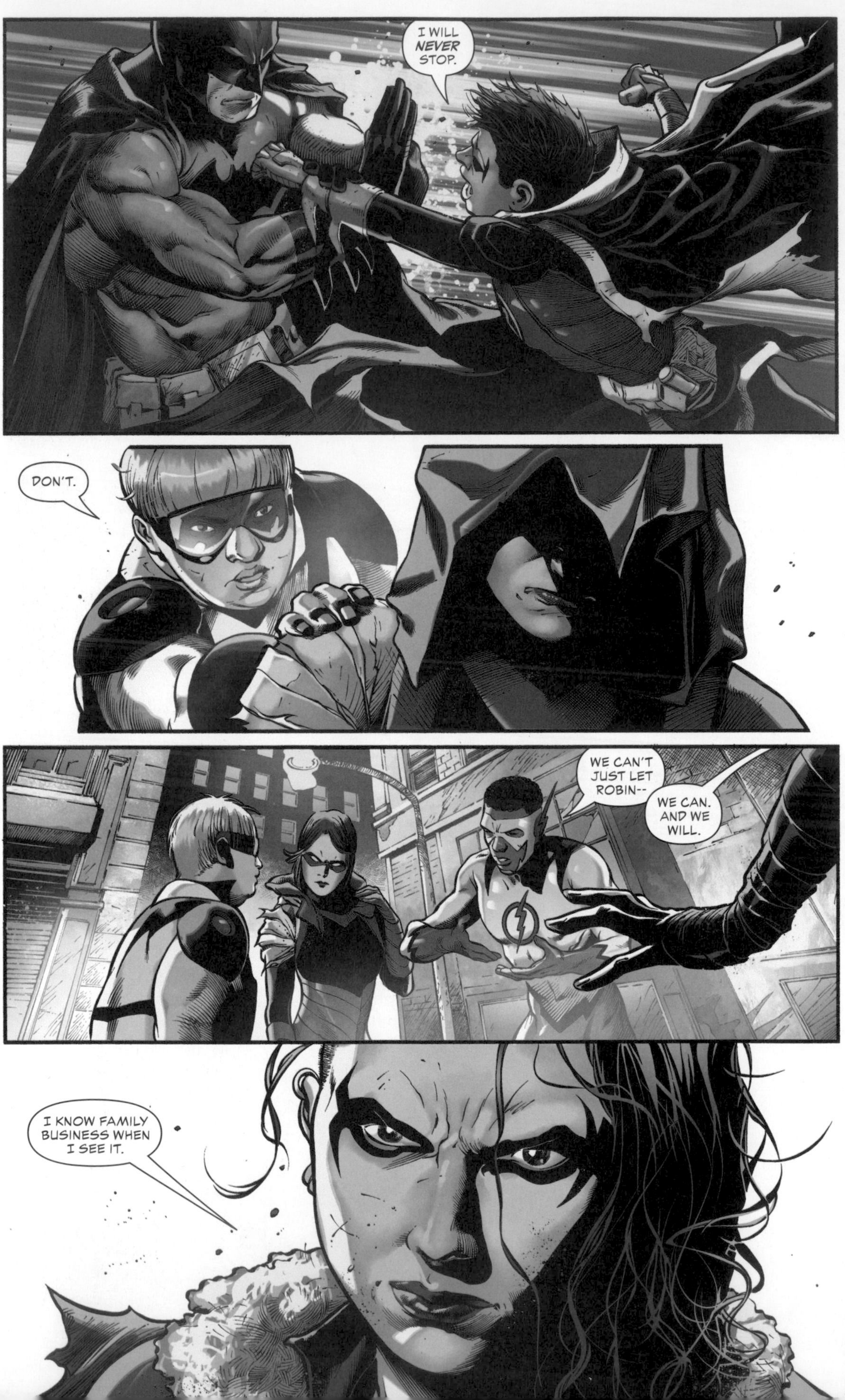
I WILL *NEVER* STOP.
DON'T.
WE CAN'T JUST LET ROBIN--
WE CAN. AND WE WILL.
I KNOW FAMILY BUSINESS WHEN I SEE IT.

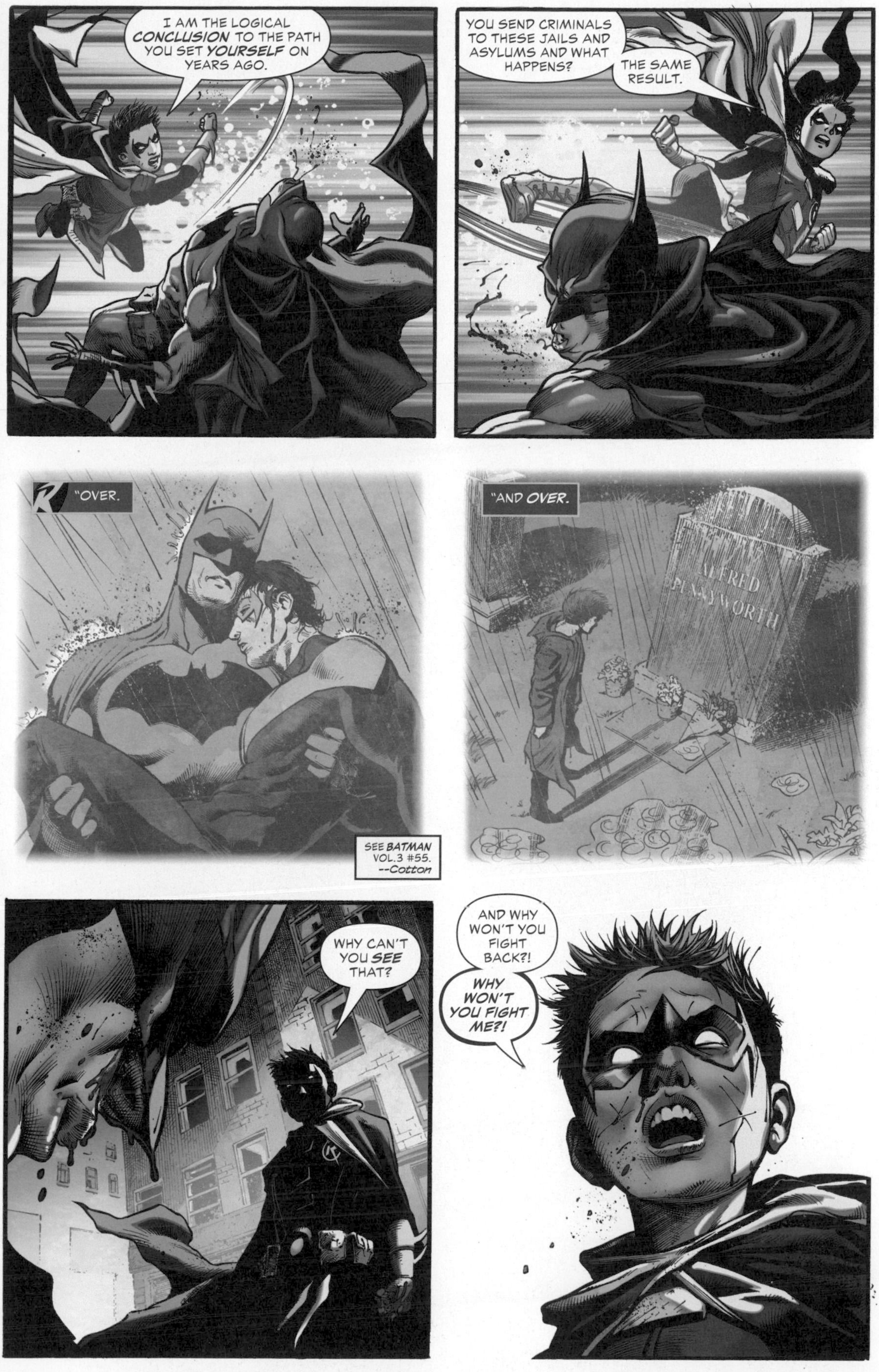
I AM THE LOGICAL CONCLUSION TO THE PATH YOU SET YOURSELF ON YEARS AGO.
YOU SEND CRIMINALS TO THESE JAILS AND ASYLUMS AND WHAT HAPPENS?
THE SAME RESULT.
"OVER.
"AND OVER.
ALFRED PENNYWORTH
SEE BATMAN VOL.3 #55. --Cotton
WHY CAN'T YOU SEE THAT?
AND WHY WON'T YOU FIGHT BACK?!
WHY WON'T YOU FIGHT ME?!

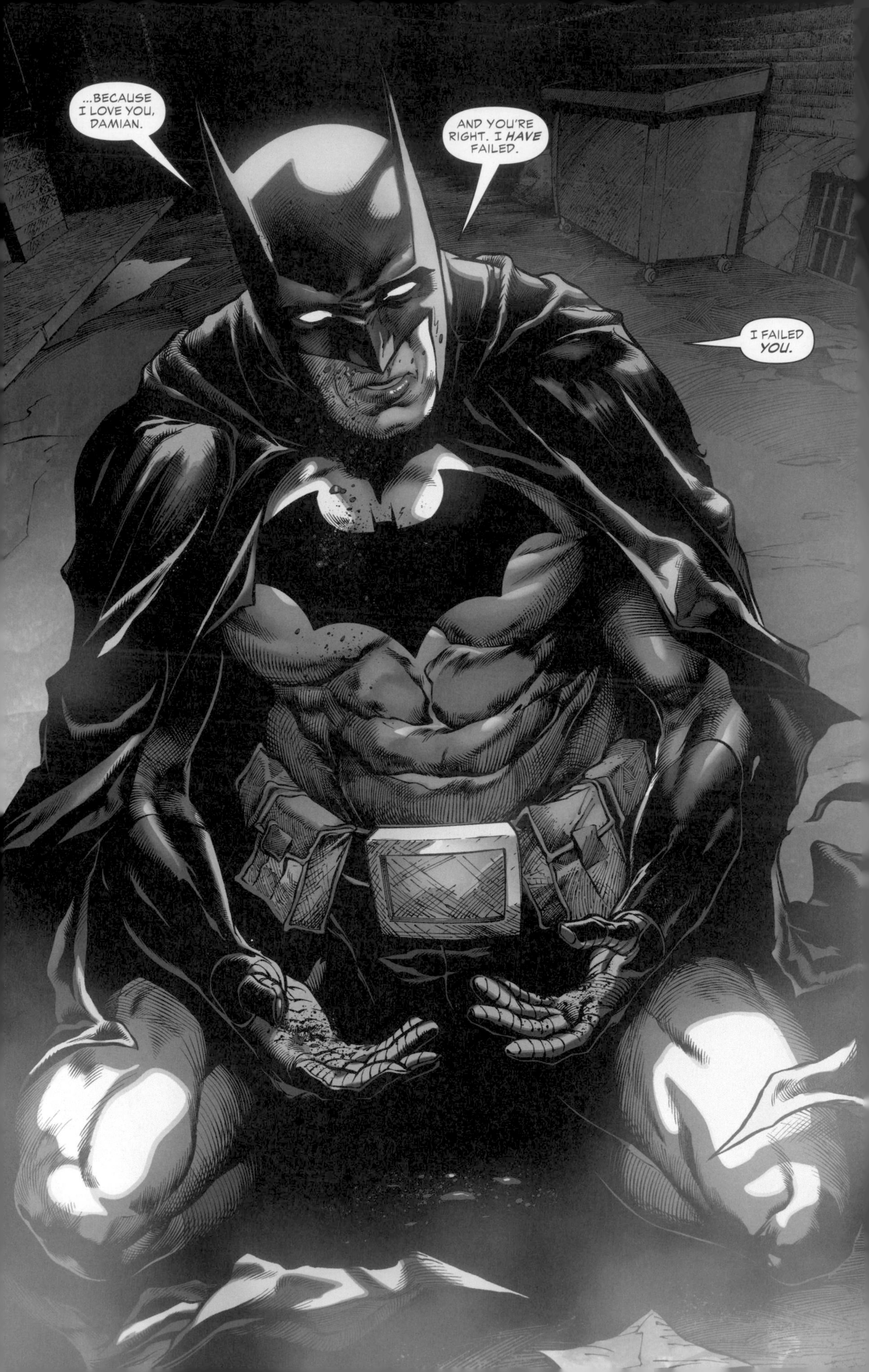
...BECAUSE I LOVE YOU, DAMIAN.
AND YOU'RE RIGHT. I *HAVE* FAILED.
I FAILED *YOU*.

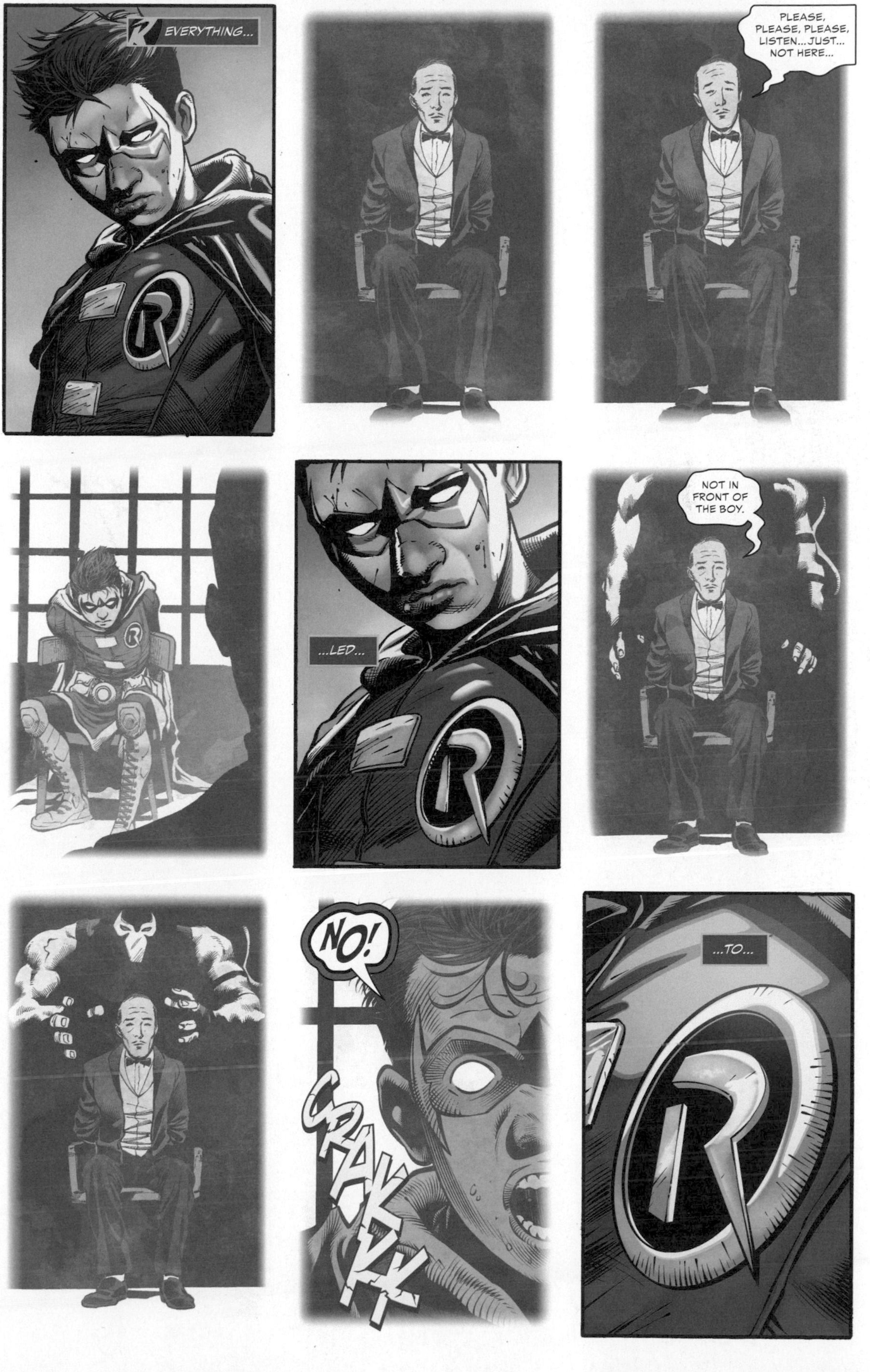
EVERYTHING...
PLEASE, PLEASE, PLEASE, LISTEN...JUST... NOT HERE...
...LED...
NOT IN FRONT OF THE BOY.
NO!
CRAKKK
...TO...

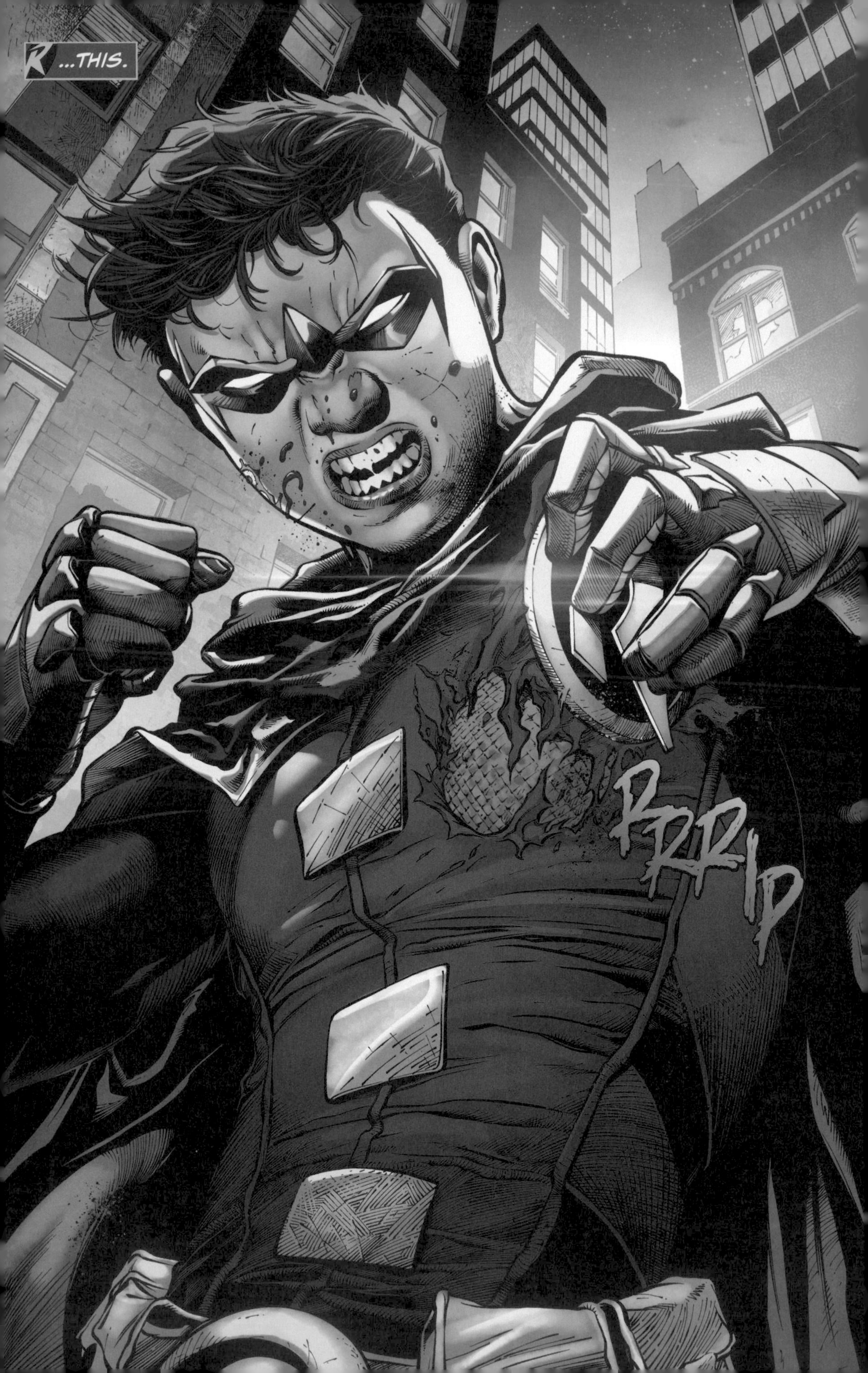
...THIS.
RRRIP

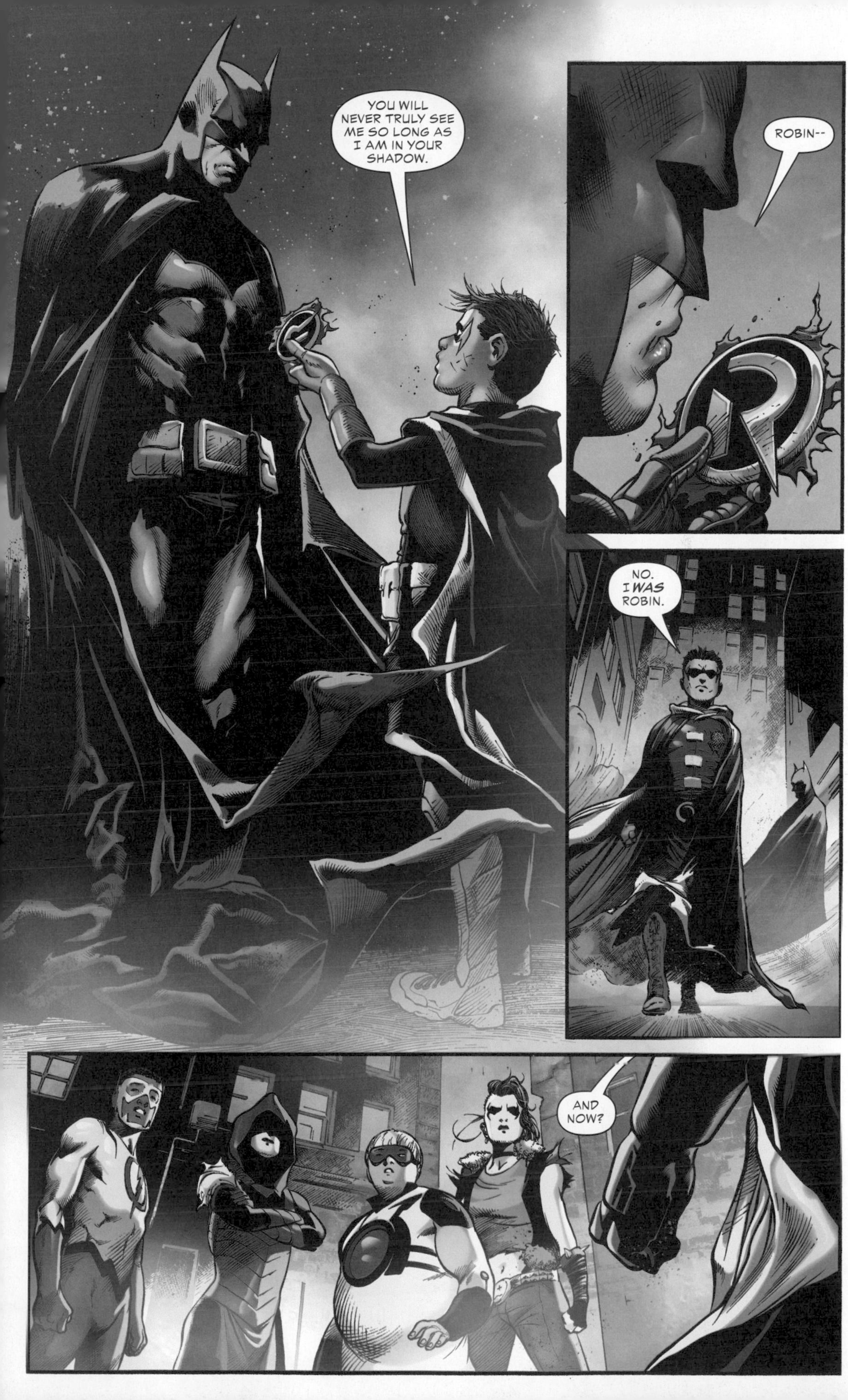
YOU WILL NEVER TRULY SEE ME SO LONG AS I AM IN YOUR SHADOW.
ROBIN--
NO. I *WAS* ROBIN.
AND NOW?

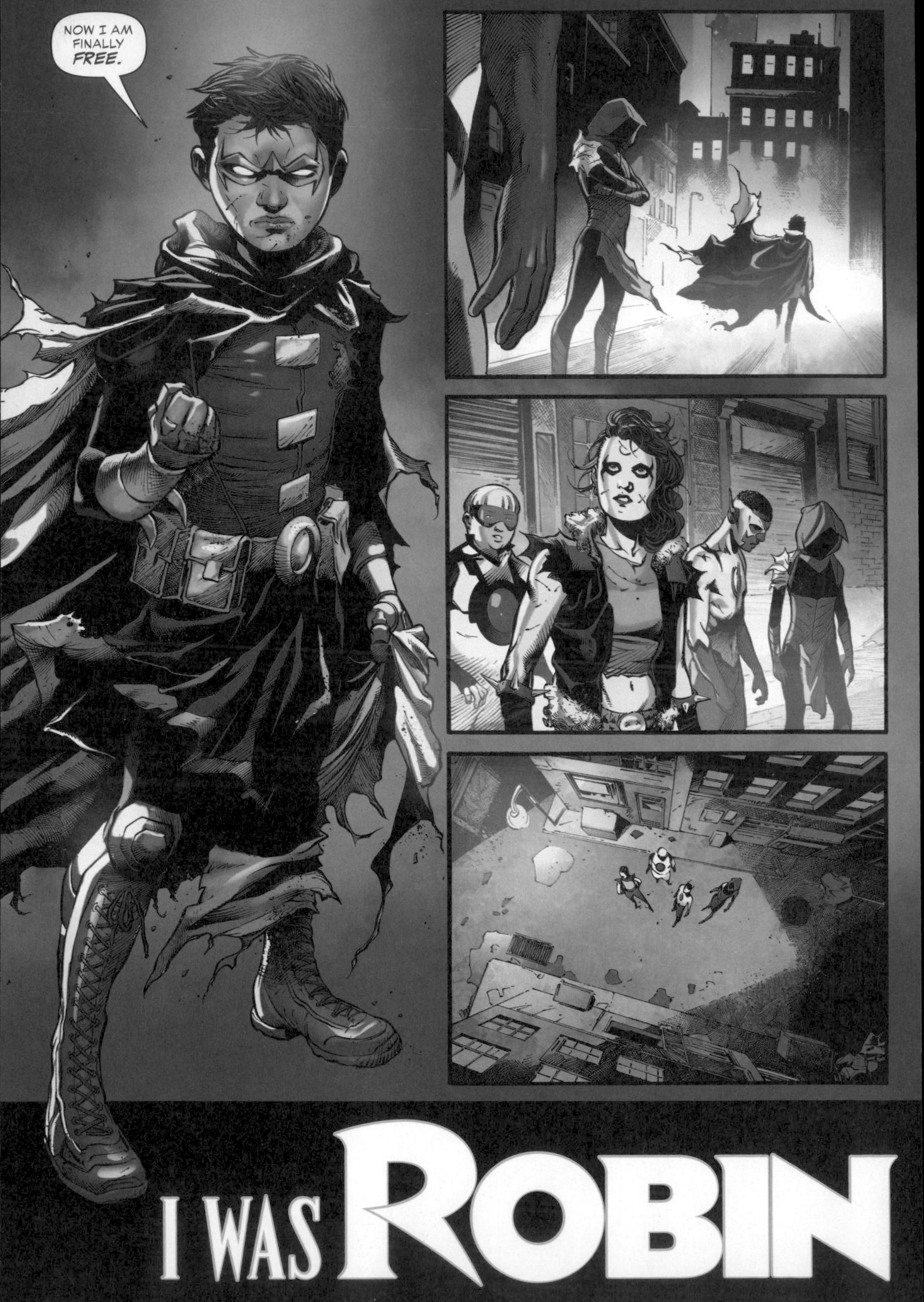
NOW I AM FINALLY FREE.

I WAS ROBIN

ROBBIE THOMPSON writer · EDUARDO PANSICA penciller · JULIO FERREIRA inker · MARCELO MAIOLO colorist · ROB LEIGH letterer · BERNARD CHANG MARCELO MAIOLO cover · MARQUIS DRAPER asst. editor · MIKE COTTON editor · ALEX R. CARR group editor

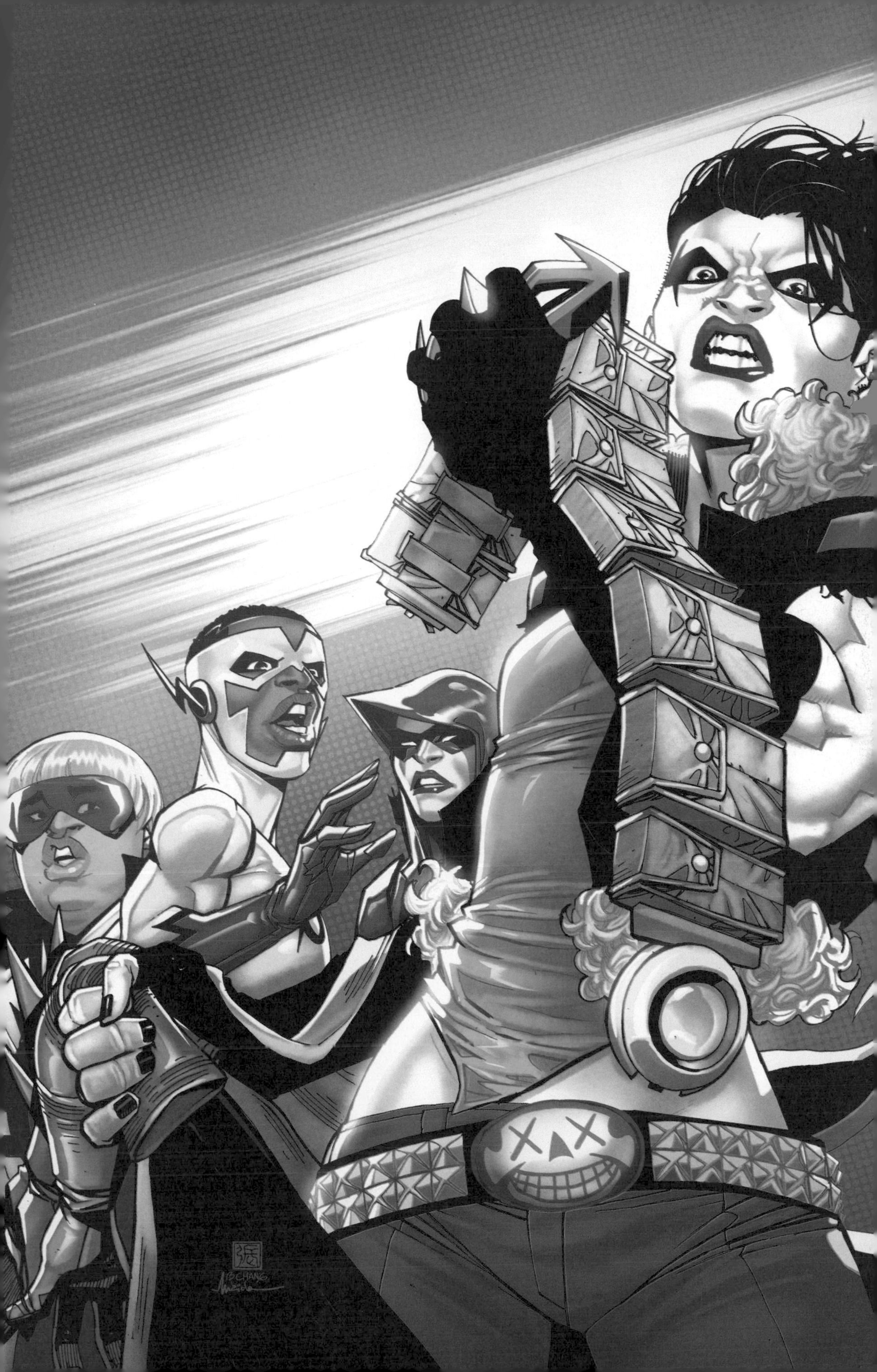

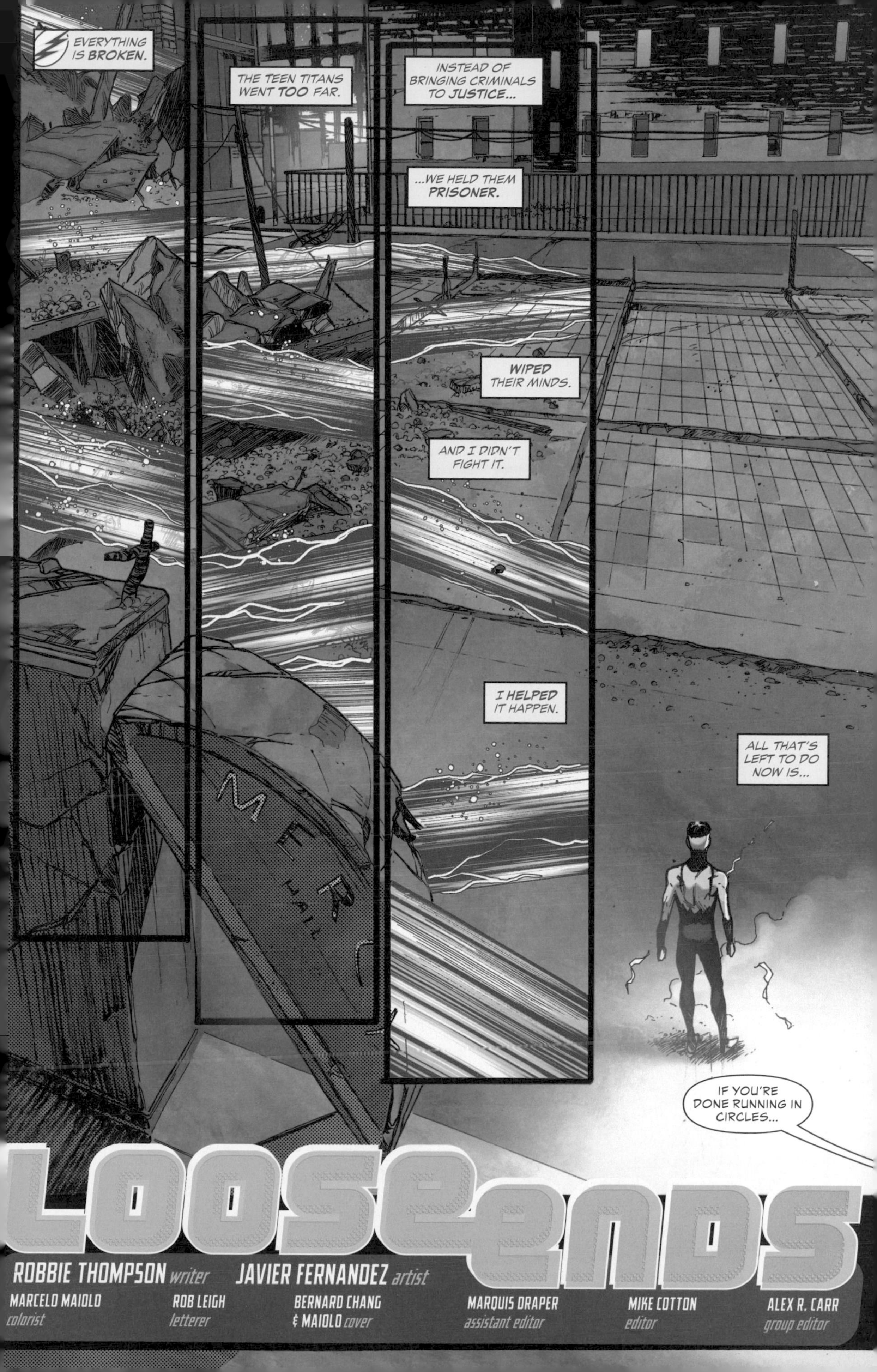
EVERYTHING IS BROKEN.
THE TEEN TITANS WENT TOO FAR.
INSTEAD OF BRINGING CRIMINALS TO JUSTICE...
...WE HELD THEM PRISONER.
WIPED THEIR MINDS.
AND I DIDN'T FIGHT IT.
I HELPED IT HAPPEN.
ALL THAT'S LEFT TO DO NOW IS...
IF YOU'RE DONE RUNNING IN CIRCLES...
LOOSE ENDS
ROBBIE THOMPSON writer JAVIER FERNANDEZ artist
MARCELO MAIOLO colorist
ROB LEIGH letterer
BERNARD CHANG & MAIOLO cover
MARQUIS DRAPER assistant editor
MIKE COTTON editor
ALEX R. CARR group editor

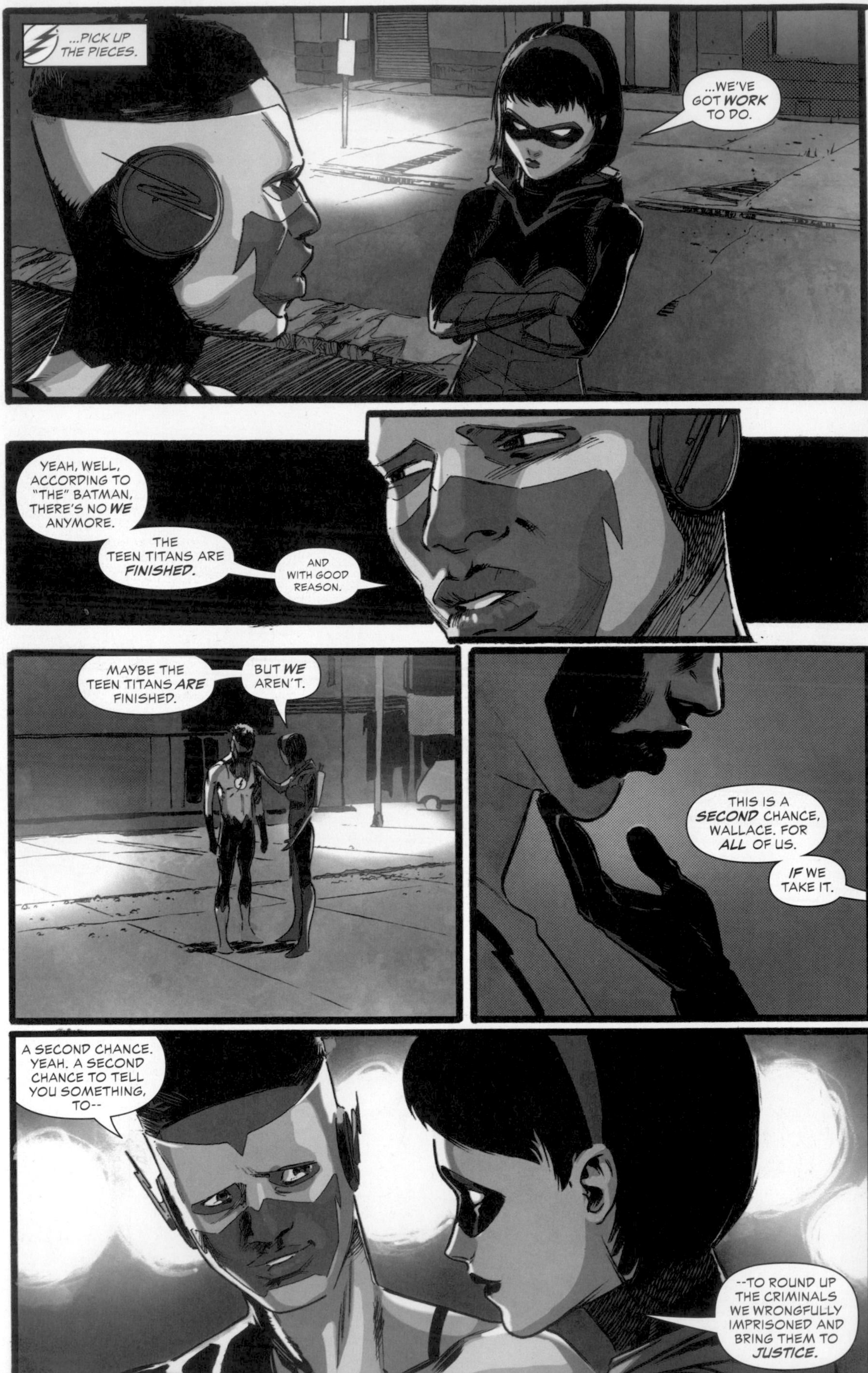
...PICK UP THE PIECES.
...WE'VE GOT WORK TO DO.
YEAH, WELL, ACCORDING TO "THE" BATMAN, THERE'S NO WE ANYMORE.
THE TEEN TITANS ARE FINISHED.
AND WITH GOOD REASON.
MAYBE THE TEEN TITANS ARE FINISHED.
BUT WE AREN'T.
THIS IS A SECOND CHANCE, WALLACE. FOR ALL OF US.
IF WE TAKE IT.
A SECOND CHANCE. YEAH. A SECOND CHANCE TO TELL YOU SOMETHING, TO--
--TO ROUND UP THE CRIMINALS WE WRONGFULLY IMPRISONED AND BRING THEM TO JUSTICE.

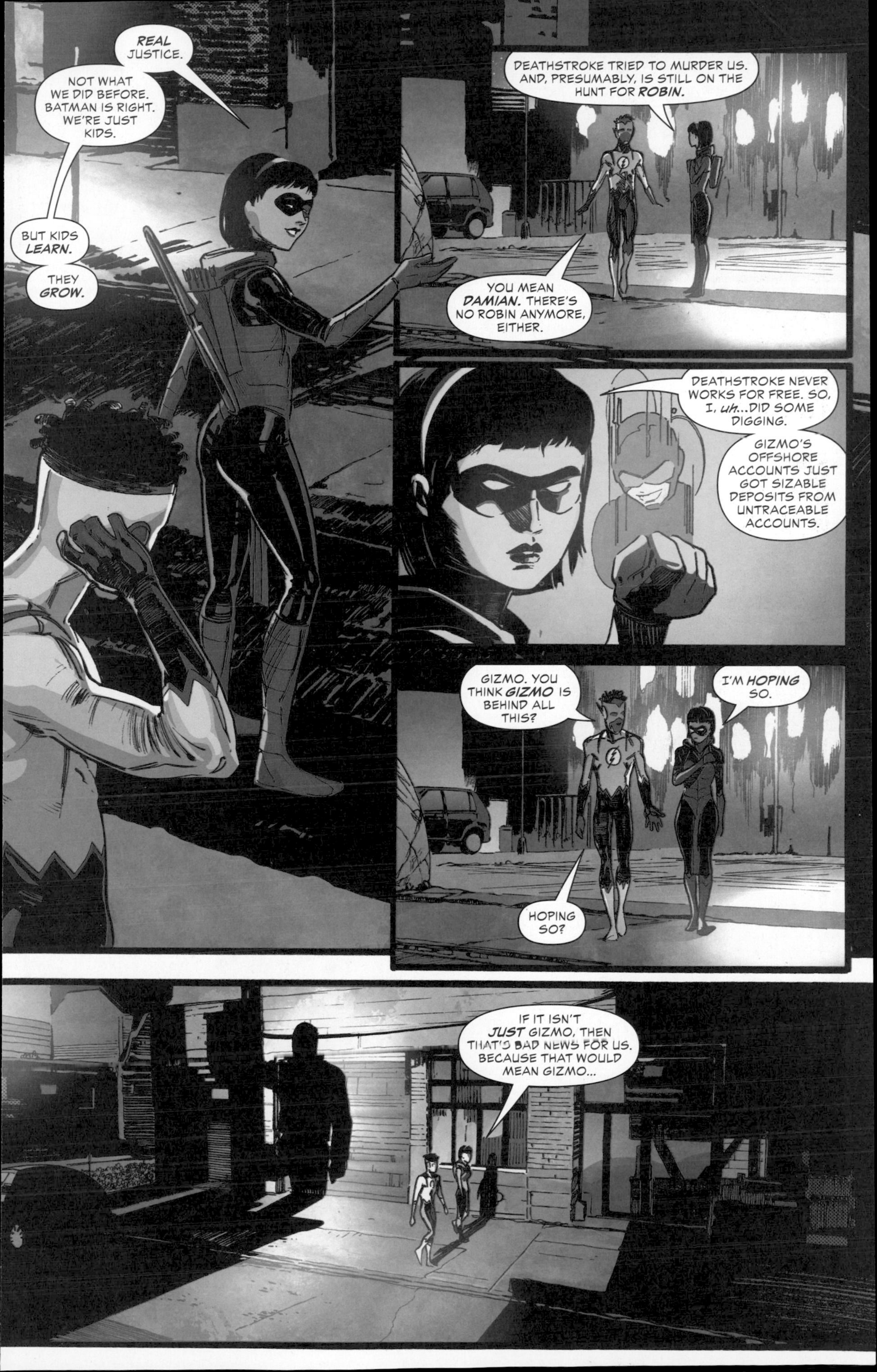
REAL JUSTICE.
NOT WHAT WE DID BEFORE. BATMAN IS RIGHT. WE'RE JUST KIDS.
BUT KIDS LEARN.
THEY GROW.
DEATHSTROKE TRIED TO MURDER US. AND, PRESUMABLY, IS STILL ON THE HUNT FOR ROBIN.
YOU MEAN DAMIAN. THERE'S NO ROBIN ANYMORE, EITHER.
DEATHSTROKE NEVER WORKS FOR FREE. SO, I, uh...DID SOME DIGGING.
GIZMO'S OFFSHORE ACCOUNTS JUST GOT SIZABLE DEPOSITS FROM UNTRACEABLE ACCOUNTS.
GIZMO. YOU THINK GIZMO IS BEHIND ALL THIS?
I'M HOPING SO.
HOPING SO?
IF IT ISN'T JUST GIZMO, THEN THAT'S BAD NEWS FOR US. BECAUSE THAT WOULD MEAN GIZMO...

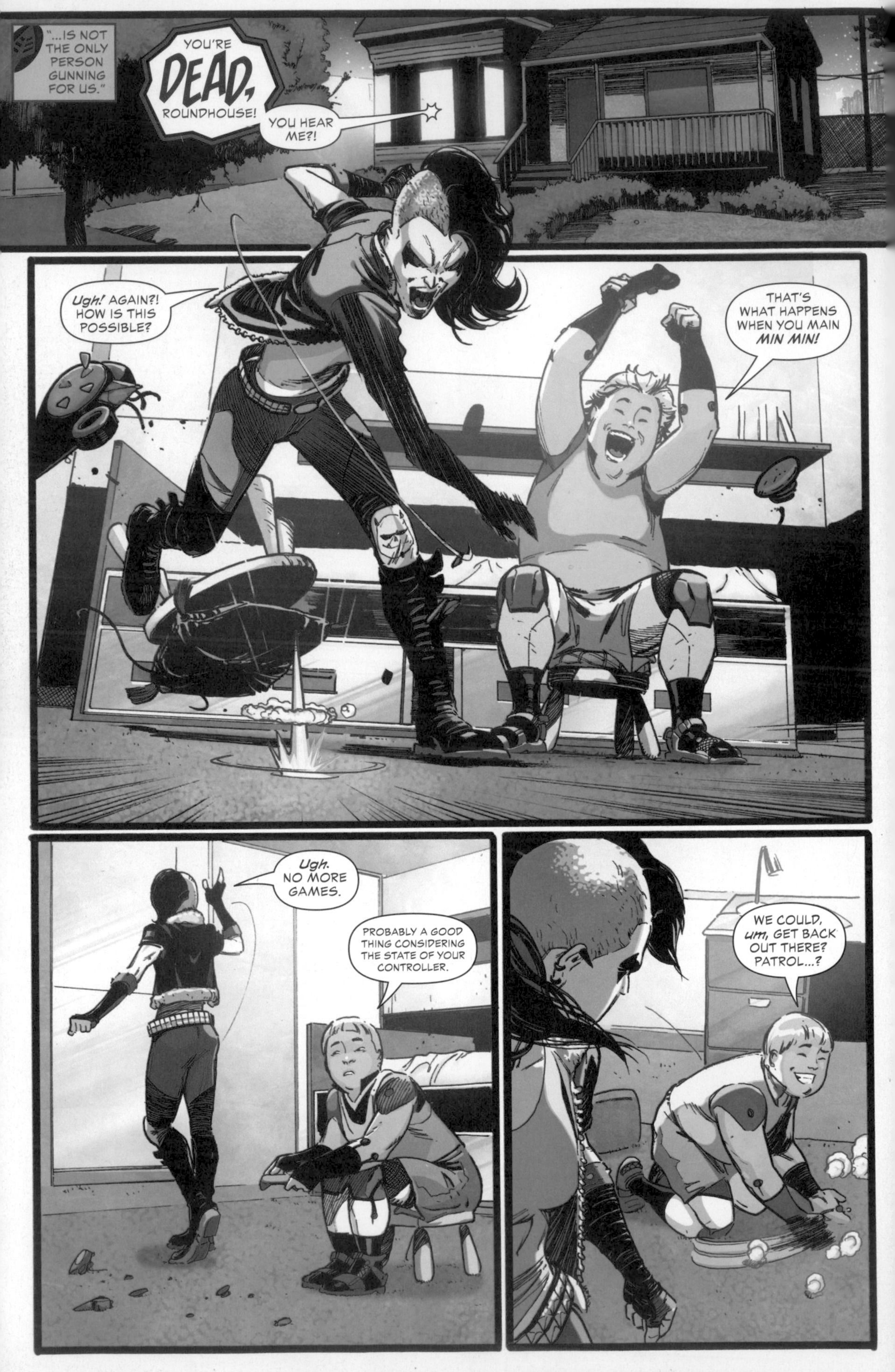
"...IS NOT THE ONLY PERSON GUNNING FOR US."
YOU'RE DEAD, ROUNDHOUSE!
YOU HEAR ME?!
Ugh! AGAIN?! HOW IS THIS POSSIBLE?
THAT'S WHAT HAPPENS WHEN YOU MAIN *MIN MIN!*
Ugh. NO MORE GAMES.
PROBABLY A GOOD THING CONSIDERING THE STATE OF YOUR CONTROLLER.
WE COULD, *um,* GET BACK OUT THERE? PATROL...?

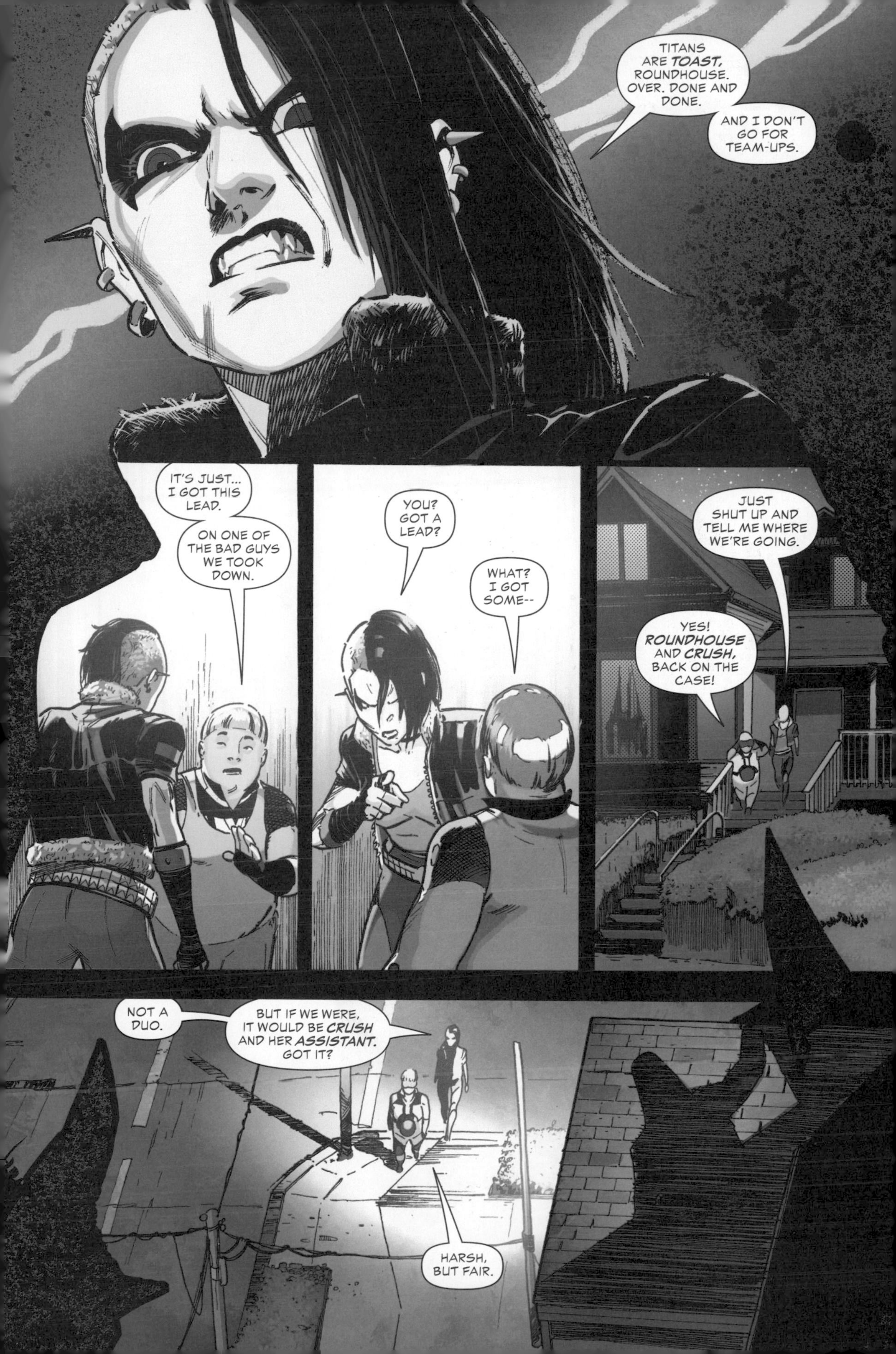
TITANS ARE **TOAST,** ROUNDHOUSE. OVER. DONE AND DONE.
AND I DON'T GO FOR TEAM-UPS.
IT'S JUST... I GOT THIS LEAD.
ON ONE OF THE BAD GUYS WE TOOK DOWN.
YOU? GOT A LEAD?
WHAT? I GOT SOME--
JUST SHUT UP AND TELL ME WHERE WE'RE GOING.
YES! ***ROUNDHOUSE*** AND ***CRUSH,*** BACK ON THE CASE!
NOT A DUO.
BUT IF WE WERE, IT WOULD BE ***CRUSH*** AND HER ***ASSISTANT.*** GOT IT?
HARSH, BUT FAIR.

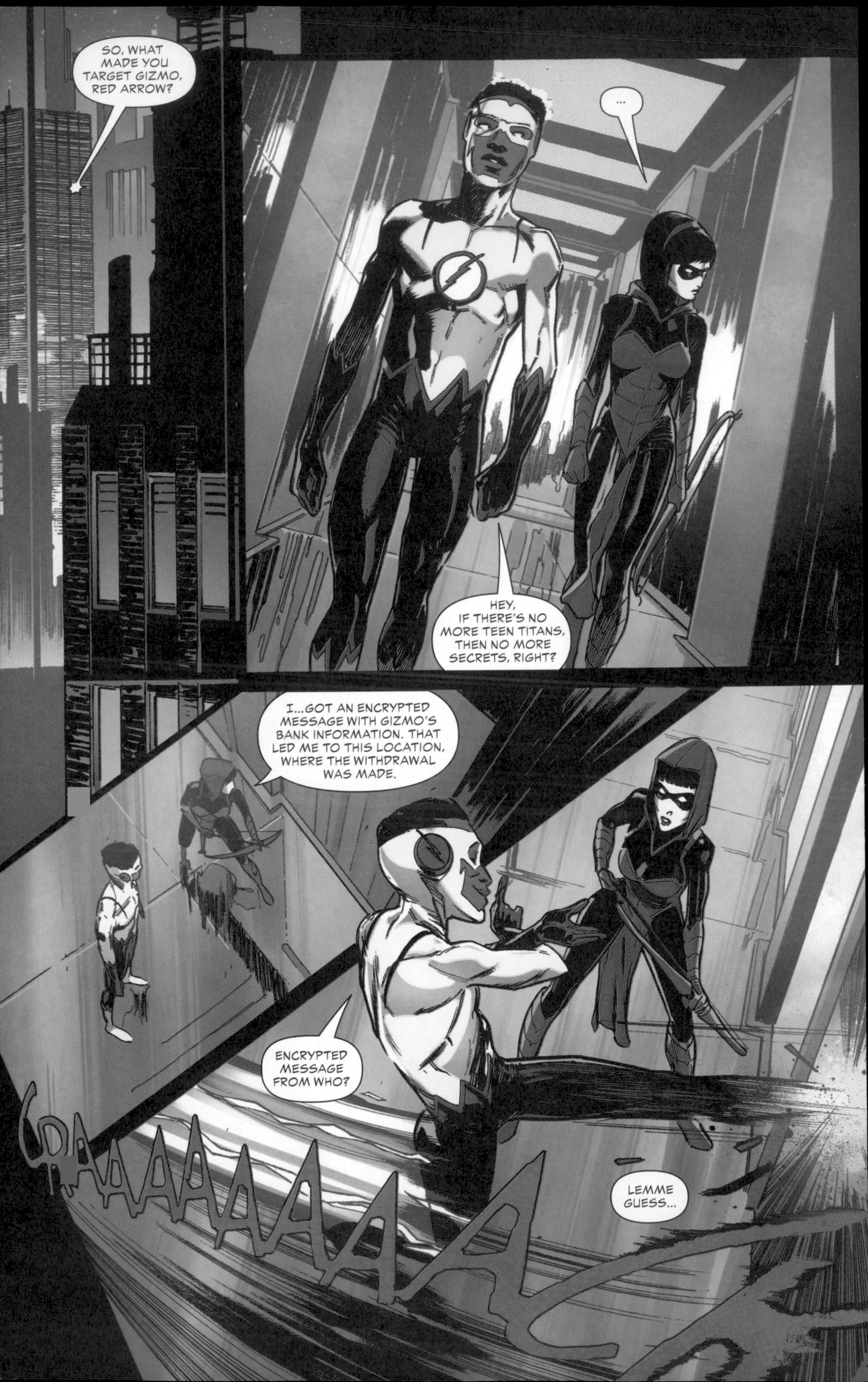
SO, WHAT MADE YOU TARGET GIZMO, RED ARROW?
...
HEY, IF THERE'S NO MORE TEEN TITANS, THEN NO MORE SECRETS, RIGHT?
I...GOT AN ENCRYPTED MESSAGE WITH GIZMO'S BANK INFORMATION. THAT LED ME TO THIS LOCATION, WHERE THE WITHDRAWAL WAS MADE.
ENCRYPTED MESSAGE FROM WHO?
LEMME GUESS...

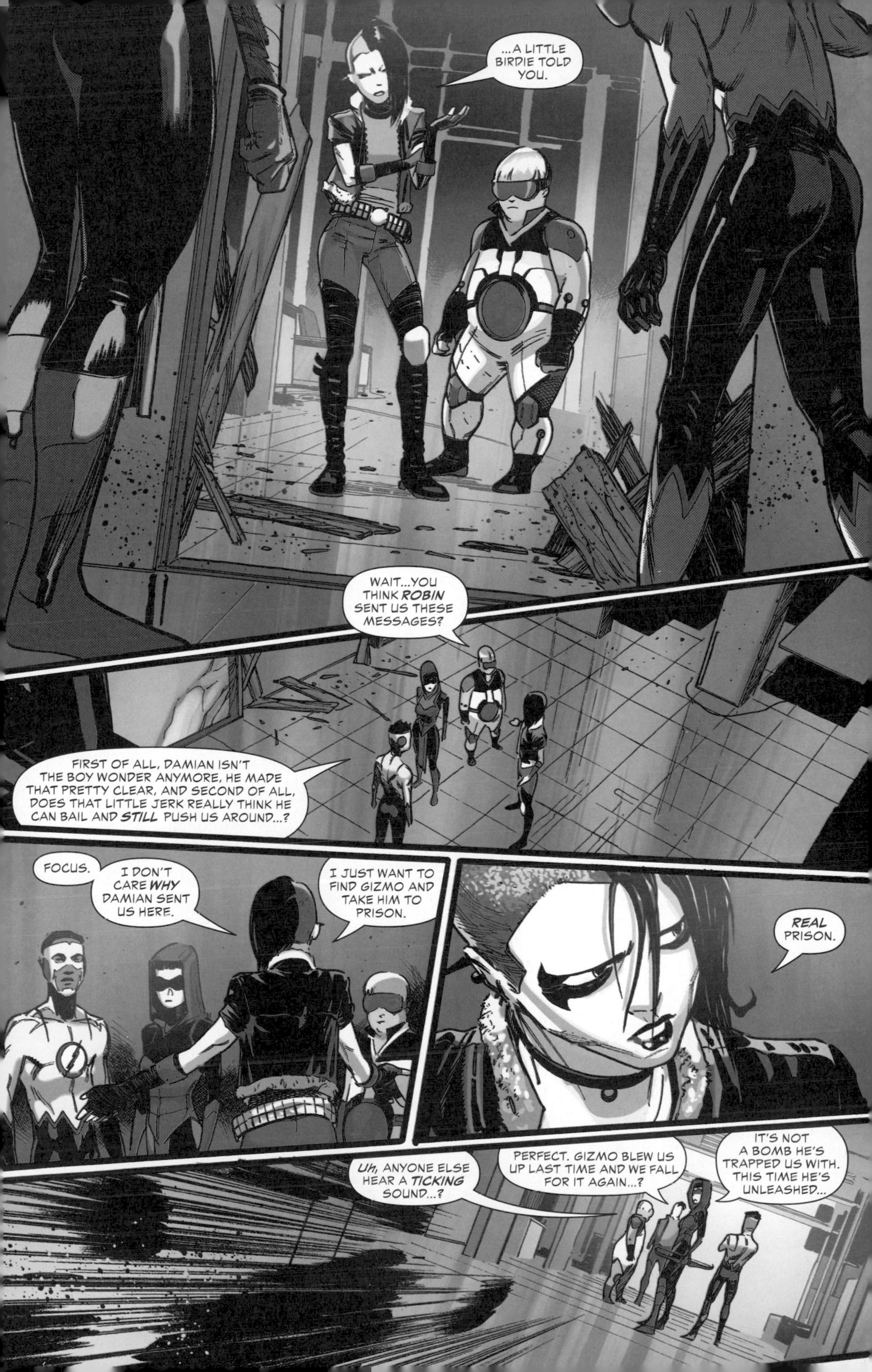
...A LITTLE BIRDIE TOLD YOU.
WAIT...YOU THINK ROBIN SENT US THESE MESSAGES?
FIRST OF ALL, DAMIAN ISN'T THE BOY WONDER ANYMORE, HE MADE THAT PRETTY CLEAR, AND SECOND OF ALL, DOES THAT LITTLE JERK REALLY THINK HE CAN BAIL AND STILL PUSH US AROUND...?
FOCUS.
I DON'T CARE WHY DAMIAN SENT US HERE.
I JUST WANT TO FIND GIZMO AND TAKE HIM TO PRISON.
REAL PRISON.
Uh, ANYONE ELSE HEAR A TICKING SOUND...?
PERFECT. GIZMO BLEW US UP LAST TIME AND WE FALL FOR IT AGAIN...?
IT'S NOT A BOMB HE'S TRAPPED US WITH. THIS TIME HE'S UNLEASHED...

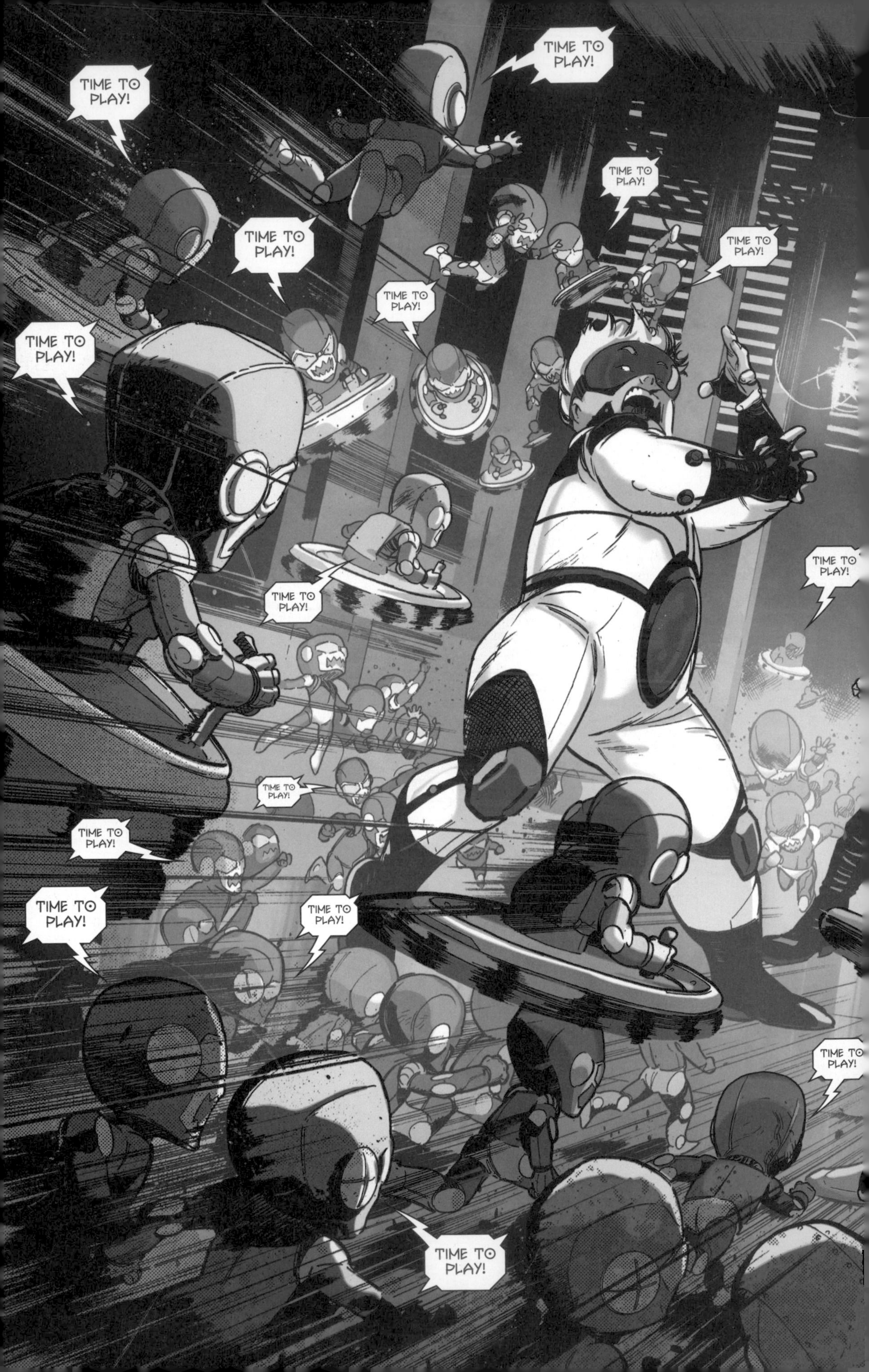
TIME TO PLAY!
TIME TO PLAY!
TIME TO PLAY!
TIME TO PLAY!
TIME TO PLAY!
TIME TO PLAY!
TIME TO PLAY!
TIME TO PLAY!
TIME TO PLAY!
TIME TO PLAY!
TIME TO PLAY!
TIME TO PLAY!
TIME TO PLAY!
TIME TO PLAY!
TIME TO PLAY!

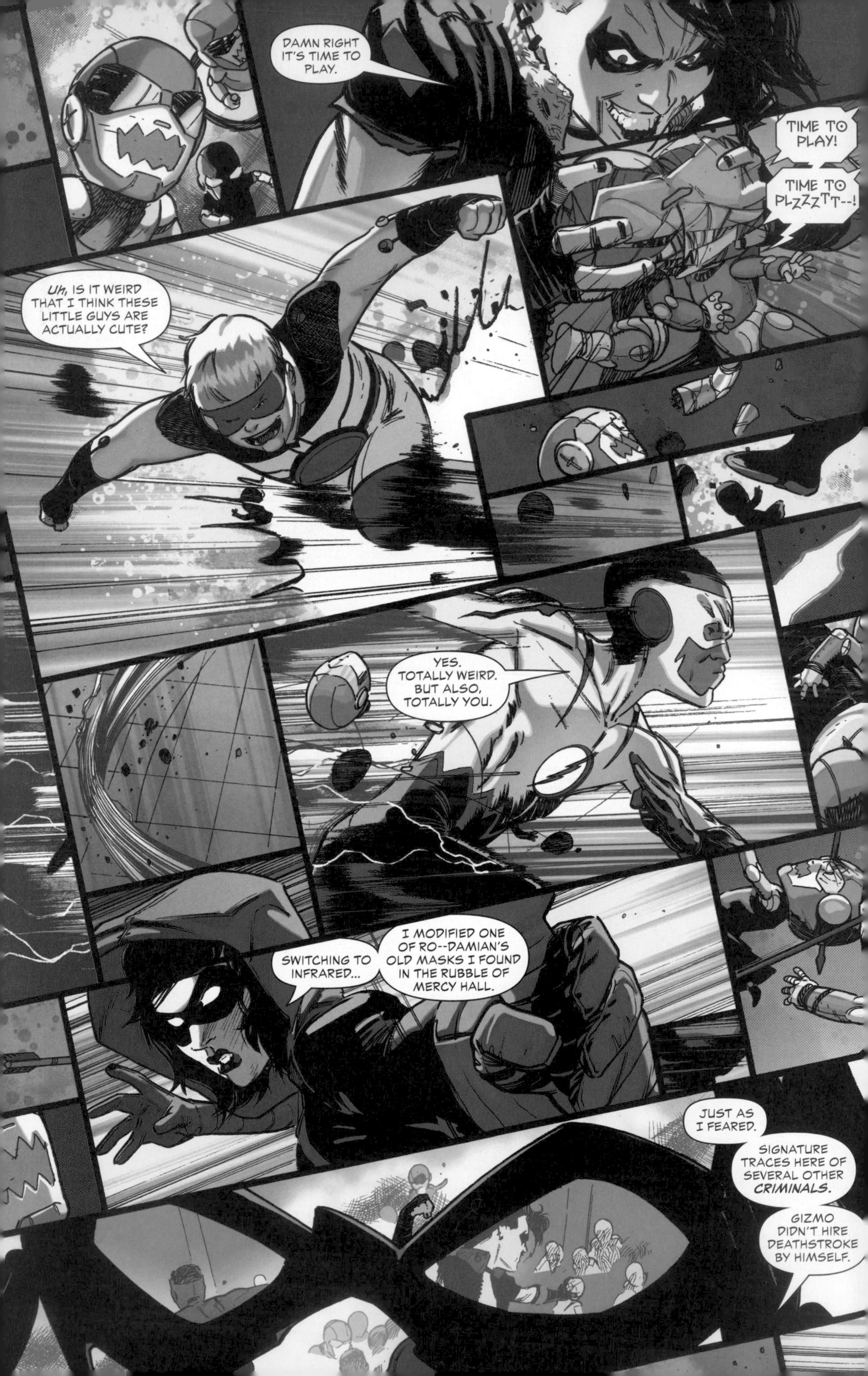
DAMN RIGHT IT'S TIME TO PLAY.
TIME TO PLAY!
TIME TO PLZZZTT--!
Uh, IS IT WEIRD THAT I THINK THESE LITTLE GUYS ARE ACTUALLY CUTE?
YES. TOTALLY WEIRD. BUT ALSO, TOTALLY YOU.
SWITCHING TO INFRARED...
I MODIFIED ONE OF RO--DAMIAN'S OLD MASKS I FOUND IN THE RUBBLE OF MERCY HALL.
JUST AS I FEARED.
SIGNATURE TRACES HERE OF SEVERAL OTHER ***CRIMINALS.***
GIZMO DIDN'T HIRE DEATHSTROKE BY HIMSELF.

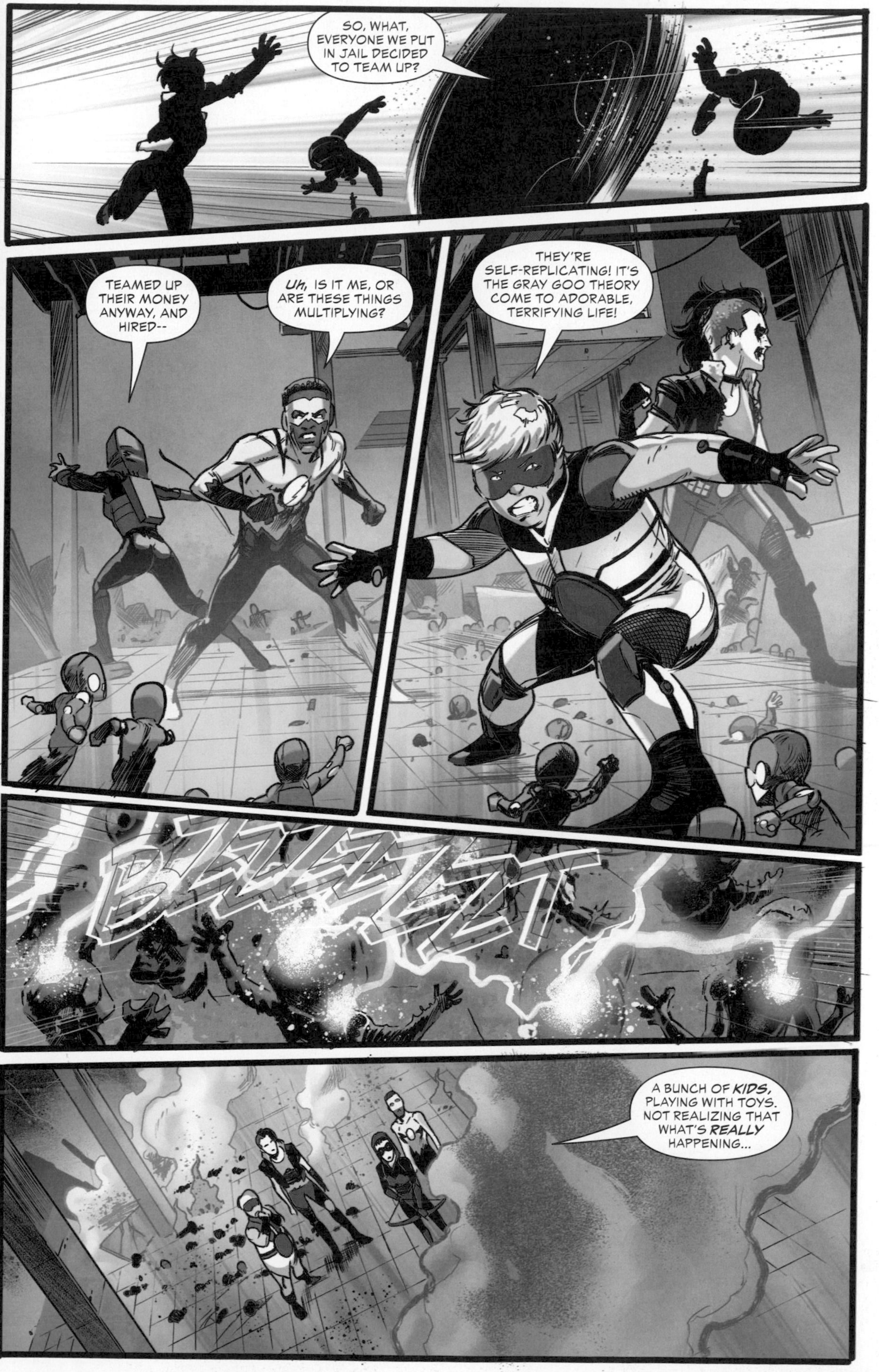
SO, WHAT, EVERYONE WE PUT IN JAIL DECIDED TO TEAM UP?
TEAMED UP THEIR MONEY ANYWAY, AND HIRED--
UH, IS IT ME, OR ARE THESE THINGS MULTIPLYING?
THEY'RE SELF-REPLICATING! IT'S THE GRAY GOO THEORY COME TO ADORABLE, TERRIFYING LIFE!
BZZZZZT
A BUNCH OF ***KIDS,*** PLAYING WITH TOYS. NOT REALIZING THAT WHAT'S ***REALLY*** HAPPENING...

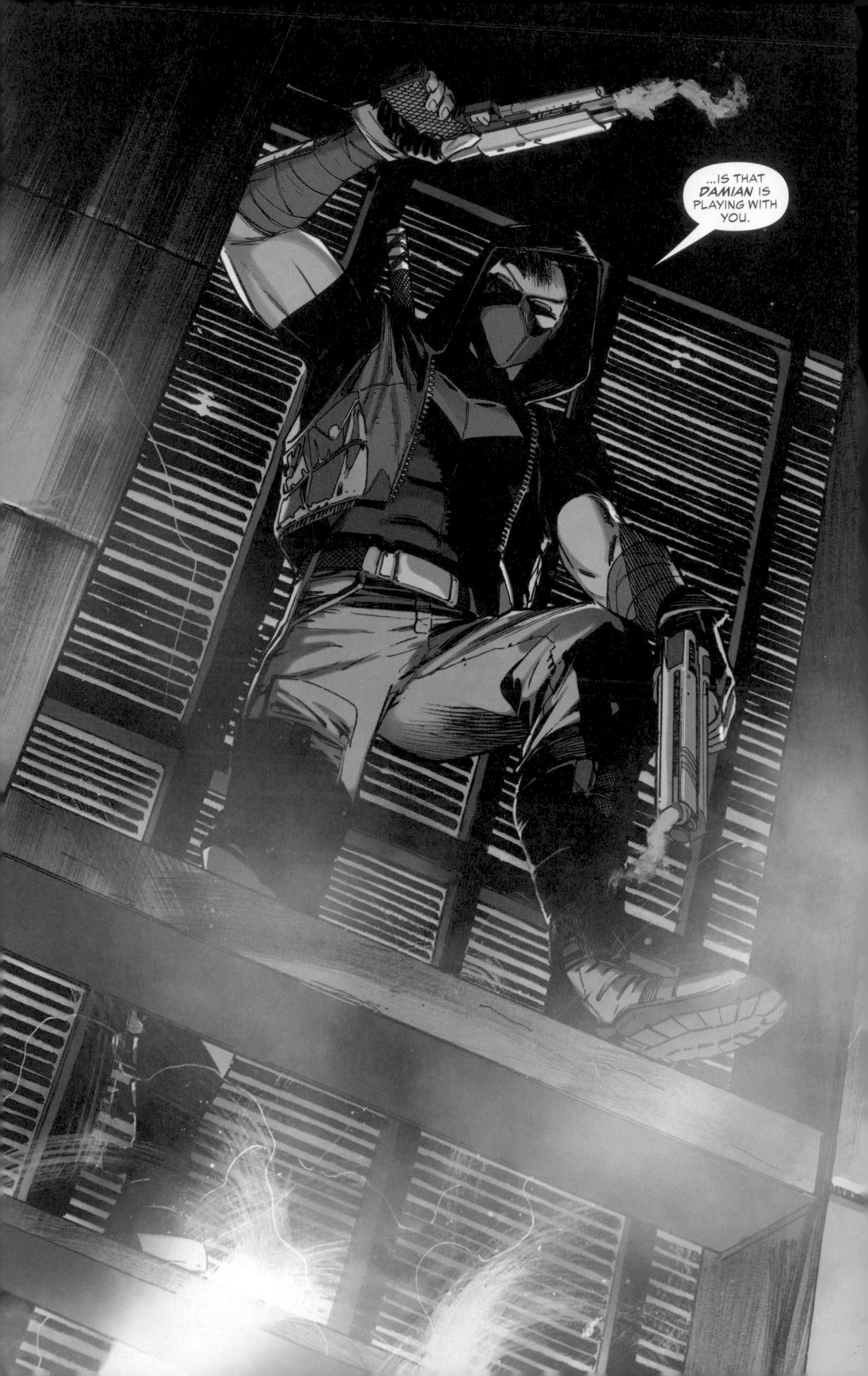
...IS THAT DAMIAN IS PLAYING WITH YOU.

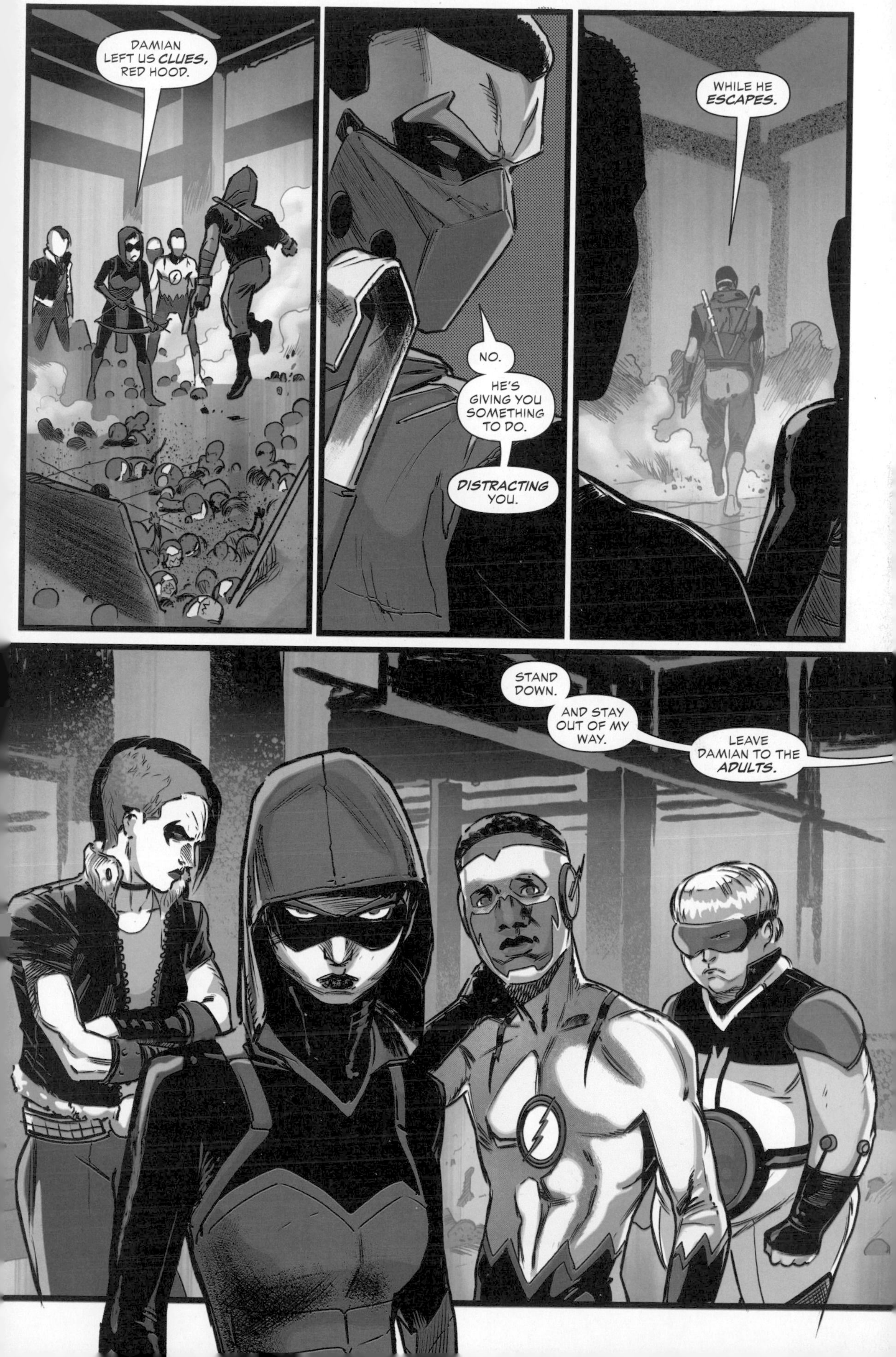
DAMIAN LEFT US CLUES, RED HOOD.
NO.
HE'S GIVING YOU SOMETHING TO DO.
DISTRACTING YOU.
WHILE HE ESCAPES.
STAND DOWN.
AND STAY OUT OF MY WAY.
LEAVE DAMIAN TO THE ADULTS.

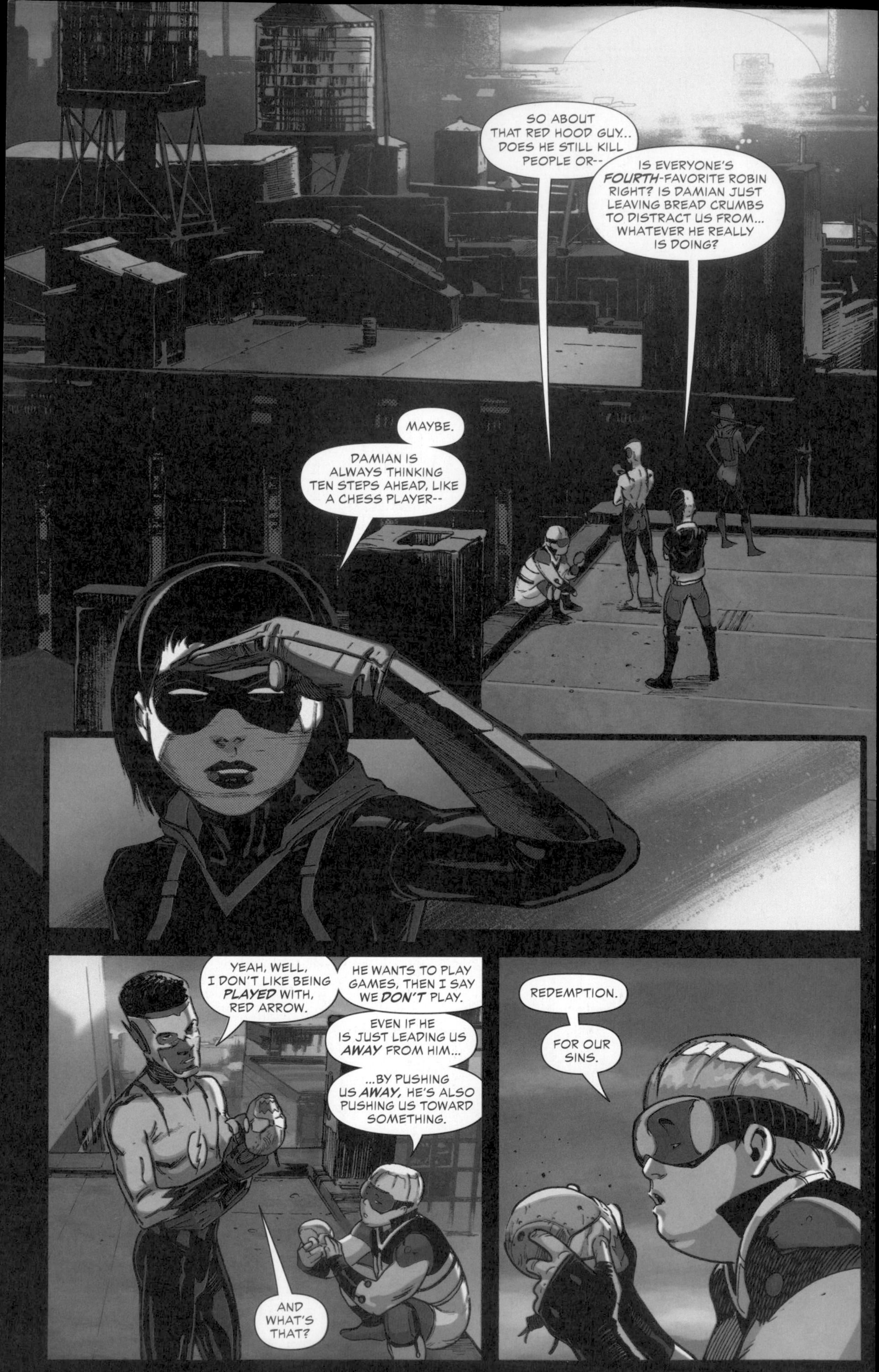
SO ABOUT THAT RED HOOD GUY... DOES HE STILL KILL PEOPLE OR--
IS EVERYONE'S FOURTH-FAVORITE ROBIN RIGHT? IS DAMIAN JUST LEAVING BREAD CRUMBS TO DISTRACT US FROM... WHATEVER HE REALLY IS DOING?
MAYBE.
DAMIAN IS ALWAYS THINKING TEN STEPS AHEAD, LIKE A CHESS PLAYER--
YEAH, WELL, I DON'T LIKE BEING PLAYED WITH, RED ARROW.
HE WANTS TO PLAY GAMES, THEN I SAY WE DON'T PLAY.
EVEN IF HE IS JUST LEADING US AWAY FROM HIM...
...BY PUSHING US AWAY, HE'S ALSO PUSHING US TOWARD SOMETHING.
AND WHAT'S THAT?
REDEMPTION.
FOR OUR SINS.

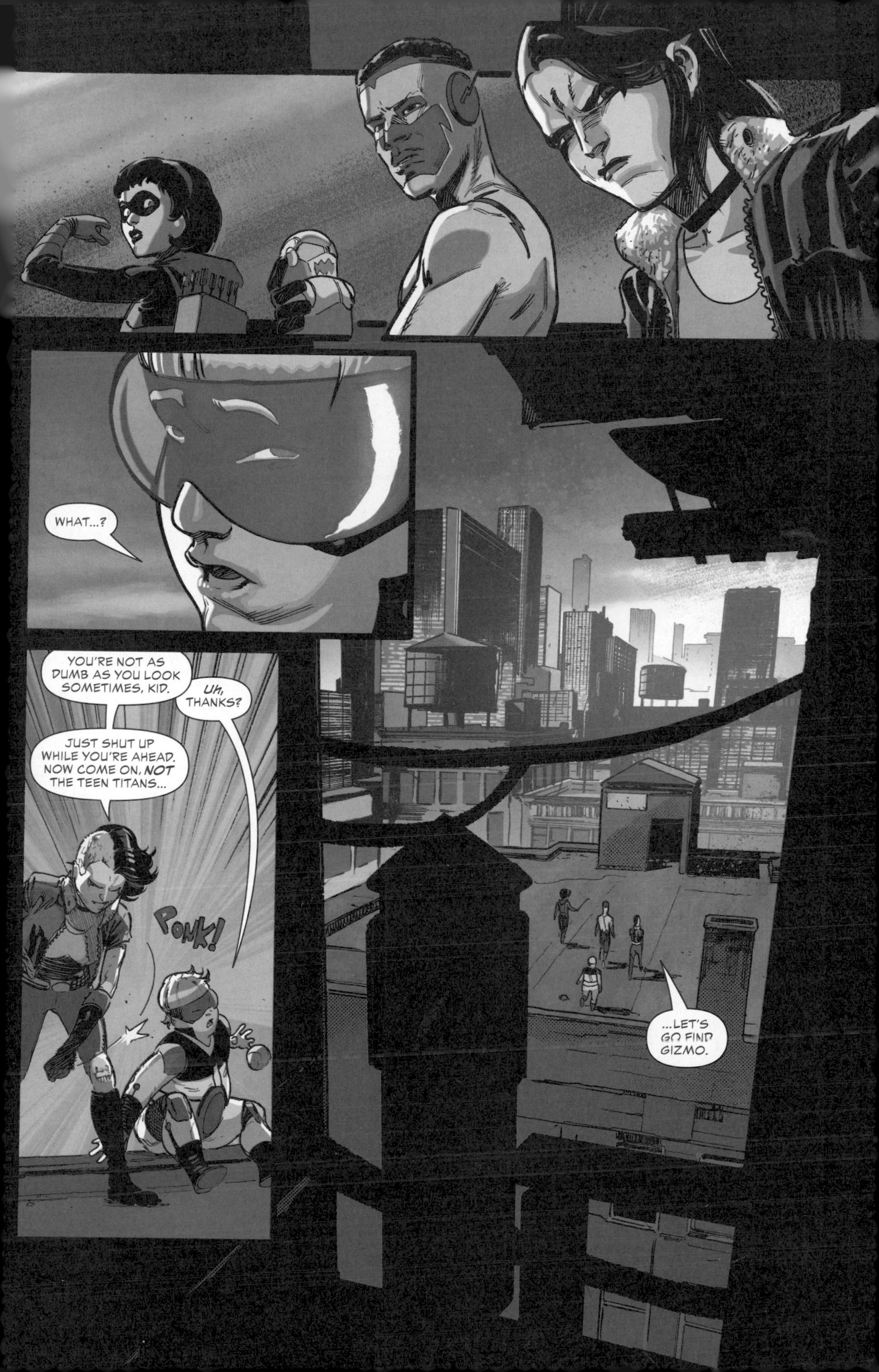
WHAT...?
YOU'RE NOT AS DUMB AS YOU LOOK SOMETIMES, KID.
UH, THANKS?
JUST SHUT UP WHILE YOU'RE AHEAD. NOW COME ON, NOT THE TEEN TITANS...
PONK!
...LET'S GO FIND GIZMO.

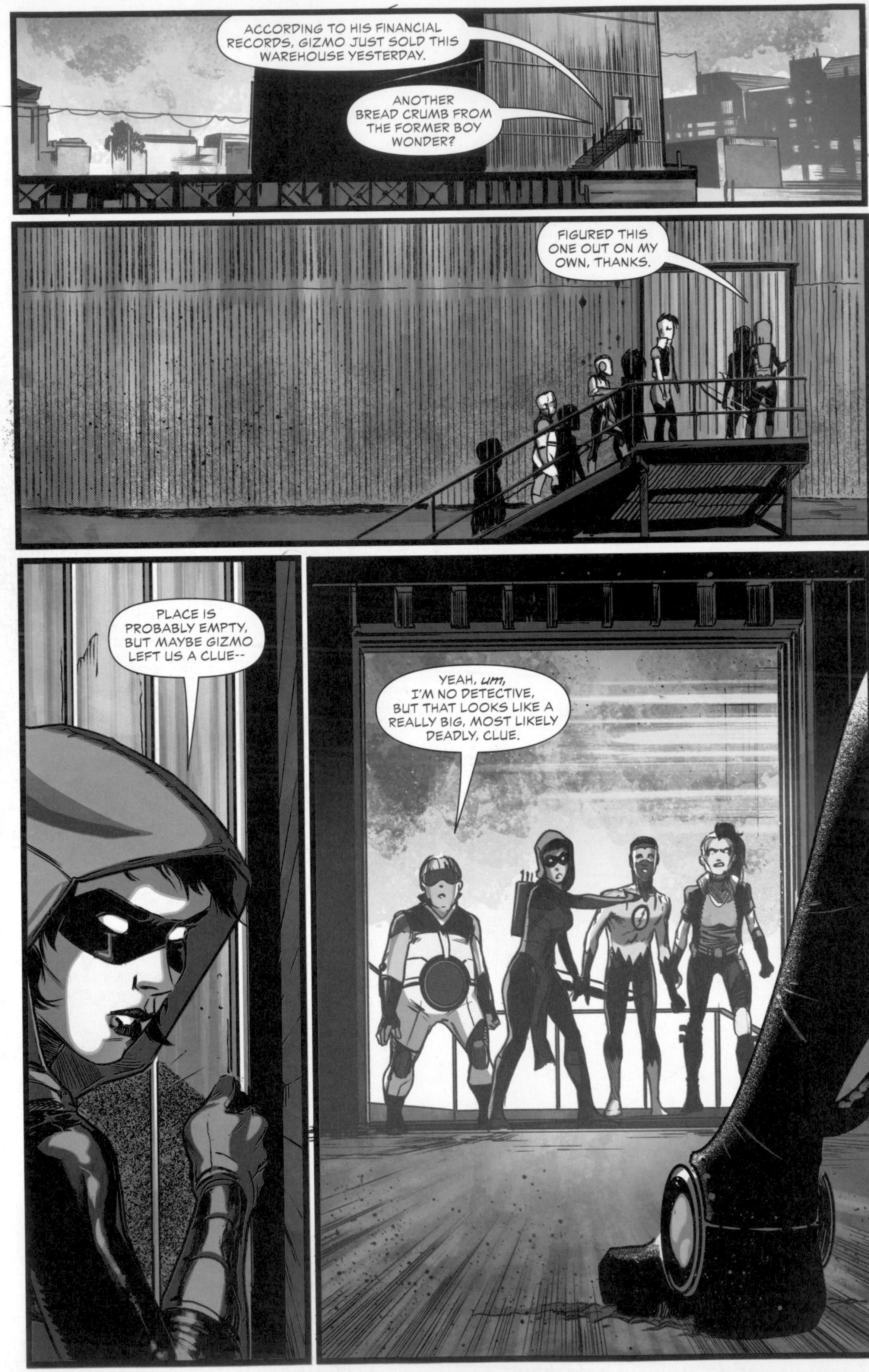
ACCORDING TO HIS FINANCIAL RECORDS, GIZMO JUST SOLD THIS WAREHOUSE YESTERDAY.
ANOTHER BREAD CRUMB FROM THE FORMER BOY WONDER?
FIGURED THIS ONE OUT ON MY OWN, THANKS.
PLACE IS PROBABLY EMPTY, BUT MAYBE GIZMO LEFT US A CLUE--
YEAH, *UM*, I'M NO DETECTIVE, BUT THAT LOOKS LIKE A REALLY BIG, MOST LIKELY DEADLY, CLUE.

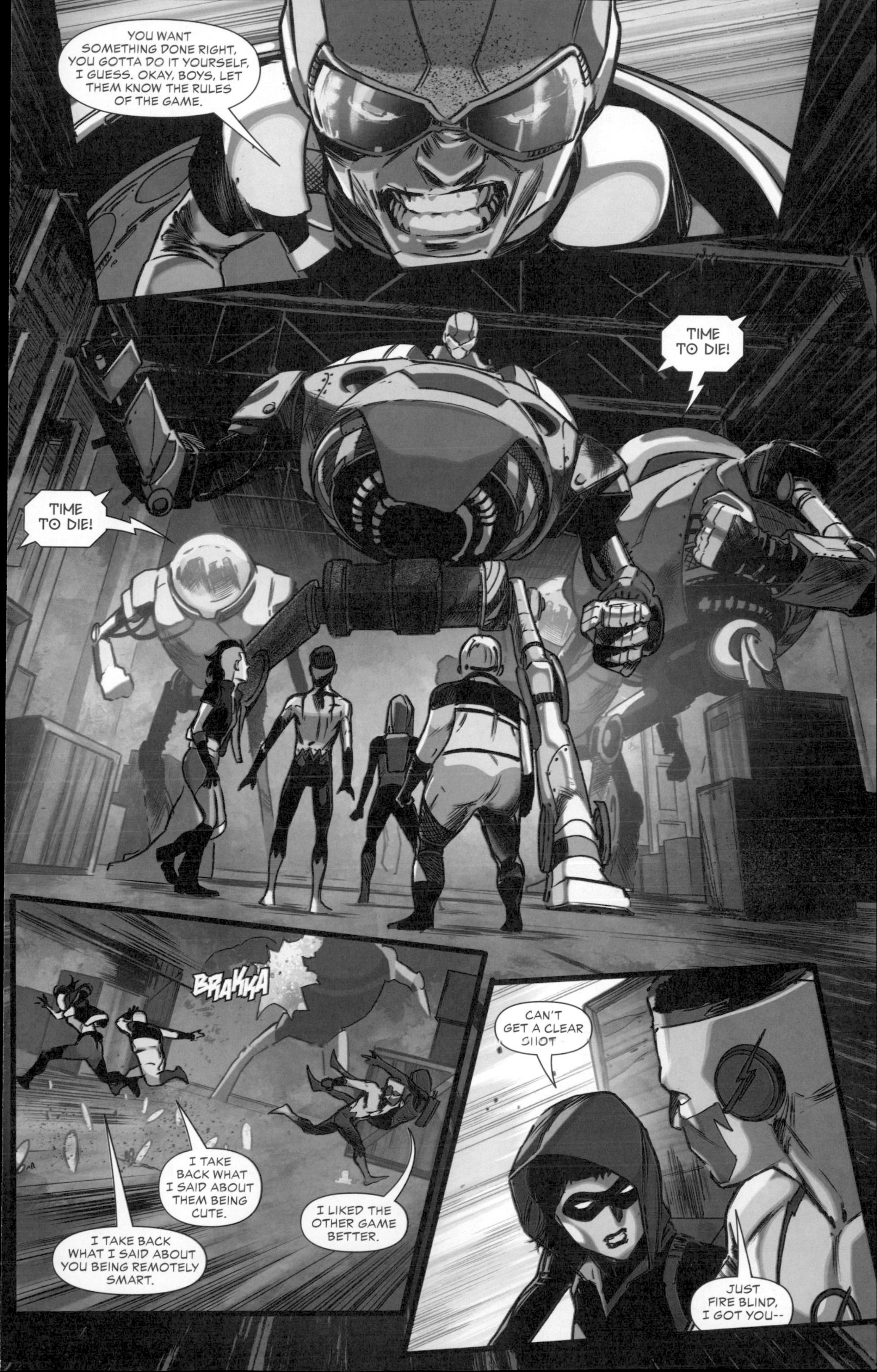
YOU WANT SOMETHING DONE RIGHT, YOU GOTTA DO IT YOURSELF, I GUESS. OKAY, BOYS, LET THEM KNOW THE RULES OF THE GAME.
TIME TO DIE!
TIME TO DIE!
BRAKKA
I TAKE BACK WHAT I SAID ABOUT THEM BEING CUTE.
I TAKE BACK WHAT I SAID ABOUT YOU BEING REMOTELY SMART.
I LIKED THE OTHER GAME BETTER.
CAN'T GET A CLEAR SHOT
JUST FIRE BLIND, I GOT YOU--

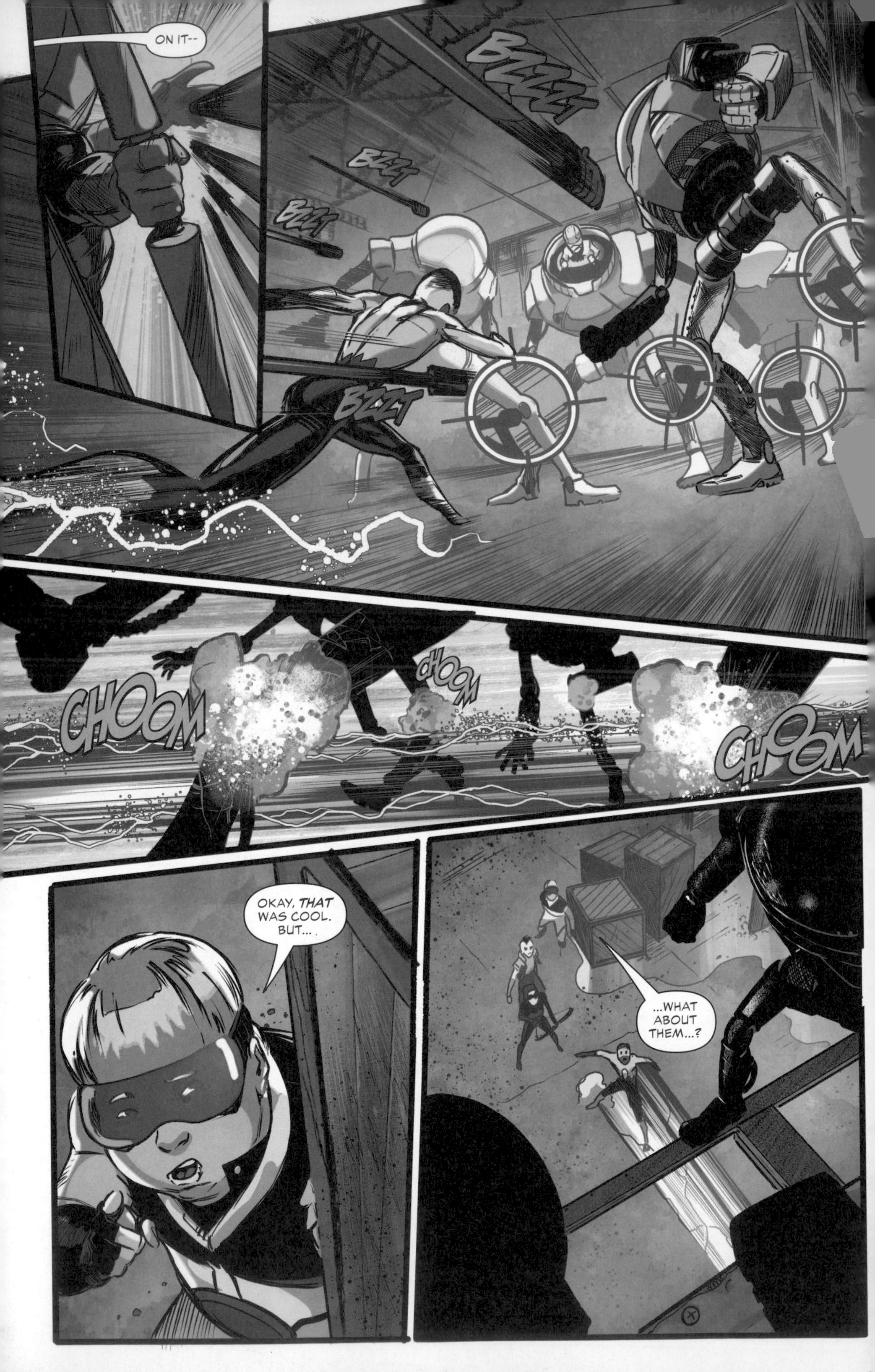
ON IT--
BZZZZT
BZZZT
BZZZT
BZZZT
CHOOM
CHOOM
CHOOM
OKAY, THAT WAS COOL. BUT...
...WHAT ABOUT THEM...?

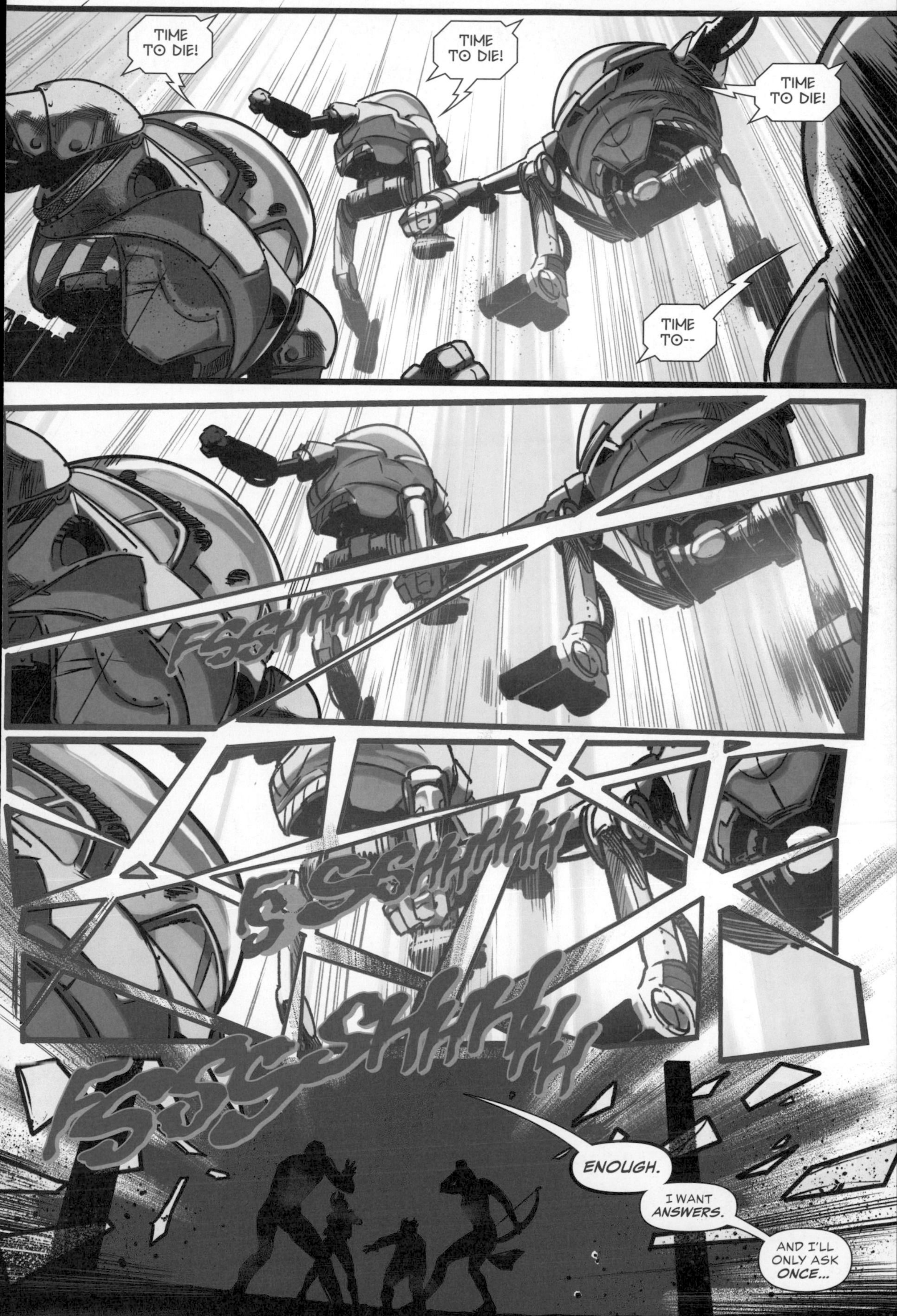

TIME TO DIE!
TIME TO DIE!
TIME TO DIE!
TIME TO--
FSSHHHH
FSSHHHHH
FSSSHHHH
ENOUGH.
I WANT ANSWERS.
AND I'LL ONLY ASK ONCE...

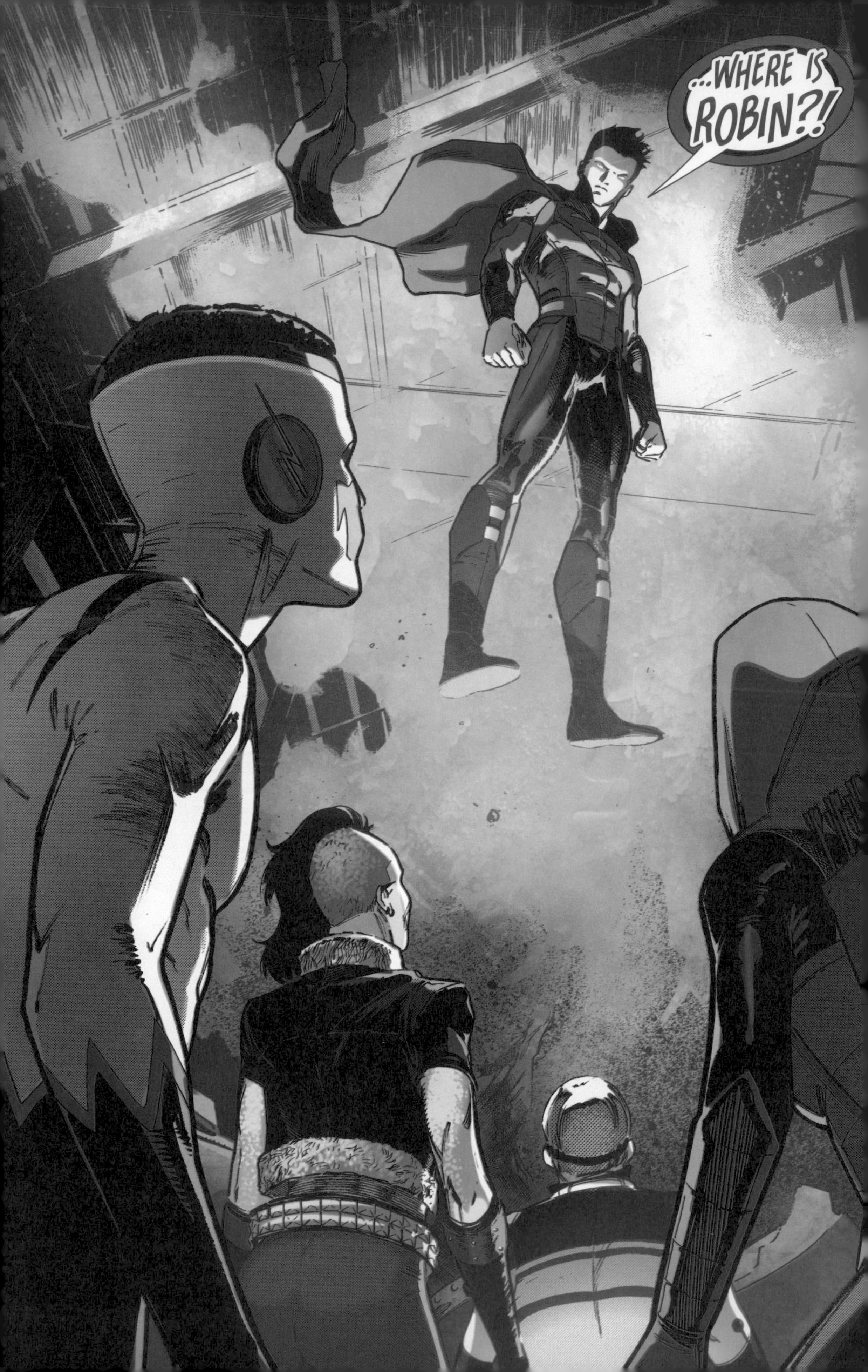
...WHERE IS ROBIN?!

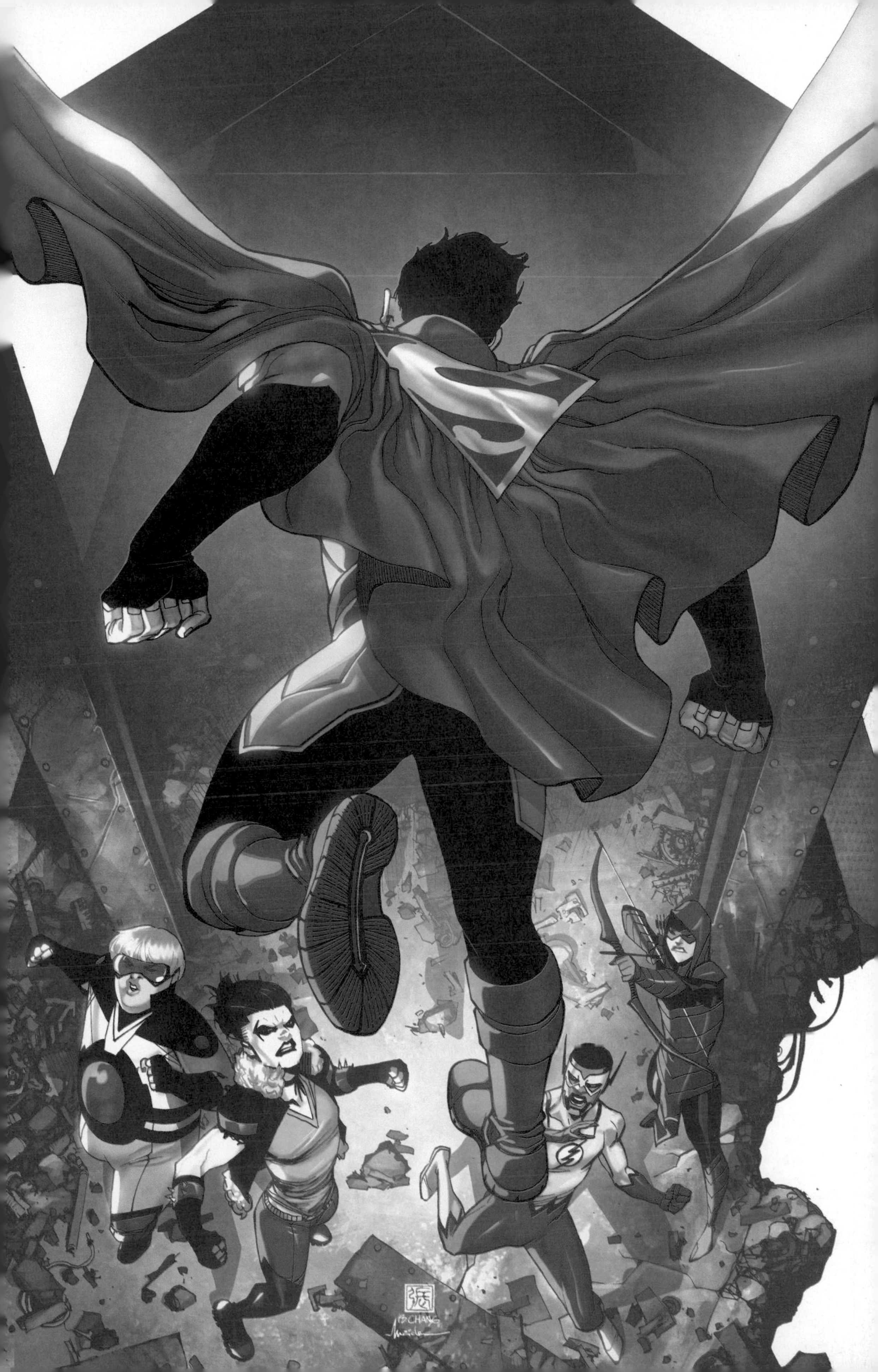
B CHANG

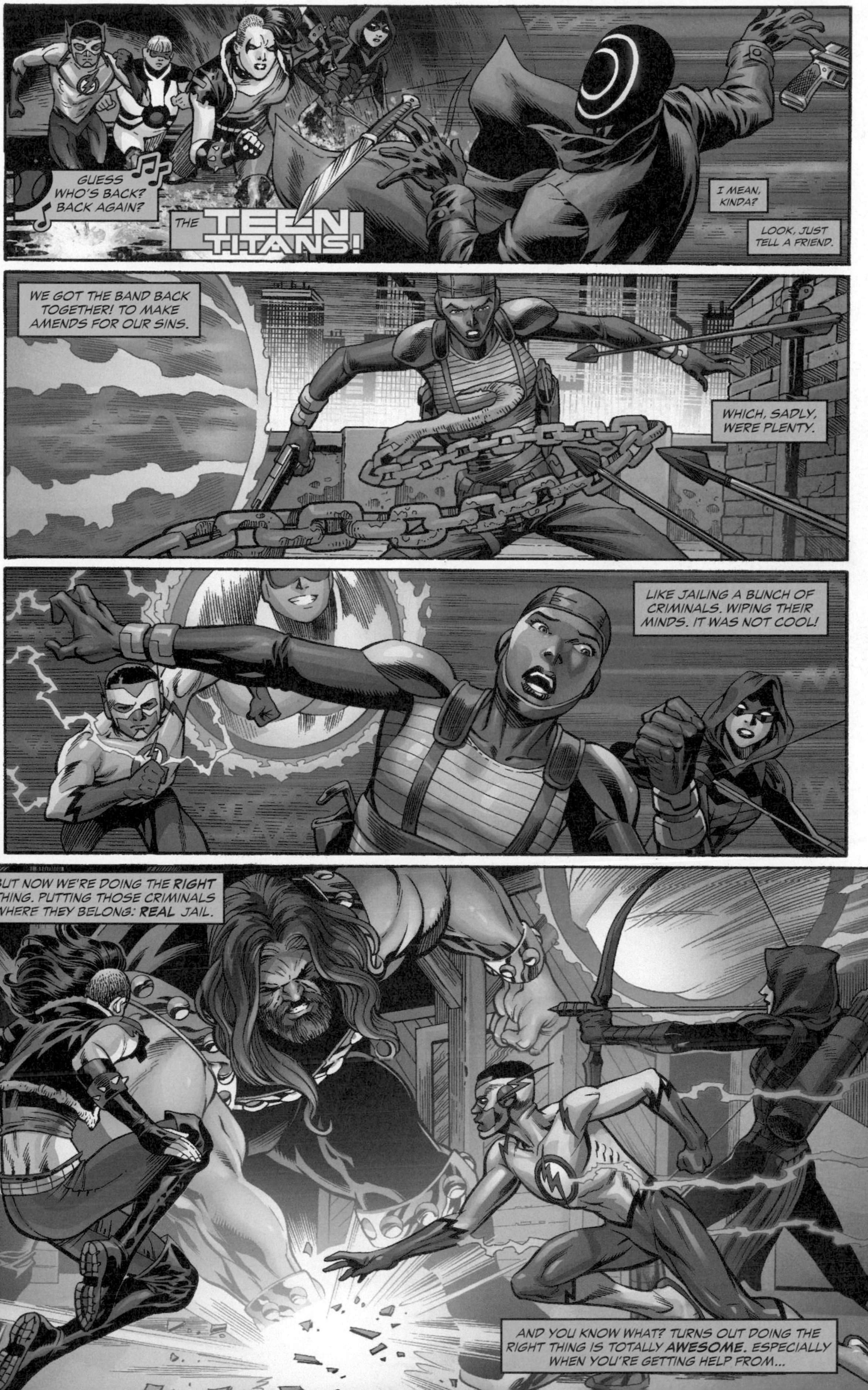

GUESS WHO'S BACK? BACK AGAIN?
THE TEEN TITANS!
I MEAN, KINDA?
LOOK, JUST TELL A FRIEND.
WE GOT THE BAND BACK TOGETHER! TO MAKE AMENDS FOR OUR SINS.
WHICH, SADLY, WERE PLENTY.
LIKE JAILING A BUNCH OF CRIMINALS. WIPING THEIR MINDS. IT WAS NOT COOL!
BUT NOW WE'RE DOING THE RIGHT THING. PUTTING THOSE CRIMINALS WHERE THEY BELONG: REAL JAIL.
AND YOU KNOW WHAT? TURNS OUT DOING THE RIGHT THING IS TOTALLY AWESOME. ESPECIALLY WHEN YOU'RE GETTING HELP FROM...

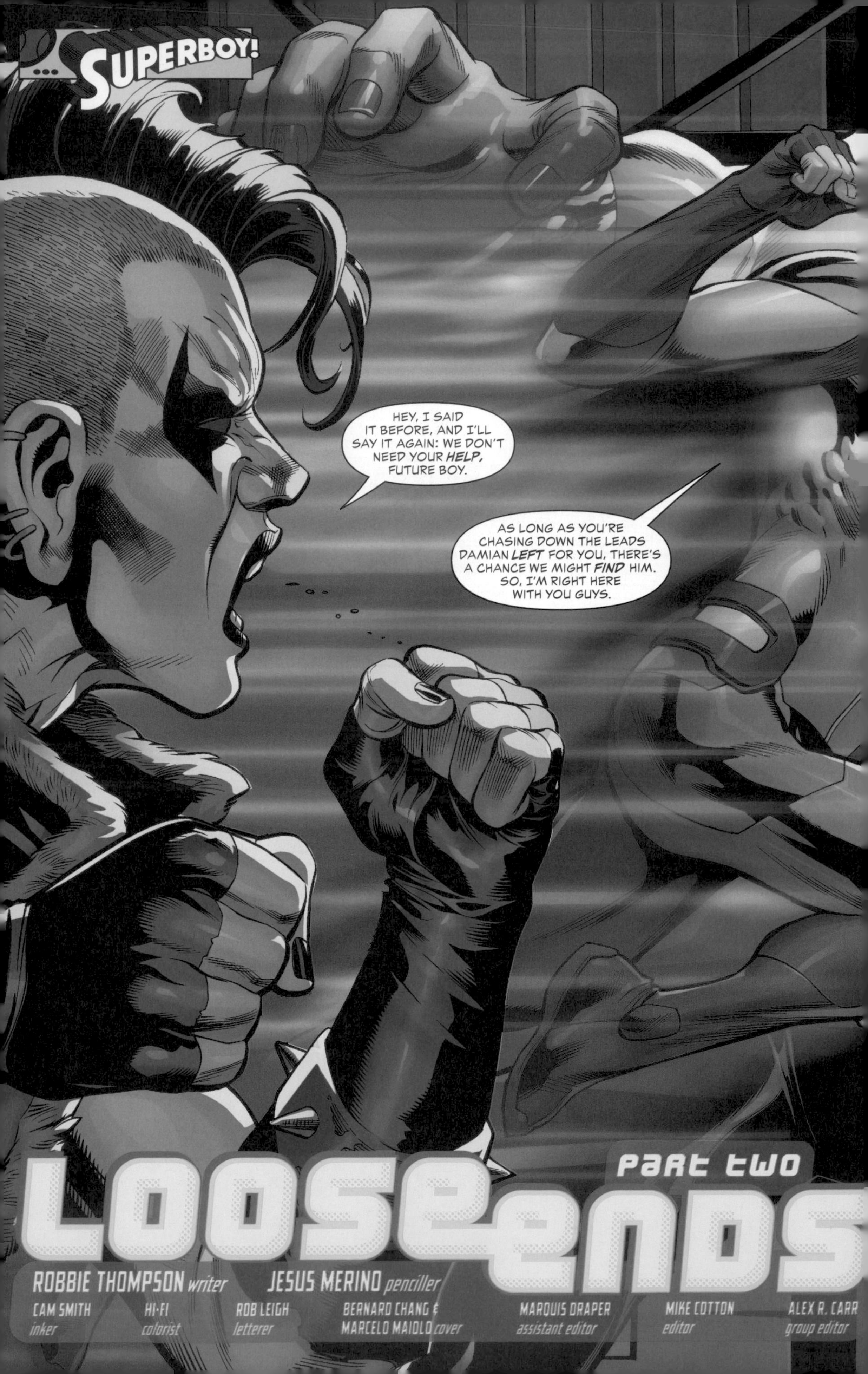

...SUPERBOY!
HEY, I SAID IT BEFORE, AND I'LL SAY IT AGAIN: WE DON'T NEED YOUR HELP, FUTURE BOY.
AS LONG AS YOU'RE CHASING DOWN THE LEADS DAMIAN LEFT FOR YOU, THERE'S A CHANCE WE MIGHT FIND HIM. SO, I'M RIGHT HERE WITH YOU GUYS.
PART TWO
LOOSE ENDS
ROBBIE THOMPSON writer JESUS MERINO penciller
CAM SMITH inker HI-FI colorist ROB LEIGH letterer BERNARD CHANG & MARCELO MAIOLO cover MARQUIS DRAPER assistant editor MIKE COTTON editor ALEX R. CARR group editor

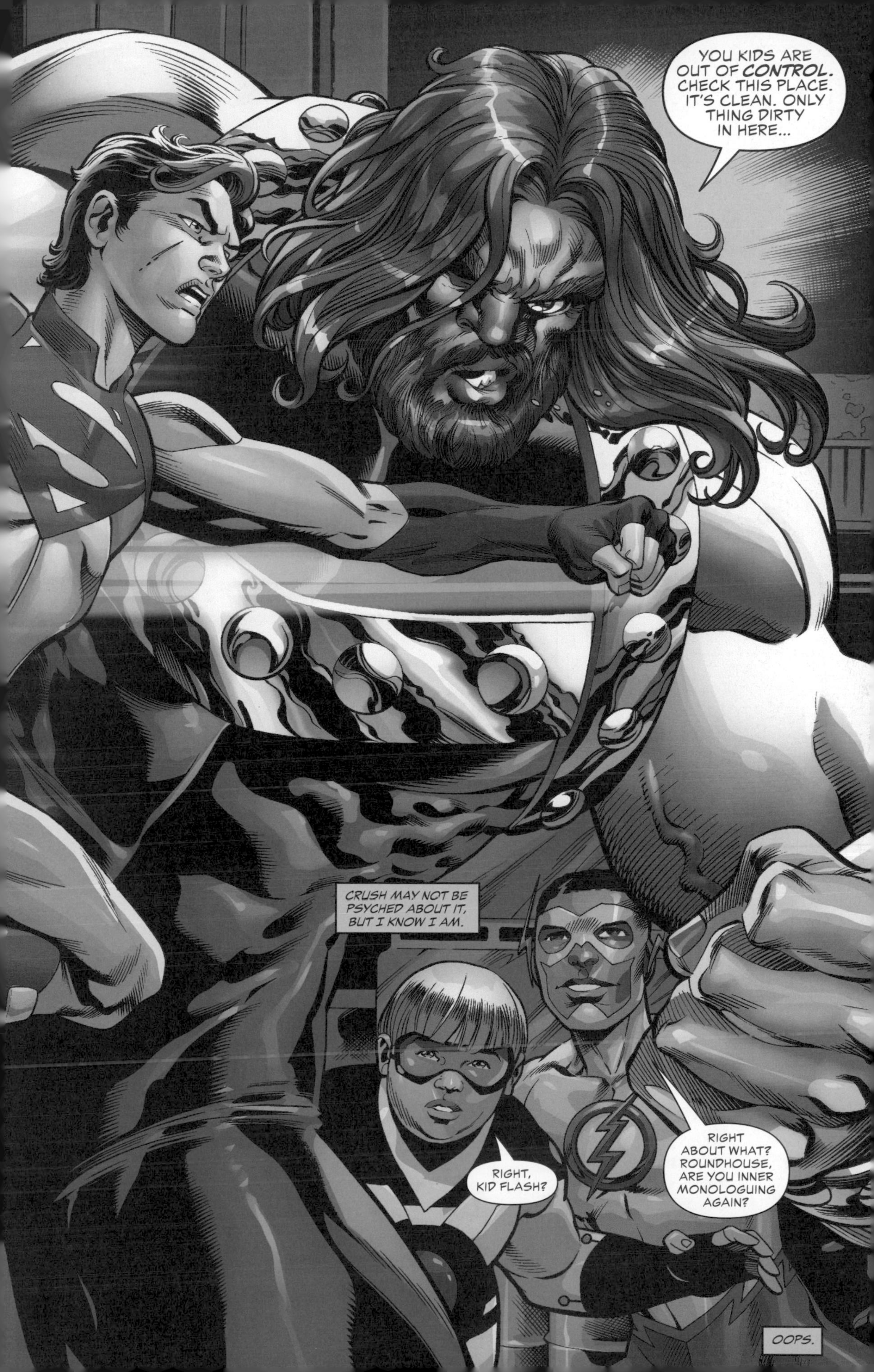
YOU KIDS ARE OUT OF **CONTROL**. CHECK THIS PLACE. IT'S CLEAN. ONLY THING DIRTY IN HERE...
CRUSH MAY NOT BE PSYCHED ABOUT IT, BUT I KNOW I AM.
RIGHT, KID FLASH?
RIGHT ABOUT WHAT? ROUNDHOUSE, ARE YOU INNER MONOLOGUING AGAIN?
OOPS.

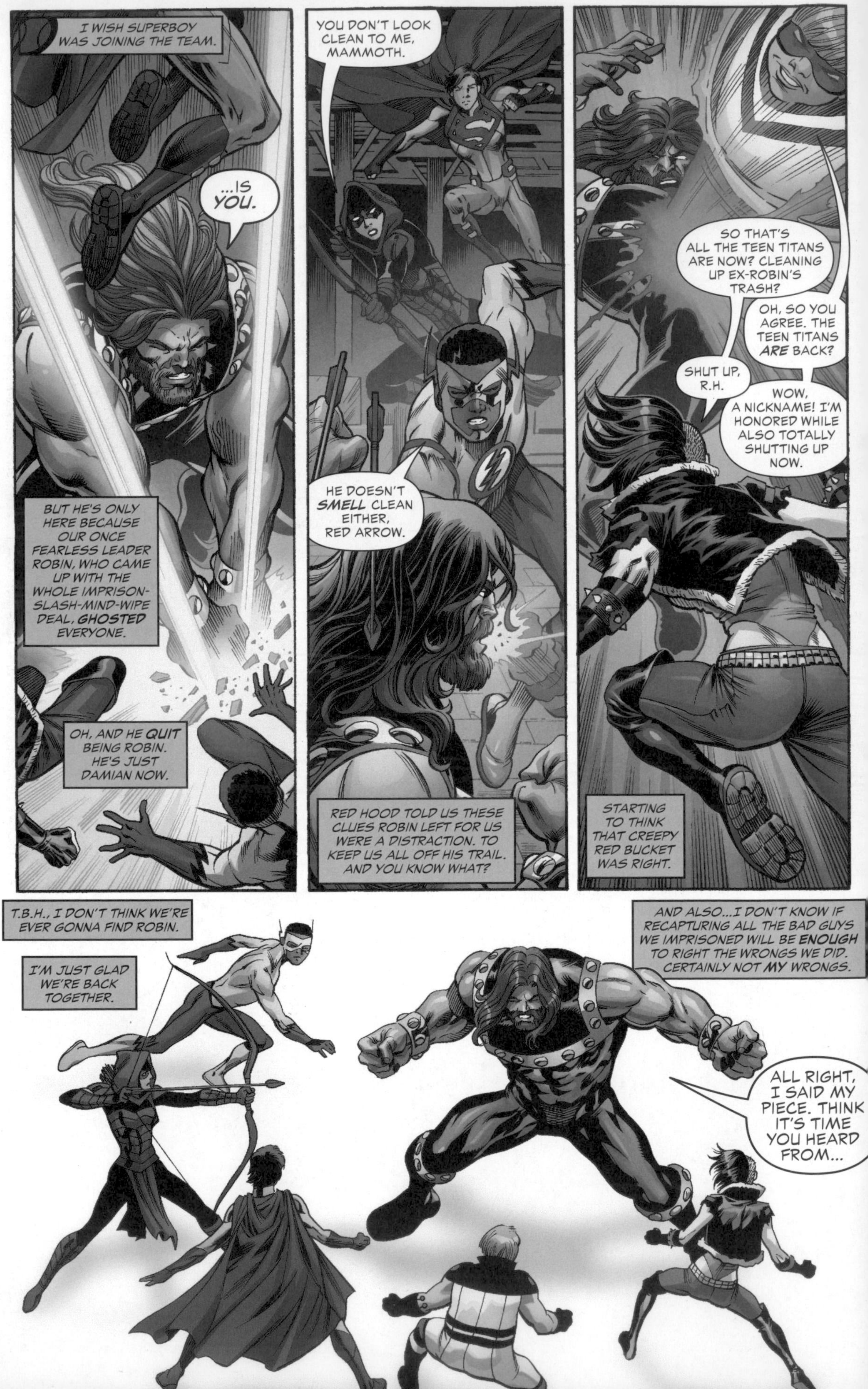
I WISH SUPERBOY WAS JOINING THE TEAM.
...IS YOU.
BUT HE'S ONLY HERE BECAUSE OUR ONCE FEARLESS LEADER ROBIN, WHO CAME UP WITH THE WHOLE IMPRISON-SLASH-MIND-WIPE DEAL, GHOSTED EVERYONE.
OH, AND HE QUIT BEING ROBIN. HE'S JUST DAMIAN NOW.
YOU DON'T LOOK CLEAN TO ME, MAMMOTH.
HE DOESN'T SMELL CLEAN EITHER, RED ARROW.
RED HOOD TOLD US THESE CLUES ROBIN LEFT FOR US WERE A DISTRACTION. TO KEEP US ALL OFF HIS TRAIL. AND YOU KNOW WHAT?
SO THAT'S ALL THE TEEN TITANS ARE NOW? CLEANING UP EX-ROBIN'S TRASH?
OH, SO YOU AGREE. THE TEEN TITANS ARE BACK?
SHUT UP, R.H.
WOW, A NICKNAME! I'M HONORED WHILE ALSO TOTALLY SHUTTING UP NOW.
STARTING TO THINK THAT CREEPY RED BUCKET WAS RIGHT.
T.B.H., I DON'T THINK WE'RE EVER GONNA FIND ROBIN.
I'M JUST GLAD WE'RE BACK TOGETHER.
AND ALSO...I DON'T KNOW IF RECAPTURING ALL THE BAD GUYS WE IMPRISONED WILL BE ENOUGH TO RIGHT THE WRONGS WE DID. CERTAINLY NOT MY WRONGS.
ALL RIGHT, I SAID MY PIECE. THINK IT'S TIME YOU HEARD FROM...

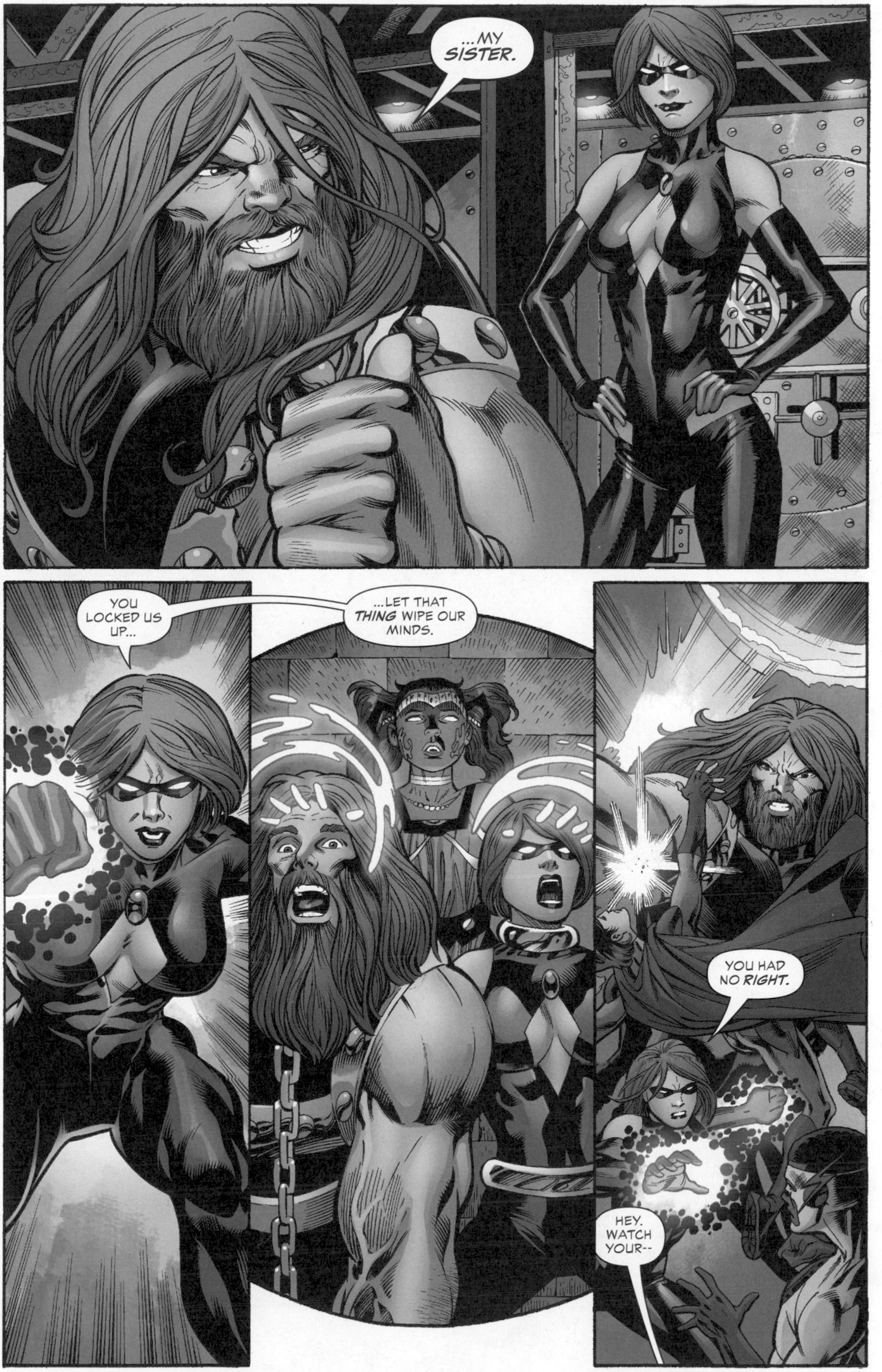
...MY *SISTER.*
YOU LOCKED US UP...
...LET THAT *THING* WIPE OUR MINDS.
YOU HAD NO *RIGHT.*
HEY. WATCH YOUR--

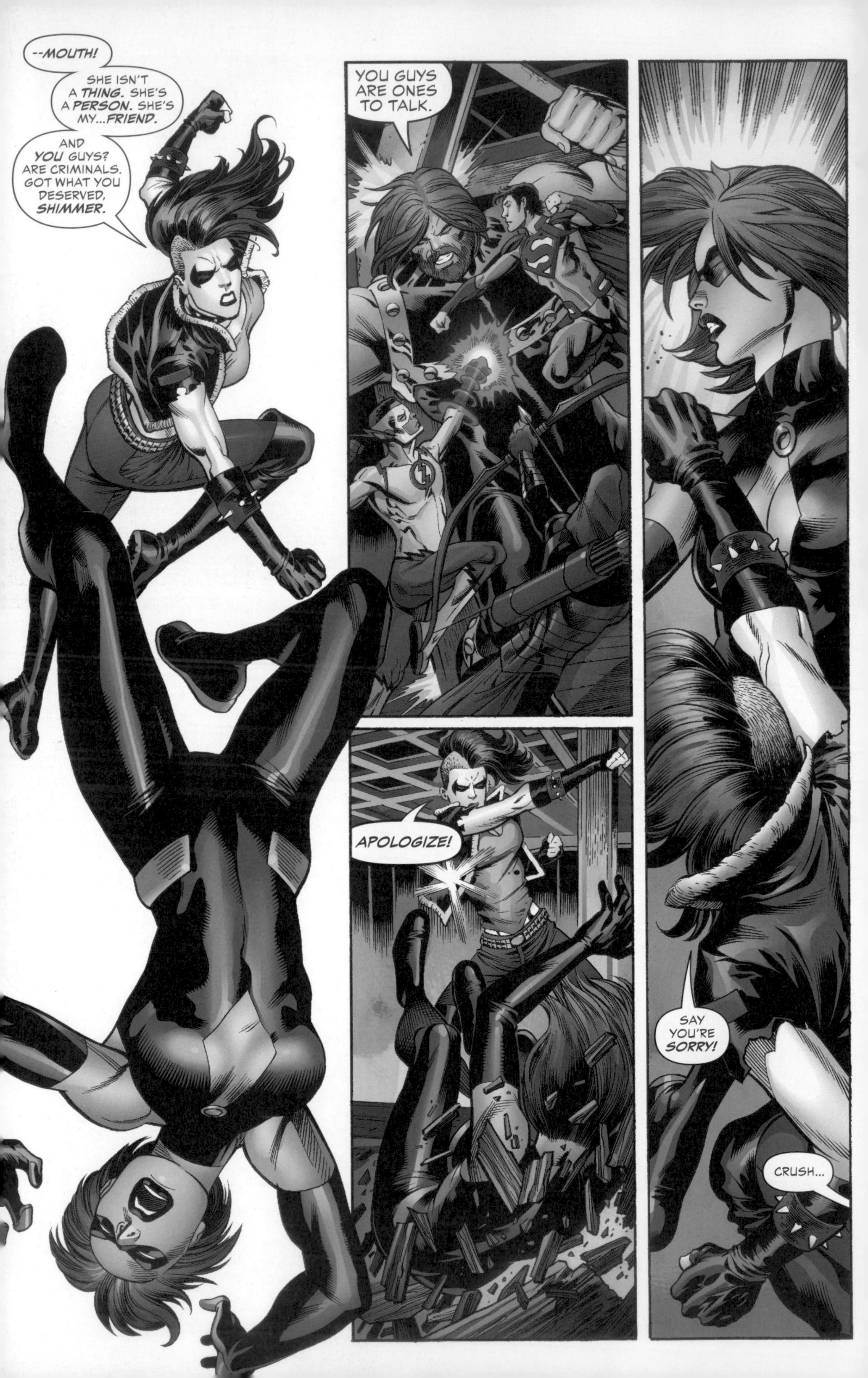
--MOUTH!
SHE ISN'T A THING. SHE'S A PERSON. SHE'S MY...FRIEND.
AND YOU GUYS? ARE CRIMINALS. GOT WHAT YOU DESERVED, SHIMMER.
YOU GUYS ARE ONES TO TALK.
APOLOGIZE!
SAY YOU'RE SORRY!
CRUSH...

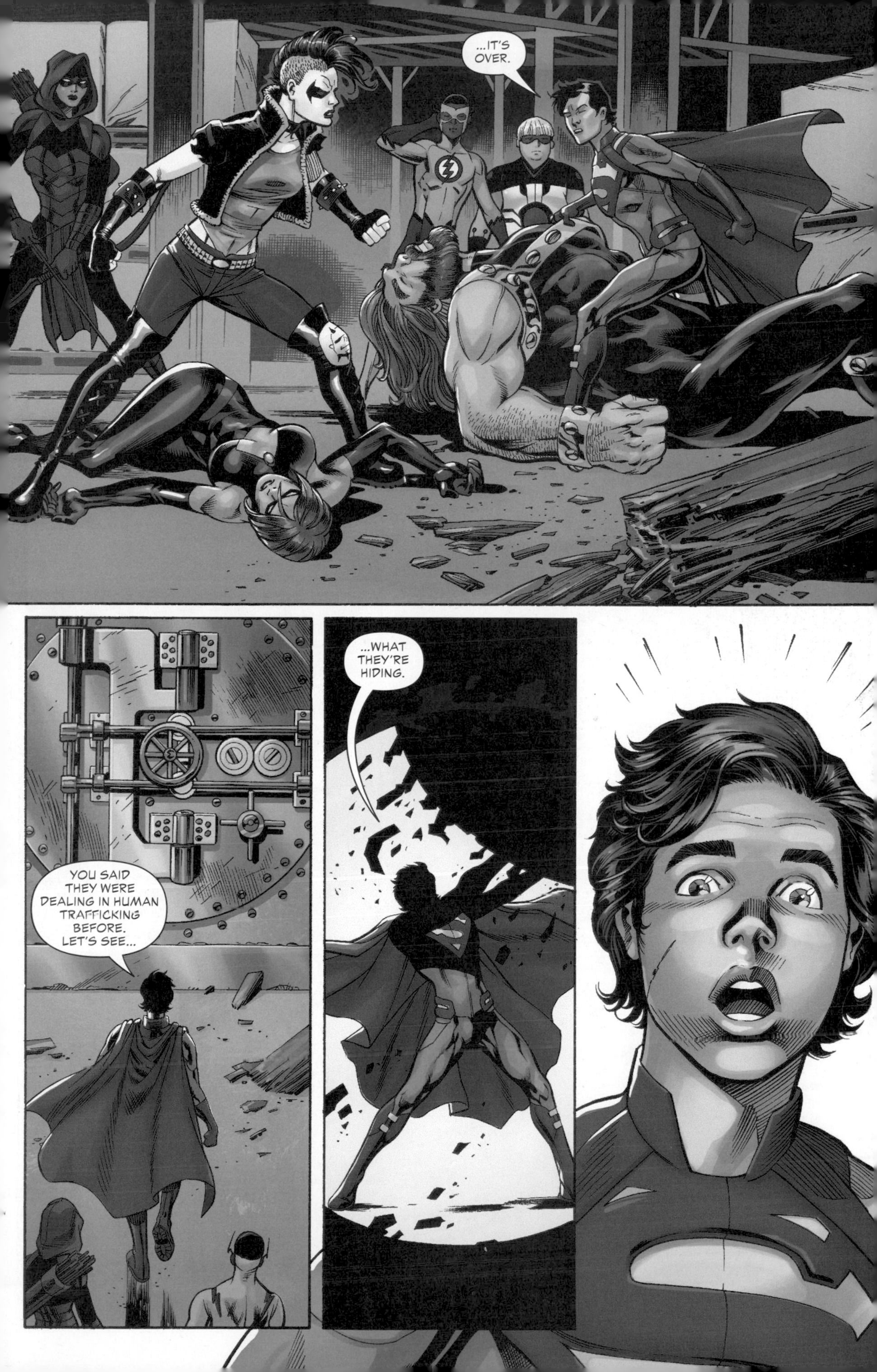
...IT'S OVER.
YOU SAID THEY WERE DEALING IN HUMAN TRAFFICKING BEFORE. LET'S SEE...
...WHAT THEY'RE HIDING.

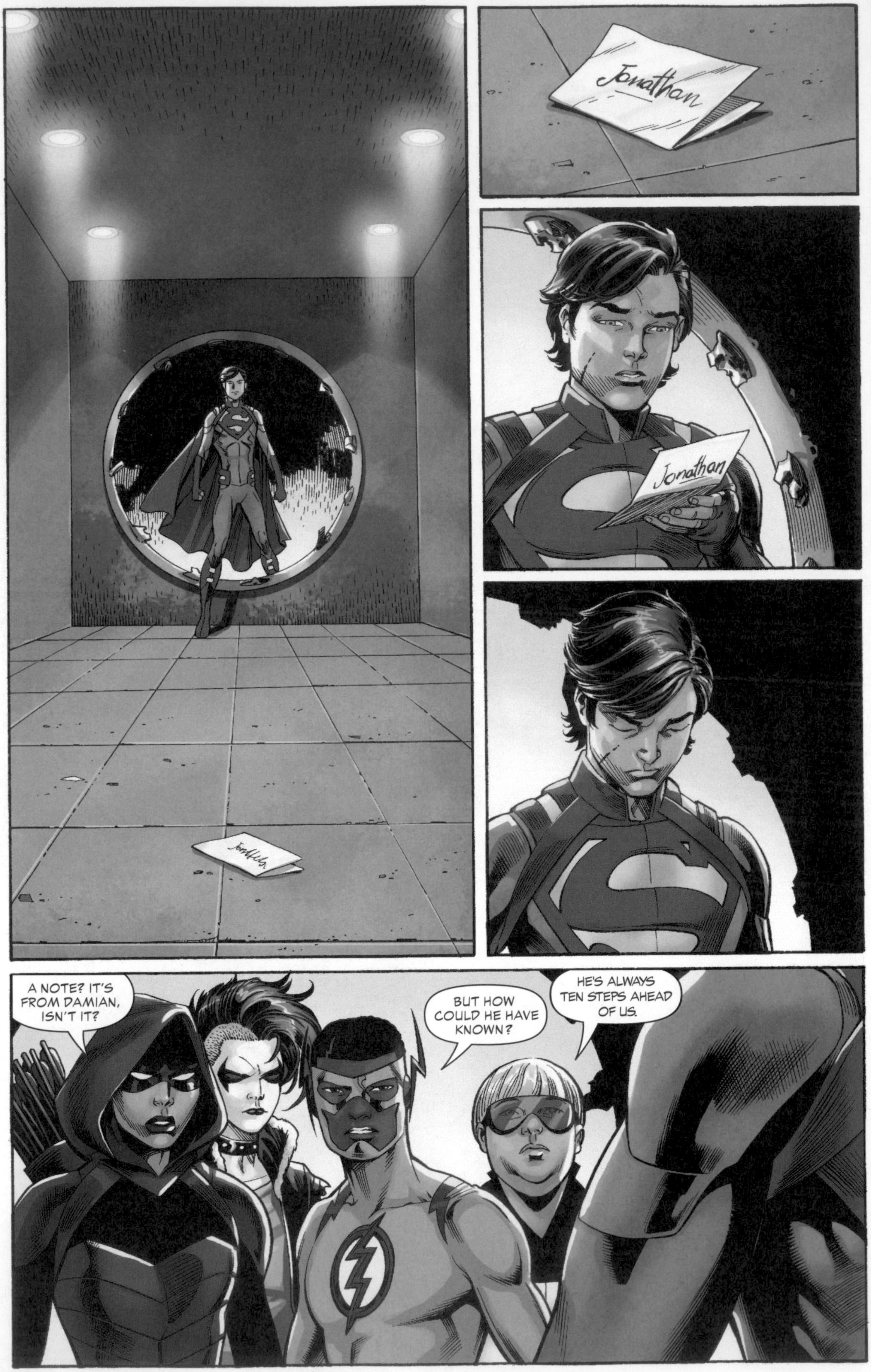
Jonathan
Jonathan
A NOTE? IT'S FROM DAMIAN, ISN'T IT?
BUT HOW COULD HE HAVE KNOWN?
HE'S ALWAYS TEN STEPS AHEAD OF US.

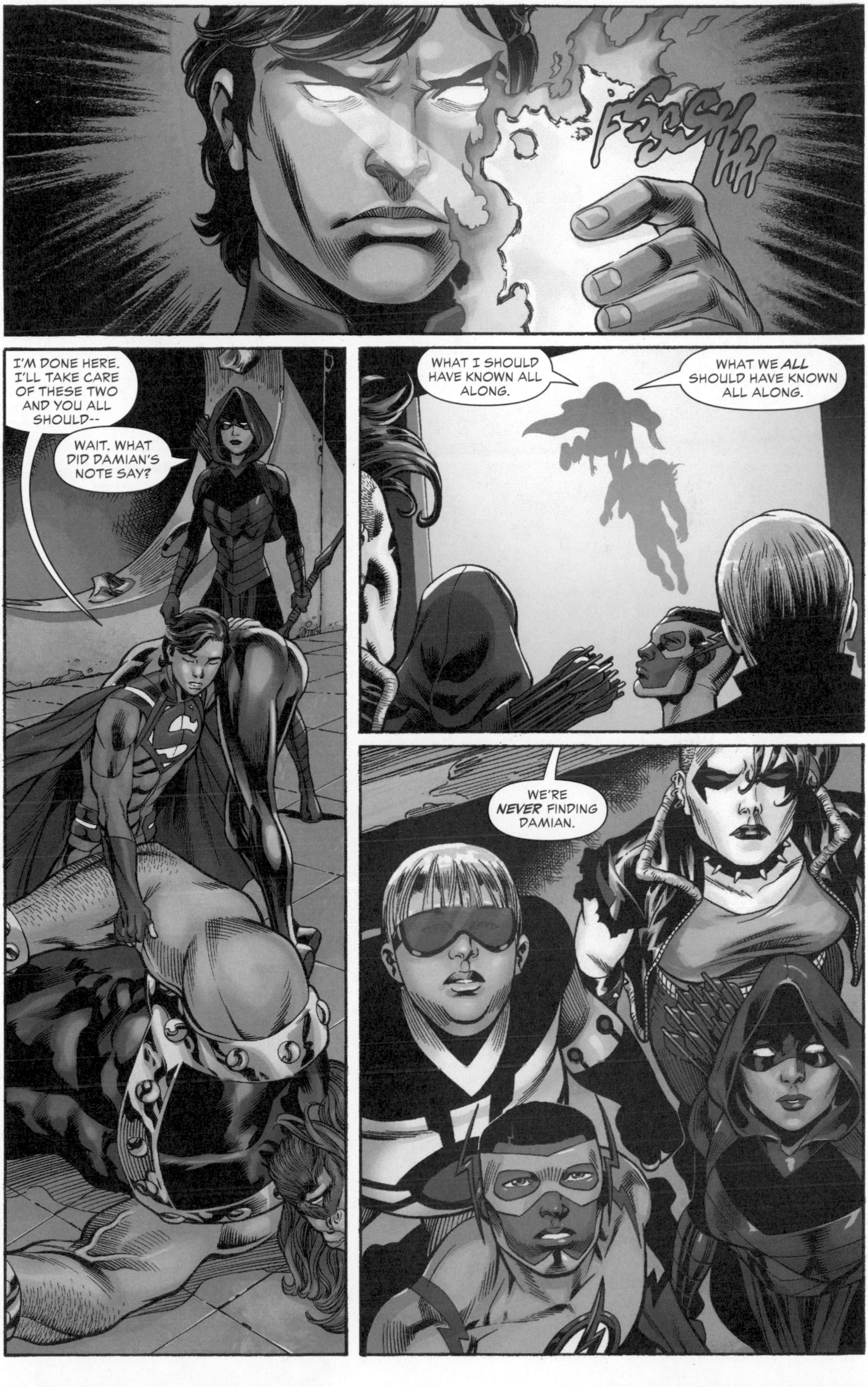
FSSSHH
I'M DONE HERE. I'LL TAKE CARE OF THESE TWO AND YOU ALL SHOULD--
WAIT. WHAT DID DAMIAN'S NOTE SAY?
WHAT I SHOULD HAVE KNOWN ALL ALONG.
WHAT WE *ALL* SHOULD HAVE KNOWN ALL ALONG.
WE'RE ***NEVER*** FINDING DAMIAN.

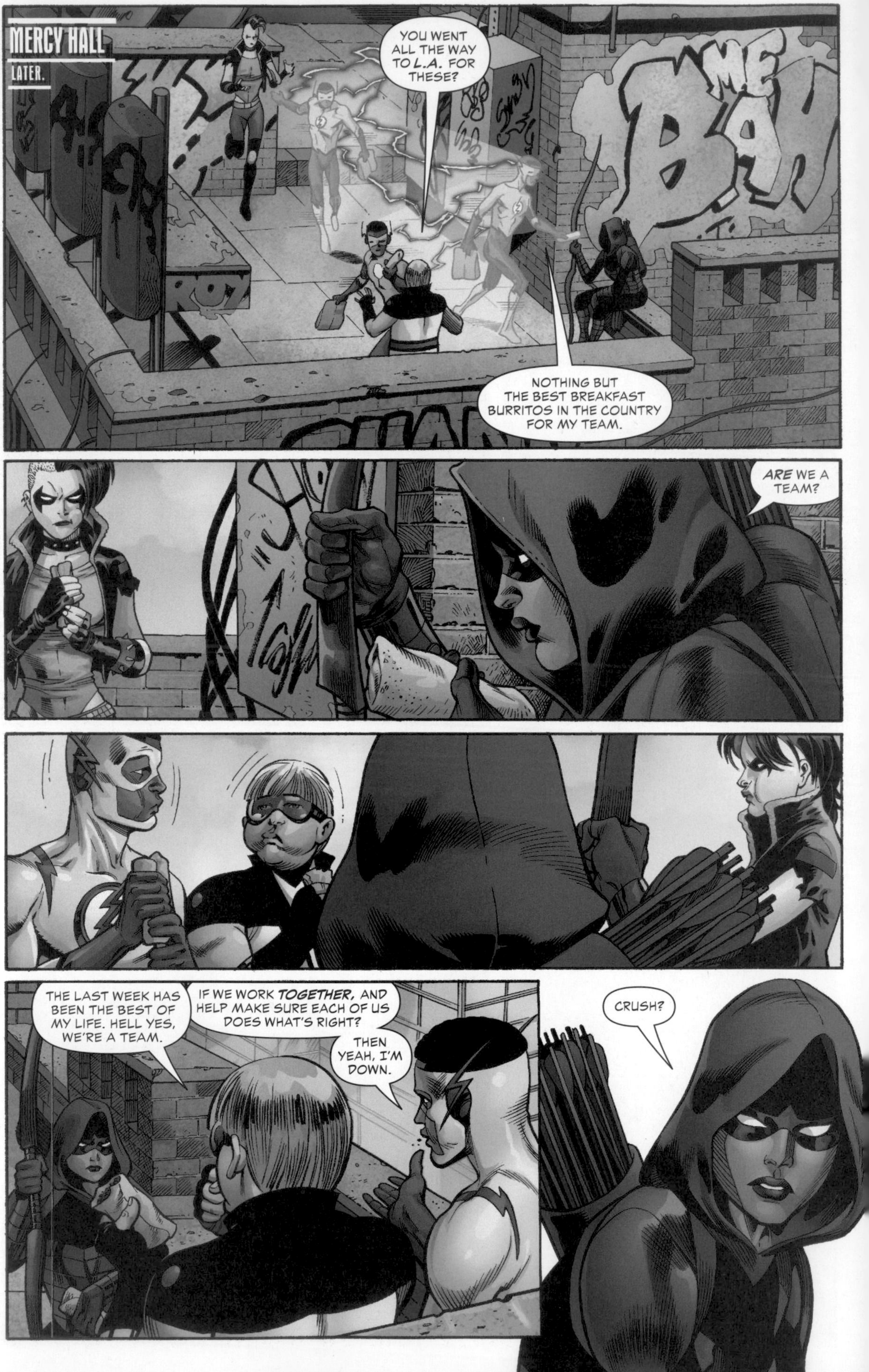
MERCY HALL
LATER.
YOU WENT ALL THE WAY TO L.A. FOR THESE?
NOTHING BUT THE BEST BREAKFAST BURRITOS IN THE COUNTRY FOR MY TEAM.
ARE WE A TEAM?
THE LAST WEEK HAS BEEN THE BEST OF MY LIFE. HELL YES, WE'RE A TEAM.
IF WE WORK TOGETHER, AND HELP MAKE SURE EACH OF US DOES WHAT'S RIGHT?
THEN YEAH, I'M DOWN.
CRUSH?

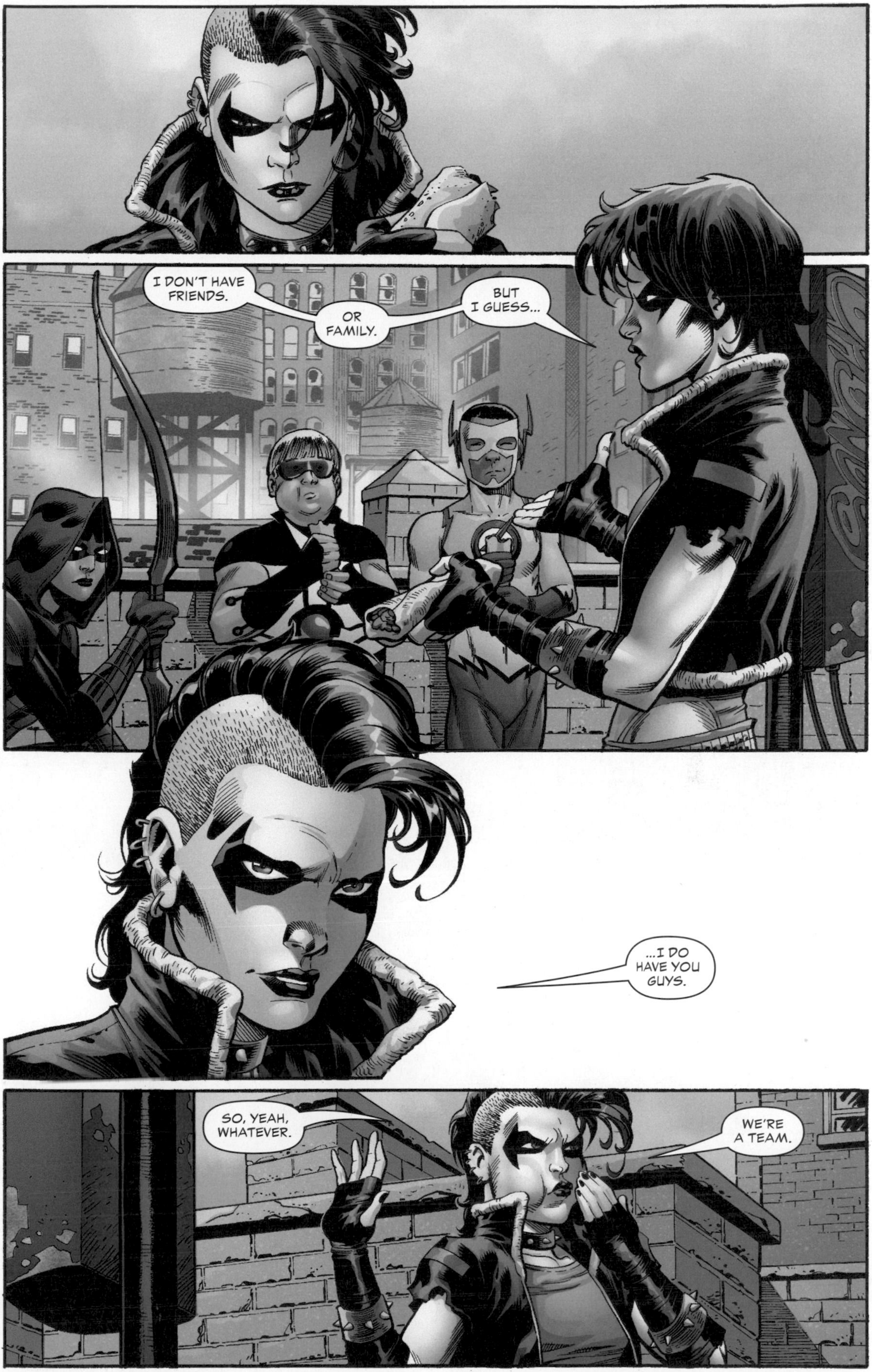
I DON'T HAVE FRIENDS.
OR FAMILY.
BUT I GUESS...
...I DO HAVE YOU GUYS.
SO, YEAH, WHATEVER.
WE'RE A TEAM.

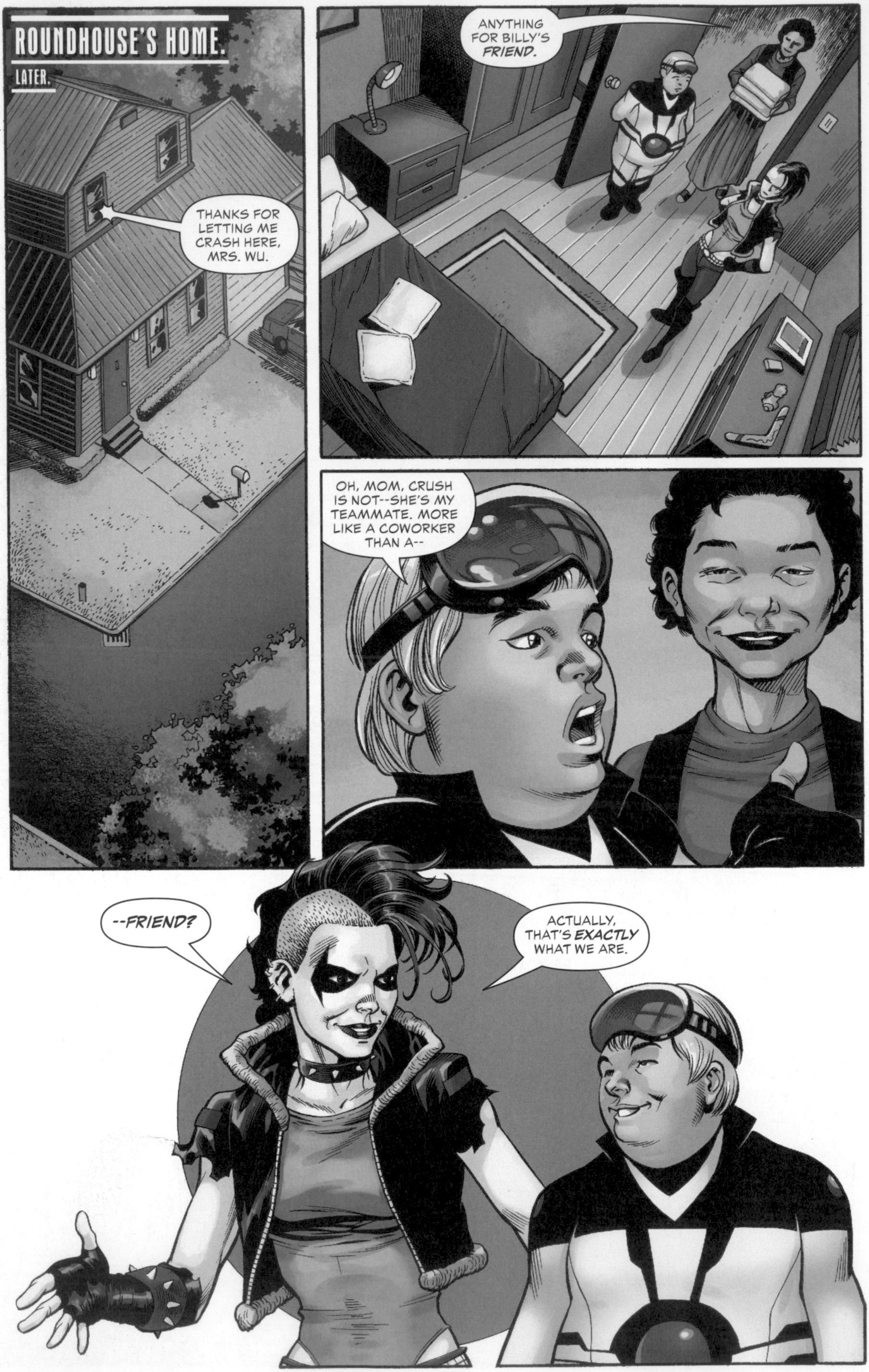
ROUNDHOUSE'S HOME.
LATER.
THANKS FOR LETTING ME CRASH HERE, MRS. WU.
ANYTHING FOR BILLY'S FRIEND.
OH, MOM, CRUSH IS NOT--SHE'S MY TEAMMATE. MORE LIKE A COWORKER THAN A--
--FRIEND?
ACTUALLY, THAT'S EXACTLY WHAT WE ARE.

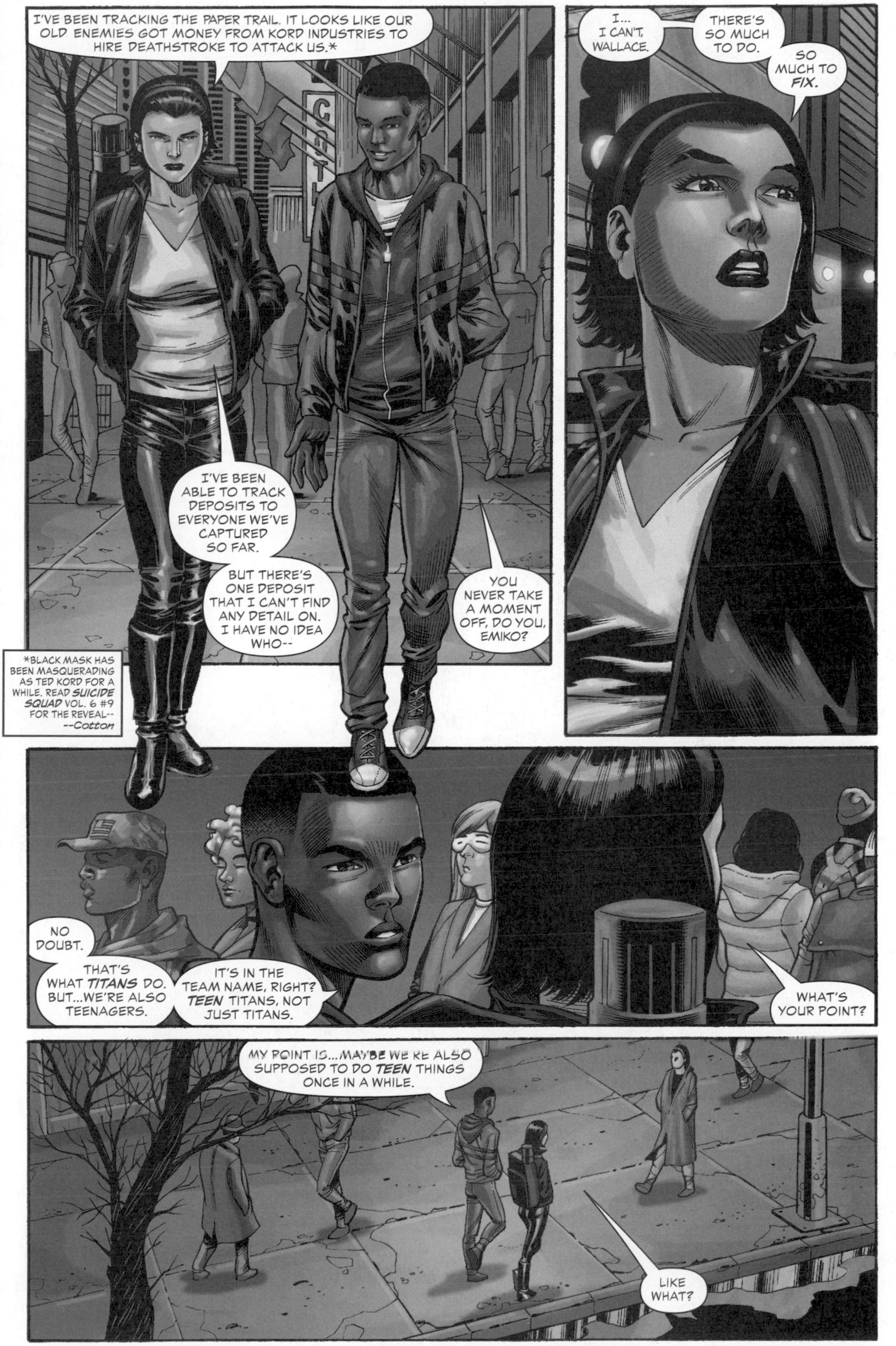
I'VE BEEN TRACKING THE PAPER TRAIL. IT LOOKS LIKE OUR OLD ENEMIES GOT MONEY FROM KORD INDUSTRIES TO HIRE DEATHSTROKE TO ATTACK US.*
I'VE BEEN ABLE TO TRACK DEPOSITS TO EVERYONE WE'VE CAPTURED SO FAR.
BUT THERE'S ONE DEPOSIT THAT I CAN'T FIND ANY DETAIL ON. I HAVE NO IDEA WHO--
YOU NEVER TAKE A MOMENT OFF, DO YOU, EMIKO?
*BLACK MASK HAS BEEN MASQUERADING AS TED KORD FOR A WHILE. READ *SUICIDE SQUAD* VOL. 6 #9 FOR THE REVEAL-- --Cotton
I... I CAN'T, WALLACE.
THERE'S SO MUCH TO DO.
SO MUCH TO *FIX.*
NO DOUBT.
THAT'S WHAT *TITANS* DO. BUT...WE'RE ALSO TEENAGERS.
IT'S IN THE TEAM NAME, RIGHT? *TEEN* TITANS, NOT JUST TITANS.
WHAT'S YOUR POINT?
MY POINT IS...MAYBE WE'RE ALSO SUPPOSED TO DO *TEEN* THINGS ONCE IN A WHILE.
LIKE WHAT?

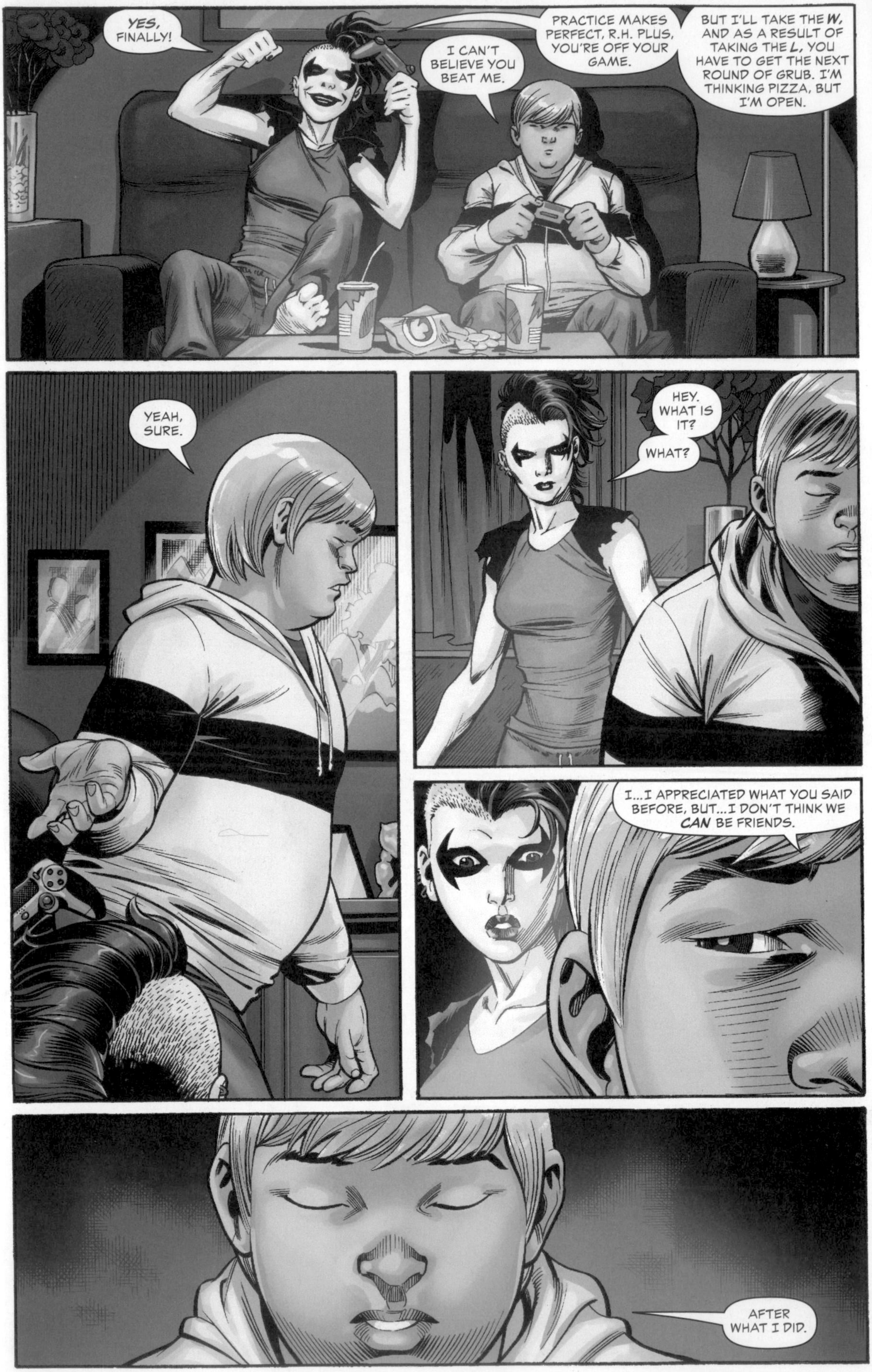

YES, FINALLY!
I CAN'T BELIEVE YOU BEAT ME.
PRACTICE MAKES PERFECT, R.H. PLUS, YOU'RE OFF YOUR GAME.
BUT I'LL TAKE THE W, AND AS A RESULT OF TAKING THE L, YOU HAVE TO GET THE NEXT ROUND OF GRUB. I'M THINKING PIZZA, BUT I'M OPEN.
YEAH, SURE.
HEY. WHAT IS IT?
WHAT?
I...I APPRECIATED WHAT YOU SAID BEFORE, BUT...I DON'T THINK WE CAN BE FRIENDS.
AFTER WHAT I DID.

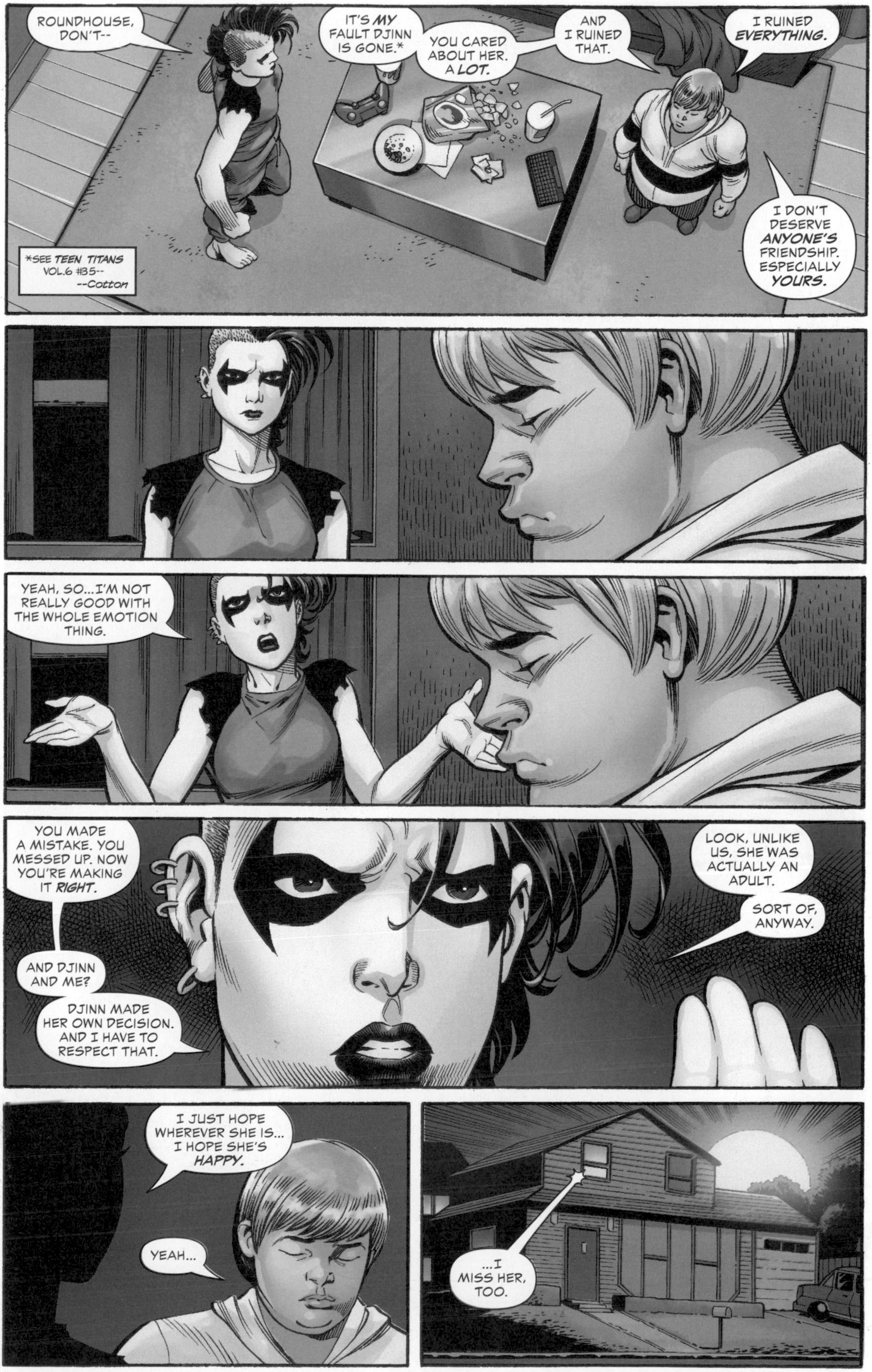
ROUNDHOUSE, DON'T--
IT'S MY FAULT DJINN IS GONE.*
YOU CARED ABOUT HER. A LOT.
AND I RUINED THAT.
I RUINED EVERYTHING.
I DON'T DESERVE ANYONE'S FRIENDSHIP. ESPECIALLY YOURS.
*SEE TEEN TITANS VOL.6 #35-- --Cotton
YEAH, SO...I'M NOT REALLY GOOD WITH THE WHOLE EMOTION THING.
YOU MADE A MISTAKE. YOU MESSED UP. NOW YOU'RE MAKING IT RIGHT.
AND DJINN AND ME?
DJINN MADE HER OWN DECISION. AND I HAVE TO RESPECT THAT.
LOOK, UNLIKE US, SHE WAS ACTUALLY AN ADULT.
SORT OF, ANYWAY.
I JUST HOPE WHEREVER SHE IS... I HOPE SHE'S HAPPY.
YEAH...
...I MISS HER, TOO.

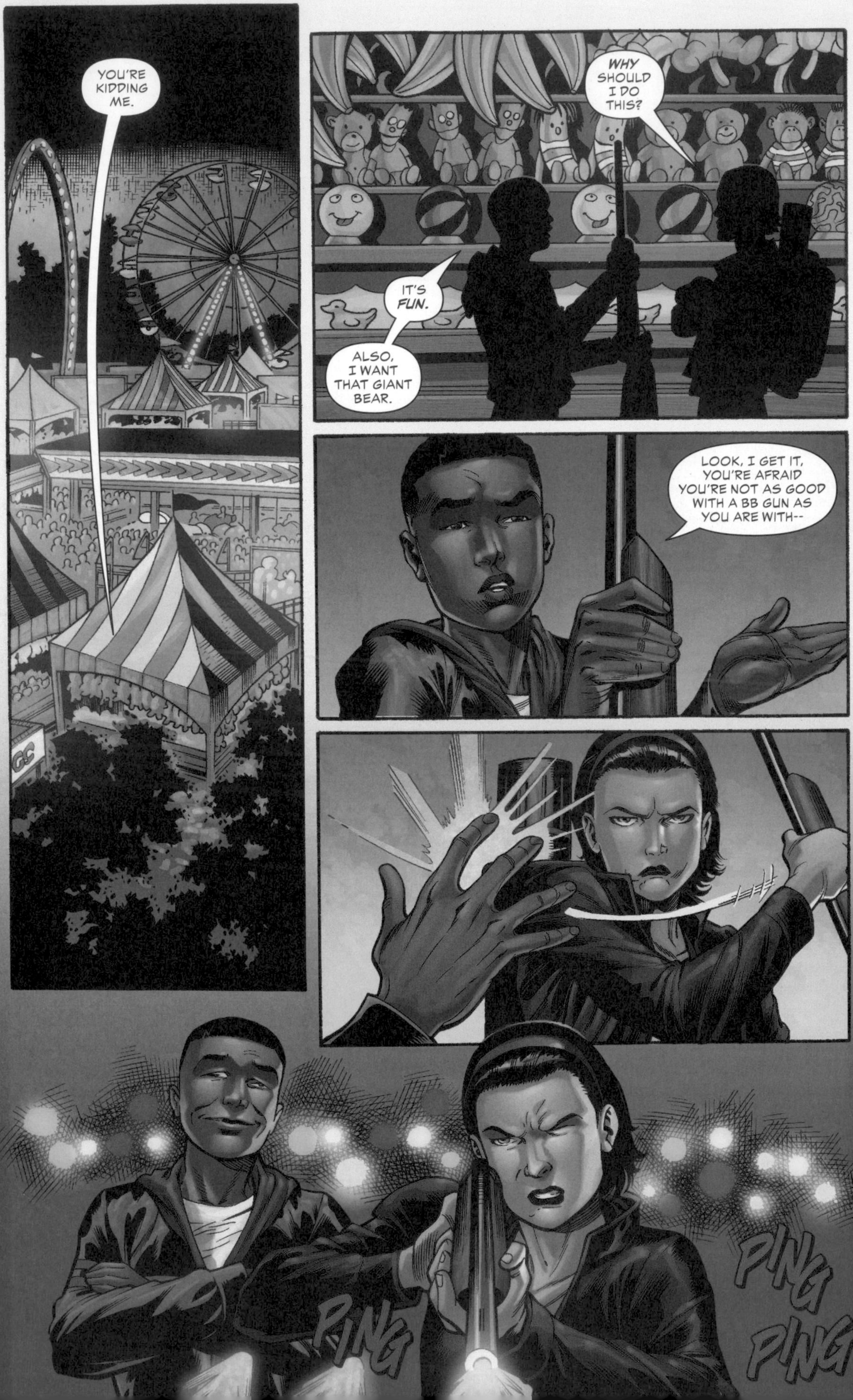
YOU'RE KIDDING ME.
WHY SHOULD I DO THIS?
IT'S FUN.
ALSO, I WANT THAT GIANT BEAR.
LOOK, I GET IT, YOU'RE AFRAID YOU'RE NOT AS GOOD WITH A BB GUN AS YOU ARE WITH--
PING
PING
PING

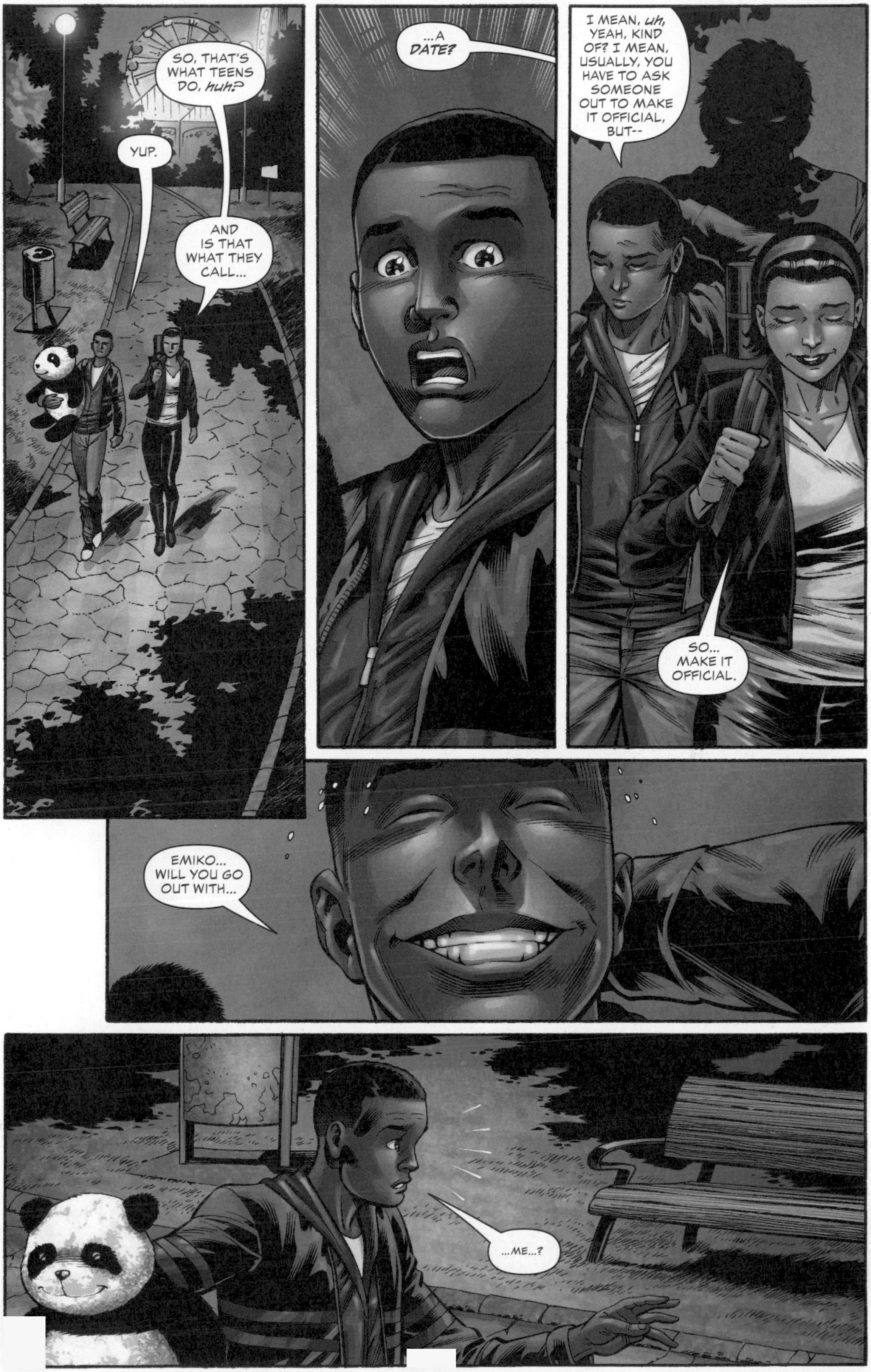
SO, THAT'S WHAT TEENS DO, *huh?*
YUP.
AND IS THAT WHAT THEY CALL...
...A *DATE?*
I MEAN, *uh,* YEAH, KIND OF? I MEAN, USUALLY, YOU HAVE TO ASK SOMEONE OUT TO MAKE IT OFFICIAL, BUT--
SO... MAKE IT OFFICIAL.
EMIKO... WILL YOU GO OUT WITH...
...ME...?

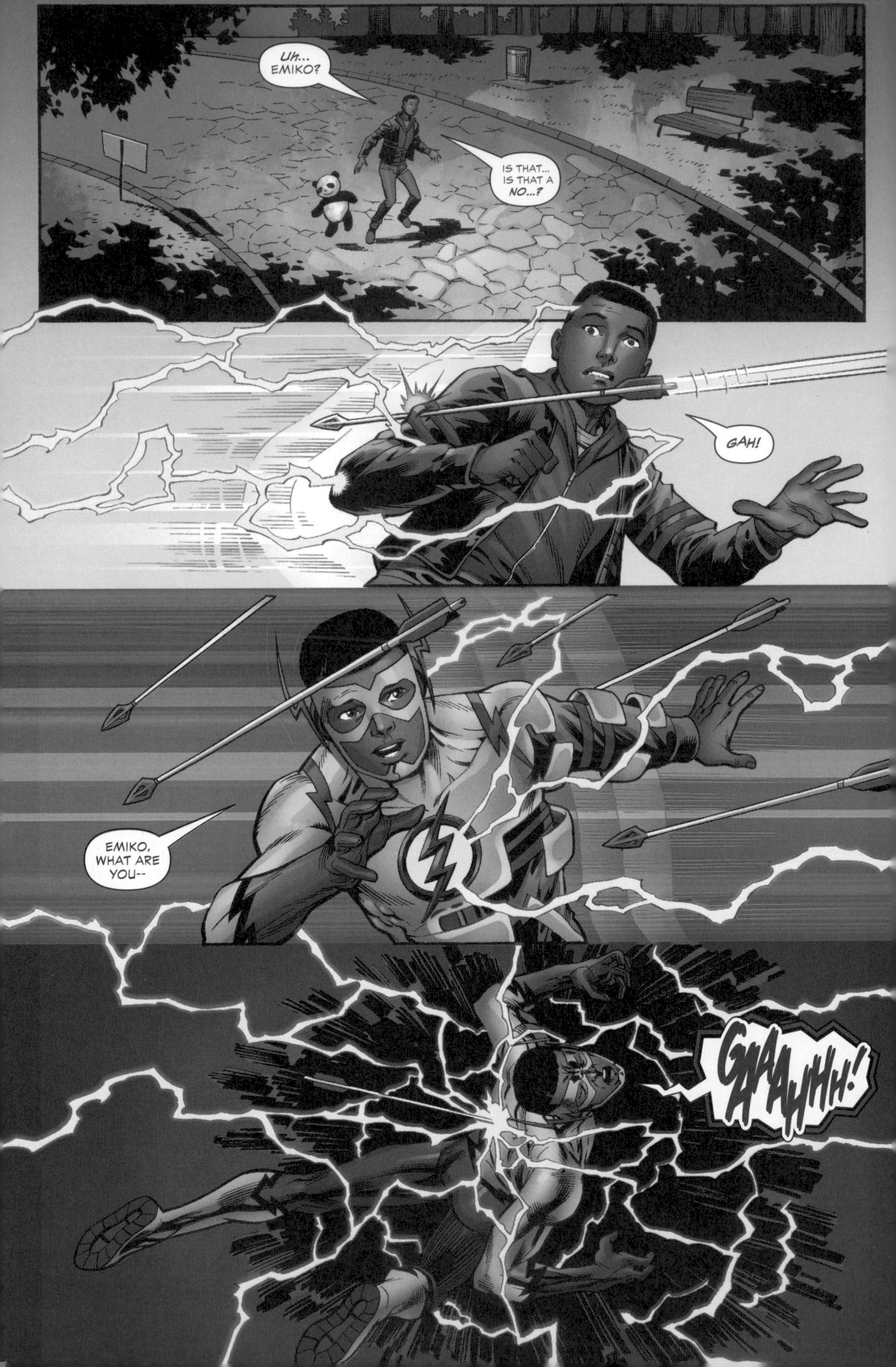
UH... EMIKO?
IS THAT... IS THAT A NO...?
GAH!
EMIKO, WHAT ARE YOU--
GAAAHHH!

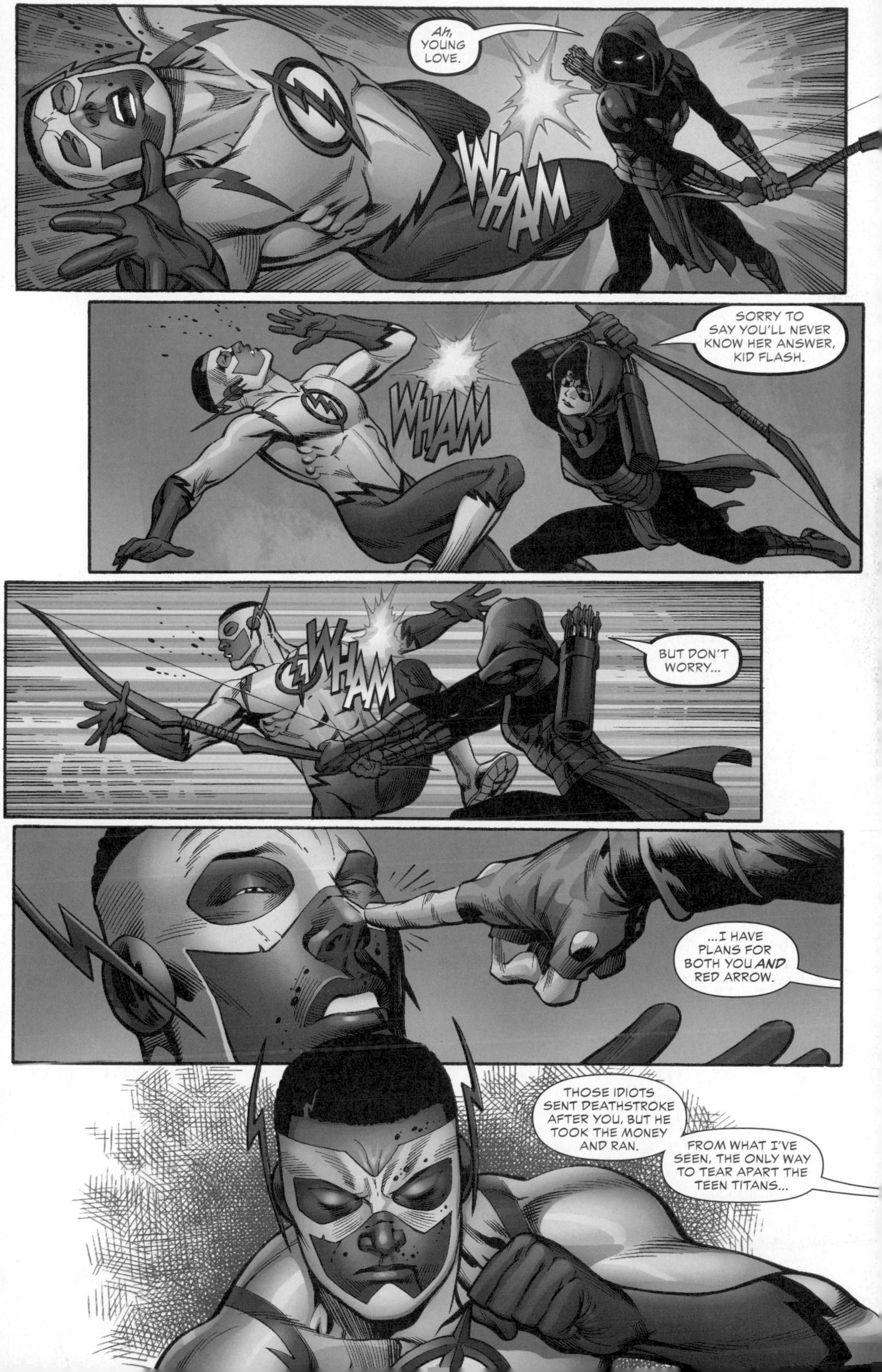
Ah, YOUNG LOVE.
WHAM
SORRY TO SAY YOU'LL NEVER KNOW HER ANSWER, KID FLASH.
WHAM
WHAM
BUT DON'T WORRY...
...I HAVE PLANS FOR BOTH YOU AND RED ARROW.
THOSE IDIOTS SENT DEATHSTROKE AFTER YOU, BUT HE TOOK THE MONEY AND RAN.
FROM WHAT I'VE SEEN, THE ONLY WAY TO TEAR APART THE TEEN TITANS...

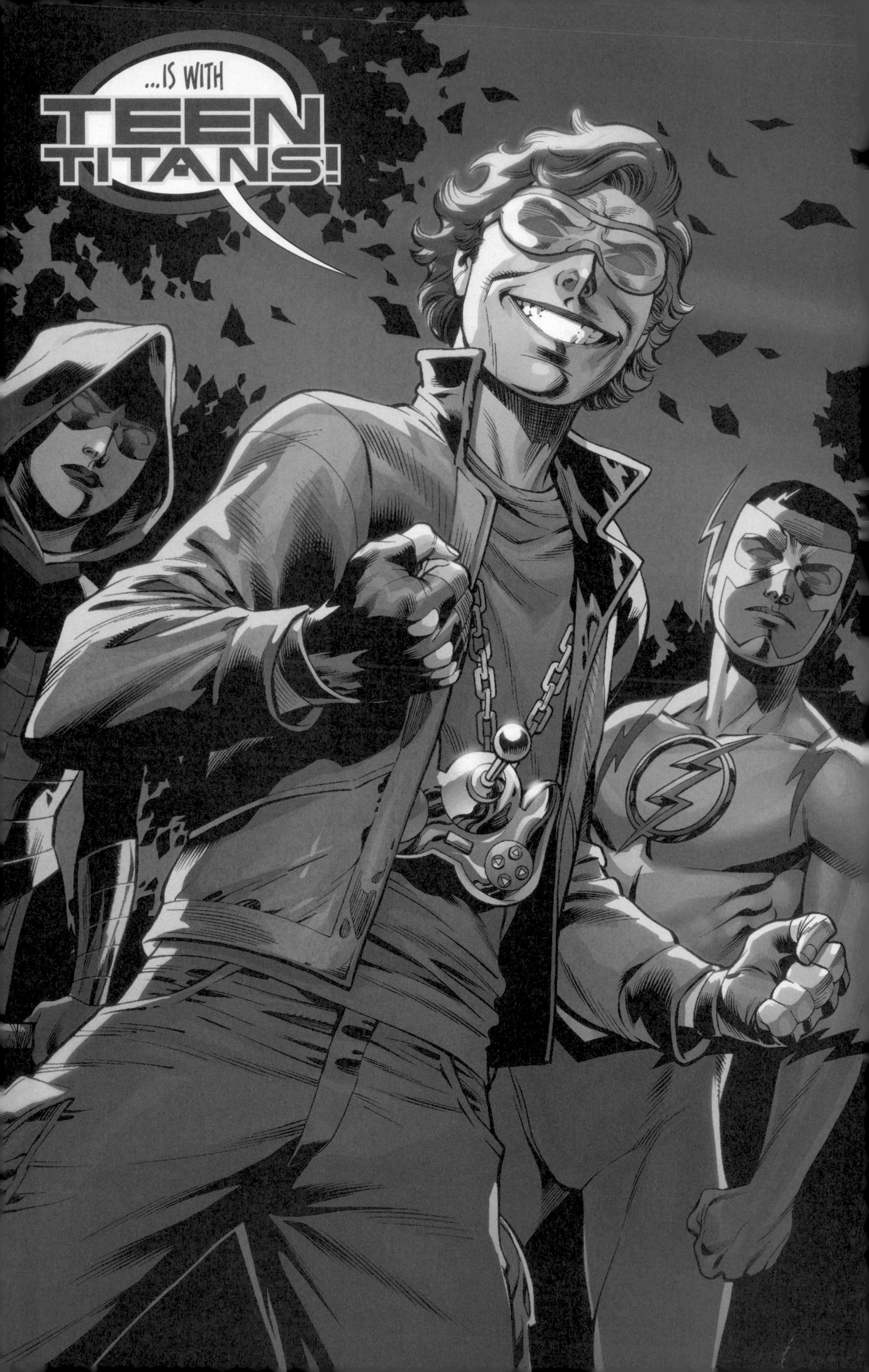
...IS WITH
TEEN TITANS!

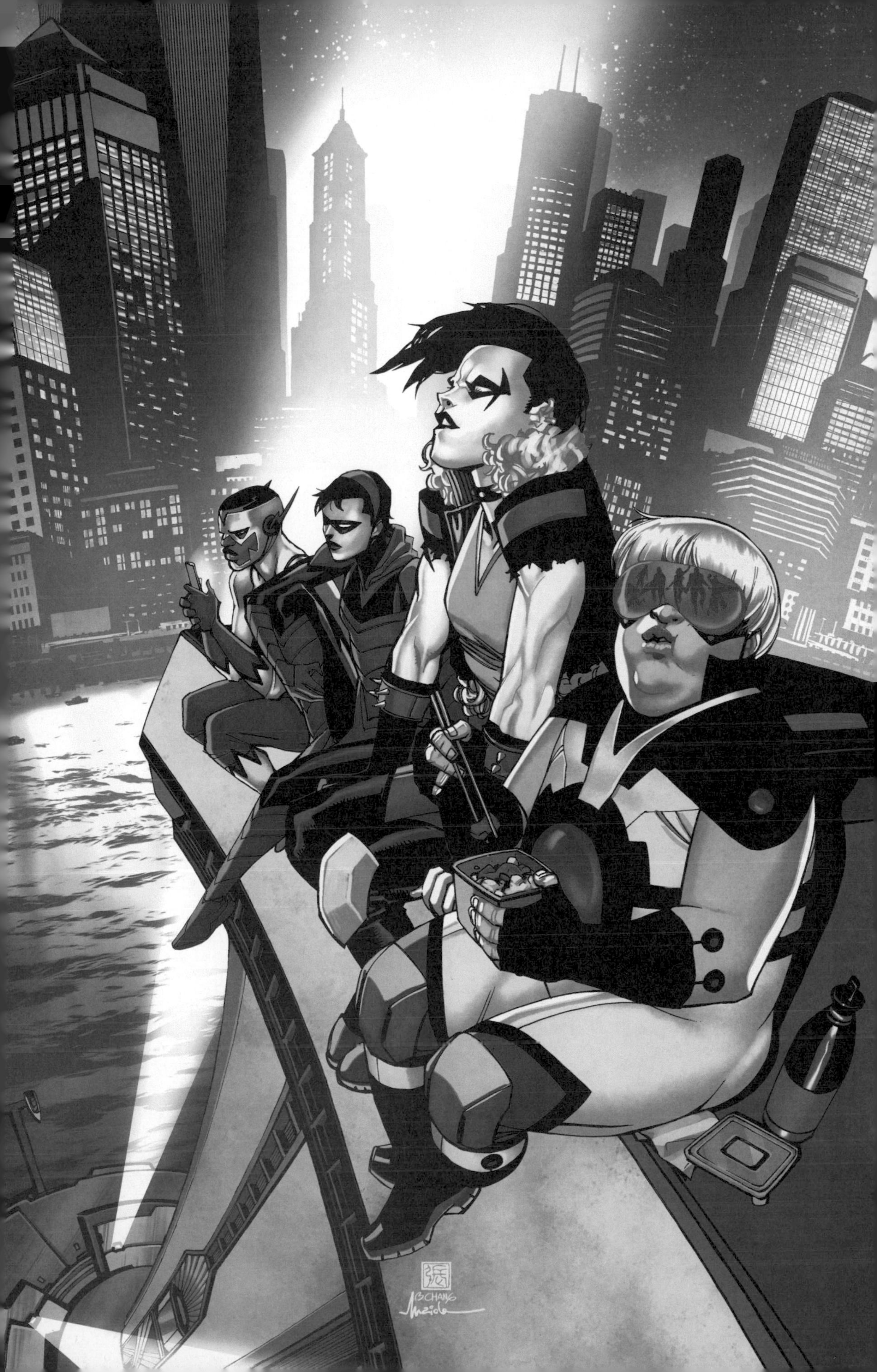
B CHANG

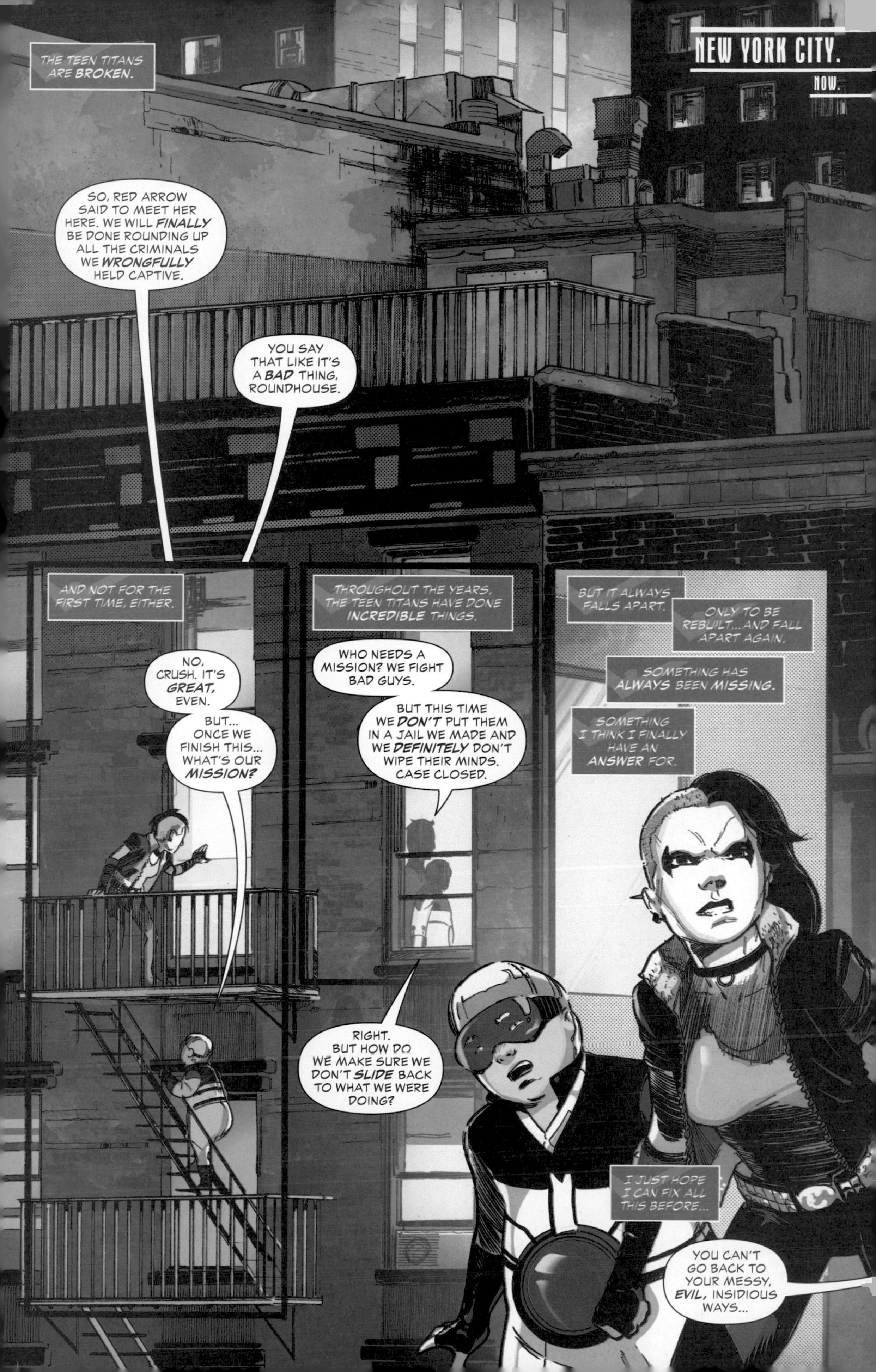
NEW YORK CITY.
NOW.
THE TEEN TITANS ARE BROKEN.
SO, RED ARROW SAID TO MEET HER HERE. WE WILL FINALLY BE DONE ROUNDING UP ALL THE CRIMINALS WE WRONGFULLY HELD CAPTIVE.
YOU SAY THAT LIKE IT'S A BAD THING, ROUNDHOUSE.
AND NOT FOR THE FIRST TIME, EITHER.
NO, CRUSH. IT'S GREAT, EVEN.
BUT... ONCE WE FINISH THIS... WHAT'S OUR MISSION?
THROUGHOUT THE YEARS, THE TEEN TITANS HAVE DONE INCREDIBLE THINGS.
WHO NEEDS A MISSION? WE FIGHT BAD GUYS.
BUT THIS TIME WE DON'T PUT THEM IN A JAIL WE MADE AND WE DEFINITELY DON'T WIPE THEIR MINDS. CASE CLOSED.
RIGHT. BUT HOW DO WE MAKE SURE WE DON'T SLIDE BACK TO WHAT WE WERE DOING?
BUT IT ALWAYS FALLS APART.
ONLY TO BE REBUILT...AND FALL APART AGAIN.
SOMETHING HAS ALWAYS BEEN MISSING.
SOMETHING I THINK I FINALLY HAVE AN ANSWER FOR.
I JUST HOPE I CAN FIX ALL THIS BEFORE...
YOU CAN'T GO BACK TO YOUR MESSY, EVIL, INSIDIOUS WAYS...

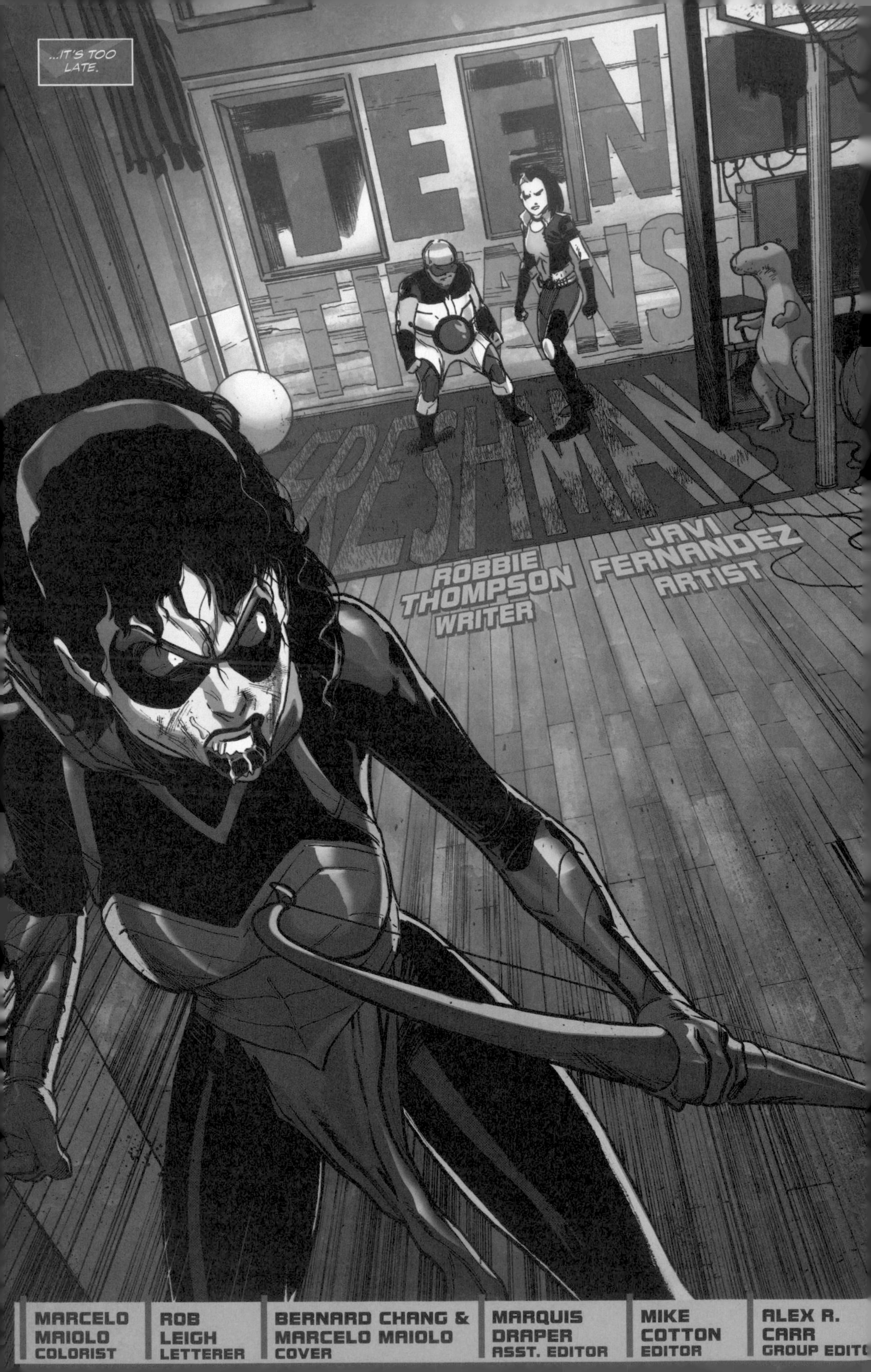

...IT'S TOO LATE.
TEEN TITANS
FRESHMAN
ROBBIE THOMPSON WRITER
JAVI FERNANDEZ ARTIST
MARCELO MAIOLO COLORIST
ROB LEIGH LETTERER
BERNARD CHANG & MARCELO MAIOLO COVER
MARQUIS DRAPER ASST. EDITOR
MIKE COTTON EDITOR
ALEX R. CARR GROUP EDITO

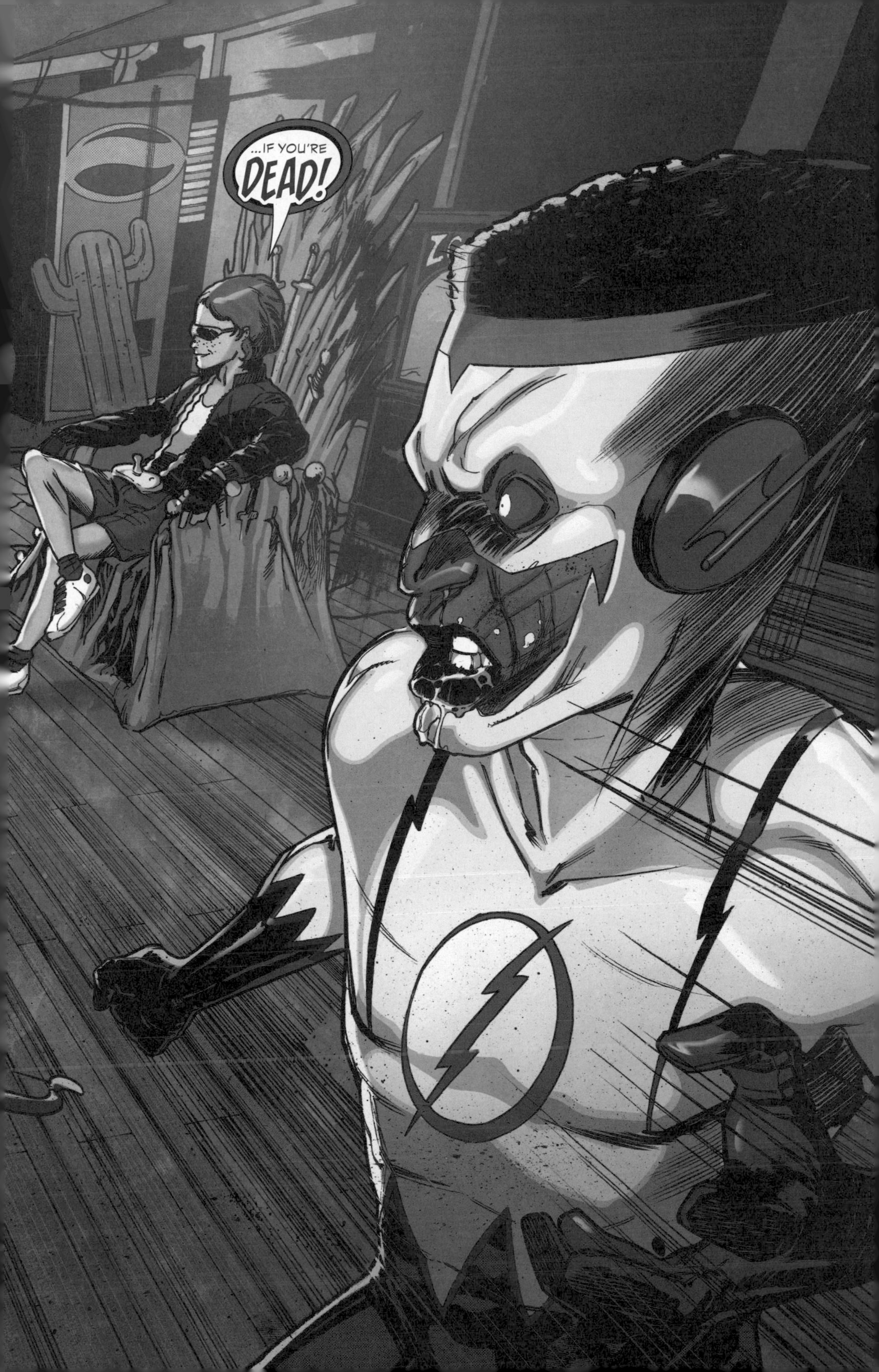
...IF YOU'RE DEAD!

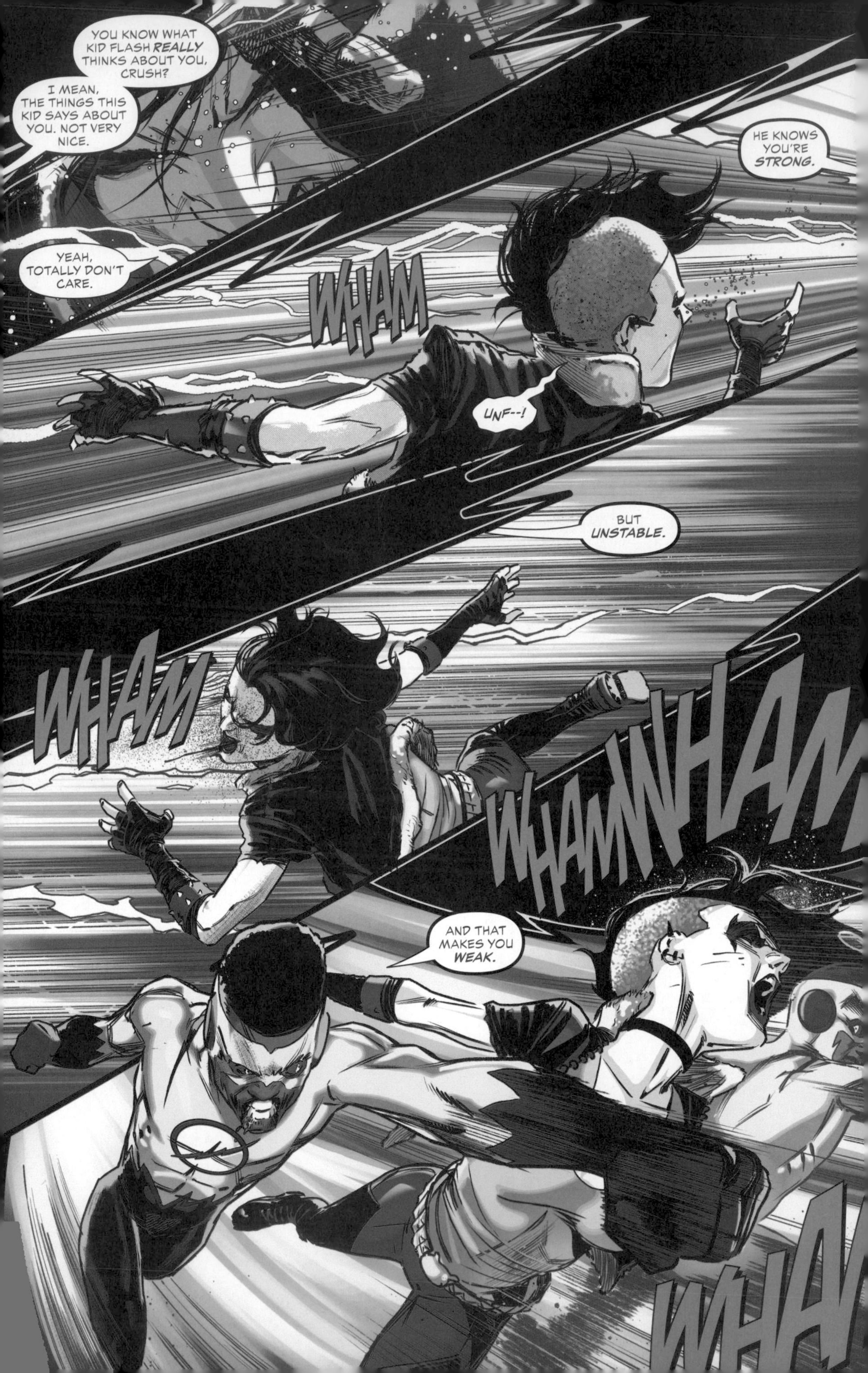

YOU KNOW WHAT KID FLASH REALLY THINKS ABOUT YOU, CRUSH?
I MEAN, THE THINGS THIS KID SAYS ABOUT YOU. NOT VERY NICE.
YEAH, TOTALLY DON'T CARE.
HE KNOWS YOU'RE STRONG.
WHAM
UNF--!
BUT UNSTABLE.
WHAM
WHAMWHAM
AND THAT MAKES YOU WEAK.

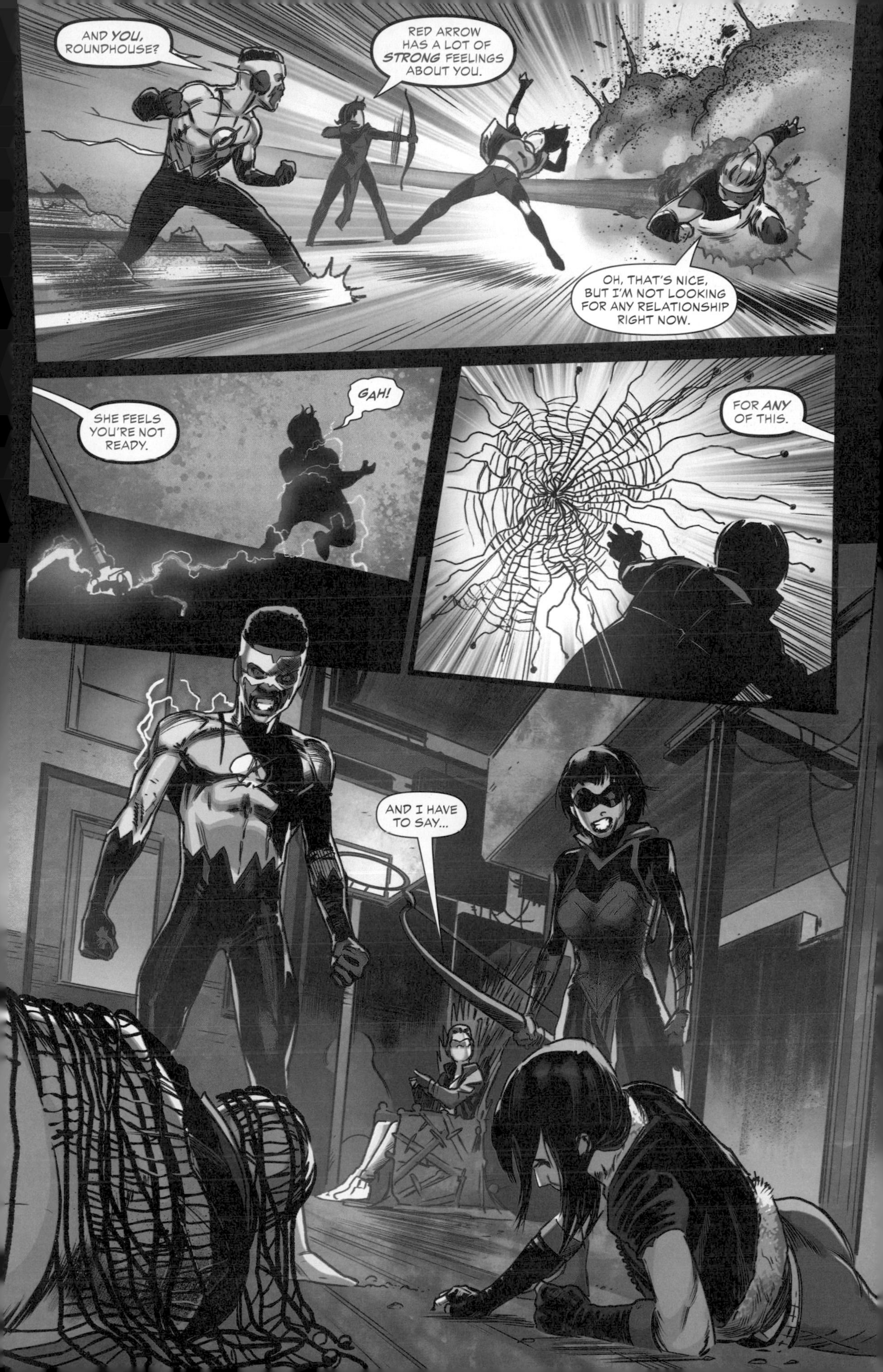
AND YOU, ROUNDHOUSE?
RED ARROW HAS A LOT OF STRONG FEELINGS ABOUT YOU.
OH, THAT'S NICE, BUT I'M NOT LOOKING FOR ANY RELATIONSHIP RIGHT NOW.
SHE FEELS YOU'RE NOT READY.
GAH!
FOR ANY OF THIS.
AND I HAVE TO SAY...

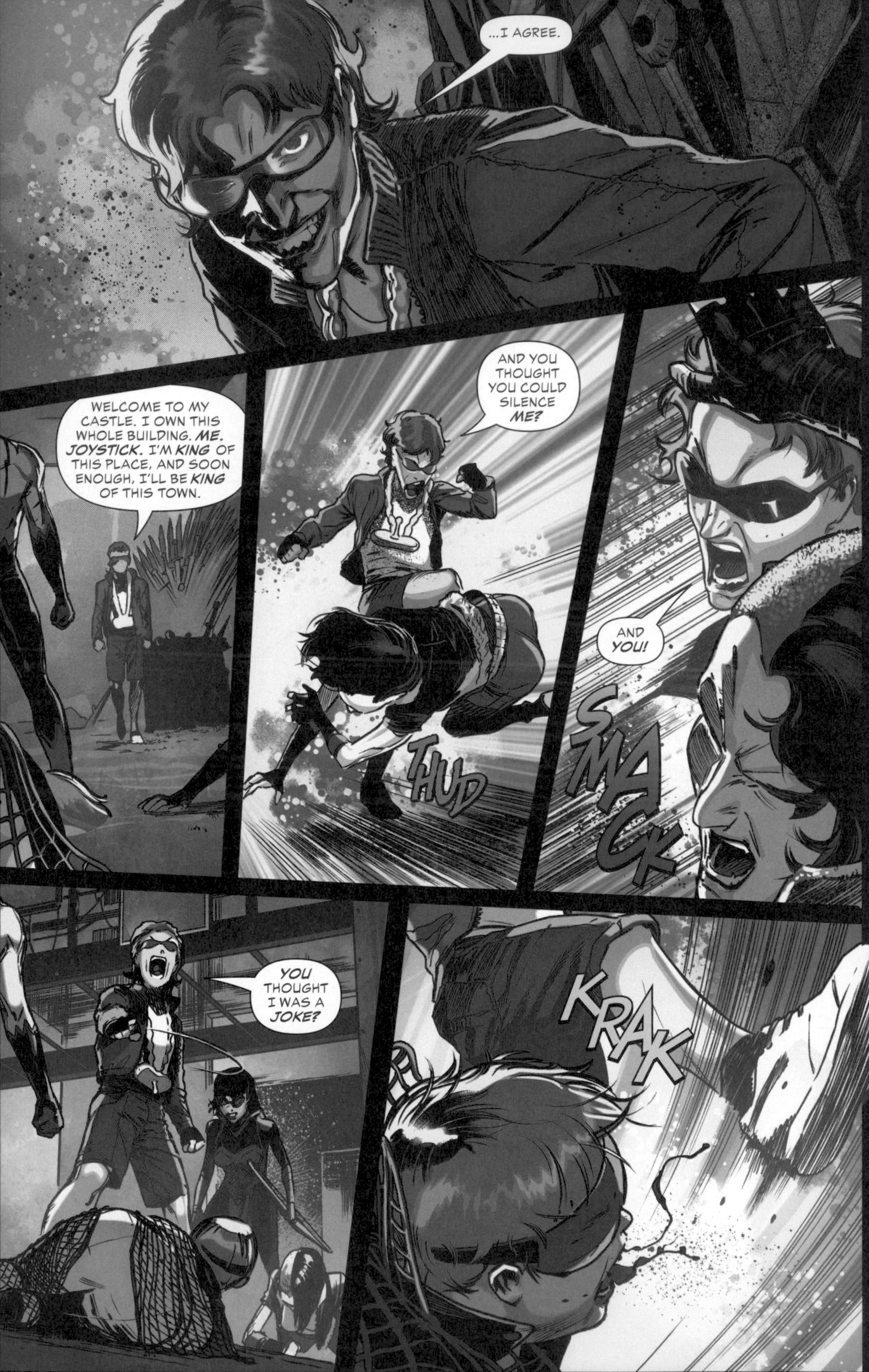
...I AGREE.
WELCOME TO MY CASTLE. I OWN THIS WHOLE BUILDING. ME. JOYSTICK. I'M KING OF THIS PLACE, AND SOON ENOUGH, I'LL BE KING OF THIS TOWN.
AND YOU THOUGHT YOU COULD SILENCE ME?
THUD
AND YOU!
SMACK
YOU THOUGHT I WAS A JOKE?
KRAK

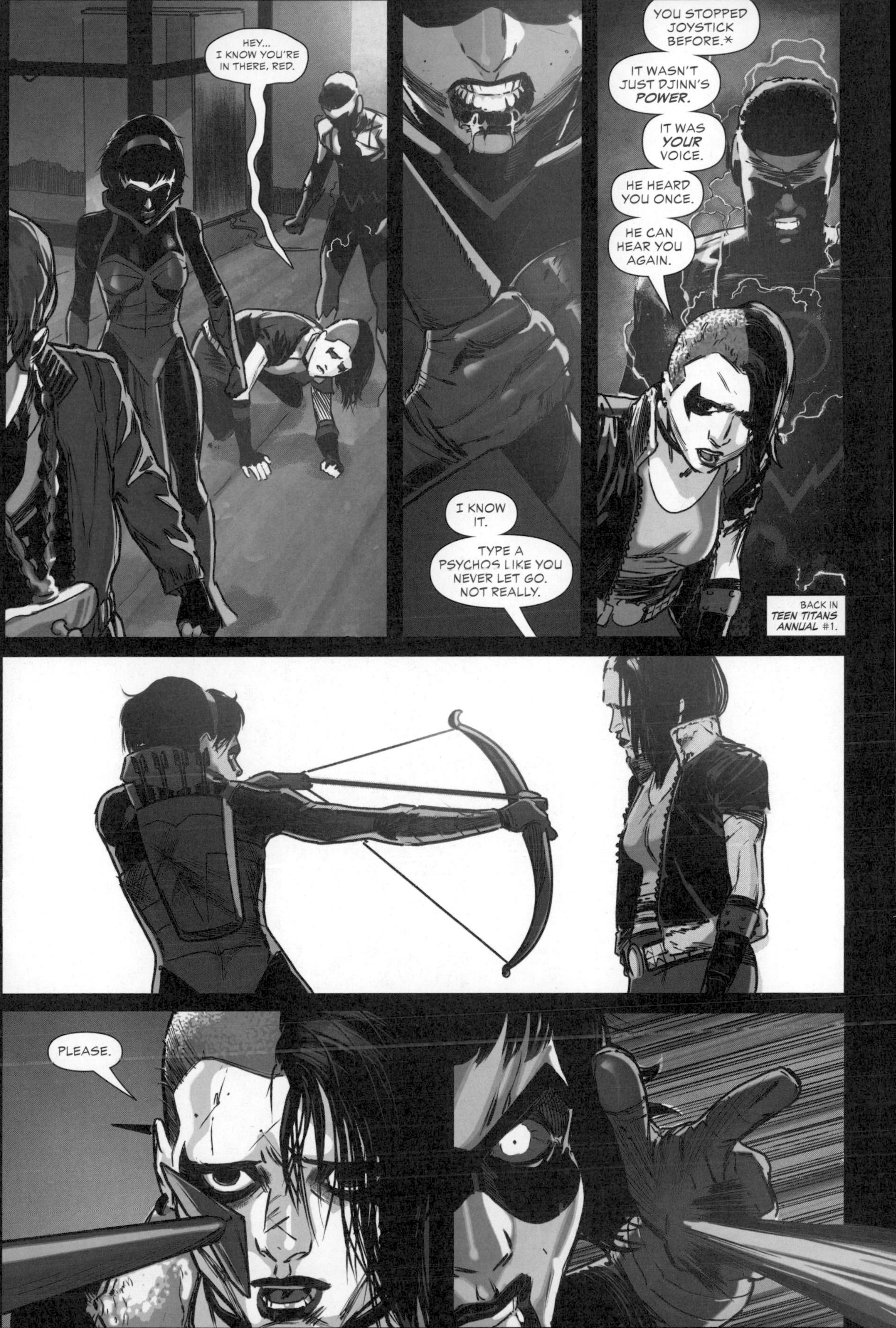
HEY... I KNOW YOU'RE IN THERE, RED.
I KNOW IT.
TYPE A PSYCHOS LIKE YOU NEVER LET GO. NOT REALLY.
YOU STOPPED JOYSTICK BEFORE.*
IT WASN'T JUST DJINN'S POWER.
IT WAS YOUR VOICE.
HE HEARD YOU ONCE.
HE CAN HEAR YOU AGAIN.
*BACK IN TEEN TITANS ANNUAL #1.
PLEASE.

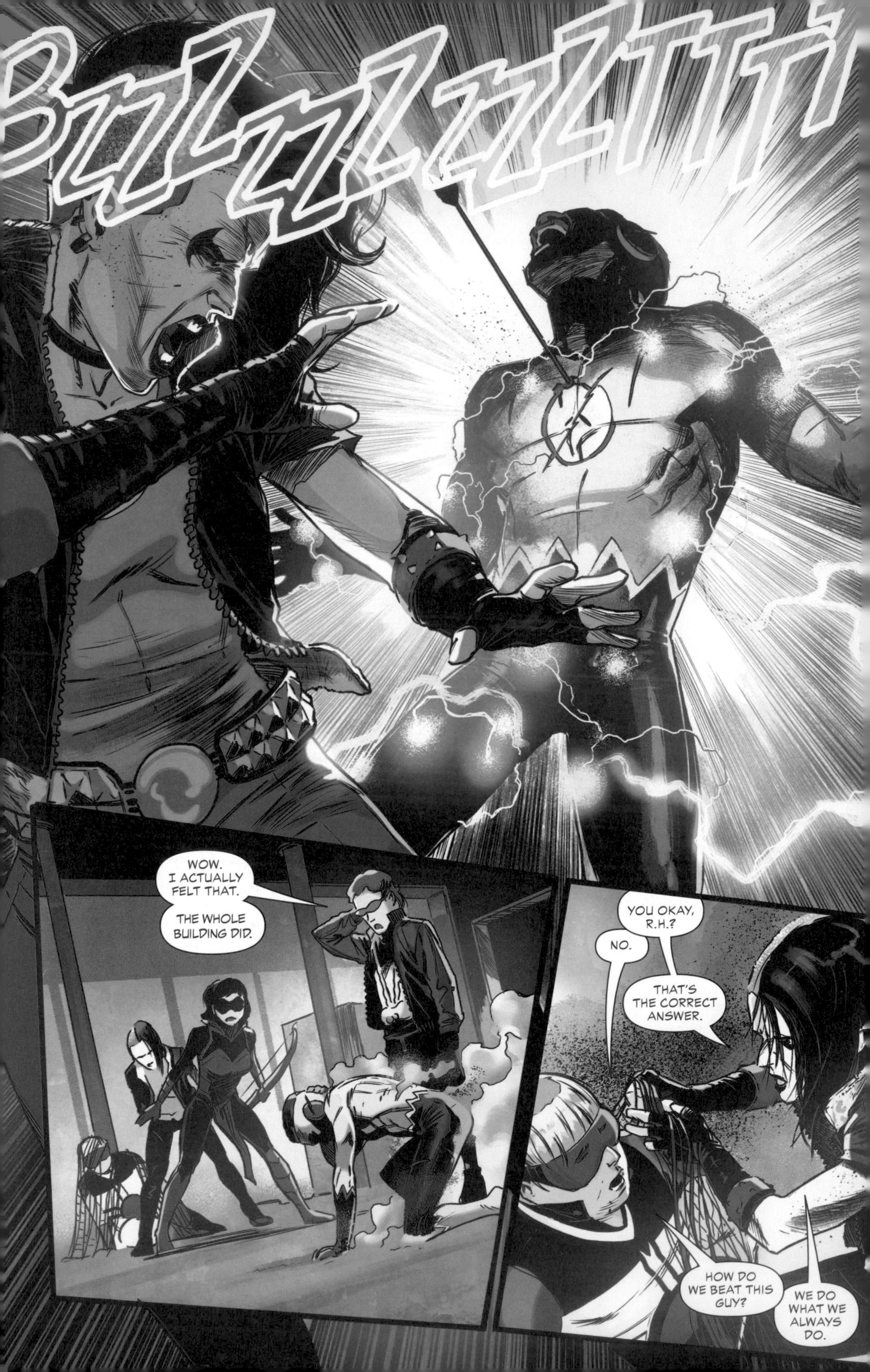
BzZZzzZTTTT
WOW. I ACTUALLY FELT THAT.
THE WHOLE BUILDING DID.
YOU OKAY, R.H.?
NO.
THAT'S THE CORRECT ANSWER.
HOW DO WE BEAT THIS GUY?
WE DO WHAT WE ALWAYS DO.

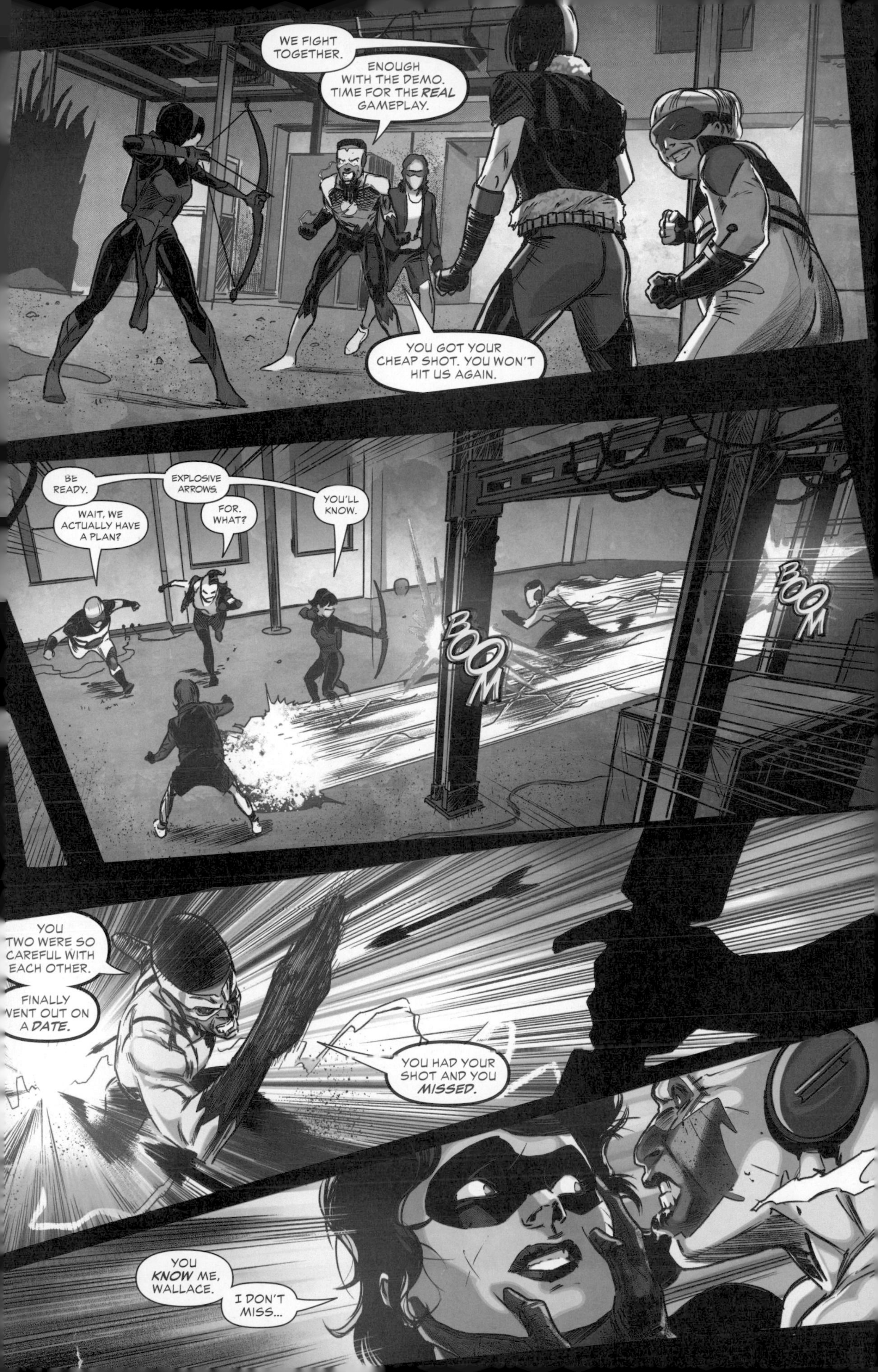
WE FIGHT TOGETHER.
ENOUGH WITH THE DEMO. TIME FOR THE *REAL* GAMEPLAY.
YOU GOT YOUR CHEAP SHOT. YOU WON'T HIT US AGAIN.
BE READY.
WAIT, WE ACTUALLY HAVE A PLAN?
EXPLOSIVE ARROWS.
FOR. WHAT?
YOU'LL KNOW.
BOOM
BOOM
YOU TWO WERE SO CAREFUL WITH EACH OTHER.
FINALLY WENT OUT ON A *DATE.*
YOU HAD YOUR SHOT AND YOU *MISSED.*
YOU *KNOW* ME, WALLACE.
I DON'T MISS...

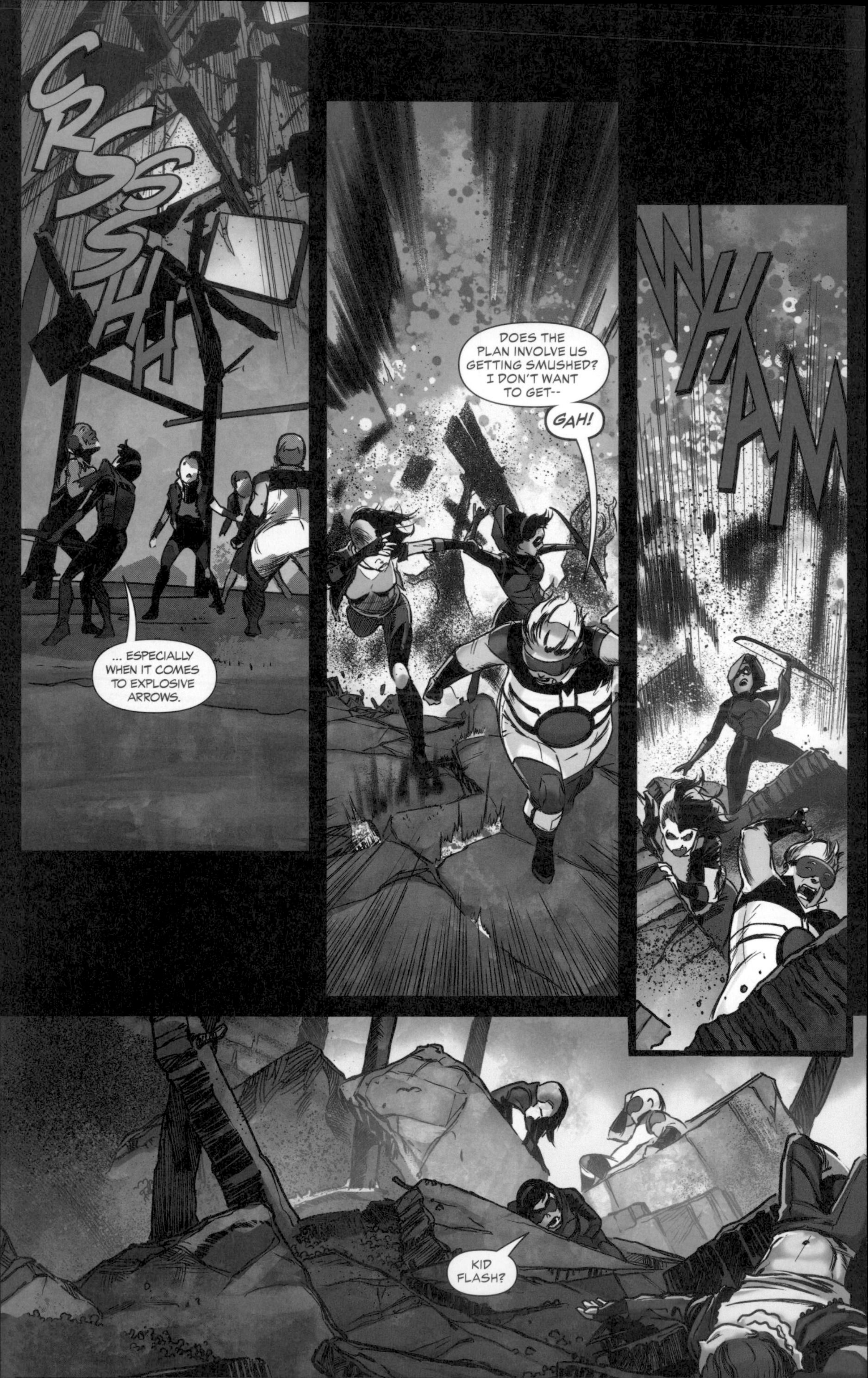
CRSSSHH
... ESPECIALLY WHEN IT COMES TO EXPLOSIVE ARROWS.
DOES THE PLAN INVOLVE US GETTING SMUSHED? I DON'T WANT TO GET--
GAH!
WHAM
KID FLASH?

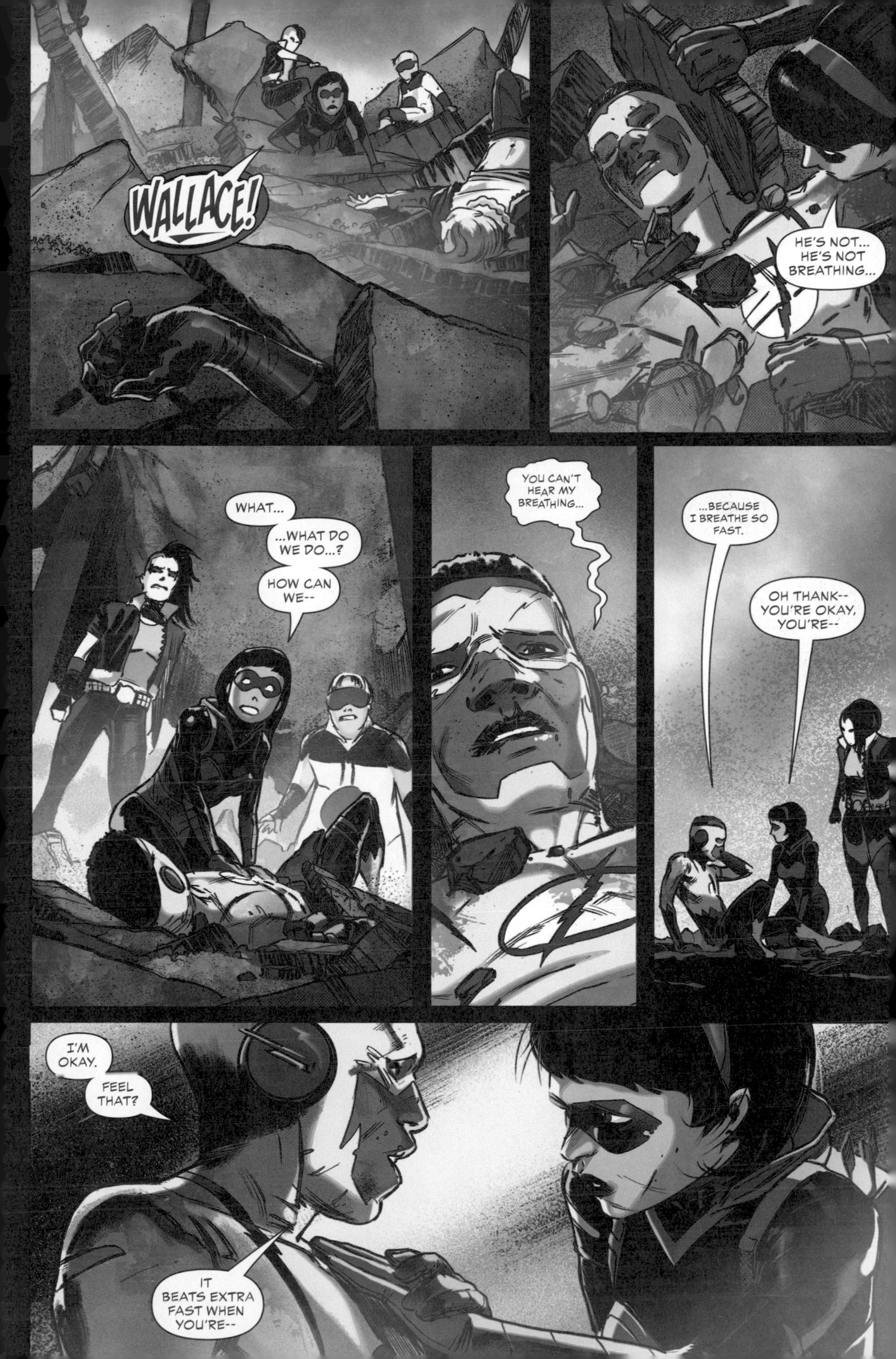
WALLACE!
HE'S NOT... HE'S NOT BREATHING...
WHAT...
...WHAT DO WE DO...?
HOW CAN WE--
YOU CAN'T HEAR MY BREATHING...
...BECAUSE I BREATHE SO FAST.
OH THANK-- YOU'RE OKAY, YOU'RE--
I'M OKAY.
FEEL THAT?
IT BEATS EXTRA FAST WHEN YOU'RE--

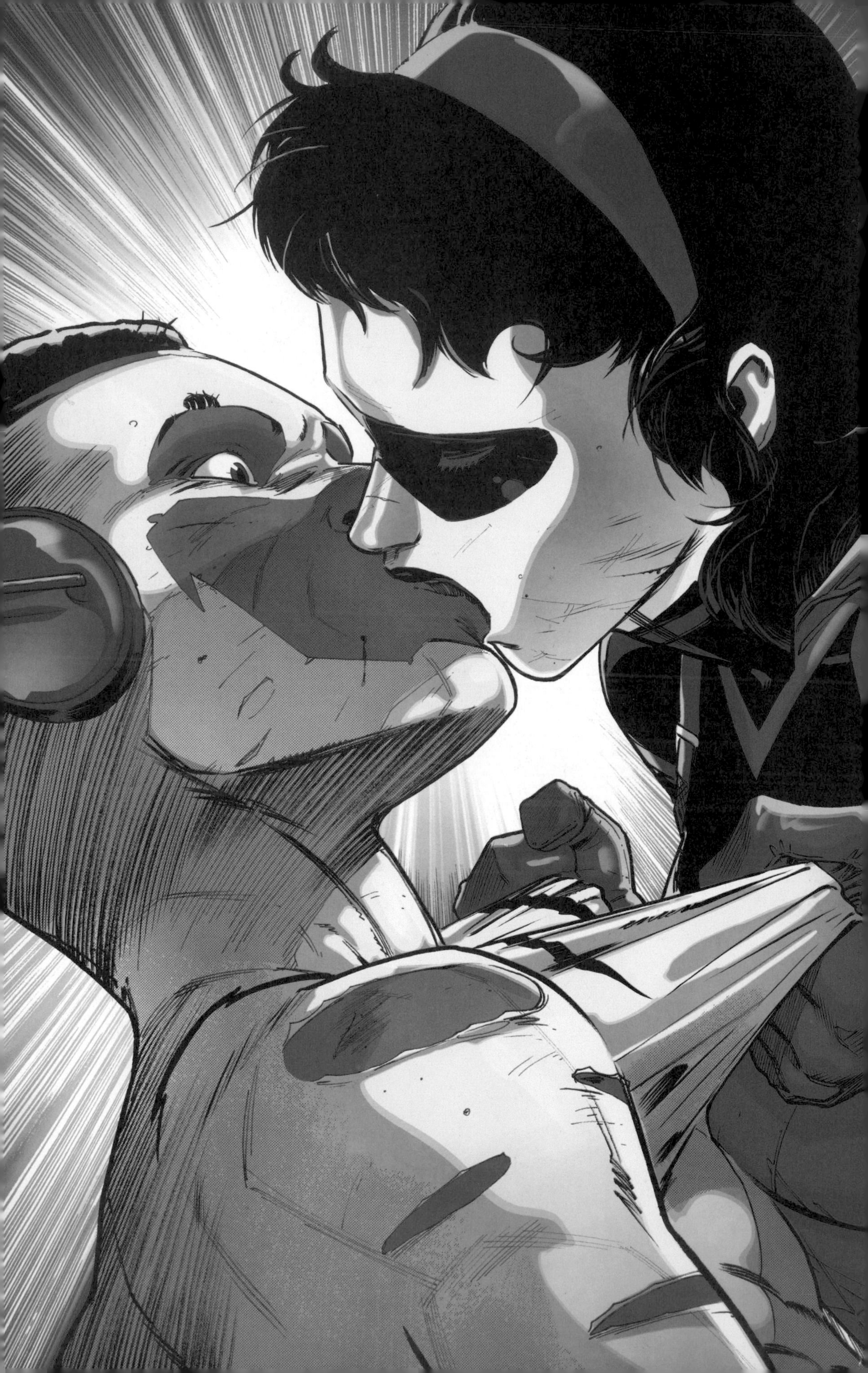

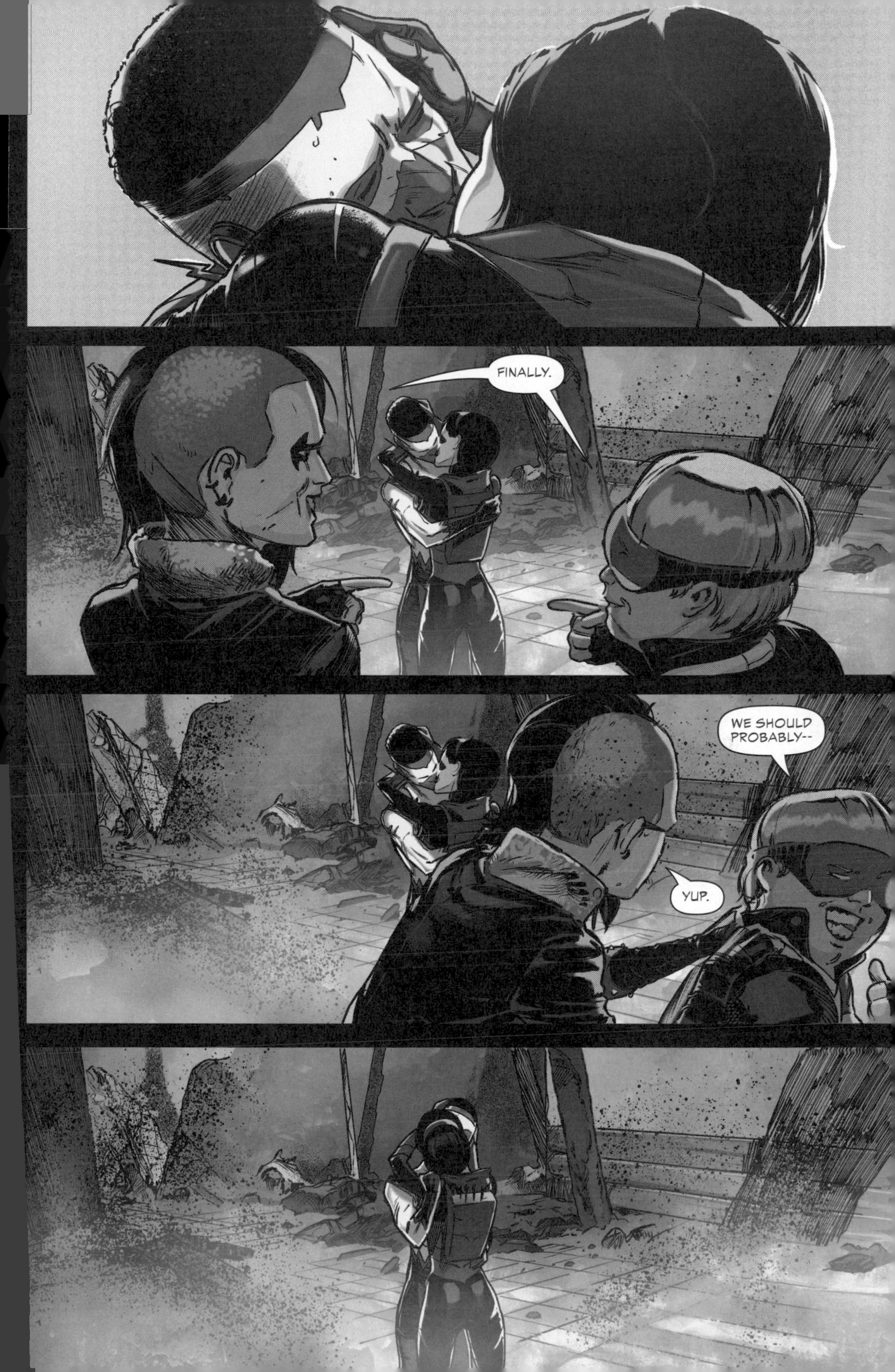
FINALLY.
WE SHOULD PROBABLY--
YUP.

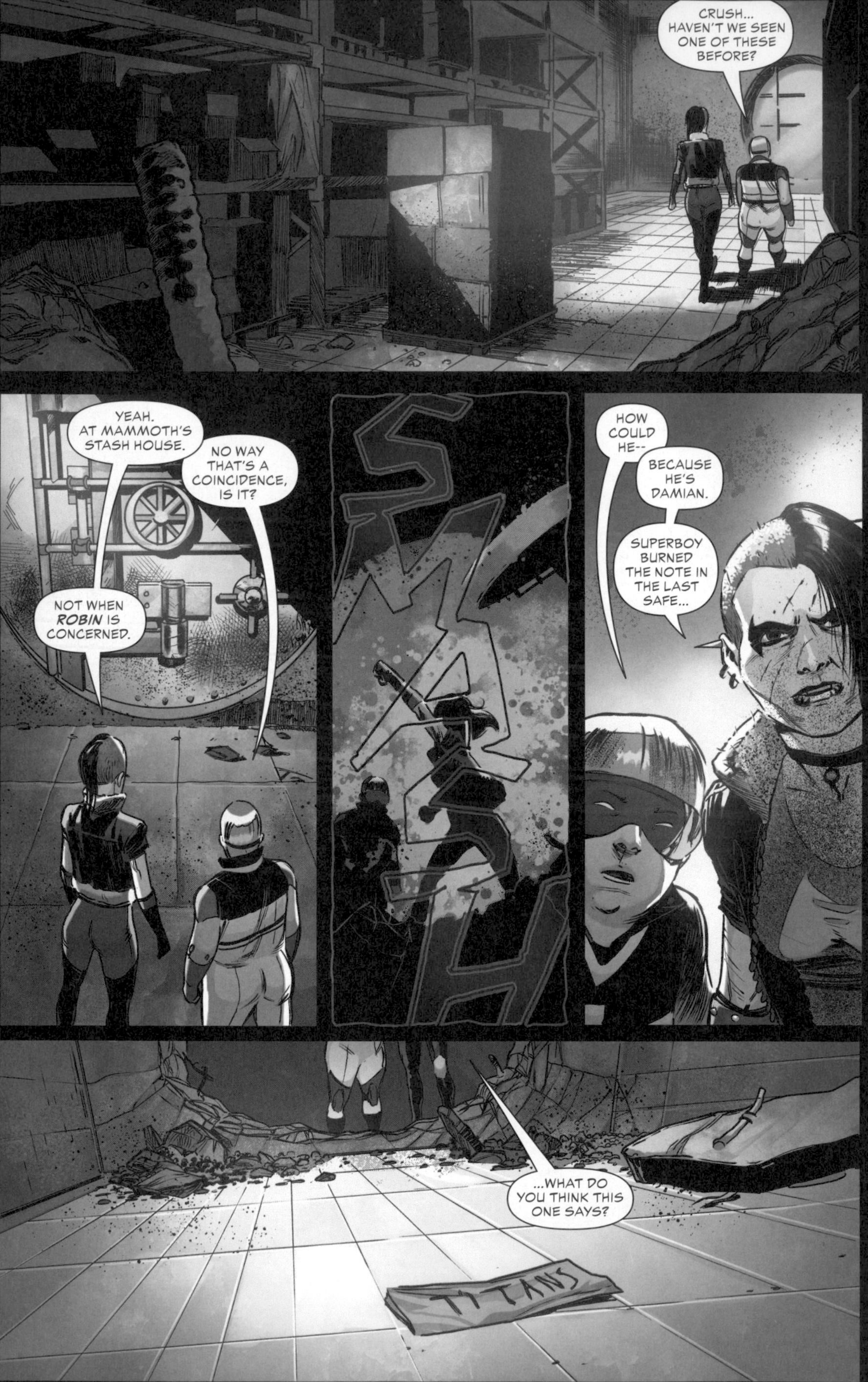
CRUSH... HAVEN'T WE SEEN ONE OF THESE BEFORE?
YEAH. AT MAMMOTH'S STASH HOUSE.
NO WAY THAT'S A COINCIDENCE, IS IT?
NOT WHEN *ROBIN* IS CONCERNED.
SMASH
HOW COULD HE--
BECAUSE HE'S DAMIAN.
SUPERBOY BURNED THE NOTE IN THE LAST SAFE...
...WHAT DO YOU THINK THIS ONE SAYS?
TITANS

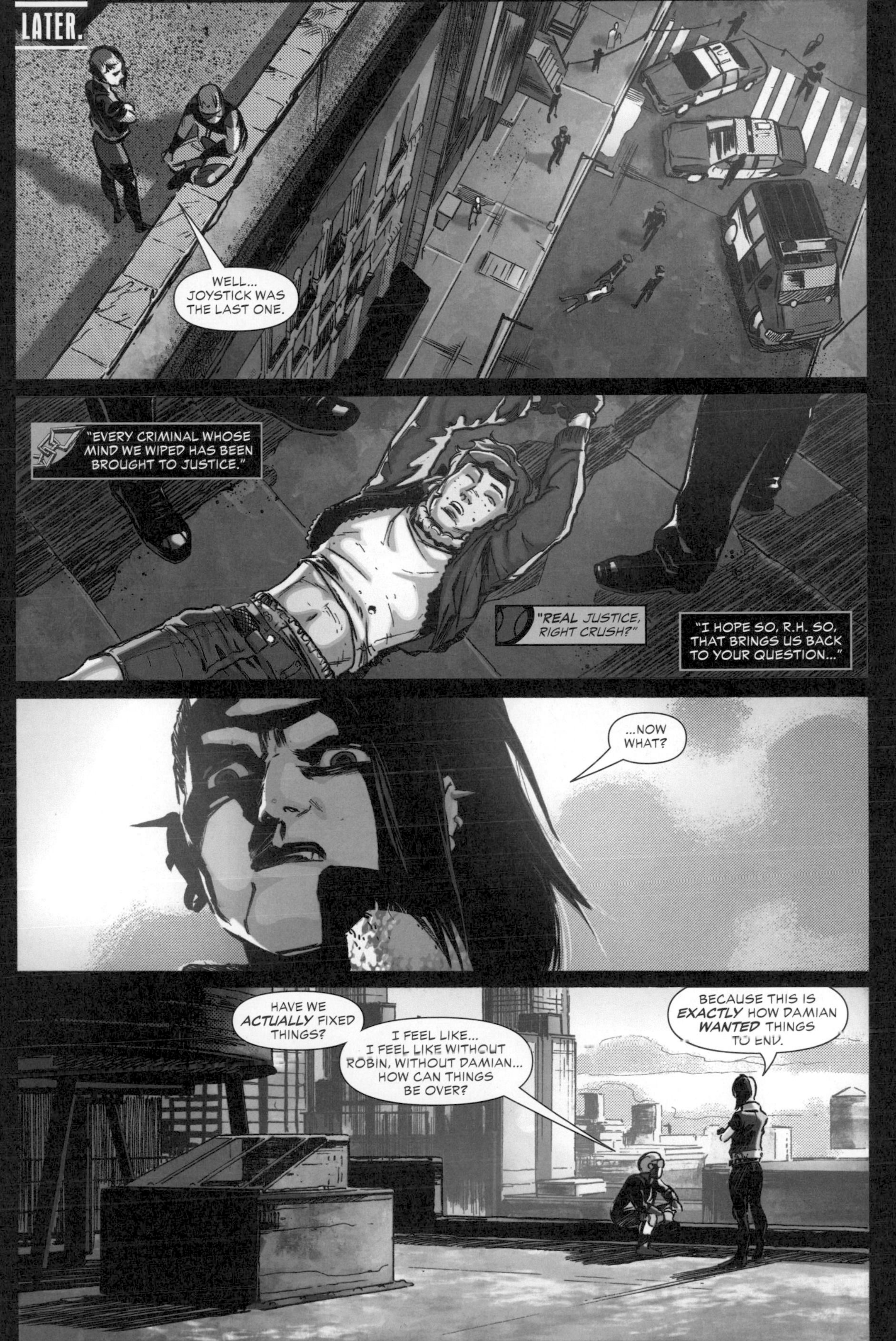
LATER.
WELL... JOYSTICK WAS THE LAST ONE.
"EVERY CRIMINAL WHOSE MIND WE WIPED HAS BEEN BROUGHT TO JUSTICE."
"REAL JUSTICE, RIGHT CRUSH?"
"I HOPE SO, R.H. SO, THAT BRINGS US BACK TO YOUR QUESTION..."
...NOW WHAT?
HAVE WE ACTUALLY FIXED THINGS?
I FEEL LIKE... I FEEL LIKE WITHOUT ROBIN, WITHOUT DAMIAN... HOW CAN THINGS BE OVER?
BECAUSE THIS IS EXACTLY HOW DAMIAN WANTED THINGS TO END.

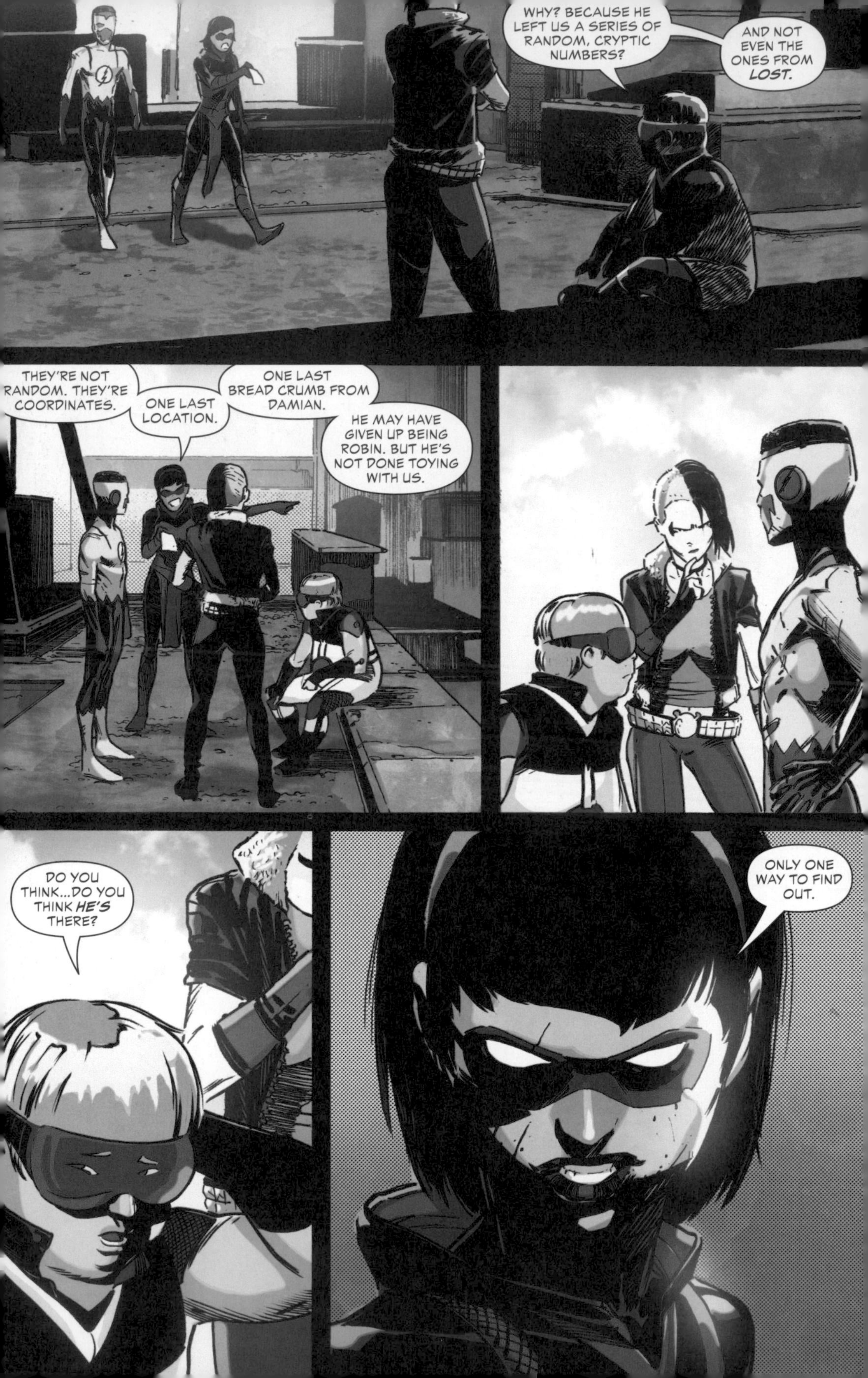
WHY? BECAUSE HE LEFT US A SERIES OF RANDOM, CRYPTIC NUMBERS?
AND NOT EVEN THE ONES FROM *LOST.*
THEY'RE NOT RANDOM. THEY'RE COORDINATES.
ONE LAST LOCATION.
ONE LAST BREAD CRUMB FROM DAMIAN.
HE MAY HAVE GIVEN UP BEING ROBIN. BUT HE'S NOT DONE TOYING WITH US.
DO YOU THINK...DO YOU THINK *HE'S* THERE?
ONLY ONE WAY TO FIND OUT.

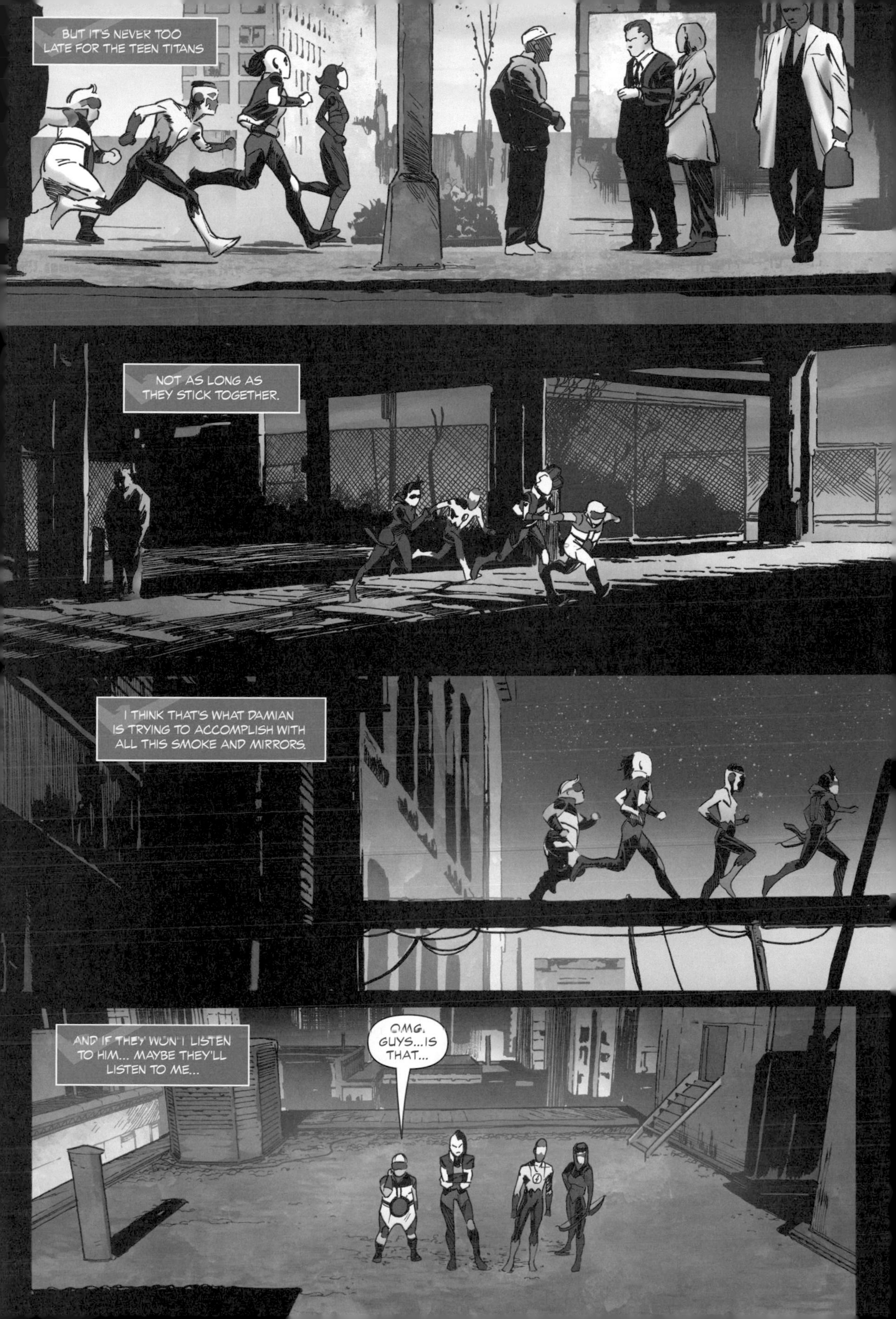
BUT IT'S NEVER TOO LATE FOR THE TEEN TITANS
NOT AS LONG AS THEY STICK TOGETHER.
I THINK THAT'S WHAT DAMIAN IS TRYING TO ACCOMPLISH WITH ALL THIS SMOKE AND MIRRORS.
AND IF THEY WON'T LISTEN TO HIM... MAYBE THEY'LL LISTEN TO ME...
OMG. GUYS...IS THAT...

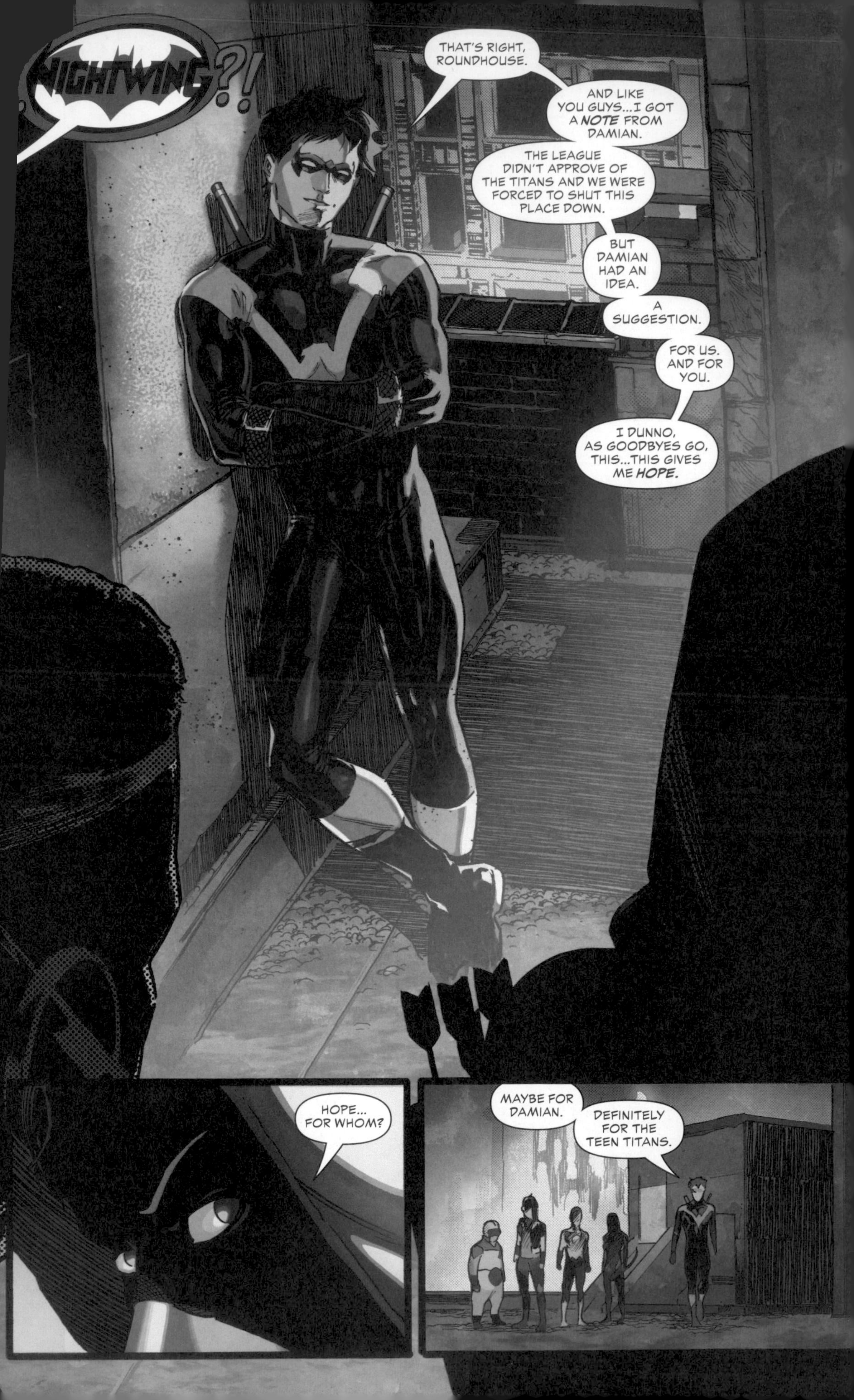
NIGHTWING?!
THAT'S RIGHT, ROUNDHOUSE.
AND LIKE YOU GUYS...I GOT A NOTE FROM DAMIAN.
THE LEAGUE DIDN'T APPROVE OF THE TITANS AND WE WERE FORCED TO SHUT THIS PLACE DOWN.
BUT DAMIAN HAD AN IDEA.
A SUGGESTION.
FOR US. AND FOR YOU.
I DUNNO, AS GOODBYES GO, THIS...THIS GIVES ME HOPE.
HOPE... FOR WHOM?
MAYBE FOR DAMIAN.
DEFINITELY FOR THE TEEN TITANS.

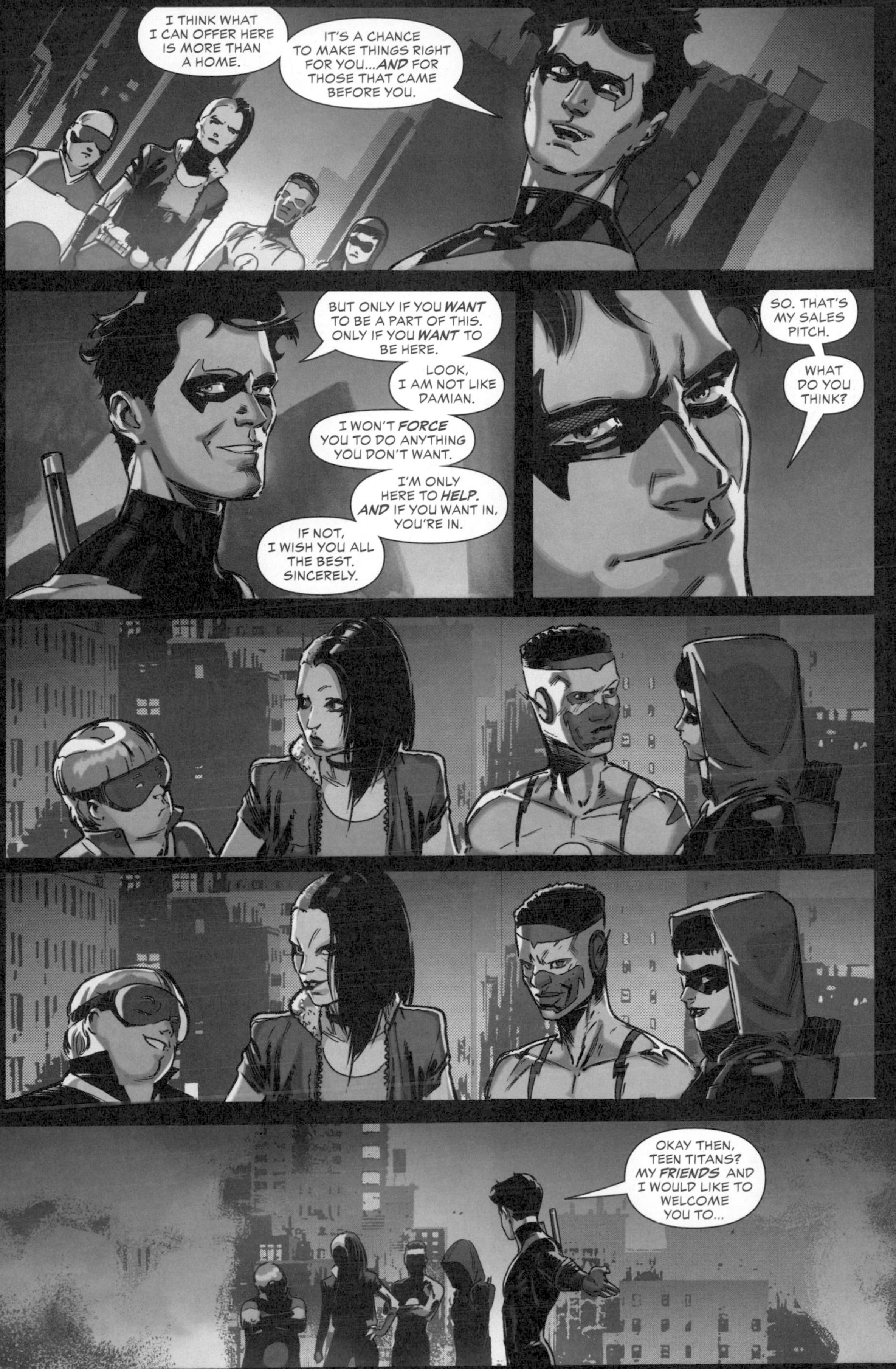
I THINK WHAT I CAN OFFER HERE IS MORE THAN A HOME.
IT'S A CHANCE TO MAKE THINGS RIGHT FOR YOU...AND FOR THOSE THAT CAME BEFORE YOU.
BUT ONLY IF YOU WANT TO BE A PART OF THIS. ONLY IF YOU WANT TO BE HERE.
LOOK, I AM NOT LIKE DAMIAN.
I WON'T FORCE YOU TO DO ANYTHING YOU DON'T WANT.
I'M ONLY HERE TO HELP. AND IF YOU WANT IN, YOU'RE IN.
IF NOT, I WISH YOU ALL THE BEST. SINCERELY.
SO. THAT'S MY SALES PITCH.
WHAT DO YOU THINK?
OKAY THEN, TEEN TITANS? MY FRIENDS AND I WOULD LIKE TO WELCOME YOU TO...

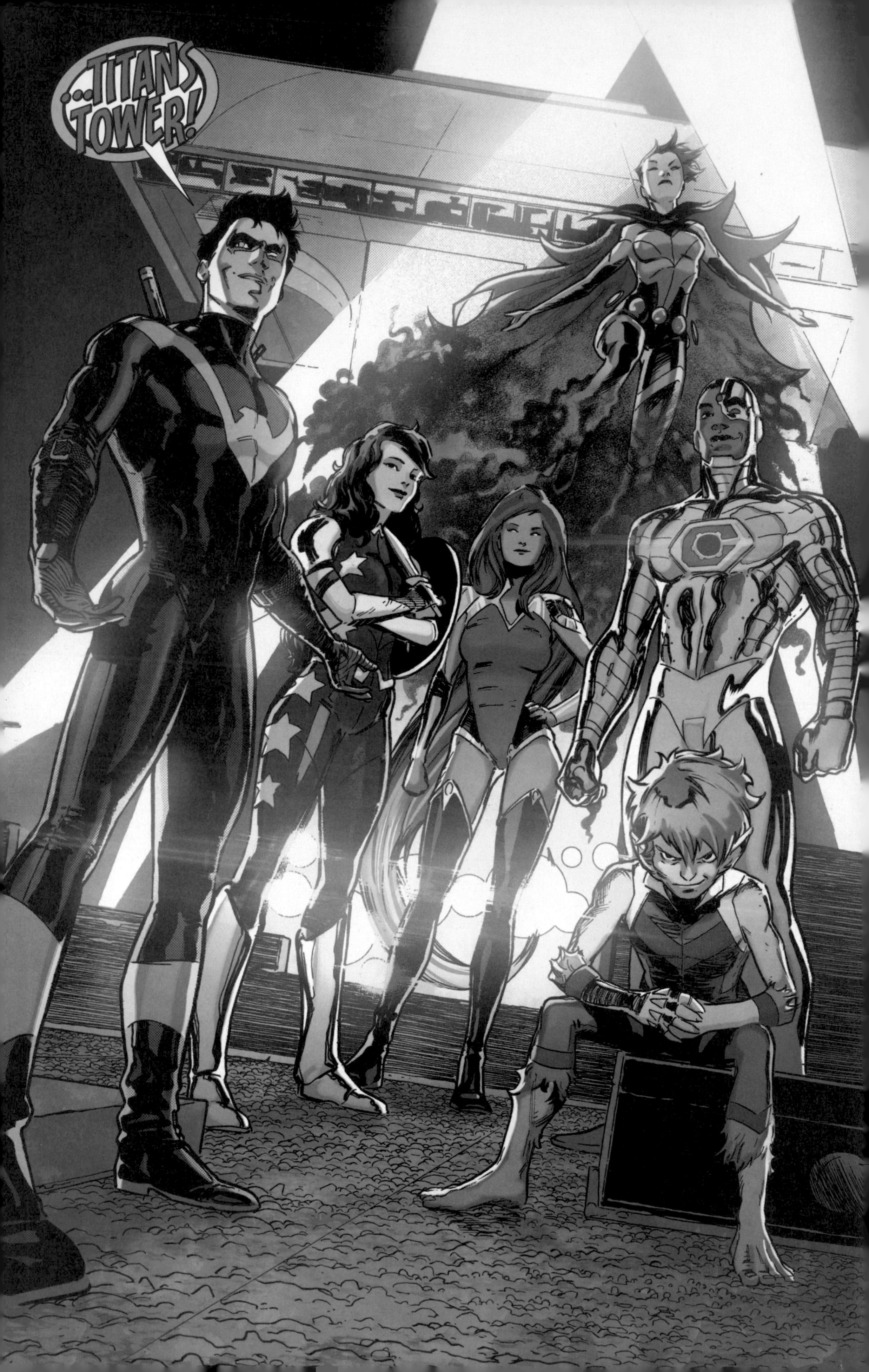
...TITANS TOWER!

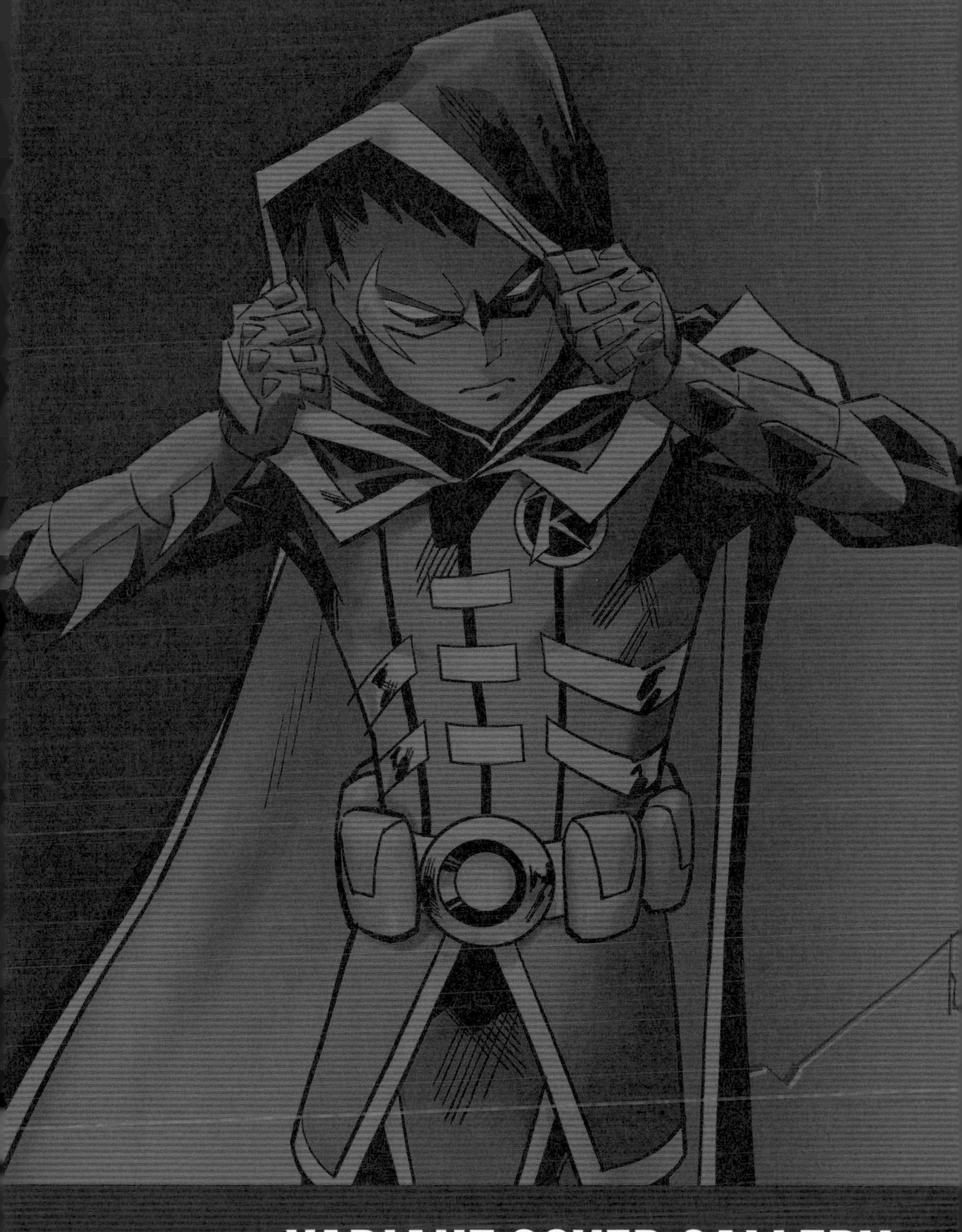

VARIANT COVER GALLERY

Teen Titans **#39** variant cover
by KHARY RANDOLPH and PETER STEIGERWALD

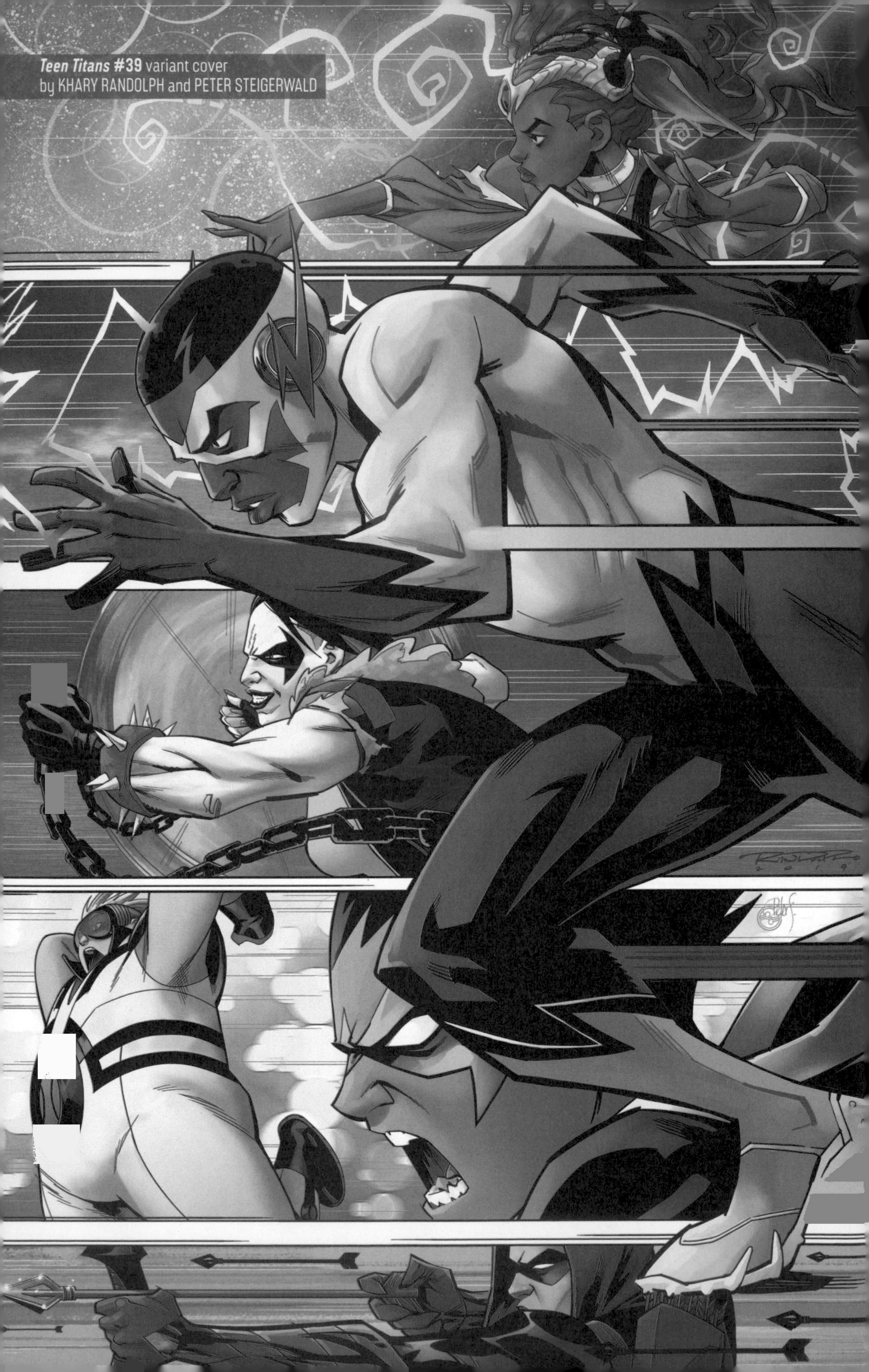

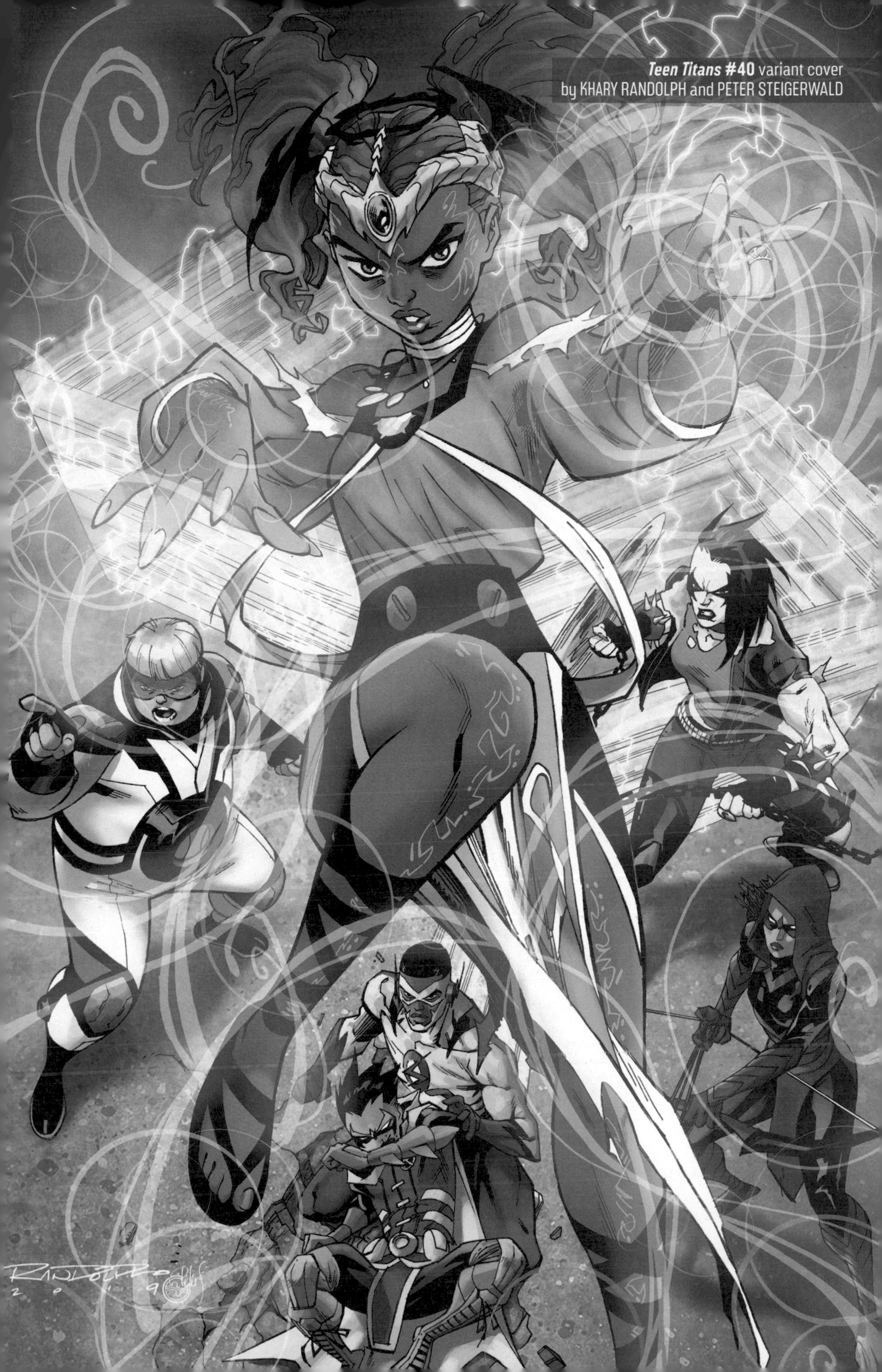

***Teen Titans* #40** variant cover
by KHARY RANDOLPH and PETER STEIGERWALD

Teen Titans **#41** variant cover
by KHARY RANDOLPH and PETER STEIGERWALD

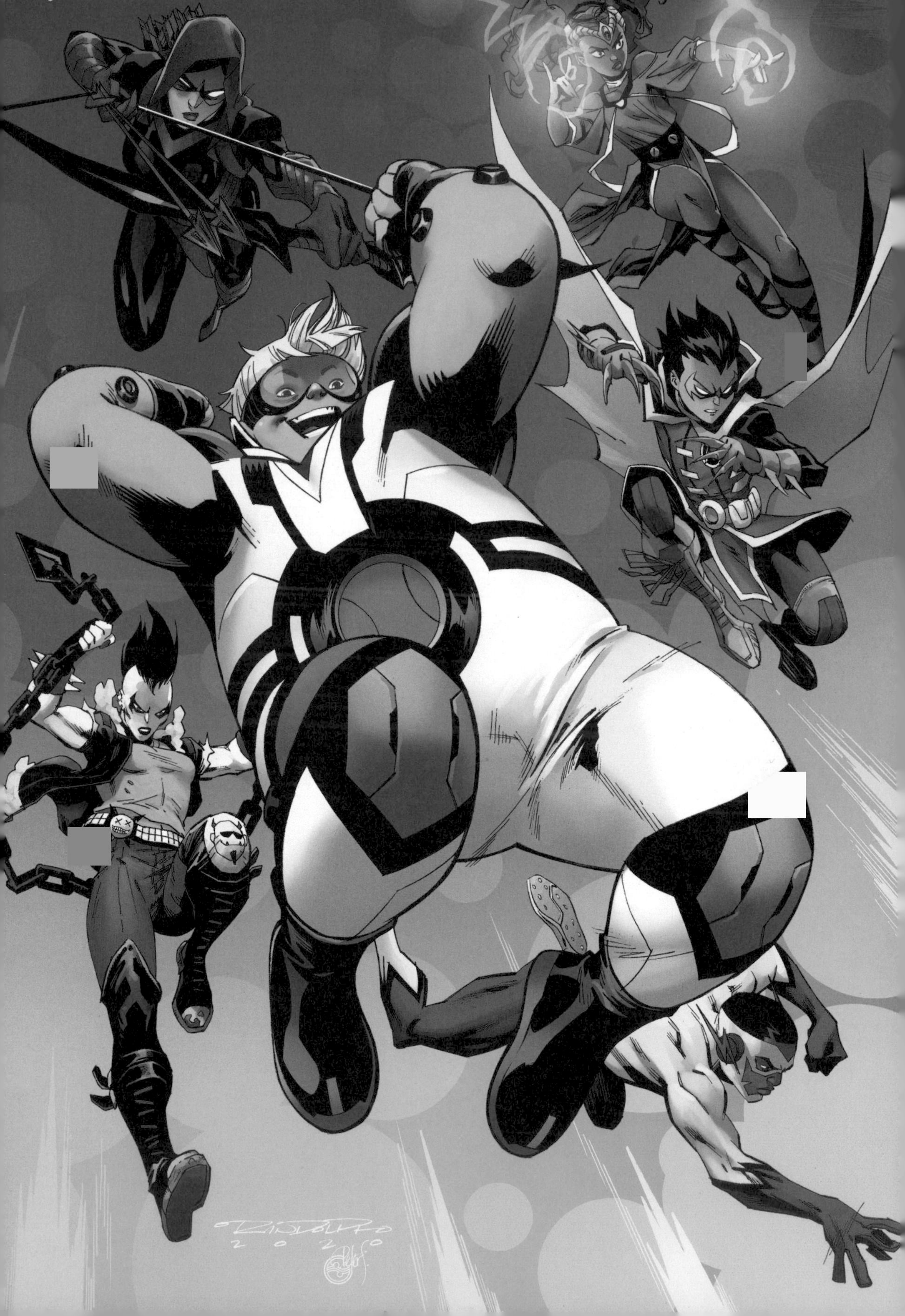

***Teen Titans* #42** variant cover
by KHARY RANDOLPH and PETER STEIGERWALD

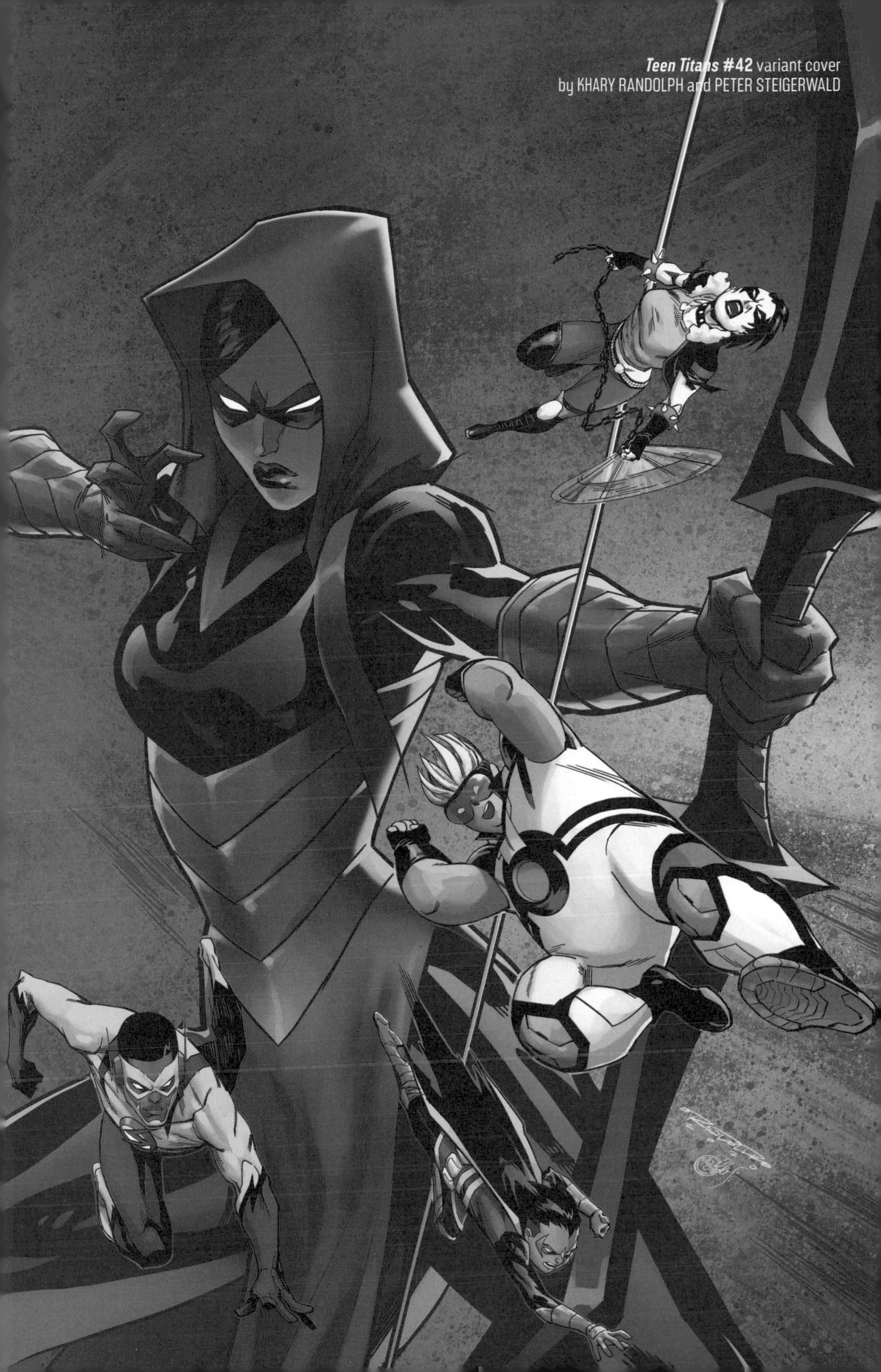

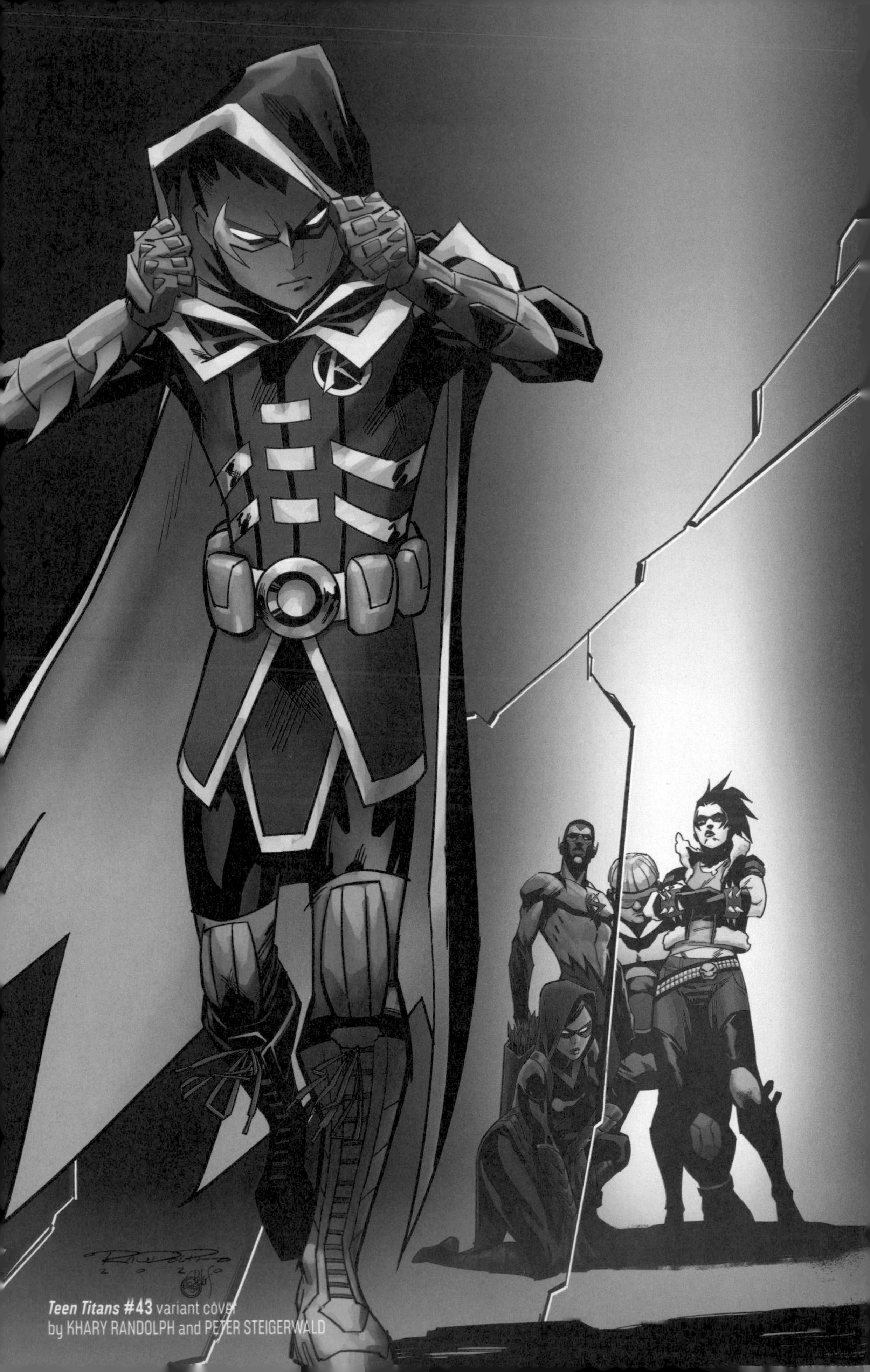

Teen Titans **#43** variant cover
by KHARY RANDOLPH and PETER STEIGERWALD

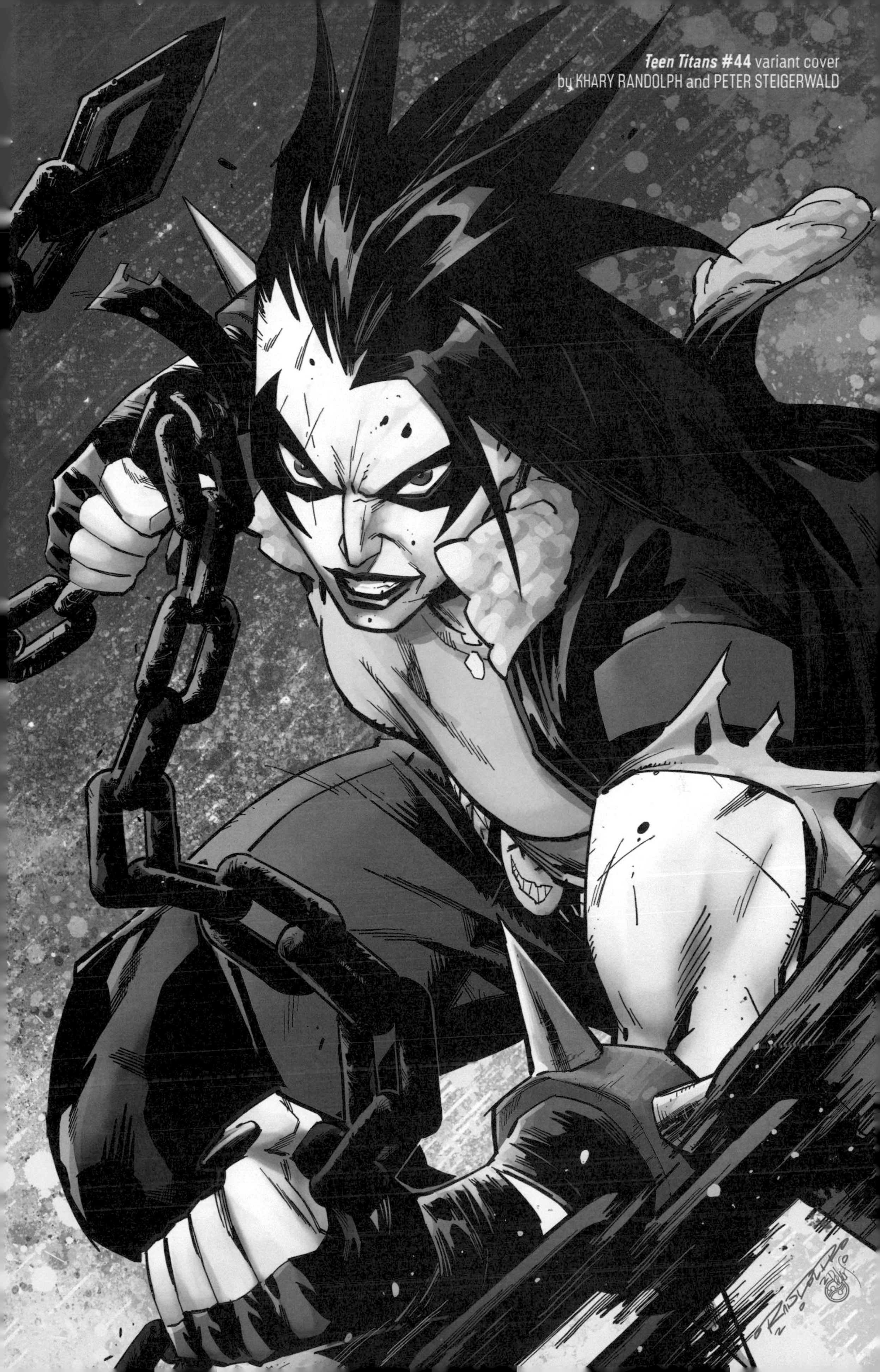

Teen Titans **#44** variant cover
by KHARY RANDOLPH and PETER STEIGERWALD

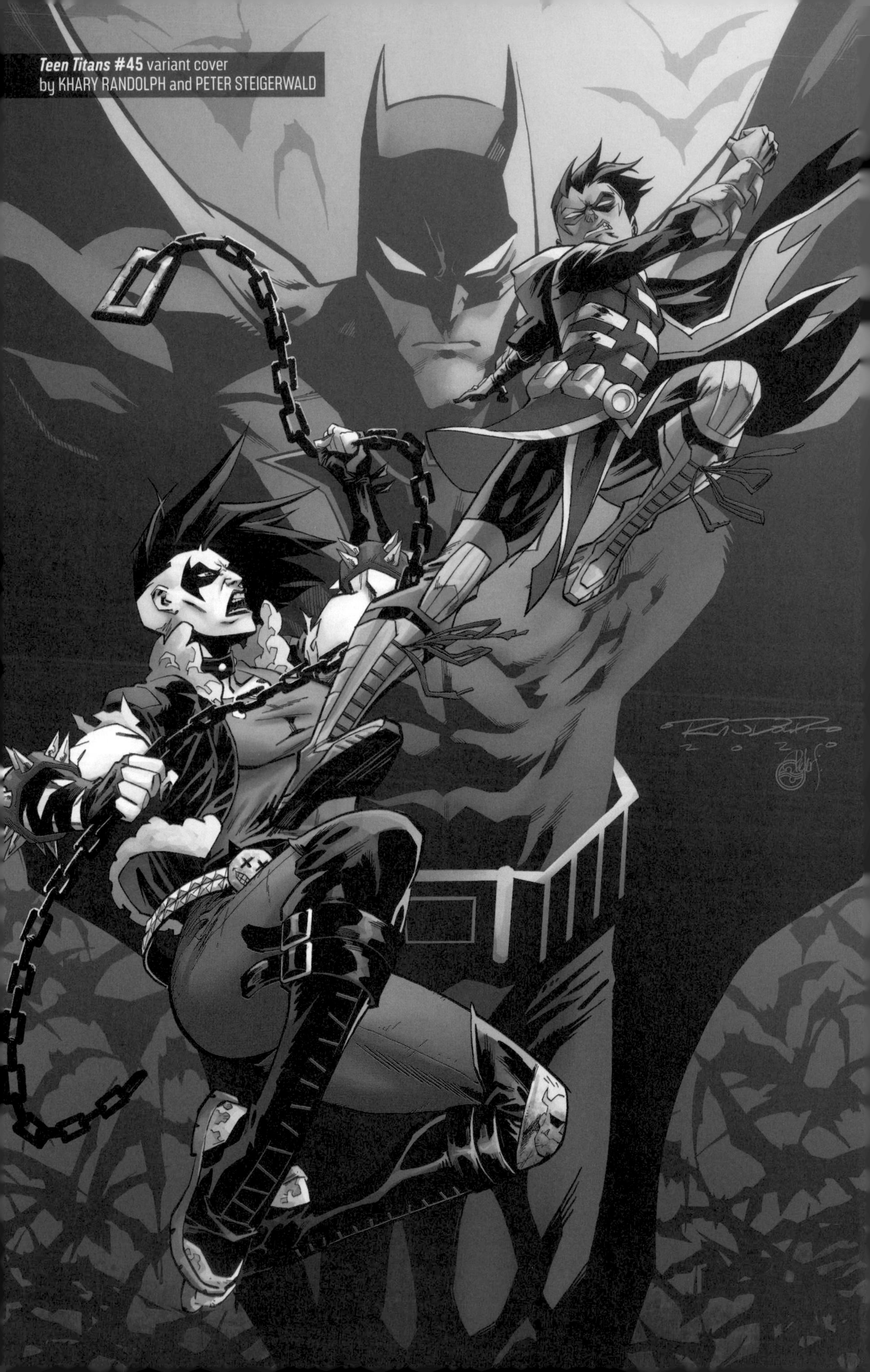

Teen Titans **#45** variant cover
by KHARY RANDOLPH and PETER STEIGERWALD

***Teen Titans* #46** variant cover
by PEACH MOMOKO

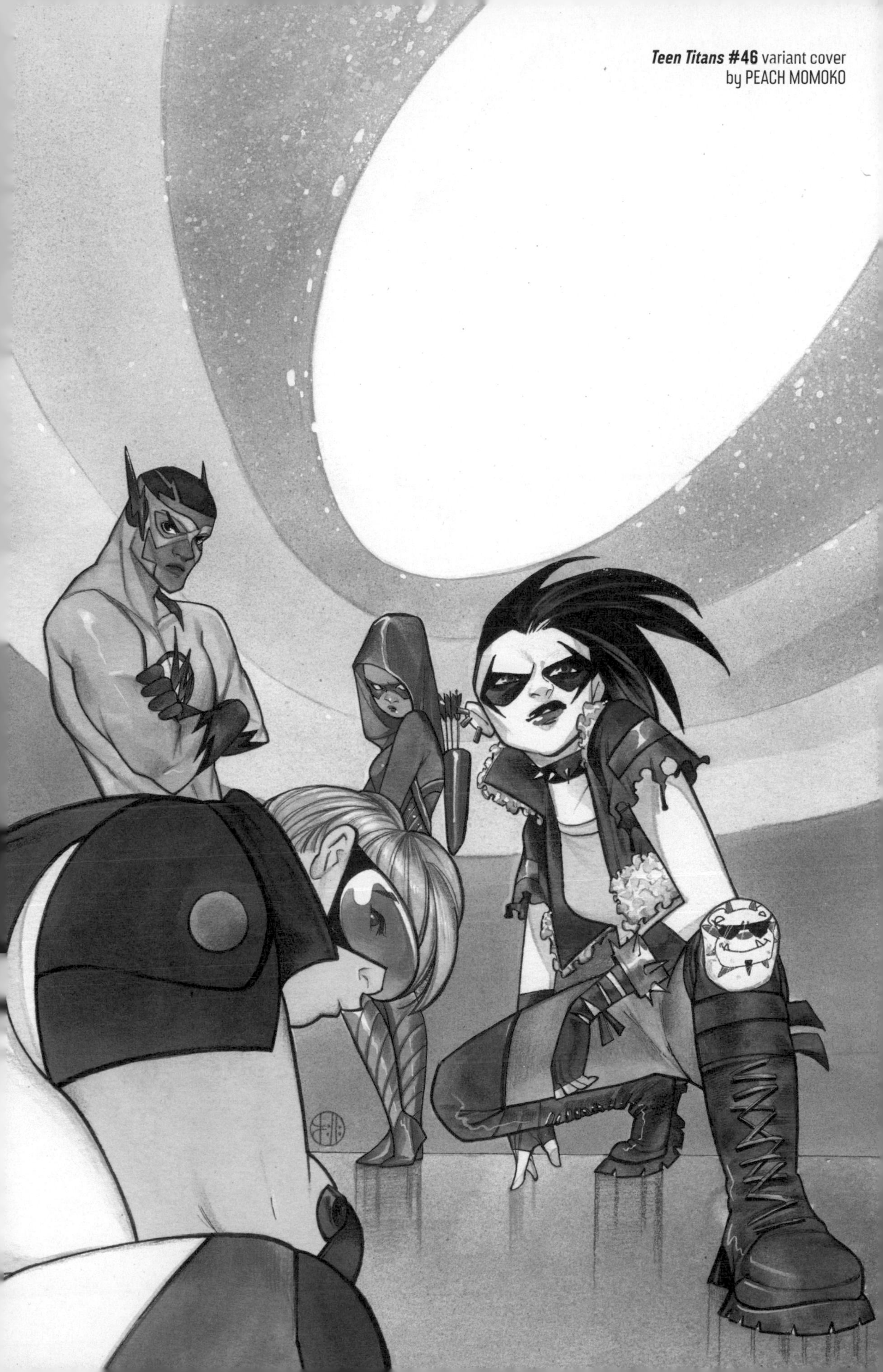

***Teen Titans* #47** variant cover
by BABS TARR

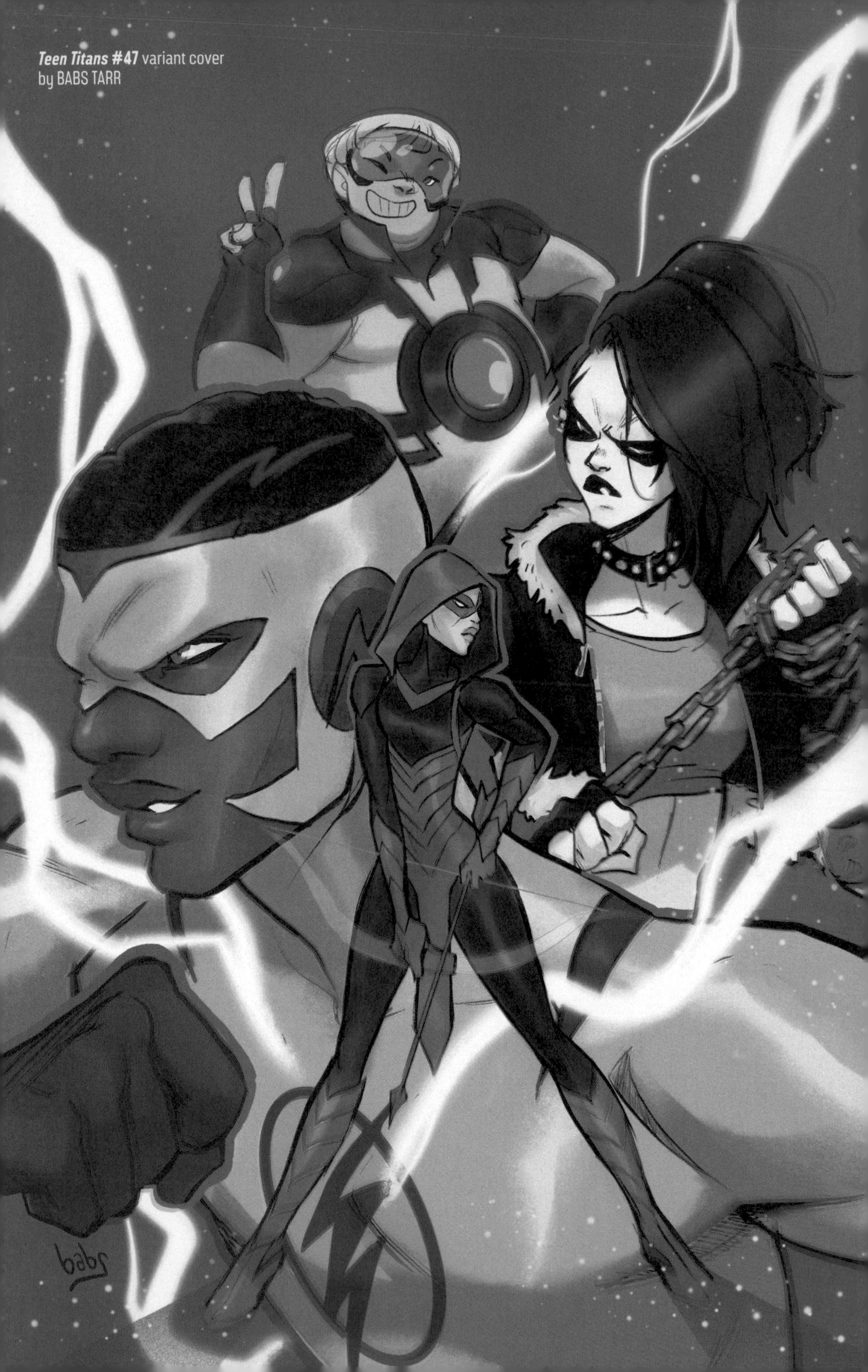
babs

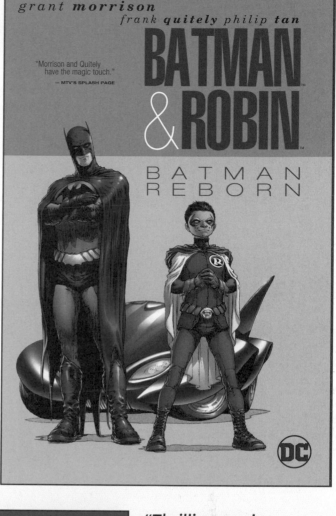
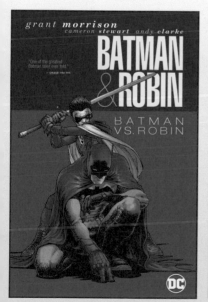
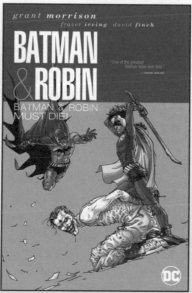

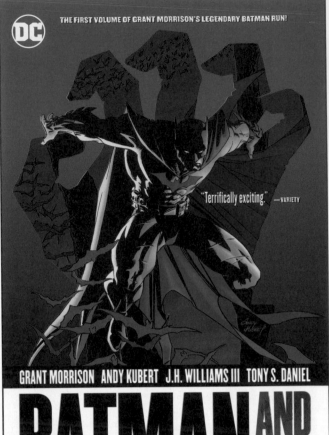

THE NEW TEEN TITANS

**MARV WOLFMAN
and GEORGE PÉREZ**
VOL. 1

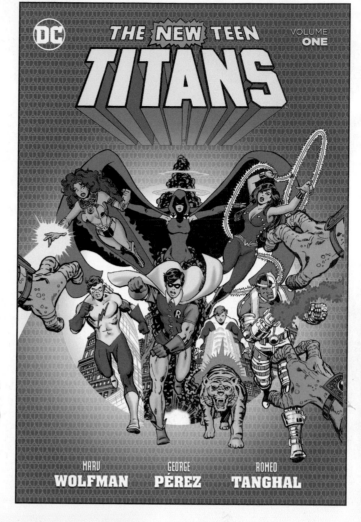

**THE NEW TEEN TITANS
VOL. 2**

**THE NEW TEEN TITANS
VOL. 3**

READ THE ENTIRE SERIES!

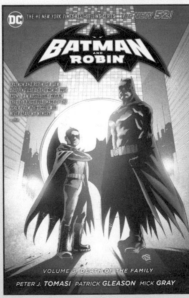